Sadlier-Oxford

NEW EDITION

PHONICS
AND WORD STUDY

D1227812

Sadlier PHONICS Reading

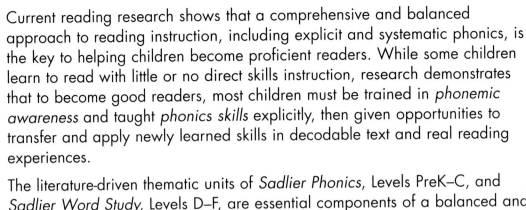

Sadlier Phonics and Word

Current reading research shows that a comprehensive and balanced approach to reading instruction, including explicit and systematic phonics, is the key to helping children become proficient readers. While some children learn to read with little or no direct skills instruction, research demonstrates that to become good readers, most children must be trained in *phonemic awareness* and taught *phonics skills* explicitly, then given opportunities to transfer and apply newly learned skills in decodable text and real reading experiences.

The literature-driven thematic units of *Sadlier Phonics*, Levels PreK–C, and *Sadlier Word Study*, Levels D–F, are essential components of a balanced and integrated approach to teaching reading. These programs contain research-based practices that meet the literacy needs of every child.

SENIOR AUTHORS

Lesley Mandel Morrow
Professor of Literacy
Rutgers University

Richard T. Vacca
Professor of Education
Kent State University

Authentic Literature

Sentence Completion

Spelling, Writing, and Speaking

T2

Study: A Balanced Approach

Phonemic Awareness

Blending

Decoding Practice

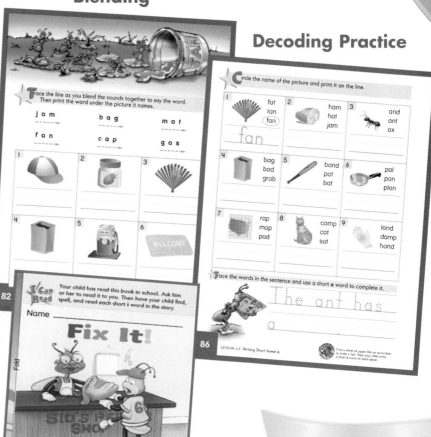

Nonfiction Photo-Essays

Decodable Readers

Research Based

"... programs including systematic instruction on letter-to-sound correspondences lead to higher achievement in both word recognition and spelling..." (Adams, 1990)

Also Available
LEVELED READERS

See pages T22–T23 for more information.

Sadlier Reading *supports* and *extends* your basal reader... call for CORRELATIONS!

	Level PreK/K	Level K	Level A
Phonemic Awareness and Auditory Discrimination	✓	✓	✓
Visual Discrimination	✓	✓	
Alphabetic Awareness	✓	✓	
Letter Recognition	✓	✓	✓
Oral Language Development	✓	✓	✓
Comprehension Skills	✓	✓	✓
Writing Skills	✓	✓	✓
Speaking and Listening Skills	✓	✓	✓
Beginning Print and Book Concepts	✓	✓	
Initial Consonants		✓	✓
Final Consonants		✓	✓
Medial Consonants			✓
Short Vowels		✓	✓
Consonant-Vowel-Consonant Blending		✓	✓
Phonograms			✓
Long Vowels			✓
y as a Vowel			✓
Spelling			✓
High-Frequency Words		✓	✓
Consonant Blends			✓
Consonant Digraphs			✓
Compound Words			✓
Contractions			✓
Inflectional Endings			✓
Soft and Hard c and g			
Syllabication			
Words ending in −le			
r-controlled Vowels			
Vowel Digraphs			
Diphthongs			
Plurals			
Suffixes			
Prefixes			
Synonyms, Antonyms, Homonyms			
Sounds of s			
Schwa			
Singular and Plural Possessives			
Dictionary Skills			
Base Words and Roots			
Thesaurus Skills			
Developing American English			
Critical Thinking	✓	✓	✓
Student Assessment	✓	✓	✓

Level B	Level C	Level D	Level E	Level F
✔				
✔	✔	✔	✔	✔
✔	✔	✔	✔	✔
✔	✔	✔	✔	✔
✔	✔			
✔	✔			
✔	✔			
✔	✔	✔	✔	✔
✔	✔	✔	✔	✔
✔	✔	✔	✔	✔
✔	✔	✔		
✔	✔	✔	✔	✔
✔				
✔	✔	✔	✔	✔
✔	✔	✔	✔	✔
✔	✔	✔	✔	✔
✔	✔	✔	✔	✔
✔	✔	✔	✔	✔
✔	✔	✔		
✔	✔	✔	✔	✔
✔	✔	✔		
✔	✔	✔	✔	✔
✔	✔	✔	✔	✔
✔	✔	✔	✔	✔
✔	✔	✔	✔	✔
✔	✔	✔	✔	✔
✔	✔	✔	✔	✔
	✔	✔		
	✔	✔	✔	✔
	✔	✔	✔	✔
	✔	✔	✔	✔
	✔	✔	✔	✔
✔	✔	✔	✔	✔
		✔	✔	✔
		✔	✔	✔
✔	✔	✔	✔	✔
✔	✔	✔	✔	✔

Literature-Driven Thematic Units

Unit Theme	Literature Selection	Skill Focus
1. Good Morning, Good Night	*Star Light*	Phonemic Awareness and Auditory Discrimination • Oral Language Development • Beginning Print Concepts • Visual Discrimination • Listening Comprehension • The Alphabet • Beginning Writing • Book Concepts
2. What's the Weather?	*Rain, Rain, Go Away*	
3. All About Bugs	*The Itsy Bitsy Spider*	
4. Let's Pretend	*Hey Diddle, Diddle*	
1. Ready, Set, Go!	*Rides* by Ilo Orleans	Early Literacy
2. Animals from A to Z	*Zoo* by John Travers Moore	The Alphabet
3. We Are Special!	*Happy Birthday to Me!* by Carmen Muñoz	Initial Consonants *f, m, s, t, h, b*
4. Off to Work!	*Work* by Babs Bell Hajdusiewicz	Initial Consonants *l, d, c, n, g, w*
5. Food, Fabulous Food!	*Yellow Butter* by Mary Ann Hoberman	Initial Consonants *p, r, k, j, q(u), v, y, z*
6. Moving Along	*Jump or Jiggle* by Evelyn Beyer	Short Vowels
1. Book Buddies	*Good Books, Good Times!* by Lee Bennett Hopkins	Phonemic Awareness and Auditory Discrimination
2. Celebrations	*Parades* by Karama Fufuka	Consonant Sounds
3. Creepy, Crawly Bugs	*Bugs* by Margaret Wise Brown	Short Vowels
4. Save Our Earth	*Yesterday's Paper* by Mabel Watts	Long Vowels
5. Sensational Senses	*Ears Hear* by Lucia & James L. Hymes, Jr.	Consonant Blends
6. Rain or Shine	*Clouds* by Christina G. Rossetti	Consonant Digraphs
7. All About Growing	*Tommy* by Gwendolyn Brooks	Word Structure: Compound Words, Contractions, Inflectional Endings
1. Friends Around the World	*A Friend* by Betsy Jones Michael	Initial, Final, and Medial Consonants
2. Splish! Splash!	*Sampan* by Tao Lang Pee	Short Vowels
3. Earth, Trees, and Me	*Trees* by Harry Behn	Long Vowels
4. In the City	*City Street* by Lois Lenski	Variant Consonant Sounds and Consonant Blends
5. Going Places	*The Museum Door* by Lee Bennett Hopkins	Syllables, Compound Words, *y* as a Vowel, Words Ending in *le*, Consonant Digraphs, *r*–controlled Vowels
6. A Rainbow of Colors	*What Is Brown?* by Mary O'Neill	Vowel Digraphs and Diphthongs
7. Numbers Count!	*Numbers, Numbers* by Lee Blair	Contractions, Plurals, Inflectional Endings
8. Outdoor Fun	*Swinging* by Irene Thompson	Suffixes; Prefixes; Synonyms, Antonyms, Homonyms

Level PreK/K

Level K

Level A

Level B

T6

Level C

Level D

Level E

Level F

Unit Theme	Literature Selection	Skill Focus
1. Fall into Autumn	*Autumn Leaves* by Aileen Fisher	Consonants and Consonant Variants
2. Sounds of Music	*Song* by Ashley Bryan	Short and Long Vowels
3. What If . . . ?	*Sunflakes* by Frank Asch	Syllables, Consonant Blends, Compound Words, *y* as a Vowel, Consonant Digraphs
4. Super Sports	*The Sidewalk Racer* by Lillian Morrison	*r*-controlled Vowels, Vowel Digraphs, Diphthongs
5. Genius at Work	*I Made a Mechanical Dragon* by Jack Prelutsky	Contractions and Word Endings
6. Space Fantasy	*Space Campers' Song* by Anastasia Suen	Suffixes, Prefixes, Multisyllabic Words
7. Wacky Words, Riddles and Rhymes	*Have You Ever Seen?* (Anonymous)	Synonyms, Antonyms, Homonyms; Dictionary Skills
1. Athletes	*Beach Volleyball* by Martin Lee and Marcia Miller	Consonant Blends and Consonant Digraphs
2. Explorers	*Meet an Underwater Explorer* by Luise Woelflein	Short, Long, and *r*-controlled Vowels; Vowel Pairs, Vowel Digraphs, Diphthongs, and Phonograms
3. Artists and Composers	*Twisted Trails* from *Time for Kids*	Word Endings, Contractions, Plurals, Possessives, and Compound Words
4. Making a Difference	*It's Our World, Too!* by Phillip Hoose	Prefixes, Roots, and Syllables
5. Scientists	*Your Future in Space* by Alan L. Bean	Suffixes and Syllables
6. People and Government	*Everybody's Uncle Sam* by Lester David	Dictionary and Thesaurus Skills; Synonyms, Antonyms, Homonyms; Clipped, Blended, and Borrowed Words; Idioms and Analogies
1. The Northeast	*Native Peoples of the Northeast* by Trudie Lamb Richmond	Consonant Blends, Consonant Digraphs, and Double Consonant Sounds
2. The Southeast	*Saving the Everglades* from *Time for Kids*	Vowel Pairs, Vowel Digraphs, Diphthongs, and Phonograms
3. The Middle West	*How to Grow a Painting* by Gail Skroback Hennessey	Word Endings, Contractions, Plurals, Possessives, and Compound Words
4. The Southwest	*Deep in the Heart of...Big Bend* by Bud McDonald	Prefixes, Roots, Base Words, and Suffixes
5. The West	*Catching Up with Lewis and Clark* from *Time for Kids*	Context Clues
6. The Northwest and Hawaii	*Hawaii: Then and Now* by Marcie and Rick Carroll	Dictionary and Thesaurus Skills; Synonyms, Antonyms, and Homonyms; Word Origin and Language Development
1. World Regions	*Thinking Big* by Scott Wallace	Consonant Blends and Consonant Digraphs; Vowel Pairs, Vowel Digraphs, Diphthongs, and Phonograms
2. Africa and the Middle East	*Cleopatra's Lost Palace* from *Time for Kids*	Word Endings, Contractions, Plurals, Possessives, and Compound Words
3. India and the Far East	*Science in Ancient China* by George Beshore	Prefixes, Roots, Base Words, and Suffixes
4. Ancient Greece to the Renaissance	*When Clothes Told a Story* by Linda Honan	More Prefixes, Roots, Base Words, and Suffixes
5. The Americas	*Coyote and the Stars* By Tsonakwa	Context Clues
6. The Modern World	*Can We Rescue the Reefs?* from *Time for Kids*	Dictionary and Thesaurus Skills; Synonyms, Antonyms, and Homonyms; Word Origin and Language Development

Building a Strong Foundation

Getting Ready to Read with Mother Goose is an exciting new beginning literacy program designed to build a strong foundation of skills for a lifetime of reading, writing, and learning. Throughout the program, children develop oral language, build phonemic awareness, strengthen listening skills, recognize letters of the alphabet, and even begin to write! It is the ideal program for use in preschools, or during the first few months of kindergarten, to introduce children to beginning literacy skills.

Activity Book

The *Activity Book* features activities that promote language development and beginning literacy skills.

Phonemic Awareness

Nursery rhymes invite children to have fun playing with sounds, language, and rhymes.

Oral Language Development

A *Think and Share* feature prompts class discussions and builds speaking and listening skills.

Alphabetic Knowledge

Learning About the Alphabet pages introduce the letters as children sing *The Alphabet Song,* with lyrics tailored to each theme.

Emergent Writing

Beginning to Write pages engage children in sharing their ideas through writing and drawing.

for Good Readers

Teacher's Resource Companion

The *Teacher's Resource Companion* is an easy-to-manage collection of rich literacy resources.

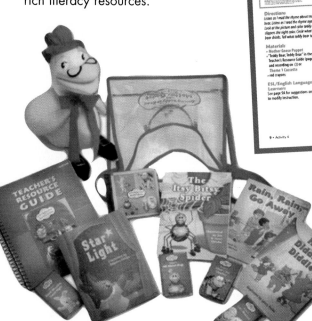

Contents

- The *Teacher's Resource Guide,* featuring 176 pages of explicit teaching plans, boasts an abundance of hands-on literacy activities.

- Four *Audiocassettes* (or one *Compact Disc*), bursting with songs, rhymes, and catchy chants, help build phonemic awareness.

- A *Mother Goose Hand Puppet,* the perfect companion for modeling language, delights children as they listen, talk, learn, and sing along with her.

- Four *Little Books,* one for each of the nursery rhymes featured in the Activity Book, introduce beginning book concepts and comprehension skills, and include a "Dear Family" letter to promote Family Literacy.

- A handy vinyl *Shoulder Bag* keeps everything organized!

Also Available
READ-ALOUD LITTLE BOOKS

Connecting Sound to Symbol

Sadlier Phonics, Level K, starts off with a review of beginning literacy skills and leads children through the alphabet, from **A** to **Z**. Children develop phonemic awareness and move from sound to symbol. They use their knowledge of letter sounds to blend and decode words. A series of decodable readers allow children to immediately apply their newly acquired phonics skills.

Authentic Literature
Engaging poetry openers provide a thematic context for phonics instruction.

Phonemic Awareness
Auditory activities help children to develop phonemic awareness. Instruction focuses on initial, final, and medial sounds in words.

Oral Language Development
Time to Talk lessons encourage children to share their ideas, experiences, and knowledge.

T10

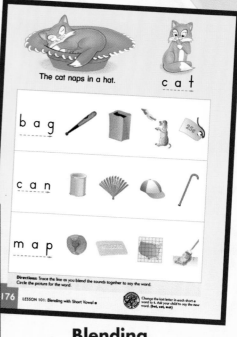

Sound–Symbol Correspondences

Extensive practice in connecting sound to symbol lays the foundation for phonics instruction.

Decodable Readers

Five colorful take-home *Decodable Readers*—included in the Student Text—contain 100% decodable text and familiar high-frequency words to help children experience the joy of reading!

Blending

Explicit instruction leads children to blend sounds into words.

Nonfiction Photo-Essays

Thematic *Look and Learn* pages at the end of each unit present phonics skills in the context of a nonfiction passage.

Writing

Time to Write pages provide children the opportunity to apply a particular phonics skill in the context of their own writing.

Also Available
LEVELED READERS

See pages T22–T23 for more information.

Practicing Phonics and

Sadlier Phonics, Level A, builds on children's proficiency in manipulating sounds, generating sounds from letters, and blending sounds into words. The focus is on decoding. Children learn to blend words with short and long vowel patterns. They progress from single consonant sounds to consonant blends and digraphs. Children also learn to use word structure to decode.

Level A

Phonemic Awareness

Catchy rhymes and tongue twisters promote phonemic awareness—a strong predictor of early reading success.

Decodable Readers

Delightful *Decodable Readers*— included in the Student Text— allow children to immediately apply their newly learned phonics skills.

Blending

Explicit instruction and practice in blending sounds into words help develop automaticity.

Authentic Literature

Engaging poetry openers set the theme of each unit. *Critical Thinking* questions prompt classroom discussion.

Decoding Skills

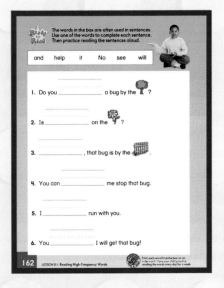

Phonograms

Exercises in which children work with high-utility phonograms, or word families, help develop fluency.

High-Frequency Words

Ready to Read lessons systematically introduce the most common words in beginning reading as sight vocabulary.

Extensive Practice

Extensive phonics practice leads to skills mastery, enabling children to decode words accurately and automatically.

"Systematic phonics instruction has been used widely over a long period of time with positive results, and a variety of systematic phonics programs have proven effective with children of different ages, abilities, and socioeconomic backgrounds." (The National Reading Panel, 1999)

Also Available
LEVELED READERS

See pages T22–T23 for more information.

Applying Advanced Phonics

Sadlier Phonics, Level B, covers more advanced phonics and word study skills, including **r**-controlled vowels, vowel digraphs and diphthongs, prefixes, suffixes, and inflectional endings. The emphasis is on fluency. Children begin to process words more efficiently as they "chunk" words, looking at larger units within both single-syllable and multisyllabic words. They also learn reliable rules to help in decoding.

Reading Comprehension

Read and Write lessons help develop comprehension skills as children find meaning in narrative and informational text.

Introductory Rhymes

Read-aloud rhymes build phonemic awareness and introduce skills in context.

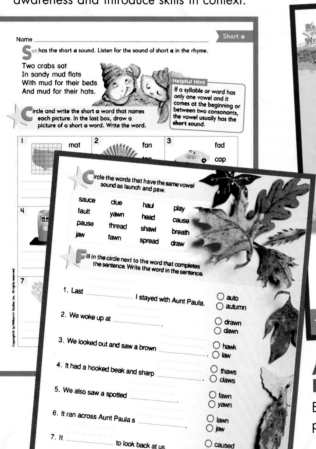

Johnny Appleseed

Johnny Appleseed lived a long time ago. Do you know the good things that he did?

Johnny wanted apple trees to grow all over America. So, as a young man, Johnny left his home. He walked across the land planting apple trees.

Johnny was nice to people. He gave them apple seeds and trees to plant. He did not make poor people pay for them. He wanted them to fruit to eat.

Years later, Johnny returned to the places he had been. He was proud to see apple trees growing there. Apple trees may still be there today.

1. What was one way Johnny Appleseed was nice to people?

2. How can you be like Johnny Appleseed?

Advanced Phonics Skills

Explicit instruction in advanced phonics skills leads to fluency.

Also Available
LEVELED READERS

See pages T22–T23 for more information.

Skills to Build Fluency

Sadlier Phonics, Level C, reviews and builds on phonics and word study skills to enable children to read for meaning. Explicit, systematic instruction and repeated practice enable children to read harder words accurately and automatically. A strong syllabication strand aids in multisyllabic word recognition. Word strategies provide guidance for decoding unfamiliar words.

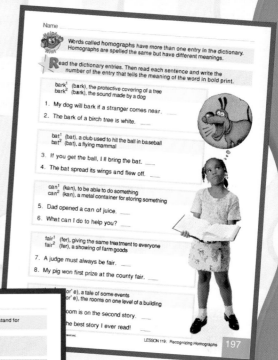

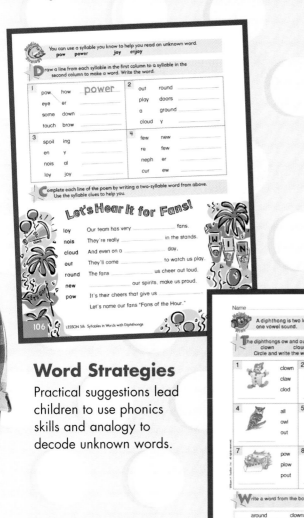

Level C

Word Strategies

Practical suggestions lead children to use phonics skills and analogy to decode unknown words.

Cloze Activities

Cloze activities promote the use of syntactic, semantic, and print cues as children focus on context to complete sentences or passages.

Word Study

Extensive word study—including structural analysis and vocabulary development—helps children become proficient readers.

"Phonics and word study skills are especially important in second and third grade as children are expected to decode and comprehend higher level text." (Morrow, 2000)

Using Word Study Skills to

Sadlier Word Study, Levels D–F, extends the development and use of phonics into the middle grades, helping students not only apply decoding skills but also develop word-meaning strategies as they read content-area materials.

The program presents a logical sequence of skills and strategies that provides students with a ready knowledge of word parts and the ability to use context clues.

With the systematic instruction provided in *Sadlier Word Study,* students learn to pronounce words and unlock their meanings more quickly and more accurately, leading to better comprehension.

Levels D–F

Word Study in Context
Nonfiction photo-essays apply word study strategies to reading comprehension and critical thinking skills.

Structural Analysis
Lessons provide students with a clear map to help analyze structural and meaning clues in parts of words.

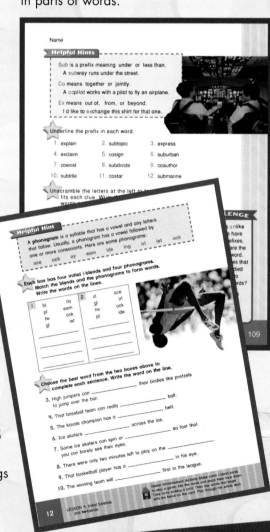

Critical Thinking
Critical Thinking questions encourage use of higher-order thinking skills.

Home Connection
A *Family Page* encourages family members to become partners in helping children become better readers.

"Chunking" Strategies
The use of phonograms, consonant blends and digraphs, and word endings helps students apply knowledge of phonics to decode difficult words.

Build Comprehension

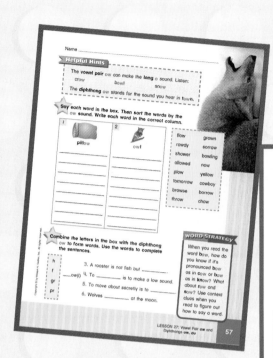

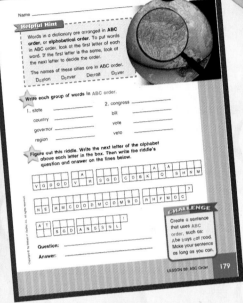

Context Clues

The Word Strategy feature shows students how to use specific context clues to unlock the meaning of unknown words.

Dictionary Usage

Practical lessons help students learn to use dictionaries and thesauruses as tools for word study.

Reading and Writing

Engaging thematic lessons help students apply word study strategies in order to better comprehend content-area reading materials.

"Students at the middle grades need to maximize their ability to analyze chunks or letters within words; analyze the structure of words for morphemic or meaning-bearing clues; use context clues not only to pronounce unfamiliar words, but also to figure out their meanings; and use dictionaries and thesauruses as tools for word study. Students develop knowledge and control over these strategies through explicit instructional activities."
(Vacca, 2000)

Providing a Complete Teacher

Sadlier Phonics and *Sadlier Word Study* Teacher's Editions provide the resources required to meet today's challenging standards. Phonics and Word Study Workshops offer built-in staff development by examining the best of today's reading research and the benefits of a balanced approach to literacy. Unit features include a Planning Resource to maintain effective classroom and curriculum management and additional activities and strategies to help teachers provide the instruction and teaching methods necessary to help all students achieve grade-level objectives.

Teacher's Editions

Unit Planner
A pre-unit planning guide for effective classroom management and lesson planning helps correlate phonics lessons with state or school curriculum.

Standards
Correlations to key national reading standards ensure grade-level objectives are being covered.

Objectives
Clearly stated objectives focus on priority skills.

4 PLANNING RESOURCE

Off to Work!
All kinds of workers do all kinds of jobs!

Initial Consonants l, d, c, n, g, w

READING/LANGUAGE ARTS STANDARDS
- Respond to a poem in a way that reflects understanding
- Identify initial and final sounds in single-syllable words
- Match consonant sounds to the appropriate letters
- Write uppercase and lowercase letters properly
- Read common, irregular sight words
- Discuss meanings of words and develop vocabulary

LESSONS
Lesson 63 . . . . Literature Introduction
                to Initial **l, d, c, n, g, w**
Lessons 64–69 . . . . Initial **l, d, c**
Lesson 70 . . . . Reviewing Initial **l, d, c**/Final **d**
Lessons 71–76 . . . . Initial **n, g, w**
Lesson 77 . . . . Reviewing Initial **n, g, w**/Final **n, g**
Lesson 78 . . . . High-Frequency Words
Lesson 79 . . . . Reviewing Initial **l, d, c, n, g, w**
Lesson 80 . . . . Integrating the Language Arts/
                Assessing Initial **l, d, c, n, g, w**
- Take-Home Book: *Workers at Work*

OBJECTIVES
▶ To enjoy a poem about work
▶ To match, identify, and isolate initial sounds
▶ To segment and blend onsets and rimes
▶ To associate the letters **l, d, c, n, g, w** with their initial sounds
▶ To associate the letters **d, n, g** with their final sounds
▶ To correctly print letter forms **Ll, Dd, Cc, Nn, Gg, Ww**

Thematic Teaching
In Unit 4, children will be introduced to the initial sounds of **l, d, c, n, g,** and **w**. As they learn to make the sound-letter associations, children will explore the world of work.

The "Off to Work!" theme presents a good opportunity for children to start a nonfiction journal or learning log. Encourage creative thinking as facts about various kinds of work and workers are discussed in the lessons. Have children express what they learn by writing or drawing. Remember to display the "Work" classroom poster.

Curriculum Integration

Math On page 118, children learn more about numbers and the letter **n**!

Social Studies Children learn about the different tools workers use to get the job done in the fun activity on page 132.

99A Unit 4 • *Initial Consonants l, d, c, n, g, w*

Support System

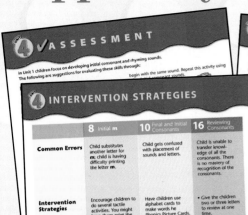

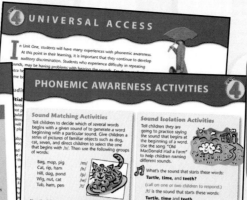

Visit us at www.sadlier-oxford.com

Additional Strategies and Activities

Strategies for assessment and activities for multiple learning styles, intervention, and universal access help meet the needs of all learners.

Internet Activities

Fun phonics activites for children, strategies for teachers, and literacy-building ideas for the entire family are available on the Sadlier-Oxford website, www.sadlier-oxford.com.

Optional Learning Activities

Multisensory Activities
Multisensory activities promoting visual, auditory, tactile, and kinesthetic learning are a regular feature of each lesson.

Multicultural Connections
Use the multicultural activities on pages 104, 106, 108, and 124 to celebrate cultural diversity.

Learning Centers
Children can participate in activities in the Math Center on page 110 and in the Science Center on page 120.

Thematic Activities
Watch for exciting thematic activities in the *Curriculum Connections* section of most lesson plans.

Babs Bell Hajdusiewicz
Author's Corner

Babs Bell Hajdusiewicz grew up in rural Indiana. Her family kept many animals and maintained a large garden. This meant that everyone in the family had lots of chores. The poet remembers singing songs with the family as everybody worked, which made each job much more fun. Her poem "Work" sets the tone for this unit, in which children learn about occupations.

Assessment

Multiple forms of assessment for each lesson help guide instruction and maintain a complete portfolio for each student.

 Assessment Strategies

Adapt and extend the suggested observational assessments, portfolio activities, and checklist methods to reflect your children's needs and progress.

Resources

These additional teaching resources are available to support phonics instruction: *Sadlier Phonics Alphabet Posters, Sadlier Phonics Picture Cards, Sadlier Reading Manipulatives, Sadlier Reading Little Books* and *Big Books,* and *Sadlier Phonics Classroom Posters.*

UNIT RESOURCES
Sadlier Reading

Student Manipulatives

Phonics Picture Cards

Alphabet Posters

Little Books and Big Books

Classroom Posters

Staff Development
Built-in staff development presents a complete phonics research base and provides "how to" strategies for using the program.

Featuring Systematic and

The *Sadlier Phonics* and *Sadlier Word Study* Teacher's Editions provide systematic and explicit skill instruction in each and every lesson. A wide variety of activities helps enable teachers to meet the diverse needs of all learners. One idea after another suggests ways for students to review, practice, and apply skills as they build confidence as readers and writers.

Objectives
Clearly stated objectives correlate to national reading standards.

Phonemic Awareness
Blending, segmenting, adding, matching, and deleting sounds are specifically taught.

Explicit Instruction
Explicit and systematic instruction helps children master essential phonics skills.

Supporting All Learners
Auditory, Visual, Kinesthetic, Extra Support, Challenge, and ESL activities for all learning styles and language needs.

LESSON 28 • UNIT 2
Student Pages 59–60

Initial Consonant /j/ Jj

Objectives
- To segment onsets and rimes
- To recognize initial /j/
- To recognize that Jj stands for /j/
- To print j to complete words

Warming Up

Reviewing Initial Sounds
Materials: **Sadlier Phonics Picture Cards** for **pig, ride, kitten**

Print on the board these sentences, and read them aloud.

Little **Ruth** is in the **parade**.

The new **king** had a big **party**.

The boy **put** a **key** in the **red** wagon.

Display the picture cards and name them with the class. Identify each beginning sound. Then have children circle words in the sentences that have the same beginning sounds as the pictures. Say each word together as it is circled.

Teaching the Lesson

Phonemic Awareness:
Segment Onsets and Rimes
Say the word **jump**. Tell children that **jump** begins with /**j**/. Then model segmenting the beginning sound from the rest of the word by saying /**j**/-/**ump**/. Say the words **jar, jeep, just, jet**. Have children repeat each word and then segment the beginning sound from the rest of the word.

Sound to Symbol
- Tell children to listen for words that begin with /**j**/ as you say this tongue twister. *The jolly clown jumps and jiggles.* Have children ___ words and then say /**j**/. ___ Explain that these ___ identify the uppercase and ___ the following words ___ **ly, jumps, jiggles, Jim**. ___ the class and ask volun- ___ letter that stands for /**j**/.

Jj

Joy starts with the sound of **j**. Listen for the sound of **j** in the rhyme.

Justin and Jasmin
Jump for joy.
The puppy in the jeep
Is theirs to keep.

Circle and color each picture that has the sound of **j** at the beginning of its name.

1 jeep	2 jam	3 bite	4 June
5 nest	6 jack-in-the-box	7 robe	8 judge
9 jacket	10 pan	11 jacks	12 jug

LESSON 28: Phonemic Awareness: Initial /j/   **59**

UNIVERSAL ACCESS
Meeting Individual Needs

Auditory • Kinesthetic
Teach the class how to do jumping jacks. Then direct children to do a single jumping jack whenever they hear you say a word that begins with /**j**/. Slowly say a list of words: **job**, gate, **jeans, jelly**, duck, hat, time, **jewel, Joe**, kangaroo, **jump, judge**, and **July**.

Visual • Kinesthetic
Materials: Sadlier Phonics Picture Cards for initial **j** (e.g., **jam, juggle, jeep**) and other initial sounds

Review the song "If You're Happy and You Know It, Clap Your Hands." Teach children to use the same melody to sing *"If the name starts with j, clap your hands."* Children should clap only if a picture card you show represents an initial **j** word.

Extra Support
Remind children that **j** stands for /**j**/. Put pictures of initial **j** objects (jacket, jelly beans, etc.) and other non-**j** objects face down. Have a child turn over two pictures. If both start with **j**, have the child write **j** on the board.

Explicit Instruction

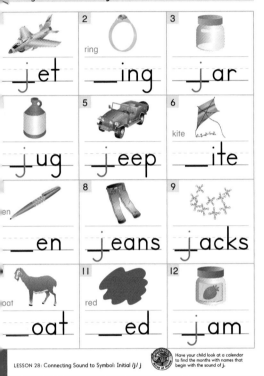

Say the name of each picture. Print **j** on the line if its name begins with the sound of **j**.

1. __jet	2. __ing (ring)	3. __jar
4. __jug	5. __jeep	6. __ite (kite)
7. __en (pen)	8. __jeans	9. __jacks
10. __oat (goat)	11. __ed (red)	12. __jam

LESSON 28: Connecting Sound to Symbol: Initial /j/ j

Have your child look at a calendar to find the months with names that begin with the sound of **j**.

Practicing the Skill

- Point to the letters **Jj** at the top of page 59. Remind children that these letters stand for /**j**/. Have them trace the letters at the top of the page and then in the air.
- Have children listen for words that begin with /**j**/ as you read the poem.
- Read aloud the directions on page 59 and identify the pictures. Model for children how to circle and color the first picture. Then tell children to complete the page.
- Read the directions for page 60. Model how to write the letter **j** to complete the first item. Then have them complete the page.

Curriculum Connections

Theme Activity: Art
Materials: *large sheets of drawing paper, crayons, magazines, catalogs, scissors, glue*

- Discuss with children the kinds of celebrations that might include jugglers. (circus, birthday parties) Let volunteers talk about their own juggling experiences.
- Distribute drawing paper and have children draw a clown in the center of it.
- Provide magazines and catalogs and have children cut out objects that begin with /**j**/. Tell children to glue the pictures around the clown so that the clown appears to be juggling the **j** pictures.

Portfolio Tell children to place their "juggling **j**" pictures in their portfolios.

Sadlier Reading
Little Books and *Big Books*
Read *J My Name Is Jess* and *In January and June* for more practice with initial consonant **j**.

Observational Assessment
*Note whether children have difficulty printing the letter **j**.*

Practice
Clear instruction, including modeling and guided practice, enables children to experience success as they practice each new skill in the Student Edition.

Curriculum Connections
Cross-curricular and learning center activities extend phonics skills into other subject areas, such as Math, Art, and Science.

Assessment
Strategies for observing, recording, and monitoring student progress are frequently highlighted in the Lesson Plans.

English Language Learners/ESL
Write **j** and **j** on the board. Tell children these letters stand for /**j**/ as in **jump**. Say /**j**/, /**j**/, -**ump** and **jump**. Tell children to watch how you form your mouth when you say /**j**/. Then ask children to mimic you and say /**j**/. Then show children an empty washed **juice** container and tell them that the word **juice** begins with the letter **j** /**j**/. Repeat this activity using a **jar**. Print labels for the juice container and the jar, and display them in the classroom.

Challenge
Have pairs of children work together to make up a short story about a **juggler**. Challenge them to use words that begin with **j** in their stories. For example, *Jo-Jo juggles bags of jelly beans. Then he jumps into his jeep.* To share stories, have one partner narrate the story, while the other acts it out. Ask listeners to raise their hands every time they hear a word that begins with **j**.

Special Strategies
For Universal Access activities, see page 13F.

60

Little Books & Big Books for

Sadlier Reading *Little Books* and *Big Books,* a series of 70 *Leveled Readers* ideal for Early Intervention and Guided Reading programs, provide children with real reading experiences while reinforcing specific phonics and comprehension skills. Children immediately apply skills as they gain fluency in reading. **Sadlier Reading** *Little Books* and *Big Books* make meaningful, skill-based reading opportunities possible in every classroom!

READ-ALOUD MOTHER GOOSE NURSERY RHYMES (PreK–1)

- 4 beautifully illustrated nursery rhyme books
- Promote beginning print and book concepts
- Encourage phonemic awareness and comprehension skills
- A "Dear Family" letter in English and Spanish in each book promotes Family Literacy

EMERGENT READERS (PreK–1)

- 40 exciting titles: 20 fiction, 20 nonfiction
- Interactive audiocassettes support independent reading as children build confidence as "readers"
- Reinforce sound-symbol correspondences by focusing on initial consonant sounds
- Develop phonemic awareness and beginning comprehension skills
- A "Dear Family" letter in each book promotes Family Literacy—also available in Spanish in the Teacher's Resource Guide
- Selected titles are available in Spanish
- Leveled for use in Guided Reading and Early Intervention programs

Real Reading Experiences

EARLY READERS (K–2)

- 20 engaging titles: 10 fiction, 10 nonfiction
- Original stories focus on short and long vowel instruction
- Encourage the transfer of phonics skills and the application of decoding strategies
- A "Dear Family" letter in each book promotes Family Literacy—also available in Spanish in the Teacher's Resource Guide
- Leveled for use in Guided Reading and Early Intervention programs

FLUENT READERS (1–3)

- 10 motivating titles: a mix of fiction and nonfiction
- Longer stories feature greater variation in both sentence structure and vocabulary
- Stories focus on more advanced phonics and comprehension skills
- A "Dear Family" letter in each book promotes Family Literacy—also available in Spanish in the Teacher's Resource Guide
- Leveled for use in Guided Reading and Early Intervention programs

SADLIER READING

**Getting Ready to Read
with Mother Goose**
Level PreK/K

Sadlier Phonics
Levels K, A, B, and C

Sadlier Word Study
Levels D, E, and F

TEACHER'S EDITION

Level A

Lesley Mandel Morrow
Senior Author

| Jane M. Carr | Emily A. Faubion | Joanne M. McCarty |

| Margaret M. McCullough | Lisa P. Piccinino | Diane M. Richner | Patricia Scanlon |

| Monica T. Sicilia | Geraldine M. Timlin | Anne F. Windle |

Program Consultants

Grace R. Cavanagh, Ed.D.
Principal, P.S. 176
Board of Education
New York, New York

Ann S. Wright
Reading Consultant
Bridgeport Public Schools
Bridgeport, Connecticut

Maria T. Driend
Reading Consultant
Cooperative Educational Services
Trumbull, Connecticut

Eydee Schultz
Staff Development Specialist
Independent Consultant
Springfield, Illinois

Melanie R. Kuhn, Ph.D.
Assistant Professor of Literacy
Rutgers University
New Brunswick, New Jersey

Maggie Pagan, Ed.S.
College of Education, ESOL Specialist
University of Central Florida
Orlando, Florida

Eleanor M. Vargas, M.A.
Resource Specialist Teacher
Los Angeles Unified School District
Los Angeles, California

Frances E. Horton
Supervisor, Title I
Cabell County Public Schools
Huntington, West Virginia

Sharon L. Suskin, M.A.
Assessment Specialist
South Brunswick Public Schools
South Brunswick, New Jersey

Donna A. Shadle
Principal
St. Mary Elementary and Preschool
Massillon, Ohio

Helen Wood Turner, Ed.D.
Deputy Director of Education
Associates for Renewal in Education
Washington, D.C.

Deborah A. Scigliano, Ed.D.
First Grade Teacher
Assumption School
Pittsburgh, Pennsylvania

Sadlier-Oxford
A Division of William H. Sadlier, Inc.

Advisors

The publisher wishes to thank the following teachers and administrators who read portions of the series prior to publication for their comments and suggestions.

Margarite K. Beniaris
Assistant Principal
Chicago, Illinois

Jean Feldman
Consultant, NCEE
Brooklyn, New York

Mary Lee Gedwill
Second Grade Teacher
North Ridgeville, Ohio

Sr. Paul Mary Janssens, O.P.
Principal
Springfield, Illinois

Sr. Francis Helen Murphy, I.H.M.
Editorial Advisor
Philadelphia, Pennsylvania

Pedro Rodriguez
First Grade Teacher
Los Angeles, California

Kathleen Cleary
First Grade Teacher
Warminster, PA

Deborah Gangstad
First Grade Teacher
Carmel, Indiana

Ana Gomez
Second Grade Teacher
Kenner, Louisiana

Stephanie Wilson
Second Grade Teacher
Knightstown, Indiana

JoAnn C. Nurdjaja
Staff Developer
Brooklyn, New York

Dawn M. Trocchio
Kindergarten Teacher
Brooklyn, New York

Noelle Deinken
Kindergarten Teacher
Thousand Oaks, California

Angela Gaudioso
First Grade Teacher
Brooklyn, New York

Patricia McNamee
Principal
Orlando, Florida

Melissa Mannetta
First Grade Teacher
Brooklyn, New York

Mary Jo Pierantozzi
Educational Consultant
Philadelphia, Pennsylvania

Rosemarie Valente
Second Grade Teacher
Newark, New Jersey

Susan Dunlap
Second Grade Teacher
Noblesville, Indiana

Sr. Dawn Gear, G.N.S.H.
Principal
Atlanta, Georgia

Laura A. Holzheimer
L.A. Resource Teacher, Title I
Cleveland, Ohio

Adelaide Hanna
Reading Resource Teacher
Brooklyn, New York

Antoinette Plewa
Principal
North Plainfield, New Jersey

Earl T. Wiggins
Program Specialist, Title I
Lehigh, Florida

Acknowledgments

Special thanks to Sr. Irene Loretta, IHM, for her advice and counsel during the early developmental stages of the *Sadlier Phonics* program.

William H. Sadlier, Inc., gratefully acknowledges the following for the use of copyrighted materials:

"Good Books, Good Times!" (text only), copyright © 1985 by Lee Bennett Hopkins. Appears in GOOD BOOKS, GOOD TIMES!, published by HarperCollins Publishers. Reprinted by permission of Curtis Brown, Ltd.

"Parades" (text only) from MY DADDY IS A COOL DUDE AND OTHER POEMS by Karama Fufuka. Copyright © 1975 by Karama Fufuka. Used by permission of Dial Books for Young Readers, a division of Penguin Putnam Inc.

"Bugs" (text only) is from *The Fish with the Deep Sea Smile* by Margaret Wise Brown, © 1966 by Roberta Rauch. Reprinted by permission of Linnet Books/The Shoe String Press, Inc., North Haven, Connecticut.

"Yesterday's Paper" (text only) by Mabel Watts. Reprinted with permission of Patricia Watts Babcock, who controls all rights.

"Ears Hear" (text only) by Lucia and James Hymes, Jr., from OODLES OF NOODLES, © 1964 by Lucia and James Hymes, Jr. Reprinted by permission of Addison Wesley Longman.

"Clouds" (text only) by Christina G. Rossetti.

"Tommy" (text only) by Gwendolyn Brooks, copyright © 1956 by Gwendolyn Brooks Blakely. Used by permission of HarperCollins Publishers.

ZB Font Method Copyright © 1996 Zaner-Bloser

Product Development and Management

Leslie A. Baranowski

Dear Teacher,

Reading ability develops in an encouraging environment where language learning is meaningful and functional. As children grow in literacy, they become proficient at recognizing semantic, syntactic, and graphophonic cues and using them to extract meaning from printed text. We believe that phonics instruction is an integral part of the total reading process.

Sadlier Phonics reflects current approaches to literacy instruction and is built upon the following sound principles:

- Early and structured phonics instruction is fundamental to a complete and effective beginning reading program.

- Phonics skills are best learned through meaningful contextual lessons that feature quality literature.

- Students need ample opportunity to practice and apply letter-sound correspondences.

- The language arts (listening, speaking, reading, and writing) are interrelated and mutually supportive.

After giving much critical attention to the latest reading research and consulting with educators across the country, we are proud to present a balanced and integrated approach to phonics instruction. Children will delight in the literature-driven, theme-based lessons, which provide an exciting context for learning decoding skills.

We hope that you and your students enjoy *Sadlier Phonics* and that it helps you inspire a lifelong love of reading!

Sincerely,

Lesley M. Morrow

Lesley Mandel Morrow, Ph.D.

Contents

Phonemic Awareness and Auditory Discrimination

THEME: Book Buddies

Consonant Sounds

THEME: Celebrations

Consonant Blends ★5

THEME: Sensational Senses

Consonant Digraphs ★6

THEME: Rain or Shine

Word Structure ★7

THEME: All About Growing

Sadlier PHONICS Reading

A Research-Based Program

Over a decade ago, the Commission on Reading's report, *Becoming a Nation of Readers* (Anderson et al., 1985), presented research which established that children who are learning to read require not only concepts about the broader purposes of printed language but also the acquisition of specific skills required to recognize letters and words and to match letters to their sounds. The use of multiple strategies to meet the individual needs of children has been referred to as a "balanced approach to literacy instruction" (Morrow, 1997). One of the ways that teachers achieve balance is to "scaffold" instruction explicitly so that students become aware of and competent in the use of skills and strategies of effective readers (Vacca and Vacca, 1999).

Today, a growing body of research confirms that a comprehensive and balanced approach to reading instruction is in children's best interests. *Sadlier Phonics*, Levels K–C, comprises a research-based program for beginning reading instruction. Current research supports the theory that beginning readers need explicit instruction and practice which lead them to an understanding that spoken words are made up of smaller units of sounds; to familiarity with spelling-sound correspondences and common spelling conventions and their use in identifying printed words; to sight recognition of frequent words; and to independent reading, including reading aloud (Snow, Burns & Griffin, 1998). All of these objectives are met in *Sadlier Phonics.*

Program Goals

It is the goal of *Sadlier Phonics* to engage young children in rich literacy experiences so that every child is reading on grade level from the start. The program provides a solid foundation of word recognition and word study skills and strategies. Repeated practice enables children to gain automaticity as decoders, which allows for both fluency and comprehension of text. *Sadlier Phonics* focuses on the key components of effective, balanced literacy instruction:

- ▶ Phonemic Awareness
- ▶ Alphabetic Knowledge
- ▶ Explicit and Systematic Phonics Instruction
- ▶ Thematic Instruction and Integration of the Language Arts
- ▶ Oral Language and Vocabulary Development
- ▶ ELL/ESL Modified Instruction

- ▶ Sight Word Instruction
- ▶ Literature Activities
- ▶ Reading Comprehension
- ▶ Spelling Instruction
- ▶ Writing
- ▶ Assessment
- ▶ Early Intervention
- ▶ Family Literacy

Phonemic Awareness

The Research

Phonemic awareness has been described as "a foundational ability underlying the learning of spelling-sound correspondences" (Stanovich, 1993). The importance of phonemic awareness and its effects on beginning readers is supported by several decades of empirical research. Early studies indicate a strong relationship between a child's ability to read and the ability to segment words into phonemes (Liberman et al., 1974). Many subsequent studies have, in fact, confirmed that there is a strong relationship between reading ability and phonemic awareness. This relationship exists not only in the early grades (Perfetti et al., 1987) but also throughout the school years (Calfee, Lindamood & Lindamood, 1973). Juel (1988) discovered that when she tracked the development of 54 children from first through fourth grade, the poorest readers at the end of fourth grade were those who started first grade with little phonemic awareness.

Research findings have concluded that the level of phonemic awareness in children is an excellent indicator of children's success in learning to read, and a better indicator than tests of general intelligence, reading readiness, and listening comprehension (Stanovich, 1986). Share and Stanovich (1995) found phonemic awareness to be the most important core and causal factor separating normal from disabled readers. Blachman (1991) states, "Children who understand the segmental nature of speech, and who understand how the phonological segments are represented by the letters of an alphabetic writing system, have been shown repeatedly to be more successful in reading and spelling acquisition than children who lack this awareness." According to Yopp (1992), activities to foster the development of phonemic awareness should be included in prekindergarten, kindergarten, and first grade.

The phonemic awareness activities in Levels K and A of *Sadlier Phonics* are based on this research. Children are given many opportunities to "play with" and "manipulate" sounds in spoken words as they participate in a wide variety of phonemic awareness tasks, including the following:

- Activities that help children understand that spoken sentences are made up of groups of separate words, that words are made up of syllables, and that words can be broken down into separate sounds

- Activities that teach children to identify rhyming words and to produce their own rhymes

- Auditory tracking activities in which children separate or segment the sounds of words, blend sounds, delete sounds, and substitute new sounds for those that are deleted

- Activities in which children identify the initial, medial, and final sounds in words

- Activities in which children count syllables and individual phonemes in words

Phonemic awareness activities are included at the beginning of daily lesson plans and follow research-based practice (Simmons and Kameenui, 1998):

- Orally modeling phonemic awareness tasks followed by children's production of the task

- Making students' cognitive manipulations of sounds overt by using concrete representations (markers and pictures) or auditory cues that signal moving from one sound to the next

- Progressing from easier phonemic awareness activities to more difficult ones

- Focusing on the combination of blending and segmenting

- Starting with initial sounds first (<u>h</u>at); then final sounds (ha<u>t</u>); and last, medial sounds (h<u>a</u>t)

Alphabetic Knowledge

The Research

The ability to name letters is a predictor of early reading success (Chall, 1967; Torgesen, 1998). Adams's (1990) review of several studies concurs with this finding, and she states, "Familiarity of the letters of the alphabet and awareness of the speech sounds, or phonemes, to which they correspond are strong predictors of the ease or difficulty with which a child learns to read." In *Preventing Reading Difficulties in Young Children* (Snow, Burns & Griffin, 1998), the authors state: "Reading is typically acquired relatively predictably by children who are given information about the nature of print via opportunities to learn letters and to recognize the sublexical structure of spoken words, as well as about the contrasting nature of spoken and written language."

A prerequisite for learning sound-symbol associations is children's ability to recognize and identify letters. In light of this, the beginning levels of the *Sadlier Phonics* program (Levels PreK/K and K) focus on letter recognition. There are numerous activities for each letter of the alphabet to teach visual recognition of both the uppercase and lowercase forms of the letter, the letter name, and how the letter is written. Children then begin to associate each letter with the sound(s) it stands for through auditory, visual, tactile, and kinesthetic activities. *Punchout Letter Cards* (with raised letters) in the back of the Student Edition (Levels K and A) provide a manipulative component to the program—ideal for hands-on alphabet activities such as naming letters, matching partner letters, and tracing letter shapes.

Explicit and Systematic Phonics Instruction

The Research

Jeanne Chall was one of the pioneers of reading research. While working on *Learning to Read: The Great Debate* (1967), Chall interviewed experts, visited classrooms, and analyzed reading programs. Her findings substantiated consistent advantages for programs that included systematic phonics, as measured by outcomes on word recognition, vocabulary, spelling, and reading comprehension at least through third grade. In her comprehensive review of reading programs and of numerous studies, Adams (1990) concluded that ". . . programs including systematic instruction on letter-to-sound correspondences lead to higher achievement in both word recognition and spelling, at least in the early grades and especially for slower or economically disadvantaged students." The study by Foorman et al. (1998) of 375 mostly disadvantaged first graders in the Houston school district yielded results which indicate that students who are given explicit and sequenced phonics instruction learn more words and score higher on standardized tests than do students in other groups.

A recent survey published in *Reading Research Quarterly* (Baumann et al., 2000) reports that 63 percent of all kindergarten through fifth grade teachers surveyed selected the statement, "I believe that phonics needs to be taught directly to beginning readers in order for students to become fluent, skillful readers." The Executive Summary of *Every Child Reading: An Action Plan* (Learning First Alliance, 1998) urges educators, policy makers, and others to adopt practices that are consistent with the research calling for explicit, systematic instruction in phonemic awareness and phonics along with early and continued exposure to rich literature and writing opportunities.

Sadlier Phonics has been designed to address the research that calls for explicit and systematic phonics instruction. The lesson plans are presented with clear, explicit instruction, such as: "This is short **a**. Short **a** stands for /**a**/. **Apple** begins with short **a**."

This program is based on all of the characteristics of "systematic instruction" outlined below.

Systematic Instruction

A Multiple lessons are provided for essential skills. Lesson plans allow time to introduce, thoroughly practice, apply, and review skills before new concepts are taught.

B Content and strategies that are likely to be confused are separated. For example, easily confused letters/sounds, such as **p** and **b,** are not grouped together.

C The majority of lessons have a single skill focus—for example, the sound of short **a**. Units are sequenced so that sounds are first presented in isolation, then in the context of words, then in decodable and connected text.

D Pretests are available at the beginning of each unit to assess prior knowledge. Phonetic skills build upon what children have previously learned. For example, before children learn consonant blends, they have learned and mastered single consonant sounds and letter-sound correspondences.

E Frequent review in the Student Edition ensures student mastery of skills. Additional review activities at the beginning of every lesson plan under *Warming Up* promote skill retention.

F Instruction emphasizes a strong foundation in the areas of phonemic awareness and sound-symbol correspondences. Students can then integrate this alphabetic knowledge as they learn more complex skills, such as blends, digraphs, and **r**-controlled vowels.

G Children first read words in isolation, then in sentence context, and finally in paragraph context.

Based on compliance with the *Reading/Language Arts Framework for California Public Schools* (1999).

Thematic Instruction and Integration of the Language Arts

The Research

Current reading research supports the use of thematic instruction. In support of a balanced approach to literacy instruction, teachers teach literacy through the use of thematic units. Themes create a "context" for learning and, by their very nature, allow for curriculum integration. Themes create meaning for students by integrating the language arts and by combining literacy instruction with other content areas (Morrow, 1997). When reading, writing, and oral language are integrated around content themes, there is no longer an unnecessary dichotomy between learning to read and reading to learn. Instead, children "learn to read *as* they read to learn" (Vacca, Vacca & Gove, 2000).

With themes, children learn about their world by engaging in genuine projects that explore topics that interest and challenge them. They learn skills and strategies as they need them in their explorations of knowledge (Dewey, 1966). The integration and concurrent teaching of the language arts—reading, writing, listening, speaking, and viewing—enables one skill area to build upon another. When children read, it helps them to write and vice versa. Listening, speaking, and viewing also help improve both reading and writing skills (Morrow, 2001).

Sadlier Phonics is a thematically-based phonics program. The phonics skills and strategies in each unit are explicitly taught in the context of high-interest, motivating themes which integrate all of the language arts. A wide range of themes from "We Are Special!" to "Creepy, Crawly Bugs" to "Numbers Count!" are used to actively engage children in learning not only about letters and sounds but also about the world around them.

Each theme not only integrates phonics, reading, writing, listening, speaking, and viewing—but it also integrates other content areas, such as math, science, social studies, art, and music. Convenient two-page thematic lessons provide flexibility for teaching skills based on the needs of children.

Oral Language and Vocabulary Development

The Research

Oral language ability plays a crucial role in a child's success in reading (Petty, Petty & Salzer, 1989). Literacy development is enhanced by language competence, since the patterns of written language represent those in oral language (Goodman, 1967). That is, a child with strong oral language abilities is better able to anticipate and verify written words in context. Language acquisition is partially dependent on developmental maturity; however, we have also learned that children actively construct language (Sulzby, 1991). Children generate language when their beginning efforts are accepted and reinforced. Environments that provide adult models for good language are rich in opportunities to practice language and receive supportive feedback from responsive listeners, and so improve a child's production of language (Morrow, 2001).

Sadlier Phonics Reading

Sadlier Phonics recognizes the importance of developing children's oral language and increasing their vocabulary. *Time to Talk* pages that prompt conversation are a regular feature in the Level K Student Edition. *Critical Thinking* questions and open-ended questions posed on the *Look and Learn* pages at all levels engage children in such activities as orally answering questions, discussing ideas, and sharing personal experiences. On *Spell, Write, and Tell* pages in the upper levels, children participate in oral presentations of a piece of writing they have completed.

Throughout the entire program, children's vocabularies increase as they learn the names of pictured objects, sight words, spelling words, and new theme-related vocabulary words. Children use these words in class discussions, in projects, in home activities, and in their writing.

ELL/ESL Modified Instruction

The Research

When English is a second language for young children, a firm foundation in their first language will support academic achievement in the second language (Cummins, 1979). Children with English as a second language are more likely to learn to read and write English when they already have a solid background in the vocabulary and concepts of their primary language. They then need to be exposed to rich English language materials and models from teachers (Wong Fillmore, 1991). English language arts standards generally emphasize the importance of oral language development and require competence in oral language on their assessment measures.

Activities for English Language Learners/English as a Second Language (ELL/ESL), a regular feature of the lesson plans, help children attach meaning to unfamiliar vocabulary through the use of concrete objects, pictures, photographs, and gestures. Learning center activities also provide hands-on experiences to make learning concrete and interactive.

Sight Word Instruction

The Research

The Committee on the Prevention of Reading Difficulties in Young Children (Snow, Burns & Griffin, 1998) recommends attention in every primary grade classroom to the full array of early reading accomplishments, including reading sight words. A sight word is a word that is immediately recognized as a whole and does not require word analysis for identification (Harris and Hodges, 1995). Words such as *the*, *of*, and *to* are examples of high-frequency sight words. The Learning First Alliance (1998) states: "By second grade, children should be able to sound out short phonetically regular words, know many 'sight words,' and have good reading comprehension skills."

Sadlier Phonics student and teacher materials from kindergarten through second grade provide lessons that explicitly teach high-frequency words by using the sight word method of instruction. In keeping with recommended practices, **Sadlier Phonics** introduces only five or six words at one time. Attention is also given to make sure that words that look alike, such as **where** and **when**, do not appear in the same lesson. Children practice and study the high-frequency words, learning to recognize them by sight, first in isolation and then in the context of sentences, so that meaning is attached to the words.

The high-frequency words are also reinforced throughout the program as children encounter them in the Student Edition on *Look and Learn* pages, which are nonfiction passages, in *Decodable Readers*, and in *Take-Home Books*.

Reading Comprehension

The Research

According to Morrow, "Understanding what is read, or comprehending text, is one of the major goals for reading instruction." For children to receive the greatest benefit and enjoyment from their reading, they must receive comprehension strategy instruction that builds on their knowledge of the world and of language (Texas Education Agency, 1997). "Learning to read is not a linear process. Students do not need to learn to decode before they can learn to comprehend. Both skills should be taught at the same time from the earliest stages of reading instruction" (Learning First Alliance, 1998).

The *Report of the National Reading Panel* (National Institute of Child Health and Human Development, 2000) explains that the rationale for the explicit teaching of comprehension skills is that comprehension can be improved by teaching students to use specific cognitive strategies or to reason strategically when they encounter barriers to understanding what they are reading.

Throughout all levels of *Sadlier Phonics* there are opportunities to teach comprehension skills and strategies. Comprehension skills are taught using materials that are read aloud to students as well as materials children read independently. Reading passages such as the *Look and Learn* and *Read and Write* lessons help to develop comprehension skills as children find meaning in narrative and informational text. Questions pertaining to the text focus in on key comprehension skills such as comparing and contrasting, drawing conclusions, and understanding cause and effect. Sometimes children are asked to respond to comprehension questions orally, and other times children are asked to write their responses.

Decodable Readers in the Student Edition (Levels K and A) and Sadlier Reading *Little Books and Big Books* introduce grade-level comprehension skills in the context of short fiction and nonfiction stories. Skills progress in difficulty from one level to the next. For example, in Level K, skills such as sequencing, recalling details, and identifying the setting are taught. More advanced skills such as making inferences, distinguishing fact from opinion, and classifying information are taught in Levels A–C. As children learn, practice, and apply comprehension skills to reading experiences they become more strategic readers.

Spelling Instruction

The Research

Poorly developed spelling knowledge is shown to hinder children's writing, to disrupt their reading fluency, and to obstruct their vocabulary development (Adams, Treiman & Pressley, 1996). "The arguments for including spelling instruction as a major component of the reading and language program are strong. As learning about spelling serves to elaborate and reinforce knowledge in the Orthographic processor, it enhances reading proficiency" (Adams, 1990). Spelling instruction supports children in learning or confirming their knowledge about the sound structure of English. Children benefit from:

▶ spelling instruction of short, regular words.

▶ learning the spelling and the meanings of prefixes, suffixes, and word roots.

▶ learning about spelling patterns.

Programmatic instruction in correct spellings should begin in the first grade and continue across the school years. In second grade, such instruction should help children "transfer spelling patterns and word analysis strategies beyond the lesson, into their own reading and writing" (Snow, Burns & Griffin, 1998).

As recommended by research, formal spelling instruction in *Sadlier Phonics* begins in first grade. After short vowels have been introduced, each unit in the Student Edition contains a spelling lesson. Within these lessons, children learn how to spell words conventionally and how to attend to spelling patterns through sorting activities. Other lessons that involve word building exercises teach the spelling patterns of common short and long vowel phonograms.

The *Sadlier Phonics* Teacher's Editions feature a *Spelling Connection* in every regular phonics lesson. Words and sentences are suggested for dictation to provide additional spelling practice. Easy spelling patterns are introduced first, gradually building to more complex spelling patterns. Children are also asked to edit their work for correct spelling when they are publishing writing to share with others.

Writing

The Research

Research supports that writing is an important aspect of beginning literacy instruction. In fact, young children want to write and often write before they can read. Through samples of children's first attempts at writing, it is clear that they have an interest in writing, that they model writing behaviors of adults, and that their scribbles, drawings, random letters, and invented spelling are very early forms of writing (Clay, 1975). Many researchers now prefer to speak of reading and writing development as virtually one process. They view reading and writing as skills that build upon each other; when they are cultivated concurrently, each adds to proficiency in the other (Morrow, 2001).

According to Adams (1990), "It seems like a good idea to exercise children's ability to print individual letters from the start. This is not only because of its potential for enhancing individual letter recognition, but further, because it will allow them to write words as soon as they are intro- duced—and, as we shall see, writing seems a solidly productive activity for the young reader." The Committee on the Prevention of Reading Difficulties in Young Children (Snow, Burns & Griffin, 1998) recom- mends that once children learn to write letters, they should be encouraged to write them, to use them to begin writing words or parts of words, and to use words to begin writing sentences. According to Pearson et al. (1992), "Good [reading] instruction includes an environment conducive to learning where the useful- ness of reading is constantly seen. Students who daily interact with print, read what others have written, and write to others develop conceptual understand- ings about the value of reading."

PHONICS Reading

In the beginning levels of the *Sadlier Phonics* series, children are taught proper letter formation and are given many opportunities to trace, write, and copy all of the letters of the alphabet. These activities add to children's letter recognition facility. Instruction moves forward, as children begin to write words independently both in and out of context. The next step is for children to complete exercises by writing complete sentences—using both decoding and encoding skills. In second and third grade, children are asked to write paragraphs and short answer responses to reading passages, an activity that is excellent preparation for standardized tests. Writing activities at the end of each unit in the Student Edition engage children in many different forms of writing, such as letter writing, journal writing, descriptive writing, and so on. As children participate in these activities, they are led step-by-step through the writing process. These pieces of writing reflect children's knowledge of newly learned phonics skills and offer insight into their understanding of beginning print concepts.

Assessment

The Research

Monitoring learners' progress calls for a variety of assessment and evaluation strategies. Teachers must constantly use keen observation of student growth and development to inform instruction (Braunger and Lewis, 1997). Phonics instruction should be "extended to include understanding of sound/symbol correspondences for both spelling and reading. . . ." (Moats, 1995).

Every Child a Reader: The Report of the California Reading Task Force (1996a) recommends that schools provide teachers with a variety of assessment tools and strategies necessary to inform daily instruction. The following types of assessments are specifically recommended by the Task Force:

▶ screening assessments (e.g., for phonemic awareness)

▶ checklists

▶ running records

▶ scoring guides for writing

▶ individual and group-administered tests

▶ comprehensive assessments

▶ collections of student work or portfolios

Recently, the incorporation of student portfolios as a means of gathering and monitoring reading development has gained in favor as performance-based assessments have been developed. Portfolios offer ways to include multiple measures taken over time of an individual's reading performance (Braunger and Lewis, 1997).

Multiple assessment strategies and diagnostic tools are incorporated in the *Sadlier Phonics* program. The Student Edition contains written assessments, some of which are in standardized test formats. Frequent assessments appear throughout each unit; for example, there is an assessment for every short and long vowel sound in the first grade book (Level A), as well as an end-of-unit comprehensive assessment. A *Student Skills Assessment Checklist*, also in every Student Edition, enables teachers to check off the skills that students have mastered.

The Teacher's Editions provide many opportunities for both formal and informal assessment. There is a *Pretest/Posttest* at the beginning of every unit. This can be used to assess prior knowledge before instruction, or it can be used to assess skill mastery after instruction. In each unit, there is also a performance-based assessment. Strategies for informal observational assessments are called out in the lesson plans, and teachers are directed so that they know exactly what reading behaviors to observe. Beginning in first grade, dictation is used on a regular basis to assess students' knowledge of sound-symbol correspondences.

Phonemic awareness assessments, administered orally, are provided in kindergarten and first grade. These assessments are particularly important because of the strong indication that phonemically aware students become better readers.

At the beginning of the year, a portfolio should be set up for each child. Throughout the year, samples of each student's work are added to his or her portfolio. These samples are reviewed with both students and parents. Writing rubrics are also included in the Teacher's Editions as a gauge for evaluating growth in students' writing.

Early Intervention

The Research

An exciting finding of recent research is that reading failure is largely preventable. Effective prevention and early intervention programs can increase the reading skills of 85–90 percent of poor readers to average levels (Torgesen, 1998). Research (Snow, Burns & Griffin, 1998) suggests that a significant number of children labeled learning disabled or dyslexic could have become successful readers had they received systematic and explicit instruction and intervention far earlier in their educational careers.

Effective early intervention and prevention includes the direct teaching of critical literacy skills, such as phonemic awareness, letter recognition, oral language, and vocabulary development. These skills should be taught as early as preschool (Good, Simmons & Smith, 1998). *The Report of the California Reading Task Force* (1996a) suggests that providing help for the lowest-performing students can be done in several ways. According to the Task Force, examples of in-class interventions include:

▶ organizing one-on-one and small-group work by the teacher.

▶ collecting diagnostic information more frequently.

▶ providing guided reading instruction.

▶ enlisting extra help from instructional aides and cross-age tutors, parents, or community members.

The *Sadlier Phonics* program is designed to help all children learn how to read. As cited earlier, the instruction is based on explicit and systematic teaching. Skills such as phonemic awareness, letter recognition, oral language, and vocabulary development are directly and systematically taught. During the course of instruction, there are many opportunities to observe, assess, and record information related to children's progress so that if intervention is needed, it can be provided.

Many of the *Extra Support Activities* are small group activities and often involve more capable students helping less capable students. The majority of *Multisensory Activities* are ideal for a teacher working one-on-one with a student to reinforce or reteach a particular concept. The Sadlier Reading *Little Books and Big Books* provide opportunities for guided reading instruction, focusing on specific phonics skills. In addition, home involvement activities throughout every unit enlist the help of parents and family members.

When students need additional practice to master a skill, *Reteaching Activities* are suggested in the teaching plans. Additionally, a reference chart for *Guided Instruction* highlights all of the *Sadlier Phonics* resources available to teach each skill. This tool pinpoints instructional materials for teachers to use for children who have not met specific reading standards.

Family Literacy

The Research

Home–school connections are critical for children learning how to read. In general, parent involvement in education is directly related to significant increases in overall student achievement (Bloom, 1985). A review of 200 studies by White (1982) showed that beginning reading achievement can be attributed more directly to family characteristics, such as the availability of reading materials, home conversations, academic guidance, cultural activities, and attitudes toward education, than to socio-economic status.

Children's attitudes about literacy practices are developed at home. Parents, other family members, and caregivers play powerful roles both as models and sources of encouragement. Their involvement through their help, guidance, and modeling of literacy behaviors is an important component of successful literacy development (Morrow, 1995). Activities such as family story-book reading promote positive feelings about books and literacy (Taylor and Strickland, 1986). Parents want to be involved in the education of their children, and they want to be informed about what their children are doing and what they can do to help (Epstein, 1990).

Sadlier Phonics is designed to actively involve caregivers and parents in their children's literacy development. Each theme in the Student Edition begins with a full-page literacy letter that explains the phonics skills in the upcoming unit and includes a reading-at-home activity and family project. The directions on these pages appear in English and Spanish. The Sadlier-Oxford web site is referenced for on-line family literacy activities.

Additional on-the-page family literacy activities that reinforce the concepts being taught in the classroom appear throughout the Student Edition, and they are identified with the logo *Phonics Alive at Home*. These activities are practical, parent-friendly, and great extra practice for kids!

Colorful *Take-Home Books* appear in the back of the Student Edition and are designed to promote family literacy. The *Take-Home Books* help parents and caregivers help their children put phonics and decoding skills into practice while sitting together for a few minutes and enjoying a good story. Easy-to-follow directions guide parents through the use of the book as a learning tool and provide questions to develop children's comprehension skills.

One Final Note

As educators ourselves, we are aware of the importance of research-based practice in today's classrooms. The **Sadlier Phonics** program reflects the most current research available and supports balanced literacy instruction. We wish you success in helping each and every child become a proficient reader.

Lesley M. Morrow

Lesley Mandel Morrow

Richard T. Vacca

Richard T. Vacca

References

Adams, M. J. 1990. *Beginning to Read: Thinking and Learning About Print*. Cambridge, MA: MIT Press.

Adams, M. J., R. Treiman, and M. Pressley. 1996. "Reading, Writing, and Literacy." In *Handbook of Child Psychology*. Edited by I. Sigel and A. Renninger, vol. 4, Child Psychology in Practice. New York: Wiley.

Anderson, R., E. Hiebert, J. Scott, and I. Wilkinson. 1985. *Becoming a Nation of Readers: The Report of the Commission on Reading*. Washington, DC: National Institute of Education, U.S. Department of Education.

Baumann, J. F., J. V. Hoffman, A. M. Duffy-Hester, and J. M. Ro. 2000. "The First R Yesterday and Today: U.S. Elementary Reading Instruction Practices Reported by Teachers and Administrators." *Reading Research Quarterly* 35: 343–353.

Blachman, B. A. 1991. *Getting Ready to Read: Learning How Print Maps to Speech*. Timonium, MD: York Press.

Bloom, B. 1985. *Developing Talent in Young People*. New York: Ballantine Books.

Braunger, J. and J. P. Lewis. 1997. *Building a Knowledge Base in Reading*. Portland, OR: Northwest Regional Educational Laboratory's Curriculum and Instruction Services.

Calfee, R. C., P. Lindamood, and C. Lindamood. 1973. "Acoustic-Phonetic Skills and Reading: Kindergarten Through Twelfth Grade." *Journal of Educational Psychology* 64(3): 293–298.

California Department of Education. 1996a. *Every Child a Reader: The Report of the California Reading Task Force*. Sacramento, CA: California Department of Education.

———. 1996b. *Teaching Reading: A Balanced, Comprehensive Approach to Teaching Reading in Prekindergarten Through Grade Three*. Sacramento, CA: California Department of Education.

———. 1999. *Reading/Language Arts Framework for California Public Schools*. Sacramento, CA: California Department of Education.

Chall, J. S. 1967. *Learning to Read: The Great Debate*. New York: McGraw-Hill.

Clay, M. 1975. *What Did I Write?* Auckland, New Zealand: Heinemann.

Cummins, J. 1979. "Linguistic Interdependence and the Educational Development of Bilingual Children." *Review of Educational Research* 49: 222–251.

Dewey, J. 1966. *Democracy and Education*. New York: The Free Press.

Epstein, J. L. 1990. "School and Family Connections: Theory, Research, and Implications for Integrating Sociologies of Education and Family." In *Families in Community Settings: Interdisciplinary Perspectives*. Edited by D. G. Unger and M. B. Sussman. New York: Haworth.

Foorman, B., et al. 1998. "The Role of Instruction in Learning to Read: Preventing Reading Failure in At-risk Children." *Journal of Educational Psychology* 90(1): 37–55.

Good, R. H., D. C. Simmons, and S. B. Smith. 1998. "Effective Academic Interventions in the United States: Evaluating and Enhancing the Acquisition of Early Reading Skills." *School Psychology Review* 27(1): 45–56.

Goodman, K. S. 1967. "Reading: A Psycholinguistic Guessing Game." *Journal of the Reading Specialist* 4: 126–135.

Harris, T. L. and R. E. Hodges, eds. 1995. *The Literacy Dictionary*. Newark, DE: International Reading Association.

Juel, C. 1988. "Learning to Read and Write: A Longitudinal Study of 54 Children from First Through Fourth Grades." *Journal of Educational Psychology* 80(4): 437–447.

Learning First Alliance. 1998. *Every Child Reading: An Action Plan*. Washington, DC: Learning First Alliance.

Liberman, I. Y., D. Shankweiler, F. W. Fischer, and B. Carter. 1974. "Explicit Syllable and Phoneme Segmentation in the Young Child." *Journal of Experimental Child Psychology* 18: 201–212.

Moats, L. C. 1995. *Spelling: Development, Disabilities, and Instruction*. Baltimore: York Press.

Morrow, L. M. 1997. *The Literacy Center: Contexts for Reading and Writing*. York, ME: Stenhouse Publishers.

———. 2001. *Literacy Development in the Early Years: Helping Children Read and Write*. 4th ed. Needham Heights, MA: Allyn & Bacon.

Morrow, L. M., ed. 1995. *Family Literacy: Connections in School and Communities*. Newark, DE: International Reading Association.

Morrow, L. M. and D. Tracey. 1997. "Strategies Used for Phonics Instruction in Early Childhood Classrooms." *The Reading Teacher* 50: 644–653.

National Institute of Child Health and Human Development. 2000. *Report of the National Reading Panel: Teaching Children to Read and Evidence-Based Assessment of the Scientific Research and Literature on Reading and Its Implications for Reading Instruction*. Washington, DC: National Institute of Child Health and Human Development.

Pearson, D. P., L. R. Roehler, J. A. Dole, and G. G. Duffy. 1992. "Developing Expertise in Reading Comprehension." In *What Research Has to Say About Reading Instruction*. Edited by J. S. Samuels and A. E. Farstrup. Newark, DE: International Reading Association.

Perfetti, C. A., I. Beck, L. Bell, and C. Hughes. 1987. "Phonemic Knowledge and Learning to Read Are Reciprocal: A Longitudinal Study of First Grade Children." *Merrill-Palmer Quarterly* 33: 283–319.

Petty, W., D. Petty, and R. Salzer. 1989. *Experiences in Language*. 5th ed. Boston: Allyn & Bacon.

Rhodes, L. and C. Dudley-Marling. 1996. *Readers and Writers with a Difference: A Holistic Approach to Teaching Struggling Readers and Writers*. 2d ed. Portsmouth, NH: Heinemann Educational Books.

Samuels, S. J. and A. E. Farstrup, eds. 1992. *What Research Has to Say About Reading Instruction*. Newark, DE: International Reading Association.

Share, D. L. and K. E. Stanovich. 1995. "Cognitive Processes in Early Reading Development: Accommodating Individual Differences into a Model of Acquisition." *Issues in Education: Contributions from Educational Psychology* 1: 1–57.

Simmons, D. C. and E. J. Kameenui, eds. 1998. *What Reading Research Tells Us About Children with Diverse Learning Needs: Bases and Basics*. Mahwah, NJ: Lawrence Erlbaum Associates.

Snow, C. E., S. M. Burns, and P. Griffin, eds. 1998. *Preventing Reading Difficulties in Young Children*. Washington, DC: National Academy Press.

Stanovich, K. E. 1986. "Matthew Effects in Reading: Some Consequences of Individual Differences in the Acquisition of Literacy." *Reading Research Quarterly* 21: 360–407.

———. 1993. "Romance and Reality." *The Reading Teacher* 47: 28.

Sulzby, E. 1991. "Roles of Oral and Written Language as Children Approach Conventional Literacy." In *Early Text Construction in Children*. Edited by M. Orsolini and C. Pontecorvo. Rome: La Nuova Italia.

Taylor, D. and D. Strickland. 1986. *Family Storybook Reading*. Portsmouth, NH: Heinemann.

Texas Education Agency. 1997. *Beginning Reading Instruction: Components and Features of a Research-Based Reading Program*. Austin, TX: Texas Education Agency.

Tierney, R. J. and T. Shanahan. 1991. "Research on the Reading-Writing Relationship: Interactions, Transactions, and Outcomes." In *Handbook of Reading Research*. Edited by R. Barr, M. L. Kamil, P. Mosenthal, and P. D. Pearson, vol. 2. New York: Longman.

Torgesen, J. K. 1998. "Catch Them Before They Fall: Identification and Assessment to Prevent Reading Failure in Young Children." *American Educator* 22 (Spring/Summer): 32–39.

Tunmer, W. E. and A. R. Nesdale. 1985. "Phonemic Segmentation Skill and Building Reading." *Journal of Educational Psychology* 77: 417–427.

Vacca, J. L., R. T. Vacca, and M. K. Gove. 2000. *Reading and Learning to Read*. New York: Addison Wesley Longman.

Vacca, R. T. and J. L. Vacca. 1999. *Content Area Reading: Literacy and Learning Across the Curriculum*. New York: Addison Wesley Longman.

White, K. 1982. "The Relation Between Socioeconomic Status and Academic Achievement." *Psychology Bulletin* 91: 461–481.

Wong Fillmore, L. 1991. "When Learning a Second Language Means Losing the First." *Early Childhood Research Quarterly* 6: 323–346.

Yopp, H. 1992. "Developing Phonemic Awareness in Young Children." *The Reading Teacher* 45: 696–703.

Phonics Workshop

What Is Phonics?

In *Beginning to Read: Thinking and Learning About Print,* Marilyn Adams defines phonics as "a system of teaching reading that builds on the alphabetic principle, a system in which a central component is the teaching of correspondences between letters or groups of letters and their pronunciations." Explicit instruction in phonics helps children make the connection between words they hear and say and words they see in print.

Explicit and Systematic Phonics Instruction

Explicit Instruction Explicit instruction reflects the dynamic interaction between the teacher and the child. It requires demonstration, participation, practice, and performance. For example, explicit instruction focusing on the phoneme /**s**/, as in the word **sat,** may proceed as follows:

▶ Model saying /**s**/, and ask children to respond by producing the sound of **s** (/**s**/) in isolation.

▶ Encourage participation by telling children to say other words that begin with /**s**/, such as **sip**, **sit**, **see**, and **sad**.

To model blending phonemes into words:

▶ Say the initial phoneme /**s**/ and then, using a similar process, identify the other phonemes in **sat**: /**s**/-/**a**/-/**t**/.

▶ Model blending /**s**/-/**a**/-/**t**/ by holding each sound as you advance to the next sound—/**ssss**/-/**aaaa**/-/**tttt**/.

After demonstrating blending, have the whole group practice by repeating /**ssss**/-/**aaaa**/-/**tttt**/ together several times.

Systematic Instruction Systematic instruction refers to the way instruction is designed and delivered. Key elements of such instruction include progressing from easier, manageable contexts to more complex contexts; building on prior knowledge and frequently revisiting previously taught skills; and following a consistent sequence when developing skills. For example, in *Sadlier Phonics*, a given vowel sound is first presented in isolation, then in the context of words, and next in the context of a *Decodable Reader* and more complex sentences. Previously learned vowel sounds are incorporated toward the end of the sequence so that children learn to discriminate among vowel sounds as they decode words.

Phonemic and Phonological Awareness

How do Phonemic and Phonological Awareness Differ?
The understanding that speech is composed of a series of individual sounds is referred to as *phonemic awareness*. Children need practice hearing and producing the sounds that make up words before they can demonstrate *phonological awareness*, which is the ability to recognize how letters represent words in print.

Strategies for Phonemic Awareness
Phonemic awareness instruction should focus on the sounds in words. For example:

Begin with simple words with easily discriminated initial consonant sounds, such as /**f**/, /**h**/, /**l**/, /**r**/, /**s**/, and /**z**/.

Model producing a specific initial sound, such as /**r**/ as in **rug**.

Have children produce /**r**/ in isolation and then as the initial sound in words of their choice.

Model blending /**r**/ with the other sounds in the word **rug**: /**r**/-/**u**/-/**g**/.

Continue in the same fashion with final sounds.

Model dividing words such as **wagon** into syllables, clapping as you say each syllable. Emphasize and identify the initial sound at the beginning and end of each syllable. Then say other words, have children listen and clap for syllables, and identify the sound at the beginning and end of syllables.

Scope of Phonemic Awareness Skills
Sadlier Phonics presents a comprehensive repertoire of phonemic awareness skills in an explicit, systematic fashion. The scope of the phonemic awareness skills developed in this program are listed below.

▸ Identify and produce rhyming words, and distinguish rhyming from nonrhyming words

▸ Alliteration and nonsense/word play
▸ Match words
▸ Divide sentences into words, and count words in a spoken sentence
▸ Identify and count syllables
▸ Divide words into syllables, and combine syllables to form words
▸ Segment and blend onsets and rimes
▸ Match initial, medial, and final sounds
▸ Identify and isolate initial, medial, and final sounds
▸ Segment initial sounds
▸ Add and delete initial sounds
▸ Substitute initial, medial, and final sounds
▸ Segment and count phonemes in a word
▸ Blend phonemes in a word

Supporting Phonological Awareness
Phonological awareness is the natural extension of phonemic awareness. A beginning reader who has developed strong listening discrimination skills can transfer these skills to recognizing and making sound-to-symbol connections. *Sadlier Phonics* concentrates on only a few letter-sound correspondences at a time, beginning first with those correspondences that have high utility in many words. Following are some strategies you can use to support children as they develop the skill of decoding written words.

As you work with children, constantly reinforce that the name of a letter does not represent the sound the letter stands for.

As you observe children's reading, remind them of letter-sound correspondences they know. Use the letter and the sound it represents to model for children how to sound out a word by blending sounds.

Model for children how you use phonograms and initial sound substitution to sound out words.

Integrating Phonics and Language Arts

Sadlier Phonics recognizes that listening, speaking, reading, and writing are interrelated and mutually supportive. The program provides explicit phonics instruction within an integrated language approach so that children apply phonics skills and strategies to listening, speaking, reading, spelling, and writing activities. These authentic experiences emphasize the importance of what children are learning and make lessons relevant and sensible.

Such integration is most evident in the *Spell, Write, and Tell* lessons in the Student Edition and in the *Integrating the Language Arts* teaching plans that accompany the *Look and Learn* lesson at the end of each unit in the Student Edition. Above all, the consistent interweaving of phonics and language arts permeates the entire program.

Listening Not only are listening activities used to introduce each unit and each skill sequence within a unit, but they are also a regular feature in the teaching plans (e.g., in the *Phonemic Awareness* and *Multisensory Activities* that accompany most lessons).

Speaking Speaking activities are provided through the *Critical Thinking* questions in the student lessons. In addition, many *Theme Activities* in the teaching plans require children to present their work orally.

Writing Writing is an integral part of most student lessons, with the exception of *Phonemic Awareness* lessons. Through writing, children master the letters of the alphabet and make a symbol-to-sound connection as a precursor to reading and spelling. Writing activities are also prominent in the Teacher's Edition, especially in the *Theme Activities* that accompany most lessons and in the *Writing Process* features that appear in the teaching plan for *Spell, Write, and Tell* lessons.

Spelling Spelling is a logical extension of phonics and is supported through activities such as starting with the phonogram **at** and adding the initial consonants **b**, **m**, **p**, and **s** to form **bat**, **mat**, **pat**, and **sat**. Spelling is reinforced through the *Spelling Connection* that appears in the teaching plans in Levels A–C.

Reading Reading independently is the goal of mastering decoding. Opportunities to read independently are provided through in-text features such as *Decodable Readers* and *Take-Home Books*. In addition, **Sadlier Reading** *Little Books and Big Books* are available to reinforce phonics and comprehension skills.

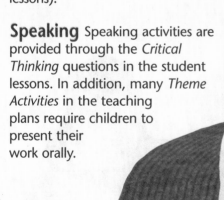

Designing a Print-Rich Environment

Children come to school with different experiences with and attitudes toward reading and print materials in general. They have varying degrees of awareness of books, magazines, newspapers, and other print materials typically found in environments outside the school. For example, some children are acutely aware of street signs, advertising posters, and other print, while others notice these things only in passing.

Regardless of children's prior experiences, you can build excitement about reading by creating a classroom rich in print and language. In such an atmosphere, children will start to understand beginning print concepts, develop phonological awareness, explore and play with language, and begin to use writing to communicate their thoughts and ideas.

Using Print Resources in the Classroom

Take a look around your classroom. Are there opportunities for children to interact constantly with print? Do children understand the significance of the print resources in the classroom? The following ideas will help children understand the significance of print in their environment and become comfortable with it in its various forms as they attempt beginning reading activities.

Begin a **class roster** during the first week of school. Have children bring in a photograph of themselves. Attach the pictures to tagboard, and write each child's name below his or her picture. Encourage children to copy their names on papers, in personal writing, on dictation worksheets, and in other materials that they use.

A **calendar** can be used to direct children's attention to temporal concepts related to print. Use a class calendar to identify the day of the week; to symbolically represent the day's weather; and to look ahead and note children's birthdays, holidays, and school events.

To introduce **schedules**, explain that a schedule can provide details about a day's activities. Write a daily schedule on the board, and read the schedule aloud. As the class completes each activity, reread the activity name aloud and check it off. Encourage children to remind you to check off completed activities. At the end of each day, return to the schedule and confirm with children that the day's plans were fulfilled.

As appropriate, display the theme-related **classroom posters**. When children have free time, read the poetry aloud to them. Track the print as you read, pointing out the left-to-right, top-to-bottom movement as well as the space between words. Encourage children to track on their own and to point out words that they recognize.

Use **signs and labels** in the classroom. Label objects, such as the pencil sharpener and the supply closet. As you use these objects or places, call attention to the labels.

Alphabet strips, **experience charts**, **message boards**, **word charts**, **maps**, and other resources that you choose to display will all contribute to children's awareness of the world of print that surrounds them both inside and outside of the classroom.

Learning Centers

An environment that fosters literacy includes Learning Centers that focus on reading, writing, listening, and language.

Organizing and Managing a Center

Learning Centers should be self-contained areas within the classroom where children can work independently or in structured groups. Such centers should be welcoming places where children can spend time comfortably and productively. To this end, you may wish to consider the following suggestions.

▶ Use carpet remnants and bookcases as dividers to clearly define each center's space. Equip centers with containers for storing materials, as well as bulletin boards for displaying the center's activities and children's work.

▶ Acquaint children with the resources in a center and in how to use them (e.g., tape recorders, computers). Model the activities in a center.

▶ Establish routines for the use of the center, and make sure children clearly understand these routines. For example, you may want to encourage children to use the center when they arrive in the morning before class begins; when they have free time after completing their work; and/or at a designated time when they can use the resources of a center of their choosing.

▶ Establish rules that might include how many children may be in the center at one time, how to use the materials, how to work and learn cooperatively, and how to clean up, keeping the center neat. Draw pictures to represent the rules, and post them for children's reference.

▶ Develop mechanisms to structure children's use of each center. Provide sign-in sheets. Develop task cards to focus children on activities, and provide logs in which children can report the work they completed.

Reading Center To nurture independent reading, set up a Reading Center that includes a wide variety of printed materials, such as books written at various reading levels, theme-related books, magazines, newspapers, plays, poetry, student-made books, and class stories. Books may be brought from children's homes, borrowed from the school or local library, or donated by parent groups. Add to and change the selection regularly.

Writing Center A Writing Center should encourage experimentation with the written word and provide opportunities for creative expression and personal communication. In setting up a Writing Center, include the following: different kinds of paper (lined and unlined, note pads, index cards, self-stick notes, stationery, construction paper), office supplies (paper clips, stapler, scissors, hole punch), pencils, pens, crayons, markers, rubber letter stamps, washable ink pads, dictionaries, a telephone book and class directory, writing journals, computers and typewriters, writing portfolios.

Listening and Language Center

To encourage verbal interaction, set up an area where children can share experiences and discuss their reading. The center should include:

▶ a tape recorder.

▶ a video recorder, if possible.

▶ blank tapes for children to record their own stories or their reading of class books.

▶ a collection of songs, stories, and poems on audio- and/or videotape.

Curriculum Integration

Sadlier Phonics provides teachers with meaningful activities for total curriculum integration.

Why Should You Integrate Phonics With Other Subject Areas?
Curriculum integration offers a balanced approach to learning that:

▶ enables children to make relevant connections to life. For example, in applying their newly acquired phonics skills to making "Save Earth" posters, children learn the importance of protecting the environment.

▶ promotes the transfer of knowledge from one subject area to other subject areas.

▶ provides for multiple intelligences by tapping into different ways of learning: kinesthetic, tactile, spatial, visual, and auditory.

▶ reinforces skills through contextual experiences.

What Curriculum Connections Can Be Made With Phonics?
Phonics is part of a total language arts program. In support of that approach, the *Sadlier Phonics* Teacher's Edition contains lesson plans with an abundance of activities that foster critical thinking and the development of oral language as listening, speaking, reading, writing, and spelling skills are enhanced. Suggested science, social studies, math, health, music, and art-related activities incorporate the relevant phonics skills and give children immediate opportunities to apply their newly learned skills.

How Is Phonics Integrated With Other Curriculum Areas?
To see how practical and enjoyable *Sadlier Phonics* makes the process of integration of curricula, look at this typical second-grade unit. The "Numbers Count!" unit begins with a fun poem. The lesson plans contain many references to trade books, songs, and purposeful writing activities. In addition, of course, a unit on numbers ties in naturally with grade-level-appropriate math concepts. While studying the inflectional endings **ed** and **ing**, second-grade children learn about time by making paper-plate clocks and by reading books such as *The Cuckoo-Clock Cuckoo* and *Around the Clock with Harriet.* In addition, children pattern their writing after a well-known author.

Thematic Instruction

Thematic instruction provides a framework and context for learning. Morrow writes both that "literacy instruction should be meaningful and taught in combination with other content areas" and that "themes create meaning for students by integrating the language arts" (Morrow, 1997). Although the main purpose of a theme is to develop and focus children's ability to read and write, the theme may also naturally encourage the easy integration of other curricula, such as science, social studies, music, math, art, and health.

Every *Sadlier Phonics* Student Edition is organized around topical themes. An engaging piece of poetry introduces each theme and presents each unit's phonics skills in context. The theme continues throughout a unit's lessons, which utilize original rhymes and/or stories, captivating artwork, and colorful photos. Each unit concludes with a theme-related photo-essay.

The time you spend on any given theme will vary, based on the expected learner outcomes. Establish a comfortable pace for you and your children, allowing time to capitalize on their particular interests and enthusiasm for the specific topic.

You may want to develop a wall chart of "theme words." Write the theme topic on a sheet of chart paper, and post it on a wall in your classroom. Have children add words to the chart throughout the unit. The chart can serve as a reference for spelling and writing activities.

The *Sadlier Phonics* Teacher's Edition provides many suggestions for theme activities. Look under *Curriculum Connections* in each lesson plan for hands-on learning activities that are related to the unit theme.

Assessment

Sadlier
PHONICS
Reading

Assessment is a continuing process that helps monitor and evaluate children's progress. To help you successfully assess students, each unit in *Sadlier Phonics* Teacher's Edition contains a section that offers multiple strategies for assessment, including blackline masters.

Suggestions for different methods of evaluation are discussed under these headings:

Pretests/Posttests These tests may be used in several ways: as a pretest to identify a starting point for individual or class instruction, as a formal end-of-unit assessment of children's mastery of the unit's content, or as a combination pretest/posttest to help you identify an appropriate starting point and to provide a basis for comparing children's mastery of the units to that starting point.

Phonemic Awareness Each pre-unit section in the Teacher's Edition contains a *Phonemic Awareness Assessment* that is to be administered orally to one child at a time. This offers you an opportunity to assess each child's phonemic awareness skills, identify problem areas, and remediate as needed.

Observational Student performance in the classroom should be observed and recorded frequently. Try to set aside five to fifteen minutes a day to observe two or three children so that you observe each child every two to three weeks. Specific instances for doing so are highlighted in the lesson plans.

Performance Classroom-based projects and activities allow you to evaluate listening skills, comprehension, and visual recognition, as well as whether children have correctly assimilated specific phonics skills. Suggestions for such activities can be found on the *Assessment* page in each pre-unit section of the Teacher's Edition.

Check-Up These assessment pages help you ascertain whether children have mastered the skills taught. If you determine that certain children need more instruction, you can use the *Reteaching Activities* in the Teacher's Edition notes. In addition, you can use the *Guided Instruction* chart in the teaching notes to identify various program resources that can help children experiencing difficulty.

Check-Up pages occur in the Student Edition at the end of each unit; in longer units, they also appear at the end of a skills sequence (e.g., at the end of each section on a given vowel in short and long vowel units, often in conjunction with a *Remember* page that serves as a review/maintenance feature).

Portfolio Icons appear in the lesson plans in the Teacher's Edition to indicate portfolio opportunities. Children keep a portfolio of drawings, writing, and other work samples that demonstrate their emergent reading and writing skills, how these skills have improved, and where children may still be experiencing difficulty. You may want each child to keep two portfolios:

A Working Portfolio would contain work-in-progress (such as graded papers, homework, projects) and should be arranged in chronological order so that the child can trace his/her growth over time.

An Assessment Portfolio would contain material selected by the child from his/her Working Portfolio to represent that child's best work. You might want to allow each child to make and attach revisions to his/her work before including the selections in the Assessment Portfolio.

Encourage self-evaluation as children progress through a unit. Explain at the beginning of the year that you will schedule individual conferences periodically to review children's work. Make sure children are aware of and understand the criteria you will apply in your evaluations. The *Assessment* page in each pre-unit section of the Teacher's Edition contains rubrics you can use to evaluate children's work.

Dictation Activities are provided in the Teacher's Edition notes that accompany each Student Edition *Check-Up,* as well as on pre-unit assessment pages. These exercises give you an opportunity to assess how well individual children can apply the phonics skills they have learned as they translate the sounds (phonemes) they hear into letters, correctly spelled words, and, eventually, complete sentences.

Technology *Technology Activities* in each pre-unit section of the Teacher's Edition provide yet another way to monitor student progress.

Family Literacy

Many parents and caretakers may want to help their children become successful readers but may not know *how* to do so. At your first school open house or teacher-parent conferences, explain the reading methods used in your classroom. Share the suggestions below with parents and caretakers. If they frequently visit your classroom, post the suggestions on a special bulletin board as reminders.

Story Time Read to your child every day! Make it a relaxed time. Bedtime is often a good time to share a favorite story or a brand-new one.

Talk it Over As you read, pause frequently to discuss the illustrations and progress of the story. When you finish a book, ask your child to summarize it or tell about his or her favorite part.

Try it Together As your child's reading skills develop, make time to read aloud together. Track the words with your finger, pausing occasionally to allow your child to read to you.

Library Time Help your child obtain a library card. Visit your local library often and allow your new cardholder to choose his or her books.

A Book of My Own Books make wonderful gifts! You might arrange times when your child can choose and purchase a book for a special occasion or as a special reward.

Review School Work Reading over phonics worksheets with your child helps reinforce what he or she has learned and provides opportunities for the child to show off knowledge. Treat errors as opportunities to teach.

Be a Role Model Make sure your child sees you reading something every day.

Bring It Home Help your child see how learning to read affects life outside of school. You might start by making your child aware of directions for playing a game or preparing a packaged food, of signs on stores and roads, and of names of items on your shopping list.

Sadlier Phonics provides a convenient take-home letter at the beginning of each unit in the Student Edition. The instructions—in English and Spanish—explain the unit skills and suggest some easy-to-do activities that will help phonics come alive at home.

Technology

Sadlier Phonics integrates technology activities in its comprehensive approach to teaching phonics. Each pre-unit section in the Teacher's Edition contains a two-page *Technology* section. *Computer Connection Activities,* which link the skills being taught with computer use, are interspersed throughout the lessons in the Teacher's Edition.

Sadlier Phonics leads you step-by-step through activities that focus on using and working with language in a variety of contexts. Through activities that involve producing audio and video files, accessing information on the Internet, and sending letters to pen pals via e-mail, students actively practice phonics skills while developing computer literacy.

Recognizing that each classroom is configured differently, *Sadlier Phonics* provides teachers with flexibility when using the material. Thus, if the number of computers in your classroom or lab is limited, all children can still participate in the

activities. Your knowledge of children's individual learning styles will help you decide whether an activity should involve children working in a small group, as partners, or working alone.

Technology can also connect school and home and help families become more involved with their children's learning. You may photocopy the *Technology* pages so that children can work on them on their home computers. In addition, each *Phonics Alive at Home* page is an opportunity for children and parents to access the Sadlier-Oxford web site for phonics activities that provide more practice or that extend the application of children's new skills.

To fully access the potential of the powerful learning tool that technology has become, you must integrate its use into the curriculum. *Sadlier Phonics* provides experiences that help guide children to the rich learning opportunities of the Internet.

ESL/ELL Students

Children who come from homes where English is spoken as a second language—or not spoken at all—face many challenges in our classrooms. In order to meet the needs of English-language learners, it is necessary to understand the five stages of second-language acquisition.

Stage 1	Pre-Production
Stage 2	Early Production
Stage 3	Speech Emergence
Stage 4	Intermediate Fluency
Stage 5	Advanced Fluency

Each of the five second-language acquisition stages can occur at different times for different children; therefore, you must select teaching strategies and materials to meet the needs of each child, depending upon his/her stage of English-language development. In the early stages of second-language acquisition, the use of total physical response strategies and of realia are key to helping children bridge the gap between their native tongues and English.

Pre-Production This stage applies to those who are totally new to the second language—in this case, English. Children at this level are nearly—if not totally—silent. They acquire language skills at the receptive level, a so-called "silent period." Shared reading activities are appropriate for this level because they do not require children to participate until they are ready.

Early Production After children have a reasonable opportunity to receive meaningful and understandable messages in English, they will begin to respond with one- or two-word answers or short utterances. Keep in mind that these children are experimenting and taking risks with the new language. Errors in grammar and pronunciation are to be expected.

Speech Emergence Learners at this level of proficiency begin to use the new language to communicate among themselves. Provide opportunities for these learners to work in small groups. Assessment includes teacher observation and frequent oral comprehension checks.

Intermediate Fluency Intermediate-level students may demonstrate near or actual native-like fluency in social settings; however, academic language is still limited. You can focus on continuing to build the vocabulary that these students understand as well as on developing higher levels of language use.

Advanced Fluency Once English-language learners reach this proficiency level, they comprehend and speak English almost as well as native English speakers. Continue to build literacy skills, to focus on improving vocabulary, and to develop higher levels of language use.

The *English Language Learners/ESL Activities* in the *Sadlier Phonics* Teacher's Edition have been designed with these five stages of second-language acquisition in mind. The goal is to help children develop both their receptive (listening, reading) and expressive (speaking, writing) abilities.

Universal Access

Sadlier Phonics offers lesson-specific methods for teaching struggling children, for those whose native language is not English, and for those who demonstrate advanced ability. *Extra Support* and *Challenge* activities and activities specially designed for English-language learners are provided in the Teacher's Edition lesson plans.

Children struggling because of learning deficits or attention deficit disorder may be harder to identify. The following is a list of behaviors to help you identify these children; the *Universal Access* pages in the pre-unit sections of the Teacher's Edition offer strategies to assist such children.

Visual/Perceptual Deficits
▶ Reversals—confuses **b** with **d**; **p** with **q**
▶ Inversions—confuses **u** with **n**; **w** with **m**
▶ Difficulty copying letters and words accurately
▶ Frequently loses place while reading
▶ Rereads or skips lines without noticing repetition or loss of an idea
▶ Experiences letter-sequencing problems (e.g., identifies **saw** as **was**; **on** as **no**)
▶ Cannot identify the main idea of a picture, and often focuses on minute details

Visual/Perceptual/Motor Deficits
▶ No space between letters or words
▶ Difficulty reading and writing similar letters, such as **b**, **p**, and **d**
▶ Letters are not written on the line but are written above or under lines, or in an uneven fashion
▶ Cannot color within lines
▶ Cannot cut or paste

Auditory Discrimination or Speech Disorders
▶ Is not able to hear or produce differences in sounds: short **i**, **e**; plosive sounds **b**, **p**, **d**, **t**, **c**, **g**, **j**, **n**, **m**; consonant digraphs **th**, **sh**, **wh**, **ch**, **kn**
▶ Difficulty identifying or producing rhyming sounds

Spatial Discrimination Deficits
▶ Has difficulty discerning the relationship between letters that form words and words that form sentences

Visual/Perceptual Memory Deficits
▶ Poor sight vocabulary
▶ Few words known at the immediate, automatic level
▶ Slow to memorize rhymes/poems
▶ Reverses letters in vowel pairs such as **oa**, **ie**, **ea**, **ui**, and **ai**
▶ Appears to know something one day, but does not know it the next

Although all children may occasionally exhibit the traits listed below, those with attention-deficit disorder (ADD) will most likely demonstrate these behaviors with greater frequency. For these children, the earlier a problem is detected and appropriate intervention given, the better the outcome will be.

Attention-Deficit Disorder
▶ Inability to sit or stand still or to follow directions for any period of time
▶ Often unable to stay on task or finish assignments in allotted time
▶ Short attention span
▶ Overreaction to stimuli; visually and auditorially easily distractable

Patty and Pop's Picnic
By Susan McCloskey   Illustrated by S. B. Sams

arly reading failure can be a powerful force in shaping children's images of themselves. The relationship between reading skills and success in all subject areas is a compelling reason for timely intervention.

At the beginning of each unit of *Sadlier Phonics* Teacher's Edition, there is a section specifically devoted to diagnosing common errors and suggesting strategies for intervention. The following describes an intervention procedure for students experiencing difficulty with phonemic awareness; however, the steps described are useful for intervention in all areas of phonics instruction.

Determine When to Intervene
When children are introduced to a new concept, they must demonstrate understanding of that concept before moving on to the next step. For example, targeted intervention at the phonemic awareness stage is often the most beneficial. Children who cannot identify the initial sound of a word in an oral activity most likely will also not be able to make the connection between that sound and its alphabetic representation. Children who demonstrate weak phonemic awareness skills need extra instructional emphasis on sound awareness *before* moving on to sound-to-symbol correspondence.

Target Students for Intervention
Your class is composed of children who have strong phonological skills as well as those who demonstrate weakness in specific areas. Activities

that are playful in nature can help you identify children who may be experiencing difficulty. Such activities do not single children out to the rest of the class, but they do provide you with an opportunity for informal evaluation. For example, when teaching identification of initial /**m**/:

▶ Model the sound /**m**/. Tell children that /**m**/ is the sound they hear at the beginning of the word **man**. Have the class produce /**m**/.

▶ In a game-like setting, have children individually produce words that begin with /**m**/. For example, you can use a circle game such as "I'm going to the **movies** and I will bring **money**." Have children repeat the sentence and add an initial **m** word to the list.

▶ Children who use words that begin with a sound other than /**m**/ can be targeted for intervention.

Use Intervention Strategies
Intervention strategies such as those below are recommended on the *Intervention* page in each pre-unit section in the Teacher's Edition.

▶ Have partners work to "read the room" or point to and say the names of objects or classmates that begin with /**m**/.

▶ Throughout the day, continue with playful activities, emphasizing a particular sound.

▶ If necessary, work individually with children. Demonstrate how it "feels" to make a sound, and use a mirror to show what a sound "looks like."

▶ Assign children to name items at home that begin with /**m**/. Have them draw pictures of some of these items; encourage them to bring the pictures to class to start an /**m**/ book.

▶ If possible, have children choose an initial /**m**/ item to bring to class for show and tell.

References
Adams, M. J. 1990. *Beginning to Read: Thinking and Learning About Print.* Cambridge, MA: MIT Press.

Morrow, L. M. 1997. *The Literacy Center: Contexts for Reading and Writing.* York, ME: Stenhouse Publishers.

PAIL

PIGGY BANK

PENCIL

Book Buddies
Good books make good friends.

Phonemic Awareness and Auditory Discrimination

READING/LANGUAGE ARTS STANDARDS

✪ Respond to a poem in a way that reflects understanding

✪ Identify rhyming words in response to an oral prompt

✪ Recognize beginning consonant sounds

OBJECTIVES

▶ To enjoy a poem about books

▶ To develop phonemic awareness by identifying, and manipulating sounds in spoken words

▶ To discriminate between words that do and do not rhyme with a given word

▶ To identify words whose beginning sounds are the same

LESSONS

Lesson 1 . . . . Phonemic Awareness and Auditory Discrimination

Lesson 2 . . . . Discriminating Rhyming Sounds

Lesson 3 . . . . Discriminating Initial Sounds

Lesson 4 . . . . Integrating the Language Arts

• Take-Home Book: *Good Books*

Thematic Teaching

In Unit 1 children make letter-sound associations by discriminating among initial consonant and rhyming sounds. The poem "Good Books, Good Times!" by Lee Bennett Hopkins reinforces the joyful experience of books and sets the tone for motivating children to become lifelong readers.

Stock your classroom library with plenty of colorful and inviting picture books. You might display the "Good Books, Good Times!" **Classroom Poster** near the library and refer to the poster throughout the unit as children choose and explore different kinds of books.

Curriculum Integration

Language Arts
Children make rhyming-word scrolls on page 8 and "same sound" drawings on page 10.

Writing On page 11 children discuss books and the kinds of stories they tell as a first step toward considering topics for their own writing.

Visit us at
www.sadlier-oxford.com
Internet

Optional Learning Activities

Multisensory Activities
Multisensory activities are a regular feature of the phonics lessons and are designed to appeal to all learning styles—visual, tactile, auditory, and kinesthetic.

Multicultural Connection
Children explore books from different cultures on page 6. On page 8 they learn about ancient Egyptian scrolls and then make their own scrolls.

Learning Centers
Children are introduced to a Reading and a Language Art Center on pages 6 and 8.

Thematic Activities
Watch for exciting thematic activities in the Curriculum Connection section of most lesson plans.

Author's Corner

Lee Bennett Hopkins
Lee Bennett Hopkins grew up poor, but he didn't know it. As a "city kid," he enjoyed playing in front of open fire hydrants on hot days. A favorite teacher taught Hopkins to love reading and theater. When he became a teacher himself, Hopkins found out that he loved poetry, too. Now he's best known for writing and collecting poems.

✓ Assessment Strategies

Assessment is an ongoing process. Multiple strategies in the Student Edition as well as the Teacher's Edition and regular use of Skills Assessment in the back of the Student Edition will help you monitor children's progress in discriminating rhyming and initial sounds.

UNIT RESOURCES

Sadlier Reading

Classroom Poster

Little Books and Big Books

Phonics Picture Cards

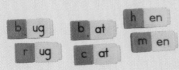

Student Manipulatives

Poetry Anthologies Selected by Lee Bennett Hopkins

Side by Side: Poems to Read Together. New York: Simon & Schuster Books for Young Readers, 1988.

Surprises. New York: Harper & Row, 1984.

Theme-Related Resources

Bunting, Eve. *The Wednesday Surprise.* Boston: Houghton Mifflin, 1991. Grandma and Anna read together every night, but who is teaching whom?

Hopkins, Lee Bennett, ed. *Good Books, Good Times!* New York: HarperCollins Children's Books, 1990. Children enjoy book adventures with some of their favorite poets.

Seuss, Dr. *Dr. Seuss's ABC.* New York: Random House Home Video, 1989. Children see how letters and sounds work together to form words.

In Unit 1 children focus on recognizing rhyming words and initial consonant sounds. Consider the suggestions on this page for assessment ideas.

Pretests/Posttests

The tests on pages 5D–5E serve as a formal end-of-unit assessment of children's mastery of rhyming and initial consonant sounds. You may choose to use them as pretests to help identify a starting point for instruction for individual children. The **Phonemic Awareness Test** on page 5J also serves as a good pretest for all children.

Observational Assessment

Specific opportunities to observe children's progress with rhyming and with initial consonant sounds are highlighted in the lesson plans. The *Student Skills Assessment Checklist* on pages 321–322 of the Student Edition will help you keep track of students' progress.

Using Technology

The activities presented on pages 5O–5P may also be used to evaluate children's progress.

Performance Assessment

Set up a station in the Art Center for children to construct a rhyming book. Show children how to put pages together to make a book. Provide magazines, drawing paper, and other art supplies. Tell children to find pictures of words that rhyme, such as **suit** and **fruit**, and **toys** and **boys**, and paste them on the drawing paper. Have children say the rhyming words. Observe whether children identify correctly words that rhyme. Display the picture books around the classroom.

Portfolio Assessment

The portfolio icon in the lesson plans indicates portfolio opportunities throughout the unit. Tell children that throughout the year they will be collecting their work in their portfolios. They will review that work periodically with you so that together you may evaluate progress and determine in what areas they need to do more work.

In Unit 1 the primary focus is on auditory discrimination. The rubrics suggested below reflect that focus. Explain to children that their work in this unit will be evaluated according to rubrics. Post the rubrics on a chart at the beginning of the unit, and review the criteria with children.

Name _____

Rubrics	Sometimes	Never	Always
Identifies rhyming words			
Identifies words that begin with like sounds			
Uses pictures to convey meaning			

Answer Key

Page 5D	Page 5E
1. hen	1. net, nail
2. well	2. door, doll
3. bug	3. rope, robot
4. boat	4. cane, cage
5. snail	5. wing, wagon

Name the first picture in each row. Then fill in the circle under the picture in the row that has a rhyming name.

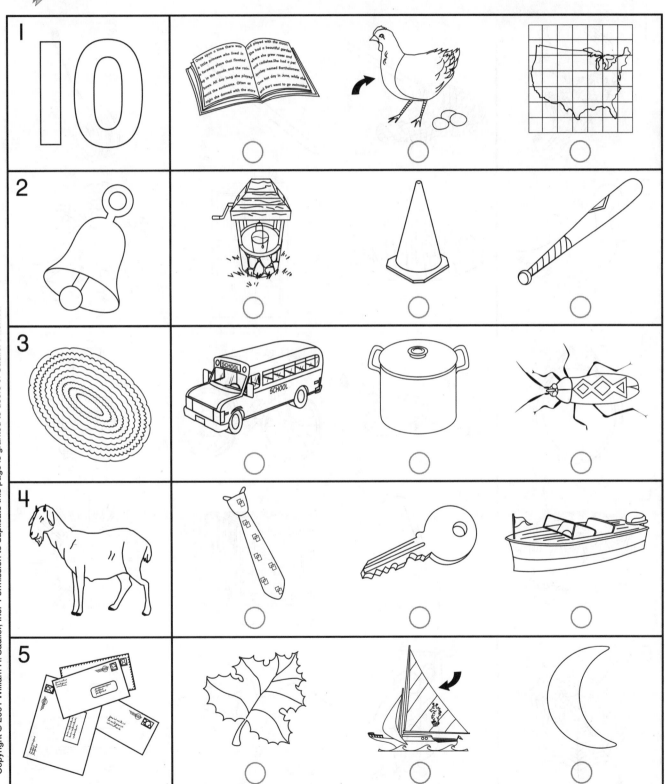

Name the first picture in each row. Then circle and color the pictures in the row that have names that begin with the same sound.

I n Unit 1 children practice phonemic awareness and continue to develop auditory discrimination. Children who struggle with this unit may manifest auditory or oral discrimination problems, perseveration, or attention deficit disorder. The following are beginning strategies you can use with these children.

Auditory/Oral Discrimination

Initial Consonant Sounds

Children with auditory discrimination difficulties or speech disorders may be unable to detect and produce differences in sounds. They may have particular problems detecting the differences between initial consonant sounds such as /**m**/ and /**n**/ or /**p**/ and /**b**/, especially when presented with words at a regular speaking speed. The following techniques may benefit these children as they proceed through the unit.

- Make a tape recording of the poem on page 5 so that children can listen to it more than once. When recording the poem, speak slowly, and emphasize initial consonant sounds.

- Have children use mirrors to observe how a given sound is formed. For example, slowly say **mat** in front of children so that they can observe how you form /**m**/ with your lips. Then say **not**, and have them notice how you position your tongue behind your front teeth to produce /**n**/. Then tell children to use mirrors to check their own mouth positioning as they mimic you to make each sound themselves. Repeat with other initial consonant sounds that children find confusing.

Rhyming

Children with auditory or pronunciation problems may have difficulty identifying or producing rhyming words. Emphasize that rhyming words have the same ending sounds (e.g., **boy** and **toy** rhyme because both end with the sound of **oy**). To further help children whose discrimination difficulties extend to rhyme:

- Say two rhyming words, such as **cake** and **lake**, and have children then repeat after you. Say the words again and add a third rhyming word, then a fourth (e.g., **cake, lake, bake; cake, lake, bake, snake**). Continue, and have children repeat the list after each addition.

- Record nursery rhymes for children to listen to more than once. As you tape yourself, emphasize the words that rhyme. For example:

  One, **two**, buckle my **shoe**.
  Three, **four**, shut the **door**.

Perseveration

Children who perseverate often have difficulty shifting to a new task and may continue working on the same task or item long after classmates have finished. As a result of their inability to complete their work in a timely fashion—even though they may be perfectly capable of doing the work—they are often perceived as being slow or lazy. To help such students move beyond the point at which they are "stuck," try these techniques.

- Encourage children to progress through items on a page or through a lesson by telling them you will affix a gold star to each row or other grouping as they complete it.

- Supply children with an hourglass that measures time in a minute denomination appropriate for the task at hand. Encourage them to monitor themselves to complete a given task within that time frame. Allow children to turn over the hourglass after completing one item or task and before beginning the next.

Attention Deficit Disorder (ADD)

Children who have attention deficit disorder have difficulty focusing and maintaining attention. They are easily distracted by external and internal stimuli. Just looking at an activity similar to the one on page 9 may overstimulate these children because they see what appear to be rows and rows of tasks. Techniques such as the following may help children concentrate on the task at hand.

- To help children focus on one task at a time, have them use a plain sheet of paper to cover all the rows on a page except the one on which they are working. Tell children to expose only one row at a time to complete the page.

- To help children focus on rhyming words, eliminate external auditory stimuli by having them use headphones to listen to a recording of the poem on page 5.

The chart below identifies problems that children may manifest as they learn the concepts and skills presented in this unit. The chart also identifies strategies to use with children who have not yet mastered the key concepts in the unit.

SKILL	Rhyming Sounds	Initial Consonant Sounds	
Observation	Child focuses on what the words mean rather than on how they sound and therefore identifies words with similar meanings (**pig**, **hog**) or opposite meanings (hot, cold) as rhyming words.	Child confuses initial consonant sounds that sound similar, such as /**m**/ and /**n**/ and /**p**/ and /**d**/.	Child has difficulty isolating the beginning sound in words.
Intervention	• Do rhyming activities using nonsense words (**mot, fot, zot**) before using real words (**hot, pot, cot**). • Sing rhyming songs with which the child is familiar, such as "Twinkle, Twinkle Little Star," leaving out a rhyming word. When the child provides the missing word, point out the word with which it rhymes.	• Have children observe how you form with your lips, the letters **m** and **n**. Distribute small mirrors and have children practice saying the different letters. • When the child begins working with words with a given initial sound that has not yet been studied in depth, avoid using a similar sound that may be a distracter. That is, if the focus is on words with initial **m**, do not present any with initial **n**. • Continue to engage children in activities that involve the sorting of pictures and objects, but be sure to add only one distracter at a time. • Encourage children to work with partners who are adept at differentiating initial sounds.	• Emphasize the initial sound in words as you ask the child to compare initial sounds. Ask: *Do /**t**/-/**t**/ **tape** and /**t**/-/**t**/ **toe** have the same beginning sound? Do /**t**/-/**t**/ **toe** and /**k**/-/**k**/ **cat** have the same beginning sound?* • Have the child repeat tongue twisters or alliterative phrases. Point out the beginning sound in each phrase. • Give the child a variety of **Sadlier Phonics Picture Cards**, making sure that most cards have the same initial sound. Instruct the child to say the initial sound before naming each card to help him or her determine which pictures have names that begin with that sound. In the case of initial **m**, model by saying: *m/ **mask**. Yes, **mask** begins with /**m**/. /**m**/ **bus**. No, **bus** does not begin with /**m**/.*

PHONEMIC AWARENESS ACTIVITIES

Children's level of phonemic awareness strongly predicts their future success in learning to read. *Phonemic awareness* is the awareness that language is made up of small units of speech that correspond to letters of the alphabet. These units are called *phonemes.* Since phonemes are the smallest functional units of speech, they are often hard to notice. Therefore explicit phonemic awareness instruction is important to help children identify, isolate, and analyze these units of speech.

The following phonemic awareness activities are designed to augment the lessons in the unit with engaging exercises that reinforce skills and encourage creativity.

Match Words

The Animal
Materials: **Sadlier Phonics Picture Cards** for **bird, kitten, duck, horse, pig, bee**

Explain that you are going to say one word that names a picture card and then some other words. Direct children to stand when they hear you say again the word with which you started. Try to use only names of animals and insects (e.g., **bird**, beetle, **bird**; **kitten**, kangaroo, **kitten**; **duck**, dog, **duck**, dinosaur; **pig**, penguin, **pig**, pup; **bee**, bunny, bird, bee, butterfly). When children stand, hold up the picture card for the first word and have them make the noise of the animal.

Group Matching
Materials: **Sadlier Phonics Picture Cards** for **boy, bus, jam, rice, grapes, lake, boat, train**

Display the cards and help children identify the names of the pictures. Then assign children to one of two groups. Distribute picture cards for **boy, jam, grapes,** and **boat** to group 1. Distribute picture cards for **bus, rice, lake,** and **train** to group 2. Read aloud the words and phrases below. When children in either group hear a word that names one of their pictures, they should hold the picture in the air and say the word.

- **boy**, ride, truck (group 1)
- hand, **bus**, cup (group 2)
- cat, box, **jam**, pen (group 1)
- banana, meat, fork, **rice** (group 2)
- cold purple **grapes** (group 1)
- light blue **lake** (group 2)
- a **boat** sails by (group 1)
- a big **train** station (group 2)

Identify Rhyming Words

Rhymes and Jingles
Say familiar rhymes and jingles with children. First say the rhyme or jingle and have children act it out. Then say it again and have children identify the rhyming words. You may wish to say each rhyme a third time, pausing before a rhyming word and asking children to supply it.

Teddy Bear, Teddy Bear
Teddy Bear, Teddy Bear, turn around;
Teddy Bear, Teddy Bear, touch the ground.
Teddy Bear, Teddy Bear, show your shoe;
Teddy Bear, Teddy Bear, that will do!
Teddy Bear, Teddy Bear, turn out the light;
Teddy Bear, Teddy Bear, say good-night!

Little Boy Blue
Little Boy Blue, come blow your horn;
The sheep's in the meadow, the cow's in the corn.
Where is the boy who looks after the sheep?
He's under a haystack, fast asleep.
Will you wake him? No, not I,
For if I do, he's sure to cry.

It's Raining, It's Pouring
It's raining, it's pouring;
The old man is snoring.
He bumped his head
As he went to bed
And he couldn't get up
in the morning.

Rhyming Activities

Rhyming Riddles

Make up and present simple riddles with clues that involve rhyming words. Here are some examples:

I am thinking of a piece of clothing. It rhymes with **clock** and **dock**. **(sock)**

I am thinking of a farm animal. It rhymes with **ten** and **men**. **(hen)**

I am thinking of a kind of weather. It rhymes with **funny** and **money**. **(sunny)**

I am thinking of a fruit you eat. It rhymes with **teach**, **reach**, and **beach**. **(peach)**

You may wish to have groups of children work together to make up their own riddles to present to other groups.

Match Initial Sounds

Initial-Sound Corner

Set aside a table in one corner of your classroom. Each day place two objects that have the same beginning sound on the table (e.g., a ball and a bat). Throughout the day have children place on the table other objects and pictures that have the same beginning sound (e.g., **book**, **bag**, **barrette**, **bell**, **boot**, **bookmark**, **box**). At the end of the day, have children name each object that is on the table. Focus on a different initial consonant sound each day.

Tongue Twisters

Read tongue twisters shown below to children. Have them identify the words that begin with the same sound.

Three **gray geese** in the **green grass** were **grazing**. **Gray** were the **geese** and **green** was the **grass**.

Betty and **Bob bought big balloons** at the **bazaar**.

Sound-Matching Song

Materials: **Sadlier Phonics Picture Cards** for **cake**, **cap**, **door**, **duck**, **peas**, **pig**, **fan**, **fox**

Display two of the picture cards, and sing the following lyrics (adjusting as needed to fit in the picture names) to the tune of "Jimmy Crack Corn and I Don't Care." Have children sing along.

Do **cake** and **cap** start the same?
Do **cake** and **cap** start the same?
Do **cake** and **cap** start the same?
They both start with the /**k**/ sound!

Repeat the song with other word pairs that do and do not have the same initial consonant sounds.

Count Words in a Sentence

Color Patterns

Materials: grid paper, crayons

Give each child a sheet of grid paper and assorted crayons. Say a sentence and tell children to use a crayon to color one square in a row for each word in the sentence. Model by slowly saying, *Ice is cold,* and then coloring three squares in a row, one for each word. Change colors for a second sentence: *Tea can be hot.* Show children how to make a pattern on the grid paper. Say the following sentences slowly as children color in squares.

Mary had a little lamb.
It had white wool.
It went to school.
The children laughed
and played.

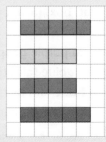

PHONEMIC AWARENESS TEST

Name _____ Date _____

Directions: Give this assessment orally to each child. Answers are in bold.

Match Words

Say: *Listen to the first word I say. Then listen as I say several other words. When you hear that first word again, raise your hand.* Then say the words below; circle the words that the child identifies.

1. apple: penny, **apple**

2. rabbit: carrot, **rabbit**

3. tree: book, **tree**

4. pencil: **pencil**, hat

5. ring: **ring**, finger

6. jump: **jump**, gate

7. book: toy, **book**

8. soup: **soup**, bike

9. green: bed, **green**

10. run: map, **run**

Identify Rhyming Words

Say: *I will say three words. Two words rhyme. You tell me which two words rhyme.* Then say the words below; circle the words that the child identifies.

11. **rain**, **mane**, tie

12. **peach**, bug, **teach**

13. mat, **pup**, **cup**

14. tire, **vine**, **line**

15. **star**, **car**, goat

16. **map**, hot, **trap**

17. see, **look**, **cook**

18. **hog**, mule, **fog**

19. **lit**, **pit**, horn

20. **play**, ten, **lay**

Book Walk

Blackline Master 4
p.5L

Objective
To name words that begin with a given consonant sound

Players
Pairs or small groups

■ Duplicate and distribute Blackline Master 4 to each pair or group.

■ Explain that the object is to help the bookworm get to the library. Ask children to find the picture of the library on the game board. Each time children name a word that begins with the same consonant sound as a specific picture, the bookworm will get closer to the library.

■ Have children name the pictures on the path. Tell them to name words that begin with the same sound as the name of each picture on the path, then have them move to the next picture.

■ Make copies of the Blackline Master for children to take home. Suggest that they look around their homes for objects having names that begin with the same sounds as the pictures on the path.

Busy Bookworm

Blackline Master 5
p. 5M

Objective
To identify rhyming word pairs

Players
Pairs

Materials
• scissors
• construction paper
• glue

■ Duplicate and distribute Blackline Master 5 to each pair. Have pairs glue it onto construction paper, name the pictures, and cut the pictures apart to make cards. Help them identify the Busy Bookworm card.

■ Have one partner deal all the cards. Tell children to match the rhyming word pair cards in their hands and to place these cards faceup in a pile. Direct children to hold the rest of the cards and to take turns drawing a card at random from their partner's cards. After each draw, have children put any new rhyming pair on their pile.

■ The winner is the child with the Busy Bookworm card after all the pairs have been matched.

Match-a-Rhyme

Blackline Master 5
p. 5M

Objective
To identify rhyming word pairs

Players
Pairs

Materials
Rhyming word pair cards made for "Busy Bookworm"

■ Have pairs remove the Busy Bookworm from the set of cards and place the remaining cards facedown in three rows of four, with the two leftover cards at the bottom of the rows.

■ Tell children to take turns turning over any two cards at a time and naming the pictures. If the picture names rhyme, the child keeps the cards; if not, the child returns the cards facedown.

■ Encourage children to remember the location of each picture card. The winner is the child who has won the greater number of cards.

Book Walk

Busy Bookworm

Blackline Master 5: Busy Bookworm

Introduction

Manipulating letters and sounds is an important part of a child's beginning reading experience. The illustrated Punchout Cards in the back of each *Sadlier Phonics* Student Edition are important tools that can help your students internalize and apply decoding and spelling strategies throughout the year.

Children can use these sturdy cards again and again in a wide variety of letter-recognition, sound-recognition, and word-building activities. Each set includes an uppercase and lowercase card for every letter, along with extra cards for vowels and for frequently used consonants. On the back of each letter card is a picture that exemplifies the letter's sound. Some blank cards are also included so that children can add letters and pictures of their own.

The activities on these pages will help you begin to incorporate Punchout Letters and Pictures into your lessons. Activities throughout the lesson plans afford children further opportunity to use the cards.

Storing the Cards

Before using the cards for the first time, plan how children will store their individual sets. You might provide a self-locking plastic bag, manila envelope, file box, or plastic jar for each child. Another idea is to punch a hole in the top of each card so that children can attach their sets to plastic curtain rings.

Mix and Match

Have children work in pairs, and have each pair take out Punchout Cards with these pictures: **ride**, **leaf**, **bug**, **rug**, **cake**, **seal**, **lamb**, **fan**, **van**, **pen**, **ten**, **cap**, **goat**, **note**, **hive**, **five**, **fox**, and **box**.

Direct children to mix up the cards and lay them down picture side up so that they can name each picture and find the six pairs of rhyming picture names. Encourage children to use the rhyming words in sentences, for example: A **goat** can't sing a **note**.

Sound of the Day

Materials: hole punch, yarn

Specify a picture card with a name that begins with a common single-consonant sound—**bug, mule, soap, ten**—and have each child take out that card. Punch a hole near the top of each card, and help children thread yarn through the hole and tie it to make a picture-card necklace.

Ask children to listen and look throughout the day for words and objects having names that begin with the same sound as the name of the picture they are wearing. Incorporate applicable words in a variety of situations throughout the day.

UNIT 1 — TECHNOLOGY

PICTURE COLLAGE

Objectives

- To reinforce the recognition of initial sounds

- To use a word-processing program with graphics features, such as Kid Pix Studio® Deluxe*, to design a collage of pictures having names that begin with the same sound

Preparation

Display the following **Sadlier Phonics Picture Cards** on the chalk ledge: **balloon**, **cake**, **pig**, and **turtle**. Have children identify each picture and name other words with the same initial sound.

One Step at a Time

1. Have children choose two picture cards from the chalk ledge. Tell them they will use computer software to create a picture collage.

2. Using Kid Pix Studio® software, have children select "Kid Pix" from the Picker screen.

3. Have children access the stamp library by selecting the stamp icon on the left toolbar. Have them scroll through the stamps at the bottom of the screen to find pictures having names that begin with the same sounds as the names of the picture cards they chose. For example, children might select pictures of a **bike** and a **bug** for initial **b** and pictures of a **cake** and **cowboy** for initial **c**. Ask them to click on their desired pictures.

4. They should place the chosen picture on the screen and click to position it in the document. Have children find several pictures that they can use to make their collages. They may wish to decorate their collages using the paintbrush icon.

5. Instruct children to print their collages.

Class Sharing

Invite volunteers to share their collages with the class. Ask them to identify the pictures on the collage and then to pair the collage with the picture card displayed on the chalk ledge. Display the collages in the classroom.

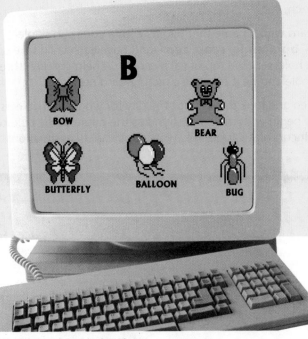

B

BOW   BEAR

BUTTERFLY   BALLOON   BUG

E-MAIL RHYMES

Objectives

- To help children discriminate rhyming sounds
- To help children use a paint program, such as Kid Pix Studio® Deluxe*, to draw a picture
- To use an on-line information service to send and receive electronic mail

Preparation

- Review rhyming words with the class. Say several one-syllable words, such as **pail**, **hat**, and **map**. Help children identify words that rhyme with each, and list them on the board.
- Set up a keypal exchange in order to trade pictures with another class on the Internet. To find a partner class, you may wish to subscribe to Classroom Connect™*.

One Step at a Time

1. Read aloud the list of words on the board, and have children draw a picture of one of these words. Instruct them to choose "Kid Pix" from the opening screen.

2. Have children use the drawing tools, colors, and stamps to illustrate their pictures.

3. Log onto your on-line service account, and access its e-mail feature. Write a message to your partner class, asking it to return pictures of words that rhyme with the names of the objects in your class's drawings.

4. Attach each drawing to a separate e-mail message. Then send the messages to your partner class.

5. Print a copy of each child's picture. Then print the pictures that are received from the partner class.

Class Sharing

Tell children to match the pictures having names that rhyme. Then have them say the rhyming words. Display the rhyme pictures on the bulletin board.

*All software referred to in this book is listed under Computer Resources on page 348.

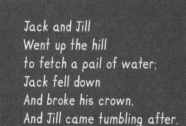

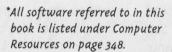

RECITE A RHYME

On the board write the rhyme "Jack and Jill" (shown at the right), and then read it aloud.

Have the class recite the rhyme with you. When most children have learned the lines, tape-record a class recitation. Listen to the recording with the class. As you play back the recording, direct children to listen for words that begin with the sounds of **j** and **f**. Then say **Jack**, and ask children to name a word in the rhyme that has the same initial sound. **(Jill)** Do the same for the word fetch. **(fell)**.

> Jack and Jill
> Went up the hill
> to fetch a pail of water;
> Jack fell down
> And broke his crown.
> And Jill came tumbling after.

Literature Introduction to Phonemic Awareness and Auditory Discrimination

Objectives
- **To enjoy a poem about books**
- **To identify rhyming words**
- **To discriminate initial sounds**

Starting with Literature

Recite "Good Books, Good Times!" Encourage children to enjoy the poem's rhythm and the fantasy drawing. Ask which word was heard most often. (**good**) Reread the poem; have children chant the word **good** along with you. Help them conclude that the poet loves to read.

Develop Critical Thinking

Read aloud the questions. Encourage children to discuss which books they like or dislike, where they like to read, and to explain why.

Introducing the Skill

Phonemic Awareness: Identify Rhyming Words

- Read aloud the first four lines of the poem "Good Books, Good Times!" Repeat the words **times** and **rhymes**. Explain that these words rhyme because they sound the same at the end. **Rhymes** and **times** both end with /īmz/. Say the following words and ask if each one rhymes with **times**: **limes, dog, dimes, fan.** Then help children identify other rhyming words from the poem: **ends/friends, facts/acts.**

Auditory Discrimination

Materials: **Unit 1 Classroom Poster**

- Say **good** and **books** as you point to the words on the poster. Explain that the words have different beginning sounds: /**g**/ and /**b**/. Have children repeat the words and beginning sounds. Continue with the word pairs **good/times** and **good/facts**.
- Ask pairs of children whose names begin with different sounds to stand. Have the class say the names and then help them identify the different beginning sounds.

5

Unit 1

GOOD BOOKS, GOOD TIMES!

Good books.
Good times.
Good stories.
Good rhymes.

Good beginnings.
Good ends.
Good people.
Good friends.

Good fiction.
Good facts.
Good adventures.
Good acts.

Good stories.
Good rhymes.
Good books.
Good times.

Lee Bennett Hopkins

Critical Thinking

Why do you like some books more than others?
Where is the best place to read a book?
outside, in my room, at school, in the library

Possible responses:
I like the characters;
I like a special subject;
I like the pictures.

LESSON 1: Phonemic Awareness and Auditory Discrimination
Phonemic Awareness: Rhyme
5

Theme Words

Book Worms Read a short story aloud. Tell children about your experiences of being read to by parents, grandparents, teachers, and others. Ask: *Who has read to you? What is your favorite story? What did you like about that story?* Elicit as many responses as possible.

Tell children you are going to build a "word wall" on which they can express the joy of reading. Start by writing the word **book** on a large sheet of chart or butcher paper. Call on volunteers to name words that are related to books. Print these words on the word wall. Refer to the word wall and add to it throughout the unit.

After touring the school library, begin a "Book Worm" display. Trace and cut out the "head" of a worm. Just below the head, add arms holding a book. Display the worm on a bulletin board titled "My Buddy the Book Worm." Every time a book is read aloud to the class, add the title onto the worm as a body segment and add new theme words to the word wall.

Name _____

Dear Family,

In this unit, your child will be listening for words that rhyme or begin with the same sound. He or she will be talking about the fun of reading books. You can enjoy this unit with your child by trying these activities at home.

• Read the poem "Good Books, Good Times!" on the reverse side of this page as your child follows along.

• Ask your child to listen as you read the poem aloud again. Name pairs of rhyming words together. (times/rhymes, ends/friends, facts/acts)

• Talk about a favorite book you have read together.

• Visit your local library and find a new book to share.

PROJECT

Have fun with beginning sounds. Say a word like **book** and ask your child to say another word that begins with the same sound, such as **bike**. Take turns thinking of words.

Apreciada Familia:

En esta unidad se enseñarán palabras que riman o que empiezan con el mismo sonido. Los niños estarán hablando de lo divertido que es leer libros. Ustedes pueden disfrutar junto al niño de esta unidad haciendo esta actividad juntos en la casa.

• Lean, en voz alta, el poema en la página 5 mientras su hijo lo repite.

• Pidan al niño que escuche el poema mientras se le lee en voz alta otra vez. Nombren pares de palabras que rimen. (times/rhymes, ends/friends, facts/acts)

• Hablen del libro que leyeron juntos y que les gustó.

• Visiten la biblioteca del vecindario y busquen un libro que puedan compartir.

PROYECTO

Diviértanse con los sonidos. Diga una palabra, por ejemplo **book** y pida al niño decir otra que empiece con el mismo sonido, tal como **bike**. Túrnense para pensar en las palabras.

Phonics Alive at Home

• The *Phonics Alive at Home* page provides an opportunity for children and their families to focus on the unit theme "Book Buddies" and to work together to further the child's auditory discrimination skills.

• Direct children to remove page 6 from their books and to take the page home to share with family members.

• Throughout the unit, provide opportunities for children to share with the class their favorite books from home or from the library. Designate a special time for children to share their books. It might be fun to extend the activity by setting aside a day for children to dress as their favorite storybook characters.

• Stimulate children's interest in using free time for reading by designing a classroom Reading Center with them. Ask children to suggest various types of reading materials and props or decorations that would personalize the corner and make it more exciting for them. You might add comfortable pillows to sit on and stuffed animals as reading companions. Make sure children know that they can check out materials from the classroom library to read at home.

Multicultural Connection

Point out to children that there are many books about people from other countries. Explain that books are one way to learn facts about different cultures. Select books from your classroom and school library that are about different cultures. Introduce these books to children. On a map, point out the areas on which these books focus. Ask children from the focus countries to talk about them. Read from the books as you continue the unit, or put them in your Reading Center.

Sadlier Reading
Little Books and Big Books

For more practice with rhyming words read *Star Light* and *The Itsy, Bitsy Spider*.

Direct children to additional activities on Sadlier-Oxford's web site: www.sadlier-oxford.com.

Take-Home Book

Include family members in activities by sending children home with a book of their own. Use the take-home component as a culminating activity for the unit or send the book home at another appropriate time. *Good Books* can be found in the student book on pages 323–24. This fold-up book provides opportunities for children to apply their newly learned phonics skills.

Student Pages 7-8

Discriminating Rhyming Sounds

Objectives
- To identify rhyming words
- To discriminate between rhyming and non-rhyming words

Warming Up

Listening Practice

Ask children to close their eyes as you make a series of sounds. For example, you might shut the door, ring a bell, or write on the board. Call on volunteers to guess each sound. Then have children take turns using classroom objects to make sounds while others guess the objects used.

Teaching the Lesson

Phonemic Awareness: Identify Rhyming Words

Materials: **Sadlier Phonics Picture Cards** for **bat, hat, fan, van, ten, pen, jet, net**

- Display the picture cards and identify the picture names. Tell children that **bat** and **hat** rhyme because they both end with /**at**/. Then have a volunteer find the two rhyming picture cards and say their names. Continue with the remaining cards.

Auditory Discrimination

- Say the words **cap** and **map**. Have children repeat them. Point out that these words rhyme because they both end with /**ap**/. Now say the words **cap** and **dig**. Explain that these words do not rhyme because they do not end with the same sounds. Say the following word pairs. Have children repeat them and then tell you if the words rhyme. Say **cap/tap, make/lake, dog/nine, five/hive, run/tree,** and **cone/bone**. If the words rhyme, help the children think of another rhyming word.

Book and **cook** are rhyming words. Listen for these rhyming words.

Dad reads the book.
I get to cook!

Name the first picture in each row. Then circle the pictures that have rhyming names.

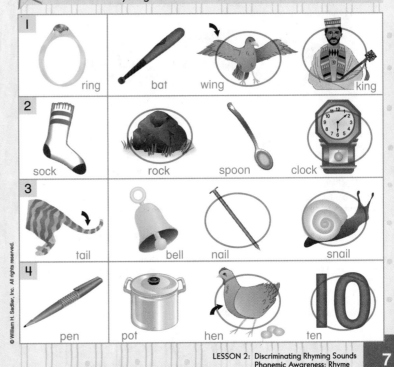

1. ring   bat   wing   king
2. sock   rock   spoon   clock
3. tail   bell   nail   snail
4. pen   pot   hen   ten

LESSON 2: Discriminating Rhyming Sounds
Phonemic Awareness: Rhyme   **7**

UNIVERSAL ACCESS
Meeting Individual Needs

Auditory
Emphasize the rhyming words as you sing the following verse to the tune of "Jingle Bells."

Read and **bead**,
Deed and **seed**,
This works every **time**.
Just change **around** the beginning **sound**,
And you can make a **rhyme**.

Have children suggest rhyming words to replace the underlined words.

Auditory • Visual
Materials: **Sadlier Phonics Picture Cards** for **ham, jam, fox, box, bug, rug**; beanbag

Display the picture cards. Hand a child the beanbag and have that child name one picture. Ask a volunteer to say the name of the picture card that rhymes with the first card's name. Have the child with the beanbag toss it to the volunteer once a correct rhyme is given. Continue until all children have participated.

Extra Support
Remind children that rhyming words always have the same ending sounds. Say groups of three words, two of which rhyme, and have volunteers identify the rhymes. Use groups of words such as **pig, cap, jig; hop, top, rail; fat, hog, log.**

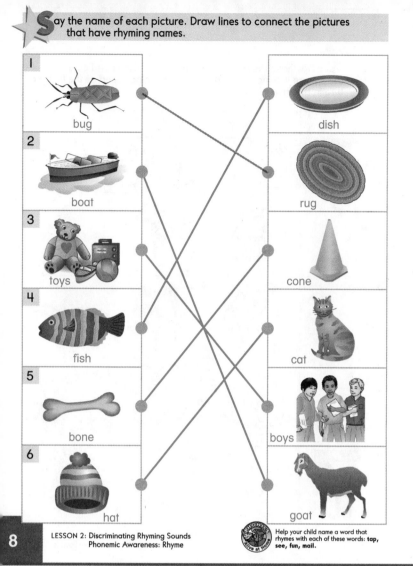

Say the name of each picture. Draw lines to connect the pictures that have rhyming names.

1 bug	dish
2 boat	rug
3 toys	cone
4 fish	cat
5 bone	boys
6 hat	goat

LESSON 2: Discriminating Rhyming Sounds
Phonemic Awareness: Rhyme

Help your child name a word that rhymes with each of these words: **tap**, **see**, **fun**, **mail**.

Practicing the Skill

- Have the class turn to page 7. Read aloud the sentences at the top and discuss the picture. Emphasize that **book** and **cook** rhyme.
- Go over the directions and together name the pictures. Be sure children understand that they should name the specific parts of the pictures indicated by the arrows.
- Model completing the first row by saying **ring** and then each picture name in the row. Explain that children should circle the **wing** and **king** because they rhyme with **ring**; **bat** does not. Model circling a picture to indicate an answer. Then have children complete the page.
- Read aloud the directions on page 8. Explain that the gray line connects picture names that rhyme: **bug** and **rug**. Identify the remaining pictures and do item 2 together. Then have children finish the page.

Curriculum Connections

Theme Activity: Multicultural
Materials: drawing paper, crayons, tape, paper towel tube

- Explain to the class that the first books were produced in Egypt and were called *scrolls*. Scrolls had to be unrolled to be read.
- Direct the class in making a rhyming-word scroll. Have children draw two objects with rhyming names on a sheet of paper. Tape the children's papers together to form a long vertical strip. Affix the top to a paper towel tube and roll the remaining length around the tube to form a scroll. Then show children how to unroll the scroll to "read" their rhyming pictures. Display the scroll in the Language Arts Center.

Sadlier Reading
Little Books and Big Books
For more practice with rhyming words read *Rain, Rain, Go Away.*

Observational Assessment

Note whether the names of the two pictures drawn by each child in the Theme Activity rhyme.

English Language Learners/ESL
Materials: pictures of a **bat** and a **cat**

Show children pictures of a **bat** and **cat**. Say /b/ - /at/, point to the picture of a **bat,** say the word and have children repeat the word after you. Repeat these steps with the picture of a **cat**. Repeat the words **bat** and **cat** and tell children that these words rhyme because they have the same ending sound /at/. Practice other rhyming words point to objects around the classroom: **mat** and **hat, chair** and **hair, book** and **hook.**

Challenge
Materials: crayons, drawing paper

Tell children they are going to make up funny rhyming sentences. As an example, say: *Ben **took** a **look** at a **book** about a **cook**.* Ask children to name the four rhyming words. Then have each child make up a funny sentence with at least three rhyming words and draw a picture to go with it. Display the pictures and have children say their sentences.

Special Strategies
For Universal Access activities, see page 5F.

Discriminating Initial Sounds

Objectives

- To match initial sounds
- To recognize initial consonant sounds
- To identify picture names with the same initial consonant sounds

Warming Up

Review Rhyming Words

Point to your eye and then wave as you say the words **eye** and **bye**. Remind children that **eye** and **bye** rhyme because they have the same ending sound. Then ask children to wave whenever they hear you say a pair of rhyming words. Use these words: **hip/lip**, **hand/band**, **book/pear**, **tie/pie**.

Teaching the Lesson

Phonemic Awareness: Match Initial Sounds

Say a word that begins with a single consonant sound, such as **book**, **page**, or **cover**. Then say just the beginning sound of that word, and have children repeat it. (**book**, /**b**/) Name other words that also begin with the same initial sound (e.g., **build, band, bat, bird, bounce**). Have children repeat the words and then work in small groups to search the room for objects with names that begin with the same sound (e.g., **book: ball, box, boy; page: pencil, paper, poster; cover: calendar, car**). Ask groups to name the objects they found.

Auditory Discrimination

Have children listen as you say the words **boy** and **bus**. Tell children that these two words begin with the same sound, /**b**/. Direct children to listen to other pairs of words and to raise their hand if the two words begin with the same sound. Use words such as **desk/door, girl/coat, light/letter, paint/fan, box/bag, table/toy**.

9

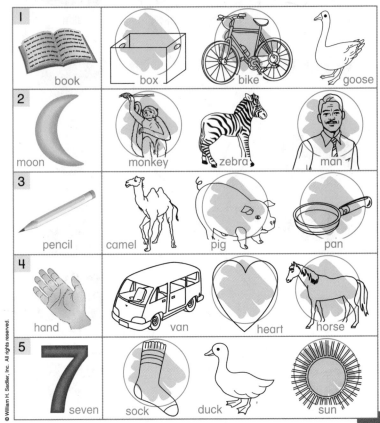

Book and **box** have the same beginning sound. Circle and color the picture if its name has the same beginning sound as the first picture in the row.

1	book	box	bike	goose
2	moon	monkey	zebra	man
3	pencil	camel	pig	pan
4	hand	van	heart	horse
5	seven	sock	duck	sun

LESSON 3: Discriminating Initial Sounds
Phonemic Awareness: Initial Sounds

9

UNIVERSAL ACCESS
Meeting Individual Needs

Visual • Auditory

Materials: picture books

Have partners find and name pictures of things that begin with the same consonant sound. Children who speak languages other than English can also say the names in those languages.

Discuss whether the beginning sound of various words changes with the different languages.

Kinesthetic • Auditory

Say an action word such as **run**. Then say three words, two of which begin with the same sound as **run**. You might use **read, ring**, and **page**. Tell children to run in place whenever they hear you say a word that begins with the same sound as **run**. Use a similar procedure with other action words, such as **jump, hop**, and **dance**.

Extra Support

Materials: **Sadlier Phonics Picture Cards** for **bus, bunny, mask, mitten, seal, seven, tub, hat**

Review that some words, such as **bug** and **bat**, have the same beginning sound. Show pairs of picture cards and say their names. Direct children to say "yes" if the names begin with the same sound and "no" if they do not.

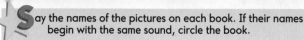

Say the names of the pictures on each book. If their names begin with the same sound, circle the book.

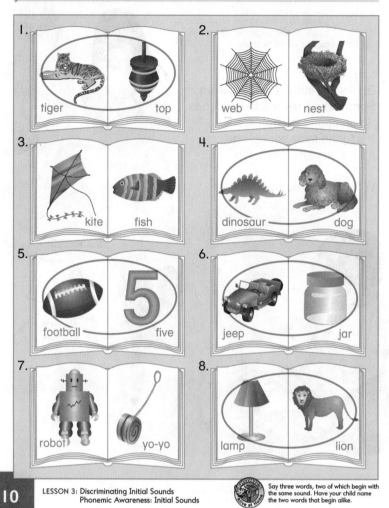

1. tiger   top
2. web   nest
3. kite   fish
4. dinosaur   dog
5. football   5   five
6. jeep   jar
7. robot   yo-yo
8. lamp   lion

LESSON 3: Discriminating Initial Sounds
Phonemic Awareness: Initial Sounds

PHONICS Alive at Home

Say three words, two of which begin with the same sound. Have your child name the two words that begin alike.

- Read aloud the directions on page 9 and help children identify the pictures in the first row. Model how to circle the pictures having names that begin with the same sound as **book**. Then work with children to identify the remaining pictures and to complete the page.
- Read aloud the directions on page 10. Guide children to realize that the first book should be circled because **tiger** and **top** both begin with the same sound. Identify each picture pair and work through the page with children.

Curriculum Connections

Theme Activity: Language Arts/Art
Materials: magazines, scissors, glue, construction paper, crayons

- Model the activity by displaying a picture of a bird glued on a sheet of construction paper. Say: *Here is a picture of a bird. The word* **bird** *begins with the same sound as many other words.* **Boy** *has the same beginning sound as* **bird**, *so I'll draw a picture of a boy.* **Book**, **ball**, *and* **box** *also have the same beginning sound.* Then draw pictures of those objects on the same sheet of construction paper.
- Have children cut out a picture from a magazine, name it, and glue it on construction paper. Then ask them to draw pictures of objects that have names that begin with the same sound as the name of the picture.

Portfolio   *Materials:* manila folders, crayons

Have each child decorate and label a manila folder. Explain to children that they will put some of their work in this portfolio. Tell children to put their "same beginning sound" drawings in their portfolios.

Sadlier Reading
Little Books and Big Books

For more practice recognizing initial consonant sounds read *Hey Diddle, Diddle.*

Hey Diddle Diddle

Observational Assessment

Note whether children have drawn objects with the same initial consonant sound as their magazine pictures.

English Language Learners/ESL
Materials: Sadlier Phonics Picture Cards for **zebra, pig, dog, bird, horse, lion, duck**

Point to the picture of a **pig** and ask children to say the word for **pig** in their native language. Repeat that word and stretch out the initial sound. Tell children that this is the beginning sound. Then say the word **pig** and stretch out the **p**, /**p**/ - /**p**/ - /**p**/ - /**ig**/. Tell children that /**p**/ is the beginning sound of the word **pig**. Practice with the picture cards and objects around the classroom to help children identify the initial sounds of words.

Challenge
Materials: drawing paper, crayons

Remind children that many words begin with the same sound. Tell children to think of a sentence in which every word begins with the same sound. As an example, say: **Big books belong behind Bob.** Have children make up a sentence and illustrate it. Then have them say their sentences as they show their drawings.

Special Strategies
For Universal Access activities, see page 5F.

Integrating the Language Arts

Objectives
- To divide sentences into words
- To use oral language to extend the theme concept
- To demonstrate the ability to discriminate similar initial sounds

Teaching the Lesson

Phonemic Awareness: Divide Sentences into Words

Materials: buttons or counters

- Tell children that a sentence is made up of individual words. Demonstrate this by tapping the top of your head for each word as you say: *I am a teacher.*
- Give each child five buttons. Tell children to listen as you say a sentence and to put aside a button for each word they hear. Then call on volunteers to count the buttons to tell how many words they heard in the sentence. Use these sentences:

  We like school.

  We count to ten.

  We read books.

  We all have fun.

Skills in Context

- Read aloud the text on page 11. Have children identify things in the picture they use at school.
- Read aloud the question on page 11. Encourage volunteers to recall books they have read (or books that have been read to them) and to talk about the stories those books told.

Comprehension Skill: Recalling Details

Ask children to choose a favorite character from a story. Then have children tell what the character looks like, what the character likes to do, and what kind of family the character has.

Look and Learn Listen as the page is read aloud. Look at the pictures. Then talk about what you see.

Look at a good book.
Books are stories written down.
Some books tell made-up stories.
Some books tell true stories.
It's fun to read books, and
it's fun to write them, too.

What stories do books tell?
Some books tell made-up stories.
Some books tell true stories.

LESSON 4: Phonemic Awareness and Auditory Discrimination in Context
Comprehension: Recalling Details

11

U N I V E R S A L A C C E S S
Meeting Individual Needs

Reading and Writing Connection

Materials: crayons or colored pencils

Suggest that children work with a partner to make a book. Have them decide what will happen at the beginning, middle, and end of the story. Ask them to fold a sheet of paper in half. Have them write or dictate a title for the book cover and decorate it. Then tell them to draw a picture of the story's beginning, middle, and end on each of the remaining three pages. Have partners use the pages to share their stories in small groups.

Language Arts Connection

This would be a good time to introduce children to the school library. Have the librarian speak to the class as part of their visit. Make sure children know where to find books that are the most appropriate for their age group. Encourage each child to take out a book during the visit. Use this opportunity to discuss with children some parts of a book: the front and back covers, the title page, the spine, and the names of the author and illustrator.

Circle and color the picture if its name has the same beginning sound as the first picture in the row.

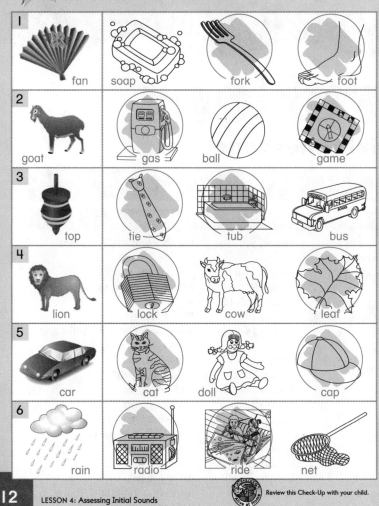

1	fan	soap	fork	foot
2	goat	gas	ball	game
3	top	tie	tub	bus
4	lion	lock	cow	leaf
5	car	cat	doll	cap
6	rain	radio	ride	net

12 LESSON 4: Assessing Initial Sounds

Review this Check-Up with your child.

Assessing the Unit

Skills Review Review beginning consonant sounds by saying a child's name that begins with a consonant. Then have volunteers suggest other words that begin with the same sound. Read aloud the directions on page 12. Help children name each picture. Then have them complete the page on their own. For additional assessment see pages 5C–5E.

Observational Assessment Note children's pronunciation of initial sounds and their ability to suggest words that begin with the same sound.

Portfolio Assessment Meet with individual children to discuss the "same beginning sound" drawings they made in Lesson 3. Guide children to review their own work by having them ask themselves, "Do the names of the pictures I drew have the same beginning sound?" See the Auditory Rubrics on page 5C.

Student Skills Assessment After observing children complete the assessment page, record your evaluation of each child's skills on pages 321-322 of the Student Edition.

Take-Home Book Remind children to complete at home the *Take-Home Book* page for Unit 1.

Additional Assessment See pages 5C–5E.

Guided Instruction

Skills	Resources
Discriminate rhyming sounds	Instruction on pages 7–8
Discriminate initial sounds	Instruction on pages 9–10
Auditory discrimination	Phonemic Awareness Strategies on pages 5H–5I Take-Home Book *Good Books*

PLANNING RESOURCE

UNIT 2

Celebrations
Celebrate special times together.

Consonant Sounds

READING/LANGUAGE ARTS STANDARDS
- Respond to a poem in a way that reflects understanding
- Recognize initial, medial, and final sounds in single-syllable words
- Understand that as the letters of words change, so do the sounds

OBJECTIVES
- To enjoy a poem about parades
- To develop phonemic awareness by identifying, matching, and manipulating sounds in spoken words
- To associate consonants with their sounds
- To identify initial, medial, and final consonant sounds in words
- To write uppercase and lowercase consonant letters
- To print initial, medial, and final consonants to complete words

Thematic Teaching

In Unit 2 children share special family and cultural celebrations. As they participate in multicultural activities and learn about traditional American holidays, they begin to associate each consonant letter with its sound.

This is a good time to approach parents about sharing cultural traditions, costumes, and food with the class. You might want to display the "Parades" **Unit 2 Classroom Poster** where all children can see it so that they can periodically locate words that begin with particular consonant sounds.

LESSONS
Lesson 5 . . . . Introduction to Consonant Sounds
Lessons 6–8 . . . . . . Initial **f, m, s**
Lesson 9 . . . . Final **f, ff, m, s, ss**
Lessons 10–12 . . . . Initial **t, h, b**
Lesson 13 . . . . Final **t, tt, b**
Lesson 14 . . . . Reviewing/Assessing Initial and Final **f, m, s, t, h, b**
Lessons 15–17 . . . . Initial **l, d, c**
Lesson 18 . . . . Final **l, ll, d, dd**
Lessons 19–21 . . . . Initial **n, g, w**
Lesson 22 . . . . Final **n, g, gg**
Lesson 23 . . . . Reviewing/Assessing Initial and Final **l, d, c, n, g, w**
Lessons 24–26 . . . . Initial **p, r, k**
Lesson 27 . . . . Final **p, r, k**
Lessons 28–29 . . . . Initial **j, q(u), v**
Lesson 30 . . . . Reviewing Initial and Final **p, r, k, j, q(u), v**
Lesson 31 . . . . Initial **y, z** and Final **x, zz**
Lesson 32 . . . . Reviewing/Assessing Initial and Final **p, r, k, j, q(u), v, x, y, z**
Lesson 33 . . . . Reviewing/Assessing Final **ff, ss, tt, ll, dd, gg, zz**
Lesson 34 . . . . Medial Consonants
Lesson 35 . . . . Integrating the Language Arts
Lesson 36 . . . . High-Frequency Words
Lesson 37 . . . . Assessing Initial, Medial, and Final Consonants
- Take-Home Book: *I Love Parades*

Curriculum Integration

Math Children use calendars and count the number of words that start with the same sound on pages 26, 30, and 60.

Science Children explore animals, nature, the seasons, and other science-related topics on pages 20, 22, 34, 42, and 64.

13A Unit 2 • *Consonant Sounds*

Optional Learning Activities

Multisensory Activities
Multisensory activities are a regular feature of the phonics lessons and appeal to all learning styles—visual, tactile, auditory, and kinesthetic.

Multicultural Connection
Help children appreciate cultural diversity by enjoying together the multicultural activities on pages 14, 18, 24, 38, 44, and 52.

Thematic Activities
Watch for other fun and meaningful thematic activities in the *Curriculum Connections* section of most lesson plans.

Karama Fufuka
Author's Corner

Using Karama Fufuka as a pseudonym, Sharon Antonia Morgan writes for both children and adults. A contributor to magazines such as *Ebony Jr.* and *Essence,* she has also been a secretary, receptionist, and newspaper editor. She is listed in *Who's Who Among Black Americans.* Morgan was born in Chicago in 1951 and has one son.

Assessment Strategies
Assessment is an ongoing process. Multiple strategies in the Student Edition as well as the Teacher's Edition and regular use of the Skills Assessment Checklist on pages 321–322 will help you monitor children's progress in recognizing initial, medial, and final consonant sounds.

UNIT RESOURCES

Sadlier Reading

Classroom Poster

Phonics Picture Cards

Little Books and Big Books

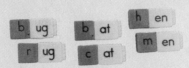

Student Manipulatives

Other Poems by Karama Fufuka
My Daddy Is a Cool Dude, and Other Poems. New York: Dial Press, 1975. Book is out of print but is available in local libraries.

Theme-Related Resources
Hopkins, Lee Bennett, ed. *Ring Out, Wild Bells.* FL: Harcourt Brace, 1992.

Leokum, Arkady. *Customs and Superstitions.* New York: Penguin Video, 1990. Find out about holidays, weddings, and other celebrations.

In Unit 2 children focus on initial, medial, and final consonant sounds and the letters associated with those sounds. The assessment ideas on this page are for use throughout the chapter.

Pretests/Posttests

The tests on pages 13D–13E serve as a formal end-of-unit assessment of children's mastery of initial, medial, and final consonant sounds. In some cases you may choose to use them as pretests to help you identify a starting point for instruction for individual children. The Phonemic Awareness Test on page 13J may also be used as a pretest.

Observational Assessment

Specific opportunities to observe the children's progress with initial, medial, and final consonant sounds are high-lighted in the lesson plans. The *Student Skills Assessment Checklist* on pages 321–322 of the Student Edition will help you keep track of students' progress.

Dictation

Dictate words and have children write the letter that stands for the sound they hear:

- at the beginning of **hot**, **queen**, **girl**, **yell**, **jug**.
- at the end of **park**, **Tom**, **give**, **six**, **road**.
- in the middle of **melon**, **tiny**, **begin**, **cider**, **woman**.

Using Technology

The activities on pages 13O–13P may also be used to evaluate children's progress.

Performance Assessment

Set up a station in the Reading Center with directions to children to draw and label a picture of a celebration that is important or means something to them. On large sheets of oaktag, print the directions using pictures. Tell children that they may go to the station during free time. Be sure to mention that children may also go to the Art Center for any materials needed to complete their pictures.

Then tell children that they will each have a turn telling about their individual celebration. Notice whether children correctly recognize and write the initial consonants. Also note whether children's written displays match their oral presentations. Use the *Student Skills Assessment Checklist* on pages 321–322 to record your observations.

Portfolio Assessment

The portfolio icon in the lesson plans indicates portfolio opportunities throughout the unit. Use rubrics like those below as a means of evaluating children's progress in Unit 2. Post the rubrics on a chart at the beginning of the unit, and review the criteria with children.

Discuss with children how they can select work from their portfolios that best represents their progress in a given area. For example, for the rubric "forms lowercase letters correctly," suggest that children compare the letters they have written with those in the student book or on an alphabet chart. Model by posing questions such as: *Of the letters you have written, which look like the letters in the student book? Which do you need to practice writing?*

Name _____

Writing Rubrics

	Sometimes	Never	Always
Phonics Skills			
Associates a sound with its corresponding consonant letter			
Distinguish between initial, medial, and final sounds			
Writing Skills			
Forms lowercase letters correctly			
Forms uppercase letters correctly and uses them appropriately			
Uses words and pictures to convey meaning			
Spells high-frequency words appropriate to grade level			

Answer Key

Page 13D		Page 13E	
1. l	7. j	1. x	7. g
2. b	8. f	2. j	8. ll
3. n	9. v	3. l	9. v
4. c	10. s	4. d	10. r
5. qu	11. w	5. b	11. y
6. h	12. r	6. k	12. d

Say the name of each picture. Circle the letter or letters that stand for its beginning sound. Print the letter or letters on the line.

1 l v d	2 j b t	3 w n f
4 g s c	5 qu n h	6 m k h
7 t j q	8 c l f	9 v z y
10 s z p	11 m w v	12 r d b

Say the name of each picture. Fill in the circle in front of the letter or letters that stand for the missing sound. Print the letter or letters on the line.

1	○ x ○ s ○ c	2	○ s ○ j ○ m	3	○ l ○ z ○ h
fo___		___ug		ru__er	

4	○ t ○ l ○ d	5	○ h ○ b ○ p	6	○ d ○ k ○ n
___esk		ro__ot		hoo___	

7	○ b ○ t ○ g	8	○ dd ○ ll ○ gg	9	○ j ○ w ○ v
wa__on		ba___		___ine	

10	○ r ○ x ○ f	11	○ g ○ j ○ y	12	○ t ○ m ○ d
ca___		___ard		ra__io	

In Unit 2 children learn to recognize initial, medial, and final consonant sounds and to associate those sounds with letters. Children who experience difficulty with this unit may manifest auditory, visual, perceptual, or motor skill problems or an attention deficit disorder (ADD). The following are beginning strategies you can use with these children.

Auditory/Oral Discrimination

Consonant Sounds

Children with speech disorders or auditory discrimination difficulties may be unable to detect and/or produce differences in sounds. The following techniques may benefit these children as they proceed through the unit.

- Children often have difficulty saying initial /**r**/ and may pronounce it as /**w**/. This may be particularly frustrating for children who can hear the difference in the two sounds but are unable to produce that difference. Say **way** slowly and distinctly so that children can see how your tongue stays flat when you make the **w** sound. Then say **ray** so that they can see how the tip of your tongue curls back to produce the **r** sound. Repeat with **wag**/**rag** and **wed**/**red**. Then allow children to mimic making each sound, and check whether each child is properly positioning the tip of his or her tongue.

- Children can learn how to pronounce similar sounds, such as **p**, **b**, **t**, **d**, by checking the airflow as they make each sound. Model for children how to put their hand about three inches in front of their mouths. Ask them to notice the difference in the puff of air when they say /**p**/ and then /**b**/. Remind children that in Unit 1 they used a mirror to notice that their lips make the same shape for /**p**/ and /**b**/. Help them notice now that the puff of air is greater when they make the sound /**p**/. Repeat with /**t**/ and /**d**/.

Visual, Perceptual, Motor Skills

Discerning Between Similar Letters

Children with visual, perceptual, and/or motor skill problems may have difficulty reading or writing similar letters such as **b**, **d**, **p**; **h**, **m**, **n**, **r**; **j**, **g**; and **v**, **w**. Letter-sound association activities can assist these children.

- Give children disposable aluminum pie pans, each one filled with about half an inch of sand (or salt). Hold up a classroom object or a picture that begins with one of the previously mentioned letters and say its name, accentuating the initial sound. Have children identify the letter that stands for the word's beginning sound. Write that letter on the board, and have children do the same in the sand in their aluminum pans. Direct them

to check their letters against the one on the board. Continue with another picture that starts with a letter visually similar to the letter on the board. For example, first hold up a **bat**, write **b** on the board, and have children write **b** in the sand; then hold up a picture with a **d** sound; then a **p** sound; then repeat.

- Provide sheets of mural paper and finger paints. Have children form two or more groups, with at least six children per group. Say a word, and tell children to identify the initial, medial, or final sound as well as the letter that stands for that sound. Focus on the previously mentioned visually confusing letters. Then direct children in each group to a section of the mural paper. Have each group form a large letter. Display the completed letter mural.

Attention Deficit Disorder (ADD)

Children who have ADD have difficulty focusing and maintaining attention. Lessons such as the assessment lesson on pages 75 and 76 may overwhelm such children because of the sheer number of exercises and the need to shift focus among initial, medial, and final sounds. As a result children may not pay attention to details and may make careless mistakes. The following techniques may help children concentrate on the task at hand.

- Break each page into two or three smaller sections. Have children complete a section and then stop to check their work with you. Only after one section has been completed and checked should children move on to the next set of items.

- Encourage children to establish a routine for completing each item in a given set. For pages 75 and 76, for example, direct children to say the picture name first. Then have them say that word again and compare what they hear themselves say with the letters given to determine whether an initial, medial, or final sound is missing. Next have children say the word a third time to determine the specific missing sound. Finally have them write the letter for that missing sound. Together rehearse the routine for the first few exercises so that children can commit it to memory. This type of routine approach will help children focus on the task at hand and have a clearer understanding of what they are to do.

The chart below identifies problems that children may manifest as they learn the concepts and skills presented in this unit. The chart also identifies strategies to use with children who have not yet mastered the key concepts in the unit.

SKILL	Consonants	Consonant Sound Positions	Hard and Soft g and c
Observation	Child confuses consonants, demonstrating a lack of mastery of the auditory and visual recognition of, as well as the writing of, consonants.	Child gets confused distinguishing initial, medial, and final consonant sounds.	Child cannot determine when to say the hard or soft **c** or **g**.
Intervention	• Give the child two or three letters to review at one time. • Start with one letter, and do singing activities, reading activities, and then writing activities involving words that begin with the sound of that letter. • Gradually add one letter at a time to help the child remember more than one or two letters at a time. • Have children work with a partner to write two different letters and name things that begin with each letter.	• Write **camel** on the board. Say: *The beginning sound in a word is the first sound you hear. /k/-amel What's the first sound?* Circle the **c** and write 1st under it. Continue in a similar fashion, writing 2nd and 3rd for the medial and final sounds in **camel**. • Have children work in pairs using **Sadlier Phonics Picture Cards** for **balloon, kitten, lemon, mitten, seven, salad, wagon**. Have one child pick a card, name it, and place it faceup on a desk. The other child writes the letter for the initial sound and places it before the card, writes the letter for the medial sound and places it above the card, and writes the letter for the final sound and places it after the card. • Partners check each other's work.	• Although only the hard **c** sound and the hard **g** sound are presented in Level A, the child may have been exposed to situations in which he or she encountered a soft **c** and/or **g**. • Explain that there are rules to help people remember which sound to say. Explain that if **c** is followed by **a**, **o**, or **u**, the **c** sound is /k/; if it is followed by an **e** or **i**, the sound is /s/. Say and write these words to illustrate the rules: **can, cot, cut, cent**. • Explain that if **g** is followed by **a**, **i**, **o**, or **u**, the **g** sound is usually /g/; if it is followed by an **e**, the sound is usually /j/. Say and write these words: **game, girl, got, gum, gentle**.

These activities are designed to augment the lessons in the unit with engaging exercises that reinforce skills and encourage creativity.

Match Initial Sounds

Memory Match
Materials: Sadlier Phonics Picture Cards for **doll, door, feet, fan, hat, hand, jam, jet, mitten, mule**

Have children work in pairs to play a phonics version of Concentration. Begin by viewing the picture cards together and naming them. Then have partners lay a set of the cards facedown in two rows of five cards each. Direct children to alternate turning over two cards, naming the pictures, and deciding whether both names have the same initial sound. If they do and the child can name the initial sound, he or she keeps the cards. If the initial sounds are different, the child returns the cards to their facedown position and lets his or her partner take a turn. The game continues until all cards are matched.

Match Final Sounds

Tag Team Endings
Have children play this game in teams, with two or three children on a team. Explain that the first team will say a word that ends with one of these consonant sounds: **/b/, /d/, /g/, /k/, /l/, /m/, /n/, /p/, /t/**. The other team must suggest another word that ends with the same sound. Give this example: *Team 1 says* **red***; team 2 says* **seed***.* If the responding team says a word with a matching final sound, it takes a turn at saying the first word. Have teams continue, alternating roles only after a correct match is given.

Which Doesn't Belong?
Materials: Sadlier Phonics Picture Cards

Tell children that in this game they choose which picture card name begins with a sound that is different from the beginning sound of the other cards. This is the card that does not belong in the group.

Display four pictures on the chalk ledge, three with names that begin with the same sound (e.g., **bike, bus, bug, duck**). Have children work in teams to decide which picture does not belong. The first team to correctly identify the picture with the different initial sound scores a point. Continue with new sets of cards until one team scores 10 points. If time permits, play again with the winning team acting as "game host" by selecting the sets of cards to be shown, displaying them, and awarding points.

Identify and Isolate Initial Sounds

Match Attack!
Materials: **Sadlier Phonics Picture Cards**

Assign each child one of the following sounds: /**f**/, /**m**/, /**s**/, /**t**/, /**h**/, /**b**/, /**l**/, /**d**/, /**k**/, /**n**/, /**g**/, /**w**/, /**p**/, /**r**/, /**j**/, /**kw**/, /**v**/, /**y**/, and /**z**/. Tell children you will hold up pictures of things that begin with one of these sounds. When children see a picture that begins with their assigned sound, they are to stand up, say the word, and identify its initial sound. For example, if you hold up the card for **zebra**, the child assigned /**z**/ should stand and say, "**Zebra**. **Zebra** begins with /**z**/."

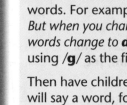

Hold up picture cards, one at a time, of objects having names that begin with one of the above sounds (for /**k**/, use only words beginning with a hard **c** or **k**). Continue until all children have had at least one turn.

What's the Answer?
Say the following questions:

What do cowboys ride? **(horses)**

What do bulls have on their heads? **(horns)**

Ask children to identify the initial sound of each answer and tell whether the initial sounds are the same. Then have children work in small groups to generate similar pairs of questions with answers that have the same initial sound. Have each group present its questions to the class.

Substitute Final Sounds

Have children focus on final sounds by showing them how inserting various final sounds forms new words. For example, say: ***Dot*** *and* ***bat*** *end with* /**t**/. *But when you change the ending sound to* /**l**/, *the words change to* ***doll*** *and* ***ball***. Ask children to try using /**g**/ as the final sound (**dog, bag**).

Then have children sit in a circle. Explain that you will say a word, for example, **hat**, to the child on your right. The child should tell the child to his or her right what final sound to substitute, for example, "**Hat**—change the ending sound to /**m**/," and the next child should respond accordingly, for example, **ham**. Then that child gives the next direction for how to change the ending sound to the child on his or her right. Play continues in a similar fashion around the circle. If a child incorrectly substitutes the final sound, the child to his or right gets a chance to respond. At first, allow children to work with nonsense words (for example, change the ending sound in **cap** to /**g**/). Then have children progress to naming real words.

Name _____ Date _____

Directions: Give this assessment orally to each child. The correct answers are boldfaced.

Match Initial Sounds

Say: *Listen to the first word I say. When you hear a word that begins with the same sound, raise your hand.* Circle the words that the child identifies.

1. jar: nail, sun, **jeep**   4. vase: deer, **vine**, bird
2. horse: cap, **hat**, band   5. bug: ten, **box**, crib
3. soup: **sock**, bowl, rope

Identify and Isolate Initial Sounds

Say: *Listen to the beginning sound in the words I say. After you hear all the words, tell me what that beginning sound is.* Write the sound that the child identifies.

6. nail, none, net   _____ /**n**/   9. lake, lamp, lid   _____ /**l**/
7. book, band, boot   _____ /**b**/   10. seed, sell, sun   _____ /**s**/
8. fish, fin, fence   _____ /**f**/

Add Initial Sounds

Say: *I will say the ending part of a word and three beginning sounds. You choose the beginning sound that forms a word.* Circle the sound the child chooses. You might say each sound with the ending part of the word, e.g., /l/-in, /p/-in, /n/-in.

11. _in   /l/   /**p**/   /n/   13. _ish   /b/   /n/   /**d**/   15. _ell   /**b**/   /p/   /v/
12. _ave   /**k**/   /m/   /t/   14. _eam   /**t**/   /w/   /z/

Match Final Sounds

Say: *I will say three words. Two words have the same ending sound. Which two words have the same ending sound?* Circle the words that the child identifies.

16. **cat**, dog, **pet**   18. **cook**, night, **bake**   20. **run**, **nine**, car
17. **frog**, **pig**, sneaker   19. **rub**, bat, **cab**

Substitute Final Sounds

Say: *I will say a word and three endings. Choose the ending sound that can replace the ending sound in the word to form a new word.* Circle the sound the child picks.

21. pan   /**t**/   /b/   /g/   23. mat   /z/   /f/   /**p**/   25. hot   /s/   /g/   /**f**/
22. pig   /h/   /m/   /**t**/   24. web   /**p**/   /t/   /g/

Join My Parade

Blackline Master 9
p.13L

Objective
To identify initial consonant sounds

Players
Individuals

Materials
- glue
- construction paper
- scissors

■ Duplicate and distribute Blackline Master 9 to each child.

■ Have children glue Blackline Master 9 onto construction paper and cut the letters and pictures into cards. Together identify all letters and pictures.

■ Tell children that all the letters decided to have a parade to celebrate a special day. Explain that each letter asked a friend whose name begins with the sound of that letter to join the parade.

■ Have children place the letter cards faceup on their desks. Then have them place to the right of each letter card the picture with a name that begins with the sound of that letter.

Join My Parade, Too

Blackline Master 9
p.13L

Objective
To identify final consonant sounds

Players
Individuals

Materials
- letter and picture cards made for "Join My Parade"

■ Have children use the cards from "Join My Parade." Tell them they will use the cards to practice recognizing ending consonant sounds.

■ Ask children to imagine that the picture cards would like a chance to lead the parade. Have them place the picture cards faceup on their desks.

■ Direct children to place the card with the letter that stands for the ending sound of a given picture name to the right of that picture card.

Rows of Dominoes

Blackline Master 10
p.13M

Objective
To identify initial and final consonant sounds

Players
Small groups

Materials
- construction paper
- scissors
- glue

■ Duplicate and distribute Blackline Master 10 to each group.

■ Name the pictures together. Have volunteers identify each initial and final sound. Direct children to glue the page onto construction paper and cut apart the cards.

■ Tell children to follow these steps:

1. Start with the clown that faces left. Say the word **clown**, and name its final consonant sound.

2. Find the picture whose name begins with the sound you just said. That picture comes next.

3. Continue until all the cards have been used.

4. Complete the row of dominoes by placing the clown that faces right at the end of the row.

Join My Parade

Rows of Dominoes

The Name Game

Have the class work in groups. Ask each group to spread out one set of Punchout Cards picture side up. Direct one child in each group to hold up a consonant letter from his or her individual set of Punchout Cards and say: "My name is (name that begins with chosen letter)." Tell children to use their real name if it begins with a consonant sound. Then have group members scan the pictures shown for a picture with a name that begins with the same letter. When a child finds an appropriate picture, she or he should hand it to the child with the consonant card and say a sentence that mentions both the picture and the child's name (e.g., "a **balloon** for **Bernie**"). Continue until each member of the group has had a chance to start the game.

Big and Small, Find Them All

Remove the vowels and extra consonants from children's sets of Punchout Cards. Then have the class work in groups of three. After stressing how important it is that each group member complete a different task, direct the groups to choose one member to be in charge of upper-case letters; another, lowercase letters; and a third, pictures.

Have each child spread out the cards so that his or her assigned category is displayed. Ask children assigned to pictures to begin the group activity by holding up a picture and naming it. Direct the other members of each group to locate the letter that stands for the picture name's beginning sound. When both uppercase and lowercase responses have been given, have children turn over the letter cards to check their work. One card will be the same as the original picture; the other card will show a different picture that begins with the same sound. Encourage children to switch tasks as they continue.

Picture Search

Ask children to spread out their consonant Punchout Cards picture side up. Direct them to scan the pictures for answers to riddles you give. Say riddles that include both meaning and sound clues. For example:

I'm an animal that swims and flies. My name begins with /**d**/. What am I? (**duck**)

I'm something you ride in or pull. My name begins with /**w**/. What am I? (**wagon**)

I'm a home for a swarm of bees. My name begins with /**h**/. What am I? (**hive**)

Trading Cards

Have children work in pairs. Ask one child in each pair to choose five different consonant letter cards and to show them to her or his partner. Then have each remaining partner spread a complete set of cards, picture side up, and find pictures with names that begin or end with the sound of the chosen letters.

LETTER-SENTENCE DESIGNS

Objectives

- To strengthen consonant sound recognition
- To use a writing and painting program such as Kid Works™ Deluxe* to write and illustrate a simple sentence

Preparation

Write the letters **b, c, d, f, g, h, j, k, l, m, n, p, q, r, s, t, v, w, x, y,** and **z** on the board. Have children identify each letter. Then help them generate a list of words that begin with each consonant. Write the words on the board.

One Step at a Time

1. Write this sentence on the board: I love the **b** in **beach**. Then read the sentence to the class.

2. Tell children to choose a letter and a word that begins with that letter from the list on the board. Have them use these letters and words to add a new sentence to the board. Then have each child say his or her new sentence.

3. Help children click on the pink "New Book" icon on the opening screen and then the white arrow at the bottom of the red book on the next screen. This will take them to two blank pages of an opened book.

4. Tell children to click on the Paint Brush icon on the left page to create a paint page.

5. Guide children to click on the Silly Scribbler icon (the pencil) on the shelf to enter their sentences.

6. Have children access the various drawing tools to design an illustration to accompany their sentences. Or, children can choose from a selection of coloring book pictures by clicking on the Picture Book icon. Show children how to scroll through the picture categories and to select a picture to color.

7. When all children have finished, have them print their illustrated sentences.

Class Sharing

Encourage volunteers to read their sentences to the class. You may wish to display the children's sentences on a bulletin board so the class can enjoy them when they are "reading the room."

CONSONANT PICTORIALS

Objectives

- To reinforce the recognition of initial, medial, and final consonant sounds
- To use a paint program such as Kid Pix Studio® Deluxe* to design a consonant pictorial

Preparation

Write the letters **b, c, d, f, g, h, j, k, l, m, n, p, q, r, s, t, v, w, x, y,** and **z** on the board. Have volunteers choose a letter, name it, and say a word that demonstrates its initial, medial, or final sound. Then assign a consonant to each child or group.

All software referred to in this book is listed under Computer Resources on page 348.

One Step at a Time

1. Have children select "Kid Pix" from the opening screen. Guide them to use the Typewriter icon from the side menu to enter the assigned consonant at the top of the screen.

2. Tell children to select "Pick a Stamp Set" under the "Goodies" menu to access different sets of decorative stamps.

3. Direct children to scan through the stamps for pictures having names that demonstrate the assigned sound in initial, medial, or final position. For example, for the sound of initial **c**, children might include pictures of a **carrot** and **cat**.

4. Have children also use the paint tools from the side menu to illustrate words that have their sound in initial, medial, or final position.

5. If a microphone is available, have children select "Record a Sound" under the "Goodies" menu and record themselves saying the illustrated words.

6. Have children print their pictorials.

Class Sharing

Invite volunteers to present their pictorials to the class. After each presentation, direct the class to identify the initial, medial, and final consonant illustrated. You may wish to display the pictorials around the room so children can refer to them periodically.

CELEBRATE!

Ask children to describe their favorite holiday. List the holidays on chart paper.

Write the word *customs* on the board, and explain what it means. Ask children to name different customs they follow. Then write the word *superstitions* on the board and say the word. Give the class examples of superstitions, such as don't open an umbrella in the house or don't walk under a ladder. Then show children the video *Customs and Superstitions.* Ask children to name holidays, customs, and superstitions that they learned about on the video. Add these words to the list. Help children identify the initial, medial, and final consonant sounds in all the words.

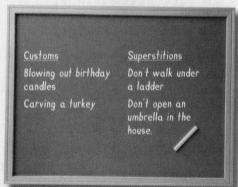

Customs	Superstitions
Blowing out birthday candles	Don't walk under a ladder
Carving a turkey	Don't open an umbrella in the house.

Literature Introduction to Consonant Sounds

Objectives

- To enjoy a poem about parades
- To produce rhyming words
- To associate consonants with their sounds

Starting with Literature

Read aloud "Parades." Use the illustration as a springboard for a discussion about parades and other celebrations children have attended or would like to attend.

Developing Critical Thinking

Read aloud the Critical Thinking questions and have children respond. Discuss with children the reasons and occasions for holding parades and other celebrations.

Introducing the Skill

Phonemic Awareness: Produce Rhyming Words

- Explain that rhyming words have the same ending sounds, such as **sing/ring**. Say groups of three words, two of which rhyme. Begin with **big, bands**, and **hands** from the poem. Have volunteers identify the words that rhyme.
- Ask one volunteer to name something he or she might see at a parade, such as a **flag**. Call on another volunteer to supply a word that rhymes with the first one, for example, **bag**. Continue with other words.

Consonant Sounds

Materials: **Unit 2 Classroom Poster**

- Print the word **bands** on the board, and circle the letter **b**. Explain that the letter **b** stands for /**b**/, the sound heard at the beginning of **bands**.
- Display the **Unit 2 Classroom Poster**. Tell children to listen for other words that begin with /**b**/ as you reread the poem's first stanza. Point to the **b** words on the poster as each is identified.

13

PARADES

I like to see parades
with the marching bands
and big bass drums;
They make me want to dance
and clap my hands.

People ride in convertible cars
and smile and wave at you
and clowns come down the street
and make you laugh.

A parade makes everybody happy;
people talk and dance and sing—
I like to watch parades
more than any other thing.

Karama Fufuka

Critical Thinking

Why do people have parades? Possible responses: to celebrate holidays, to honor or to welcome people
What other kinds of celebrations are fun? parties, shows, picnics

LESSON 5: Consonant Sounds
Phonemic Awareness: Rhyme

13

Theme Words

Words on Parade Describe to the class parades you have seen. Then ask children to share their parade experiences. Ask who and what they saw in each parade. Then make a word wall by recording key words from their responses on chart paper. Include words from the poem "Parades" and tell children they will add to the word wall throughout the unit.

Return to the earlier Critical Thinking discussion concerning other kinds of celebrations that are fun. Have children describe these celebrations, and then add new words from their responses to the word wall. Refer to the word wall and add to it regularly.

At the end of the unit, display a picture of a parade or celebration and have children tell a story about the picture. Encourage them to use words from the word wall. Write the class story on a separate chart and display it in the classroom as a model for future stories.

Dear Family,

In this unit about celebrations, your child will learn the sounds of the consonant letters. As your child progresses through this unit, you may wish to try these activities together at home.

• The consonant letters of the alphabet are shown below. Help your child find the consonants in his or her name.

bcdfghjklmnpqrstvwxyz

• Read the poem "Parades" on the reverse side of this page.

• Help your child identify some of the consonants in the poem.

• With your child, think of words that rhyme with **band** and **sing**. (hand/land/sand, bing/ding/king/ping/ring/wing)

Apreciada Familia:

Esta unidad es sobre las celebraciones. Los niños aprenderán el sonido de las consonantes. A medida que se avanza en la unidad, pueden hacer estas actividades con su hijo.

• Las consonantes son mostradas abajo. Ayude al niño a encontrar las consonantes en su nombre.

• Lea el poema "Parades" en la página 13.

• Ayude al niño a identificar las consonantes en el poema.

• Junto con su niño piensen en palabras que rimen con **band** y **sing**. (hand/land/sand, bing/ding/king/ping/ring/wing)

PROJECT

What kinds of celebrations are special for your family? Look at a calendar together and mark the dates of a few of them. Talk about why these days are important. How does your family celebrate them? Help your child find and name some consonants in the names of these celebrations.

PROYECTO

¿Cuáles celebraciones son especiales en su familia? Juntos busquen en un calendario las fechas de algunas. Hablen sobre esos días importantes. ¿Cómo celebra la familia esos días? Ayude al niño a encontrar algunas consonantes en los nombres de esas celebraciones.

14   LESSON 5: Consonant Sounds—Phonics Alive at Home

Phonics Alive at Home

• The *Phonics Alive at Home* page promotes family involvement in children's reading and writing progress. As family members work together on the activities, they actively participate in their child's language and phonics learning.

• Activities on the *Phonics Alive at Home* page for Unit 2 focus on the unit theme "Celebrations" and on consonant sounds.

• Direct children to remove page 14 from their books and take the page home so that their families can participate in *Phonics Alive at Home* activities.

• Make a class calendar of special days. Encourage children to add to the class calendar any special days they talked about at home with their families.

• Throughout the unit, connect school and home activities by providing opportunities for children to share photos, stories, and books from home that deal with holidays and celebrations.

Sadlier Reading
Little Books and Big Books

Read several poems in Worlds of Poetry from *Around the Neighborhood* to practice recognizing initial consonant sounds.

Direct children to additional activities on Sadlier-Oxford's web site: www.sadlier-oxford.com.

Multicultural Connection

Explain that cultures around the world may celebrate the same holiday differently. In some Asian cultures, it's a custom to eat noodles on one's birthday because noodles represent long life. Ask children to tell what special things they do on their birthday. Then have a birthday celebration. Brainstorm ideas, such as making hats or decorations. During the celebration, sing variations of "Happy Birthday to You" by replacing all initial consonant sounds with one sound, such as /**b**/, making it "Bappy Birthday Bo Bou."

Take-Home Book

The Unit 2 Take-Home Book, *I Love Parades,* is found on student pages 325–326. This fold-up book may be enjoyed by children and family members alike and can be used to reinforce the phonics skills of consonant recognition taught in Unit 2. Choose an appropriate time in the unit to send this component home with each child.

Initial /f/ Ff

Objectives
- To match initial sounds
- To recognize initial /f/
- To recognize that **Ff** stands for /f/
- To print **f** to complete words

Warming Up

Reviewing Rhyming Words

Remind children that rhyming words have the same ending sounds. Tell children that **sing** and **ring** are rhyming words. Have children stand up when they hear you say two words that rhyme. Use these words: **cake/bake**, **mop/top**, **bed/jog**, **sun/fun**, **cat/big**.

Teaching the Lesson

Phonemic Awareness: Match Initial Sounds

Say the word **fair**. Tell children that **fair** begins with /f/. Then say the words **fair**, **food**, and **ball**. Tell children that **fair** and **food** begin with /f/ but that **ball** begins with a different sound. Together, say **five**, **nose**, and **fork**. Have children say the two words that begin with the same sound.

Sound to Symbol

- Say /f/, and have children repeat /f/. Say **Fannie**, **found**, **fish**, **fair**, **face.** Then explain that the words all begin with /f/. Tell children to listen to a sentence and point to their face when they hear a word that begins with /**f**/. Say: *Find a funny fan for me.*
- On the board, print **Ff**. Point to and identify the uppercase and lowercase letters. Tell children that both letters stand for /**f**/. Print these words on the board: **Follow**, **farm**, **Find**, **fish**. Read the words. Then ask a volunteer to underline the letter that stands for /f/ in each word. Ask another volunteer to tell whether the underlined letter is uppercase or lowercase.

Ff

Fair starts with the sound of **f**. Listen for the sound of **f** in the rhyme.

Follow me to the fair,
Be the very first one there!
Find your favorite foods to eat,
Or find a funny clown to meet!

Circle and color each picture that has the sound of **f** at the beginning of its name.

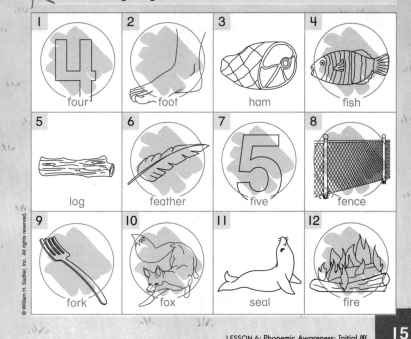

1 four	2 foot	3 ham	4 fish
5 log	6 feather	7 five	8 fence
9 fork	10 fox	11 seal	12 fire

LESSON 6: Phonemic Awareness: Initial /f/

15

UNIVERSAL ACCESS
Meeting Individual Needs

Auditory • Visual
Materials: drawing paper, crayons

Have children draw a picture of something that begins with /f/ and then turn the picture into a fan. After pictures are drawn, model folding the paper back and forth to make a fan. Ask children to open their fans to share their pictures.

Auditory • Kinesthetic
Materials: fans from preceding activity

Remind children that the letter **f** stands for /**f**/. Say aloud a list of words, some of which begin with /**f**/. Have children wave their fans in the air whenever they hear a word that begins with /**f**/. Your list of words might include **fox, band, fun, fix, go, fire, field, horse, four.**

Extra Support
Have children say **finger** and tell them that it begins with /**f**/. Review how to write the letter **f** in the air with one finger and direct children to do that each time they hear you say an initial **f** word. Say these words: **fast, fin, fog, get, fun, cap, fit.**

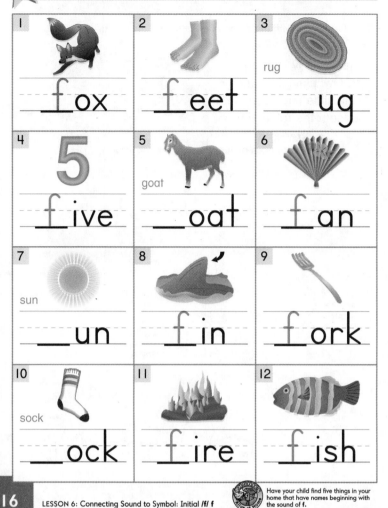

Say the name of each picture. Print **f** on the line if its name begins with the sound of **f**.

1	2	3
f͟o͟x͟	f͟e͟e͟t͟	rug __͟u͟g͟
4 five	**5** goat	**6**
f͟i͟v͟e͟	__͟o͟a͟t͟	f͟a͟n͟
7 sun	**8**	**9**
__͟u͟n͟	f͟i͟n͟	f͟o͟r͟k͟
10 sock	**11**	**12**
__͟o͟c͟k͟	f͟i͟r͟e͟	f͟i͟s͟h͟

16

LESSON 6: Connecting Sound to Symbol: Initial /f/ f

Have your child find five things in your home that have names beginning with the sound of f.

Practicing the Skill

- Point to the letters **Ff** at the top of page 15. Remind children that these letters stand for /**f**/. Tell children to trace the letters on the page and then write them in the air.
- Ask children to look at the picture at the top of the page. Explain that the picture takes place at a **fair** and discuss what happens at a fair. Then instruct children to listen for /**f**/ as you read the rhyme at the top of the page.
- As a class, go over the directions and identify the pictures. Model for children how to circle and color the first picture. Then tell children to complete the page.
- Read the directions for page 16. Have children trace the **f** under the first picture before they complete the page.

Curriculum Connections

Theme Activity: Social Studies
Materials: construction paper, scissors, crayons

- Tell children about the Japanese holiday Children's Day, celebrated on March 5. On this day, once called Boys' Day, families fly a banner in the shape of a carp, a powerful fish that can leap up a waterfall. Both boys and girls are encouraged to be strong and brave like the carp.
- Have children make fish banners that are decorated with pictures of initial **f** words.

Portfolio

Tell children to place their fish banners in their portfolios.

Sadlier Reading
Little Books and Big Books

Read *Felix, the Very Hungry Fish* (fiction) and *Who Has Four Feet?* (nonfiction) for more practice with initial consonant **f**.

Observational Assessment

*Note whether children draw pictures of initial **f** words on their fish banners.*

English Language Learners/ESL
As you read the rhyme on page 15, add these gestures to help children understand the rhyme.

- line 1: beckon with hand
- line 2: put up one index finger
- line 3: mimic eating something delicious
- line 4: turn to a child to shake hands

Repeat the rhyme, using gestures, and tell children to listen for words that begin with /**f**/ as in **fair**.

Challenge
Tell children that they are going to make up riddles with answers that begin with **f**. Model the following riddle and ask children to give the answer.

I have five toes.
You use me to stand on and to hop.
What am I? (**foot**)

Have children work in pairs to make up riddles for words such as **farmer**, **fog**, or **five**. Then have the class solve the riddles.

Special Strategies
For Universal Access activities, see page 13F.

16

Initial /m/ Mm

Objectives

- To match initial sounds
- To recognize initial /m/
- To recognize that **Mm** stands for /m/
- To print **m** to complete words

Warming Up

Reviewing Rhyming Words

- Recite the following verse.
  Let's all play a rhyming **game**.
  Stand up for words that sound the **same**.
  Like **boy** and **joy**, and **force** and **horse**.
  But not like bread and milk, of **course**.

- Repeat the verse and have children identify the rhyming words.

Teaching the Lesson

Phonemic Awareness: Match Initial Sounds

Materials: a mask or picture of a mask

Display a mask or a picture of a mask. Identify the object as a mask, and tell children that **mask** begins with /m/. Have children say **mask** and /m/. Then say **music**, **moon**, and **tub**, and have children repeat the words. Ask children to tell which words begin with /m/—the sound at the beginning of **mask**. Repeat with the words **man**, **mop**, **fill**.

Sound to Symbol

- Say /m/. Have children repeat /m/. Explain that /m/ is the sound at the beginning of **mop**. Say: ***Mike makes music***. Tell children that every word in the sentence begins with /m/. Have children pretend to mop the floor when they hear a word that begins with /m/ in this sentence: ***My mom** looked at the **moon***.

- Print **Mm** on chart paper. Tell children that these letters stand for /m/. Point to and name uppercase and lowercase **m**, and then print the following words on the chart: **mop**, **me**, **mess**, **Mike**. Have children say the words with you while volunteers underline the letters that stand for /m/.

17

Mm

Moon starts with the sound of **m.** Listen for the sound of **m** in the rhyme.

One Monday in May,
Mr. Owl played a tune
While little mice danced
Beneath the full moon.

Circle and color each picture that has the sound of **m** at the beginning of its name.

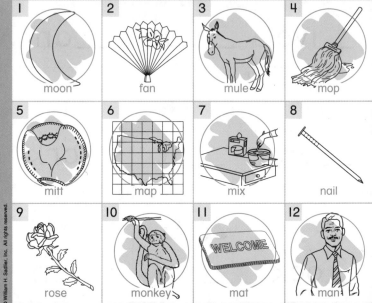

1	2	3	4
moon	fan	mule	mop

5	6	7	8
mitt	map	mix	nail

9	10	11	12
rose	monkey	mat	man

LESSON 7: Phonemic Awareness: Initial /m/   **17**

UNIVERSAL ACCESS
Meeting Individual Needs

Auditory • Visual

Say: ***Magical Max makes music***. Write the words on the board, leaving out each **m**. Invite volunteers to fill in the missing letters. Help them with the uppercase **M** that begins the sentence and the name. Repeat the activity using ***Matt misses Marcy***.

Visual • Kinesthetic

Materials: Sadlier Phonics Picture Cards for **mask, mitten, mix, mule,** and for words beginning with other sounds

Have children stand still and pretend to be statues. Tell the "statues" to change position only when they see a picture card that begins with /m/. Mix the cards up and then display them one by one.

Extra Support

Review that **m** stands for /m/ as in **most**. Then write the following on the board: -om, -an, -op, -ud, -ust, and -ad. Have children rewrite each word by replacing the dash with an **m**. Then say the words together.

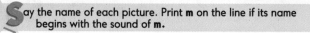

Say the name of each picture. Print **m** on the line if its name begins with the sound of **m**.

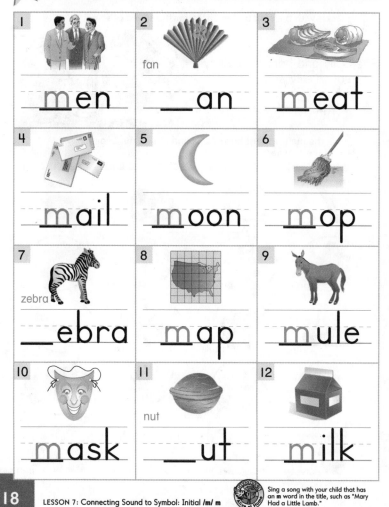

1 __m__en	2 fan __an	3 __m__eat
4 __m__ail	5 __m__oon	6 __m__op
7 zebra __ebra	8 __m__ap	9 __m__ule
10 __m__ask	11 nut __ut	12 __m__ilk

18

LESSON 7: Connecting Sound to Symbol: Initial /m/ m

Sing a song with your child that has an **m** word in the title, such as "Mary Had a Little Lamb."

Practicing the Skill

● Ask children to point to **Mm** at the top of page 17. Review that the letters stand for /**m**/. Then have children trace the letters on the page and write them in the air. Have children listen for words beginning with /**m**/ as you read the rhyme.

● Read aloud the directions. Ask if the first picture should be circled and colored. Name the rest of the pictures and then have children complete the page.

● Go over the directions on page 18 and name the pictures. Model the first item before having children complete the page.

Curriculum Connections

Theme Activity: Multicultural
Materials: paper plates, craft sticks, tape

● Tell children that people all over the world sometimes dress up in costumes and masks to celebrate. Point out that traditionally, Native American nations have often used animal masks as props to tell stories.

● Tell children that they are going to make a mask with a picture of a /**m**/ word. Punch eyeholes in plates for children. Ask children to draw a picture on the "face" side of the plate. Suggest words such as **man**, **moth**, **monkey**, **moon**, and **monster**. Help children tape craft sticks to the finished masks. Have children show their masks and name their drawings.

Portfolio Tell children to place their masks in their portfolios.

Sadlier Reading
Little Books and Big Books

Read *Messy Moose* (fiction) and *Who Is My Mom?* (nonfiction) for more practice with initial consonant **m**.

English Language Learners/ESL
Materials: milk carton

Point to a milk carton and say /**m**/ and tell children that /**m**/ is the sound at the beginning of the word **milk**. Have children repeat the word **milk** after you. Write the word **milk** on chart paper and circle the **m**. Then say the word again, moving your hand from left to right along the word as you say it. Repeat this procedure using objects around the classroom that begin with **m**, e.g., **me**, **map**, **meal**, **mail**, and any children's names that begin with **m**.

Challenge
Materials: drawing paper, crayons

Say **menu** and have children repeat it. Mention that **menu**, as well as some food names, begin with **m**. Give the examples **macaroni**, **muffin**, **melon**, and **milk**. Then ask children to work with a partner to design a menu of **m** foods. Children can draw the foods. Display the menus and let partners read aloud the foods listed on them.

Special Strategies
For Universal Access activities, see page 13F.

Observational Assessment

*Note children who easily recognize words that begin with **m**.*

18

Initial /s/ Ss

Objectives
- To match initial sounds
- To recognize initial /s/
- To recognize that **Ss** stands for /s/
- To print **s** to complete words

Warming Up

Reviewing /f/ and /m/

Materials: Punchout Letter Cards for **Ff** and **Mm**

Tell children they will review words beginning with /f/ and /m/. Ask children to hold up the **f** or the **m** letter card that stands for the beginning sound they hear. Use words such as **fan**, **fox**, **mask**, **mom**, **feet**, and **Mark**.

Teaching the Lesson

Phonemic Awareness: Match Initial Sounds

Say the word **song** and have children repeat it. Explain that **song** begins with /s/. Then say: **song**, **see**, **girl**. Have children say the words and identify which two begin with /s/. Continue the activity using the following words: **mud**, **sand**, **soap**; **sister**, **sail**, **read**; **sat**, **map**, **see**.

Sound to Symbol

- Ask children to listen as you say: *Every Sunday Sally sings songs* about **seals**. Have children repeat the sentence. Explain that **Sunday**, **Sally**, **sings**, **songs**, and **seals** begin with /s/. Have children repeat each word after you and then say /s/.
- Print **Ss** on the board. Point to the uppercase and lowercase letters and explain that they stand for /s/. Print these words on the board: **Sunday**, **Sally**, **sings**, **songs**, **seals**. Read aloud the words. Ask volunteers to underline the letter that stands for /s/ at the beginning of each word. Have the class identify the uppercase **S** in two of the words.

19

Ss

Sing starts with the sound of **s**. Listen for the sound of **s** in the tongue twister.

See Sally and her sister Suzy sing seven silly songs.

Circle the pictures that have the sound of **s** at the beginning of their names.

1	seven	safe	milk	five
2	seed	sock	moon	soap
3	fire	mule	six	saw
4	sun	suit	fan	seat
5	monkey	sail	sink	men

LESSON 8: Phonemic Awareness: Initial /s/   **19**

U N I V E R S A L   A C C E S S
Meeting Individual Needs

Visual • Kinesthetic

Materials: Sadlier Phonics Picture Cards for **fan, feet, fox, mask, mitten, mule, seal, six, sun**

Have children work in two teams. Distribute picture cards representing **f, m,** and **s** beginning sounds. Have each team sort its picture cards into initial **f, m,** and **s** words.

Auditory • Kinesthetic

Arrange chairs, backs facing inward, in a circle; include a chair for each child. Direct children to march around the circle of chairs as you say a list of words, some of which begin with /s/. Tell children that when they hear an **s** word, they should sit in the nearest chair. Use words such as **sink, sit, fox, man, seven, fall, socks**.

Extra Support

Materials: Sadlier Phonics Picture Cards for **seal, seven, salad, six, sun,** and cards with other initial sounds.

Review that **s** stands for /s/, as in **sip**. Display a picture card. Have a volunteer say the name. If its name begins with /s/, have the child write **s** on the board.

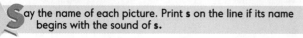

Say the name of each picture. Print **s** on the line if its name begins with the sound of **s**.

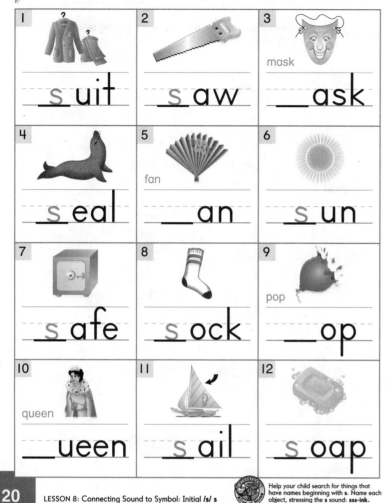

1	2	3
<u>s</u> uit	<u>s</u> aw	<u>__</u> ask (mask)
4	5	6
<u>s</u> eal	<u>__</u> an (fan)	<u>s</u> un
7	8	9
<u>s</u> afe	<u>s</u> ock	<u>__</u> op (pop)
10	11	12
<u>__</u> ueen (queen)	<u>s</u> ail	<u>s</u> oap

LESSON 8: Connecting Sound to Symbol: Initial /s/ **s**

Help your child search for things that have names beginning with **s**. Name each object, stressing the **s** sound: **sss-ink**.

Practicing the Skill

● Ask children to identify the letters at the top of page 19. Remind children that the letters stand for /**s**/. Then have children use clay to form an uppercase and lowercase **s**. Have children listen for initial /**s**/ as you read the tongue twister.

● Go over the directions with children and name the pictures. Have children trace the gray circles around the first two pictures because they have names that begin with /**s**/. Have children finish the page.

● Read aloud the directions on page 20. Say the names of the pictures with children. Model writing **s** to complete the first word. Then have children complete the page.

Curriculum Connections

Theme Activity: Science/Art

● Explain to children that the circus is a special kind of celebration. Have children tell about the circus.

● Tell the class that a seal is a circus animal known for its tricks and that **seal** begins with /**s**/. Describe tricks that a seal might do, such as clapping or balancing a ball on its nose. Have children draw a picture of a seal performing and print a caption for the picture, using some words with initial **s**.

Portfolio Have children add their seal pictures to their portfolios.

Sadlier Reading

Little Books and Big Books

Read *What Do You See by the Sea?* (nonfiction) and *What Does Sam Sell?* (fiction) for more practice with initial consonant **s**.

English Language Learners/ESL

Say /**s**/ and tell children to listen for that sound. Then say: *See Sally and her sister Suzy.* Print **Ss** on the board and tell children these letters stand for /**s**/. Repeat the sentence several times, and encourage children to join in as they trace an **s** on their desks each time they hear an initial **s** sound. Repeat the activity, using names of children in the class.

Challenge

Reread the tongue twister on page 19 with children. Challenge them to write their own tongue twister with as many words as they can that begin with /**s**/. Children can print their tongue twisters on strips of paper, get together with a partner, and read them. Have children determine which tongue twister(s) contain the most **s** words.

Special Strategies

For Universal Access activities, see page 13F.

Observational Assessment

*Note whether children are able to include initial **s** words in their captions.*

Final /f/ f, ff; /m/ m; /s/ s, ss

Objectives
- To match final sounds
- To recognize final /**f**/, /**m**/, and /**s**/
- To recognize that **f** and **ff** stand for /**f**/, that **m** stands for /**m**/, and that **s** and **ss** stand for /**s**/
- To print **f**, **ff**, **m**, **s**, and **ss** to complete words

Warming Up

Reviewing Rhyming Words

Have children form a line facing you. Ask them to say words that rhyme with words you say. Use the words **fan**, **sun**, **mat**, **hill**, and **pot**. When children give a rhyming word, have them take one giant step forward.

Teaching the Lesson

Phonemic Awareness:
Match Final Sounds

Materials: **Sadlier Phonics Picture Cards** for **leaf**, **drum**, **bus**

Display picture card **leaf**. Name it and explain that **leaf** ends with /**f**/. Say **off**, **pail**, **roof**. Have children raise their hands if they hear /**f**/ at the end of a word. Use picture cards **drum** and **bus** to introduce final /**m**/ and /**s**/. Say **ham**, **Pam**, **bead**, and have children identify words with final /**m**/. For final /**s**/, say **class**, **good**, **gas**.

Sound to Symbol

Say **roof**. Explain that roof ends with /**f**/. Have children repeat /**f**/. Write the word **roof**, circle the letter **f**, and explain that this letter stands for /**f**/ at the end of **roof**. Write the word **off**, and circle the letters **ff**. Explain that /**f**/ is also the sound of **ff**. Repeat the process with /**m**/ **m** (using **ham**) and /**s**/ **s**, **ss** (using **lips** and **dress**).

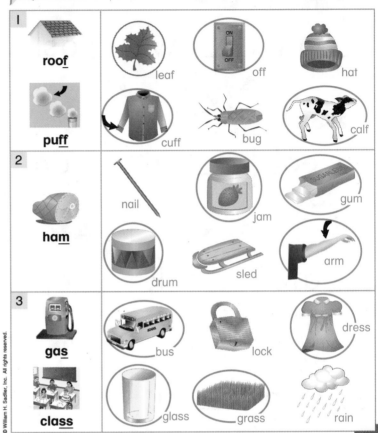

Circle the pictures if their names have the same ending sound as the first picture or pictures in the box.

1 | roof | puff | leaf | off | hat | cuff | bug | calf

2 | ham | nail | jam | gum | drum | sled | arm

3 | gas | class | bus | lock | dress | glass | grass | rain

LESSON 9: Phonemic Awareness: Final /**f**/, /**m**/, /**s**/   **21**

UNIVERSAL ACCESS
Meeting Individual Needs

Auditory • Kinesthetic

Remind children of the big, bad wolf who, in the well-known tale, huffed and puffed at the houses of the three little pigs. Have children role-play the wolf. Direct them to **huff** and **puff** whenever they hear a word you say that ends in /**f**/. Say **stuff**, **cat**, **calf**, **leaf**, **sniff**, **book**, **roof**.

Auditory • Tactile

Materials: shoe box lid for each child, with a layer of sand or flour

Tell children that you are going to say some words. Ask children to print the letter **f**, **m**, or **s** in the sand (or flour) to identify the ending sound. Use these words: **leaf**, **drum**, **bus**, **ham**, **gas**, **hum**, **leaf**.

Extra Support

Have children say **puff**, **hum**, and **hiss**. Identify each ending sound with them as /**f**/, /**m**/, or /**s**/. Ask children to identify the same ending sounds in other words you say: **room**, **elf**, **glass**, **off**, **bus**.

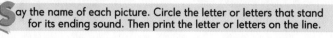

Say the name of each picture. Circle the letter or letters that stand for its ending sound. Then print the letter or letters on the line.

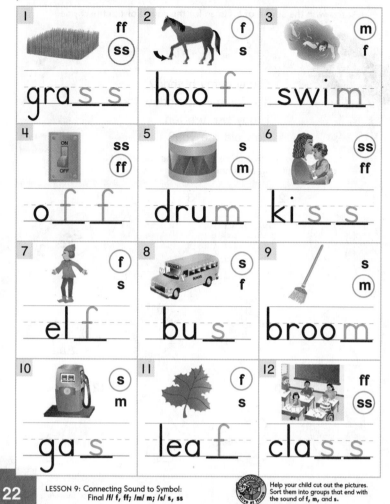

1. (ff) (ss) — gra**ss**
2. (f) s — hoo**f**
3. (m) f — swi**m**
4. (ss) (ff) — o**f**f
5. (s) m — dru**m**
6. (ss) ff — ki**ss**
7. (f) s — el**f**
8. (s) f — bu**s**
9. s (m) — broo**m**
10. (s) m — ga**s**
11. (f) s — lea**f**
12. ff (ss) — cla**ss**

22 | LESSON 9: Connecting Sound to Symbol: Final /f/ f, ff; /m/ m; /s/ s, ss

Help your child cut out the pictures. Sort them into groups that end with the sound of f, m, and s.

Practicing the Skill

● Have children turn to page 21. Read the directions aloud. Identify the ending sound of the first picture in each row. Model completing the first set of pictures with children. Together identify the rest of the pictures before having children complete the page.

● Read aloud the directions on page 22. Go over the first item with children. Identify the final /s/ in **grass** and then have children trace the gray circle. Model writing **ss** to complete the first word. Identify the other pictures with children and have them complete the page.

Curriculum Connections

Theme Activity: Science

Materials: drawing paper, crayons

● Tell children they will be marching in a nature parade. Ask children to brainstorm nature words that end in /**f**/, /**m**/, and /**s**/ (e.g., **leaf**, **reef**, **cliff**, **ram**, **clam**, **moss**, **grass**). Write the nature words on the board. Have volunteers circle the letter or letters that stand for the final sound.

● Have each child illustrate one of the nature words, copy the word from the board, and circle the letter or letters that stand for the final sound.

● Have children parade around the room displaying their nature pictures.

Portfolio — Have children place their completed nature drawings in their portfolios.

English Language Learners/ESL

Help children recognize and say final /**f**/, /**m**/, and /**s**/. Direct children to page 21. Point to each final **f** picture on the page, say its name, and have children repeat it several times. Remind children that these words end with /**f**/ as in **leaf**. Continue in the same manner with the picture names involving final **m** and then final **s**.

Challenge

Distribute to children the word puzzles shown below. Point out how to read the words across and down. Challenge children to solve each word puzzle by filling in **f**, **m**, or **s** to complete the words. Children might like to make up a word puzzle of their own for others to solve.

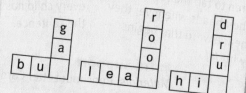

Special Strategies

For Universal Access activities, see page 13F.

Observational Assessment

Note whether children are able to identify final /f/, /m/, and /s/ in the auditory activities.

22

Initial /t/ Tt

Objectives
- To identify and isolate initial sounds
- To recognize initial /t/
- To recognize that **Tt** stands for /t/
- To print **t** to complete words

Warming Up

Reviewing Initial Consonant Sounds

Materials: **Sadlier Phonics Picture Cards** for initial /**f**/, /**m**/, /**s**/ (e.g., **fan**, **feet**, **mask**, **mitten**, **seal**, **sun**)

Have children stand up. Tell them that you will show pictures of objects whose names start with /**f**/, /**m**/, or /**s**/. As you show the picture cards, ask children to fan themselves to identify initial **f** words; to march in place for initial **m** words; and to sit down for initial **s** words.

Teaching the Lesson

Phonemic Awareness: Identify and Isolate Initial Sounds

Say the word **ten**. Repeat the word and then isolate the initial sound: **ten**, /**t**/. Explain that /**t**/ is the beginning sound in **ten**. Then have children identify and isolate the initial sound for each of these words: **top**, /**t**/; **tub**, /**t**/; **fan**, /**f**/; **sod**, /**s**/; **map** /**m**/.

Sound to Symbol

- Say: ***Tommy took a toy toad to town.*** Tell children that /**t**/ is the sound they hear at the beginning of **Tommy**, **took**, **toy**, **toad**, **to**, and **town**. Have children repeat the words and say /**t**/ after each one. Say the sentence again, and have children tap their toes each time they hear /**t**/ at the beginning of a word.
- Write **Tt** on the board. Point to the lowercase and the uppercase letters, and explain that both letters stand for /**t**/. Write the sentence about Tommy on the board. Read the sentence together. Have volunteers underline the letters that stand for /**t**/ at the beginning of words.

23

Tt

Ten starts with the sound of **t**. Listen for the sound of **t** in the rhyme.

Today is my birthday.
It's Tammy's birthday, too.
Today we turn ten.
How old are you?

Circle and color each picture that has the sound of **t** at the beginning of its name.

1 ten	2 map	3 toe	4 tag
5 two	6 top	7 sun	8 fish
9 tire	10 tools	11 robe	12 tie

LESSON 10: Phonemic Awareness: Initial /t/   **23**

UNIVERSAL ACCESS
Meeting Individual Needs

Auditory • Kinesthetic
Tell children they will play a game called Tap-Top **T**. Say a list of words such as **ten**, **men**, **table**, **toy**, **first**, **two**, **save**, **top**, **tie**, **meal**, **seal**, **talk**, and **toad**. Direct children to tap the tops of their heads whenever they hear a word that begins with /**t**/.

Auditory • Kinesthetic
Materials: picture of a circus tent

Have children sit in a circle. Show a picture of a **tent** and ask children to identify the beginning sound. Hand one child the picture and say: *In my circus tent, I have a. . . .* Tell the child to complete the sentence with a word that starts with /**t**/. Then pass the picture and continue until every child has had a turn to complete the sentence.

Extra Support
Materials: Punchout Letter Card **t**

Review that /**t**/ is the beginning sound in **tub** and that **t** stands for initial /**t**/. Have children hold up the letter card **t** for the words that begin with /**t**/. Say groups of words such as: **man, top, tip; tin, bat, tie; net, ten, tan.**

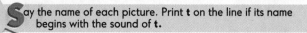

1. **t**oys	2. __ork (fork)	3. **t**ail
4. __ix (six)	5. **t**oad	6. **t**ape
7. **t**ack	8. **t**oes	9. __oon (moon)
10. **t**eam	11. __eal (seal)	12. **t**ub

24

LESSON 10: Connecting Sound to Symbol: Initial /t/ t

Help your child find things in your home that have names beginning with the t sound. Set them on a table.

Practicing the Skill

● Call attention to the letters **Tt** at the top of page 23. Review that they stand for /**t**/. Have children trace the letters. Discuss the top picture. Have children listen for words beginning with /**t**/ in the rhyme.

● Read the directions and identify all pictures. Go over the first item with children before they complete the page.

● Read the directions on page 24. Identify all pictures. Then model writing **t** for the first item before children complete the page.

Curriculum Connections

Theme Activity: Multicultural

Materials: small envelopes, ribbon or yarn, glue, magazines or catalogs

● Tell children that unlike a baby born in the United States, a baby born in China is considered one year old the day he or she is born. One year after their births, the American baby and the Chinese baby would celebrate their birthdays on the same day but the Chinese baby would be two years old and the American baby would be one.

● Let volunteers explain how their families celebrate birthdays. Have each child decorate an envelope so that it looks like a present. Then have children fill their "presents" with cutout magazine pictures of objects whose names begin with /**t**/. Have children exchange "gifts" with partners and discuss the pictures inside.

Sadlier Reading

Little Books and Big Books

Read *Show and Tell* (fiction) and *Tina's Toys* (nonfiction) for more practice with initial consonant **t**.

English Language Learners/ESL

Materials: pictures of birthday party celebrations

Some children may come from countries where they do not celebrate birthdays, but rather celebrate their name day. Explain that in this country, birthdays are celebrated each year on the date of one's birth and involve parties with cake, ice cream, and presents; show pictures of such parties. Teach the birthday song. Help children find their birthday on a calendar.

Special Strategies

For Universal Access activities, see page 13F.

Challenge

On the board, write the following poem:

> I like all **toys**!
> **Toy tops** that spin,
> And little cars
> Made out of **tin**.
> But one I love
> The best of all—
> My **teddy** bear!

Read aloud the poem. Have children identify the words that begin with **t**. Then have them copy the poem, write their own last line, and read their poems aloud.

Observational Assessment

*Note whether children are easily able to determine which words begin with **t**.*

Student Pages 25–26

Initial /h/ Hh

Objectives

- To identify and isolate initial sounds
- To recognize initial /h/
- To recognize that **Hh** stands for /h/
- To print **h** to complete words

Warming Up

Reviewing Initial f, m, s, and t

Materials: beach ball or other soft ball

Direct children to stand in a circle, and then give one child the ball. Tell this child to say **f**, **m**, **s**, or **t** as he or she passes the ball to another child. Tell the child who receives the ball to name a word that begins with the sound of the designated letter. Repeat using the other letters. Make sure each child has a chance to participate.

Teaching the Lesson

Phonemic Awareness: Identify and Isolate Initial Sounds

Say **hot**. Repeat the word, isolating the initial sound, /**h**/. Explain that /**h**/ is the beginning sound in **hot**. Then have children say the following words and identify and isolate the initial sound for each of them: **hat**, /**h**/; **ham**, /**h**/; **bat**, /**b**/; and **seal**, /**s**/.

Sound to Symbol

- Say the words **hand** and **horn**, emphasizing /**h**/. Point out that **hand** and **horn** both begin with /**h**/. Have children repeat each word and say /**h**/. Then say these words and have children raise their hands if they hear /**h**/ at the beginning: **hum, hill, top, heart**.
- Print **Hh** on the board and explain that these letters stand for /**h**/. Point out uppercase **H** and lowercase **h**. On the board, print: **Harry held** a **horn** in his **hand**. Read each word aloud. Ask a volunteer whether the word begins with /**h**/. If it does, have him or her circle the letter in the word that stands for /**h**/.

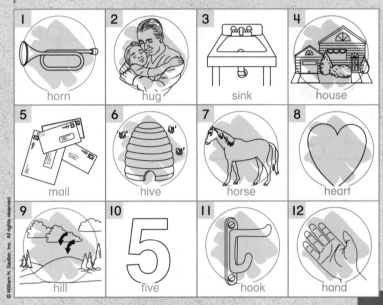

Hh

Horn starts with the sound of **h**. Listen for the sound of **h** in the rhyme.

Honk your horn
And shout, "Hooray!"
Have a happy holiday.

Circle and color each picture that has the sound of **h** at the beginning of its name.

1 horn	2 hug	3 sink	4 house
5 mail	6 hive	7 horse	8 heart
9 hill	10 five	11 hook	12 hand

LESSON 11: Phonemic Awareness: Initial /**h**/   **25**

U N I V E R S A L A C C E S S
Meeting Individual Needs

Visual • Kinesthetic

Materials: magazines, tape

Cut out and tape pictures on the floor in a random arrangement. Include several whose names begin with /**h**/. Ask children, one at a time, to hop from picture to picture and, as they do so, to name each picture and tell whether it begins with /**h**/.

Visual • Kinesthetic

Materials: Sadlier Phonics Picture Cards for **ham, hand, hat, horn**; other picture cards; construction paper

Direct each child to roll a sheet of paper into a cone shape to represent a party horn. Then present the picture cards. Ask children to say "honk" through their horns when they see a picture beginning with /**h**/.

Extra Support

Materials: drawing paper, crayons

Review that **hat** begins with /**h**/. Have children draw a party hat and write **h** on it. Then have them think of three things that begin with initial /**h**/, say them, and draw them on their hats.

26

Say the name of each picture. Print **h** on the line if its name begins with the sound of **h**.

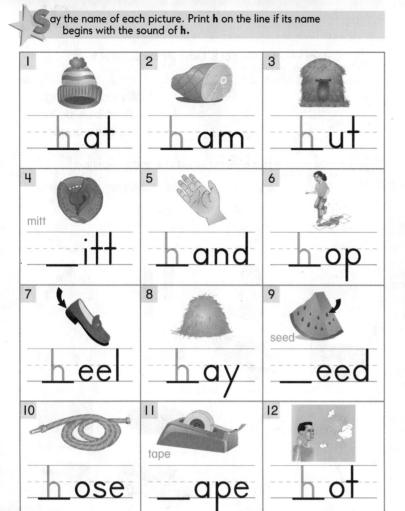

1	2	3
h at	h am	h ut

4	5	6
mitt		
_itt	h and	h op

7	8	9
		seed
h eel	h ay	_eed

10	11	12
	tape	
h ose	_ape	h ot

26

LESSON 11: Connecting Sound to Symbol: Initial /h/ h

Randomly point to a picture. Have your child give you a high five if its name begins with the sound of **h**.

Practicing the Skill

● Have children turn to page 25 and say /**h**/ while tracing the letters **Hh**. Discuss what the top picture shows, and read the rhyme. Tell children to listen for words beginning with /**h**/ in the rhyme.

● Together read the directions and do the first item. Name the pictures with children; then have them complete the page.

● Read aloud the directions on page 26 and model writing **h** to complete the first item. Be sure all pictures are identified before having children complete the page.

Curriculum Connections

Computer Connection

Challenge children to explore consonant sounds in Froggy Phonics (Ingenuity). Have children use the software for additional practice with /**h**/. Help children select **h** when presented with the alphabet. The children will then practice recognizing words that begin with **h**.

Theme Activity: Social Studies

Materials: calendar, drawing paper, crayons, streamers, tape

● Display a calendar. Explain that we celebrate the New Year on January 1. Mention that many people celebrate the New Year with a party, during which they might throw streamers, blow horns, and shout, "Happy New Year!"

● Have children make "Happy New Year" decorations by illustrating words that begin with the same sound as **horn**. Attach streamers to their pictures and display them. Then have children name the **h** words they illustrated.

Sadlier Reading
Little Books and Big Books

Read *Harry's Hat* (fiction) and *How Many Are Here?* (nonfiction) for more practice with initial consonant **h**.

English Language Learners/ESL
Tell children to listen for the sound /**h**/ as in **hat**. Model using Total Physical Response commands as you say the words **hair, heart, hand, heel, head** (e.g., *Raise your* **hand**. *Put your* **hand** *on your* **heart**.). Have children repeat after you. Then have volunteers give commands so they practice saying initial /**h**/.

Challenge
Materials: drawing paper, crayons

Direct children to fold a sheet of drawing paper in half to make a holiday greeting card. Let children choose the holiday, decorate the card, and write a message on the inside. Challenge children to include at least three **h** words in the message. Give children a chance to deliver their cards to classmates. Have children read the cards and identify the **h** words.

Special Strategies
For Universal Access activities, see page 13F.

26

Initial /b/ Bb

Objectives
- To recognize alliteration
- To recognize initial /**b**/
- To recognize that **Bb** stands for /**b**/
- To print **b** to complete words

Warming Up

Reviewing Partner Letters

Materials: Punchout Letter Cards for partner letters **Ff**, **Mm**, **Ss**, **Tt**, and **Hh**

Distribute the letter cards. Then invite the children to play Beat the Clock. Direct them to find the classmate who has the partner letter that corresponds to their own card. Children "beat the clock" by finding their "partner" in 30 seconds. Repeat until all children have had a chance to play.

Teaching the Lesson

Phonemic Awareness: Alliteration

Say: *Big bugs buzzed by the barn*. Explain to children that **Big**, **bugs**, **buzzed**, **by**, and **barn** all begin with /**b**/. Say the sentence again, and have children repeat each word beginning with /**b**/. Tell children to make up their own silly sentences using words that begin with /**b**/.

Sound to Symbol

- Say the words **big**, **balloon**, **Betty**, **bugs**, and **boat**, emphasizing /**b**/. Tell children that all the words begin with /**b**/. Have children say each word after you and then say /**b**/.
- Print **Bb** on the board, and explain that these letters stand for /**b**/. Identify each letter as uppercase or lowercase. Then list the following words on the board: **big**, **balloon**, **Betty**, **bugs**, and **boat**. Have children say the words with you as a volunteer underlines the letter that stands for /**b**/.

Bb

Baby starts with the sound of **b**. Listen for the sound of **b** in the tongue twister.

Bobby Baxter bought a bunch of blue balloons for his baby brother.

Circle the pictures that have the sound of **b** at the beginning of their names.

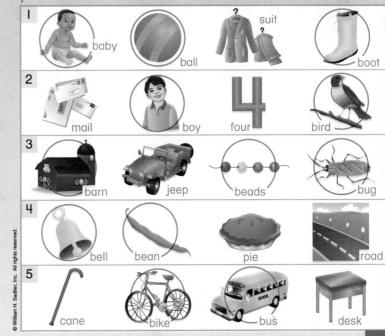

1. baby | ball | suit | boot
2. mail | boy | four | bird
3. barn | jeep | beads | bug
4. bell | bean | pie | road
5. cane | bike | bus | desk

LESSON 12: Phonemic Awareness: Initial /b/

UNIVERSAL ACCESS
Meeting Individual Needs

Auditory • Visual

Materials: Sadlier Phonics Picture Cards for initial **b** (**balloon**, **bunny**, **bus**, **bat**) and other initial sounds

Have children sit in a circle. Distribute a card to each child. Then go around the circle, calling on each child to hold up the picture, name it, and buzz like a bee if the name begins with /**b**/.

Auditory • Kinesthetic

Explain that the Bunny Hop is a dance people do at celebrations. Teach children to do the Bunny Hop. (Extend your left leg to the side, touch your left heel to the floor, and bring the leg back to the center; do the same with your right leg. Hop forward once, backward once, and forward three more times.) Have children take turns calling out, with each sequence of hops, initial **b** words.

Extra Support

Review that **bat** begins with /**b**/. Display objects that begin with /**b**/, such as **balloon**, **ball**, **basket**, **bus**, and **boat**. Name the objects, emphasizing the /**b**/. Have children repeat the words with you as they write the letter **b** in the air with a finger.

Say the name of each picture. Print **b** on the line if its name begins with the sound of **b**.

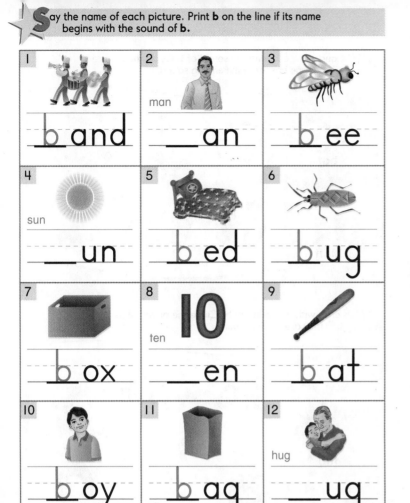

1. b and	2. man __ an	3. b ee
4. sun __ un	5. b ed	6. b ug
7. b ox	8. ten __ en	9. b at
10. b oy	11. b ag	12. hug __ ug

28   LESSON 12: Connnecting Sound to Symbol: Initial /b/ b

Help your child fill a bag with household objects and pictures that have names beginning with the sound of **b**.

Practicing the Skill

- Ask children to find **Bb** at the top of page 27 and say the sound that the letters stand for. Have children trace the letters on the page.
- Direct children's attention to the picture at the top of the page. Ask them to listen for words that start with /**b**/ as you read a tongue twister about the picture.
- Read the directions and model circling the first picture. Identify pictures before having children complete the page.
- Go over the directions on page 28 and model writing **b** to complete the first item. Name the pictures with children, and then have them complete the page.

Curriculum Connections

Theme Activity: Language Arts

Materials: catalogs and supermarket flyers, glue, scissors

- Ask children to cut out pictures of things that begin with /**b**/ and could be used at a party, such as gifts, decorations, and food. Have children group their pictures and make a collage.
- Ask children the following questions about a **b** party.

Who could come to a **b** party? (**Betsy, Billy, Barbara, Bobby, Ben**)

What gifts could you give? (**bike, bag, bear, ball**)

What could you eat? (**beans, burgers, biscuits, bananas, berries**)

What could you use to decorate? (**balloons, bows**)

Sadlier Reading
Little Books and Big Books

Read *A Basket Full of Surprises* (fiction) and *The Best Ride* (nonfiction) for more practice with initial consonant **b**.

English Language Learners/ESL

Tell children to listen for initial /**b**/ as in **boy**. Write **boy** on the board and the letters **Bb**. Say the word **boy** again and exaggerate the initial sound and the way you use your mouth to form a **b**. Then say **big, toy, sail** and have children identify the word that begins with /**b**/. Use other sets of three words, and ask children to identify the word that begins with initial /**b**/. Use **horn, bat, mop; fun, moon, buy; ball, nose, soap**.

Special Strategies

For Universal Access activities, see page 13F.

Challenge

Materials: drawing paper, crayons

Discuss with children TV commercials and advertisements. Ask children to make up an ad to get people to buy an object that begins with **b**. Children can write sentences using as many **b** words as they can. Give this example:

The **Big Ben Basketball** is the **best ball** to **buy**!
It **bounces** high.
You will make a lot of **baskets** with it!

Observational Assessment

*Note whether children are able to identify and suggest words starting with **b**.*

Final /t/ and /b/

Objectives

- To match final sounds
- To recognize final **/t/** and **/b/**
- To recognize that **t** and **tt** stand for **/t/** and that **b** stands for **/b/**
- To print **t**, **tt**, and **b** to complete words

Warming Up

Reviewing Final m

Remind children that **/m/** is the sound heard at the end of **hum**. Direct children to **hum** each time they hear you say a word that ends in **/m/**. Say: **jam**, **cap**, **ham**, **team**, **swim**, **feet**, **leaf**, **drum**, **gum**.

Teaching the Lesson

Phonemic Awareness:
Match Final Sounds

Materials: **Sadlier Phonics Picture Cards** for **web, cub, van, tub, net, jet, pot, log**

Say the word **web**. Tell children **web** ends with **/b/**. Display the cards for **web**, **cub**, and **van**. Name each picture. Have children repeat the names. Point out that **web** and **cub** both end with **/b/** but that **van** does not. Display **tub**, **net**, and **cub**. Have children say the two names with the same ending sound. Repeat with **jet**, **pot**, and **log**.

Sound to Symbol

- Say **cat**. Explain that **cat** ends with **/t/**. Have children say **/t/**. Write **cat** and circle the letter **t**. Explain that this letter stands for **/t/** at the end of **cat**. Write **mitt** and circle the letters **tt**. Tell children that **/t/** is also the sound of the letters **tt** at the end of **mitt**.
- Print **-t**, **-tt** at the top of one column and **-b** on another. Say the following words: **hat**, **cob**, **get**, **boot**, **tab**, **mitt**, **hub**, **cab**, **nut**, **job**. Have children name the ending sound of each word and tell you under which letter(s) to write the word. Ask volunteers to circle the letter(s) that stand for the final sound.

Bat and **Matt** end with the sound of **t**. Circle the picture if its name has the same ending sound.

ba**t**

Ma**tt**

pot   man   feet

mitt   book   cat

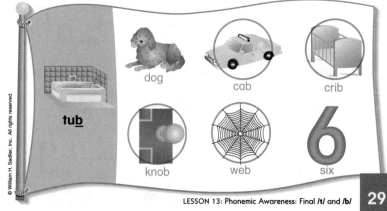

Tub ends with the sound of **b**. Circle the picture if its name has the same ending sound.

tu**b**

dog   cab   crib

knob   web   six

LESSON 13: Phonemic Awareness: Final **/t/** and **/b/**

U N I V E R S A L A C C E S S
Meeting Individual Needs

Visual • Kinesthetic

Materials: **Sadlier Phonics Picture Cards** for **cub, tub, web, feet, fruit, hat**

Point out that **pat** ends with **/t/** and **rub** ends with **/b/**. As you show the picture cards one at a time, have children pat their heads if the name of the picture ends in **/t/** or rub their tummies if it ends in **/b/**.

Visual • Kinesthetic

Materials: large bag, collection of items or pictures that end in **/t/** or **/b/**, for example, **boat**, **bib**, **crib**, **cub**, **hat**, **net**

Put all the items into the bag. Ask children what sound they hear at the end of **grab**. Tell them they will be playing a grab bag game. Give each child a chance to grab an item from the bag and to tell whether it ends in **/b/** or **/t/**.

Extra Support

Materials: pictures of a **pot** and a **bib**

Review that **t** stands for **/t/** as in **hat** and **b** stands for **/b/** as in **Rob**. Display the pictures of a pot and a bib. Ask children to name the objects and identify the ending sounds. Then have them name other words that end in **/t/** or **/b/**.

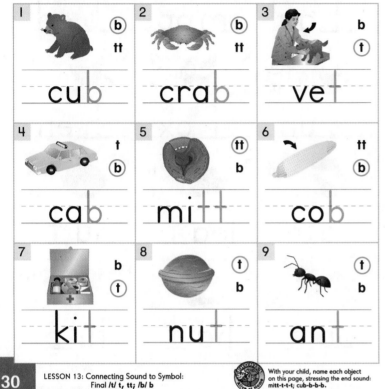

Say the name of each picture. Circle the letter or letters that stand for its ending sound. Then print the letter or letters on the line.

1	ⓑ tt	cu_b_	2	ⓑ tt	cra_b_	3	ⓑ ⓣ	ve_t_
4	t ⓑ	ca_b_	5	ⓣⓣ b	mi_tt_	6	tt ⓑ	co_b_
7	b ⓣ	ki_t_	8	ⓣ b	nu_t_	9	ⓣ b	an_t_

30

LESSON 13: Connecting Sound to Symbol: Final /t/ t, tt; /b/ b

With your child, name each object on this page, stressing the end sound: mitt-t-t-t; cub-b-b-b.

Practicing the Skill

- Read aloud the directions at the top of page 29. Together, say the name of each picture on the first flag. Model circling a picture, such as pot, that ends with /**t**/. Have children complete the first flag.
- Use the same procedure to have children find final **b** pictures on the second flag.
- Read aloud the directions on page 30. Model circling the **b** and writing it at the end of the word in the first item. Be sure children can identify each picture. Then ask them to complete the page.

Curriculum Connections

Theme Activity: Math/Language Arts

Materials: calendar, paper, crayons, catalogs and advertising flyers, scissors, glue

- Display a calendar, and name each month. Ask each child in the class to tell his or her birthday month.
- Ask children to wish themselves a happy birthday—regardless of when their birthday really is—by giving themselves "presents" with names that end with /**t**/ and /**b**/. Direct children to print **t**, **tt** on one piece of paper and **b** on the other. Then have them draw "presents" or glue on advertising pictures of "presents" that end with /**t**/ or /**b**/.
- On a third sheet, have children write themselves birthday messages. Staple each child's pages together to make "Happy Birthday" books.

Portfolio
Have children place their "Happy Birthday" books in their portfolios.

English Language Learners/ESL

Materials: index cards, magazines, catalogs, scissors, paste

Help children with the names for the pictures on pages 28 and 29. Together with children make picture cards for those words with final **t** and **b**. Direct children to find other examples of those words in the picture sources, cut them out, and paste them on index cards. Help them say the name of each picture, emphasizing the final **t** and **b**. Have children sort the cards by final sound. Have children take these cards home to practice.

Special Strategies

For Universal Access activities, see page 13F.

Challenge

Materials: drawing paper, crayons

Make sure that children know how to play Tic-Tac-Toe. Have children work with a partner to draw grids on paper and play games of Tic-Tac-Toe using **t** and **b** instead of **X** and **O**. Tell children that before each move, they must say a word that ends with the sound of their letter. You may want to have partners list their words.

Observational Assessment

Observe whether "presents" are correctly grouped according to ending sounds.

30

Reviewing and Assessing Initial and Final f, m, s, t, h, b

Objectives
- To identify and print initial or final **f**, **m**, **s**, **t**, **h**, and **b** to complete words

Warming Up

Reviewing Final Consonants

Materials: **Sadlier Phonics Picture Cards** for final **f**, **m**, **s**, **t**, and **b**, such as **leaf**, **jam**, **bus**, **jet**, **tub**

Remind children that words have ending sounds. Tell them that **pot** ends with /t/. Place ten or more picture cards on the chalk ledge. Ask a volunteer to name each picture and identify the consonant that stands for each picture name's final sound.

Teaching the Lesson

- Print **f**, **m**, **s**, **t**, **h**, and **b** on the board, and say the letters with children. Then say **face**. Tell children that **face** begins with /f/, and point to **f**. Ask children what sound they hear at the beginning of **fence**. Review the remaining initial consonant sounds.

- Write **_ork** on the board. Say **fork**. Have a volunteer identify the initial sound and write it on the board to complete the word. Repeat this activity with these words: **four, mail, sink, toy, hook, bell**.

- Say **leaf** and remind children that **leaf** ends with /f/. Point to **f**. Then write **chie_** on the board, and say **chief**. Have a child identify the final sound and write it to complete the word. Repeat using these words: **drum, gas, cat, cub**.

- Have children turn to page 31. Read the directions aloud, and help children name each picture. Do the first item together. Then have children finish the page.

Say the name of each picture. Circle the letter that stands for the missing sound. Then print the letter on the line.

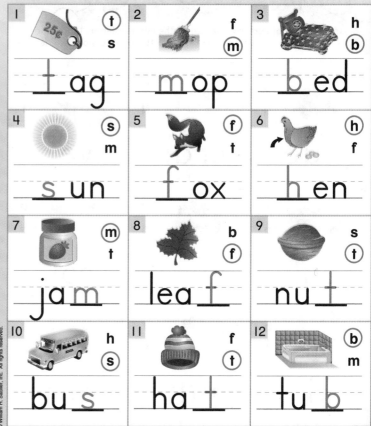

LESSON 14: Reviewing Initial and Final Consonants f, m, s, t, h, b

31

UNIVERSAL ACCESS
Reteaching Activities

Activity 1

Materials: paper, crayons

Tell children that **ball** begins with /b/. Ask them what beginning sound they hear in **horn**. Then tell children that **drum** ends with /m/. Ask them what ending sound they hear in **bat**. Have children think of a toy they have that begins or ends with **f**, **m**, **s**, **t**, **h**, or **b**. Have each child draw a picture of the toy and write its beginning or ending sound. Scatter the pictures, or toys, on the floor and have children group them by their initial and then final sound.

Activity 2

Draw a picture of a hat on the board. Remind children that **hat** begins with /h/ and ends with /t/. Have children work in small groups. Assign each group a consonant letter: **f**, **m**, **s**, **t**, **h**, or **b**. Have groups work together until each child has named a word to draw that begins or ends with the assigned letter. Have children name their picture, say their letter, and tell if it is the beginning or ending sound. Then have each group parade around the classroom with its completed pictures.

Check-Up Say the name of each picture. Find the letter in the box that stands for the missing sound. Then print the letter on the line.

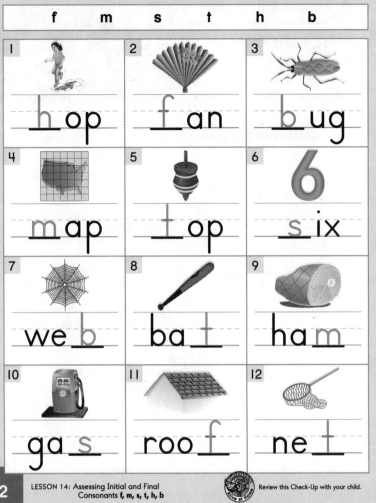

f	m	s	t	h	b

1. h op
2. f an
3. b ug
4. m ap
5. t op
6. s ix
7. we b
8. ba t
9. ha m
10. ga s
11. roo f
12. ne t

32 LESSON 14: Assessing Initial and Final
Consonants **f, m, s, t, h, b**

Review this Check-Up with your child.

Check-Up Before administering the written assessment on page 32, conduct a final class review of initial and final consonants **f**, **m**, **s**, **t**, **h**, and **b**. Write the consonants on the board. Have volunteers choose a letter, name it, and say a word that begins or ends with its sound. Write each word on the board under the appropriate letter, and underline the initial or final consonant.

Ask children to turn to page 32. Read the directions aloud. Then identify the pictures together. Have children complete the page.

Observational Assessment During the Check-Up activity, take notes on the ability of individual children to suggest words with a particular beginning or ending sound.

Dictation Tell children that you will say some words and that they will write the letter that stands for the beginning sound they hear in each word. Say these words: **fish**, **mask**, **sock**, **toad**, **hat**, **bag**. Continue in the same way for final sounds. Say these words: **leaf**, **peas**, **nut**, **hum**, **crab**.

Student Skills Assessment Use the checklist on Student Edition pages 321–322 to record your observations of individual children.

Guided Instruction

Skills	Resources
Initial consonants **f, m, s**	Instruction on pages 15–20
Initial consonants **t, h, b**	Instruction on pages 23–28
Final consonants **f, ff, m, s, ss**	Instruction on pages 21–22
Final consonants **t, tt, b**	Instruction on pages 29–30
Initial and final consonants **f, m, s, t, h, b**	Phonemic Awareness Activities pages 13H–13I Punchout Cards page 13N

Initial /l/ Ll

Objectives
- To segment initial sounds
- To recognize initial /l/
- To recognize that **Ll** stands for /l/
- To print **l** to complete words

Warming Up

Reviewing Initial Sounds
Materials: **Sadlier Phonics Picture Cards** for initial /f/, /m/, /s/, /t/, /h/, and /b/ (e.g., **fox**, **mitten**, **seven**, **top**, **hand**, **bus**)

Ask children to name each picture card and its beginning sound.

Teaching the Lesson

Phonemic Awareness: Segment Initial Sounds
Materials: **Sadlier Phonics Picture Cards** for **log**, **leaf**, **lemon**, **lake**, **lamp**

Display the cards and name each picture. Then repeat the name, separating the initial sound from the rest of the word: /l/-/og/. Have children follow your model as they say each picture name.

Sound to Symbol
- Say /l/, and have children repeat /l/. Tell children that /l/ is the sound at the beginning of **like**. Write **like** on the board, and trace over the **l** with colored chalk. Explain that **l** stands for /l/. Write **lips**, **loaf**, and **leap**, and read the words with children. Ask volunteers to draw a vertical line to separate the beginning /l/ from the rest of the word: **l/ips**, **l/oaf**, **l/eaf**.
- Print **Ll** on the board. Point out the uppercase and the lowercase letter. Tell children that both letters stand for /l/. On the board, write: **Lee likes** the **lake**. Read it together. Ask volunteers to circle the letter that stands for /l/ at the beginning of the words. Ask a volunteer to tell which circled letter is uppercase **L**.

Lunch starts with the sound of **l**. Listen for the sound of **l** in the rhyme.

Lunch, lunch, lunch,
There's lots to eat.
Let's sit by the lake
And munch, munch, munch.

Circle and color each picture that has the sound of **l** at the beginning of its name.

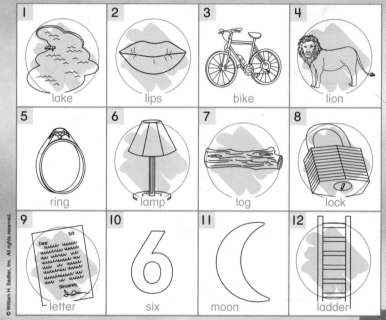

1 lake	2 lips	3 bike	4 lion
5 ring	6 lamp	7 log	8 lock
9 letter	10 six	11 moon	12 ladder

LESSON 15: Phonemic Awareness: Initial /l/   33

UNIVERSAL ACCESS
Meeting Individual Needs

Auditory • Kinesthetic
Tell the class about the comic-strip *Little Orphan Annie* and her favorite expression: "Leaping lizards!" Have children leap up and call out "Leaping lizards!" each time they hear you say an initial **l** word: **leaf, Max, leg, lemon, fun, listen, lock, sit, baby, lake, ham, low.**

Auditory • Kinesthetic
Teach children to say the following tongue twisters that have words that begin with /l/:

Little Lil likes to **lead** parades.
Louie learned letters lickety-split.
Larry laughs loudly at the **lions**.

Have pairs of children make up their own **l** tongue twisters and act them out.

Extra Support
Review that **l** stands for /l/ as in the beginning sound in **lion**. Have children think of other words that begin with /l/. Write the suggestions on the board and have a volunteer circle the letter **l**.

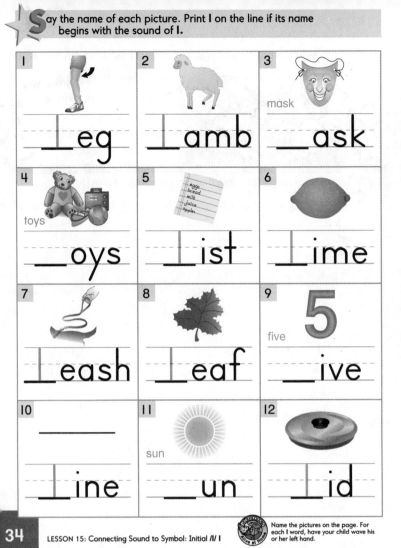

Say the name of each picture. Print **l** on the line if its name begins with the sound of **l**.

1. _Leg	2. _Lamb	3. __ask (mask)
4. __oys (toys)	5. _List	6. _Lime
7. _Leash	8. _Leaf	9. __ive (five)
10. _Line	11. __un (sun)	12. _Lid

34

LESSON 15: Connecting Sound to Symbol: Initial /l/ **l**

Name the pictures on the page. For each **l** word, have your child wave his or her left hand.

Practicing the Skill

● Point out the letters **Ll** at the top of page 33. Review that they stand for /l/. Have children trace the letters with their fingers. Have children listen for words beginning with /l/ as you read the rhyme.

● Read the directions aloud. Ask whether the first picture should be circled and colored. Help children name all the pictures. Then have children complete the page.

● Read aloud the directions on page 34. Model writing **l** to complete the first item. Then have volunteers name each picture. Ask children to complete the page.

Curriculum Connections

Theme Activity: Science

Materials: construction paper in fall colors, magazines, scissors, glue, yarn

● Ask children what they like about the fall and what special holidays they celebrate during this season.

● Distribute materials and have children work alone or in pairs to make **l** books. Guide children to cut leaf shapes out of paper. Then have children cut out pictures of things from the magazines that begin with **l** and glue them on the leaves.

● Punch a hole in the stem of each leaf and tie bunches together to make books. Have children place their books in the library corner.

Sadlier Reading
Little Books and Big Books

Read *What Does Lucy Like?* (fiction) and *Looking at Lizards* (nonfiction) for more practice with initial consonant **l**.

English Language Learners/ESL

Display a sandwich, a piece of fruit, and a glass of milk. Tell children this is your **lunch**. Write the word **lunch** on the board, point to it and say /l/-/l/-/l/-**unch**. Explain that **lunch** begins with the letter **l**. Point to objects or pictures of objects that begin with the sound of /l/ such as **lips, lock, lamp, leg, list, letter** and help children identify them.

Challenge

Have children write a story about a picnic party. Have them tell about children **laughing** and **leaping** by a lake. Encourage children to use as many initial **l** words as they can. Have children read their stories aloud. You might also have children illustrate their stories.

Special Strategies

For Universal Access activities, see page 13F.

For Universal Access activities, see page 13F.

Observational Assessment

*Be sure children are able to identify pictures that begin with **l** for their leaf pages.*

34

Initial /d/ Dd

Objectives
- To segment onsets and rimes
- To recognize initial /d/
- To recognize that **Dd** stands for /d/
- To print **d** to complete words

Warming Up

Reviewing Initial Sounds

Materials: Punchout Letter Cards for **Ff**, **Mm**, **Ss**, **Tt**, **Hh**, **Bb**, and **Ll**; Sadlier Phonics Picture Cards for **fox**, **feet**, **mask**, **mitten**, **seal**, **seven**, **toys**, **tub**, **hat**, **horn**, **balloon**, **bus**, **leaf**, and **log**

Hold up letter cards for uppercase and lowercase **f**, **m**, **s**, **t**, **h**, **b**, and **l**. Have children say the sound of each letter. Then display the picture cards. Give each child a letter card and have the child match it to a picture card.

Teaching the Lesson

Phonemic Awareness: Segment Onsets and Rimes

Say the word **dig**. Tell children that **dig** begins with /d/. Then model segmenting the beginning sound from the rest of the word by saying /d/-/ig/. Say the words **dip**, **dive**, **dune**, **date**. Have children repeat each word and then segment the beginning sound from the rest of the word.

Sound to Symbol

- Say the word **dance**. Explain that **dance** begins with /d/. Have children repeat the word and say /d/. Now say **dime**, **dot**, **quack**, **dash**, **walk**. Have children dance when they hear a word beginning with /d/.
- Write **Dd** on the board. Point out the uppercase and lowercase letters. Tell children that both letters stand for /d/. Then write ***Ducks dive down***. Read the sentence together. Ask a volunteer to underline the letter that stands for /d/ in each word. Ask another child to tell whether the underlined letter is uppercase or lowercase.

35

Dd

Dance starts with the sound of **d**. Listen for the sound of **d** in the rhyme.

> Dance, dance, dance,
> Get on your feet.
> Dance, dance, dance,
> Don't miss a beat.

Circle and color each picture that has the sound of **d** at the beginning of its name.

1 deer	2 box	3 dime	4 dog
5 door	6 kite	7 feet	8 dinosaur
9 doll	10 cat	11 dive	12 heart

LESSON 16: Phonemic Awareness: Initial /d/   **35**

UNIVERSAL ACCESS
Meeting Individual Needs

Auditory • Kinesthetic
Designate one child "Big Duck," and have other children sit in a circle. Explain that Big Duck will walk around the circle and tap one person lightly on the shoulder. If the child who is tapped can say a word that begins with **d**, he or she may take over as Big Duck.

Auditory • Kinesthetic
Materials: plastic dish

Have children sit in a circle. Give one child a plastic dish and ask him or her to complete this sentence with a **d** word: ***In my dish I have a. . . .*** Ask this child to pass the dish to the right. As a child receives the dish, he or she must say the same sentence with a new initial **d** word.

Extra Support
Review that **dinosaur** and **dance** begin with /d/. Have children move like a dinosaur or do a little dance each time you say a word that begins with /d/.

1	2 bug	3
<u>d</u> uck	__ug	<u>d</u> esk

4	5 top	6
<u>d</u> oor	__op	<u>d</u> ig

7 hug	8	9
__ug	<u>d</u> ish	<u>d</u> og

10	11 fire	12
<u>d</u> ive	__ire	<u>d</u> oll

36

LESSON 16: Connecting Sound to Symbol: Initial /d/ d

Take turns with your child naming words that begin with the sound of **d**.

Practicing the Skill

● Discuss what the dinosaurs at the top of page 35 are doing. Ask children to find the letters on this page that stand for the beginning sound of **dance**. Have children trace the letters on the page and in the air.

● Tell children to listen as you read the rhyme. Repeat the rhyme and have children name the initial **d** words they heard.

● Read the directions aloud. Ask children to identify the first picture and tell whether it should be circled and colored. Say the names of the other pictures on the page. Direct children to complete the page.

● Read aloud the directions on page 36. Model writing **d** to complete the first item. Then have children name all the pictures. Tell children to complete the page.

Curriculum Connections

Theme Activity: Art
Materials: paper, scissors, crayons, oaktag cutouts of a mother duck and ducklings

● Remind the class of how ducklings walk and swim behind the mother duck.

● Show children the mother duck cutout and label it with the partner letters **D** and **d**. Then distribute duckling cutouts. Have children trace, cut out, and decorate a duckling with a picture of an item whose name begins with /**d**/.

● Arrange the mother duck and ducklings on the wall in a line formation. Have children parade past the ducklings and name each picture as they pass.

Sadlier Reading
Little Books and Big Books

Read *The Dinosaur Dance* (fiction) and *Do You See a Dozen?* (nonfiction) for more practice with initial consonant **d**.

English Language Learners/ESL
Materials: chart paper, crayons

Tell children they will be learning words that begin with the sound /**d**/ as in **daisy**. Show children how to make the **d** sound. Have them repeat /**d**/ after you. Draw a large daisy on chart paper. Tell children a daisy is a kind of flower. Show pictures of flowers. Then say sets of words, for example, **duck, ten; dog, kite; dad, leaf.** Have children identify the word that begins with /**d**/ and print the word on a petal of the daisy.

Challenge
Ask children what sound they hear at the beginning of **diary**. Discuss the purpose of a diary. Then ask children to imagine that they are dancing ducks. Have children write about their dance and the music. Ask children to underline all the words they used that begin with /**d**/.

Special Strategies
For Universal Access activities, see page 13F.

Observational Assessment

*Notice whether children choose picture names that begin with **d**.*

Student Pages 37–38

Initial /k/ Cc

Objectives
- To add initial sounds
- To recognize initial /k/
- To recognize that **Cc** can stand for /k/
- To print **c** to complete words

Warming Up

Reviewing Initial Consonants
Materials: large square box, **Sadlier Phonics Picture Cards** for initial **f, m, s, t, h, b** (e.g., **fan, mask, seal, tub, hat, bus**)

On each face of a box, print **f, m, s, t, h, b**. Display the box and picture cards. As a group, name each picture. Then call on a child to choose a picture, name it, and turn the box so that the beginning letter of the picture name faces up.

Teaching the Lesson

Phonemic Awareness: Add Initial Sounds
*Note: In this lesson children will learn only the hard sound of **c** (**cake**), not the soft sound (**city**).*

Tell children that you are going to say the end of a word and they are going to add /k/ to the beginning to say the entire word. Model this by saying /**ap**/ and then /**k**/-/**ap**/ **cap**. Say the phonograms -**ane**, -**at**, -**up**, -**all**, -**ut**, -**amp,** and have children add /k/ to the beginning to say the whole word.

Sound to Symbol
- Say: **Cassie** *has a* **cute car.** Point out that /k/ is the sound at the beginning of **Cassie**, **cute**, and **car**. Have children repeat each word and then say /k/.
- Print **Cc** on the board. Tell children that both letters can stand for /k/. Write: **Casey can paddle a canoe at camp.** Read the sentence aloud. Point to each word. Have children tell whether or not it begins with /k/. If so, have a volunteer underline the letter that stands for /k/.

37

Caps starts with the sound of **c**. Listen for the sound of **c** in the rhyme.

> Casey comes in.
> And so does her twin.
> Our caps go up,
> The Cubs win!

Circle and color each picture that has the sound of **c** at the beginning of its name.

1 cap	2 bell	3 cob	4 car
5 six	6 cow	7 box	8 leaf
9 coat	10 cup	11 mask	12 coins

LESSON 17: Phonemic Awareness: Initial /k/ c   **37**

UNIVERSAL ACCESS
Meeting Individual Needs

Auditory • Kinesthetic
Explain that "Calico Cat" is having a party and has planned a special game similar to Simon Says. Tell children to respond only to commands that include the sound of initial **c**. For example:

Meow like a **cat**.
Walk like a dog.
Catch a fly ball.

Auditory • Visual
Materials: drawing paper, crayons

Guide children to fold a sheet of paper to make four boxes. Then say: *In the top-left box, draw a* **cow**. *In the top-right box, draw a* **coat**. *In the bottom-left box, draw a* **coin**. *In the bottom-right box, draw your own picture that begins with /k/.* Have children name their pictures.

Extra Support
Materials: large cutout paper birthday cake, large cutout paper candles

Review that **cake** begins with /k/. Give each child a paper candle, and have them draw a picture beginning with /k/ on it. Let children name their picture and put it on the cake.

Cc

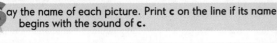

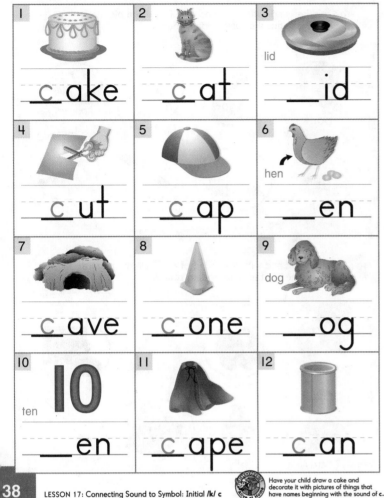

1 c ake	2 c at	3 lid __id
4 c ut	5 c ap	6 hen __en
7 c ave	8 c one	9 dog __og
10 ten __en	11 c ape	12 c an

38

LESSON 17: Connecting Sound to Symbol: Initial /k/ c

Practicing the Skill

● Have children turn to page 37. Point out the letters **Cc**. Have children say /**k**/ while tracing the letters **Cc** with their fingers.

● Discuss the picture at the top of the page. Ask children to listen for words beginning with /**k**/ as you read the rhyme.

● Read aloud the directions. Help children name all the pictures. Then ask a volunteer whether the first picture should be circled and colored. Have children complete the page.

● Read the directions on page 38 and model writing **c** to complete the first item. Be sure all pictures are identified before having children complete the page.

Curriculum Connections

Theme Activity: Multicultural

Materials: grocery flyers, food magazines, construction paper, glue, scissors, crayons

● Display flyers and food magazines to show pictures of foods and spices, including ones that begin with **c** as /**k**/ (e.g., **carrot**, **curry**, **cantaloupe**, **couscous**, **coconut**).

● Have children talk about family foods served on special occasions. Ask children of diverse cultural backgrounds to tell about the particular foods enjoyed in their homes.

● Have children work in small groups to find pictures of foods that start with **c** as /**k**/. Have them make a collage with their pictures. Tell children to print **Cc** at the top of their collages.

Sadlier Reading

Little Books and Big Books

Read *Count with Me* (nonfiction) and *Cats! Cats! Cats!* (fiction) for more practice with initial consonant **c**.

English Language Learners/ESL

Materials: index cards

Distribute index cards with **c** printed on each. Tell children that this letter sometimes stands for /**k**/. Then say the name of each object on page 37 as you point to it. Have children hold up their **c** cards if the name begins with /**k**/. Repeat the process for page 38 before children complete the pages.

Challenge

Materials: drawing paper, crayons

Discuss the parts of a comic strip. Have children work in groups to create a comic strip about a party or holiday celebration. Have children draw a picture for each "frame" of their comic. Then have them include in their characters' speech bubbles some initial **c** words. Tape the "frames" together to form a comic strip. Let children underline words that begin with **c**.

Special Strategies

For Universal Access activities, see page 13F.

Observational Assessment

*Observe children's group work to determine which individuals are able to identify words with initial **c**.*

Final /l/ l, ll and /d/ d, dd

Objectives

- To identify and isolate final sounds
- To recognize final /l/ and /d/
- To recognize that **l** and **ll** stand for /l/ and that **d** and **dd** stand for /d/
- To print **l**, **ll**, **d**, and **dd** to complete words

Warming Up

Reviewing Initial Cc

Write **Cc** on the board. Remind children that these letters can stand for /k/ in some words, as in **cap** and **cake**. Ask children to "pop up" each time they hear /k/ at the beginning of words you will say. Say **cup**, **cat**, **milk**, **card**, **can**, **dot**, **cough**.

Teaching the Lesson

Phonemic Awareness: Identify and Isolate Final Sounds

Say a word and have children repeat the sound they hear at the end of the word. Model by saying: **pal** /l/, **sad** /d/. Say these words, and have children repeat the final sounds: **smell**, **add**, **tall**, **head**, **meal**, **Bill**, **need**, **fell**.

Sound to Symbol

- Say the words **sail** and **rail**. Explain that **sail** and **rail** both end with /l/. Have children say /l/. Write **rail** and **sail** on the board. Circle the letter **l** in each word. Explain that this letter stands for /l/ at the end of **rail** and **sail**. Write the word **ball**, and circle the letters **ll**. Tell children that /l/ is also the sound of the letters **ll** at the end of **ball**. Repeat the process with /d/ **d**, **dd**, using **nod** and **add**.
- Print -**l**, -**ll** at the top of one column and -**d**, -**dd** at the top of the other. Under the appropriate letters print **sail**, **feel**, **Nell**, **kid**, **head**, **Todd**. Read the words with children as volunteers underline the letter(s) that stand for final /l/ or final /d/.

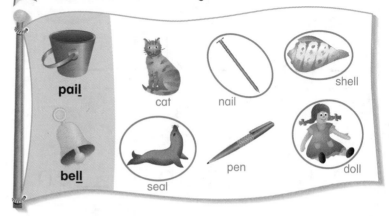

Pail and bell end with the sound of **l**. Circle the picture if its name has the same ending sound.

pail
bell
cat
nail
shell
seal
pen
doll

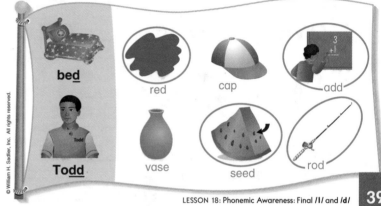

Bed and Todd end with the sound of **d**. Circle the picture if its name has the same ending sound.

bed
Todd
red
cap
add
vase
seed
rod

LESSON 18: Phonemic Awareness: Final /l/ and /d/   **39**

UNIVERSAL ACCESS
Meeting Individual Needs

Auditory • Kinesthetic

Have children stand in a circle. Tell children to pretend to bounce a ball when they hear a word that ends with /l/ and to raise one hand when they hear a word that ends with /d/. Say **pail**, **feel**, **lid**, and **odd**.

Auditory • Visual

Materials: party horns, **Sadlier Phonics Picture Cards** for **red, seal, yard, doll, bed, pail**

Remind children that noisemakers are sometimes used at parties. Tell children you will show picture cards. Ask children to toot once if the picture ends in /l/ and toot twice if it ends in /d/.

Extra Support

Review that final **l** and **ll** stand for /l/ as in **pal** and **sell** and **d** and **dd** stand for /d/ as in **bed** and **add**. Write **bell**, **pail**, **hid**, **add** on the board. Read the words. Have children say the final sound in each word and then circle the letter or letters that stand for the final sound.

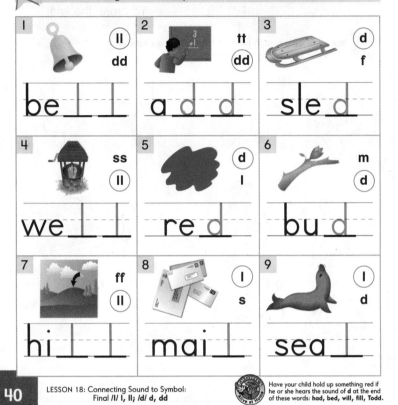

Say the name of each picture. Circle the letter or letters that stand for its ending sound. Then print the letter or letters on the line.

1	ⓛⓛ dd	2	tt ⓓⓓ	3	ⓓ f
be l l		a d d		sle d	

4	ss ⓛⓛ	5	ⓓ l	6	m ⓓ
we l l		re d		bu d	

7	ff ⓛⓛ	8	ⓛ s	9	ⓛ d
hi l l		mai l		sea l	

40

LESSON 18: Connecting Sound to Symbol: Final /l/ l, ll; /d/ d, dd

Have your child hold up something red if he or she hears the sound of **d** at the end of these words: **had, bed, will, fill, Todd.**

- Read aloud the directions at the top of page 39. Identify the pictures on the first flag. Stress the ending sound of each picture name. Then model identifying the ending sounds in **cat** and **nail** and circling the picture of the **nail** because it has the same ending sound as **pail** and **bell**. Have children complete the activity on the first flag.

- Repeat the same procedure for the pictures on the second flag. Have children complete the page.

- Read aloud the directions on page 40. Have children name the pictures. Model completing the first item, and then have children complete the page.

Curriculum Connections

Theme Activity: Language Arts

Materials: eight large bell shapes cut from two colors of construction paper, catalogs, scissors, glue, long piece of ribbon

- Tell children that bells are sometimes used in celebrations. Point out examples such as ringing bells on Independence Day and at weddings.

- Have children work in four groups. Give two different colored bell shapes to each group. Have a member of each group print **l**, **ll** on one bell and **d**, **dd** on the other. Have group members cut out pictures of things ending in **l**, **ll**, and **d**, **dd** from catalogs. Tell children to paste the pictures on the appropriate bell.

- Have group members name the pictures on their bells. Then tape the bells to ribbon, and hang them in the classroom.

English Language Learners/ESL

Materials: drawing paper, crayons

Say the name of each picture on page 40, emphasizing the final **l** or **d**, and have children repeat. Then count off children from one to nine, and have them draw a picture for that numbered word. Encourage them to put themselves in the picture. Ask them to show the picture to the group, say its name, and tell about it.

Challenge

Materials: drawing paper, crayons

Point out to children that flags are often used in parades and celebrations. Have children make a final **l**, **ll** flag and final **d**, **dd** flag to celebrate these sounds. Let children draw pictures of things that end in each sound and label each one. Display the flags, and have children name the pictures.

Special Strategies

For Universal Access activities, see page 13F.

Observational Assessment

*Notice whether children can find pictures representing final **l**, **ll**, **d**, and **dd** to paste on their bells.*

Initial Consonant /n/ Nn

Objectives

- To segment onsets and rimes
- To recognize initial /n/
- To recognize that **Nn** stands for /n/
- To print **n** to complete words

Warming Up

Reviewing Initial Consonants

Draw ten bowling pins on the board. Write one of the consonants **f, m, s, t, h, b, l, d,** and **c** on each of nine pins. Mark the tenth with a question mark. Then ask children to take turns "bowling." To "knock over" (erase) a pin, they must name two words that begin with the sound the consonant stands for. Let children choose a mystery consonant for the tenth pin.

Teaching the Lesson

Phonemic Awareness: Segment Onsets and Rimes

Tell children to listen while you separate the beginning sound of **net** from the rest of the word. Say **net**, /**n**/-/**et**/. Have children repeat after you. Continue with **nap**, /**n**/-/**ap**/; **not**, /**n**/-/**ot**/; and **nut**, /**n**/-/**ut**/.

Sound to Symbol

- Say /**n**/. Have children repeat /**n**/. Explain that /**n**/ is the sound at the beginning of the word **nest**. Then write **nest** on the board. Circle the letter **n**. Tell children that the letter **n** stands for /**n**/. Write the words **not, nap, net,** and **nut** on the board. Say the words together, and ask volunteers to circle the letter that stands for /**n**/.
- Print **Nn** on the board and point out the uppercase and lowercase letters. Explain that both letters stand for /**n**/. Say the following words: **nose, nail, fit, note, leg, nest.** Ask a volunteer to come to the board and write **n** if the word begins with /**n**/.

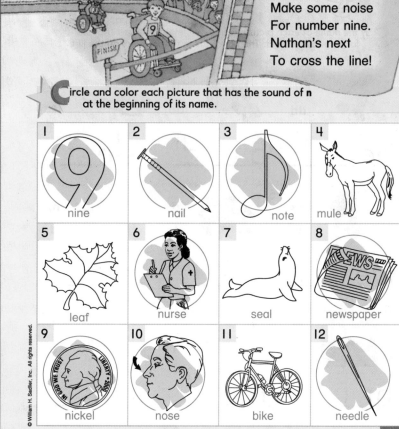

Nn

Noise starts with the sound of **n**. Listen for the sound of **n** in the rhyme.

Make some noise
For number nine.
Nathan's next
To cross the line!

Circle and color each picture that has the sound of **n** at the beginning of its name.

1 nine	2 nail	3 note	4 mule
5 leaf	6 nurse	7 seal	8 newspaper
9 nickel	10 nose	11 bike	12 needle

LESSON 19: Phonemic Awareness: Initial /n/   **41**

UNIVERSAL ACCESS
Meeting Individual Needs

Auditory • Kinesthetic

Tell children they will have an **n** race. Put several objects that start with **n** (e.g., **nickel, napkin**) on four tables. Set up four teams. When you say, "Go," the first child in each line picks up an item, says its name, and puts it aside. The next child then picks up the next item on the table, names it, and so on.

Auditory • Kinesthetic

Materials: tape recording of different animal sounds

Play the recording and ask children to name the animals. Say that the sound a horse makes is "neigh." Say *neigh* and have children repeat it. Tell children to neigh like a horse when they hear you say a word that begins with **n**. Use words such as **nice, nail, marble, napkin, needle, lip,** and **note**.

Extra Support

Review that **nap** begins with /**n**/ and that the letter **n** can stand for /**n**/. Have children write **n** on the board when they hear a word that begins with /**n**/. Say these words: **note, new, dog, next, noise, red, not.**

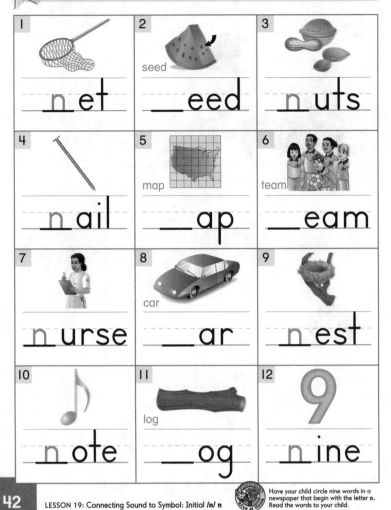

Say the name of each picture. Print **n** on the line if its name begins with the sound of **n**.

1. <u>n</u> et	2. seed __eed	3. <u>n</u> uts
4. <u>n</u> ail	5. map __ap	6. team __eam
7. <u>n</u> urse	8. car __ar	9. <u>n</u> est
10. <u>n</u> ote	11. log __og	12. <u>n</u> ine

42

LESSON 19: Connecting Sound to Symbol: Initial /n/ n

Practicing the Skill

- Point out the **Nn** at the top of page 41. Remind children that these letters stand for /**n**/. Ask children to trace these letters on the page and then in the air. Then tell children to listen for words that begin with /**n**/ as you read the rhyme.
- Read aloud the directions. Talk about whether the first picture should be circled and colored. Identify the other pictures before having children complete the page.
- Read aloud the directions on page 42. Model writing **n** to complete the first item. Name the pictures before having children work on their own.

Curriculum Connections

Theme Activity: Science/Art

Materials: picture of a bird's nest with baby birds, calendar, large manila envelope for each child, crayons, paper egg shapes

- Tell children that spring is a season for many kinds of celebrations. Explain that there are celebrations that mark the beginning of new life. Show spring months on a calendar and the picture of a bird's nest. Talk about signs of spring. (baby animals, flowers blooming)
- Give an envelope to each child. Have them write **Nn** on it and draw a picture of a bird's nest under the letters.
- Give three paper eggs to each child. Have children decorate the eggs by drawing pictures that begin with /**n**/ and writing **Nn** on the reverse side.
- Let children work with a partner to name the pictures on each other's eggs and place them in their envelope nests.

Sadlier Reading

Little Books and Big Books

Read *Nora Plays All Day* (fiction) and *A Party for Nine* (nonfiction) for more practice with initial consonant **n**.

English Language Learners/ESL

Materials: noisemakers

Add these gestures to the rhyme on page 41 to help children understand the rhyme. Have them repeat after you.

line 1: end line with noisemaker

line 2: hold up nine fingers

line 3: take a large step forward

To help children increase their vocabulary, substitute the numbers 1–10 in line 2. Encourage children to join in.

Challenge

Have children work in pairs to write two different tongue twisters that include words beginning with **n**. Give children one example. Say: **Nosey Nick** paid **nine nickels** to see **Ned's new necktie**. When pairs finish composing their tongue twisters, challenge them to have a race to see which partner can read each tongue twister more quickly.

Special Strategies

For Universal Access activities, see page 13F.

Initial /g/ Gg

Objectives
- To add initial sounds
- To recognize initial /g/
- To recognize that **Gg** stands for /g/
- To print **g** to complete words

Warming Up

Reviewing Initial s

Review initial **s** by having children answer riddles such as:

I come up in the morning and go down at night. (**sun**)

I am what your eyes do. (**see**)

Teaching the Lesson

Phonemic Awareness:
Add Initial Sounds

*Note: In this lesson children will learn only the hard sound of **g** (**goat**), not the soft sound (**giant**).*

Materials: gift-wrapped box

Say the word **ate**. Tell children that they can make a new word by adding /g/ before **ate**, such as /g/ -**ate**, **gate**. Help them add other sounds to the beginning of **ate** to make new words (e.g., **late**, **fate**, **mate**, **date**, **rate**).

Sound to Symbol

- Say the following sentence: **Gertie Gorilla gave** a **gift** to a **goose**. Explain that /g/ is the sound at the beginning of **Gertie, Gorilla, gave, gift, goose**. Have children say /g/ after you. Reread the sentence, having children clap each time they hear /g/.
- Write **Gg** on the board. Identify the uppercase and lowercase letters. Explain that both letters stand for /g/. On the board, print **Gail got** a **good gift**. Read each word aloud. Ask a volunteer whether the word begins with /g/. If it does, have him or her circle the letter in the word that stands for /g/. Ask a child to point to the word beginning with the uppercase **G**.

Gift starts with the sound of **g**. Listen for the sound of **g** in the rhyme.

Getting a gift
Is good, it is true.
But giving a gift
Is very good too.

Circle and color each picture that has the sound of **g** at the beginning of its name.

1 gift	2 gum	3 lake	4 gate
5 girl	6 fork	7 gas	8 tie
9 mask	10 goat	11 game	12 goose

LESSON 20: Phonemic Awareness: Initial /g/

43

UNIVERSAL ACCESS
Meeting Individual Needs

Auditory • Kinesthetic

Materials: green and red paper circles, craft sticks, glue

Have each child glue a red circle, for "stop," to one craft stick and a green circle, for "go," to another. Ask children to hold up their "go" signals if a word you say begins with **g** and their "stop" signals for any other initial sound. Use words such as **get, goat, lot,** and **give**.

Auditory • Kinesthetic

Direct two volunteers to face each other and hold hands to form a gate. The gate is "open" when children's arms are raised; the gate is "closed" when they are lowered. Have children line up in front of a closed gate. Say a word that begins with **g** to let children walk through an open gate.

Extra Support

Review that **g** stands for /g/ as in **good**. Then write the following on the board: **gas, gift, gum, game**. Read aloud each word and have volunteers circle the letter that stands for /g/.

Say the name of each picture. Print **g** on the line if its name begins with the sound of **g**.

1. __g__ um	2. cane __ane	3. __g__ as
4. desk __esk	5. __g__ old	6. sail __ail
7. meat __eat	8. __g__ ate	9. __g__ irl
10. __g__ oat	11. __g__ ame	12. lock __ock

LESSON 20: Connecting Sound to Symbol: Initial /g/ **g**

Say, "Give me a **g**!" Then have your child say a word from the page that begins with the sound of **g**.

Practicing the Skill

● Have children turn to page 43, and say /**g**/ while tracing the letters **Gg** with their fingers in the palms of their hands. Discuss the top picture and read the rhyme. Ask children to listen for words that start with /**g**/.

● Read aloud the directions, and go over the first item with children. Have them name each picture and then complete the page.

● Go over the directions on page 44 and model writing **g**. Name the pictures, and have children complete the page.

Curriculum Connections

Theme Activity: Multicultural
Materials: magazines and catalogs, scissors, small boxes, ribbon

● Have children talk about holidays when people exchange gifts, such as Christmas, Hanukkah, or Kwanzaa. Explain that Kwanzaa is an African-American holiday that began in 1966. The main purpose of Kwanzaa is to celebrate African-American history, heritage, ideas, and beliefs.

● Have each child cut out from a magazine or catalog a picture of an object that begins with **g**.

● Have each child put his or her picture in a box and decorate it as a holiday gift. Have children exchange gifts with partners and then show them to the class.

Sadlier Reading
Little Books and Big Books

Read *Goldilocks and the Three Bears* (fiction) and *Good Pets* (nonfiction) for more practice with initial consonant **g**.

English Language Learners/ESL
Materials: wrapped gift, paper, crayons

Wrap a gift and display it in the classroom. Tell children this is a gift. It begins with /**g**/. Write the word on chart paper and have children repeat the word. Underline the letter **g**. Brainstorm to name everything that might be a gift, e.g., **game, gate, gum, goat**. Model using Total Physical Response giving a gift to one child saying: *I **give** you the **gift gate***. Then have that child turn to another and say, "I give you the gift" and use another **g** word.

Challenge
Ask children to choose a holiday they celebrate and write a few sentences about it. Tell children to use as many words that begin with **g** as they can, and to underline those words. Have children make and attach a cover for their work. Have children share their work with the class.

Special Strategies
For Universal Access activities, see page 13F.

Observational Assessment

*Note children who confuse /g/ with similar sounds, such as hard **c**, and provide help.*

Initial /w/ Ww

Objectives
- To recognize alliteration
- To recognize initial /w/
- To recognize that **Ww** stands for /**w**/
- To print **w** to complete words

Warming Up

Reviewing Initial d
Remind children that **dance** begins with /**d**/. Have children stand and do a dance as you say some words to them. Tell them to stop dancing if they hear a word that does not begin with /**d**/. Have them start dancing again at the next **d** word. Say: *dog, deer, Dale, four, doll, me, duck, door, hat.*

Teaching the Lesson

Phonemic Awareness: Alliteration
Say: *Willy went in the wild wet wave.* Explain to children that **Willy, went, wild, wet,** and **wave** all begin with /**w**/. Have children say /**w**/ and each word with you. Now say: *Big Bob builds a blue boat.* Have children tell what sound is repeated. Then have them make up their own silly sentence and say it to the class. Ask volunteers to identify the repeated sound.

Sound to Symbol
- Say the words **wet, well,** and **wait**. Tell children that all the words begin with /**w**/. Ask children to repeat each word after you and then say /**w**/.
- Print **Ww** on the board. Explain that these letters stand for /**w**/. Point out the uppercase and lowercase letters. Then list the following words on the board: **Willy, went, wild, wet, wave.** Have children say the words with you as volunteers underline the letter that stands for /**w**/. Ask a child to find the word beginning with the uppercase **W.**

Ww

Waves starts with the sound of **w.** Listen for the sound of **w** in the rhyme.

> Willy wiggles and giggles.
> Willy watches and waves.
> Willy's next!
> Will he be brave?

Circle and color each picture that has the sound of **w** at the beginning of its name.

1 wagon	2 dinosaur
3 window	4 wave
5 well	6 windmill
7 lion	8 wallet
9 corn	10 watermelon
11 wig	12 watch

LESSON 21: Phonemic Awareness: Initial /**w**/   **45**

UNIVERSAL ACCESS
Meeting Individual Needs

Visual • Kinesthetic
Point out that **wiggle** begins with /**w**/. Have children say **wiggle** and then stand beside their desks and act out the word. Direct the class to wiggle when they hear you say a word that begins with /**w**/. Say words such as **wet, watch, bell, worm, got,** and **web.**

Auditory • Kinesthetic
Have the class work in two teams, the Wavers and the Others. Have the teams line up facing one another. Tell the Wavers to wave at the Others when they hear a word that begins with **w.** Direct the Others to wave at the Wavers when they hear a non-**w** word. Say a list of **w** and non-**w** words. Then switch team names and say more words.

Extra Support
Review that **w** stands for /**w**/, as in the beginning sound in **web.** Then have pairs of children look through their science or social studies books for objects that begin with /**w**/ and make a list. Have children share their lists.

1. w eb	2. w ig	3. tooth / __ooth
4. w orm	5. w ell	6. hook / __ook
7. w ax	8. boy / __oy	9. w ink
10. tent / __ent	11. w ing	12. w ave

46

LESSON 21: Connecting Sound to Symbol: Initial /w/ w

Print **Welcome** on a sheet of paper. Let your child trace the W and decorate the sign.

Practicing the Skill

- Direct children to the letters at the top of page 45. Review that they stand for /**w**/. Have the children trace the letters on the page.
- Discuss the picture at the top of the page. Tell children to listen for words that start with /**w**/ as you read the rhyme.
- Read the directions. Ask if the first picture should be circled and colored. Identify the other pictures before having children complete the page.
- Go over the directions on page 46 and identify each picture. Model the first item, and then have children complete the page.

Curriculum Connections

Theme Activity: Language Arts

- Remind children that celebrations are sometimes held at an amusement park. Reread the rhyme about Willy at the amusement park, and ask children to identify the things that Willy does: **wiggles**, giggles, **watches**, **waves**. Have children tell which words start with **w**.
- Compose a class story about Willy at an amusement park. Ask each child to suggest a sentence. Write contributions on the board, adding necessary transitions to shape a simple narrative. Record the story on chart paper. Reread the story with children, and give it a title. Have volunteers underline words that begin with **w**. Have children illustrate parts of the story.

Sadlier Reading
Little Books and Big Books

Read *Wait for Me* (fiction) and *Weather Wise* (nonfiction) for more practice with initial consonant **w**.

English Language Learners/ESL

Add gestures to the rhyme on page 45 to help children understand the words. Tell children to listen for words that begin with /**w**/ as in **window**. Encourage children to join in on subsequent repetitions.

- line 1: wiggle and cover your mouth as if giggling
- line 2: peer through hands/wave
- line 3: step forward with one foot
- line 4: stand tall with hand on hips

Special Strategies

For Universal Access activities, see page 13F.

Challenge

Materials: drawing paper, crayons

Have children brainstorm names for amusement park rides whose names start with **w**, such as **Wiggly Worm** and **Wonder Wagon**. Then ask children to choose one name, draw a picture of the ride, and write three sentences about it. Tell children to underline all **w** words.

Observational Assessment

*Note any children who are having difficulty identifying words that begin with **w**.*

Final /n/ n and /g/ g, gg

Objectives

- To identify and isolate final sounds
- To recognize final /n/ and /g/
- To recognize that **n** stands for final /n/ and **g** or **gg** stands for final /g/
- To print final **n**, **g**, and **gg** to complete words

Warming Up

Reviewing Rhyming Words

Have children name rhymes for words they have studied. Ask what word:

starts with **n** and rhymes with **game**; starts with **g** and rhymes with **hot**; starts with **d** and rhymes with **time**.

Teaching the Lesson

Phonemic Awareness: Identify and Isolate Final Sounds

Tell children you will say a word, and they will repeat the sound they hear at the end of the word. Model the process by saying: *pen*, /n/; *pig*, /g/. Say these words and have children repeat the final sounds: *dig*, *hen*, *log*, *egg*, *ran*, *sun*, *wag*.

Sound to Symbol

- Display a can. Ask children to name the object. Explain that /n/ is the last sound in **can**. Say **can** again, stressing /n/, and have children say it with you. Write the word **can** on the board, and circle the letter **n**. Explain that this letter stands for the ending sound, /n/, in **can**. Point to the **n** and say /n/ with the class.
- Repeat the process with /g/ **g**, **gg**, using the words **bag** and **egg**.
- Write two columns on the board. Print **-n** at the top of one, and **-g**, **-gg** at the top of the other. Under the appropriate letters, print **pen, fun, Jon, pan, Meg, bag, flag, egg**. Have children say the words with you as volunteers underline the letter or letters that stand for final /n/ or final /g/.

Pan ends with the sound of **n**. Circle the picture if its name has the same ending sound.

pan · man · cot · ten · bean · run · bus

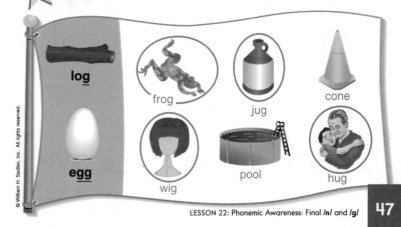

Log and **egg** end with the sound of **g**. Circle the picture if its name has the same ending sound.

log · egg · frog · jug · cone · wig · pool · hug

© William H. Sadlier, Inc. All rights reserved.

LESSON 22: Phonemic Awareness: Final /n/ and /g/

47

UNIVERSAL ACCESS
Meeting Individual Needs

Auditory • Kinesthetic

Review that **fan** ends in /n/ and **flag** ends in /g/. In response to words you say, have the class wave an imaginary flag to identify words ending in /g/, and use their hands to fan themselves to identify words that end in /n/. Use words such as **bag, pan, big, tag, men, egg, run, Jane, done,** and **hog.**

Auditory • Visual

Materials: Sadlier Phonics Picture Cards for **balloon, fan, van, lemon, horn, pig, tag, log, bug, rug**

Say **pin** and **rag**, and have children identify the ending sounds. Give out the picture cards. Tell children to hold up a card to match the ending sound of a word you say. Say these words: **dog, moon, frog, train, sag, pain, wig, son, bag, fin.**

Extra Support

Review that **n** stands for /n/ as in **pan** and **g** stands for /g/ as in **log**. Ask children to listen and then tell the ending sounds and letters for these words: **fog, pin, can, jog, lag, fin, Dan.**

Say the name of each picture. Circle the letter or letters that stand for its ending sound. Then print the letter or letters on the line.

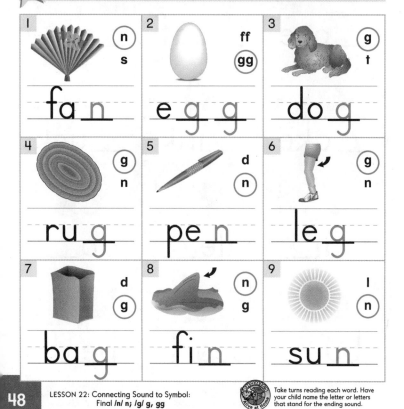

1. (n) s — fa_n_	2. ff (gg) — e_g__g_	3. (g) t — do_g_
4. (g) n — ru_g_	5. d (n) — pe_n_	6. (g) n — le_g_
7. d (g) — ba_g_	8. (n) g — fi_n_	9. l (n) — su_n_

LESSON 22: Connecting Sound to Symbol:
Final /n/ n; /g/ g, gg

Take turns reading each word. Have your child name the letter or letters that stand for the ending sound.

Practicing the Skill

● Read aloud the directions at the top of page 47. Have children point to the picture of the pan on the first flag and say its name. Identify the ending sound in **pan** (/**n**/). Then model identifying the ending sound in **man** and circling the picture because it matches the ending sound in **pan**. Have children complete the first flag.

● Have children point to the pictures of the log and the egg on the second flag, say the words, and identify the ending sound. Be sure children can name the other pictures on the flag before they work on their own.

● Read aloud the directions on page 48. Have them name each picture. Model completing the first item before having children complete the page.

Curriculum Connections

Theme Activity:
Art/Physical Education
Materials: unlined index cards, crayons

● Point out that party prizes are often small, fun gifts. Then give each child two index cards. Ask children to draw a prize that ends in /**n**/ on one card and a prize that ends in /**g**/ on the other. Tell children to put their names on the backs of the cards.

● Put all the cards in a pile. Play Simon Says with the children. When six players are left standing, declare them winners and hand out "prizes" (the cards). Have winners hold up their cards so the class can identify the items and tell their ending sounds. Play several rounds until all "prizes" are given out.

Portfolio
After playing the game, sort the cards according to the names on the back and have children put them in their portfolios.

English Language Learners/ESL
Some children may have difficulty with similar sounding words (e.g., **pen, pin, pan; pig, leg, log**). Use realia, pictures, and pantomime to help them learn and use the words in context. For example, say: *Print your name with the* **pen**. *Cook the egg in a* **pan**. *Point to your* **leg**. *Oink like a* **pig**. Then have children give commands.

Challenge
Have children work in pairs. Partner A thinks of a word that ends in **n, g,** or **gg**, and writes it down. Then Partner A uses clues to describe the word so Partner B can identify the word. Then have children reverse roles.

Special Strategies
For Universal Access activities, see page 13F.

Observational Assessment

Note whether children are correctly identifying the ending sounds for **n, g,** *and* **gg** *on the prize cards.*

Reviewing and Assessing Initial and Final
l, d, c, n, g, w

Objectives
● To identify and print initial or final **l**, **d**, **c**, **n**, **g**, and **w** to complete words

Warming Up

Reviewing Initial Consonants

Materials: **Sadlier Phonics Picture Cards** for initial **f**, **m**, **s**, **t**, **h**, and **b**, such as **feet**, **mask**, **seal**, **toys**, **horn**, **balloon**; Punchout Letter Cards

Remind children that words have beginning sounds. Tell them that **fan** begins with /**f**/. Ask children what beginning sound they hear in **bike**. Display the picture cards on the chalk ledge, and place the letter cards facedown on a desk. Have volunteers name each picture. Then have volunteers pick a letter card and scan the chalk ledge for pictures with names that begin with that letter.

Teaching the Lesson

● Write _**amp** on the board. Say the word **lamp**. Tell children that **lamp** begins with /**l**/. Write **l** on the board to complete the word. Next write _**eaf** on the board. Say the word **leaf**. Have a volunteer identify the beginning sound in **leaf** and write it on the board to complete the word. Continue in this way for other initial sounds. Use these words: **door**, **cap**, **nest**, **gate**, and **wave**. Repeat the activity for ending sounds using these words: **sad**, **rag**, **seal**, **fun**.

● Have children turn to page 49. Read aloud the directions and name each picture. Together complete the first two items. Have children finish the page.

Say the name of each picture. Circle the letter that stands for the missing sound. Then print the letter on the line.

LESSON 23: Reviewing Initial and Final Consonants **l, d, c, n g, w**

UNIVERSAL ACCESS
Reteaching Activities

Activity 1

Materials: **Sadlier Phonics Picture Cards** for initial **l, d, c, n, g,** and **w** and final **l, d, n,** and **g**

Write the letters **l, d, c, n, g,** and **w** on the board, and review the sound each letter stands for. Have children stand in a line facing you. Spread the picture cards facedown on a table. Ask a child to take a card and tell whether the picture name has the sound of initial or final **l, d, c, n, g,** or **w**. Children with initial sounds go to the head of the line (your left); those with final sounds go to the end (your right).

Activity 2

Materials: **Sadlier Phonics Picture Cards** for initial **l, d, c, n, g,** and **w** and final **l, d, n,** and **g**

Divide chart paper into six sections. Label sections with one of these letters: **l, d, c, n, g,** and **w**. Display the picture cards. Have children tape to the chart a picture card whose initial sound matches a letter. Repeat for final sounds with a chart divided into quarters and labeled with: **l, d, n,** and **g**.

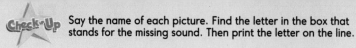

l	d	c	n	g	w

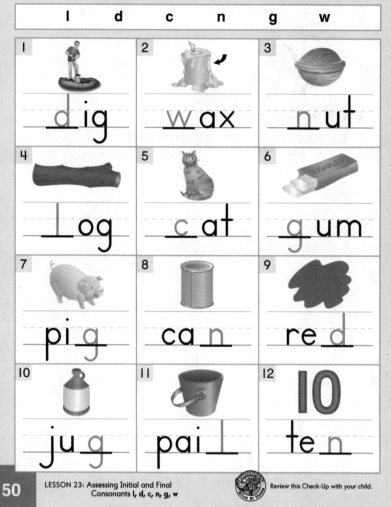

1. d ig
2. w ax
3. n ut
4. l og
5. c at
6. g um
7. pi g
8. ca n
9. re d
10. ju g
11. pai l
12. te n

50

LESSON 23: Assessing Initial and Final
Consonants l, d, c, n, g, w

Review this Check-Up with your child.

Assessing the Skills

Check-Up Use page 50 to help assess how well children have learned the sounds of consonants **l**, **d**, **c**, **n**, **g**, and **w**. Tell children that together they will review these sounds orally.

Write on the board **log**, **dime**, **cat**, **net**, **goat**, and **worm**. Read each word aloud. Have volunteers come to the board, underline the initial letter in one of the words, and then say the word and its initial letter. Repeat for the final sounds using these words: **seal**, **bird**, **van**, **mug**.

Read aloud the directions on page 50, and identify the pictures together. Have children complete the page.

Observational Assessment To note children's progress, observe them as they complete page 50. Also, refer to notes you took while observing children complete written and oral activities throughout the lessons dealing with these consonants.

Dictation Tell children they will write the letter that stands for the beginning sound they hear in each word you say. Then say the words **lamp**, **dish**, **car**, **not**, **gum**, **wet**. Then have them write the final sounds of each word you say. Say **rail**, **mud**, **sun**, **rug**.

Student Skills Assessment Use the checklist on Student Edition pages 321–322 to record your observations of individual children.

Guided Instruction

Skills	Resources
Initial consonants **l, d, c**	Instruction on pages 33–38
Final consonants **l, ll, d, dd**	Instruction on pages 39–40
Initial consonants **n, g, w**	Instruction on pages 41–46
Final consonants **n, g, gg**	Instruction on pages 47–48
Initial and final consonants **l, d, c, n, g, w**	Phonemic Awareness Activities on pages 13H–13I Punchout Cards on page 13N

Initial /p/ Pp

Objectives
- To add initial sounds
- To recognize initial /**p**/
- To recognize that **Pp** stands for /**p**/
- To print **p** to complete words

Warming Up

Reviewing Initial /w/

Remind children that the letter **w** stands for the beginning sound /**w**/, as in **web**. Show children how to form a **w** by holding up three fingers on one hand. Tell children to hold up a **w** when they hear you say a word that begins with /**w**/. Say **wind**, **with**, **wool**, **full**, **wag**, **run**, **wash**, **wet**, **wall**, **van**, **well**.

Teaching the Lesson

Phonemic Awareness: Add Initial Sounds

Tell children that you are going to say the end of a word and they are going to add the sound /**p**/ to the beginning to say the entire word. Model this by saying /**an**/ and then /**p**/-/**an**/ **pan**. Say these phonograms one at a time: **–it**, **-ot**, **-ig**, **-ad**, **-at**, **-al**, and ask children to add /**p**/ to the beginning to say the entire word.

Sound to Symbol

- Say these words: **pet**, **Patty**, **pole**, **peel**. Tell children that all these words begin with /**p**/. Have children say each word with you, and then say /**p**/.
- Print **Pp** on the board. Point out the uppercase and lowercase letters. Explain that these letters stand for /**p**/. Then print **pick**, **pail**, **Polly**, **part**, **Peter**, **pond**, and **Paul** on the board. Have children say the words with you as a volunteer circles the letter that stands for /**p**/. Ask a child to find the three words that begin with an uppercase **P**.

Pp

Ponies starts with the sound of **p**. Listen for the sound of **p** in the rhyme.

> Ponies and poodles
> And parakeets, too.
> They're having a pet parade
> Just for you.

Circle and color each picture that has the sound of **p** at the beginning of its name.

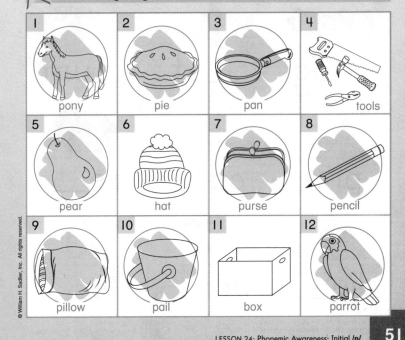

1 pony	2 pie	3 pan	4 tools
5 pear	6 hat	7 purse	8 pencil
9 pillow	10 pail	11 box	12 parrot

LESSON 24: Phonemic Awareness: Initial /**p**/   **51**

UNIVERSAL ACCESS
Meeting Individual Needs

Auditory • Kinesthetic

Introduce "pop up" as an action name that begins with **p**. Direct children to crouch down and then pop up whenever they hear you say a word that begins with **p**. Say **pet**, **bow**, **parade**, **meal**, **party**, **point**, **tall**, **people**, **sing**, **panda**, **have**, **pie**.

Visual • Kinesthetic
Materials: piggy bank, pennies

Place a piggy bank on a desk and give each child four pennies. Tell children that **piggy** and **penny** begin with /**p**/. Have volunteers deposit a penny in the bank when you say a word that begins with **p**. Say: **Peter**, **popcorn**, **desk**, **horn**, **peas**, **marbles**, **pencil**. After several rounds, count the coins in the bank.

Extra Support
Materials: Sadlier Phonics Picture Cards for **pig**, **pen**, **pot**, **pail**, **pie**

Review that **pig** begins with /**p**/. Display the picture cards and ask volunteers to say the picture name and then the beginning sound.

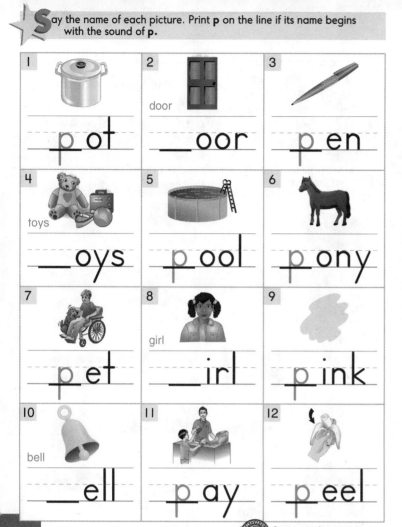

Say the name of each picture. Print **p** on the line if its name begins with the sound of **p.**

1 __p__ ot	2 door __oor	3 __p__ en
4 toys __oys	5 __p__ ool	6 __p__ ony
7 __p__ et	8 girl __irl	9 __p__ ink
10 bell __ell	11 __p__ ay	12 __p__ eel

52   LESSON 24: Connecting Sound to Symbol: Initial /p/ **p**

Practice saying this tongue twister together: Peter Piper picked a peck of pickled peppers for Paula's party.

Practicing the Skill

● Direct children to trace the letters **Pp** at the top of page 51 while saying /**p**/.

● Identify the animals at the top of the page that have names beginning with /**p**/—**ponies, poodles,** and **parakeets.** Then have children listen for words beginning with /**p**/ as you read the rhyme.

● Read aloud the directions and name the pictures. Model how to circle and color the first item with children. Then have them finish the page.

● Read aloud the directions on page 52. Model writing **p** to complete the first word. Be sure children can identify all the pictures before having them complete the page.

Curriculum Connections

Theme Activity: Multicultural
Materials: chart paper, crayons

● Point out that a world's fair provides a chance for people from around the world to come together and learn about their own country and the countries of others.

● Read the theme book listed below. Then have children plan a United States exhibit for a world's fair. Ask them to list what they want to show and tell the world about the United States. Have children suggest foods, toys, crafts, and so on. Guide the planning to include items from different cultures. List items under headings on chart paper. Have children underline words that begin with **p.**

Theme Book Reese, Bob. *Field Trip.* New York: Children's Press, 1992. A rhyming story about a field trip to a fair.

Sadlier Reading
Little Books and Big Books

Read *Patty and Pop's Picnic* (fiction) and *Pumpkin Days* (nonfiction) for more practice with initial consonant **p.**

English Language Learners/ESL
Initial /**p**/ and /**f**/ are often confusing for children learning English. Show children how you say /**p**/ and the difference for /**f**/. Display pictures of words with initial **p** such as **pig, pot,** and **pan.** Modify the rhyme on page 51; in the first two lines, substitute the names of the pictures. End by saying: *We're having a parade with the sound of p/Just for you and me.* Then use **f** pictures, such as **fan, fox,** and **fur,** and repeat the activity, adjusting it for initial **f.** Review all pictures, and have children identify those that begin with /**p**/.

Challenge
Mention that pie is often served at a party and that **pie** and **party** begin with **p.** Explain that to make a pie, people follow a recipe, which is a list of foods to put in a pie and the directions for making it. Show children an example of a recipe and then have them write a funny recipe for a pie with **p** words, such as **peaches, pears, peas,** and **pickles.** Tell children to read aloud their recipes to the rest of the class.

Special Strategies
For Universal Access activities, see page 13F.

52

Student Pages 53-54

Initial /r/ Rr

Objectives
- To use nonsense and word play
- To recognize initial /r/
- To recognize that **Rr** stands for /r/
- To print **r** to complete words

Warming Up

Reviewing Initial c

Say **call** and review that it begins with /k/. Have children clap each time you say a word that begins with /k/. Words may include: **cat**, **come**, **fill**, **cup**, **cake**, **house**, **coat**.

Teaching the Lesson

Phonemic Awareness: Nonsense and Word Play

Tell children that the sound heard at the beginning of **red** and **run** is /r/. Have children repeat the sound. Then ask them to make up some silly words by replacing the first sound in words you say with /r/. Give an example: **sit—rit**. Say: **bike** (*rike*), **juggle** (*ruggle*), **cone** (*rone*), **hill** (*rill*), **mop** (*rop*), **lunch** (*runch*).

Sound to Symbol

- Say to children: *Raise your right hand.* Explain that **raise** and **right** both begin with /r/. Direct children to raise their right hands each time they hear a word that starts with /r/. Say: **Rita rode Rosa's** *bike near the rocks.*

- Print **Rr** on the board and tell children these letters stand for /r/. Identify the uppercase and lowercase letters. Under the letters write the words **raise**, **right**, **Rita**, **rode**, **Rosa**, **rocks**. Have children say the words as volunteers underline the letter that stands for initial /r/. Ask volunteers to identify uppercase and lowercase letters and tell what sound they make.

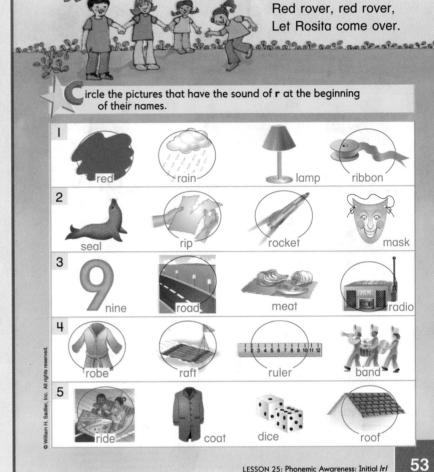

Rr

Red starts with the sound of **r**. Listen for the sound of **r** in the rhyme.

Red rover, red rover,
Let Rosita come over.

Circle the pictures that have the sound of **r** at the beginning of their names.

1. red | rain | lamp | ribbon
2. seal | rip | rocket | mask
3. nine | road | meat | radio
4. robe | raft | ruler | band
5. ride | coat | dice | roof

LESSON 25: Phonemic Awareness: Initial /r/   **53**

UNIVERSAL ACCESS
Meeting Individual Needs

Auditory • Kinesthetic
Materials: large, soft ball

Have children sit on the floor in a circle. Give the ball to one child. Say that whoever has the ball calls out a word that begins with /r/ and then rolls the ball to another child, who does the same. Make sure everyone names an **r** word before rolling the ball.

Visual • Kinesthetic
Materials: Sadlier Phonics Picture Cards, including several for initial **r** words such as **red**, **ride**, **rug**, **rose**

Have children stand in a circle singing "Ring Around the Rosy." Have children say, "Look at this!" instead of "We all fall down" at the end. Show a picture card. Children fall down if the name begins with **r**.

Extra Support
Say: *Red starts with /r/.* Write **red** on the board. Help children look around to find items that start with **r**, including children's names. Write the **r** words on the board, read them aloud, and then have volunteers circle the letter **r** in each word.

Say the name of each picture. Print **r** on the line if its name begins with the sound of **r**.

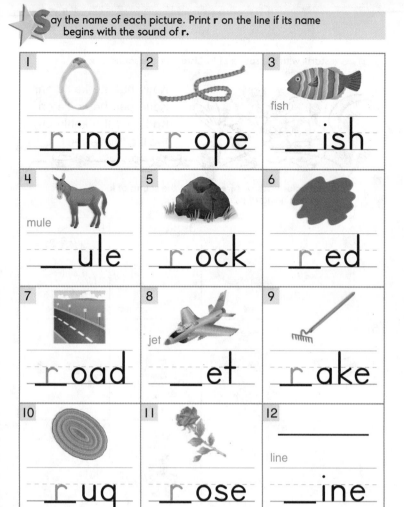

1 __r__ing	2 __r__ope	3 fish __ish
4 mule __ule	5 __r__ock	6 __r__ed
7 __r__oad	8 jet __et	9 __r__ake
10 __r__ug	11 __r__ose	12 line __ine

LESSON 25: Connecting Sound to Symbol: Initial /r/ r

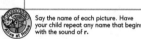

Say the name of each picture. Have your child repeat any name that begins with the sound of r.

Practicing the Skill

● Direct children to trace the letters **Rr** at the top of page 53 while saying /**r**/. Ask children to listen for words that begin with /**r**/ as you read the rhyme.

● Read the directions. Identify the pictures on the page and model circling the first item. Then have children complete the page.

● Read aloud the directions on page 54. Model writing **r** in the first item. Then have children name all pictures and complete the page.

Curriculum Connections

Theme Activity: Science

Materials: toy cars with moving wheels, blocks, wood and cardboard scraps, cardboard tubes, tape

● Raise one end of a book on blocks and roll a toy car down the **ramp**. Then have children work in small groups to make roller coaster slides for toy cars. Provide scrap materials listed above. Then hold roller-coaster races. Have two children in each group position their cars at the top of their ramps. Tell them to send cars down the ramp only when they hear a word that begins with **r**. If they start on a different sound, they lose the race. Start each race by saying three words, one of which begins with **r**.

● Have the class confirm that **roller coaster**, **ramp**, and **race** each begin with **r**.

Sadlier Reading

Little Books and Big Books

Read *Here Comes the Rain!* (fiction) and *I Love to Read* (nonfiction) for more practice with initial consonant **r**.

English Language Learners/ESL

Tell children to listen for /**r**/. Play the Red Rover game by saying: *Red rover, red rover, let [use a child's name] come over.* Repeat, substituting the verbs **run** and **rush**, and then with other verbs (**skip**, **walk**, **hop**, etc.) Guide children in acting out the verbs. Use this opportunity to introduce school commands and rules: *Don't **run** in the halls. Don't **rush** to the cafeteria.*

Challenge

Materials: large ball

Have children say the following chant using **r** words, and bounce the ball on each **r** word. For example: "R my name is **Risa**, my mother's name is **Rose**; we come from **Russia**, and we sell **rabbits**." Tell children they can make up nonsense names and place names if they get stuck.

Special Strategies

For Universal Access activities, see page 13F.

Observational Assessment

*Note whether children have problems recognizing **r** words during the roller-coaster race.*

Initial Consonant /k/ Kk

Objectives
- To use nonsense and word play
- To recognize initial /k/
- To recognize that **Kk** stands for /k/
- To print **k** to complete words

Warming Up

Reviewing Initial n

Point to your nose and say **nose**. Remind children that **nose** begins with /n/. Write **Nn** on the board, say the letter names, and review that these letters stand for /n/. Have children point to their noses when they hear a word that begins with /n/. Say: **name, nuts, napkin, dot, nest, neck, mat.**

Teaching the Lesson

Phonemic Awareness: Nonsense and Word Play

- Tell children that you will recite a nursery rhyme, but you are going to change the beginning sound of some words to /k/. Have them guess the rhyme.

    /K/ary had a /k/ittle /k/amb.

    Its /k/leece was /k/ite as snow.

- Have children replace /k/ with a different beginning sound, such as /b/, to make new nonsense words.

Sound to Symbol

- Tell children to listen as you say: *Kevin is kind to his kitten*. Explain that /k/ is the sound at the beginning of **Kevin, kind** and **kitten**. Say each word, and have children repeat the word and /k/ after you.
- Print **Kk** on the board. Identify the uppercase **K** and lowercase **k**. Tell children that these letters make the sound /k/. Then list these words: **Kevin, kind, key, kitten, kitchen, Kim.** Have children say the words with you as volunteers underline the letter that stands for /k/ at the beginning of each word. Ask a child to find the two words beginning with uppercase **K**.

55

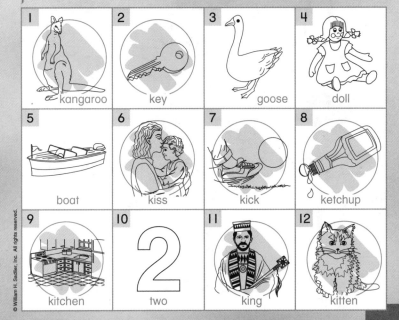

Kettle starts with the sound of **k.** Listen for the sound of **k** in the rhyme.

Katie put the kettle on,
Katie put the kettle on,
Katie put the kettle on,
We'll all have tea.

Circle and color each picture that has the sound of **k** at the beginning of its name.

1 kangaroo	2 key	3 goose	4 doll
5 boat	6 kiss	7 kick	8 ketchup
9 kitchen	10 two	11 king	12 kitten

LESSON 26: Phonemic Awareness: Initial /k/ **k**   **55**

UNIVERSAL ACCESS
Meeting Individual Needs

Kinesthetic • Auditory
Materials: Sadlier Phonics Picture Cards for **king, kitten, horn, toe, kite, lemon**; six keys

Give two children each three keys. Place six picture cards faceup. Tell one child to place keys on initial **k** pictures. The second child may place keys on the pictures to confirm or revise.

Kinesthetic • Auditory
Materials: drawing paper, ribbon, crayons

Remind children that **kite** begins with **k**. Model cutting a kite from drawing paper and attaching a ribbon tail. Then have each child make a kite. Have children decorate their kites with pictures beginning with **k**. Have children name the **k** pictures on their kites.

Extra Support
Materials: paper cutouts of keys, magazines

Say **key** and identify its beginning sound as /k/. Provide children with magazines and several key cutouts. Ask them to place a key on pictures that start with **k**.

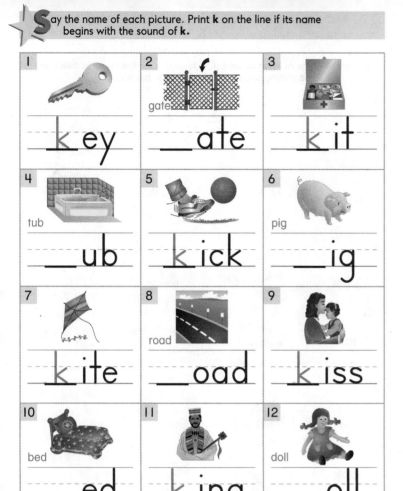

Say the name of each picture. Print **k** on the line if its name begins with the sound of **k**.

1 key	2 gate __ate	3 kit
k ey	__ate	k it

4 tub	5	6 pig
__ub	k ick	__ig

7	8 road	9
k ite	__oad	k iss

10 bed	11	12 doll
__ed	k ing	__oll

56

LESSON 26: Connecting Sound to Symbol: Initial /k/ k

Name the pictures. Let your child shake a set of keys after each word that begins with the sound of **k**.

56

Final /p/ p, /r/ r, and /k/ k

Objectives

- To identify and isolate final sounds
- To recognize final /p/, /r/, and /k/
- To recognize that **p** stands for final /p/, **r** stands for final /r/, and **k** stands for final /k/
- To print final **p**, **r**, and **k** to complete words

Warming Up

Reviewing Ending Sounds

Materials: **Sadlier Phonics Picture Cards** for **leaf**, **drum**, **queen**, **red**, **hill**; pocket chart

Place the cards in the chart. Ask children to identify the pictures that match the ending sounds of these words. Say: **roof**, **Sam**, **bean**, **food**, **call**.

Teaching the Lesson

Phonemic Awareness: Identify and Isolate Final Sounds

Tell children to repeat the sounds they hear at the end of words you will say. Model by saying: **cup**, /p/; **bear**, /r/; **cake**, /k/. Then say: **book**, **nap**, **deer**, **lip**, **park**, **hair**.

Sound to Symbol

- Say the word **nap**. Explain that /p/ is the sound at the end of **nap**. Have children say **nap** and then /p/. Write **nap** on the board. Circle the letter **p**. Tell children the letter **p** stands for /p/ at the end of **nap**. Repeat the process to point out the final sounds of **r** and **k** in the words **car** and **book**.
- Write **-p**, **-r**, and **-k** at the top of three columns. Under the appropriate letters, write **cap**, **top**, **fair**, **deer**, **hook**, **look**. Have children say each word with you as volunteers underline the letter that stands for final /p/, /r/, or /k/.

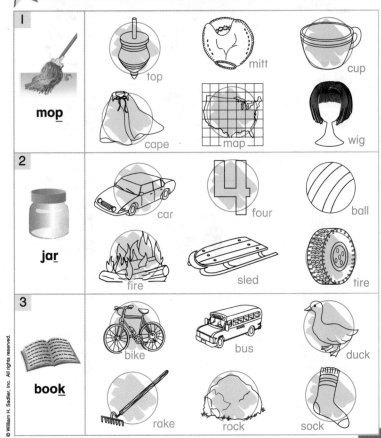

Say the name of each picture. Circle and color the pictures that have the same ending sound as the picture in the box.

1. mop — top, mitt, cup, cape, map, wig
2. jar — car, four, ball, fire, sled, tire
3. book — bike, bus, duck, rake, rock, sock

LESSON 27: Phonemic Awareness: Final /p/, /r/, /k/   **57**

UNIVERSAL ACCESS
Meeting Individual Needs

Kinesthetic • Auditory

Have children work in pairs to become pretend cars. The "passenger" stands behind, with his or her hands on the "driver's" shoulders. Explain that these "cars" will move forward one step at a time, but only when the driver or passenger says a word that ends in **r**. Repeat with **p** and **k**.

Auditory • Visual

Say: *I'm thinking of something that ends in **p**. What do you think it could be?* After one guess is made, provide positive feedback and offer a second hint, such as, "I wash my floor with it." Repeat with words ending in **r**, and **k**. After the word is guessed, write it on the board and circle the final letter.

Extra Support

Display objects ending with **p**, **r**, and **k** (e.g., a **cup**, a toy **car**, a **book**). Have children name the objects and the ending sounds. Hold up the cup and model by saying: *cup, /p/. Cup ends with **p**.* Have children repeat in a similar way with other items. Help them find other objects ending in **p**, **r**, or **k**.

Say the name of each picture. Circle the letter that stands for its ending sound. Then print the letter on the line.

1. (p) / r — to__p__

2. (l) / k — hoo__k__

3. (r) / n — ja__r__

4. (p) / m — ca__p__

5. (p) / g — cu__p__

6. (k) / f — coo__k__

7. (r) / m — doo__r__

8. d / (k) — mil__k__

9. k / (p) — mo__p__

LESSON 27: Connecting Sound to Symbol:
Final /p/ p, /r/ r, /k/ k

Say the name of each picture. Have your child clap if its name ends with the sound of **p**.

Practicing the Skill

- Direct children's attention to the pictures and words on the left side of page 57. Help children identify the final sound for each.
- Read aloud the directions. Model identifying the final sound in **top** and circling and coloring the picture. Explain that the final sound in **top** matches the final sound in **mop**. Be sure children can name the other pictures before completing the page.
- Direct children's attention to page 58. Point out that **top** ends with /**p**/. Read aloud the directions and model completing the first item. Identify all pictures. Then have children complete the page.

Curriculum Connections

Theme Activity: Art/Language Arts
Materials: nine large triangular flags cut from construction paper, three 3-foot lengths of yarn, markers, tape, poster board

- Have children work in three groups. Give each group three flags and one length of yarn.
- Have each group write the letter **r** on one flag, **p** on another, and **k** on the last flag.
- Have the class brainstorm things they might do or see at a school picnic, fair, or park. Suggest activities, rides, games, and exhibits.
- As children respond, ask if each word belongs under any of their banners. Lead them to realize that only words whose ending sound matches the letter on a banner belong under that banner.
- Have children illustrate their "Fun Fair" ideas on the flags.
- String each group's flags together and display them. Have children identify the objects they drew.

English Language Learners/ESL
Children may need help with some of the names for the objects pictured in the lesson. Direct children to page 57. Point to each final **p** picture on the page, say its name, and have children repeat the word several times. Ask a volunteer to tell you what is the ending sound for all these words. Continue with the picture names for words with final **r** and then final **k**.

Special Strategies
For Universal Access activities, see page 13F.

Challenge
Have children make up riddles whose answers end in **p**, **r**, or **k**. Provide the following model riddles:

I spin and spin and spin. (**top**)

You can ride in me. (**car**)

You can read me. (**book**)

Then have children pose their riddles to the class for them to answer.

Observational Assessment

Note any children who have difficulty determining whether /p/, /r/, or /k/ is the final sound.

Student Pages 59–60

Initial Consonant /j/ Jj

Objectives
- To segment onsets and rimes
- To recognize initial /j/
- To recognize that **Jj** stands for /j/
- To print **j** to complete words

Warming Up

Reviewing Initial Sounds
Materials: **Sadlier Phonics Picture Cards** for **pig**, **ride**, **kitten**

Print on the board these sentences, and read them aloud.

Little **Ruth** is in the **parade**.

The new **king** had a big **party**.

The boy **put** a **key** in the **red** wagon.

Display the picture cards and name them with the class. Identify each beginning sound. Then have children circle words in the sentences that have the same beginning sounds as the pictures. Say each word together as it is circled.

Teaching the Lesson

Phonemic Awareness: Segment Onsets and Rimes
Say the word **jog**. Tell children that **jog** begins with /j/. Then model segmenting the beginning sound from the rest of the word by saying /j/-/og/. Say the words **jar, jeep, just, jet**. Have children repeat each word and then segment the beginning sound from the rest of the word.

Sound to Symbol
- Tell children to listen for words that begin with /j/ as you say this tongue twister: *The jolly clown jumps and jiggles.* Have children name the initial **j** words and then say /j/.
- Print **Jj** on the board. Explain that these letters stand for /j/. Identify the uppercase and lowercase letters. Write the following words under the letters: **jolly, jumps, jiggles, Jim**. Read each word with the class and ask volunteers to point to the letter that stands for /j/.

59

Jj

Joy starts with the sound of **j**. Listen for the sound of **j** in the rhyme.

Justin and Jasmin
Jump for joy.
The puppy in the jeep
Is theirs to keep.

Circle and color each picture that has the sound of **j** at the beginning of its name.

1 jeep	2 jam	3 bite	4 June
5 nest	6 jack-in-the-box	7 robe	8 judge
9 jacket	10 pan	11 jacks	12 jug

LESSON 28: Phonemic Awareness: Initial /j/   **59**

U N I V E R S A L   A C C E S S
Meeting Individual Needs

Auditory • Kinesthetic
Teach the class how to do jumping jacks. Then direct children to do a single jumping jack whenever they hear you say a word that begins with /j/. Slowly say a list of words: **job**, gate, **jeans, jelly**, duck, hat, time, **jewel, Joe**, kangaroo, **jump, judge**, and **July**.

Visual • Kinesthetic
Materials: **Sadlier Phonics Picture Cards** for initial **j** (e.g., **jam, juggle, jeep**) and other initial sounds

Review the song "If You're Happy and You Know It, Clap Your Hands." Teach children to use the same melody to sing *"If the name starts with j, clap your hands."* Children should clap only if a picture card you show represents an initial **j** word.

Extra Support
Remind children that **j** stands for /j/. Put pictures of initial **j** objects (**jacket, jelly beans**, etc.) and other non-j objects facedown. Have a child turn over two pictures. If both start with **j**, have the child write **j** on the board.

Say the name of each picture. Print **j** on the line if its name begins with the sound of **j**.

1 j et	2 ring ___ing	3 j ar
4 j ug	5 j eep	6 kite ___ite
7 pen ___en	8 j eans	9 j acks
10 goat ___oat	11 red ___ed	12 j am

60

LESSON 28: Connecting Sound to Symbol: Initial /j/ j

Have your child look at a calendar to find the months with names that begin with the sound of **j**.

Practicing the Skill

● Point to the letters **Jj** at the top of page 59. Remind children that these letters stand for /**j**/. Have them trace the letters at the top of the page and then in the air. Have children listen for words that begin with /**j**/ as you read the poem.

● Read aloud the directions on page 59 and identify the pictures. Model for children how to circle and color the first picture. Then tell children to complete the page.

● Read the directions for page 60. Model how to write the letter **j** to complete the first item. Identify all pictures. Then have them complete the page.

Curriculum Connections

Theme Activity: Art/Math

Materials: large sheets of drawing paper, crayons, magazines, catalogs, scissors, glue

● Discuss with children the kinds of celebrations that might include jugglers. (circus, birthday parties) Let volunteers talk about their own juggling experiences.

● Distribute drawing paper and have children draw a clown in the center of it.

● Provide magazines and catalogs and have children cut out objects that begin with /**j**/. Tell children to glue the pictures around the clown so that the clown appears to be juggling the **j** pictures.

● When children are finished, have them count the items their clown is juggling and print the number on the back of the paper. Then have partners exchange drawings and count and name each other's **j** pictures.

Portfolio — Tell children to place their "juggling **j**" pictures in their portfolios.

Sadlier Reading
Little Books and Big Books

Read *J My Name Is Jess* (fiction) and *In January and June* (nonfiction) for more practice with initial consonant **j**.

English Language Learners/ESL

Write **J** and **j** on the board. Tell children these letters stand for /**j**/ as in **jump**. Say /**j**/, /**j**/, -**ump** and **jump**. Tell children to watch how you form your mouth when you say /**j**/. Then ask children to mimic you and say /**j**/. Then show children an empty, washed **juice** container and tell them that the word **juice** begins with the letter **j** /**j**/. Repeat this activity using a **jar**. Print labels for the juice container and the jar, and display them in the classroom.

Challenge

Have pairs of children work together to make up a short story about a **juggler**. Challenge them to use words that begin with **j** in their stories. For example, *Jo-Jo* **juggles** *bags of* **jelly** *beans. Then he* **jumps** *into his* **jeep**. To share stories, have one partner narrate the story, while the other acts it out. Ask listeners to raise their hands every time they hear a word that begins with **j**.

Special Strategies

For Universal Access activities, see page 13F.

60

Initial Consonants /kw/ Q(u), q(u) and /v/ V v

Objectives

- To identify and isolate initial sounds
- To recognize initial /**kw**/
- To recognize initial /**v**/
- To recognize that **Q(u) q(u)** stands for /**kw**/ and **Vv** stands for /**v**/

Warming Up

Reviewing the Sounds of Hard g and Hard c

Materials: **Sadlier Phonics Picture Cards** for **cap, gift, game, cub, cake**

Have children sort the cards into two groups—picture names beginning with **g** and with **c**.

Teaching the Lesson

Phonemic Awareness: Identify and Isolate Initial Sounds

Say the word **quack**. Repeat the word and then isolate the initial sound: **quack**, /**kw**/. Explain that /**kw**/ is the beginning sound in **quack**. Have children say /**kw**/. Then say **quiet, queen**, and **quilt** and have children say the beginning sound in each word. Repeat with /**v**/ using the words **van, vase**, and **valentine**.

Sound to Symbol

- Say /**kw**/, and have children repeat /**kw**/. Say **quick, questions, quart**. Explain that the words begin with /**kw**/. Have children clap when they hear a word that begins with /**kw**/. Say: *The* **quiet queen** *made a* **quilt**. Repeat the process for /**v**/ using the words **van, visit, violin**, and the sentence: *Val ate very big* **vegetables**.
- On the board, print **Qu** and **qu**. Point to and identify the uppercase and lowercase letters. Explain that both pairs of letters stand for /**kw**/. Print these words on the board: **quarter, quack, Quinn, quail**. Read the words. Then ask a child to underline the letters that stands for /**kw**/. Repeat the process for **Vv** using **vanilla, Victor, very, volcano**.

61

Qu qu

Quiet starts with the sound of **qu**. Listen for the sound of **qu** in the rhyme.

"Shh! Quiet!" said the queen.
"Quick! Hide!" said the king.
Here comes Farmer Green!

Circle the pictures that have the sound of **qu** at the beginning of their names.

1	queen	robot	lion	quilt
2	fire	quiet	wagon	doll
3	heart	question mark	quack	nuts
4	gift	puzzle	quart	ball
5	rope	quarter	yellow	saw

LESSON 29: Phonemic Awareness: Initial /**kw**/   **61**

UNIVERSAL ACCESS
Meeting Individual Needs

Auditory • Kinesthetic

Teach the class to pantomime ducks by bending over, placing their fists on their hips, and holding their elbows out behind them. Have children waddle around in a circle. Tell them to stop and say **"quack"** when they hear you say a word that begins with /**kw**/. Say words such as **queen, quiet, quiz, quilt**.

Auditory • Kinesthetic

Ask children to answer these riddles with words that begin with /**v**/:

I'm bigger than a car and smaller than a truck. What am I? (**van**)

You can eat us to be healthy. We include carrots, beans, and peas. What are we? (**vegetables**)

I'm the time when you don't come to school. What am I? (**vacation**)

Extra Support

Remind children that **qu** stands for /**kw**/ and **v** stands for /**v**/. Draw nine squares on the board. Have children write **qu** or **v** in each square as you say words such as **queen, vanilla, quiet, vegetable, question, quick, vet, quart**, and **quit**.

Vase starts with the sound of **v**. Listen for the sound of **v** in the rhyme.

Vv

A big vase of violets
And velvet hearts, too,
Are the Valentine gifts
I'd like to give to you.

Circle and color each picture that has the sound of **v** at the beginning of its name.

1 vase	2 jack-in-the-box	3 violin	4 van
5 vacuum	6 watermelon	7 vine	8 kangaroo
9 queen	10 vegetables	11 volcano	12 volleyball

62

LESSON 29: Phonemic Awareness: Initial /v/

Help your child cut out a Valentine heart. Write words that begin with **v** on it.

Practicing the Skill

- Have children point to and trace the letters **Qu qu** at the top of page 61. Remind children that these letters stand for /**kw**/.
- Have children listen for words that begin with /**kw**/ as you read the rhyme.
- Read aloud the directions on page 61 and identify the pictures. Model for children how to circle the first picture. Then tell children to complete the page.
- Have children trace the letters **Vv** at the top of page 62. Remind children that these letters stand for /**v**/. Have children listen for words that begin with /**v**/ as you read the rhyme.
- Read aloud the directions on page 62 and identify the pictures. Model for children how to circle and color the first picture. Then tell children to complete the page.

Curriculum Connections

Theme Activity: Art/Language Arts

Materials: large brown-paper grocery bags, scissors, crayons or markers

- Ask children how they spend vacations from school. Have them share memories from family trips they may have taken.
- Prepare for children paper bag vests by slitting the front of the bag from top to bottom and cutting arm and neck holes. Distribute the paper bags and tell children to decorate the fronts of their vests with the letter **v** printed in various sizes and colors and with drawings of objects that begin with the same sound as the beginning sound in **vacation**.

Sadlier Reading

Little Books and Big Books

Read *I Have a Question* (nonfiction) and *Violets and Vegetables* (nonfiction) for more practice with initial consonants **q(u)** and **v**.

Observational Assessment

*Note children who are easily able to decorate their vests with initial **qu** and **v** pictures.*

English Language Learners/ESL

Materials: pictures of initial **v** words such as **van**, **vacuum** (cleaner), **vegetables**, **vest**

Some children will have difficulty with initial /**v**/. Model for children how to put your front teeth over your bottom lip to produce /**v**/, and have them practice doing the same. Then present the pictures and say the word stretching out the /**v**/, and have children repeat after you.

Challenge

Ask children what sound **quiz** begins with. Tell children to pretend that they are going to be the host of a TV quiz show. Challenge children to write two questions to ask on the show. Ask children to include as many words as they can that begin with **qu** and **v** in their questions and to underline those words. Let children present their quiz show and ask contestants the questions they wrote.

Special Strategies

For Universal Access activities, see page 13F.

Final Consonant /v/ v
Reviewing Initial and Final Consonants
p, r, k, j, q(u), and v

Objectives

- To substitute final sounds
- To recognize final /v/
- To print initial and final consonants to complete words

Warming Up

Reviewing Partner Letters

Materials: Punchout Letter Cards

Have partners place uppercase and lowercase letter cards facedown. Direct partners to take turns turning two letters faceup. If the letters are partner letters, the child takes them. If not, the child turns the letters face down. The one with the most cards at the end wins.

Teaching the Lesson

Phonemic Awareness: Substitute Final Sounds

Say **map** slowly: /m/-/a/-/p/. Point out that the last sound in **map** is /p/. Explain that you are going to make a new word by replacing the last sound in **map**, /p/, with /n/. Say the new word slowly /m/-/a/-/n/. Now have children say /m/-/a/-/p/. Tell them to change the last sound to /n/ and have them say /m/-/a/-/n/. Repeat with **jar/jam** and **pop/pot**.

Sound to Symbol

Materials: **Sadlier Phonics Picture Cards** for **pig, cap, book, jam, queen, vine, red, door**

- Tell children that /v/ is the sound they hear at the end of **wave**. Ask them to wave when they hear /v/ at the end of a word. Say: *Dave and **five brave** friends went into a **cave**.*
- Display the picture cards. On the board write: **p___, ___p, ___k, j___, qu___, v___, r___, ___r.** Have children place each picture card on the chalk ledge beneath its corresponding final or initial letter pattern.

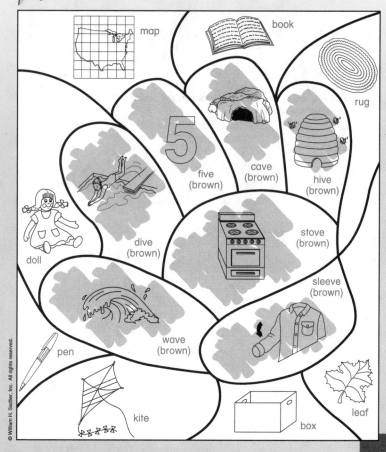

☆ ay the name of each picture. Color the space brown if the name ends with the sound of **v**. What picture do you see?

map

book

rug

five (brown)

cave (brown)

hive (brown)

dive (brown)

stove (brown)

sleeve (brown)

doll

wave (brown)

pen

kite

box

leaf

LESSON 30: Phonemic Awareness: Final /v/   **63**

UNIVERSAL ACCESS
Meeting Individual Needs

Auditory • Visual

Materials: Punchout Letter Cards for **p, r, k, j, q, u, v**

Recite the verse below:

It's a **party**, lots of fun!
Sing songs, **jump**, and **run**.
Choose a **king** and a **queen**.
Join a **very** happy scene!

Have children hold up the appropriate letter or letters for words beginning with **p, r, k, j, qu,** or **v**.

Visual • Auditory

Materials: six paper plates, **Sadlier Phonics Picture Cards** for **peas, pig, pot, red, ride, rain, king, kitten, jam, juggle, queen, quilt, vine, vine, valentine**

Label six paper plates **p, r, k, j, qu,** and **v**. Have children say each picture's initial sound and place the picture on the plate with the letter that stands for that sound.

Extra Support

Draw a train with six cars labeled **p, r, k, j, qu, v**. Have the class listen for final sounds as you say: *cup, flower, silk, have, car.* Have children say in which cars to write the words. Repeat with initial sounds and **king, pot, jam, quiz, violin, run.**

Say the name of each picture. Circle the letter or letters that stand for the missing sound. Then print the letter or letters on the line.

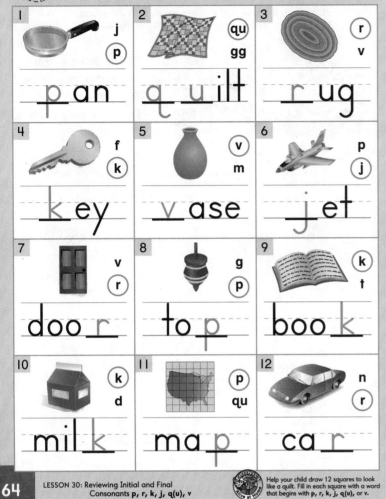

1	j / p	p an
2	qu / gg	q uilt
3	r / v	r ug
4	f / k	k ey
5	v / m	v ase
6	p / j	j et
7	v / r	doo r
8	g / p	to p
9	k / t	boo k
10	k / d	mil k
11	p / qu	ma p
12	n / r	ca r

64

LESSON 30: Reviewing Initial and Final
Consonants p, r, k, j, q(u), v

Help your child draw 12 squares to look like a quilt. Fill in each square with a word that begins with p, r, k, j, q(u), or v.

Initial Consonants
/y/ Y y and /z/ Z z
Final Consonants
/ks/ x and /z/ zz

Objectives
- To identify and isolate initial sounds
- To recognize initial /y/ Y y and /z/ Z z
- To recognize final /ks/ x and /z/ zz

Warming Up

Reviewing Initial and Final v

Have children say **vest** and **wave**. Remind them that **v** stands for /v/. Then have them form a **v** with their fingers and say *beginning* or *end* to identify initial or final **v** words you say, such as **vine**, **hive**, **leave**, **very**, **vest**, **cave**.

Teaching the Lesson

Phonemic Awareness:
Identify and Isolate Initial Sounds

Say: *Zooming zebras zig zag*. Then tell children: *Now I will say the beginning sound of each word and then the word: /z/-/z/-Zooming /z/-/z/-zebras /z/-/z/-zig /z/-/z/-zag*. Repeat with children saying the sounds and words with you. Then have the class try the process with this sentence: **Yellow yaks yell, "Yahoo!"**

Sound to Symbol

Materials: **Sadlier Phonics Picture Cards** for **yard**, **yo-yo**, **zebra**, **zipper**, **fox**, **box**

- Display the pictures and have children identify them. Help children recognize which picture names begin with /y/ or /z/ and which end with /ks/. Tell children that some words also end with /z/, such as **buzz**.
- On the board, write **x**, **Yy**, **Zz**. Point out the uppercase and lowercase letters and tell children that these letters stand for final /ks/, initial /y/, and /z/. Explain that words ending with /z/ usually have two **z**'s at the end, such as **buzz**.

65

Year starts with the sound of **y**. Zero starts with the sound of **z**. Listen for the sounds of **y** and **z** in the rhyme.

Count down to zero.
Yell out a loud cheer.
The old year is out.
The new year is here.

First color each picture that has the sound of **y** at the beginning of its name ▭. Then color each picture that has the sound of **z** at the beginning of its name ▭.

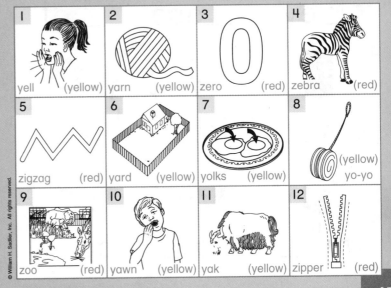

1 yell (yellow)	2 yarn (yellow)	3 zero (red)	4 zebra (red)
5 zigzag (red)	6 yard (yellow)	7 yolks (yellow)	8 yo-yo (yellow)
9 zoo (red)	10 yawn (yellow)	11 yak (yellow)	12 zipper (red)

LESSON 31: Phonemic Awareness: Initial /y/ and /z/   **65**

UNIVERSAL ACCESS
Meeting Individual Needs

Visual • Auditory

Direct children to say **yum** if the sentence you say contains a word that begins with the sound of **y**, and **zoom** if it contains a word that begins with the sound of **z**. You might say:

Zack got a new **yellow yo-yo**.

He played with the **yo-yo** in his **yard**.

Then he went to the **zoo** to see **zebras**.

Auditory • Kinesthetic

Remind children that the word **mix** ends with /ks/. Direct them to pantomime mixing something in a bowl when they hear you say a word that ends with /ks/. Say these words: **ax, ran, Max, sax, wave, wax, Rex, fix, box, hat, fox.**

Extra Support

Materials: **Sadlier Phonics Picture Cards** for **yard, yo-yo, zebra, zipper, fox, box**

Have children sort the cards into three groups: initial **y**, initial **z**, and final **x**. Then ask children to say other words that begin or end with those sounds.

Box ends with the sound of **x**. **Fuzz** ends with the sound of **z**. Listen for the sounds of **x** and **z** in the rhyme.

A toy with fuzz,
Bugs that buzz,
A box of clay, a sax to play,
I love a fun piñata day!

Put an **X** on each picture that has the sound of **x** at the end of its name. Then circle each picture that has the sound of **z** at the end of its name.

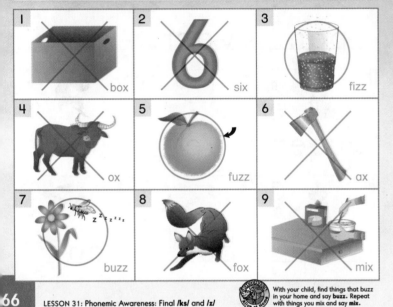

1 box	2 six	3 fizz
4 ox	5 fuzz	6 ax
7 buzz	8 fox	9 mix

LESSON 31: Phonemic Awareness: Final /ks/ and /z/

With your child, find things that buzz in your home and say **buzz**. Repeat with things you mix and say **mix**.

● Point to the letters **Yy** and **Zz** at the top of page 65. Remind children that these letters stand for /**y**/ and /**z**/. Have them trace the letters at the top of the page.

● Have children listen for words that begin with /**y**/ and /**z**/ as you read the rhyme.

● Read aloud the directions on page 65 and identify the pictures. Explain that children will use a yellow crayon for **y** because **yellow** begins with the sound of **y**. Decide together what color to make the first picture. Then have children complete the page.

● Follow the same procedure for page 66. Before you read the poem, make sure children know what a *piñata* is.

Curriculum Connections

Theme Activity: Language Arts
Materials: chart paper, crayons

Write a class story about a zebra who comes uninvited to a backyard celebration. Brainstorm words that begin with /**y**/ and /**z**/ to use in the class story. Suggest that children might measure the **zebra** with a **yardstick,** ride it to the **zoo,** or feed it **yummy yogurt**. Call on volunteers to dictate sentences that use **y** and **z** words. Record sentences on chart paper. Then have each child copy and illustrate a favorite sentence.

Portfolio Have children place their sentences and illustrations in their portfolio.

Sadlier Reading
Little Books and Big Books

Read *Yes, You Can* (nonfiction) and *Zack Can Fix It!* (fiction) for more practice with initial consonants **y** and **z** and final **x**.

Yes, You Can

Zack Can Fix It!

English Language Learners/ESL
Materials: 10 blocks or counters

Say the numbers from 0 to 10, holding up a corresponding number of counters. Have children count with you. Point out that one number (**zero**) begins with /**z**/ and one number (**six**) ends with /**ks**/. When teaching the verse on page 65, count down from 10 to 0 after saying the first line, "Count down to zero." Have children clap when they hear the number beginning with /**z**/ and give the thumbs-up signal when they hear the number ending with /**ks**/.

Special Strategies
For Universal Access activities, see page 13F.

Challenge

Tell children to pretend they are selecting four gifts to take to an **XYZ** party. Explain that each gift must begin with **y** or **z**, or end with **x** or **zz**. Challenge children to write four sentences describing their gifts. Give this example: *My gift is a **yellow yo-yo**.* Have children underline appropriate words and read their sentences aloud.

Observational Assessment

*Note children who cannot easily distinguish the sounds of initial **y** and **z**, and the final sounds of **x** and **zz**.*

Reviewing and Assessing Initial and Final
p, r, k, j, q(u), v, x, y, z

Objectives
- To identify and print initial or final **p, r, k, j, q(u), v, x, y,** and **z** to complete words

Warming Up

Reviewing Partner Letters

Materials: Punchout Letter Cards for uppercase and lowercase **Pp, Rr, Kk, Jj, Qq, Vv, Xx, Yy, Zz**

Have children play Letter Go Fish in pairs. Ask one child to shuffle the letter cards, deal seven cards to each player, and place the remaining cards facedown. Explain these rules: Child A asks Child B for a specific letter that Child A already holds. If Child B holds either form of the letter, she or he must pass it over. Otherwise, Child A "goes fishing" among the facedown cards. When a player gets a set of partner letters, she or he lays them down. The first child to lay down all of his or her cards wins the game.

Teaching the Lesson

- Print **p, r, k, j, q(u), v, x, y, z** on the board, and say the letters with children. Tell children that **jet** begins with /j/. Ask children what sound they hear at the beginning of **juggle**. Then write _am on the board and say **jam**. Have a volunteer identify the initial sound and write the letter that stands for that sound on the board to complete the word. Repeat the activity with these words: **pig, ride, king, quilt, vine, yet, zipper**. Continue this process for ending sounds, using the words **cap, door, look, fox**.
- Have children turn to page 67. Read the directions aloud, and help children name each picture before completing the page.

Say the name of each picture. Circle the letter or letters that stand for the missing sound. Then print the letter or letters on the line.

1	k, (v)	van
2	(z), y	zoo
3	f, (k)	key
4	(p), j	pen
5	qu, (y)	yarn
6	(r), z	rug
7	g, (qu)	queen
8	(j), p	jet
9	v, (x)	fox
10	(p), k	top
11	(k), t	book
12	(r), x	car

LESSON 32: Reviewing Initial and Final Consonants **p, r, k, j, q(u), v, x, y, z**   67

UNIVERSAL ACCESS
Reteaching Activities

Activity 1

Materials: masking tape; **Sadlier Phonics Picture Cards** for **peas, ride, pin, pen, rose, prize, ring,** and other initial **p** and **r** words

Use masking tape to define a tic-tac-toe grid on the floor. Display picture cards for initial **p** and **r**. Appoint one child to be **p** and another **r**. Have the two children take turns naming and placing on the grid picture cards that begin with the sound of their letters. The first child to complete a row wins. Adapt the game for the other letters being assessed in this lesson.

Activity 2

Materials: magazines, scissors, glue, long paper strips

Review the initial and final sounds of **p, r, k, j, q(u), v, x, y, z**. Have children work in groups to turn paper strips into "parades of sound." Ask each group to cut out pictures that begin with **p, r, k, j, q(u), v, x, y,** or **z** and glue them onto a paper strip until the entire length is covered. Then have them repeat for the ending sounds (**p, r, k, x**). Have groups present their "parades" to the class.

Say the name of each picture. Find the letter or letters in the box that stand for the missing sound. Then print the letter or letters on the line.

p	r	k	j	qu	v	x	y	z

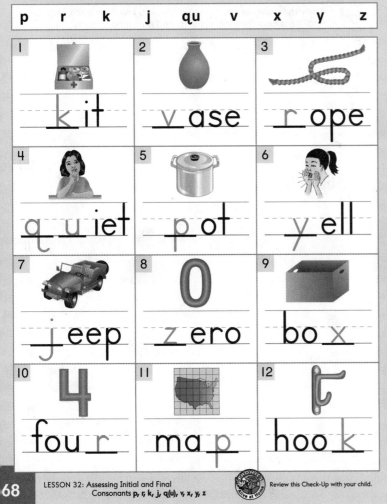

1. k it
2. v ase
3. r ope
4. q u iet
5. p ot
6. y ell
7. j eep
8. z ero
9. bo x
10. fou r
11. ma p
12. hoo k

LESSON 32: Assessing Initial and Final
Consonants p, r, k, j, q(u), v, x, y, z

Review this Check-Up with your child.

Assessing the Skills

Check-Up Before administering the assessment on page 68, briefly review the consonants involved. Write on the board **book**, **job**, **quiz**, **van**, **six**, **pen**, **car**, **yard**, and **zoom**. Say each word; have the class repeat each after you. Ask volunteers to identify the underlined letters as beginning or ending sounds. Then have them name another word with the same beginning or ending sound.

Have children turn to page 68. Point out the *Check-Up* logo. Remind children that this is not a test but a special page used to check how well they understand and remember what they have learned.

Read aloud the directions. Identify each picture together. Have children complete the page.

Observational Assessment Watch children complete the assessment page. Note whether children confuse letters or are unable to identify letters.

Dictation Have children write the letter or letters that stand for the beginning sound they hear in each word. Say these words: **jelly**, **roof**, **zoom**, **yes**, **pet**, **voice**, **kite**, **quit**. Have children write the letter that stands for the final sound of each word. Then say **wax**, **cook**, **car**, **cup**

Student Skills Assessment Use the checklist on Student Edition pages 321–322 to record your observations of individual children.

Guided Instruction

Skills	Resources
Initial and final consonants **p, r, k, j, q(u), v**	Instruction on pages 51–63
Initial and final consonants **x, y, z**	Instruction on pages 65–66
Initial and final consonants **p, r, k, j, q(u), v, x, y, z**	Phonemic Awareness Activities on pages 13H–13I Game Time on pages 13L–13M Punchout Cards on page 13N

Reviewing and Assessing Double Final ff, ss, tt, ll, dd, gg, zz

Objectives

- To match pictures with their double final consonant sound
- To identify and print double final consonants to complete words

Warming Up

Reviewing Initial Consonants

Materials: paper strips cut into 6-inch sections (two per child), crayons

Have children write their first names on one paper strip and their last names on the other. Say consonants in random order. Have children raise the correct strip when you say a letter that begins one of their names.

Teaching the Lesson

Materials: pictures or objects that end with double consonants (e.g., pictures of a **cliff**, a **glass**, a **mitt**, a **ball**, a plastic **egg**, and a bee buzzing for **buzz**); seven index cards, each printed with one of the double final consonants **ff**, **ss**, **tt**, **ll**, **dd**, **gg**, or **zz**.

- Display the items on a table. Place the letter cards in random order on the chalk ledge. Point to the glass. Remind children that **glass** ends with **ss**. Place the **ss** card in front of the glass. Ask a volunteer to choose another card and place it in front of the picture or object that has that ending sound. When finished, rearrange the pictures or objects and repeat the activity.
- Have children turn to page 69. Read the instructions aloud with children, and say the name of each picture. Do the first item together and then have children complete the page.

Say the name of each picture. Draw a line from each picture to the letters that stand for its ending sound.

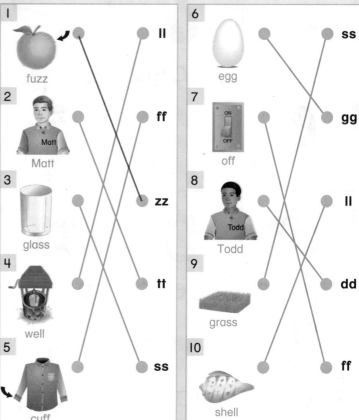

1. fuzz
2. Matt
3. glass
4. well
5. cuff

6. egg
7. off
8. Todd
9. grass
10. shell

ll, ff, zz, tt, ss

ss, gg, ll, dd, ff

LESSON 33: Reviewing Double Final Consonants **ff, ss, tt, ll, dd, gg, zz**   **69**

UNIVERSAL ACCESS
Reteaching Activities

Activity 1

Materials: 25–30 cards with double final consonant words written on them, tape player, tape of lively music

Tell children that **egg** ends with **gg**. Ask them what they hear at the end of **fuzz**. Tape the cards to the floor to form a circle. Play "double final letter walk." As the music plays, children walk along the index cards. When the music stops, the children stop at the word they are near. Call out one of the double final consonant sounds. Any child standing on a word that ends with that sound wins the round.

Activity 2

Materials: word cards used in Reteaching Activity 1

Remind children about words that end with two of the same letter. Tell them that the name **Todd** ends with **dd**. Have them identify the ending letters in the name **Matt**. Make up riddles for each word printed on the word cards. Choose a card; say a riddle such as: *I am round. You can play catch with me. I end with /l/. What am I?* (**ball**) Have children guess the word. Show children the card; point out the double final consonants.

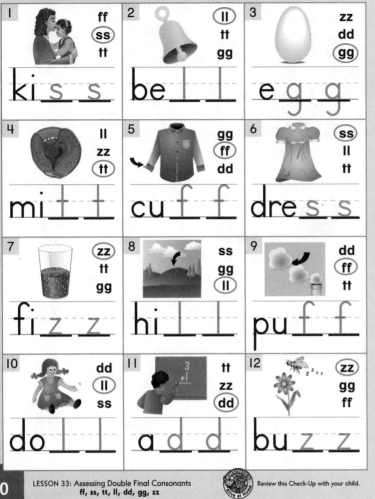

1.
ff
(ss)
tt

ki s s

2.
(ll)
tt
gg

be l l

3.
zz
dd
(gg)

e g g

4.
ll
zz
(tt)

mi t t

5.
gg
(ff)
dd

cu f f

6.
(ss)
ll
tt

dre s s

7.
(zz)
tt
gg

fi z z

8.
ss
gg
(ll)

hi l l

9.
dd
(ff)
tt

pu f f

10.
dd
(ll)
ss

do l l

11.
tt
zz
(dd)

a d d

12.
(zz)
gg
ff

bu z z

LESSON 33: Assessing Double Final Consonants
ff, ss, tt, ll, dd, gg, zz

70

Review this Check-Up with your child.

Assessing the Skill

Check-Up Review the double final consonants presented in the lessons. Write these words on the board: **odd**, **buzz**, **miss**, **egg**, **tell**, **cuff**, and **Matt**. Underline the final double letters. Say each word, and have children repeat each after you. Have volunteers identify the underlined letters as the ending sound.

Ask children to turn to page 70. Read aloud the directions, and have volunteers identify each picture. Point out that there are three answer choices for each picture. Have children complete the page.

Observational Assessment As children complete the Check-Up activity, note whether they have difficulty with any of the final double consonant letters.

Dictation Write the following letters on the board: **ff**, **ss**, **tt**, **ll**, **dd**, **gg**, **zz**. Tell children you are going to say some words that have these ending sounds. Have children write the letters of the ending sound they hear in each word. Say these words: **add**, **ball**, **egg**, **mitt**, **cuff**, **buzz**, **grass**.

Student Skills Assessment Use the checklist on Student Edition pages 321–322 to record your observations of individual children.

Guided Instruction

Skills	Resources
Double final consonants **ff**, **ss**	Instruction on pages 21–22
Double final consonants **tt**	Instruction on pages 29–30
Double final consonants **ll**, **dd**	Instruction on pages 39–40
Double final consonants **gg**	Instruction on pages 47–48
Double final consonants **zz**	Instruction on page 66

Medial Consonants

Objectives
- To identify and isolate medial sounds
- To recognize the sound of the medial consonant
- To print medial consonants to complete words

Warming Up

Reviewing Initial and Final Consonants

Remind children that they can identify the beginning and ending sounds—and their corresponding letters—of many words. Ask children to identify the beginning and ending sound of words you say, such as **tub**, **jam**, **fan**, **lid**, **wet**, and **map**. As children say the sounds, write the letters on the board with a blank in between: **t_b**. Then add the appropriate vowel to complete the word.

Teaching the Lesson

Phonemic Awareness: Identify and Isolate Medial Sounds

Say the word **wagon**. Segment the word: /w/-/a/-/g/-/o/-/n/ **wagon**. Have children repeat after you. Explain that /**g**/ is the sound in the middle of the word **wagon**. Say the following words and have children identify the middle sound for each: **tiger**, /**g**/; **lemon**, /**m**/; **seven**, /**v**/; **kitten**, /**t**/.

Sound to Symbol

Say **cabin**, and have children repeat after you. Explain that /**b**/ is the consonant sound in the middle of the word **cabin**. Then write **cabin** on the board. Circle the letter **b**. Write the words **melon**, **rider**, **paper**, and **river** on the board. Say each word together. Ask volunteers to name the middle sound, then circle the letter that stands for that sound.

Summer has the sound of **m** in the middle. Listen for the middle consonant sounds in the rhyme.

Bobbing for apples,
A three-legged run,
And riding on ponies,
Make summer great fun!

Circle the letter that stands for the middle consonant sound.

1 apple	2 kitten	3 hammer	4 zipper
m (p) n	j p (t)	(m) n w	(p) f v

5 ribbon	6 tiger	7 ladder	8 peanut
l (b) n	x v (g)	c (d) q	x (n) h

9 vacuum	10 juggle	11 mitten	12 robot
d f (c)	m (g) p	s (t) l	(b) k f

LESSON 34: Phonemic Awareness: Sounds of Medial Consonants   71

U N I V E R S A L   A C C E S S
Meeting Individual Needs

Visual • Auditory
Materials: Sadlier Phonics Picture Cards for **balloon**, **mitten**, **kitten**, **juggle**, **salad**, **wagon**; Punchout Letter Cards

Display the picture cards. Direct children to work in groups to identify each picture and to choose letter cards that match the middle sound of each picture name.

Visual • Kinesthetic
Materials: Sadlier Phonics Picture Cards for **lemon**, **seven**, **zipper**; index cards

Display the picture cards. Have children work in groups of three. Each child chooses a picture and prints on an index card the beginning, medial, and final consonant sounds.

Extra Support
Review that in some words, consonants stand for the middle sound. For example, the word **rabbit** has /**b**/ as the middle sound. Have children write the letter that stands for the middle sound for the following: **button**, **ladder**, **paper**, **funny**, **tulip**, and **juggle**.

71

1 wa g on	2 spi d er	3 tu l ip
4 ca m el	5 ca b in	6 wa t er
7 se v en	8 ru l er	9 le m on
10 sa l ad	11 ro b in	12 po n y

LESSON 34: Recognizing and Writing Medial Consonants

Say **l, d, g, m, b, n, v,** or **t,** and have your child point to a picture with that letter in the middle of its name.

Practicing the Skill

● Have children listen as you read aloud the rhyme on page 71. Together identify the middle consonant sounds in the rhyme. Then read aloud the directions. Help children identify all the pictures. Then go over the first item as a class.

● Read the directions on page 72, and review all the picture names. Model the first item before having children complete both pages.

Curriculum Connections

Theme Activity: Language Arts/Art
Materials: *drawing paper, crayons, chart paper or cardboard boxes*

● Read aloud the poem "Parades" on page 13. Print the title on the board, and ask a volunteer to circle and name the middle sound. (/**r**/)

● Write these consonants on the board: **b, c, d, g, l, m, n, p, t, v.** Help children brainstorm words that have these medial consonants. List the words on the board. Then have children draw a picture of one of the words to be placed on a middle consonant float. For example, a **bunny** for the medial **n** float.

● Draw several floats on chart paper, or construct simple ones from cardboard boxes. Print one of the listed consonants on the side of each.

● Have children display their pictures on the appropriate floats. Then lead children in a parade around the room.

English Language Learners/ESL
To help children identify medial consonants, first say **cat, dog,** clapping once for each word. Say: *These words have one part.* Then clap for each syllable as you say **kitten, puppy.** Say: *These words have two parts.* Then say **ribbon,** emphasizing the medial **b** as you clap on the second syllable. Ask: *Do you hear the /**b**/ when I clap for the second part?* Explain that the sound that divides the two parts is the medial sound. Repeat with other words until children are able to identify the medial sounds.

Challenge
Materials: index cards

Make word cards for words with medial consonants, such as **parade, tuba,** and **balloon.** Have children work together in groups. Give each group several word cards. Direct groups to tell or write a story about a celebration that includes the words on their cards.

Special Strategies
For Universal Access activities, see page 13F.

Integrating the Language Arts

Objectives

- To divide sentences into words
- To use oral and written language to extend the theme concept
- To demonstrate recognition of initial, final, and medial consonant sounds

Teaching the Lesson

Phonemic Awareness: Divide Sentences into Words

Tell children that sentences are made up of words. Toss a bean bag in the air each time you say a word in this sentence: *I have a dog.* Then have children stand in a circle. Toss a bean bag to one child, who says the first word of the sentence. Then he or she tosses it to the next child, who says the second word, and so on, until the sentence is complete. Continue with:

My dog is brown.

He wags his tail at me.

He barks at cats.

Skills in Context

- Read aloud the text on page 73. Discuss what is happening in the pictures. Tell children about Chinese New Year. Explain that people celebrate a new year in different ways.
- Reread the text, pausing to have children chime in with key words. Ask them to identify initial, final, and—when possible—medial consonants in the key words.
- Have children tell about their favorite celebrations and what special things they do to celebrate.

Comprehension Skill: Comparing and Contrasting

Ask pairs of children to talk about how they celebrate their birthdays. Have them tell the class how the celebrations are alike and how they are different.

Listen as the page is read aloud. Look at the pictures. Then talk about what you see.

We can celebrate in many ways. We can have a parade. We can also make food, sing songs, and wear costumes. The people in the pictures are celebrating the new year. They made a big dragon.

How do you celebrate special times?
Encourage children to discuss preparations for celebrations and how they participate.

LESSON 35: Initial, Final, and Medial Consonants in Context
Comprehension: Comparing and Contrasting

73

UNIVERSAL ACCESS
Meeting Individual Needs

Reading and Writing Connection

Have children draw a picture of their favorite holiday as a prewriting activity. Then have them write a story about the special day.

Invite volunteers to read their stories to the class and then place the completed stories in their portfolios.

Computer Connection

Have children practice the letter sounds with *Let's Go Read, An Island Adventure®* (Edmark). Have children say sounds, and tell them to listen as the computer repeats what they pronounced.

The words in the box are often used in sentences. Use one of the words to complete each sentence. Then practice reading the sentences aloud.

| by | funny | Let | ride | Stop | walk |

1. The **dogs** run ___by___ me.

2. The **bears** ___ride___ by me.

3. The **clowns** ___walk___ by me.

4. I like the ___funny___ **clowns**.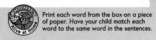

5. ___Stop___! Let me walk with you.

6. ___Let___ me be funny, too!

74

LESSON 36: Reading High-Frequency Words

Print each word from the box on a piece of paper. Have your child match each word to the same word in the sentences.

Objectives
- To recognize and read high-frequency words
- To write high-frequency words to complete sentences

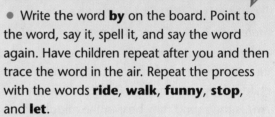

Teaching the Lesson

- Write the word **by** on the board. Point to the word, say it, spell it, and say the word again. Have children repeat after you and then trace the word in the air. Repeat the process with the words **ride**, **walk**, **funny**, **stop**, and **let**.
- Write these sentences on the board, and underline the words as shown:

  I like to <u>ride</u> my bike.

  Sometimes I <u>stop</u> in the park.

  Yesterday I saw a <u>funny</u> dog.

  A man wanted to take it for a <u>walk</u>.

  The dog pulled the man right <u>by</u> me.

  The dog did not <u>let</u> the man stop!

Point to the uppercase letter that begins each sentence and the period that ends each sentence as you read the sentences aloud. Write the words **ride, stop, funny, walk, by, let** on the board. Read the words with the class. As you read each sentence again, call on a volunteer to find and spell the word in the list that matches the underlined word.

Practicing the Skill

Read aloud the directions at the top of page 74. Have children read each word in the box. Be sure children can read the sentences before having them complete the page. Remind children that the first word in a sentence begins with an uppercase letter.

U N I V E R S A L A C C E S S
Meeting Individual Needs

Extra Practice
Write the words **sunny, pet, hop, hide, talk,** and **my** on the board. Write a second list of words on the board: **by, funny, let, ride, stop,** and **walk.** Tell children you are going to say a word from the first list and they should find a rhyming word from the second list. As you say each word, call on a volunteer to repeat the word you said and then say and circle the rhyming word. Have the child spell the rhyming word aloud. Tell the rest of the class to write each word as it is spelled aloud. Then ask children to say other rhyming words.

Review
Materials: index cards

Write the words **I, like, my, not,** and **run** on index cards, repeating words so that each child gets a card. Review saying the words with children.

As you read aloud the story that follows, have children stand each time they hear the word on their card. When each group stands, call on a volunteer to say, spell, and write the word on the board.

It was **my** birthday. **I** wanted to sleep late. **My** mom would **not** let me. She told **my** brother to **run** in and wake me. **I** did **not like** getting up. My brother said **I** had better **run** downstairs to the kitchen for **my** breakfast. **I** would **like** what **I** found. He was **not** kidding. **I** really did **like my** presents!

74

Assessing Initial, Final, and Medial Consonants

Objectives

- To recognize and print initial, final, or medial consonants to complete words

Warming Up

Reviewing Medial Consonants

Materials: 2" by 2" pieces of paper

Write the word **camel** on the board, and say **camel**, stressing the medial consonant. Have children repeat after you. Remind them that /**m**/ is the sound they hear in the middle of **camel**. Ask a volunteer to name the letter that stands for /**m**/ and to underline it on the board. Continue with **tiger**, **robot**, **seven**, and **tulip**. Have children write the middle letter they hear in each word on a paper and hold it up.

Teaching the Lesson

Materials: Punchout Letter Cards

- Display the letter cards on the chalk ledge. Say **jet**. Write _et on the board. Say the word again, stressing the initial sound. Remind children that /**j**/ is the sound they hear at the beginning of the word **jet**. Tape the **j** card on the board to complete the word.
- Say another word and write it on the board, leaving a space for the initial, final, or medial consonant. Say the word again. Then have a volunteer choose the missing letter and tape it on the board to complete the word. Include these words: **pig**, **book**, **fork**, **rider**, **bed**, **food**, **ruler**, **nest**.

Say the name of each picture. Print the letter that stands for the missing sound on the line.

1. lemon
2. seal
3. fish
4. rug
5. log
6. cabin
7. zoo
8. spider
9. web
10. peanut
11. pot
12. jeep

LESSON 37: Assessing Initial, Final, and Medial Consonants   **75**

U N I V E R S A L   A C C E S S
Reteaching Activities

Activity 1

Materials: **Sadlier Phonics Picture Cards** for **lemon**, **seven**, **wagon**, and other words

Say **lemon**, and have children repeat after you. Write _e_o_ on the board, with blanks for l, m, and n. Fill the blanks, saying: *l stands for the beginning sound in lemon; m stands for its middle sound; and n stands for its ending sound.* Underline the three letters. Then have children work in pairs. Distribute cards to partners. Have one partner say the picture name; have the other say the initial, final, and medial letters.

Activity 2

Review with children initial, medial, and final consonants. Work with small groups of children who need extra practice with consonant sounds. Say a list of words, and have children print on the board the consonants they hear in each word. Tell children not to be concerned with sound position at this time. Say these words: **bus, cabin, water, ten, dog, seven, yes, zip, tulip, hum, jet, kid, loop, camel, quiz, fox, lemon.**

Check-Up Say the name of each picture. Print the letter that stands for the missing sound on the line.

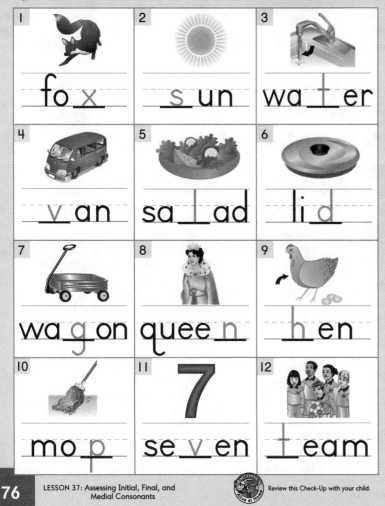

1. fo_x_
2. _s_un
3. wa_t_er
4. _v_an
5. sa_l_ad
6. li_d_
7. wa_g_on
8. quee_n_
9. _h_en
10. mo_p_
11. se_v_en
12. _t_eam

76 LESSON 37: Assessing Initial, Final, and Medial Consonants

Review this Check-Up with your child.

Check-Up Tell children they will review beginning, ending, and middle consonants. Say several two-syllable words (e.g., **robin**, **pedal**, **paper**, and **water**). Say each word three times. Each time, have children name a sound (initial, medial, and final). Then have the class turn to pages 75 and 76. Read aloud the directions. Name each picture. Do the first item on each page together, and then have children complete the activities.

Observational Assessment Throughout the lesson, identify any children who have not mastered the skills.

Portfolio Assessment Arrange student-teacher conferences to assess portfolios. Help children review their own work, guiding them to distinguish their best efforts from other work. Children should begin to recognize how their work has improved. See the Writing Rubrics on page 13C.

Dictation Tell children you are going to say some words. Have them write the letter that stands for the beginning sound they hear in each word. Say these words: **band**, **summer**, **monkey**, **vest**, **farm**. Continue in the same way for final sounds. Say these words: **dress**, **foot**, **tub**, **sun**, **hug**. Continue in the same way for medial sounds. Say these words: **tiger**, **cabin**, **robot**, **tulip**, **ruler**.

Student Skills Assessment Use the check-list on Student Edition pages 321–322 to record your observations of individual children.

Take-Home Book Remind children to complete at home the *Take-Home Book* page for Unit 2.

Additional Assessment See pages 13C–13E.

Guided Instruction

Skills	Resources
Initial, final, and medial consonants	Instruction on pages 15–30, 33–48, 51–66, 71–73 Phonemic Awareness Activities on pages 13H–13I Game Time on pages 13L–13M Punchout Cards on page 13N Technology on pages 13O–13P Take-Home Book *I Love Parades*

Creepy Crawly Bugs
Big bugs, little bugs, all kinds of bugs!

Short Vowels

READING/LANGUAGE ARTS STANDARDS

- ✪ Respond to a poem in a way that reflects understanding
- ✪ Match short vowel sounds to the appropriate letters
- ✪ Blend short vowels with initial and final consonants to sound out words
- ✪ Write short vowel words
- ✪ Read simple one-syllable and high- frequency words

OBJECTIVES

- ▶ To enjoy a poem about bugs
- ▶ To develop phonemic awareness by identifying, matching, segmenting, blending, and manipulating sounds in spoken words
- ▶ To recognize **Aa**, **Ii**, **Oo**, **Uu**, and **Ee**
- ▶ To identify short vowel words
- ▶ To use short vowel concepts to decode words
- ▶ To read and write short vowel words and high-frequency words in context

LESSONS

Lesson 38 . . . . Introduction to Short Vowels
Lessons 39–44 . . . . Short Vowel **a**
Lesson 45 . . . . Reviewing/Assessing Short Vowel **a**
Lessons 46–52 . . . . Short Vowel **i**
Lesson 53 . . . . Assessing Short Vowel **i**
Reviewing Short Vowels **a, i**
Lessons 54–60 . . . . Short Vowel **o**
Lesson 61 . . . . Assessing Short Vowel **o**
Reviewing Short Vowels **a, i, o**
Lesson 62 . . . . Assessing Short Vowels **a, i, o**
Lessons 63–69 . . . . Short Vowel **u**
Lesson 70 . . . . Assessing Short Vowel **u**
Reviewing Short Vowels **a, i, o, u**
Lessons 71–77 . . . . Short Vowel **e**
Lesson 78 . . . . Assessing Short Vowel **e**; Reviewing Short Vowels **a, i, o, u, e**
Lesson 79 . . . . Connecting Spelling, Writing, and Speaking
Lesson 80 . . . . Integrating the Language Arts
Lesson 81 . . . . High-Frequency Words
Lesson 82 . . . . Assessing Short Vowels **a, i, o, u, e**
- Take-Home Book: *Is It a Bug?*

Thematic Teaching

In Unit 3 children learn short vowels as they learn about creatures that are familiar to all of us—bugs! Find out what children know and want to know about bugs. Keep their interests in mind as you follow these plans.

Display the "Bugs" **Unit 3 Classroom Poster** and refer to it often as children learn to blend phonograms, to discriminate among short vowel words, and to read and write short vowel words in context.

Curriculum Integration

Spelling A *Spelling Connection* appears in most lesson plans. Children also practice short vowel high-frequency words on page 162.

Science Science-related activities appear on pages 80, 84, 96, 98, 106, 136, 140, 148, and 150.

Optional Learning Activities

Multisensory Activities
Multisensory activities promoting visual, auditory, tactile, and kinesthetic learning are a regular feature of each lesson.

Multicultural Connection
Use the mulitcultural activities on pages 78, 90, 94, 128, and 156 to celebrate cultural diversity.

Learning Centers
Children put together short vowel **i** jigsaw puzzles and make their own grouchy bugs in the Art Center.

Thematic Activities
Look for other exciting thematic activities in the *Curriculum Connections* section of most lesson plans.

Margaret Wise Brown

Author's Corner

Margaret Wise Brown wrote not only poetry but over ninety picture books as well. Her short books may seem easy to write, but she once said that although it only took about fifteen or twenty minutes to write a book, it took more than a year to "polish" the book by trying it out over and over again with groups of children.

Assessment Strategies
Assessment is an ongoing process. Multiple strategies in the Student Edition as well as the Teacher's Edition and regular use of the *Skills Assessment Checklist* on pages 321–322 will help you monitor children's progress in reading and writing words with short vowels.

UNIT RESOURCES

Sadlier Reading

Classroom Poster

Phonics Picture Cards

Little Books and Big Books

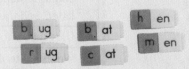

Student Manipulatives

Books by Margaret Wise Brown

Goodnight Moon. New York: Harper & Row, 1947.

The Runaway Bunny. New York: Harper & Row, 1942.

Theme-Related Resources

Insect. Dorling Kindersley, 1995. An informative, enriching, fast-paced video.

Murphy, Jane. *Songs About Insects, Bugs and Squiggly Things.* Kimbo Educational, 1993. Facts and fun about bugs!

Dobkin, Bonnie. *The Great Bug Hunt.* Chicago: Children's Press, 1993. Bugs, bugs everywhere!

In Unit 3 children focus on developing the ability to recognize short vowel sounds. The assessment ideas on this page are for use throughout the unit.

Pretests/Posttests

The tests on pages 77D–77E can serve as a formal end-of-unit assessment of children's mastery of short vowel sounds. In some cases you may choose to use them as pretests to help you identify a starting point for instruction for individual children. The Phonemic Awareness Test on page 77J also serves as a pretest.

Observational Assessment

Specific opportunities to observe children's progress in recognizing short vowel sounds are highlighted in the lesson plans. The *Student Skills Assessment Checklist* on pages 321–322 of the Student Edition will help you keep track of students' progress.

Dictation

Dictate the following words and have children write each word on a sheet of paper: **map**, **bed**, **mix**, **dog**, **pig**, **bug**, **hot**, **jam**, **jet**, **tub**. Then have children write the following sentences: I see the **bat**. The **mop** is in the **van**. In addition to assessing short vowels, observe whether children begin each sentence with an uppercase letter and end with a period.

Using Technology

The activities on pages 77O–77P may also be used to evaluate children's progress.

Performance Assessment

Have children pretend to be ants at a picnic and write a story about their adventures. You might want to read **Sadlier Reading** *Little Books and Big Books* *Patty and Pop's Picnic* (fiction) or *Count How Many!* (nonfiction). Tell children that they may also use any of the materials in the Reading or Writing Centers to help them write their stories. Allow time for children to practice their stories with a partner and present their stories to the rest of the class. Use the *Students Skills Assessment Checklist* on pages 321–322 to record your observations.

Portfolio Assessment

The portfolio icon in the lesson plans indicates portfolio opportunities throughout the unit. Post the rubrics on a chart at the beginning of the unit, and review the criteria with children. Discuss with children how they can select work from their portfolios that best represents their progress. For example, for "begins sentences with an uppercase letter and uses correct end punctuation," model by posing questions such as: *What should a sentence begin with? What should it end with?* Then ask: *What work do you have in your portfolio that shows you know how to write sentences properly?*

Answer Key

Page 77D			Page 77E	
1. pin	5. bed	9. rip	1. bug	4. lid
2. hat	6. bag	10. crib	2. cat	5. net
3. dog	7. cup	11. sun	3. top	
4. sock	8. hen	12. ham		

Name _____

Writing Rubrics

	Sometimes	Never	Always
Phonics Skills			
Associates short vowel sounds with their corresponding letters			
Recognizes picture names with a given short vowel sound			
Blends sounds to form short vowel words			
Supplies rhyming words with a given short vowel sound			
Reads short vowel words in context			
Writing Skills			
Spells short vowel words and sight words appropriate to grade level			
Traces words to write a sentence			
Formulates and writes sentences using short vowel words			
Begins sentences with upper case letters and uses correct punctuation			
Uses spaces to separate words			
Writes left to right			

Say the name of each picture. Circle the word and print it on the line.

1 pan / pin / pond	2 hill / hot / hat	3 dog / dig / dad
4 sick / sock / sack	5 bat / bed / bad	6 bag / big / box
7 cot / cap / cup	8 hen / hat / hop	9 rip / rap / rot
10 crab / crib / cab	11 sand / sit / sun	12 ham / him / hop

Say the name of the picture. Read the sentence. Then fill in the circle in front of the missing letters.

1		
	There is a big red **b**_____.	○ ag ○ eg ○ ug
2	Did it hop on the **c**_____?	○ at ○ ot ○ ut
3	No, it is on the **t**_____.	○ ap ○ op ○ up
4	Now it is on the **l**_____.	○ ad ○ ed ○ id
5	Get it in the **n**_____.	○ et ○ ot ○ ut

In Unit 3 children learn the short vowel sounds while practicing phonemic awareness and continuing to develop auditory discrimination. While teaching this unit, you may notice that some children manifest auditory discrimination or speech problems, perseveration, and/or attention deficit disorder (ADD). Techniques to help these children are presented here.

Auditory/Oral Discrimination

Discriminating between the short vowel sounds may be especially difficult for children with auditory discrimination problems or speech disorders. They may have particular difficulty detecting or producing the differences between /**e**/ and /**i**/. The following techniques may benefit these children as they proceed through the unit.

- It is important for children to learn the different positions of the mouth when forming these sounds. As you say /**e**/, have children observe how you form the sound with your mouth. Call attention to the way your lips flatten and pull back at the corners. Also point out the position of your tongue. Then have children watch in the mirror as they say /**e**/. Next have children watch as you say /**i**/. Point out how the mouth positioning for /**i**/ differs from the position for /**e**/; that is, your lips are more rounded. Have children say the sound as they watch themselves in the mirror.

- Move from the isolated short vowel sounds to words containing /**e**/ and /**i**/. For example, say **leg**, stressing the /**e**/. Then segment the word into phonemes, again stressing the /**e**/: /**l**/-/**e**/-/**g**/. Have children repeat the word and the phonemes. Each time they say /**e**/, have them note the position of their mouths. Then say a word with /**i**/, such as **pig**, stressing the /**i**/. Repeat the word, saying each phoneme slowly and calling attention to the position of your mouth as you say /**i**/. Have children repeat after you.

- Begin a list of words for short vowels **e** and **i**. Encourage children to listen for words with short **e** and **i** in the course of each day. When they hear a word that contains either /**e**/ or /**i**/, have them repeat the word and add it to the list. When the list has several words for each vowel, have children read the words into a tape recorder. Play back the recording, and ask them to identify the short vowel in each word.

Perseveration

Children who tend to perform the same task over and over again even though a change is required may not simply be careless. They may be perseverating or acting compulsively. For example, once a child understands how to complete the activity on page 83 of Lesson 41, the child will transfer the same method to page 84, even though that page needs to be completed in a different fashion. Children who exhibit this behavior may benefit from guidance in comparing the pages to be completed.

Help children compare pages 83 and 84, and guide them to notice the differences in the layouts. Read the directions on page 83. Have children repeat them in their own words. Make sure they understand that they should circle the two pictures that have rhyming names and then write a letter to complete a word that rhymes with the two pictures circled. Next go over the directions on page 84, and again encourage children to restate the task in their own words. Help them verbalize the specific differences in what should be done for each page.

Attention Deficit Disorder (ADD)

Children who have ADD may have difficulty focusing and maintaining attention while completing tasks. These children can benefit from carefully planned modifications to the activities and exercises in the unit. The following strategies may help them stay on task and successfully complete assignments.

- Read the instructions with children. Have them use a highlighter to underscore the steps that need to be taken to complete the assignment.

- To help children stay on task, give them an hourglass timer. Have them aim to finish a certain portion of a written exercise, such as one row, before time runs out.

- Have children work under conditions that better meet their needs or learning styles. For example, have them stand while working or allow them to complete the assignment orally or with a partner.

The chart below identifies problems that children may manifest as they learn the concepts and skills presented in this unit. The chart also identifies strategies to use with children who have not yet mastered the key concepts in the unit. The problems addressed in the first two columns can be extended to other short vowel sounds, and intervention strategies can be modified accordingly.

SKILL	Saying Short a Words	Identifying Short a in Words	Writing Vowels
Observation	Child focuses on the letter name rather than on the sound and therefore pronounces short **a** words with /ā/ instead of /a/.	Child has difficulty hearing and identifying the short vowel **a** in words presented orally.	Child has difficulty printing the vowels **a**, **i**, **o**, **u**, **e**.
Intervention	• Select several **Sadlier Phonics Picture Cards** for short **a**. Have child say the name of each picture; then write the word on the board. • Give child extra practice reading words with the consonant-short vowel-consonant pattern. Try to avoid giving child words with more than three phonemes. • When reading words in context, have child use contextual clues to determine vowel sound.	• Give child several **Sadlier Phonics Picture Cards** for short **a**. Have child record himself or herself saying the words, stressing the short vowel sound. Have child replay the tape and listen to the short **a** words. • Have child think of a familiar short **a** word, such as **cat**. Tell child to use that word as a comparative guide for identifying the short **a** sound in other words you say.	• Have child complete several tactile activities, beginning with "writing" **a** in the air with a finger. Progress to "writing" the letter in sand or salt, followed by tracing the letter **a** on paper. • Provide child with unlined paper. Encourage him or her to concentrate on forming the letter without the added restriction of printing on a line.

These activities are designed to augment the lessons in the unit with engaging exercises that reinforce skills and encourage creativity.

Match Medial Sounds

Can You Match This?

Have children identify and match middle sounds. Tell them that you will say a word followed by a sentence and that they are to listen for a word in the sentence that contains the same middle sound as the "clue" word. Direct children to hold up two thumbs when they hear that word and to say "Yes!". As children become more proficient, include in the sentence more than one word with the target medial sound. Use sentences such as these:

cat A bug is on my **cap**.

hop The **fox** is fast.

mix My baby brother wears a **bib**.

rug Let's have some **fun** in the **sun**.

net Let me **get** a **pen**.

Identify and Isolate Medial Sounds

Listen Up

Tell children to listen for sounds heard in the middle of words. Sing the following song to the tune of "The Wheels on the Bus":

What's the sound in the middle of these words: **bit, pit, fit; bit, pit, fit**?

What's the middle sound in these words?

/**i**/ is the middle sound.

Repeat for /**a**/, using **cat, fan, ham**. Continue with other medial short vowel sounds.

Substitute Medial Sounds

Silly Stories

Teach this chant to children:

A **pig, pig, pig**

Sat on a **log, log, log**.

It had a **pan, pan, pan**

And was in a **band, band, band**.

When children know the words, have them change the middle sound in each repeated word to /**e**/.

A **peg, peg, peg**

Sat on a **leg, leg, leg**.

It had a **pen, pen, pen**

And was in a **bend, bend, bend**.

Make up similar repetitive nonsense chants. Have children change the medial short vowel sounds in the repeated words and then tell whether the words they come up with are real words.

What's the Word?

Say **ham, pan**, and **bug**; and have children repeat the words. Call on volunteers to substitute the middle sound in each word with /**i**/. Have children repeat the new words. Continue with the following:

fin, top, hit; /a/

hat, net, bib; /o/

bill, pit, chick; /e/

sink, not, trick; /u

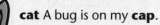

Segment Phonemes

Phoneme Race
Materials: word cards for **cup**, **hot**, **pan**, **kit**, **ten**, **pill**, **den**, **mom**, **tug**, **bed**, **cat**, **bib**, **hop**, **sun**, **sick**, **ran**; masking tape

Play this game with three teams: On the floor in front of each team, place 10 pieces of masking tape at one-foot intervals. Have each team line up just behind its "starting line." Choose a word card, and say the word. Have the team going first consult to decide what phonemes make up the word and then say them as a group. Give this example: *If the word is* **bug**, *say* /**b**/-/**u**/-/**g**/.

For each correctly identified sound in the word, the team moves up one line. Repeat with different words for the other two teams. Continue the process until all members of one team reach the "finish line."

Charades
Explain to children how to play charades; adjust the rules so that sounds and actions may be used but not words. For example, a child acting out **dog** may bark. Call on a volunteer to act out a word, and then whisper the word to the child. Use the following categories and words:

Animals: **dog**, **cat**, **cow**, **hen**, **duck**, **pig**

Feelings: **mad**, **sad**

Things you wear: **hat**, **sock**

Things you play with: **bat**, **top**, **doll**

Before the volunteer begins, tell the class the category to which the word belongs. Direct children who guess correctly to say the word and then the phonemes that make up the word (e.g., **dog**, /**d**/-/**o**/-/**g**/).

Blend Phonemes

Name That Word
Choose three volunteers. Whisper /**m**/ to the first child, /**a**/ to the second, and /**t**/ to the third. Have each child repeat the sound. Direct the class to blend the sounds together to say the word **mat**. Continue with different volunteers, using **leg**, **paw**, **hog**, **lid**, **pal**, **bun**, **jog**, **help**, **fan**, **kid**, **nut**.

The Ant That Can't
Read aloud the poem below, slowly articulating each segmented word. Then have children blend the sounds together to say the segmented words.

There was a /**b**/-/**u**/-/**g**/

　　/**u**/-/**p**/ in the air.

It saw a /**r**/-/**u**/-/**g**/

　　and flew over there.

There was a /**b**/-/**a**/-/**t**/

　　/**u**/-/**p**/ in the air.

It saw a /**h**/-/**a**/-/**t**/

　　and flew over there.

Down on the ground

　　there was an /**a**/-/**n**/-/**t**/.

　　It said, "I want to fly around,

　　but I just can't!"

PHONEMIC AWARENESS TEST

Name _____ Date _____

Directions: Give this assessment orally to each child. The correct answers are boldfaced.

Identify and Isolate Medial Sounds

Say: *Listen as I say three words. All three words have the same middle sound.*
What is the middle sound you hear in the words? Write the sound the child identifies.

1. box, pop, not   _____ /o/   4. tin, lit, Jim   _____ /i/
2. let, fed, leg   _____ /e/   5. tub, hunt, hut   _____ /u/
3. pad, fat, can   _____ /a/

Match Medial Sounds

Say: *Listen to the middle sound in the first word I say. Then listen as I say three more*
words. Which word has the same middle sound as the first word? Circle the word the
child identifies.

6. can: **lap**, hen, fun   8. run: pig, **cut**, gas   10. fox: **hot**, king, fed
7. wet: from, duck, **web**   9. pin: cat, **lid**, fun

Substitute Medial Sounds

Say: *I am going to say a word. Then I will say a sound. Change the middle sound in*
the word to the new sound and say the new word. Write the word the child says.

11. ham; change the /a/ to /i/ _____**him**   14. rod; change the /o/ to /e/ _____**red**
12. lug; change the /u/ to /e/ _____**leg**   15. pet; change the /e/ to /a/ _____**pat**
13. pit; change the /i/ to /o/   _____**pot**

Blend Phonemes in a Word

Say: *I am going to say some sounds. Tell me what word you get when you*
blend the sounds together. Write the word the child says.

16. /k/-/i/-/d/ _____**kid**   18. /j/-/a/-/m/ _____**jam**   20. /f/-/u/-/n/ _____**fun**
17. /t/-/o/-/p/ _____**top**   19. /n/-/e/-/t/ _____**net**

Segment Phonemes in a Word

Say: *I will say a word. Say each of the sounds you hear in the word.* Write the sounds
the child says.

21. **rag** _____ /r/-/a/-/g/   23. **ten** _____ /t/-/e/-/n/   25. **dot** _____ /d/-/o/-/t/
22. **rub** _____ /r/-/u/-/b/   24. **lid** _____ /l/-/i/-/d/

Do You Have a ...?

Blackline Master 14
p. 77L

Objective
To identify short vowel rhyming words

Players
Small groups

Materials
• construction paper
• glue
• scissors

■ Duplicate and distribute one copy of Blackline Master 14 to each group.

■ Have one child in each group glue Blackline Master 14 onto construction paper and cut out the cards.

■ Appoint dealers, and ask them to deal out the cards. Have children place on the table any rhyming pairs in their hands.

■ The dealer then asks the child to his or her left if that child has a card with a name that rhymes with the name of a card in the dealer's hand, for example, "Do you have a card that rhymes with (**bug**)?" The child answers either "No" or "Yes, I have (**rug**), and it rhymes with (**bug**)." The child gives that card to the dealer, who lays down the pair.

■ The child who answered then asks the next child for a rhyming card. Play continues until one child has no cards. The child with the most rhyming pairs wins.

Hungry Bugs

Blackline Master 14
p. 77L

Objective
To generate short vowel words

Players
Pairs

Materials
• scissors
• construction paper
• glue
• crayons
• scraps of paper

■ Duplicate and distribute Blackline Master 14 to each pair.

■ Have one child in each pair glue the blackline master onto construction paper and cut out the cards while the other draws a large bug on a sheet of construction paper and cuts a hole for its mouth.

■ Tell children to take turns choosing a card, saying the picture name, and then telling the vowel sound in the name. If children say the correct sound, have them "feed" the bug by dropping the picture into its mouth.

■ Encourage children to print more short vowel words on scraps of paper, say the sounds, and feed them to the bug.

Ant Hill Crawl

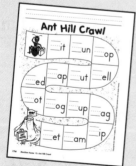

Blackline Master 15
p. 77M

Objective
To add initial consonants to short vowel phonograms to build words

Players
Pairs or small groups

Materials
• markers
• Punchout Letter Cards

■ Distribute a copy of Blackline Master 15 to each group.

■ Have children locate the ant and anthill. Explain that they will help the ant get home by using the phonograms to make words.

■ Ask children to print a letter at the beginning of each word part to make a word. Then have them say the new word. The ant has arrived at home when every space has been filled.

■ Tell children to use Punchout Letter Cards to help them remember the consonants.

■ Give the groups extra copies of Blackline Master 15 so they can repeat the game with different words.

Do You Have a ...?

Ant Hill Crawl

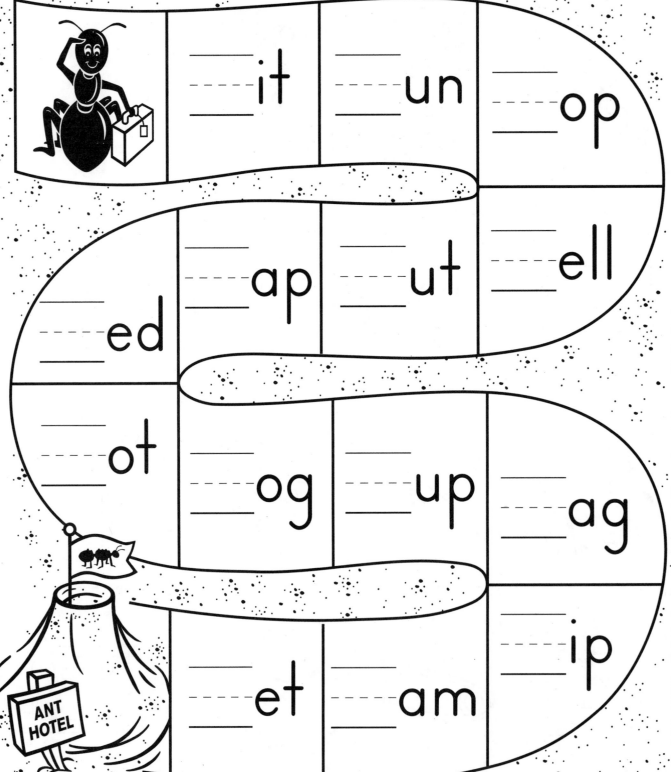

____ it

____ un

____ op

____ ell

____ ut

____ ap

____ ed

____ ot

____ og

____ up

____ ag

____ et

____ am

____ ip

ANT HOTEL

Change a Word

Have children place the Punchout Letter **a** card in the center of their desks and arrange cards for all the consonants around it. Then direct them to find the **t** letter card, place it to the right of **a**, and read in unison the phonogram that they have spelled. Next, have children place the **b** letter card before the phonogram -**at** and say the new word (**bat**). Continue to give directions for forming new words by replacing one letter at a time. After each change, have children sound and say the new word.

Replace **b** with **h**. (**hat**)

Replace **t** with **d**. (**had**)

Replace **d** with **m**. (**ham**)

Replace **h** with **r**. (**ram**)

Replace **m** with **p**. (**rap**)

Replace **r** with **c**. (**cap**)

Replace **c** with **t**. (**tap**)

Replace **p** with **n**. (**tan**)

Replace **t** with **f**. (**fan**)

Replace **f** with **v**. (**van**)

Repeat this activity building words around other short vowels.

Letter Search

Have children take out their Punchout Letters. Say one of the spelling words from Unit 3 (**bug**, **six**, **bed**, **hat**, **log**, **fun**, **sit**, **get**, **had**, **not**), and use it in a sentence. Ask children to spell the word with their letter cards. Call on volunteers to use the word in a sentence. Continue with more of the spelling words.

Short Vowel Hunt

Materials: **Sadlier Phonics Picture Cards** for **bat**, **web**, **pin**, **top**, **sun**

Tell children to spread out the following short vowel Punchout Cards, picture side up, on their desks: **ant**, **box**, **bug**, **cap**, **cup**, **doll**, **duck**, **fan**, **fox**, **gift**, **inch**, **king**, **lamb**, **lamp**, **mask**, **net**, **ox**, **pen**, **pig**, **rug**, **six**, **ten**, **tent**, **van**, and **yell**. Then hold up the **Sadlier Phonics Picture Cards** for **bat**, **web**, **pin**, **top**, and **sun** one at a time. Call on volunteers to say the picture name, identify its vowel sound, and hold up a Punchout Card that has the same short vowel sound.

Short Vowel Bingo

Materials: bingo markers (game pieces, buttons, or paper clips), index cards

Have each child arrange the following short vowel picture cards in three rows of three: **cap**, **van**, **net**, **pen**, **pig**, **six**, **fox**, **bug**, and **cup**. Give out bingo markers. On separate index cards, write the words **lap**, **fan**, **get**, **hen**, **big**, **mix**, **box**, **rug**, and **pup**.

Call on children one at a time to choose one of the words on an index card, and have them read aloud the word while the rest of the class places a marker over the picture having a name that rhymes with the word. Explain that the first child to cover three cards in a row and call out "Bingo!" gets to be the caller for the next game. Make sure children rearrange their cards after each round.

SHORT VOWEL PICTURE DICTIONARY

Objectives

- To help children recognize and build words that contain short vowel sounds
- To make a picture dictionary that illustrates short vowel sound words using a writing and painting program such as Kid Pix Studio® Deluxe*

Preparation

- Help the class recall the short vowel sounds of **a**, **e**, **i**, **o**, and **u**. Say words that contain them, and have children identify the short vowel sounds they hear. On the board write the words under each corresponding vowel.
- Have children work in groups. Assign a vowel to each group.

One Step at a Time

1. Have children select "Kid Pix" from the opening screen.

2. Tell children to click on the Typewriter icon and then to type in their assigned vowel.

3. Have children select "Pick a Stamp Set" from the "Goodies" menu. Tell them to scan the Adventures, City, Home, and Nature categories for words that illustrate their assigned short vowel sound and to stamp those pictures on their dictionary page. For example, for short vowel **a**, children might include a picture of a **hat**.

4. You may wish to have children go back to the Typewriter icon and to enter words for their assigned vowel on their dictionary page.

5. When all pages have been finished, have children print them and start a new dictionary page for another vowel.

Class Sharing

Display an alphabet chart and assist children in arranging their dictionary pages in alphabetical order. Read the picture dictionary together, allowing each child to tell about the page he or she constructed.

RHYMING STORIES

Objectives

- To help children recognize and write words that have short vowel sounds
- To use a writing program such as Storybook Weaver® Deluxe* to write and illustrate a book of rhymes

Preparation

Review short vowel sounds in the context of a story by reading aloud a book such as *A Bug in a Jug & Other Funny Rhymes* by Gloria Patrick. Have children identify words from the story that contain short vowel sounds. Then brainstorm to come up with some rhyming short vowel words. List them on the board or on chart paper.

All software referred to in this book is listed under Computer Resources on page 348.

One Step at a Time

1. Have children work individually or in small groups. Using Storybook Weaver® Deluxe, direct children to select "Start a New Story" from the opening screen.

2. Have children select "Title" and enter "My Rhyme Book." Then have them select "Author" to enter their names and "Border" to include a decorative border for their title pages.

3. On the board write the following:
   This is a _____. (**hat**)
   This is a _____. (**cat**)
   This is a _____ in/on a _____. (**hat, cat**)

4. Tell children to choose a pair of rhyming words from the list to complete the sentences.

5. For each sentence have children select "Picture and Text" and enter their sentences. Then have children choose from "Scenery," "Objects," and "Color" to illustrate each page. Inform them that they may also add music or sound effects to accompany each page by selecting the Musical Note icon.

6. Direct children to print the pages of their rhyme books.

Class Sharing

Encourage volunteers to read their rhyme books to the class. You may also wish to have children choose "Read a Story" from the opening screen and use an LCD (liquid crystal display) plate and overhead projector to display their rhyme books.

SING A SONG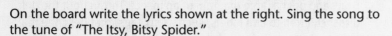

On the board write the lyrics shown at the right. Sing the song to the tune of "The Itsy, Bitsy Spider."

Invite children to sing with you. When all have learned the words, tape-record the class singing the song. As you play back the recording, direct children to listen for words that demonstrate short vowel sounds.

The funny little red bug
Went up the water spout.
Plop went the rain drops
And washed the red bug out.

Out came the sun
And dried up all the rain.
And the funny little red bug
Went up the spout again.

Literature Introduction to Short Vowels

Objectives
- To enjoy a poem about bugs
- To segment phonemes in a word
- To identify short vowels **a, i, o, u, e**

Starting with Literature

Read aloud "Bugs." As children enjoy the illustration, discuss bugs with which they are familiar and whether any of them are in the drawing. Reread the poem and have children chant the word **bugs** with you.

Developing Critical Thinking

Ask the Critical Thinking questions at the bottom of page 77. Guide children to consider a variety of differences among the bugs, including size, shape, color, body parts, habitat, and living habits.

Introducing the Skill

Phonemic Awareness: Segment Phonemes in a Word

Say the word **bug**. Tell children that words are made up of separate sounds. Tell children that there are three sounds in the word **bug**. Segment the word by saying: /b/-/u/-/g/ **bug** and have children repeat after you. Repeat the process using short vowel words from the poem.

Short Vowels
- Print the letters **a, i, o, u, e** in a column on the board. Have children repeat their names after you. Explain that these letters, called *vowels*, will be studied in Unit 3. Point to the title "Bugs" on the **Unit 3 Classroom Poster** and identify its vowel **u**.
- In another column, write the words **bug**, **fat**, **on**, **net**, **big**. Read the words aloud. Have volunteers draw a line from each vowel to a word that contains it.

BUGS

Read-Aloud

Unit 3

I like bugs.
Black bugs,
Green bugs,
Bad bugs,
Mean bugs,
Any kind of bug,

A bug in a rug,
A bug in the grass,
A bug on the sidewalk,
A bug in a glass—
I like bugs.

Round bugs,
Shiny bugs,
Fat bugs,
Buggy bugs,
Big bugs,
Ladybugs,
I like bugs.

Margaret Wise Brown

Critical Thinking
How are these bugs different? different sizes, colors, and shapes
How do different kinds of bugs move? crawl, fly, jump, hop

Possible responses:

LESSON 38: Short Vowels
Phonemic Awareness: Segmenting Words
77

Theme Words

Sharing Feelings Reread the poem "Bugs" aloud. Ask children how they think the poet feels about bugs. Then ask children to share their own opinions and feelings about bugs. Point out that bugs can be a helpful part of the environment by carrying pollen from one plant to another.

Direct children to describe a bug they have seen. Print the words **bug** and **insect**, as well as descriptive words children suggest, on a word wall. Refer to the word wall and add to it throughout the unit.

Draw and post a large diagram of an insect. Throughout the unit, direct children to add labels, such as **six legs**, that describe real insects. Call attention to short vowels in the labels.

Dear Family,

In this unit, your child will learn the sounds of the short vowels. She or he will also be thinking and reading about bugs. As your child progresses through this unit, you can make phonics come alive at home with these activities.

• Look at the pictures below. Say each letter and picture name with your child. Listen to the vowel sound.

Apreciada Familia:

En esta unidad los niños aprenderán los sonidos cortos de las vocales. También pensarán y leerán sobre insectos. A medida que se avanza ustedes pueden revivir los fonemas en la casa con estas actividades.

• Miren los grabados. Pronuncien juntos cada letra y el nombre del objeto. Escuchen el sonido de la vocal.

a	i	o	u	e
	6			
cat	six	box	bug	bed

• Read the poem "Bugs" on the reverse side of this page as your child follows along. Talk about the bugs you see.

• Help your child find some of the short vowel words in the poem, such as **bugs, black, bad, rug, on, glass, fat,** and **big.**

• Say these words one at a time: **bug, fat,** and **big.** Ask your child to say the three sounds heard in each word. (b-u-g, f-a-t, b-i-g)

• Lea el poema "Bugs" en la página 77 mientras su hijo lo repite. Hablen acerca de los insectos que ven.

• Ayude al niño a encontrar algunas vocales de sonido corto en las palabras del poema, tales como: **bugs, black, bad, rug, on, glass, fat** y **big.**

• Pronuncie estas palabras una por una: **bug, fat** y **big.** Pida al niño decir el sonido en cada palabra. (b-u-g, f-a-t, b-i-g)

PROJECT

Use your imagination to draw a "never seen before" bug. Will it have spots? What kind of wings will it have? Give your new bug a name. Next to your picture, print five or six words that describe it.

PROYECTO

Dibujen un "insecto nunca visto". ¿Tendrá motitas? ¿Qué tipo de alas tendrá? Pónganle un nombre al nuevo insecto. Escriban cinco o seis palabras para describirlo.

Phonics Alive at Home

• The *Phonics Alive at Home* page is intended to actively involve families in their children's language learning. For Unit 3, the page provides activities related to the unit theme, "Creepy Crawly Bugs," and short vowels.

• Have children remove page 78 from their books and take the page home to share with family members.

• Throughout the unit, provide frequent opportunities for children to share projects and resources related to bugs, including pictures they've drawn, stories they've written, and books they've read at home. Welcome fictional or nonfictional additions to your classroom library of bug books.

 Direct children to additional activities on Sadlier-Oxford's web site: www.sadlier-oxford.com.

Sadlier Reading
Little Books and Big Books

Read the poem "Stars" on page 13 in Worlds of Poetry *Families, Families* and have children listen for words with short vowel sounds.

Multicultural Connection

Tell the class that children throughout Europe and the Americas play "snail" hopscotch. On a hard surface outdoors, draw squares in a spiral pattern to represent the shape of a snail's shell. Direct children to write in each square a short vowel word describing bugs. To play, have children hop on each square, without touching any border lines, and read the word in each square. Have any child who completes a successful round choose a square and write his or her name in it. Other players must then hop over that square.

Take-Home Book

The Take-Home Book for Unit 3, *Is It a Bug?*, is found on student pages 327–328. This fold-up book encourages children to apply their newly learned short vowel phonics skills while learning about bugs. Use this take-home component as a culminating activity for the unit or send the book home at another appropriate time.

Student Pages 79–80

Phonemic Awareness /a/

Objectives
- To match medial sounds
- To recognize the sound of short **a**
- To discriminate between short **a** words and other words

Warming Up

Reviewing Initial Sounds
Materials: first-name cards

Provide a first-name card for each child. Say the consonants in random order, and ask children to raise their hands when they hear you say the first letter of their first names. Tell children to point to that letter on their name cards and say the sound.

⭐ Teaching the Lesson

Phonemic Awareness: Match Medial Sounds

Say **map** and **tag**, and ask children to repeat after you. Explain that /a/ is the sound in the middle of both words. Have children say /a/. Ask children to raise both hands when they hear two words that have /a/ in the middle. Say **hat, pan; log, tag; cap, bat.**

Sound to Symbol
- Say the words **cat**, **bag**, and **pal**. Explain that these words have /a/ in the middle. Have children repeat the words and say /a/ after each one. Tell children that /a/ is the sound for short vowel **a**. Ask children to listen for words with short **a** in the following sentence: *Dan had an ant on his van.* Have children repeat the sentence and clap each time they hear a short **a** word.
- On the board, print **a**. Explain that **a** can stand for /a/. Under the **a**, print **Dan**, **had**, **an**, **ant**, and **van**. Read the words together as a volunteer underlines the **a** in each one. Add **mat**, **tag**, **ham**, and **pass** to the list, and repeat the procedure.

Listen Listen as the page is read aloud. Talk about the short **a** words you hear, such as **can** and **pack.** Then act out the story.

I Can

I **can** pack a **bag.**
An **ant** can't.

I **can** tag a **pal.**
An **ant** can't.

I **can** clap my **hands.**
An **ant** can't.

I **can** hide in the **grass.**
And an **ant** can, too!

Critical Thinking   Possible answer:
An ant can hide in the sand.
What are some things an ant can do that you can't?

LESSON 39: Phonemic Awareness: /a/   **79**

U N I V E R S A L A C C E S S
Meeting Individual Needs

Visual • Auditory
Materials: Punchout Letter Cards, grocery bag

Place letter cards for all lowercase consonants in a bag. Have children take turns selecting and displaying a card and naming the letter. Ask volunteers to name words that begin with that letter and have the short **a** sound.

Kinesthetic • Auditory
Remind children that **ant** and **can** have a short **a** sound. Ask children to move their fingers like a crawling ant whenever they hear a word that has the sound of short **a**. Then slowly say words such as **man, desk, cap, van, top, six, fan, fox, has, kit, sat, flat, bed,** and **lamp.**

Extra Support
Materials: Sadlier Phonics Picture Cards for **ant, bat, ham, hand, fan, hat, tag, van, box, rug, mix, net,** and **bus**

Place picture cards facedown. Have children turn over a card, name the picture, and say if they hear short **a** in the picture name.

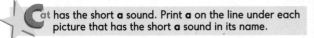
Cat has the short **a** sound. Print **a** on the line under each picture that has the short **a** sound in its name.

Short a

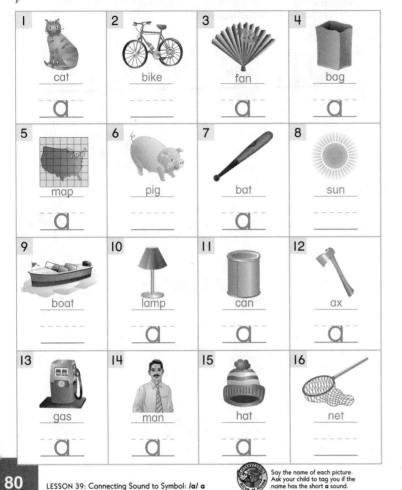

1 cat — a	2 bike	3 fan — a	4 bag — a
5 map — a	6 pig	7 bat — a	8 sun
9 boat	10 lamp — a	11 can — a	12 ax — a
13 gas — a	14 man — a	15 hat — a	16 net

LESSON 39: Connecting Sound to Symbol: /a/ a

Say the name of each picture. Ask your child to tag you if the name has the short **a** sound.

Practicing the Skill

- Discuss the picture on page 79. Then read aloud the directions and the story. Help children identify the short **a** words. You might do the Critical Thinking section before children act out the story.
- Point out that **cat**, the Key Picture Cue on page 80, has the short **a** sound. Tell children to use the picture to check whether the words on the page have the same vowel sound. Then review the directions and identify the pictures with children. Model the first example before children work on their own.

Curriculum Connections

Theme Activity: Science
Materials: chart paper

- Read the theme book to the class. Ask what children have learned about ants and the way they live. Record children's responses on the board, and use the information to develop a class story. Write the story on chart paper.
- Read the completed story aloud. Have volunteers repeat the short **a** words.

Dorros, Arthur. *Ant Cities.* New York: HarperCollins Children's Book, 1987. Explore how ants, like people, live and work closely together.

English Language Learners/ESL
Materials: Sadlier Phonics Picture Cards for **ant, bat, ham, hand, tag, van,** and cards for other short vowel sounds

To introduce vocabulary that will be used in this short **a** section, hold up a short **a** picture card and say its name, exaggerating the /**a**/ sound. Have children repeat. Continue with the remaining short **a** cards. Then show a picture card involving another short vowel, say its name, and ask if that word has the /**a**/ sound. Alternate between the short **a** picture cards and the others until children can distinguish the /**a**/ sound.

Challenge
Materials: drawing paper, crayons

Point out that ants seem to like picnics as much as people do. Ask children to draw a picture of a picnic and to include animals and objects that have the short **a** sound in their names. After they draw the scene, help children label the items. Then compile a group list of all the short **a** words used.

Special Strategies
For Universal Access activities, see page 77F.

Observational Assessment

*Note whether children can identify short **a** sounds in words.*

Blending with Short Vowel a

Objectives
- To blend phonemes in a word
- To blend short **a** words
- To identify and write short **a** words

Warming Up

Reviewing the Sound of Short Vowel a

Say the words **fan**, **bag**, **tap,** and have children repeat after you. Ask: *What sound do you hear in the middle of each word?* (short **a**) Then ask children to fan themselves with their hands each time they hear a word with the short **a** sound. Say: **cat**, **map**, **sun**, **lamp**, **pan**.

Teaching the Lesson

Phonemic Awareness: Blend Phonemes in a Word

Materials: **Sadlier Phonics Picture Cards** for **bat**, **ham**, **tag**; three counters

Display the picture cards. Explain that to say each picture name, we blend together the sounds in the word. Move three counters, one at a time, as you say /b/-/a/-/t/. Then bring the counters together as you say **bat**. Have children use counters as they repeat what you said and did. Ask a volunteer to point to the appropriate picture card. Repeat for **ham** and **tag**.

Blending

Tell children you are going to blend the sounds of letters to read a word. Write **fan** on the board, leaving a space between each letter. Point to **f** and say /f/. Point to **a** and say /a/. Point to **n** and say /n/. Then slide your finger under the letters as you say /f/-/a/-/n/. Finally, say **fan**. Repeat the entire process with children. Then repeat for the words **bag** and **jam**.

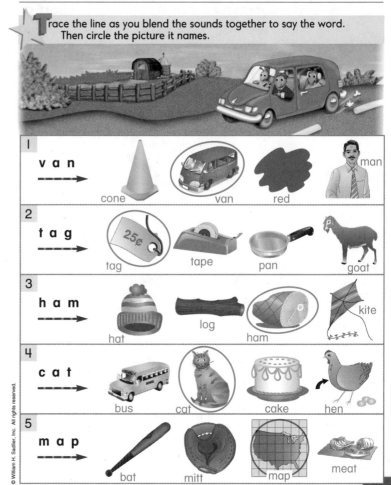

Trace the line as you blend the sounds together to say the word. Then circle the picture it names.

1 v a n → cone | van | red | man

2 t a g → tag | tape | pan | goat

3 h a m → hat | log | ham | kite

4 c a t → bus | cat | cake | hen

5 m a p → bat | mitt | map | meat

LESSON 40: Blending with Short Vowel a   **81**

UNIVERSAL ACCESS
Meeting Individual Needs

Kinesthetic • Visual
Materials: oaktag, scissors, marker

On oaktag strips, write short **a** words, such as **cab** or **tag**, leaving extra space between letters. Ask children to cut apart each word, letter by letter, in a zigzag pattern to make puzzle pieces. Have children put together the word puzzle as they blend the sounds to say the word.

Kinesthetic • Visual
Materials: Punchout Letter Cards

Use letter cards to make short **a** words, such as **bat**, **dad**, **bag**, and **jam**. Show children how to run their finger from left to right beneath the letters to blend the sounds and say the word.

Extra Support
Materials: construction paper

Have children make a fan with three pleats and print one letter of a short **a** word on each pleat, for example, **c-a-t**, **j-a-m**, **c-a-p**. Ask children to fold the fan and then open it slowly, blending the sounds the letters make to say the word.

Trace the line as you blend the sounds together to say the word. Then print the word under the picture it names.

j a m →   b a g →   m a t →

f a n →   c a p →   g a s →

1	2	3
cap	jam	fan
4	5	6
bag	gas	mat

Clap hands with your child as he or she says the three sounds heard in each word on this page: **j-a-m**.

● Go over the directions on page 81 with children, and help them identify all pictures. Work through the first item together. Then have children complete the page.

● Discuss what is happening in the picture on the top of page 82. Then read aloud the directions and together identify the pictures. Guide the class in tracing the line beneath **jam**, blending the sounds together, and printing the word beneath the picture.

Curriculum Connections

Spelling Connection

Read aloud the words and sentences below. Call on a volunteer to spell each word or to print it on the board.

mat   The cat is on the **mat**.

ham   I put the **ham** in a pan.

pan   Put the **pan** on the stove.

rag   Sam can use this **rag**.

sad   Jan is never **sad**.

Theme Activity: Language Arts

● Point out that Anansi the Spider is a character in several folktales, and share the theme book listed below.

● Read the story aloud for children's enjoyment. Then read it again, asking children to move their fingers like a creepy-crawly insect whenever they hear a short **a** word.

● Have children draw a picture and write a sentence to tell about the story. Children can draw a line under each short **a** word they use.

Theme Book

McDermott, Gerald. *Anansi the Spider.* New York: Henry Holt, 1972. A classic folktale about a mischievous spider.

Sadlier Reading
Little Books and Big Books

Read *Alexander Ant Cools Off* (fiction) for more practice with short **a**.

English Language Learners/ESL
Materials: Punchout Letter Cards

Before completing the student pages, help children practice blending sounds to form a word. Use letter cards to form words for the short **a** pictures in this lesson. Help children make the corresponding sound for each letter as you point to it and then blend the sounds together to say the word, for example, /h/-/a/-/m/ **ham**.

Challenge
Materials: Punchout Letter Cards for lowercase consonants and the vowel **a**

Display the letter cards. Ask children to take the **a** card and two consonant cards and form a short **a** word. Have children first blend the sounds to say the word and then write the word on a sheet of paper. Have children repeat to form other short **a** words. Allow time to share word lists.

Special Strategies
For Universal Access activities, see page 77F.

Short Vowel a Phonograms

Objectives
- To distinguish rhyming words from non-rhyming words
- To recognize short **a** phonograms
- To blend initial consonants with short **a** phonograms

Warming Up

Reviewing Initial Consonant Sounds
Read aloud the tongue twisters below. Have children identify the initial consonant sound repeated in each one.

> A big bug buzzes by a busy bus.

> Moths munched my mom's mittens.

Teaching the Lesson

Phonemic Awareness: Distinguish Rhyming Words from Non-Rhyming Words
Materials: Sadlier Phonics Picture Cards for **fan, van, hat, bat, ham, jam**; other cards with picture names that do not rhyme

Remind children that rhyming words sound the same at the end (e.g., **ran/pan** both end with **/an/**). Display pairs of picture cards. Have children tell if the picture names rhyme.

Phonograms
Materials: Sadlier Phonics Picture Cards for **bat** and **pan**

- On the board, write the phonogram **at**. Under it write **mat, cat, sat**. Read aloud the phonogram and then each word. Point out that all the words end with the phonogram **at**. Ask children to circle **at** in each word.
- Write **at** on the board. Show the picture of the bat and say **bat**. Explain that to write **bat**, you need to add the letter that stands for **/b/** to the beginning of **at**. Write **b** in front of **at** and read the word. Then read it together.
- Repeat these steps for the phonogram **an**, using the words **man, can, ran**, and the picture card for **van**.

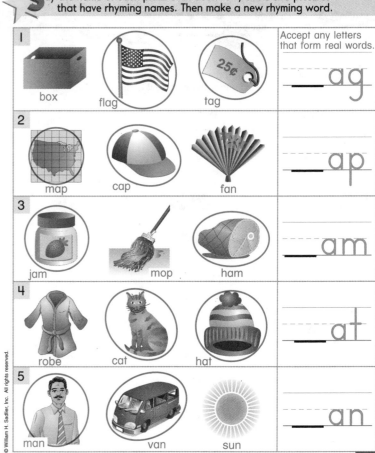

Say the name of each picture. In each row, circle two pictures that have rhyming names. Then make a new rhyming word.

Accept any letters that form real words.

1. box — flag — tag — _ag
2. map — cap — fan — _ap
3. jam — mop — ham — _am
4. robe — cat — hat — _at
5. man — van — sun — _an

LESSON 41: Short Vowel **a** Phonograms   **83**

U N I V E R S A L   A C C E S S
Meeting Individual Needs

Visual • Tactile
Draw a tic-tac-toe grid on the board. Have two teams each choose a short **a** phonogram, such as **ad, ag, an,** or **at**. See which team is first to fill a tic-tac-toe row with three words that end with the chosen phonogram. Make sure teams rotate players.

Kinesthetic • Visual
Materials: Punchout Letter Cards

Place letter cards in a path on the floor so that they spell words with short **a** phonograms (e.g., **bat, dad, fan, cap**). Have children walk from letter to letter and say the sound of each letter as they walk on it. Have children blend the letters to say each completed word when they reach its final letter.

Extra Support
Materials: Punchout Letter Cards

Write the phonograms **ad, ag, an,** and **at** on the board. Help children choose a letter card, tape it before a phonogram, blend the word parts, and say the word.

Trace the line as you blend the sounds together to say the word.
Print the word on the line. Then circle the picture it names.

1. b ag → **bag**
   bag   tag   tack

2. c ap → **cap**
   cap   pan   lamp

3. c an → **can**
   cat   fan   can

4. h am → **ham**
   map   ham   hat

5. b at → **bat**
   gas   lamb   bat

6. v an → **van**
   ant   hand   van

84

LESSON 41: Blending with Short Vowel **a** Phonograms

Have your child select one word on the page and together build a list of rhyming words.

● Read aloud the directions on page 83 and help children identify the pictures, row by row. Have the class say each phonogram with you before completing the page.
● Read aloud the directions and identify the pictures on page 84. Then model the first item. Remind children to trace the lines as they blend the sounds. Have children complete the page.

Practicing the Skill

● Read aloud the directions on page 83 and help children identify the pictures, row by row. Have the class say each phonogram with you before completing the page.
● Read aloud the directions and identify the pictures on page 84. Then model the first item. Remind children to trace the lines as they blend the sounds. Have children complete the page.

Curriculum Connections

Spelling Connection

Read aloud the words and sentences below. Call on a volunteer to spell each word or print it on the board.

hat Jan has a red **hat**.
bat **Bat** the ball to me.
man Sam is a big **man**.
cap Can Pat get the **cap**?
ant The **ant** is in the bag.

Theme Activity:
Language Arts/Science

● Explain that a safari is a trip taken to explore a place. Take children on a safari of the school grounds to search for objects with the short **a** sound in their names. Ask children to use "mental cameras" to remember the items.
● Back in the classroom, compile a list of short **a** objects. Sort the words by phonogram. Then have each child draw and label a picture of one short **a** word. Display the pictures on a bulletin board titled "Short **a** Safari."

Portfolio Have children add their short **a** safari drawings to their portfolios.

English Language Learners/ESL

As an additional warm-up activity, review with children the names of all the pictures on pages 80–82. Have children clap their hands whenever they name a picture with a short **a** sound. Then say one of the short **a** words again, and have children work with a partner to identify a word that rhymes with that short **a** word. Allow partners to share their rhyming words with the group.

Challenge

Materials: drawing paper, crayons, scissors

On the board write the phonograms **an**, **at**, **ap**, **am**, and **ag**. Challenge children to choose a phonogram and use it in a rhyme about a kind of bug or bugs in general. Have children draw and cut out a large bug on which they can copy their completed rhyme.

Special Strategies

For Universal Access activities, see page 77F.

Observational Assessment

*Note whether children can blend initial consonants with short **a** phonograms to form new words.*

Short Vowel a

Objectives

- To blend onsets and rimes
- To use phonograms to read short **a** words
- To recognize short **a** words

Warming Up

Reviewing Phonograms

Say a series of short **a** words such as **cat**, **bag**, **fan**, and **map**. Ask children to name words that rhyme with each given word.

Teaching the Lesson

Phonemic Awareness: Blend Onsets and Rimes

Say these word parts: /**p**/-/**at**/. Tell children you are going to blend these two parts to say a word. Model by again saying /**p**/-/**at**/ and then **pat**. Now say /**k**/-/**at**/ and ask a volunteer to blend the two parts. Repeat with /**b**/-/**ag**/, /**r**/-/**an**/, /**t**/-/**ap**/.

Phonograms

Materials: Punchout Letter Cards

- Have children use their letter cards to make the phonogram **am**. Read it aloud with children. Then tell them to place the letter **j** in front of **am**, leaving a space between **j** and **am**. Show children how to run their finger from left to right beneath the word parts as you say together /**j**/-/**am**/, and then **jam**.
- Explain that other words can be made with the **am** phonogram by changing the initial consonant. Tell children to replace the **j** with **h**. Ask a volunteer to read the word by blending /**h**/ with /**am**/.
- Have volunteers suggest other words that have the phonogram **am**. Tell children to make the words and then read them aloud.
- Repeat the procedure using phonograms **at**, **ap**, **an**, **ag**.

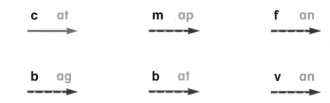

Trace the line as you blend the sounds together to say the word. Then print the word under the picture it names.

c at →
m ap →
f an →
b ag →
b at →
v an →

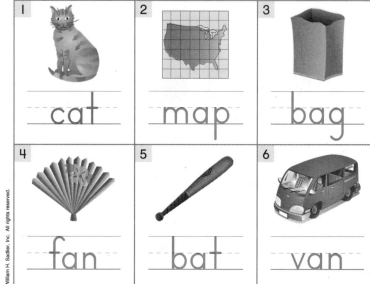

1	2	3
cat	map	bag
4	5	6
fan	bat	van

LESSON 42: Blending with Short Vowel **a** Phonograms

U N I V E R S A L   A C C E S S
Meeting Individual Needs

Visual • Kinesthetic

Have children write the phonogram **am** in the center of a page, circle it, and draw four "spokes" from the circle. Direct children to add initial sounds to the phonogram **am** to make four words, then write each word on a spoke. Repeat with **at**, **ap**, **an**, and **ag**.

Auditory • Kinesthetic

Have the class work in two teams to answer riddles that involve rhyming words with short **a** phonograms. After responding, children can act out the riddles. Use riddles and ask for responses like these:

I cool the air. I rhyme with **tan**.
 What am I? (**fan**)
I can hit a ball. I rhyme with **cat**.
 What am I? (**bat**)

Extra Support

Materials: Sadlier Phonics Picture Cards for **fan**, **ham**, **tag**

On the board write **f an**, **h am**, **t ag**. Remind children that we blend parts of a word together to say it. Have children first say the word parts and then the whole word, and finally match the appropriate picture card to the word.

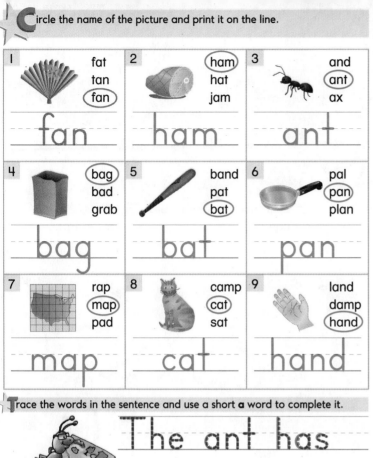

Circle the name of the picture and print it on the line.

1	fat tan (fan)	2	(ham) hat jam	3	and (ant) ax
	fan		ham		ant

4	(bag) bad grab	5	band pat (bat)	6	pal (pan) plan
	bag		bat		pan

7	rap (map) pad	8	camp (cat) sat	9	land damp (hand)
	map		cat		hand

Trace the words in the sentence and use a short a word to complete it.

The ant has

a map .

Fold a sheet of paper like an accordion to make a fan. Help your child write a short a word on each pleat.

LESSON 42: Writing Short Vowel a

Practicing the Skill

● Read the directions on page 85, and together identify all pictures. Guide children through the first item. Remind them to trace the lines as they blend the sounds to read the words.

● Read the directions on page 86, and help children identify all pictures. Model the first item. Have children complete the page.

Curriculum Connections

Spelling Connection

Read aloud the words and sentences below. Call on a volunteer to spell each word or print it on the board.

ran	Tashi **ran** a hard race.
sat	Jack **sat** on the swing.
rag	Use a **rag** to wash the car.
map	Is our street on the **map**?
ham	Put the **ham** in the pot.

Theme Activity: Language Arts

Share poems about bugs from the theme book. Select those that include words with short **a** phonograms. On the second reading, have children identify short **a** words. List the words on the board, and sort them by phonogram. Model writing a rhyme, using words from the list. Then have children work in pairs to write and illustrate their own rhymes.

Theme Book

Schulz, Lillian. "Fuzzy Wuzzy, Creepy Crawly." *Read-Aloud Rhymes for the Very Young.* New York: Alfred A. Knopf, 1986. Over 200 short poems for children.

Portfolio

Have children add their rhymes and illustrations to their portfolios.

English Language Learners/ESL
Materials: oaktag cards

To give children more practice in blending sounds, tell them they will "become" parts of a word that they will put together. Write the letters **c, b, m,** and **v** and the phonograms **at, ag, ap,** and **an** on individual oaktag cards, and give each child a card. In turn, help children say their sound as they hold up their card. Form words by having children link arms. Ask children to say their sounds separately and to then blend the sounds to say the word.

Special Strategies
For Universal Access activities, see page 77F.

Challenge
Have children work in small groups and use the symbols **–, +,** and **=** to form words with the phonograms **at, ad, ag,** and **an**. Have children follow these models.

$$mat - m + c = cat$$
$$lad - l + m = mad$$
$$rag - r + n = nag$$
$$fan - f + t = tan$$

Observational Assessment

*Note whether children can identify short **a** words in their rhymes.*

Short Vowel a
Decodable Reader

Objectives
- To read short a words and high-frequency words in context
- To read the story fluently
- To recall details

Introducing the Story Words

Short a Decodable Words   Remind children that the sound of short **a** is /**a**/. On the board, write **Pat** and point out that the word has the short **a** sound. Model blending the sounds /**p**/-/**a**/-/**t**/ to read the word. Then write the words **tap**, **nap**, **bat**, **can** on the board and have children read the words by blending the letter sounds.

High-Frequency Words   *Materials: six* index cards

On index cards, write the high-frequency words **This**, **is**, **run**, **ride**, **jump**, **stop**. Read each card with children. Then direct children to spell each word aloud as they write the word in the air.

Reading the Book

Reading Together   Have children remove pages 87 and 88. Show them how to cut and fold the pages into a book. Read aloud the title, "Pat." Tell children that they will read a story about what Pat can do. Ask children to follow along in their books as you read aloud.

Responding   Ask children to describe what Pat did in the story.

Reading for Fluency   Have children read the story along with you. Direct children to take turns reading alternate pages with a partner. Finally, have children read the story independently.

Observational Assessment

Note whether children can decode the short a words and read the story fluently.

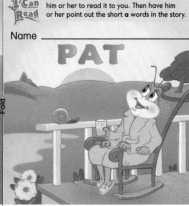

Your child has read this book in school. Ask him or her to read it to you. Then have him or her point out the short **a** words in the story.

Name _____

PAT

Pat can nap.

This is Pat.

8

Pat can tap.

Pat can ride.

6

3

Directions: Cut and fold the book. Then read the story. Tell all of the different things Pat does in the story.

LESSON 43: Short Vowel **a** Decodable Reader
Comprehension: Recalling Details

87

U N I V E R S A L A C C E S S
Meeting Individual Needs

Visual • Kinesthetic
Materials: slips of paper, container

Print short **a** words, such as **cat, hat, pat, tap, nap**, on slips of paper. Have children choose a slip from the container and act out the word for the class. Ask the child who guesses the word to spell it aloud.

Auditory • Tactile
Materials: colored index cards, glue

Display the high-frequency words on a word wall. Have children print each word in large letters on an index card and then trace the word with glue. After the glue dries, have children trace the letters with their fingers as they read the word.

Extra Support
Materials: index cards, empty can

Write **Pat, can, tap, nap, bat** on cards. Say /k/-/a/-/n/ as you show the card. Blend to say **can** and drop the card in the can. Have children do the same for each card.

Pat can run.

Pat can stop.

2

7

Pat can jump.

Pat can bat.

4

5

88

LESSON 43: Short Vowel **a** Decodable Reader
Comprehension: Recalling Details

Comprehension Strategy

Recalling Details Explain to children that details are small parts of a story that make up the whole story. Tell children that details tell us specific information about people, places, and things. Ask for details from the story "Pat." Point out that one way to recall the details of a story is to think of questions to ask a friend about what happened in the story.

Phonics and Decoding

Learning About Short a On the board write this sentence from the story: **Pat can bat**. Read it aloud. Ask children what vowel sound is in each word. (/**a**/) Have children read aloud other sentences from the story. Direct children to act out the sentence if the last word has the short **a** sound.

Word Building *Materials:* Punchout Letter Cards for **a, b, c, m, n, p, s, t**

Show children how to use letter cards to build the word **bat** from the phonogram **at**. Write **at** on the board. Add the **b** letter card in front of **at** to make **bat**. Ask children to make new words by choosing letter cards to add to the front of **at**. (**cat, mat, pat, sat**) Repeat with the phonogram **ap**. (**cap, map, nap, tap**)

Curriculum Connections

Writing and Sharing Guide children in writing about a character who is Pat's friend, Matt. Together, decide what kind of bug Matt will be. Direct each child to print action words to complete this sentence frame: "**Matt can ___.**" Have children illustrate their sentences and orally present their work. Then bind children's work into a class book.

English Language Learners/ESL
Prepare children for the *Decodable Reader* with a pantomime game. List the actions—**run, ride, jump, bat, tap, stop, nap**—on the board. Read each word aloud as you point to it, pantomime the action, and ask children to repeat after you. Then form two teams and have a child from one team pantomime one of the actions while the other team guesses it and points to the corresponding word on the board.

Challenge
Materials: oaktag, index cards, markers, stapler

Have children write "A bug can" on the oaktag. On separate cards, have them write short **a** words that could complete the sentence. Model how to staple the word cards to the end of the sentence strip, and flip through the stapled stack to read the sentence with different words.

Special Strategies
For Universal Access activities, see page 77F.

88

Short Vowel a in Context

Objectives
- To count words in a spoken sentence
- To complete sentences by writing short **a** words
- To recognize short **a** words in context

Warming Up

Reviewing Short a Words
- Have children print answers to these short **a** riddles on a sheet of paper:

  I'm something you do with your feet when you hear music. I rhyme with **map**. (**tap**)

  You have me when you sit, but not when you stand. I rhyme with **cap**. (**lap**)

- Choose volunteers to print the correct answers on the board, and check spelling.

Teaching the Lesson

Phonemic Awareness: Count Words in a Spoken Sentence

Materials: counters

Tell children you are going to count words in a sentence. Place six counters in a row for each child. Say this sentence: *Sal had an ant farm.* Make a mark on the board each time you say a word. Count the marks. Tell children there are five words in the sentence. Repeat the sentence, and tell children to slide up a counter each time you say a word. Ask how many words children heard. Then have them use their counters to count words as you say: *Look at my ants.*

Phonics in Context

Write this sentence on the board: An ant _____ up the hill. Write the words **pan**, **ran**, and **man** next to the sentence. Read aloud the sentence and the word choices. Then read the sentence three times, each time filling in the blank with one of the word choices. Circle the word **ran**, and tell children that it best completes the meaning of the sentence. Now have children complete this sentence: An ant ___ on a mat. (**pat**, **cat**, **sat**)

89

Look at each picture. Circle the word that completes the sentence. Then print it on the line.

1. Dan got his __bat__ .
   fat
   (bat)
   bad

2. He __ran__ up the hill.
   rap
   pan
   (ran)

3. His __cap__ fell off.
   (cap)
   cat
   can

4. Dan __sat__ on the log.
   (sat)
   rat
   mat

5. He felt a bug on his __hand__ .
   ham
   sand
   (hand)

6. It was just a little __ant__ .
   ax
   (ant)
   tan

LESSON 44: Short Vowel **a** in Sentences

89

UNIVERSAL ACCESS
Meeting Individual Needs

Kinesthetic • Auditory
Materials: small beanbag

Direct children to stand in a circle. Tell them that you have a beanbag bug that flies when it hears a short **a** word. Say a short **a** word and toss the beanbag to a child. Have that child say a short **a** word and toss the beanbag to another child.

Kinesthetic • Visual
Materials: construction paper, scissors, marker

Cut large footprints from colored paper, and print a short **a** word on each footprint. Place the footprints on the floor to make a path. Then invite children, one at a time, to walk along the path and read each word aloud before stepping on it. Use words such as **wax**, **van**, **tag**, **sat**, and **pal**.

Extra Support
Materials: short **a** word cards **ant**, **ran**, **bat**, **cap**, **sat**, **hand**

Display word cards, three at a time, and read them with children. Have children pick a card and use the word in a sentence.

Listen as the poem is read aloud. Then use short **a** words to complete the sentences.

My Ant Farm

My pet ants
Snack on jam.
Their names are
Ann, Pam, and Sam.

I hand them
Scraps and grass.
Then I watch them
In the glass.

1. Jam is a ___snack___ for the ants.

2. The ants are Ann, Pam, and ___Sam___.

3. You can watch them in the ___glass___.

LESSON 44: Short Vowel **a** in Context
Comprehension: Recalling Details

Read the poem to your child. Talk about other things Ann, Pam, and Sam might do.

Practicing the Skill

● Read aloud the directions on page 89. Model the first sentence before asking children to complete the page.
● Go over the directions on page 90, and read aloud the poem. Review the incomplete sentences with children before having them complete the page.

Curriculum Connections

Spelling Connection

Read aloud the words and sentences below. Call on a volunteer to spell each word or print it on the board.

cap   An ant crawled on my **cap**.

ax   Dad cut the tree with an **ax**.

had   The ants **had** a big meal.

lap   The cat sat on my **lap**.

Multicultural Connection

● Tell children that long ago the Native Americans in the Southwest desert grew little of their own food because the climate was hot and dry. They fished and hunted, but mostly they ate seeds and roots—and even insects.
● On a map, show the class where these Native Americans lived. Compare and contrast where they lived and what they ate to where you live and what you eat.

Computer Connection

Have children learn about the alphabet using Bailey's Book House® (Edmark). Tell them to select the letter machine graphic and choose a letter. Words that begin with the sound of that letter are animated on the screen.

Sadlier Reading
Little Books and Big Books

Read *Who Can Run Fast?* (nonfiction) for more practice with short **a**.

English Language Learners/ESL

Display and read one or more books about ants such as *The Little Red Ant and the Great Big Crumb*, a Mexican fable, retold by Shirley Climo (Clarion Books) or *Ant Cities* by Arthur Dorros (Let's-Read-&-Find-Out Science Book). Then ask questions such as: *Can an ant be a pet? What is an ant farm? Where do ants usually live? What do ants eat?* Encourage discussion and exchange of experiences.

Challenge
Materials: writing paper, crayons

Ask children to write a sentence using two rhyming short **a** words and to draw a picture to go with it. Allow time for children to share their sentences and pictures.

Special Strategies
For Universal Access activities, see page 77F.

Observational Assessment

*Note whether children can identify the short **a** word that belongs in the sentence.*

Reviewing and Assessing Short Vowel a

Objectives
- To review short **a** words
- To identify and write short **a** words

Warming Up

Reviewing Short Vowel a Phonograms

Remind children that we blend together the sounds in a word when reading. Say /m/-/at/, and ask a volunteer to name the word you blended. Write **m at** on the board and say **mat** again. Draw an arrow from left to right under the letters as you blend the sounds. Then write **n ap**, **s at**, and **c an** on the board. Have a volunteer draw an arrow under each word as she or he blends the sounds together to say the word.

Teaching the Lesson

Short Vowel a

Materials: Punchout Letter Cards, pocket chart

- Remind children that the short vowel sound of **a** is the sound they hear in **hat**. Place the letter cards **h** and **t** in a pocket chart, leaving a space in the middle for a vowel. Have children identify the beginning and ending consonants and tell what sounds they stand for. Ask a volunteer to insert an **a** card in the space and read the word. (**hat**) Use final consonant **t** from **hat** to begin the new word **t_p**. Continue in the same way with **pal** and **lap**, **pat**, and **tan**.

- Have children turn to page 91. Explain how to use the picture clues and the letters from completed words to fill in each word. Have children identify the clue pictures. Show where they will write the 3 and 5 Across words and the 2 and 4 Down words. Have children complete the page.

 Use the pictures to complete the puzzle. Start in the box with the same number as the clue. Print one letter in each box.

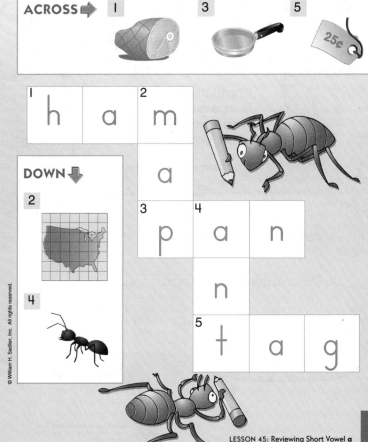

LESSON 45: Reviewing Short Vowel **a** 91

UNIVERSAL ACCESS
Reteaching Activities

Activity 1

Materials: **Sadlier Phonics Picture Cards** for **cap, fan, hat, jam, salad, wagon, ant, bat, ham, hand, tag, van, clap, glass, band, lamp;** paper, markers

Display the picture cards on the chalk ledge. Have children name the picture cards, and then ask: *What rhymes with **glass**?* (**class**) Ask children to suggest rhymes for the other picture cards, and list their words on the board. Then ask children to draw a picture illustrating one of the rhyming words they suggested, and label the picture with its picture name.

Activity 2

Remind children that the sound of short **a** is /a/. Have children think of things to pack for a vacation trip that have short **a** vowels. Play a cumulative game in which each person names one or more already mentioned items and adds a new one. Have children say: *I went on a trip in the **van**, and in my **bag** I packed a* [**bat**]. Keep a list of their words, but let children try to remember the list. At the end of the game, write their words on the board. Have children copy the list and illustrate some things they took on the trip.

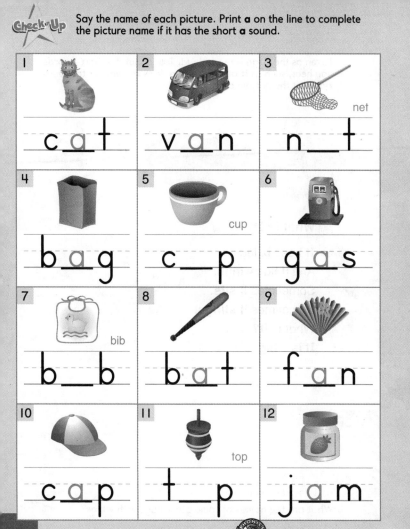

Check-Up Say the name of each picture. Print **a** on the line to complete the picture name if it has the short **a** sound.

1 c a t	2 v a n	3 net n _ t
4 b a g	5 cup c _ p	6 g a s
7 bib b _ b	8 b a t	9 f a n
10 c a p	11 top t _ p	12 j a m

92

LESSON 45: Assessing Short Vowel **a**

Review this Check-Up with your child.

Assessing the Skill

Check-Up Before administering the written assessment on page 92, review some words with the short **a** sound. Write **zap** on the board, and ask children to think of some other short **a** words that rhyme with it. (**nap**, **lap**, **tap**)

Ask children to turn to page 92. Read the directions aloud. Point out that the beginning and ending consonants for each word are already in place. Suggest that children try to say each word with the short **a** sound and then check to see that the word is real and names the picture above it. If so, children will write **a** to complete the word. Do one item together, and have children complete the page on their own.

Observational Assessment As children write throughout the day, check to see whether any children misspell short **a** words.

Dictation Tell children you are going to say some short **a** words. Have them write the short **a** words as you dictate them. Say these words: **plan, gas, pat, cap, bad**.

Student Skills Assessment Use the check-list on Student Edition pages 321-322 to record your observations of individual children.

Guided Instruction	
Skills	**Resources**

Short vowel **a**	Instruction on pages 79–90
	Phonemic Awareness Activities on
	    pages 77H–77I
	Little Books *Alexander Ant Cools Off*;
	    Who Can Run Fast?

92

Phonemic Awareness /i/

Objectives

- To match medial sounds
- To recognize the sound of short **i**
- To discriminate between short **i** words and other words

Warming Up

Reviewing Initial and Final Consonants

Print **hat** on the board and say the word. Point to **h** and say: /h/ is the beginning sound. Point to **t** and say: /t/ is the final sound. Repeat this with children. Then have children identify beginning and ending letters and sounds in **cap**, **bag**, **sad**, **pal**, and **jam**.

Teaching the Lesson

Phonemic Awareness: Match Medial Sounds

Say **dig** and **fin**. Tell children that both words have /i/ in the middle. Demonstrate by saying /d/-/i/-/g/, emphasizing /i/. Have children say /i/ before repeating the words **dig** and **fin**. Now say pairs of words and ask children to pretend to dig if the words both have /i/ in the middle (e.g. **hit/pin**, **hot/fish**, **lip/dig**, **mitt/sit**, **fix/bag**).

Sound to Symbol

- Say the words **sit**, **mix**, **fill**. Explain that these words have /i/ in the middle. Have children say /i/ before repeating each word with you. Explain that /i/ is the sound for short vowel **i**. Ask children to listen for short **i** words in this sentence: **This big** bug has **six** legs. Have children clap each time they hear a word with /i/.

- Print **i** on the board. Explain that **i** can stand for /i/. Under the **i** print **pig**, **bib**, **mitt**, **lid**. Read the words aloud. Say the words again with children and ask a volunteer to underline the letter that stands for /i/ in each word. Repeat with **pin**, **sip**, **will**, **him**.

Listen as the page is read aloud. Talk about the short **i** words you hear, such as **it** and **sits**. Then draw the answer to the riddle at the bottom of the page.

What Is It?

It has **six** legs,
And **it** has **wings**.
Sometimes **it sits**.
Sometimes **it stings**.
What **is it**?
It **is** a **big**…

Accept any drawing that looks like a bug.

Critical Thinking

Possible answers: fly, butterfly, moth, etc.

What are the names of some other bugs with wings?

LESSON 46: Phonemic Awareness: /i/   93

UNIVERSAL ACCESS
Meeting Individual Needs

Auditory • Kinesthetic

Remind children that **six** has the short **i** sound. Read the poem below and have children hold up six fingers when they hear a word with the short **i** sound.

Six little bugs,
They fly and **flip**;
They play a game
Of dart and **nip**.

Visual • Kinesthetic

Materials: Sadlier Phonics Picture Cards for short **a** and short **i**

Have children work in small groups. Give each group a stack of cards for short **a** and short **i** words. Tell group members to identify the pictures and sort them into two groups according to vowel sound.

Extra Support

Remind children that the short **i** sound is /i/. Then point to your chin and say **chin**. Tell children to do the same. Say some short vowel words such as **chick**, **pit**, **rag**, **dish**, **crab**. Have children point to their chin when they hear a short **i** word.

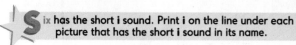

Six has the short **i** sound. Print **i** on the line under each picture that has the short **i** sound in its name.

Short i

1 — 6 — six	2 — van	3 — fish	4 — kiss
5 — leaf	6 — pig	7 — tube	8 — bib
9 — mitt	10 — fox	11 — nail	12 — fist
13 — bone	14 — crib	15 — rip	16 — hut

LESSON 46: Connecting Sound to Symbol /i/ i

Say the name of each picture. Ask your child to hold up six fingers if the name has the short **i** sound.

Practicing the Skill

● Read aloud the directions on page 93. Read aloud the poem and help children answer the riddle. Together discuss the Critical Thinking question and have children name other winged bugs.

● Point to the Key Picture Cue **six** on page 94. Review that **six** has a short **i** sound. Have children trace with a finger the letter **i** at the top of the page. Read aloud the directions and identify each picture. Model how to write **i** in the first item. Have children complete the page.

Curriculum Connections

Spelling Connection

Materials: Punchout Letter Cards

Read aloud the words and sentences below. Have children use their letter cards to spell each short **i** word.

bit	The bug **bit** me.
did	Tim **did** it!
big	Look at this **big** bug!
fix	Mom can **fix** it.
win	Who will **win** the race?

Theme Activity: Multicultural

Materials: pull-down map; pictures of Mexican, British, and Indian flags; paper; crayons

● Tell children there are different kinds of butterflies in different parts of the world. On a pull-down map, point to Mexico, Britain, and India and say each country's name. Explain that different types of butterflies live in these countries. Then say each name in separate syllables and have children identify the short **i** sound.

● Display pictures of Mexican, British, and Indian flags. Have children draw three butterflies and decorate the wings with the three different flag designs.

● Write "Wings of the World" on the board. Point to each word as you read it and have children repeat. Direct them to copy on their drawings the short **i** word **wings**.

Observational Assessment

*Note whether children are able to recognize the sound of short **i** in spoken words.*

English Language Learners/ESL
Display several books about insects. You might read *About Bugs* by Sheryl Scarborough (Treasure Bay, Inc.). This book shows about 20 different insects. Ask children to tell what they know about different kinds of insects. Then help children identify the parts of an insect and count the six legs. Make sure children understand that the words **insect** and **bug** are used interchangeably.

Challenge
Remind children that the **i** in words such as **big** and **wing**, has a short **i** sound. Have children draw an insect with big wings. Then have children decorate the wings by drawing items on the wings that have the short **i** sound.

Special Strategies
For Universal Access activities, see page 77F.

94

Blending with Short Vowel i

Objectives

- To substitute final sounds
- To blend short **i** words
- To identify and write short **i** words

Warming Up

Reviewing the Sound of Short Vowel i

On the board write **big**, **pit**, **six**. Say each word and have children repeat it. Review that these words have the short **i** sound. Underline the **i** in each word. Then say **hill**, **lid**, **map**, **sit**, **fix**, and **box**. Have children hold up six fingers each time they hear a word with the short **i** sound.

Teaching the Lesson

Phonemic Awareness: Substitute Final Sounds

Say **hid** slowly. Point out that the last sound in **hid** is /d/. Explain that you are going to make a new word by replacing the last sound in **hid**, /d/, with /m/. Say the new word—**him**. Now have children say **hid**. Tell them to change the last sound to /m/ and have them say **him**. Repeat with **pin/pit** and **dig/dip**.

Blending

Materials: Sadlier Phonics Picture Cards for **lid**, **pin**, **bib**, **six**.

Show the **lid** picture card. Say its name and write the word **lid** on the board, leaving a space between each letter. Tell children you are going to blend the sounds of these letters to read the word **lid**. Point to **l** and say /l/. Point to **i** and say /i/. Point to **d** and say /d/. Then slide your finger under the letters as you say /l/-/i/-/d/. Finally say **lid**. Repeat the entire process with children. Then repeat with the words **pin**, **bib**, and **six**.

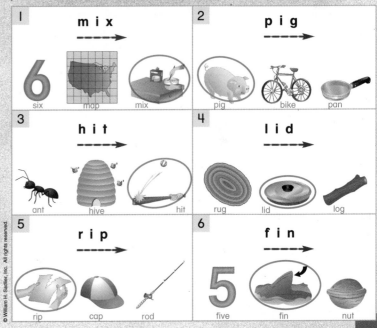

Trace the line as you blend the sounds together to say the word. Then circle the picture it names.

1	mix ➡		2	pig ➡	
	six map mix			pig bike pan	
3	hit ➡		4	lid ➡	
	ant hive hit			rug lid log	
5	rip ➡		6	fin ➡	
	rip cap rod			five fin nut	

LESSON 47: Blending with Short Vowel **i**   **95**

UNIVERSAL ACCESS
Meeting Individual Needs

Auditory • Kinesthetic

Review that /i/ is the sound of short vowel **i**. Say the following nursery rhyme and ask children to jump when they hear the short **i** sound in a word.

Jack be **nimble**;
Jack be **quick**.
Jack jump over
the **candlestick**.

Visual • Tactile

Materials: fabric, yarn, glue, crayons

Have children glue fabric or yarn onto paper to form an **i**. Together, list short **i** words on the board. Direct children to write a letter before and after their crafted **i** to form a word and then finger-trace the letters as they read the word.

Extra Support

Materials: Punchout Letter Cards

Review that **i** can stand for /i/. Write **big**, **tip**, **rib**, and **lid** on the board. Read the words aloud. Then have children use their letter cards to form each word. Have them blend the letter sounds to say each word.

95

Trace the line as you blend the sounds together to say the word.
Then print the word that names each picture.

1.
t i p
w i g

wig

2.
p i n
d i d

pin

3.
f i t
b i b

bib

4.
s i x
b i g

six

5.
h i m
k i t

kit

6.
z i p
w i n

zip

Have your child retrace the arrow
slowly with a pencil or crayon as
you blend each word.

LESSON 47: Blending with Short Vowel **i**

Practicing the Skill

● Have children turn to page 95. Talk about the action in the top picture. Be sure they notice the bug **mixing** the batter.

● Read aloud the directions. Model how to blend the sounds in the word **mix** as you trace the line. Then identify the pictures in the first box and model how to circle the picture for **mix**. Help children name remaining pictures before they complete the page.

● Discuss the picture at the top of page 96. Ask children what the bugs are wearing. (**wigs**) Go over the directions and do the first item with children. Identify remaining pictures before having children complete the page.

Curriculum Connections

Spelling Connection
Materials: Punchout Letter Cards

Read aloud the words and sentences below. Have children use letter cards to spell each word as they hear it.

sit   I need to **sit** down.

bib   Put the **bib** on the baby.

hill   A bug is on the **hill**.

dig   Let's **dig** a hole here.

Theme Activity: Art/Science
Materials: paper, crayons

● Tell children that many insects have wings but some do not. Ask children to name winged insects. List names such as **bee**, **fly**, and **butterfly** on the board and have each child choose one and draw a picture of it. Display drawings in the classroom.

● Direct children to become their insects and flap their "wings" whenever they hear you say a short **i** word. Then say words with and without the short **i** sound. You can say **pit**, **fill**, **pat**, **tin**, **lift**, **mix**, **pal**, and **sip**.

English Language Learners/ESL
Materials: Sadlier Phonics Picture Cards for **bib**, **pig**, **lid**, **pin**, **six**, and **mix**; large index cards; crayons

Use the picture cards to help children recall some of the short **i** words presented in the lesson. Display a card, call on a child to say its name, and write the word on the board. Model saying the sound represented by each letter and blending the sounds to say the word. Then have children work in groups to identify and illustrate other short **i** words.

Challenge
Ask children if they have ever visited websites on the Internet. Point out that each website has a Home Page, or a main starting point. Have children design a "Home Page" (on paper) about bugs. Children can write a welcome message, list some facts about bugs, and draw a picture. Have children underline any short **i** words they use. Display the pages on the bulletin board so that classmates can read them.

Special Strategies
For Universal Access activities, see page 77F.

Observational Assessment

*Note whether children can recognize short **i** words as they are spoken aloud.*

Short Vowel i Phonograms

Objectives

- To distinguish rhyming words from non-rhyming words
- To recognize short **i** phonograms
- To blend initial consonants with short **i** phonograms

Warming Up

Reviewing Final Consonant Sounds

Have children answer riddles, like those below, targeting final consonant sounds.

It's a baby's bed. It ends with /b/. (**crib**)

It's a purple fruit. It ends with /m/. (**plum**)

Teaching the Lesson

Phonemic Awareness: Distinguish Rhyming Words from Non-Rhyming Words

Tell children that they will help you find out who went swimming yesterday. Only children whose names rhyme with **swim** went swimming. Remind children that rhyming words sound the same at the end (e.g. **him/dim** both end with /**im**/). Ask: *Did Kim swim?* Repeat with other rhyming and non-rhyming names, such as **Tim**, **Bob**, **Pat**, and **Jim**.

Phonograms

Materials: **Sadlier Phonics Picture Card** for **pig**

- On the board, write the phonogram **ig**. Under it write **big**, **wig**, and **dig** in one column. Read aloud the phonogram and then each word. Point out that all the words end with the phonogram **ig**. Ask volunteers to circle **ig** in each word and say /**ig**/.
- Write **ig** on the board. Show the picture card for pig and say **pig**. Explain that to write **pig** you need to add the letter that stands for /p/ to the beginning of **ig**. Write **p** in front of **ig** and read the word. Then read the word together.
- Repeat this process for the phonogram **id** using **did**, **hid**, **rid**, and **lid**.

97

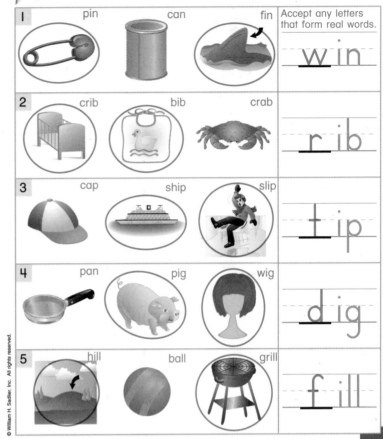

Say the name of each picture. In each row, circle two pictures that have rhyming names. Then make a new rhyming word.

				Accept any letters that form real words.
1	pin	can	fin	w in
2	crib	bib	crab	r ib
3	cap	ship	slip	t ip
4	pan	pig	wig	d ig
5	hill	ball	grill	f ill

LESSON 48: Short Vowel **i** Phonograms

97

UNIVERSAL ACCESS
Meeting Individual Needs

Auditory • Visual
Materials: Sadlier Phonics Picture Cards for short **i**

Seat children in a circle with picture cards face-down in the middle. Direct one child to pick up a card and name the picture. Call on children to say words that rhyme with the name. Repeat.

Auditory • Kinesthetic
Materials: assortment of hats

Model the act of tipping a hat. On the board, write a list of short-vowel words with space before the phonogram. Include **t ip, t in, m at, k it, p ig, b ag,** and **l ip.** Direct children to read the words by blending the sounds and to tip their hats when they read a word with /**i**/.

Extra Support
Materials: Punchout Letter Cards

Help children use letter cards to make the phonogram **in.** Say /in/ together. Have children place a **t** in front of **in.** Model how to blend /t/ and /**in**/ to say **tin.** Have children make and say new words with **in** using **b, f, p,** and **w.**

Trace the line as you blend the sounds together to say the word. Then print the word on the line.

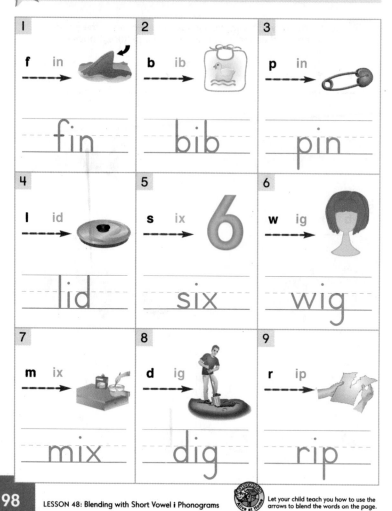

1 f → in	**2** b → ib	**3** p → in
fin	bib	pin
4 l → id	**5** s → ix	**6** w → ig
lid	six	wig
7 m → ix	**8** d → ig	**9** r → ip
mix	dig	rip

LESSON 48: Blending with Short Vowel i Phonograms

Let your child teach you how to use the arrows to blend the words on the page.

Practicing the Skill

• Read aloud the directions on page 97. Help children identify the pictures. Remind children that rhyming words have the same ending sound. Model how to identify and circle the two rhyming pictures in the first row. Give an example of a rhyming word for the first item. Then have children complete the page.

• Read aloud the directions for page 98. Model how to blend the initial consonant sound with the phonogram to read the word that names the first item pictured. Then have children blend the sounds and write the remaining picture names.

Curriculum Connections

Spelling Connection

Read aloud the words and sentences listed below. Then call on a volunteer to spell the word or print it on the board.

tip Don't **tip** the glass over.
fib Never tell a **fib**.
lid The **lid** is on the pan.
lit The firefly **lit** up.

Theme Activity: Physical Education/Science

• Tell children that insects have six legs. Direct them to work in groups of three to become six-legged "bugs" by standing one behind the other, with the second and the third children holding the shoulders of the child in front of them.

• Explain that the bugs can only take a step when they hear a word with /i/. Slowly say a string of words that includes short **i** words. You might say **quiz**, **bag**, **kiss**, **nest**, **win**, **six**, **did**, **dip**, and **hop**.

Sadlier Reading
Little Books and Big Books

Read *All Mixed Up* (fiction) for more practice with short **i**.

Observational Assessment

Note whether children are able to blend short i phonograms to read words.

English Language Learners/ESL

Help build children's confidence in themselves by allowing them to use previous pages in the short **i** section as a resource when completing this lesson. For example, if they are having difficulty thinking of new rhyming words, encourage them to "rediscover" rhyming words from previous short **i** pages.

Challenge

Have children work in groups. Give each group a short **i** phonogram, such as **in**, **ig**, or **ip**. Direct the groups to brainstorm a list of rhyming words that contain their phonogram. Have the group use one of the words from their list to write a question about insects. For example, the group with the phonogram **in** might write: Does an insect have a **fin**? Gather groups together and have them pose their questions to one another.

Special Strategies

For Universal Access activities, see page 77F.

Objectives

- To blend onsets and rimes
- To use phonograms to read short **i** words
- To recognize short **i** words

Warming Up

Reviewing Short a and i

Materials: Punchout Letter Cards **a**, **i**

Give children **a** and **i** letter cards. Tell them to hold up the card for the vowel sound they hear. Say words with short **a** and short **i** phonograms, such as **hat**, **hit**, **tan**, **tin**.

Teaching the Lesson

Phonemic Awareness: Blend Onsets and Rimes

Lead children in a call and response game. Model the game by saying: *I say /p/-/in/; you say* **pin**. Repeat the phrases and have children chime in on the last word—**pin**. Continue with /l/-/ip/ (**lip**); /m/-/iks/ (**mix**); /f/-/an/ (**fan**); /s/-/at/ (**sat**).

Phonograms

- Write the word **pin** on the board, leaving a space between **p** and **in**. Model how to read the word. Point to the letter **p** and say /p/. Slide your finger under **in** and say /in/. Then blend the two parts to say **pin**.
- Ask a volunteer to draw an arrow beneath the parts from left to right as he or she blends the two parts /p/-/in/.
- Write **tin** beneath **pin** and read the word. Point out that both **tin** and **pin** have the same phonogram—**in**. Ask a volunteer to read the word **tin** in the same way the last volunteer read the word **pin**. Write **win** under **tin** and repeat the process again.
- Follow the same procedure for the phonogram **ip** using the words **rip**, **sip**, **tip**, and **lip**.

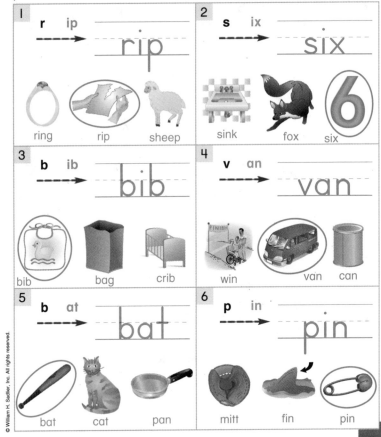

Trace the line as you blend the sounds together to say the word. Print the word on the line. Then circle the picture it names.

1   r   ip   ___   rip

ring   rip   sheep

2   s   ix   ___   six

sink   fox   six

3   b   ib   ___   bib

bib   bag   crib

4   v   an   ___   van

win   van   can

5   b   at   ___   bat

bat   cat   pan

6   p   in   ___   pin

mitt   fin   pin

LESSON 49: Blending with Phonograms   **99**

U N I V E R S A L   A C C E S S
Meeting Individual Needs

Auditory • Kinesthetic

Tell children they are going to play a game of Short **i** Says. Direct them to follow only those directions that contain a short **i** word. Use directions such as these:

Touch your **chin**.

Sit down.

Stand up.

Lick your **lips**.

Auditory

Ask children to pretend that the class is taking a trip and can only bring along objects with short **i** sounds. Say: *I'm taking a trip, and I'm bringing a* **pig**. Have children take turns repeating your words and adding on other short **i** items to extend the list. For example: *I'm taking a trip, and I'm bringing a* **pig** *and a* **wig**.

Extra Support

Materials: Punchout Letter Cards

Help children make the phonogram **ip** using letter cards. Read it aloud together. Help children add a **t** to the beginning. Read **tip** together. Continue making and reading other words with **ip**. Repeat with **in**, **ix**, and **ig**.

Circle the word that names each picture.

1 (win) will tin	**2** fit sink (six)	**3** hill gift (grill)
4 pin fix (fin)	**5** (ham) hit hat	**6** pit (pig) wig
7 bit fib (bib)	**8** pit pan (pin)	**9** cat bit (bat)
10 (hill) will him	**11** wag (wig) win	**12** pin (pan) pat
13 (bag) big bug	**14** (mitt) mat milk	**15** laps sip (lips)

LESSON 49: Practicing Short Vowel **i**

Read a circled word. Have your child say the word slowly, separating the initial sound from the rest of the word: w in.

● Read aloud the directions on page 99. Help children identify the names of all the pictures. Model tracing the line and blending the initial consonant and phonogram in the first item. Show children how to print the word and circle the picture it names. Then have them complete the page.

● Read aloud the directions for page 100. Help children name the pictures. Guide them to blend the sounds to read the words in the first item and circle the picture name. Then have children complete the page.

Curriculum Connections

Spelling Connection

Materials: Punchout Letter Cards

Read aloud the words and sentences below. After saying each word and sentence, call on a volunteer to spell the word aloud or use letter cards to spell it.

hid The bug **hid** under the leaf.

pin Will you **pin** the tail on the donkey?

kit Please bring the first aid **kit**.

mix Can you **mix** the batter?

tin Put the **tin** can in the bin.

ART CENTER

Materials: chart paper, oaktag, crayons, scissors, envelopes

● Ask children to name short **i** words they can draw, such as **bib**, **crib**, **fin**, **hill**, **lips**, **lid**, **mitt**, **pig**, **pin**, **six**, **wig**. Record answers on chart paper.

● In the Art Center, have each child choose one short **i** word to illustrate on oaktag. Direct children to write the word on the back of their illustrations, cut the drawings into jigsaw puzzle pieces, and place the pieces in envelopes.

● Have children put together one another's puzzles, name the pictures, and then check that the name matches the word on the back.

 Portfolio

Have children put their puzzle pieces back into the envelopes and then place them in their portfolios.

English Language Learners/ESL
Materials: pocket mirrors

Before children do the lesson, help them distinguish between the short vowel sounds /**a**/ and /**i**/. Write word pairs such as **mat**/**mit** and **pan**/**pin** on the board. As you point to each word in a pair, model saying the word, exaggerating the way you use your mouth to form each short vowel sound. Discuss how the shape and opening of the mouth are different. Then have children practice saying the words while watching their mouths in a mirror.

Special Strategies
For Universal Access activities, see page 77F.

Challenge
Remind children that insects have six legs. Have children work in groups to draw and write about insects. Show them how to draw an insect body and head. Rather than drawing each leg, have children write a short sentence in its place. Direct children to underline any short **i** words they use.

Student Pages 101-102

Writing Short Vowel i

Objectives
- To delete initial sounds
- To recognize short **i** words
- To write short **i** words

Warming Up

Reviewing Medial Consonants

Ask children to solve riddles involving medial consonant sounds. For example:

You can swim in me. My middle consonant is **t**. (**water**)

I'm the number after six. My middle consonant is **v**. (**seven**)

I'm a yellow fruit. My middle consonant is **m**. (**lemon**)

Teaching the Lesson

Phonemic Awareness: Delete Initial Sounds

Say the word **tin**. Then say the beginning sound in **tin**, /**t**/. Explain that you are going to say a new word by taking away /**t**/ from **tin**. Say: *Take away the /**t**/ from* **tin***, you will hear the new word,* **in***.* Have children repeat after you. Continue making new words by having children take away the beginning sounds from **cat, pan, fin, hat, hill**. Have children identify the beginning sound in each word before taking it away.

Sound to Symbol

Materials: **Sadlier Phonics Picture Cards** for **pin, bib, lid, pig**

Show the **pin** picture card. Say the name slowly: /**p**/-/**i**/-/**n**/. Tell children you are going to write the word by writing the letter that stands for each sound you say. Say /**p**/ and write a **p**, say /**i**/ and write **i**, say /**n**/ and write **n**. Then read the word **pin**. Have children write the word on a piece of paper and say **pin**. Repeat with **bib, lid**, and **pig**.

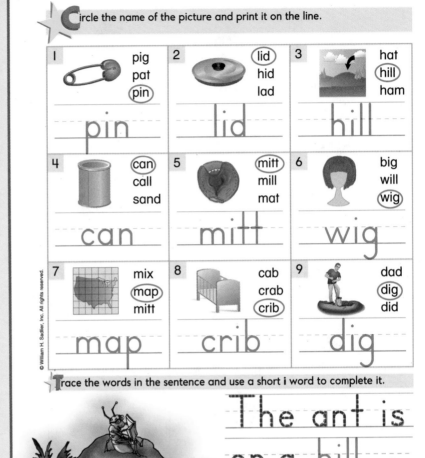

Circle the name of the picture and print it on the line.

1. pig / pat / **pin** — pin	2. **lid** / hid / lad — lid	3. hat / **hill** / ham — hill
4. **can** / call / sand — can	5. **mitt** / mill / mat — mitt	6. big / will / **wig** — wig
7. mix / **map** / mitt — map	8. cab / crab / **crib** — crib	9. dad / **dig** / did — dig

Trace the words in the sentence and use a short **i** word to complete it.

The ant is on a hill .

UNIVERSAL ACCESS
Meeting Individual Needs

Visual • Kinesthetic

Materials: **Sadlier Phonics Picture Cards** for short **a** and short **i**

Say **sit** and **stand** and have children identify the vowel sound in each word. Direct children to **sit** when you show a picture card for a short **i** word and to **stand** for a short **a** picture.

Auditory • Kinesthetic

Have the class work in two teams. Designate three bases and a home plate in the classroom. Direct children to play a baseball game in which batters move to first base by saying short **i** words. Instead of keeping track of outs, end each inning after six children "bat." Guide batters in advancing around the bases and keeping score.

Extra Support

Materials: **Sadlier Phonics Picture Cards** for **lid, pin, bib, six**

Show a picture card. Write its name with a missing letter for children to fill in. Help children idenify the sound of the missing letter and then print the letter. Progress to leaving out two letters.

1 bib	2 pig	3 dig	4 mix
5 hill	6 six	7 lid	8 win
9 crib	10 rip	11 fin	12 mitt
13 pin	14 wig	15 milk	16 sink

102 LESSON 50: Writing Short Vowel **i**

Ask your child to read the words. Work together to make up sentences for three of the words.

Practicing the Skill

● Read aloud the directions on page 101 and help children identify the pictures. Remind them to blend sounds to read each word. Model completing the first item and have children complete the first part of the page. Then read aloud the directions for the bottom part of the page and guide children in tracing the first word. Remind them that a sentence begins with an uppercase letter and ends with a period. Then have children complete the sentence.

● Read aloud the directions for page 102. Together, identify the pictures. Then have the children complete the page.

Curriculum Connections

Spelling Connection

Read aloud the words and sentences below. Call on a volunteer to spell each word aloud.

dim	The light is too **dim**.
fit	Does your coat still **fit?**
Jim	A bee stung **Jim**.
kid	Don't **kid** me!
pit	Don't eat a peach **pit**.

SCIENCE CENTER

Materials: construction paper, scissors, crayons, pipe cleaners or drinking straws, clay

● Review different kinds of bugs with wings (e.g., flies, butterflies, bees). Have children cut wing shapes from construction paper and decorate each wing by drawing a picture of a short **i** word. Have children print the word beneath the picture.

● Model how to attach the wings to six pipe cleaners or straws for legs and to a clay body to form a bug. Tell children to make their completed bugs "fly" by carrying them to visit classmates. Have children identify one another's pictures and words. Set up an exhibit of winged insects in the Science Center.

Sadlier Reading

Little Books and Big Books

Read *Look at the Pictures* (nonfiction) for more practice with short **i**.

English Language Learners/ESL
Materials: Punchout Letter Cards

To help children spell and write words, allow them to use letter cards to spell out each word on page 102 before writing it. Have them show and read their words to you, and work with them to correct any misspellings before asking them to print the words on the student page.

Challenge
Share the following traditional finger-play with children:

One, two, three,
There's a bug on me!
  [Pretend to brush off bug.]
Where did it go?
  [Cup hands and look around.]
I don't know!

Have children try to use one or more short **i** words to write a silly answer to the question.

Special Strategies
For Universal Access activities, see page 77F.

102

LESSON 51 • UNIT 3
Student Pages 103–104

Short Vowel i Decodable Reader

Objectives
- To read short **i** words and high-frequency words in context
- To read the story fluently
- To identify problem/solution

Introducing the Story Words

Short i Decodable Words Remind children that the sound of short **i** is /i/. Write **fix** on the board and model blending the sounds /**f**/-/**i**/-/**ks**/ to read the word. On the board write the following: **S_d, f_x, m_tt, d_d, _t, w_g, b_g, r_p, l_d.** Tell children that each of these words is missing a short **i**. Direct volunteers to print **i** in each blank. Then guide children in blending and reading each word.

High-Frequency Words Write **can** and **the** on the board. Read and spell each word, and have children repeat after you.

Reading the Book

Reading Together Have children remove pages 103 and 104. Show them how to cut and fold the pages into a book. Read aloud the title, "Fix It!" Tell children they will read a story about a character who fixes things. Direct them to follow along in their books as you read aloud.

Responding Ask children to identify all the things Sid fixed. Ask them what they would take to Sid to have fixed.

Reading for Fluency Have children track the words with a finger as you read aloud. Then have them read pages 1–4 to a partner and the partner read pages 5–8. Finally, have children read the story on their own.

Observational Assessment

*Note whether children can decode short **i** words and read the story fluently.*

103

Your child has read this book in school. Ask him or her to read it to you. Then have your child find, spell, and read each short **i** word in the story.

Name _____

Fix It!

8 Sid did fix it!

Can Sid fix the mitt? 1

6 Sid did fix it!

Can Sid fix the wig? 3

Directions: Cut and fold the book. Read the story. Tell about each problem and how it was solved.

LESSON 51: Short Vowel **i** Decodable Reader
Comprehension: Identifying Problem/Solution   103

UNIVERSAL ACCESS
Meeting Individual Needs

Visual • Tactile
Materials: chart, alphabet rubber stamps, paper

Write the decodable words from the story on a chart. Direct children to use the alphabet stamps to build each word. Model reading each word by blending the letter sounds as each letter is stamped.

Auditory • Kinesthetic
Write the high-frequency words **the** and **can** on the board. Say each word, spell it, and have children repeat it after you. As children spell, direct them to write the words in the air.

Extra Support
Materials: decodable words on index cards, Punchout Letter Cards

Blend and read each decodable word card with children. Then have them build each word with letter cards and use each word orally in a sentence.

| 2 Sid did fix it! | Can Sid fix the big rip? 7 |

| 4 Sid did fix it! | Can Sid fix the lid? 5 |

104

LESSON 51: Short Vowel **i** Decodable Reader
Comprehension: Identifying Problem/Solution

Comprehension Strategy

Identifying Problem/Solution Explain to children that one way of better understanding a story is to think about what problems the characters have and how those problems are solved. Help children identify the problems and solutions in "Fix It!" Ask children to talk about or draw a picture of what each character could do once Sid "fixed" his or her problem.

Phonics and Decoding

Learning About Short i On the board write these story words: **mitt**, **wig**, **lid**, **big**, **rip**. Have children read the words aloud. Ask children to name the vowel sound in each word. (/i/) Then have children write **i** on a paper and tell them to hold up the **i** each time you say a word that has /i/. Read these words: **crib**, **ship**, **map**, **dish**, **bag**, **drill**.

Word Building *Materials:* Punchout Letter Cards for **f**, **i**, **m**, **s**, **x**

Use letter cards to build the phonogram **ix**. Tell children to choose letters to put in front of the phonogram to spell words with these meanings: *a number higher than five; to repair something; to stir something.*

Curriculum Connections

Writing and Sharing Tell children to imagine that Sid's sister Jill was also working in the fix-it shop. Guide children in writing a group story on the chalkboard, telling what Sid and Jill fixed together. Ask children to draw illustrations and then read aloud sentences from the story.

English Language Learners/ESL

Materials: tape and a ripped sheet of paper; a book positioned upside down on the chalk ledge; an unsharpened pencil and a pencil sharpener

Before introducing the story, demonstrate how to "fix" the ripped sheet of paper. Then display the other items listed above and ask children to identify them. Ask for volunteers to "fix" the items so they can be used. For each successful outcome, say: *You solved the problem. You're a fix-it boy/girl!* Ask children to talk about things they have fixed, such as a broken bicycle or a toy that did not work.

Special Strategies

For Universal Access activities, see page 77F.

Challenge

Materials: paper, scissors, markers

Direct children to cut out an inchworm shape for a creepy crawly bookmark. Point out that **inch** has the short **i** sound. Ask children to write the short **i** words from "Fix It!" on their bookmark. Tell them to add new short **i** words as they read other books.

Short Vowel i in Context

Objectives

- To count phonemes in a word
- To complete sentences by writing short **i** words
- To recognize short **i** words in context

Warming Up

Reviewing Rhyming Words

Write the following short **i** rhymes on the board. Have volunteers name the unfinished rhyming words.

> Wouldn't a pig
> Look odd with a **w__**? (**wig**)
> Do you think the ant will
> Walk up the **h__**? (**hill**)

Teaching the Lesson

Phonemic Awareness: Count Phonemes in a Word

Materials: counters

Tell children you are going to count sounds in a word. Place four counters in a row for each child. Say the word **sit**. Then say each sound one at a time: /s/-/i/-/t/. Make a mark on the board each time you say a sound. Count the marks. Tell children there are 3 sounds in the word **sit**. Repeat the sounds and tell children to slide up a counter each time you say a sound. Ask how many sounds children heard. Then have them use their counters as you slowly say the words **lip**, **in**, and **kit**.

Phonics in Context

Write this sentence on the board: I will _____ a hole. Write the words **wig**, **dig**, **dip** next to the sentence. Read aloud the sentence and the word choices. Then read the sentence three times, each time filling in the blank with one of the word choices. Circle the word **dig**, and tell children that it best completes the meaning of the sentence. Now have children complete this sentence: This is a ___ bug. (**bib**, **bag**, **big**)

Look at each picture. Circle the word that completes the sentence. Then print it on the line.

1		Lin ___sits___ still.	hits / six / (sits)
2		A bug ___is___ in the grass.	(is) / kiss / as
3		Lin is ___quick___ to grab it.	bib / sink / (quick)
4		Lin has the bug ___in___ the jar.	is / (in) / it
5		Lin looks at ___it___.	(it) / in / an
6		She lifts the ___lid___.	lad / (lid) / Lin

LESSON 52: Short Vowel **i** in Sentences **105**

U N I V E R S A L   A C C E S S
Meeting Individual Needs

Auditory • Kinesthetic

Explain that a **jig** is a dance. Model how to improvise a **jig**. Ask children to listen to a list of words, such as **Bill, bake, like, man, kids,** and **hat**. Direct them to dance a **jig** when they hear a word with /i/ and to stop when they hear a word with another vowel sound.

Visual • Tactile

Materials: twigs, oaktag, glue, crayons

Have each child glue a twig in the middle of a sheet of oaktag. Model how to turn the twig into the letter **i** and write letters on either side of it to spell a short **i** word. Have children write their own short **i** words. Then have them read one another's words.

Extra Support

Materials: index cards

Write the words **pig, mix, will, sit, in,** and **hid** on index cards. Read the words with children. Then ask a child to pick a card, read it, spell it, and use it in a sentence.

Listen as the poem is read aloud to find out about bugs. Then use short **i** words to complete the sentences.

What Is a Bug?

Some bugs have six legs,
Not more than six!
Some bugs have odd names,
Like walkingsticks.

Insects can have wings,
And some can sting!
It seems bugs can do
All kinds of things.

1. Some bugs have _____ **six** _____ legs.

2. Bugs with **wings** can fly.

3. Look out for bugs that can _____ **sting** _____ .

106

LESSON 52: Short Vowel **i** in Context
Comprehension: Setting a Purpose for Reading

Have your child use a
yellow crayon to highlight
short **i** words in the poem.

Practicing the Skill

● Read aloud the directions on page 105. Together with children read the first incomplete sentence and word choices. Model how to use the picture to help choose the correct missing word. Then read aloud the remaining incomplete sentences and word choices, discuss the pictures, and have children complete the page.

● Read aloud the directions on page 106. Then read the poem several times. Encourage children to read with you. Then direct children to circle the short **i** words in the poem and use them to complete the sentences.

Curriculum Connections

Spelling Connection
Materials: Punchout Letter Cards

Read aloud the words and sentences below. Call on volunteers to spell the words aloud or use their letter cards to spell the words.

rig	Dad can drive a big **rig**.
sip	Do you want a **sip** of milk?
quit	Lil did not **quit**.
Miss	Our teacher is **Miss** Smith.
fin	The fish flapped its **fin**.

Theme Activity: Science/Language Arts
Materials: picture books about bugs, chart paper

● Show pictures and read aloud from the theme book cited below. Have children work in groups to look through the theme book and other books about bugs. Ask groups to use the pictures and text to make statements about bugs, such as "Some bugs have six legs," or "Some bugs are green."

● Have each child draw a picture that shows something about bugs. As each child explains his or her drawing to the class, make a word map of bug characteristics on chart paper. Have volunteers circle any short **i** words.

Theme Book

Royston, Angela. *Insects and Crawly Creatures.* New York: Macmillan, 1992. Photographs and simple facts about bugs.

English Language Learners/ESL
Materials: sentence strips, index cards

Model how to fill in the correct word to complete the sentence. Copy the sentence on a sentence strip with a blank space for the answer. Write the answer choices on index cards and help children read each choice. Model how to read the sentence, saying the word **blank** for the missing word in the sentence. Have volunteers hold an answer choice in the space and read the sentence. Discuss which answer makes the most sense.

Special Strategies
For Universal Access activities, see page 77F.

Challenge
Have each child draw a bug. Direct children to draw a speech bubble to show something that their bug is saying. Have them write in the bubble a fill-in sentence with a short **i** word missing. Then have children exchange papers and complete the sentences.

106

Assessing Short Vowel i
Reviewing Short Vowels a and i

Objectives

- To identify and complete words with short **i**
- To review short **a** and short **i** words

Warming Up

Reviewing Final Consonants

Say **bat**, **tag**, and **car**, and ask volunteers to name the ending sound in each word. Then on the board print the incomplete words given below. Say the initial consonant and short vowel sound. Have children print final consonants to complete as many words as possible and then say the words.

ha_ (had, hag, ham, has, hat)

bi_ (bib, bid, big, bin, bit)

Teaching the Lesson

Short Vowel i

Materials: **Sadlier Phonics Picture Cards** for **ant**, **bat**, **ham**, **van**, **bib**, **hill**, **pin**

- Say **six**, and have children repeat after you. Write **s_x** on the board, and say: */i/ is the short vowel i sound you hear in the middle of six.* Fill in the blank with the letter **i**.
- Show the picture cards, one at a time, and have children say **six** and the name of the picture (e.g., **six/ant**, **six/pin**). If the picture name has the same vowel sound as **six**, children should say: *short i sound.*

Short Vowels a and i

Say **mat** and **mitt**, and have children name the short vowel sound in each word. Write these consonant patterns on the board: **b_d**, **b_g**, **h_p**, **c_t**, **p_g**, **t_p**. Ask volunteers to print **a** in each blank and then say the word. Ask children to tell whether the letters stand for a real word. Then repeat for **i**.

107

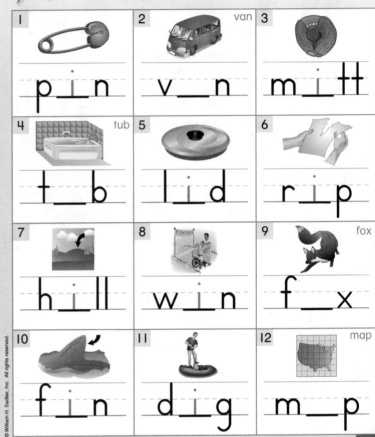

Check-Up Say the name of each picture. Print **i** on the line to complete the picture name if it has the short **i** sound.

1. p_in 2. v_n (van) 3. m_tt
4. t_b (tub) 5. l_d 6. r_p
7. h_ll 8. w_n 9. f_x (fox)
10. f_n 11. d_g 12. m_p (map)

UNIVERSAL ACCESS
Reteaching Activities

Activity 1

Materials: various children's books and magazines

Tell children to look through books and magazines to find and list words that have the same short vowel **i** sound as in the word **list**. Appoint one child to list the words as children dictate them. Set a time limit for the activity, and then make a chart of the words listed. Display the chart as a short **i** word reference. Repeat for short **a** words.

Activity 2

Materials: index cards (two for each child)

Ask children to draw a **pig** on one index card and a **bag** on the other. Tell children that you will say some short **i** and short **a** words. Have children hold up their **pig** drawing when you say a short **i** word and their **bag** drawing when you say a short **a** word. Use words such as **jazz**, **mix**, **him**, **Sam**, **Liz**, **mask**, **tap**, **lips**, **tax**, **lick**, **sad**, **van**, **rip**, **ham**, and **hid**.

Print **a** or **i** in each center box to make two words. Read the words across and down. Say the rhyming word part used in both words.

1.
```
    b
c a t
    t
```

2.
```
    l
d i p
    p
```

3.
```
    w
p i g
    g
```

4.
```
    b
t a g
    g
```

5.
```
    p
c a n
    n
```

6.
```
    b
r i b
    b
```

7.
```
    h
p a d
    d
```

8.
```
    s
m i x
    x
```

LESSON 53: Reviewing Short Vowels **a** and **i**

Use word pairs from the puzzles to make up silly rhymes with your child.

Guided Instruction

Skills	Resources
Short vowel **a**	Instruction on pages 79–90 Little Books *Alexander Ant Cools Off; Who Can Run Fast?*
Short vowel **i**	Instruction on pages 93–106 Little Books *All Mixed Up; Look at the Pictures*
Short vowels **a, i**	Phonemic Awareness Activities on pages 77H–77I

Assessing the Skill

Name the pictures on page 107 with children. Read aloud the directions, and have children complete the page on their own.

Cumulative Review

On the board, draw a box puzzle like the ones on page 108. Print the letter patterns **h_t** and **g_s**, leaving a blank for the middle letter. Tell children they will have to choose between **i** or **a** when they fill in the middle letter. Call on a volunteer to write **i** in the blank and read the words. Explain that **i** is the wrong choice because although **hit** is a real word, **gis** is not a real word. Then have the volunteer write **a** in the blank and read the words to confirm that **a** completes the puzzle correctly. Then read aloud the directions on page 108, and have children complete the page.

Observational Assessment   Observe children as they complete the pages and as they read and write in other subjects. Note whether any children have difficulty with short **a** and short **i** words.

Dictation   Tell children you are going to say some short **a** words. Have them write the short **a** words as you dictate them. Say these words: **pad, ham, fad, tan, lad.** Repeat the activity with short **i** words **fin, hid, rig, fix, kid.**

Student Skills Assessment   Use the checklist on Student Edition pages 321–322 to record your observations of individual children.

Student Pages 109–110

Phonemic Awareness /o/

Objectives

- To match medial sounds
- To recognize the sound of short **o**
- To discriminate between short **o** words and other words

Warming Up

Reviewing Initial Consonants

Have children work with partners to list or draw pictures of words that begin with an assigned consonant sound. Set a timer for three minutes. After the timer sounds, ask volunteers to read their lists. Use these consonants: **b, h, d, p, s, m, t, l.**

Teaching the Lesson

Phonemic Awareness: Match Medial Sounds

Say **top** and **lot**, and ask children to repeat. Explain that /o/ is the sound they hear in the middle of both words. Then pair the word **top** with other short vowel words such as **jog, stick, pat, box, fix,** and **sock.** Say each word pair. Tell children to touch the top of their heads if the two words have the same middle sound.

Sound to Symbol

Materials: **Sadlier Phonics Picture Cards** for **box, ox, log, pot, top, doll, jam, lamp, bib, pin;** colored chalk; box

- Display the picture cards for **box, top,** and **doll.** Have children name each picture and say the vowel sound they hear. (/o/) Explain that /o/ is the sound for short vowel **o.**
- On the board, print **o.** Tell children that **o** can stand for /o/. Write **box, top,** and **doll** on the board and have volunteers trace the **o** with colored chalk.
- Work with children to sort the remaining picture cards by vowel sound and place those with /o/ in a box.

Short **o**

Listen Listen as the page is read aloud. Talk about the short **o** words you hear, such as **hop** and **stop.** Then hop like a bug and stop like one, too.

Hop and Stop

Hop! Hop! Hop!
Time to **stop.**

Hop to the **box.**
Time to **stop.**

Jog in place.
Time to **stop.**

Isn't it fun
To **hop** and **stop!**

Critical Thinking
What are some other ways bugs can move?

Possible answers: Some bugs can fly and some can swim.

LESSON 54: Phonemic Awareness: /o/   109

UNIVERSAL ACCESS
Meeting Individual Needs

Auditory • Kinesthetic
Materials: box of Sadlier Phonics Picture Cards, several for short **o** words

Have children take turns reaching into the box, taking out a picture, and naming it. Direct them to crow **cock-a-doodle-do** like a rooster if they choose a short **o** word.

Auditory • Kinesthetic
Materials: shopping bags; short **o** objects such as **socks, blocks**

Give groups of children a shopping bag. Ask each group to collect short **o** objects in the classroom. Have available objects such as **tops, blocks, boxes,** and **dolls.** Have groups share their collections with the class.

Extra Support
Say **hop, stop,** and **mop,** emphasizing the /o/ in each word. Remind children that this is the short **o** sound. Ask them to **hop** when they hear another word with the same short **o** sound. Say **block, bug, pot, fog,** and **pet.**

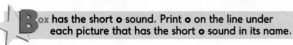

Box has the short **o** sound. Print **o** on the line under each picture that has the short **o** sound in its name.

Short o

1 box ○	2 dog ○	3 hat ○	4 clock ○
5 bat ○	6 knot ○	7 sock ○	8 log ○
9 doll ○	10 blocks ○	11 pot ○	12 six ○
13 top ○	14 bib ○	15 mop ○	16 ox ○

110

LESSON 54: Connecting Sound to Symbol: /o/ o

Say the name of each picture. Then have your child point to the picture of the box when he or she hears the short **o** sound.

Practicing the Skill

● Read aloud the directions and the poem on page 109. Then guide children to **hop** and **stop** as you read the poem again. Together read the Critical Thinking question and discuss other ways bugs move.

● Read aloud the directions on page 110 and point to the picture cue as you say **box**. Help children name the pictures on the page. Model completing the first item; then direct children to complete the page.

Curriculum Connections

ART CENTER

Materials: assorted materials for making bugs, including small boxes, paper cups, markers or crayons, pipe cleaners, scissors, buttons, glue

● Read aloud the theme book cited below. Then have children work in pairs in the Art Center to craft their own grouchy bug.

● Have children name their bugs and describe them to the class in a sentence or two. Display children's work in the Art Center.

Theme Book

Carle, Eric. *The Grouchy Ladybug.* New York: Thomas Y. Crowell, 1977. A bug looking for trouble!

English Language Learners/ESL
Materials: realia for **box, sock, doll, block, top, pot**

Present the poem on page 109 as a Total Physical Response activity. Demonstrate how to perform the movements as you say the poem, emphasizing the short **o** words, before having children do the movements. Then direct children to hop to a box that contains the objects listed above. Ask each child to choose an object, and help him/her name the object. Say: **Box** has the /**o**/ sound. Does ____ have the /**o**/ sound?

Challenge
Repeat for children the following story.

There was a bug named ____. He was very ____. One day, ____ wanted to ____. But he could not ____ because his ____ said. . . .

Have children suggest short **o** words to complete the story.

Special Strategies
For Universal Access activities, see page 77F.

Blending with Short Vowel o

Objectives
- To blend phonemes in a word
- To blend short **o** words
- To identify and write short **o** words

Warming Up

Reviewing Rhyming Words

Remind children that rhyming words have the same ending sound. Say the following rhyme, and help children identify the rhyming words.

Ladybug, you have a **spot**.

I will call you Lady **Dot**.

I hope you like this name a **lot**.

Let me know if you do **not**.

Teaching the Lesson

Phonemic Awareness: Blend Phonemes in a Word

Slowly say /l/-/o/-/g/. Then blend the sounds together to say **log**. Explain that words are sounds blended together. Have children repeat /l/-/o/-/g/ **log** with you. Segment other /o/ words, such as **fox**, **sock**, **mop**, and **pot**, and have children follow your model to blend the sounds into words.

Blending

- Say the sentences below, segmenting the final word. Repeat and have children blend the sounds to complete the word.

The bug can /h/-/o/-/p/.

It hops on the /d/-/o/-/g/.

It hops in the /b/-/o/-/ks/.

- Write **hop** on the board, leaving space between letters. Draw a right-pointing arrow beneath the word, and say /h/-/o/-/p/ as you slide your hand along the arrow. Repeat, this time moving your hand quickly as you say **hop**. Repeat with other short **o** words and have children blend the sounds.

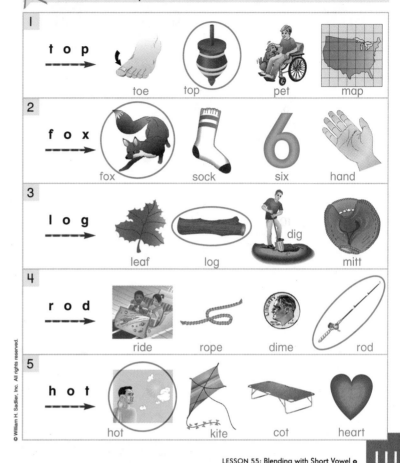

Trace the line as you blend the sounds together to say the word. Then circle the picture it names.

1. **t o p** — toe, top, pet, map
2. **f o x** — fox, sock, six, hand
3. **l o g** — leaf, log, dig, mitt
4. **r o d** — ride, rope, dime, rod
5. **h o t** — hot, kite, cot, heart

LESSON 55: Blending with Short Vowel o

111

UNIVERSAL ACCESS
Meeting Individual Needs

Visual • Kinesthetic
Materials: large letter cards

Give children working in groups of three a set of cards to spell a short **o** word, such as **dog**. Have children stand apart, and tell each child to say the sound of the letter on his or her card. Then have children move in closer, blend the sounds by saying them quickly, and together say the blended word.

Auditory • Tactile
Materials: Punchout Letter Cards

Have children take out the letters **b, o,** and **x** and say the sound for each letter. Then have children arrange the letters to spell **box**. Tell children to slide a finger from left to right beneath the letters as they blend and then say the word. Repeat with other short **o** words.

Extra Support
Materials: highlighting markers

Distribute lists of short **o** words with blending arrows under the letters. Point out the /o/ in each word, and use a highlighter to model blending sounds to read the words.

111

Trace the line as you blend the sounds together to say the word. Then print the word under the picture it names.

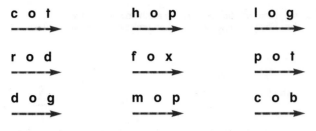

c o t →   h o p →   l o g →

r o d →   f o x →   p o t →

d o g →   m o p →   c o b →

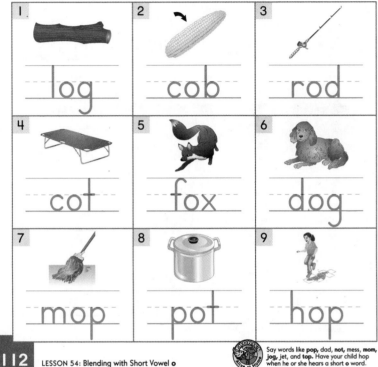

1	2	3
log	cob	rod
4	**5**	**6**
cot	fox	dog
7	**8**	**9**
mop	pot	hop

Say words like **pop,** dad, **not,** mess, **mom, jog,** jet, and **top.** Have your child hop when he or she hears a short **o** word.

112   LESSON 54: Blending with Short Vowel **o**

Practicing the Skill

• Read aloud the directions on page 111, and help children identify the pictures. Model item 1, and remind children how to blend sounds to say a word. Then have children complete the page.

• Read the directions on page 112. Help children identify all the pictures. Work through the first item with children. Then have them complete the page.

Curriculum Connections

Spelling Connection

Read aloud each word and sentence below. Then call on a volunteer to spell the word or print it on the board.

dot   Don't forget to **dot** your **i**!

fog   The **fog** made it hard to see.

pod   There are no peas in this **pod.**

not   I did **not** see that movie.

Bob   **Bob** took a nap**.**

Theme Activity: Art/Language Arts

Materials: pipe cleaners, **Unit 3 Classroom Poster,** construction paper, crayons, tape

• Give each child two pipe cleaners with which to craft a bug.

• Display the classroom poster. Ask: *Where can you find bugs? Could you find a bug on top of a rock?* Write **on top of a rock** on the board. Have children suggest other places they might find bugs. Write their ideas on the board and have children identify the short **o** words on the board.

• Direct children to draw a place for their bug and put their pipe cleaner bug on it. Help them tape their bugs in place. Provide assistance as they write captions to go with their pictures. Direct them to use short **o** words, such as **on**, **log**, and **hop**, and to underline those words.

Portfolio   Have children save their bugs and sentences in their portfolios.

English Language Learners/ESL

To extend vocabulary development, preview the pictures on student pages 111 and 112 with children and ask general questions to promote oral language development. For example, to focus children on the short **o** words, ask: *Do you have a _____ (top, cot, dog, sock)? What do you do with your _____ (top, cot, dog, sock)?* You may wish to expand the activity to include other vocabulary words from the lesson that do not have the short **o** sound.

Challenge

Materials: drawing paper, crayons

Have children work in small groups to draw a bug cartoon. Direct them to draw speech bubbles and to include and underline short **o** words in the bugs' dialogue.

Special Strategies

For Universal Access activities, see page 77F.

Short Vowel o Phonograms

Objectives

- To substitute initial sounds
- To recognize short **o** phonograms
- To blend initial consonants with short **o** phonograms

Warming Up

Reviewing Initial Consonant Sounds

Write the tongue twisters below on the board, and read them aloud. Have children identify the repeated initial consonants.

Harry Hippo hums happily.

Zelda Zebra zigzags around the zoo.

Sammy Seal sings silly sea songs.

Teaching the Lesson

Phonemic Awareness: Substitute Initial Sounds

Tell children that we can change the beginning sound in a word to make a new one. Identify the beginning sound in **pot**, /p/. Then say: *If we change the /p/ in pot to /h/, we get hot.* Have children practice this with you. Then have children answer the following:

What word do we get if we. . .

change the /**f**/ in **fox** to /**b**/? (**box**)

change the /**j**/ in **jog** to /**h**/? (**hog**)

change the /**h**/ in **hop** to /**p**/? (**pop**)

change the /**d**/ in **dock** to /**l**/? (**lock**)

Phonograms

Say: *Crickets hop.* Repeat the word **hop**, emphasizing /**op**/. Write **op** on the board. Tell children that the letters **op** stand for /**op**/ in **hop**. Add an **h** to **op** to form **hop**. Help children blend the sounds to say the word. Generate a list of **op** words, and read it with the class. Point out that words ending with the same sound rhyme. Repeat the activity with other short **o** phonograms such as **ox**, **og**, and **ot**. Have children blend and say the words.

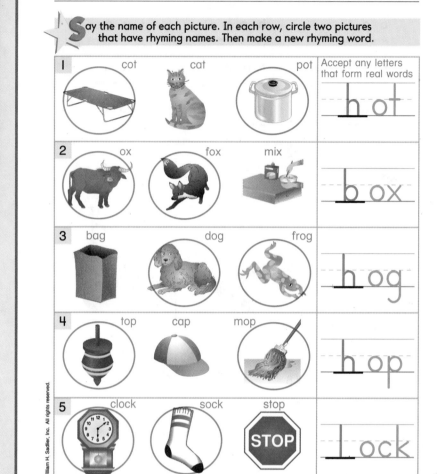

Say the name of each picture. In each row, circle two pictures that have rhyming names. Then make a new rhyming word.

				Accept any letters that form real words
1	cot	cat	pot	hot
2	ox	fox	mix	box
3	bag	dog	frog	hog
4	top	cap	mop	hop
5	clock	sock	stop	lock

LESSON 56: Short Vowel o Phonograms   **113**

UNIVERSAL ACCESS
Meeting Individual Needs

Auditory • Kinesthetic

Have the class line up facing you. Direct children to take a giant step forward when they hear you say two words that rhyme, and to stand still when they hear word pairs that do not rhyme. Use the following pairs: **Bob/job, jog/jig, lock/dock, dog/log, tip/top, box/fox.**

Auditory • Kinesthetic

Write this poem on the board:

Bugs **hop**

On **top** of a **mop**.

They **hop** on a log.

They **hop** near a frog.

Uh-oh! **Hop**, bug! Don't **stop**!

Read the poem aloud. Direct children to hop when they hear the **op** phonogram.

Extra Support

Materials: index cards

Remind children that **ot** stands for /**ot**/. Write the short **o** phonogram **ot** on the board. On index cards write the consonants **h, p, c, g,** and **d**. Have children place a consonant at the beginning of the phonogram and blend the sounds to say the word.

113

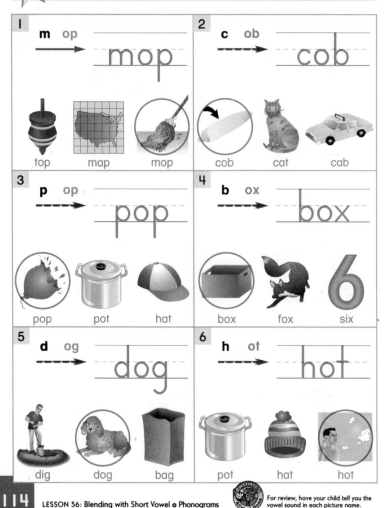

Trace the line as you blend the sounds together to say the word.
Print the word on the line. Then circle the picture it names.

1   m op
mop
top   map   mop

2   c ob
cob
cob   cat   cab

3   p op
pop
pop   pot   hat

4   b ox
box
box   fox   six

5   d og
dog
dig   dog   bag

6   h ot
hot
pot   hat   hot

114

LESSON 56: Blending with Short Vowel o Phonograms

For review, have your child tell you the vowel sound in each picture name.

114

Objectives
- To blend onsets and rimes
- To use phonograms to read short **o** words
- To build short **o** words

Warming Up

Reviewing Short i Words

Say the following sentences:

Can the ant **win** the race?

Bugs have **six** legs.

After each sentence, have children name the word with the short **i** sound. Direct a volunteer to write the word on the board. Ask other children to say rhyming words (e.g., **fin** and **mix**).

Teaching the Lesson

Phonemic Awareness: Blend Onsets and Rimes

Materials: puppet

Tell children they can blend word parts to say a word. Move a puppet from left to right as you blend /t/-/op/ to say **top**. Have children repeat. Continue with /h/-/op/ **hop**, /n/-/ot/ **not**, /d/-/og/ **dog**, /g/-/ot/ **got**.

Phonograms

- On the board, write **ot** and read the phonogram aloud. Add a **p** to the **ot**, leaving a space between word parts. Tell children you will blend the two word parts to read a word. Slide a finger from left to right as you say /p/-/ot/ and then **pot**.
- Ask a volunteer to circle the word part **ot**. Tell children that other words can be made with this word part. Replace **p** with **h** and have children blend /h/ with /ot/ and read the new word, **hot**.
- Continue building words by replacing the initial consonant with **c, d, g, l,** and **n**.

Trace the line as you blend the sounds together to say the word. Then print the word under the picture it names.

p	ot		c	ap		f	ox
s	ix		l	og		c	ot
t	op		h	op		c	at

1	2	3
six	hop	log
4	5	6
cot	top	cap
7	8	9
fox	pot	cat

LESSON 57: Blending with Phonograms

115

UNIVERSAL ACCESS
Meeting Individual Needs

Auditory • Visual

On the board draw crossword puzzle frames with three connected boxes going down and three going across. Write **o** in the middle box. Direct volunteers to fill in the other boxes with consonants that will form rhyming words. Have partners make and complete their own puzzle boxes.

Visual • Tactile

Materials: Punchout Letter Cards for **c, d, h, l, p, t**; phonogram cards for **op, ot, ob, og**

Have children working in pairs take turns choosing a letter card and a phonogram card and blending the sounds into words. Tell children to record the real words that they form and then compare words with classmates.

Extra Support

Tell children to listen for words with short **o** as in **box**. Direct children to follow your commands as you blend the words.

/h/-/op/ up and down.

Spin like a /t/-/op/.

/j/-/og/ in place.

Say each word part. Say the name of each picture. Print the word on the line. Then add your own rhyming word and picture.

_op	_ot	_ock
1 pop	4 cot	7 sock
2 hop	5 hot	8 lock
3 Accept any answers that will form new words.	6 Accept any answers that will form new words.	9 Accept any answers that will form new words.

LESSON 57: Word Building with Short Vowel **o** Phonograms

Read any two words. Have your child tell whether or not the words rhyme.

Practicing the Skill

• Read aloud the directions on page 115, and help children identify all the pictures. Remind children to trace the arrow to help them blend and say the words. Do the first item together. Then have children complete the page.

• Read the directions on page 116. Help children identify the pictures on the page. Do the first item together. Then have children complete the page.

Curriculum Connections

Spelling Connection
Read aloud each word and sentence below. Then call on volunteers to spell the word or print it on the board.

cob I like to eat corn on the **cob**.

mop Please **mop** up the mess.

log Bugs live under the **log**.

ox The **ox** can pull the plow.

rod Bring your fishing **rod**.

Theme Activity: Language Arts/Art
Materials: **Unit 3 Classroom Poster**, drawing paper, crayons

• Together recite the poem "Bugs." Copy the second stanza on the board. Then erase the words **rug** and **sidewalk**.

• Direct children to name different words that have the sound of short **o** to replace the words you have erased. List each response on the board beneath the corresponding blank space.

• Instruct children to copy on drawing paper the two lines completed with their suggested words and to illustrate each. Have children share their work.

Sadlier Reading
Little Books and Big Books

Read *How to Make a Crocodile* (fiction) for more practice with short **o**.

English Language Learners/ESL
Materials: Sadlier Phonics Picture Cards for **box, doll, log, ox, pot, top, block**

Display the picture cards and help children name each picture. Then write **op** on the board and say: */op/—Which picture name ends with the same sound?* As children say **top**, say: *So we add /t/ to /op/ to make **top**.* Write a **t** at the beginning of **op**. Continue in a similar fashion with **ot** and **ock**.

Challenge
Materials: Sadlier Phonics Picture Cards for **fox, box, doll, log, pot, top**

Invite children to use the picture cards to help them answer riddles like these:

I begin with /f/ and I end like **box**. Who am I? (**fox**)

I begin like **lip** and I end with /og/. What am I? (**log**)

Special Strategies
For Universal Access activities, see page 77F.

116

Writing Short Vowel o

Objectives
- To blend phonemes in a word
- To recognize short **o** words
- To write short **o** words

Warming Up

Reviewing Short a, i, and o

Materials: Punchout Letter Cards

Give groups of children nine cards: **a, i, o,** and six consonants. Have the groups use the letters to spell as many three-letter words as possible. Instruct children to practice blending sounds to say each word.

Teaching the Lesson

Phonemic Awareness: Blend Phonemes in a Word

Remind children that they can blend sounds to say a word. Together sing the words below to the tune of "Are You Sleeping?"

Here are three sounds: (repeat)

/h/-/o/-/p/, /h/-/o/-/p/.

Blend the sounds together. (repeat)

Make a word. (repeat)

Repeat with other short **o** words.

Sound to Symbol

Materials: Punchout Letter Cards

- Remind children that they can blend sounds of letters or word parts to read words. Ask children to take out the letters **l, o,** and **g,** then say and blend the sounds to read the word **log**. Repeat for other short **o** words.
- On the board, print the following:

   Where is the bug?

   Is it under a glo, **(log)**

   Or on top of the odg? **(dog)**

   Is it in the black tpo, **(pot)**

   Or under the toc? **(cot)**

Have children working in pairs use letter cards to unscramble the short **o** words.

117

Circle the word that names each picture.

1	2	3
(hop) mop hip	log lock (block)	ox fix (fox)
4	5	6
pot (pond) pan	pit (pot) pat	(stop) top tip
7	8	9
(top) tap pot	rock sick (sock)	log (dog) dig
10	11	12
mop (pop) pin	(lock) lick sock	map top (mop)

LESSON 58: Practicing Short Vowel o   **117**

UNIVERSAL ACCESS
Meeting Individual Needs

Auditory • Kinesthetic
Materials: beanbag, music

Direct children to stand in a circle. Play music as they pass a beanbag. Stop the music, and instruct the child holding the beanbag to say a short **o** word. Continue the process.

Auditory • Kinesthetic
Materials: list of short **a, i, o** words

Have children line up for a spelling bee. Give players one-syllable short **a, i,** or **o** words to print on the board. If the word is spelled correctly, have the child go to the end of the line for another turn. If not, have the child sit near you and help call out words from the list.

Extra Support
Materials: word cards

Point out the /**o**/ in **hop, mom,** and **cot.** Give pairs of children nine word cards, three for short **o**. Have them sort and read the short **o** words.

☆ Circle the name of the picture and print it on the line.

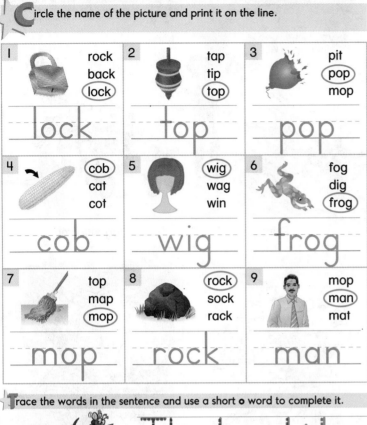

1	rock back **(lock)**	2	tap tip **(top)**	3	pit **(pop)** mop

lock   top   pop

4	**(cob)** cat cot	5	**(wig)** wag win	6	fog dig **(frog)**

cob   wig   frog

7	top map **(mop)**	8	**(rock)** sock rack	9	mop **(man)** mat

mop   rock   man

☆ Trace the words in the sentence and use a short **o** word to complete it.

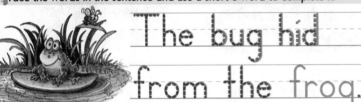

The bug hid from the frog.

118   LESSON 58: Writing Short Vowel **o**

Have your child read the sentence and name the short **o** word in it.

Practicing the Skill

- Read aloud the directions on page 117, and help children identify all the pictures. Do the first item together; then have children complete the page.
- Read aloud directions for page 118, and identify pictures. Point out that this time children must circle and then print the picture names. Go over directions for the bottom of the page. Remind children that a sentence begins with an uppercase letter and ends with a period. Then have children complete the page.

Curriculum Connections

Spelling Connection

Read aloud each word and sentence below. Then call on volunteers to spell each word or print it on the board.

fox   They say a **fox** is sly.
job   Whose **job** is making honey?
nod   If you mean "yes," **nod**.
pot   The lid is on the **pot**.
cot   Do you sleep on a **cot**?

Theme Activity: Physical Education/ Language Arts

Materials: masking tape, index cards

- Use masking tape to outline a simple hopscotch diagram or zigzag path. Make each square large enough to contain several index cards.
- Ask children to name short **o** words. List the words on the board so that children can copy them onto index cards and tape the cards along the path.
- Direct children to hop like a bug along the path, reading each short **o** word as they land on it.

English Language Learners/ESL

Do a quick oral check of children's proficiency with vocabulary before having them complete the lesson. Have them turn to page 117 and say: *Point to the [name a picture]. Point to the [name another picture].* If they have difficulty naming a picture, say its name as you point to it, and have children repeat. Come back to the picture again later on. Continue in this manner with the pictures on page 118.

Challenge

Materials: pictures of bugs, reference materials

Show children pictures of bugs such as mosquitoes, spiders, and dragonflies in pond environments. Have children look at reference materials about bugs and ponds and list words that might describe the bugs and their environment. Tell them to underline all the short **o** words in their lists.

Special Strategies

For Universal Access activities, see page 77F.

Observational Assessment

*As children prepare the cards for the Theme Activity, note whether any have difficulty writing short **o** words.*

118

Short Vowel o
Decodable Reader

Objectives

- To read short **o** words and high-frequency words in context
- To read the story fluently
- To summarize

Introducing the Story Words

Short o Decodable Words Remind children that the sound of short **o** is /**o**/. On the board, write **jog** and explain that it has the short **o** sound. Model how to read the word by blending /**j**/-/**o**/-/**g**/. On the board write **not**, **log**, **dog**, and **mop**. Ask children to read the words by blending the sounds of the letters.

High-Frequency Words On the board, write the words **with**, **me**, **do**, **walk**, **by**, **a**, **funny**, **stop**, and **run**. Read the words with children. Direct them to copy each word on a card and use the cards as flashcards with a partner.

Reading the Book

Reading Together Have children remove pages 119 and 120, and show them how to cut and fold the pages into a book. Read aloud the title, "Jog with Me." Have children follow in their books as you read the story.

Responding Ask children how they would feel if they had been the bugs in the story.

Reading for Fluency Have children track the print as you read. Then have them read each page with a partner. Finally, have children read the story independently.

Observational Assessment

*Notice whether children are able to decode the short **o** words and read the story fluently.*

119

Your child has read this book in school. Ask him or her to read it to you. Then see if he or she ca spot all of the short **o** words in the story.

Name

Jog with Me

8   Run!   Jog with me.

6   Stop! Stop! Stop!   Jog by a big log.   3

Directions: Cut and fold the book. Then read the story. Tell what happens to the bugs in the book.

LESSON 59: Short Vowel **o** Decodable Reader
Comprehension: Summarizing

119

UNIVERSAL ACCESS
Meeting Individual Needs

Visual
Materials: paper, crayons

Write the high-frequency words from the story on a chart. Direct children to use a crayon to write a word and to outline it twice in different colors to create "rainbow words." Ask children to use the word in a sentence.

Auditory • Kinesthetic
Materials: construction paper

Write the words **not**, **dog**, **mop**, **log**, **jog** on pieces of construction paper. Also write some words with short **a** and short **i**. Tack up the words around the classroom. Direct children to jog to each word that has the short **o** sound, to touch the word, and to read the word aloud.

Extra Support

Write **not**, **dog**, **mop**, **log**, and **jog** on a chart. Remind children that each word has the short **o** sound. Ask them to read the words by blending the sounds of the letters. Highlight each correctly read word. Have children practice until all words are read correctly.

2   Do not walk.   Do not jog.   7

4   Jog by a funny dog.   Jog by a pig with a mop.   5

120

LESSON 59: Short Vowel o Decodable Reader
Comprehension: Summarizing

Comprehension Strategy

Summarizing Explain to children that you can keep track of story events by asking yourself what has happened so far. After reading a story, you can also sum up the whole story. Ask children to tell in a few words what happened in "Jog with Me." Have them draw pictures to show the story's main events.

Phonics and Decoding

Learning About Short o *Materials:* index cards

On the board write these story words: **jog**, **mop**. Read them aloud. Tell children that both words have the short **o** sound. Show a variety of word cards, some with short **o** words (**pop**, **box**, **top**) and some with short **a** (**cat**, **map**, **pal**) or short **i** (**pin**, **mitt**, **wig**). Tell children to read each word aloud and jog in place if it has the short **o** sound.

Word Building *Materials:* paper plates, metal fastener, paper clip

Divide a paper plate into five sections. Write one of these letters in each section: **d**, **f**, **h**, **j**, **l**. Poke a fastener through the middle of the plate and then attach a paper clip to the fastener so that it acts as a spinner. On the board write the phonogram **og**. Model for children how to spin the spinner. In front of the phonogram, write the letter that the paper clip points to. Blend and read the word. Have volunteers spin the spinner and do the same.

Curriculum Connections

Writing and Sharing On the board write the title, "Hop with Me." Read it aloud. Direct partners to work together to replace **jog** with **hop** and write a variation on the story "Jog with Me." Have partners read their completed stories to the class.

Sadlier Reading
Little Books and Big Books

Read *Stop by a Pond* (nonfiction) for more practice with short **o**.

English Language Learners/ESL
Use the *Decodable Reader* as an opportunity to review movement words with children. Play a Simon Says game with commands such as **hop**, **walk**, **jog**, **run**, **skip**, **bend**, **stretch**. If necessary, say each word and model the movement for children before beginning the game.

Challenge
Have children work in pairs to write a list of rules that begin with **Do not**. Have them underline all the short **o** words on the list. Then have them choose one rule with a short **o** word in it and illustrate it. Ask the pairs to share their illustrated rule with the class.

Special Strategies
For Universal Access activities, see page 77F.

Short Vowel o in Context

Objectives
- To match words
- To complete sentences by writing **o** words
- To recognize short **o** words in context

Warming Up

Reviewing Short i Words

Pose riddles for which the answers are short **i** words. For example:

This helps a fish move. It begins with /**f**/. (**fin**)

When you run a race, you hope to do this. It begins with /**w**/. (**win**)

This farm animal makes an "oink" sound. It begins with /**p**/. (**pig**)

Teaching the Lesson

Phonemic Awareness: Match Words

Materials: **Sadlier Phonics Picture Cards** for **fox, doll, pot, ox**

Display the cards on the chalk ledge, and name each picture. Then ask children to point to the appropriate picture card when they hear the picture name in a sentence. Use a sentence like this: *My **doll** has brown eyes.*

Phonics in Context

Materials: pen, box, block

Place a pen on top of a box. Write the following on the board: The pen is _____. Next to the sentence write these phrases: on the log, on the box, on the doll. Then read the sentence three times, each time filling in the blank with one of the choices. Circle the phrase "on the box," and tell children that it best describes what they are seeing. Then place the pen on a block and write the following on the board: The pen is ____. Repeat the process with these phrases: on the dog, on the lock, on the block.

121

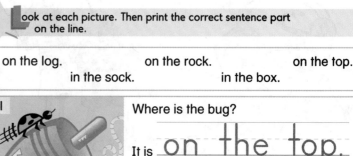
Look at each picture. Then print the correct sentence part on the line.

| on the log. | on the rock. | on the top. |
| in the sock. | in the box. | |

1 — Where is the bug?
It is on the top.

2 — Where is the bug?
It is in the box.

3 — Where is the bug?
It is on the rock.

4 — Where is the bug?
It is on the log.

5 — Where is the bug?
It is in the sock.

LESSON 60: Short Vowel o in Sentences   **121**

UNIVERSAL ACCESS
Meeting Individual Needs

Visual • Kinesthetic

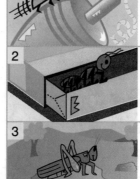

Materials: slips of paper, container

Print on slips of paper short **o** words, such as **box, doll, hop, mop, jog, dog,** and **top.** Direct volunteers to choose a slip from the container and pantomime the word. Have the class try to guess the word.

Auditory • Kinesthetic

Direct children to **pop** up when they hear you say a short **o** word. Tell this story:

A big bug flew by. It landed **on** Lin's head. "Go away!" said Lin. It flew to Bud's **sock.** "Scram," said Bud. It buzzed to Jed's cup and fell in with a **plop.** It **got** out and flew to a flower to rest **on top.**

Extra Support

Review the short **o** sound in **pond.** Share a finger play with children:

A little bug in a **pond** am I,

Hop! Hop! Hop!

See me **hop** up so high.

Hop! Hop! Hop!

Listen as the story is read aloud. Look at the picture. Number the sentences at the bottom to show the correct order.

POP'S

Hop, Bug, Hop!

Hop, Bug, hop!
1 Hop past Pop.
2 Hop to the blocks.
3 Hop in the box.
4 Hop over the dog.
5 Hop up on the log.

Stop, Bug, stop!
Don't hop in the pond.

__4__ The bug hops over the dog.

__2__ The bug hops to the blocks.

__1__ The bug hops past Pop.

__5__ The bug hops up on the log.

__3__ The bug hops in the box.

122 LESSON 60: Short Vowel o in Context
Comprehension: Sequencing

Read the story aloud. Stop before the last word in each line to let your child say the short o word.

Practicing the Skill

● Read aloud the directions on page 121. Ask children to repeat after you: *Where is the bug?* and the response phrases at the top of the page. Model the first item for children, pointing out why "**on** the **top**" is the correct answer. Then have them complete the page.

● Read aloud the poem on page 122, instructing the class to join in with you. Direct children to trace the grasshopper's route in the picture as you recite the poem again. Go over the directions, and have volunteers read aloud the sentences below the poem. Together identify the sentence that should be marked number 1. Then have children complete the page.

Curriculum Connections

Spelling Connection
Materials: Punchout Letter Cards

Read aloud each word and sentence below. Then call on volunteers to spell the word aloud or use letter cards to spell it.

Don **Don** saw a bug at the pond.

jog Let's **jog** down the trail.

top There's a bug on **top** of your head.

rot Fruit may **rot** in the sun.

hog The **hog** is in the pen.

Computer Connection
Have children explore short vowel sounds in JumpStart Phonics (Knowledge Adventure). Use the Read 'n' Respond feature to help children reinforce short vowel sounds through on screen dialogues with characters.

English Language Learners/ESL
Materials: sentence strips

Copy the phrases and sentences in the lesson onto sentence strips for children to use. Children can arrange and rearrange their answers before committing pencil to paper. Have children read aloud their sentences. Provide assistance as needed, and check their answers before they write in their books.

Challenge
Brainstorm with children a list of things bugs do. Then direct children to write and illustrate a story about a day in the life of a bug. Have children share their work and point out any short o words.

Special Strategies
For Universal Access activities, see page 77F.

Observational Assessment

Note whether children can easily distinguish the short o sound from other vowel sounds.

122

Assessing Short Vowel o
Reviewing Short Vowels a, i, and o

Objectives
- To identify and complete words with short **o**
- To review short **a**, **i**, and **o** words

Warming Up

Reviewing Final Consonants

Materials: index cards, pocket chart

Print these names on cards: **Dan**, **Deb**, **Jill**, **Tom**, **Peg**, **Sid**. Place the cards in a pocket chart. Ask the questions below, and have children answer them by choosing the name card that ends with the same consonant sound as the last word in the question.

Who caught the **bug**? (**Peg**)

Who dropped the **pen**? (**Dan**)

Who did the **job**? (**Deb**)

Who hopped out of **bed**? (**Sid**)

Who rang the **bell**? (**Jill**)

Who likes to **swim**? (**Tom**)

Teaching the Lesson

Short Vowel o

Materials: **Sadlier Phonics Picture Cards** for **ham**, **ox**, **hill**, **six**, **log**, **top**

Remind children that **dot** and **nod** have the short **o** sound. Show the picture cards one at a time, and call on a child to name the picture. If the name has the short **o** sound, the child writes **o** on the board.

Short Vowels a, i, and o

Say **tan**, write it on the board, and tell children this word has the short **a** sound. Review short **i** and **o** in a similar manner using the words **pin** and **cot**. Then write **bat** on the board, and call on a volunteer to read the word. Replace **t** with **d**, and have children read the new word. Continue by changing one sound at a time to form **bag**, **big**, **pig**, **pit**, **pot**, **not**, **nod**.

123

Say the name of each picture. Print **o** on the line to complete the picture name if it has the short **o** sound.

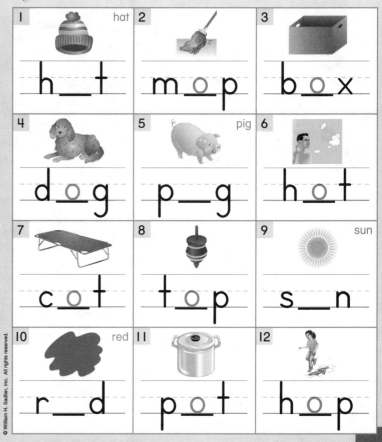

LESSON 61: Assessing Short Vowel o **123**

U N I V E R S A L   A C C E S S
Reteaching Activities

Activity 1

Materials: **Sadlier Phonics Picture Cards** for **log, ox, pot, top, ant, van, six, bib**; a box

Remind children that the short **o** sound is the sound they hear in **box**. Place the box at the front of the room and give each child a picture card. Have children come up one at a time, stand beside the box, and name the picture on their picture cards. If the picture has the short **o** sound, children put it in the box. If the picture has a different vowel sound, they place the card beside the box.

Activity 2

Materials: index cards; pocket chart; Punchout Letter Cards **a, i, o**

Review with children that **can** has the short **a** sound, **sit** the short **i** sound, and **hop** the short **o** sound. On index cards, print consonant combinations that become words when short vowels **a**, **i**, and **o** are inserted in the middle. Use combinations such as **b_g, f_x, h_t, m_ss, t_p, p_t**. Place the cards in a pocket chart. Give children the letter cards, and have them form words. Have children list the words they form.

Read the words in the box. Color the picture each word names.

fox	log	rock	hat
pond	man	fin	frog

124

LESSON 61: Reviewing Short Vowels a, i, o

Help your child point out pictures of short o words on the page and tell a story about the scene.

Help children identify the pictures on page 123. Read aloud the directions, and ask a volunteer to explain how he or she knows whether or not to complete the picture name in the first item. Have children complete the page on their own.

Cumulative Review

Point out the Remember logo on page 124, and tell children that the elephant does not want them to forget short **a**, **i**, and **o**. Read aloud the directions. Point to the word **fox**, and help children read the word. Ask a volunteer to point to the picture of the fox. Then have children complete the page.

Observational Assessment   Observe children as they complete the pages and during oral reading activities throughout the day. Note which children confuse words with short vowel **a**, **i**, or **o**.

Dictation   Tell children you will say some short **a** words. Have them write the short **a** words as you dictate them. Say these words: **man**, **cat**, **cab**, **tag**, **fan**. Repeat with the short **i** words **win**, **hit**, **lip**, **six**, **did** and the short **o** words **top**, **fox**, **dog**, **doll**, **hot**.

Student Skills Assessment   Use the checklist on Student Edition pages 321–322 to record your observations of the progress of individual children.

Guided Instruction

Skills	Resources
Short vowel **a**	Instruction on pages 79–90 Little Books *Alexander Ant Cools Off; Who Can Run Fast?*
Short vowel **i**	Instruction on pages 93–106 Little Books *All Mixed Up; Look at the Picture*
Short vowel **o**	Instruction on pages 109–122 Little Books *How to Make a Crocodile; Stop by a Pond*
Short vowels **a, i, o**	Phonemic Awareness Activities pages 77H–77I

Assessing Short Vowels a, i, o

Objectives
- To read words with short **a**, **i**, **o**
- To write words with short **a**, **i**, **o**

Warming Up

Reviewing Final Consonants x and zz

Write **fox** and **buzz** on the board. Remind children that the word **fox** ends with the sound /**ks**/ and the word **buzz** ends with the sound /**z**/. Tell children you are going to say some words. Ask them to wave an arm like a fox wagging its tail when they hear a word that ends in the sound /**ks**/, and to buzz like a bee when they hear a word that ends in the sound /**z**/. Say these words: **six**, **ox**, **fuzz**, **mix**, **jazz**, **sax**.

Teaching the Lesson

Short Vowels a, i, o

Materials: **Sadlier Phonics Picture Cards** for **ant**, **lid**, **box**; red crayon

- Say **pot**, and write the word on the board. Tell children that **pot** has the short **o** sound. Erase the **o** and replace it with an **a**. Ask children to name the new short **a** word. (**pat**) Then erase the **a** and replace it with **i**. Ask children to name the new short **i** word. (**pit**)
- Write **short a**, **short i**, and **short o** on the board. Display the picture cards and ask volunteers to match each card to one of the headings. Ask children to name other words with the short vowel sounds. Suggest that they get ideas from pictures and objects in the room and by recalling words they used on earlier phonics pages. Record their words under the headings. Point out words that are almost the same but have different vowels, such as **dig** and **dog**.

 Check-Up Say the name of each picture. Circle the word and print it on the line.

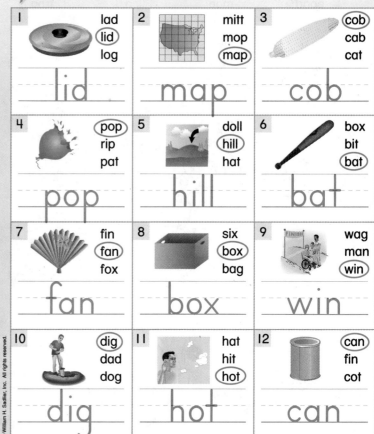

1 lad / **(lid)** / log — **lid**	2 mitt / mop / **(map)** — **map**	3 **(cob)** / cab / cat — **cob**
4 **(pop)** / rip / pat — **pop**	5 doll / **(hill)** / hat — **hill**	6 box / bit / **(bat)** — **bat**
7 fin / **(fan)** / fox — **fan**	8 six / **(box)** / bag — **box**	9 wag / man / **(win)** — **win**
10 **(dig)** / dad / dog — **dig**	11 hat / hit / **(hot)** — **hot**	12 **(can)** / fin / cot — **can**

LESSON 62: Assessing Short Vowels a, i, o **125**

UNIVERSAL ACCESS
Reteaching Activities

Activity 1

Materials: **Sadlier Phonics Picture Cards** for **cap, mask, king, kitten, fox, pot,** and other words with short vowels **a, i, o**

Remind children of the key words **ant, six,** and **top** that they can use to remember the short **a, i,** and **o** sounds. Then turn the picture cards face down. Have children take turns picking a card and looking at the picture without letting the class see it. Have other children ask questions about the picture name's vowel sound and about the pictured object to guess what the card shows.

Activity 2

Materials: construction paper, markers

Write **ant, six,** and **top** on the board. Have volunteers underline the short vowels and say each sound. Then divide the class into three groups: the short **a**'s, short **i**'s, short **o**'s. Have children work in pairs. Have one partner say a word with the short vowel sound of his or her group (e.g., **sand**); have the other partner say a rhyming word (e.g., **hand**). Have partners write and illustrate a rhyme (e.g., **hand** in the **sand**).

Say the name of each picture. Circle the word and print it on the line.

1	mat (circled) / mop / mitt	2	tip / tap / top (circled)	3	dog / wig (circled) / wag
	mat		top		wig
4	cot (circled) / cat / can	5	pot / pin / pan (circled)	6	six (circled) / fox / sat
	cot		pan		six
7	cob / bat / bib (circled)	8	lap / pig / log (circled)	9	top / tag (circled) / wig
	bib		log		tag
10	fix / fox (circled) / fan	11	pig (circled) / bag / pot	12	cap (circled) / lip / cob
	fox		pig		cap

126   LESSON 62: Assessing Short Vowels a, i, o

Review this Check-Up with your child.

Assessing the Skills

Check-Up   Write **tap**, **tip**, and **top** on the board in a column. Ask the questions below, and have a child point to and read the word that answers the question.

Which word means, "a toy you spin"? (**top**)

Which word means, "to hit something lightly"? (**tap**)

Which word means, "the end of your pencil"? (**tip**)

Read aloud the directions on page 125, and have a volunteer tell what children will do first, next, and last. Work through the first item together. Explain that the directions for pages 125 and 126 are the same. Have children complete the pages independently.

Observational Assessment   As children read aloud, note whether they have difficulty blending words with short **a**, **i**, or **o**.

Portfolio Assessment   Have children choose a writing sample to discuss. Ask if they would make any changes now that they have learned about short vowels **a**, **i**, and **o**. Add new notes to children's portfolios. See the Writing Rubrics on page 77C.

Dictation   Tell children you are going to say some short **a** words. Have them write the short **a** words as you dictate them. Say these words: **has, am, at, fan, as**. Continue the activity with short **i** words (e.g., **his, will, fit, dip, nip**) and short **o** words (e.g., **on, not, lot, fog, Tom**).

Student Skills Assessment   Use the checklist on Student Edition pages 321–322 to record your observations of individual children.

Guided Instruction

Skills	Resources
Short vowel **a**	Instruction on pages 79–90 Little Books *Alexander Ant Cools Off*; *Who Can Run Fast*
Short vowel **i**	Instruction on pages 93–106 Little Books *All Mixed Up*; *Look at the Pictures*
Short vowel **o**	Instruction on pages 109–122 Little Books *How to Make a Crocodile*; *Stop by a Pond*
Short vowels **a, i, o**	Phonemic Awareness Activities on pages 77H–77I

Student Pages 127–128

Phonemic Awareness /u/

Objectives
- To divide words into syllables
- To recognize the sound of short **u**
- To discriminate between short **u** words and other words

Warming Up

Reviewing Initial Consonants
Materials: Punchout Letter Cards for consonants studied in Unit 2

Have children take turns flipping the top letter card from a stack placed facedown. Children keep the card if they name a word that begins with the same sound as the consonant shown.

⭐ Teaching the Lesson

Phonemic Awareness: Divide Words into Syllables
Tell children that words are made up of one or more syllables or word parts, with each syllable having one vowel sound. Model clapping out the syllables for these words: **ant**, **beetle**, **cricket**, **bee**, **butterfly**. Say the words again and have children clap with you.

Sound to Symbol
- Say the words **cub**, **fun**, **tub**. Explain that these words have /**u**/ in the middle. Have children say /**u**/ after repeating each word with you. Explain that /**u**/ is the sound for short vowel **u**. Ask children to listen for short **u** words in this sentence: The **bug** sleeps on the **rug** in the **sun**. Have children clap each time they hear a word with /**u**/.
- Print **u** on the board. Explain that **u** can stand for /**u**/. Under the **u**, print **fun**, **rug**, **nut**, **cub**. Read the words aloud. Say the words again with children and ask a volunteer to underline the letter that stands for /**u**/ in each word. Repeat with **cut**, **jug**, **run**, **hug**, **cup**.

Short u

Listen Listen as the page is read aloud. Talk about the short **u** words you hear, such as **bug** and **rug**. Then color the bugs.

A Snug Bug

One little **bug**
In the middle of a **rug**.
Poor little **bug**
Isn't very **snug**.

Tug, bug, tug!
Roll up the **rug**.
Soon you'll be
Cozy and **snug**.

Critical Thinking
Where else would a bug feel cozy and snug?
Possible answers: on a bed; on clothes, etc.

LESSON 63: Phonemic Awareness: /u/ **127**

UNIVERSAL ACCESS
Meeting Individual Needs

Kinesthetic • Visual
Materials: Sadlier Phonics Picture Cards for short **a, i, o, u**

Have children stand in a semicircle. Flash picture cards, one at a time, and have volunteers name them. Tell children to **jump** in place for pictures that have a short **u** sound.

Auditory • Kinesthetic
Ask one child to play the role of **bus** driver. Have that child walk around the classroom, stopping at each desk. Seated children may board the "bus" by paying the "fare" — saying one short **u** word. Each child who gives a correct word lines up behind the bus driver. Continue until all children are aboard the bus.

Extra Support
Materials: Sadlier Phonics Picture Cards for **ant, bib, cup, rug, ten, jet, log, hill, bug, lid, sun**

Place picture cards face down. Have children turn over a card, name the picture, and say if they hear short **u** in the picture name.

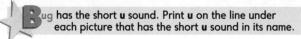

Bug has the short **u** sound. Print **u** on the line under each picture that has the short **u** sound in its name.

1	2	3 six	4 cone
bug	cup	6	
u	u		

5 cage	6	7	8 five
	drum	bun	5
	u	u	

9	10 bat	11	12
truck		rug	cut
u		u	u

13 robe	14	15 jeep	16
	gum		sun
	u		u

128

LESSON 63: Connecting Sound to Symbol /u/ u

Name the pictures on the page. Let your child drum on a table when he or she hears a word with the short u sound.

Practicing the Skill

● Have children follow along as you recite the poem about the **snug bug** on page 127. Then have them identify the short **u** words and color the bugs, as directed. Discuss the Critical Thinking question about other places a bug might feel cozy and **snug**.

● Read aloud the directions on page 128. Point out the **u** under the picture cue at the top right of the page. Have children use it as a guide to draw a **u** in the air with their finger. Together, do items 1, 2, and 3; guide children in printing a **u** beneath the first two pictures. Identify remaining pictures and have children complete the page.

Curriculum Connections

Theme Activity: Multicultural
Materials: picture of monarch butterfly, world map

● Show a picture of a monarch butterfly. Say the word **butterfly** in separate syllables: **but-ter-fly**. Ask children which part of the word has the short **u** sound.

● Explain that monarch butterflies like warm climates. Point out your city and Mexico on a map. Explain that Mexico has warm weather all year. Have volunteers trace a route from your city to Mexico.

● Discuss why a monarch might migrate to Mexico in winter. Then have children draw pictures of **butterflies** enjoying the **sun**. Have children talk about the short **u** words in their pictures.

Portfolio Have children include their butterfly pictures in their portfolios.

English Language Learners/ESL
Materials: a small sweater and a big sweater

Ask children to describe how they feel when they are cold. Then have them tell what they could do to feel **warm** and **cozy** and **snug**. Put on a soft sweater and tell children you feel **warm** and **cozy** and **snug**. Show children the difference between a **big** sweater and a **snug** sweater.

Challenge
Materials: drawing paper, crayons

Remind children that **bug** and **rug** are short **u** words. Tell each child to draw a picture of a bug. Then challenge children to turn their drawings into a scene with pictures of other short **u** words, for example, a **bug** crawling on a **cup** or eating a **bun**. When children have finished, have them name the short **u** words in their drawings.

Special Strategies
For Universal Access activities, see page 77F.

128

Blending with Short Vowel u

Objectives
- To blend phonemes in a word
- To blend short **u** words
- To identify and write short **u** words

Warming Up

Reviewing Medial Consonants
- Say the word **seven**. Tell children /**v**/ is the medial consonant sound in **seven**. Write **seven** on the board and underline the **v**.
- Ask children riddles involving medial consonant sounds. For example:

  I bloom in spring. My middle consonant is **l**. (**tulip**)

  I am a sour, yellow fruit. My middle consonant is **m**. (**lemon**)

Teaching the Lesson

Phonemic Awareness: Blend Phonemes in a Word
Explain that when we say words such as **hum** and **fun**, we blend together the sounds of consonants and vowels. Demonstrate by saying /**h**/-/**u**/-/**m**/ and then the whole word, **hum**. Have children practice blending with you. Then repeat the process with **fun**, **cut** and **dug**.

Blending
- Tell children that we can blend the sounds of letters together to read words. Write **mud** on the board, leaving space between letters. Aloud, blend /**m**/-/**u**/-/**d**/ as you trace with your finger under the word, letter by letter.
- Trace along with your finger again and have children blend /**m**/-/**u**/-/**d**/. Together, say the whole word, **mud**.
- Repeat the process for two more short **u** words, such as **nut** and **bus**.

Trace the line as you blend the sounds together to say the word. Then circle the picture it names.

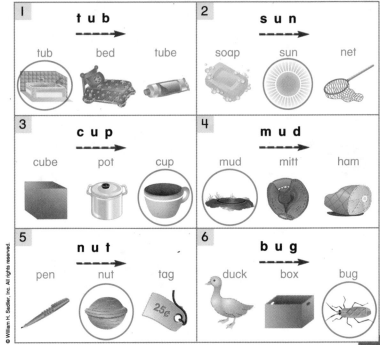

1 **t u b**	2 **s u n**
tub bed tube	soap sun net
3 **c u p**	4 **m u d**
cube pot cup	mud mitt ham
5 **n u t**	6 **b u g**
pen nut tag	duck box bug

LESSON 64: Blending with Short Vowel **u** 129

U N I V E R S A L   A C C E S S
Meeting Individual Needs

Auditory • Kinesthetic
Materials: small paper cups, pennies or other tokens

Have students listen as you blend short **u** words, such as **bud, mud, buzz, nut, sun, tub**. Tell them to put a token in the cup for each sound they hear in each word.

Auditory • Kinesthetic
Materials: index cards; Sadlier Phonics Picture Cards for **bug, cub, cup, rug, sun**

Write the words **bug, cub, cup, rug** and **sun** on index cards. Display the picture and word cards. Ask volunteers to pick a word card, blend the sounds to say the word, and find the matching picture.

Extra Support
Say /**b**/-/**u**/-/**s**/, holding up a finger for each sound. Ask children how many sounds they heard and what word the sounds make when put together. Then write **bus** on the board. Help children say the sound of each letter /**b**/-/**u**/-/**s**/ and then the whole word **bus**. Continue with **cup, hug, up**.

Trace the line as you blend the sounds together to say the word.
Then print the word that names each picture.

1 h u t
    t u g
    __hut__
	2 g u m
	    b u n
	    __gum__

3 c u p
    b u s
    __bus__
	4 b u d
	    j u g
	    __jug__

5 r u n
    d u g
    __run__
	6 h u m
	    c u b
	    __cub__

130 LESSON 64: Blending with Short Vowel **u**

Say the three sounds in each word, for example, c-u-p. Have your child put a button into a cup for each sound.

● Have children turn to page 129. Ask what they see in the picture at the top and have them identify the short **u** words they used. (**bug, tub, bubbles**)

● Read aloud the directions. Help children identify the pictures. Then model the first item by tracing the arrow with your finger as you blend the sounds in **tub**. Have children circle the correct picture and then complete the page independently.

● Read aloud the directions on page 130 and identify the pictures. Model how to complete the first item. Then have children complete the page.

Curriculum Connections

Spelling Connection

Read aloud each word and sentence below. Ask a volunteer to spell the word aloud. Have another volunteer print the word on the board.

hum	Can you **hum** the tune?
bus	The school **bus** is late.
dug	The dog **dug** the hole.
mug	The milk is in the **mug**.

Theme Activity: Language Arts/Art

Recite the nursery rhyme "Humpty Dumpty." Write the title on the board and have children listen for the short **u** sound in the words **Humpty Dumpty** as you repeat the rhyme. Then recite "Little Miss Muffet." Write **Miss Muffet** and **tuffet** on the board; explain that a tuffet is a stool. Tell children to listen carefully for the sound of short **u** as you repeat the rhyme. Afterward have children draw a picture and write an accompanying sentence for one of these nursery rhymes.

Portfolio Have students add their nursery rhyme pictures to their portfolios.

English Language Learners/ESL

Materials: Sadlier Phonics Picture Cards for **cub, cup, rug, sun, umbrella, duck, bunny, tub, brush,** and **drum**; large index cards; colored pencils

Review the names of the picture cards with children, and remind them they all have the /**u**/ sound. Help children locate additional short **u** words in the lessons in the short **u** section, and have them draw pictures on the index cards. These cards can be used as a vocabulary bank of words to be practiced each day with a partner until easily identified.

Special Strategies

For Universal Access activities, see page 77F.

Challenge

Materials: drawing paper, crayons, pencils

Have students retell the story of "The Three Little Pigs" and help them recall these words: "I'll huff, and I'll puff, and I'll blow your house down." Point out that **huff** and **puff** rhyme and that both words have the short **u** sound. Have children draw a picture of the wolf and write his famous lines in a speech bubble.

Short Vowel **u** Phonograms

Objectives

- To substitute initial sounds
- To recognize short **u** phonograms
- To blend initial consonants with short **u** phonograms

Warming Up

Reviewing Final Consonants

Materials: Punchout Letter Cards

Hold up a letter card. Say a sentence, and tell children to listen for and then say the words with the same final sound. For example:

d Bugs are **good** for us all.

n Ants **clean** up messes.

g Watch the **frog** catch a **bug**.

Teaching the Lesson

Phonemic Awareness: Substitute Initial Sounds

Say the word **hut** and then /h/-/ut/. Point out that the beginning sound in **hut** is /h/; the rest of the word is /ut/. Tell children that by changing the beginning sound in a word, we can sometimes make a new word. Have children repeat after you as you say: /h/-/ut/ **hut** and /n/-/ut/ **nut.** Point out that you changed the /h/ to a /n/ to make a new word. Repeat the procedure, changing the beginning sound in **hum** to make **sum.**

Phonograms

Materials: a cup

- On the board write the phonogram **ug.** Under it write **tug** and **jug.** Read aloud the phonogram and the words. Point out that **tug** and **jug** end with the phonogram **ug.** Ask volunteers to circle **ug** in both words and say /ug/.
- Write **up** on the board and display a cup. Explain that to write **cup** you need to add a letter that stands for /k/ to the beginning of **up.** Write **c** in front of **cup** and read the word. Have children repeat after you.
- Repeat this process for the **ub** phonogram and the words **cub, tub, sub.**

131

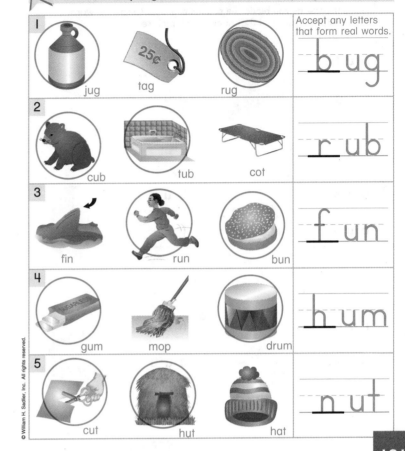

Say the name of each picture. In each row, circle two pictures that have rhyming names. Then make a new rhyming word.

Accept any letters that form real words.

1	jug	tag	rug	b u g
2	cub	tub	cot	r u b
3	fin	run	bun	f u n
4	gum	mop	drum	h u m
5	cut	hut	hat	n u t

LESSON 65: Short Vowel **u** Phonograms **131**

UNIVERSAL ACCESS
Meeting Individual Needs

Visual • Auditory

Materials: Sadlier Phonics Picture Cards for **bug, cub, cup, duck, rug, sun, tub;** other picture cards

Show children each picture card. Tell them to make a humming sound when they see a card whose name has the short **u** sound.

Kinesthetic • Auditory

Materials: yellow paper, scissors

Have each child cut out a yellow sun. Ask them to listen as you say a list of words (e.g., **sun, hop, pet, pup, man, jug**). Tell children to make the sun rise for short **u** words and set for words with other vowel sounds.

Extra Support

Have children use letter cards to make the phonogram **ug.** Read it aloud together. Help children add an **m** to the beginning. Read **mug** together. Continue making and reading other words with **ug.** Repeat with **un** and **ub.**

Trace the line as you blend the sounds together to say the word. Then print the word on the line.

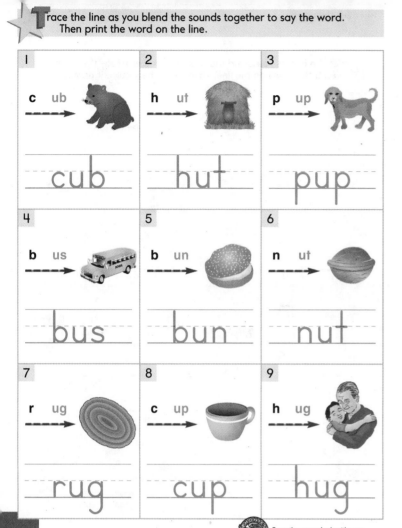

1 c ub	2 h ut	3 p up
cub	hut	pup
4 b us	5 b un	6 n ut
bus	bun	nut
7 r ug	8 c up	9 h ug
rug	cup	hug

132

LESSON 65: Blending with Short Vowel u Phonograms

Practicing the Skill

● Read aloud the directions on page 131, and identify the pictures together. Do the first item with the class. Then have children complete the page.

● Go over the directions on page 132. Model how to blend the initial consonant sound with the phonogram to read **cub**. Have children write the word on the line. Then have them complete the page.

Curriculum Connections

Spelling Connection
Materials: Punchout Letter Cards

Read aloud each word and sample sentence below. Call on a volunteer to use letter cards to spell the word. Ask another volunteer to print the word on the board.

rug	I am as snug as a bug in a **rug**.
tub	Wash the pup in the **tub**.
cup	Would you like a **cup** of soup?
mud	Do not step in the **mud**!

Theme Activity: Language Arts/Art
Materials: drawing paper, crayons

● Repeat the saying "snug as a bug in a rug." Then write "____ as a bug in/on a _____" on a sentence strip. Have children make new "buggy" comparisons using short **u** words. Start them off with examples such as these:

    bumpy as a bug on a **bus**

    funny as a bug on a **pup**

    jumpy as a bug in a **cup**

● Tell children to draw pictures to illustrate one of the expressions. Help them print the expression beneath the picture. Then have children underline the short **u** words.

Portfolio   Direct children to include their captioned pictures in their portfolios.

English Language Learners/ESL
To help students produce rhyming short **u** words, give them practice in hearing rhyming short **u** words. Tell them that **cut** and **nut** rhyme because they have the same ending sounds /u/-/t/. Have children listen as you say a series of words. Then say each word in a given series one by one, and have children repeat after you. Say the following words: **hug, jug, bug; tub, cub, rub; sun, fun, bun; gum, drum, hum; nut, hut, cut**. Use Total Physical Response to demonstrate the meaning of some of the words, and display as many of the objects referred to as possible.

Challenge
Have children work in pairs to write and illustrate a comic strip featuring a friendly bug who brings good luck wherever it goes. Have children include and underline short **u** words in their comic strips.

Special Strategies
For Universal Access activities, see page 77F.

Observational Assessment

Notice whether students can say a new word by blending an initial consonant with a phonogram.

Short Vowel u

Objectives
- To add initial sounds
- To use phonograms to read short **u** words
- To build short **u** words

Warming Up

Reviewing Rhyming Words

Materials: Sadlier Phonics Picture Cards for **fan, van, bat, hat, block, lock, fox, ox, king, ring**

Shuffle and display the picture cards. Tell children to say the picture names and sort the cards according to their ending sounds. Ask children to name other rhyming words.

Teaching the Lesson

Phonemic Awareness: Add Initial Sounds

Say the word **an** and have children repeat after you. Tell children that they can make a new word by adding /**f**/ to the beginning of **an**, such as /**f**-**an**, **fan**. Ask children to add /**m**/, /**p**/, /**r**/, /**v**/ to **an** to make new words (**man, pan, ran, van**).

Phonograms

- Write the word **fun** on the board, leaving a space between **f** and **un**. Model how to read the word. Point to the letter **f** and say /**f**/. Slide your finger under **un** and say /**un**/. Then blend the two parts /**f**-/**un**/. Ask a volunteer to draw an arrow beneath the parts from left to right as he or she blends the two parts /**f**-/**un**/.
- Write **run** beneath **fun** and read the word. Point out that both **run** and **fun** have the same phonogram—**un**. Ask a volunteer to read the word **run** in the same way the last volunteer read the word **fun**. Write **bun** under **run** and repeat the process again.
- Follow the same procedure for the phonogram **ut** using **nut, cut, hut**.

Trace the line as you blend the sounds together to say the word. Print the word on the line. Then circle the picture it names.

1. b ud → bud
   dad   bud   bat

2. p ot → pot
   hut   mop   pot

3. m an → man
   fan   man   mud

4. j ug → jug
   jug   jet   jar

5. s un → sun
   fin   bun   sun

6. l id → lid
   lid   dig   red

LESSON 66: Blending with Phonograms   **133**

UNIVERSAL ACCESS
Meeting Individual Needs

Auditory • Kinesthetic
Say **hug**: /**h**/-/**ug**/. Direct children to open their arms on the beginning sound and fold them into a self-hug on the short **u** phonogram. Say a list of short **u** words. Call on volunteers to repeat the hug motion as they say the beginning sound and short **u** phonogram for each word.

Visual • Kinesthetic
Materials: Sadlier Phonics Picture Cards for **duck, bus, rug, tub**; modeling clay

Have children choose a picture card and then stretch the clay as he or she names the picture by saying each phoneme. Then bring the clay together as he or she blends the parts and says the word.

Extra Support
Write **an, ug, id,** and **un** on the board. Have children use their punchout letter cards to add a consonant to the beginning of each phonogram and blend the words they made. Help children distinguish real words from nonsense words.

Say each word part. Say the name of each picture. Print the word on the line. Then add your own rhyming word and picture.

_ug	_un	_ut
1	4	7
tug	bun	cut
2	5	8
hug	run	hut
3 Accept any letters that form real words.	6 Accept any letters that form real words.	9 Accept any letters that form real words.

134

LESSON 66: Word Building with Short Vowel **u** Phonograms

Cut out the boxes and turn them over. With your child, take turns choosing two pictures. If the two picture names rhyme, read them aloud.

Practicing the Skill

● Read the directions on page 133 together, and help children identify the pictures. Go over the first item; then have them complete the page.

● Read aloud the directions on page 134, and identify the pictures. Go over the first column by modeling the process of finding and writing a word that rhymes with **tug** and **hug**. Then have children complete the page.

Curriculum Connections

Spelling Connection
Read aloud each word and sentence below. Then call on a volunteer to spell the word aloud.

bus   The **bus** is here.

fun   School is **fun**.

cut   **Cut** the paper in half.

jug   Bring me the **jug**.

Theme Activity: Language Arts

● Retell for children Aesop's fable "The Grasshopper and the Ant." Talk about the industrious ant who works hard to store food for the winter and the lazy grasshopper who plays all day.

● Provide a list of short **u** words that children can use to write about the grasshopper and the ant. Include words such as **fuss**, **hum**, **run**, **rush**, **must**, **nuts**, **bugs**, **summer**, **mud**, **fun**, **but**, and **up**.

● Have children write sentences about the grasshopper and the ant. Guide children by asking: *What will happen to the grasshopper in winter? What did the grasshopper learn? What will the grasshopper do next summer?* Direct children to print or dictate their sentences. Have them underline all the short **u** words they used.

Portfolio

Have children put their grasshopper stories in their portfolios.

Sadlier Reading
Little Books and Big Books
Read *What Bear Cubs Like to Do* (nonfiction) for more practice with short **u**.

English Language Learners/ESL
Materials: Sadlier Phonics Picture Cards for **bat, pin, box,** and **rug**

Review with children the short vowel sounds they have already learned. Hold up each picture card, ask children to name it and tell what sound they hear in the middle of the word. Ask a child to print the letter for that sound on the board. As you repeat the word, stretch out the beginning and ending sounds and write the corresponding letters around the vowel. Then have children suggest other words that rhyme with that word.

Challenge
Write **Dad, hut, mud, dig, big, bug, jam,** and **lid** on the board, and point out that each of these words is made up of a beginning consonant and a short vowel phonogram. Have groups of students use the word list to brainstorm and then perform a funny dramatic skit. Afterward, have the groups use the words to write sentences about the action in their skits.

Special Strategies
For Universal Access activities, see page 77F.

Writing Short Vowel u

Objectives
- To substitute medial sounds
- To recognize short **u** words
- To write short **u** words

Warming Up

Reviewing Short Vowel Phonograms

Materials: **Sadlier Phonics Picture Cards** for **fan, van, bat, hat, block, lock, fox, ox, king, ring, mix, six**

Display the picture cards. Ask volunteers to sort the words by phonogram. Then write each phonogram on the board and have children generate lists of rhyming words.

Teaching the Lesson

Phonemic Awareness: Substitute Medial Sounds

Tell children they can make new words by changing the middle sound in a word. Model by saying: *If I change the /a/ in* **cap** *to /u/, what word do I make? I make the word /k/-/u/-/p/* **cup**. Tell children to change the middle sound in these words: **pot**—change /o/ to /i/ (**pit**); **fin**—change /i/ to /a/ (**fan**); **bag**—change /a/ to /u/ (**bug**).

Sound to Symbol

Materials: **Sadlier Phonics Picture Cards** for **rug, sun, bug, cup, cub**

Show the **rug** picture card. Say the name slowly: /r/-/u/-/g/. Tell children you are going to write the word by writing the letter that stands for each sound you say. Say /r/ and write **r**, say /u/ and write **u**, say /g/ and write **g**. Then read the word **rug**. Have children write the word on a piece of paper and say **rug**. Repeat using the picture cards for **sun, bug, cup, cub**.

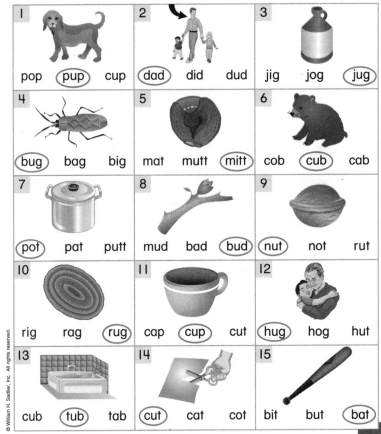

Circle the word that names each picture.

1. pop (pup) cup
2. (dad) did dud
3. jig jog (jug)
4. (bug) bag big
5. mat mutt (mitt)
6. cob (cub) cab
7. (pot) pat putt
8. mud bad (bud)
9. (nut) not rut
10. rig rag (rug)
11. cap (cup) cut
12. (hug) hog hut
13. cub (tub) tab
14. (cut) cat cot
15. bit but (bat)

U N I V E R S A L   A C C E S S
Meeting Individual Needs

Visual • Auditory
Materials: index cards

Have small groups print these short **u** words on separate index cards: **run, cub, bug, tug, jump, pup**. Tell the groups to sort the cards into two categories: animals and actions. Encourage them to add animal and action words with other vowel sounds.

Kinesthetic • Auditory
Divide the class into two teams. Then designate spots in the classroom as first, second, and third base and home plate. A "batter" gets to first base by saying a short **u** word and continues to advance as each new batter reaches first base. Instead of calling "outs," have six batters from each team bat during each inning.

Extra Support
Materials: **Sadlier Phonics Picture Cards** for **bug, rug, cub, tub, bus**

On the board write each picture name, leaving the **u** blank. Review that the **u** in **tug** stands for the short **u** sound. Have volunteers name each picture and fill in the missing **u**.

Circle the name of the picture and print it on the line.

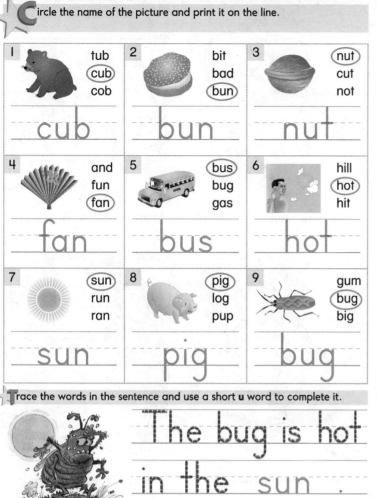

1 tub **(cub)** cob	2 bit bad **(bun)**	3 **(nut)** cut not
cub	**bun**	**nut**
4 and fun **(fan)**	5 **(bus)** bug gas	6 hill **(hot)** hit
fan	**bus**	**hot**
7 **(sun)** run ran	8 **(pig)** log pup	9 gum **(bug)** big
sun	**pig**	**bug**

Trace the words in the sentence and use a short u word to complete it.

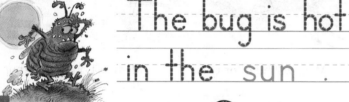

The bug is hot in the sun .

136 LESSON 67: Writing Short Vowel **u**

Point to each picture on the page. Have your child use each picture name in a sentence.

Practicing the Skill

● Read aloud the directions on page 135 and help children identify the pictures. Do the first two items together. Then have children complete the page.

● Read aloud the directions on page 136 and identify the pictures together. Point out that the sentence that they will trace and complete begins with an uppercase letter and ends with a period. Then have children complete the page.

Curriculum Connections

Spelling Connection

Read aloud each word and sample sentence below. Then call on a volunteer to spell each word orally. Ask a second volunteer to print each word on the board.

puff Did the big, bad wolf huff and **puff**?

bud I see a pretty flower **bud**.

fun It is **fun** to play tag.

hug The baby wants a **hug**.

Theme Activity: Science

Materials: photo of a chrysalis, index cards, crayons, envelopes

● Say **butterfly** and point out the short **u** sound. Have children discuss butterflies they've seen. Then read aloud the theme book listed below. Direct children to raise their hands each time they hear a short **u** word.

● Review information about a butterfly's life and display a photo of a chrysalis. Tell each child to make a chrysalis by printing a short **u** word on an index card and drawing the outline of a caterpillar around it. Have children color an envelope to look like the outer covering of a chrysalis and place their caterpillar inside.

Theme Book

Fowler, Allan. *It Could Still Be a Butterfly.* Chicago: Children's Press, 1994. Bright photos of butterflies.

Portfolio

Have children include their chrysalis models in their portfolios.

English Language Learners/ ESL

Preview the theme book, *It Could Still Be a Butterfly,* with children and elicit their prior knowledge about butterflies. Have children describe what they see on the pages and to relate it to their own experiences with nature. Supply English words, as needed, in a natural manner to help the discussion.

Challenge

Remind children of the nursery rhyme that begins "Rub-a-dub-dub, three men in a tub." Have them identify the short **u** words in those opening lines. Tell children to substitute other short **u** words for **tub** and change the rhyming nonsense words to match (e.g., "Rup-a-dup-dup, three men in a cup"). Ask children to write down and illustrate the new versions they made up.

Special Strategies

For Universal Access activities, see page 77F.

136

Short Vowel u
Decodable Reader

Objectives
- To read short **u** words and high-frequency words in context
- To read the story fluently
- To identify the setting

Introducing the Story Words

Short u Decodable Words Remind children that the sound of short **u** is /u/. Write **hug** on the board. Model blending the sounds /h/-/u/-/g/ to read the word. On the board, write **up**, **but**, **Gus**, **cup**, **pup**, **tub**, **cut**, **bus**, and **hum**. Point to a word and ask a volunteer to read it by blending the letter sounds.

High-Frequency Words Write two sets of the words **is**, **a**, **for**, **let**, **the**, **jump**, and **too** on index cards. Display each word, read it, and have children repeat it. Then distribute both sets of cards. Tell children to find a partner with the same card. Direct them to read and spell their cards to the class.

Reading the Book

Reading Together Have children remove pages 137 and 138. Show them how to cut and fold the pages into a book. Read aloud the title, "Gus and Mom." Tell children to look at the picture on page 1 and help them make predictions about the story. Have children follow along in their books as you read aloud.

Responding Revisit children's predictions. Ask them to compare what they thought might happen to the actual events.

Reading for Fluency Have children track the print while you read. Direct children to take turns reading the story to a partner. Finally, have children read the story independently.

Observational Assessment

*Notice whether children are able to decode the short **u** words and read the story fluently.*

Gus is up, but Mom is not!   8

Mom is up, but Gus is not!   1

Mom will hum for Gus.   6

Mom will not let the pup jump on Gus.   3

Directions: Cut and fold the book. Then read the story. Tell where the story happens.

LESSON 68: Short Vowel **u** Decodable Reader
Comprehension: Identifying the Setting   137

UNIVERSAL ACCESS
Meeting Individual Needs

Visual
Materials: word search puzzles

Create a simple word search puzzle with the high-frequency words **is, a, for, the, jump,** and **too.** Duplicate and distribute to children. Ask children to write each word they find.

Visual • Auditory
Write the phonograms **up, ut,** and **us** on the board. Ask children to find words from the story with these phonograms, to read them aloud, and to write them under the correct heading. Then ask children to think of other words with the same phonogram and write them on the board.

Extra Support
Materials: button, paper

Read the short **u** story words with children. Point out that **u** stands for /u/ in the words. Make a chart with the words. Have children toss a button on the chart and read the word it lands on.

Mom will fix a cup for Gus.

2

Mom will hug Gus, too.

7

Mom will fill the tub for Gus.

4

Mom will cut the bus for Gus.

5

LESSON 68: Short Vowel **u** Decodable Reader
Comprehension: Identifying the Setting

Comprehension Strategy

Identifying Setting   Explain to the class that the place where a story takes place is called the *setting*. Point out that the setting can affect details and events of a story. Help children identify the setting of "Gus and Mom."(**home**) Ask children to draw a picture that shows the setting of the story.

Phonics and Decoding

Learning About Short u   *Materials:* construction paper, markers

On the board, write these story words: **cup**, **bus**. Read them aloud. Help children notice that each word has the short **u** sound. Have children print **u** on their papers. Ask them to hold up the letter when they hear a word with /**u**/. Say these words: **up**, **hot**, **run**, **cut**, **tub**, **fill**, **leg**, **fun**. Have children write down and read the short **u** words they hear.

Word Building   Draw a ladder on the board. On the first rung, write **cut**. Direct volunteers to change the first letter to write a new word on the next rung. When children have filled up the ladder, repeat the activity with a new ladder using **bug**.

Curriculum Connections

Writing and Sharing   Direct children to write a continuation of the story. Write this rhyme on the board, and read it aloud:

Gus will help Mom, too.

This is what Gus will do:

Gus will _____.

Ask children to complete the last sentence and write it down. Have volunteers read their endings after the class reads the first two lines of the rhyme.

English Language Learners/ESL
Children may be unfamiliar with the idiom, *to be up*, and the verb, *hum*. Introduce these words by actions. For example, pretend to be sleeping and say: *I am asleep*; then open your eyes, yawn, stretch, stand, and say: *Now I am up*. Have children mimic the actions and repeat the sentences after you. After writing **up** and **hum** on the board, have children locate those words in the *Decodable Reader*.

Challenge
Ask children to write their own stories about a bug. Tell children to use as many short **u** words as possible. The bug can be on a **cup**, on a **bus**, or in a **tub**. Have children read and illustrate their stories.

Special Strategies
For Universal Access activities, see page 77F.

Short Vowel u in Context

Objectives
- To divide sentences into words
- To complete sentences by writing short **u** words
- To recognize short **u** words in context

Warming Up

Reviewing Rhymes
Say the following words and ask children to say a rhyming animal name: **mat** (**cat**); **wig** (**pig**); **log** (**dog**); **luck** (**duck**).

Teaching the Lesson

Phonemic Awareness:
Divide Sentences into Words
Explain that sentences are made up of words. Tell children that the following sentence is made up of four words: *You are my friend.* Demonstrate this by saying each word as you count them with your fingers. Ask children to listen as you say the sentences below. Then have them hold up a finger for each word they hear and then tell how many words were in the sentence.

Look at the bug.

The bug is on the rug.

He runs fast.

Phonics in Context
Write this sentence on the board: I drink milk from a ___. Write the words **fun, pup,** and **cup** next to the sentence. Read aloud the sentence and the word choices. Then read the sentence three times, each time filling in the blank with one of the word choices. Circle the word **cup**, and tell children that it best completes the meaning of the sentence. Now have children complete this sentence: The cat sat on the ___. **cut, mat, sun**

Look at each picture. Circle the word that completes the sentence. Then print it on the line.

1		The ___pup___ naps in the sun.	(pup) / pep / pop
2		"Buzz," ___hums___ the bug.	has / hams / (hums)
3		The pup looks ___up___ at it.	us / (up) / as
4		It bats at the ___bug___ .	bag / beg / (bug)
5		This is not ___fun___ .	fit / (fun) / fat
6		The pup ___runs___ off.	(runs) / suns / buns

LESSON 69: Short Vowel **u** in Sentences   **139**

UNIVERSAL ACCESS
Meeting Individual Needs

Visual • Tactile
Materials: construction paper, glue

Have children use glue to print short **u** words on paper. Have children work in pairs. After the glue dries, tell partners to take turns closing their eyes and trying to identify the words by feeling each glue letter.

Kinesthetic • Visual
Materials: oaktag, scissors, marker

On oaktag strips, write short **u** words, such as **mug, hum,** and **bun,** leaving extra space between letters. Ask children to cut apart each word letter by letter, in a zigzag pattern to make puzzle pieces. Have children put together the word puzzle as they blend the sounds to say the word.

Extra Support
Materials: Sadlier Phonics Picture Cards for **bus, cup, rug, sun, up**

Display the picture cards and ask children to name each picture, spell it, and use it in a sentence. Have children count on their fingers the number of words in each sentence.

Listen as the poem is read aloud. Then use short **u** words to complete the sentences.

A Buggy Lunch

A bug is in the cup.
A bug is on the bun.
A bug is by the pup.
Run, bugs, run.

Run, bugs, run.
Do not munch
on our lunch.

1. A bug is in the ___cup___ .

2. A bug is on the ___bun___ .

3. A bug is by the ___pup___ .

4. Do not ___munch___ on our lunch.

LESSON 69: Short Vowel **u** in Context
Comprehension: Recalling Details

Read the poem with your child. Then ask him or her to circle all of the short **u** words.

Practicing the Skill

● Read the directions on page 139 together. Have children use the pictures to help them decide which word best completes each sentence. Then read the sentences together. Guide volunteers to read the word choices. Complete the first item with children before having them complete the page.

● Read aloud the directions and the poem on page 140. Then read the sentences at the bottom of the page. Tell children to use a short **u** word from the poem to complete each sentence.

Curriculum Connections

Spelling Connection

Read aloud each short **u** word and sample sentence below. Have a volunteer spell the word orally. Have another volunteer print it on the board:

bun Put the ham on the **bun**.

bus Did you miss your **bus**?

cup The **cup** is full.

hug Mom gave me a **hug**.

nut I ate a **nut**.

Theme Activity: Science/Language Arts

● Remind children of the picnic scene pictured on page 140. Have them share good and bad experiences they have had with bugs, such as: being stung or bitten; watching fireflies or butterflies.

● Encourage children to write and illustrate a short story about an experience with bugs. Tell them to circle any short **u** words they use. Have children share their stories with their classmates.

Portfolio

Have children include their bug short stories in their portfolios.

English Language Learners/ESL
Materials: pictures of people on picnics, chart paper, crayons

Display the pictures to help children understand the term **picnic**. Discuss what the picnickers have brought with them. Then lead a group drawing project by drawing a large rectangle on chart paper with blades of grass around it and saying: *This is our picnic tablecloth.* Have children draw food and other items they would bring to a picnic that contain the short **u** sound (**jug, cup, butter, buns, nuts**). Help them label each item.

Challenge
Provide children with a story starter using words with short **u**. For example, you might say, *The **bug** sat in the **sun**.* Ask children to write two or three sentences to finish the story. Have them circle any short **u** words used.

Special Strategies
For Universal Access activities, see page 77F.

Sadlier Reading
Little Books and Big Books
Read *Funny Bugs* (fiction) for more practice with short **u**.

140

Student Pages 141–142

Assessing Short Vowel u
Reviewing Short Vowels a, i, o, and u

Objectives
- To identify and complete words with short **u**
- To review short **a**, **i**, **o**, and **u** words

Warming Up

Reviewing Initial Consonants

On the board write the phonograms listed below. Have children add initial consonants to the phonograms to make rhyming words.

at (bat, cat, fat, hat, mat, sat)

ig (big, dig, jig, pig, rig, wig)

og (bog, dog, fog, hog, log)

un (bun, fun, run, sun)

Teaching the Lesson

Short Vowel u

- Say /**u**/. Have children repeat. Remind children that /**u**/ is the short **u** sound in the word **bug**.
- On the board write the consonant patterns below. Have children print **u** in the blank, then blend the sounds of the letters together to read the word.

m_d   r_n   g_m   b_d
h_m   m_g   b_g   s_n

Short Vowels a, i, o, and u

Write the letters **a**, **i**, **o**, and **u** on the board and remind children of the short vowel sounds that each can stand for. Then write **b_g** on the board four times. Have volunteers add the short vowels **a**, **i**, **o**, and **u** to complete each word. Then have children blend the sounds, say the word, and say another rhyming word with the same short vowel sound. Have children print their words on the board.

Check-Up Say the name of each picture. Print **u** on the line to complete the picture name if it has the short **u** sound.

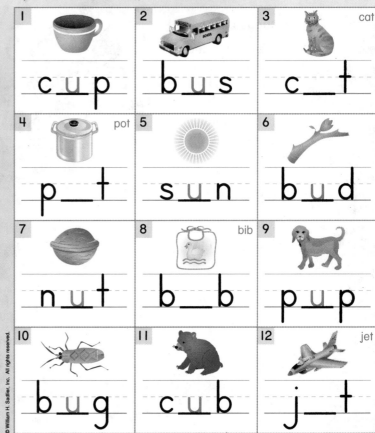

1. c u p
2. b u s
3. c _ t   cat
4. p _ t   pot
5. s u n
6. b u d
7. n u t
8. b _ b   bib
9. p u p
10. b u g
11. c u b
12. j _ t   jet

LESSON 70: Assessing Short Vowel u   **141**

UNIVERSAL ACCESS
Reteaching Activities

Activity 1

Remind children that **jump** is a short vowel **u** word. Have children jump in place when they hear a word that has the short **u** sound. Say **cat, cub, not, run, sit, nut, pop, hum, sun**. Then write the short **u** words on the board, and have children circle the **u** in each one.

Activity 2

Materials: alphabet cookie cutters, clay

Give groups of children sets of cookie cutters and some clay. Have them cut out clay letters and use the letters to spell short vowel words. (If cookie cutters are not available, mold letters by hand.) Have children trace the letters with their fingers as they read the words aloud.

Find the hidden three-letter words. Circle them. Then print the vowels that will complete the words on the lines.

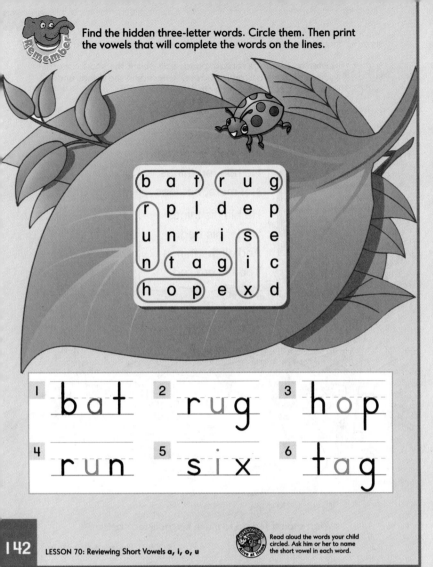

| 1 bat | 2 rug | 3 hop |
| 4 run | 5 six | 6 tag |

LESSON 70: Reviewing Short Vowels a, i, o, u

Read aloud the words your child circled. Ask him or her to name the short vowel in each word.

Read aloud the directions on page 141. Ask volunteers to name the pictures. Do the first item together, and then have children complete the page on their own.

Cumulative Review

On the board write the sample hidden-word puzzle below. Model how to read across to find the word **bun**. Circle the word. Then model how to read down to find the word **map**. Circle **map**. Have volunteers find and circle other three-letter words. (**hat, pop, nut, rod, pig**)

b	u	n	h	a	t
g	r	t	v	e	p
i	p	o	p	z	i
m	t	r	o	d	g
a	w	s	n	d	w
p	c	n	u	t	b

Then read aloud the directions on page 142. Have children complete the puzzle on their own.

Observational Assessment Observe as children read and write words with short vowels **a, i, o,** and **u**. Note which children have difficulty with a particular sound.

Dictation Tell children you are going to say some short **a** words. Have them write the short **a** words as you dictate them. Say **sat, van, jam, cab, tag**. Repeat the activity with short **i** words **bib, win, fix, pin, bit**; short **o** words **cot, box, dot, log, not**; and short **u** words **fun, rug, run, bus, bud**.

Student Skills Assessment Use the checklist on Student Edition pages 321–322 to record your observations of individual children.

Guided Instruction

Skills	Resources
Short vowel **a**	Instruction on pages 79–90 Little Books *Alexander Ant Cools Off; Who Can Run Fast?*
Short vowel **i**	Instruction on pages 93–106 Little Books *All Mixed Up; Look at the Pictures*
Short vowel **o**	Instruction on pages 109–122 Little Books *How to Make a Crocodile; Stop by a Pond*
Short vowel **u**	Instruction on pages 127–140 Little Books *What Bear Cubs Like to Do; Funny Bugs*
Short vowels **a, i, o, u**	Phonemic Awareness Activities on pages 77H–77I

Student Pages 143–144

Phonemic Awareness /e/

Objectives
- To match medial sounds
- To recognize the sound of short **e**
- To discriminate between short **e** words and other words

Warming Up

Reviewing Rhyming Words

Say each rhyme below, leaving out the underlined word. Direct children to guess the missing word that completes the rhyme.

"Hey! Look at **me!**"

Said the buzzing **bee**.

"Did you see the **fly**

That zoomed right **by?**"

★ Teaching the Lesson

Phonemic Awareness: Match Medial Sounds

Say **met** and **den** and ask children to repeat after you. Explain that /**e**/, the sound of short **e**, is the sound in the middle of both words. Have children say /**e**/. Then have children raise their hands when they hear two words with /**e**/ in the middle. Use these word pairs: **hen/log**; **let/pen**; **ran/bed**; **men/get**; **bid/set**.

Sound to Symbol

● Say the words **get**, **tell**, and **men**. Explain that these words have /**e**/ in the middle. Have children repeat the words with you and say /**e**/ after each one. Tell children that /**e**/ is the sound of short **e**. Ask them to think of names of people or things in the classroom with short **e** (e.g., **test**, **Ken**, **Ted**, **pen**, **pet**, **desk**, **leg**).

● Write the letter **e** on the board and tell children that it can stand for /**e**/. Review children's suggestions of short **e** words and write them on the board. Call on volunteers to underline the short **e** in each word.

Listen as the page is read aloud. Talk about the short **e** words you hear, such as **Ted** and **mess.** Then name the things under the bed. Color them Ted's favorite color—red.

Ted's Room

It's **Ted** the bug.

His room's a **mess.**

He has **ten** things

Not more, not **less.**

He hid his things

Under his **bed.**

And all the things

Ted hid are **red.**

All should be colored red

Critical Thinking Possible answer: He could stack his papers and put his toys in a box.
What should Ted do to make his room look better?

LESSON 71: Phonemic Awareness: /e/   **143**

UNIVERSAL ACCESS
Meeting Individual Needs

Auditory • Kinesthetic
Say a list of words, some having the short **e** sound, such as: **hen, cat, jet, pest, top, win, get, hat, desk.** Tell children to listen for the middle sounds and to nod their heads "yes" when they hear the sound of short **e** and shake their heads "no" when they don't.

Tactile • Auditory
Materials: construction paper, scissors, crayons, paper clips

Ask children which part of the word **necktie** has the short **e** sound. Have each child cut a necktie shape from paper and decorate it with drawings of short **e** words. Help children clip the ties to their shirts. Tell them to circulate around the room and talk about the pictures on one another's ties.

Extra Support
Remind children that the vowel sound in **hen** is short **e**. Then say: *Ted has a **red** pen on his **bed**.* Have children raise their hands and say /**e**/ each time they hear a short **e** word.

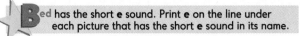

Bed has the short **e** sound. Print **e** on the line under each picture that has the short **e** sound in its name.

 Short **e**

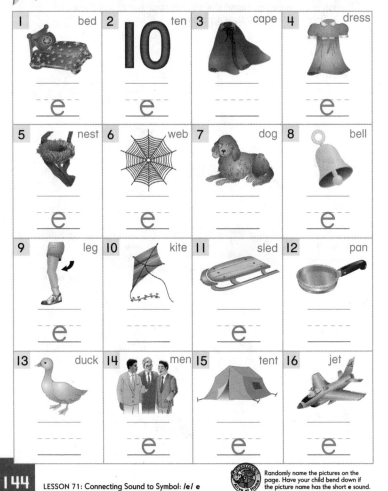

1 bed	2 ten	3 cape	4 dress
e	e		e

5 nest	6 web	7 dog	8 bell
e	e		e

9 leg	10 kite	11 sled	12 pan
e		e	

13 duck	14 men	15 tent	16 jet
	e	e	e

LESSON 71: Connecting Sound to Symbol: /e/ **e**

Randomly name the pictures on the page. Have your child bend down if the picture name has the short e sound.

Practicing the Skill

● Read aloud the directions and poem on page 143. Call on volunteers to read each short **e** word from the poem. Then direct children to color the short **e** items under the bed **red** and suggest ideas for Ted in response to the Critical Thinking question.

● Point out the picture cue **bed** at the top of page 144, and have children say the word as they trace over the **e**. Read aloud the directions, and do items 1 and 3 together. Identify the pictures, and have children complete the page.

Curriculum Connections

Theme Activity: Art/Math

Materials: construction paper, washable ink on ink pads, crayons

● Have children say short **e** words in sentences that include the words **ten bugs**. For example: **Ten** bugs **get wet**.

● Using an ink pad and paper, demonstrate how to make a thumbprint. Direct children to make ten thumbprints, decorate them to look like bugs, and draw a background that goes with one of the children's sentences.

 Portfolio

Have children place their bug prints in their portfolios.

English Language Learners/ESL

Preview the picture and poem on page 143. Name and discuss each item under the bed. Point out that all these items have the short **e** sound. Then call out a number from one to ten, and invite a volunteer to name that number of items from under Ted's bed. Repeat, in a game-like fashion, until everyone has had a turn.

Challenge

Write **insect** on the board, and ask children to draw any insect they like. When their picture is finished, have them say one or two sentences about that insect. Have them use as many short **e** words as they can.

Special Strategies

For Universal Access activities, see page 77F.

Observational Assessment

*Note whether children can easily write **e**.*

Blending with Short Vowel e

Objectives
- To blend phonemes in a word
- To blend short **e** words
- To identify and write short **e** words

Warming Up

Reviewing Initial Consonants

Materials: Punchout Letter Cards for consonants

Display letter cards. Then say: **bug**, **termite**, **leafhopper**, **butterfly**, **moth**, **caterpillar**, **ladybug**, **beetle**, **firefly**, **wasp**. Call on volunteers to find and name the letter that stands for the initial consonant sound.

Teaching the Lesson

Phonemic Awareness: Blend Phonemes in a Word

Materials: **Sadlier Phonics Picture Cards** for **net**, **ten**, **jet**, and three counters

Display the picture cards. Explain that to say each picture name, we blend together the sounds in the word. Move three counters, one at a time, as you say /**n**/-/**e**/-/**t**/. Then bring the counters together as you say **net**. Have children use counters as they repeat what you said and did. Ask a volunteer to point to the appropriate picture card. Repeat for **ten** and **jet**.

Blending

Tell children you are going to blend the sounds of letters to read a word. Write **pen** on the board, leaving a space between each letter. Point to **p** and say /**p**/. Point to **e** and say /**e**/. Point to **n** and say /**n**/. Then slide your finger under the letters as you say /**p**/-/**e**/-/**n**/ **pen**. Repeat the entire process with children. Then repeat with the words **men**, **set**, and **wet**.

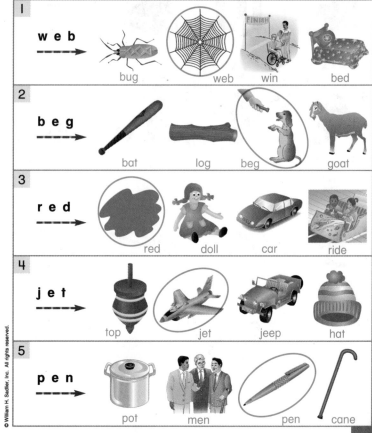

Trace the line as you blend the sounds together to say the word. Then circle the picture it names.

1. **w e b** → bug · web · win · bed
2. **b e g** → bat · log · beg · goat
3. **r e d** → red · doll · car · ride
4. **j e t** → top · jet · jeep · hat
5. **p e n** → pot · men · pen · cane

LESSON 72: Blending with Short Vowel **e** **145**

UNIVERSAL ACCESS
Meeting Individual Needs

Visual • Tactile
Materials: drawing paper, crayons, glitter, glue

Explain that when someone is sick, it's nice to send a get-well wish. Write **get well** on the board and read the words together. Have children make get-well cards that include short **e** words such as **best**, **rest**, and **bed**. Have them decorate each **e** with glitter.

Auditory • Kinesthetic
Write **ten** on the board. Point out that the middle sound in **ten** is /**e**/. Tell children to hold up all ten fingers when they hear a short **e** word. Use words such as these: **get**, **bell**, **sit**, **men**, **fun**, **box**, **web**, **did**, **hen**, **beg**, **bug**, **pep**, **mop**, **sun**, **red**, **den**.

Extra Support
Write **et** on a card. Review how to say the short **e** phonogram. Write **g, m, b, p, s, w, l** in a vertical list on the board. Show children how to hold the card next to each consonant and then read the word formed by the blending the sounds of the letters.

Trace the line as you blend the sounds together to say each word.
Then print the word under the picture it names.

p e t →

m e n →

b e d →

h e n →

l e g →

n e t →

w e b →

v e t →

t e n →

1	2	3
net	hen	pet
4	5	6
vet	web	men
7	8	9
bed	ten	leg

146

LESSON 72: Blending with Short Vowel **e**

As your child blends each word, retrace the arrow slowly with a red pen or crayon.

146

Student Pages 147–148

Short Vowel e Phonograms

Objectives

- To blend onsets and rimes
- To recognize short **e** phonograms
- To blend initial consonants with short **e** phonograms

Warming Up

Reviewing Initial Consonants

Have children identify the repeated initial consonant sounds in these tongue twisters:

Polly Parrot is a **perfect pet**.

Nick nabbed a **newt** in his **new net**.

Little ladybugs have **little legs**.

Have children make up and recite other initial consonant tongue twisters.

★ Teaching the Lesson

Phonemic Awareness: Blend Onsets and Rimes

Say the word parts /**p**/-/**et**/. Tell children you are going to blend these two parts to say a word. Model by saying /**p**/-/**et**/ and then **pet**. Now say /**r**/-/**ed**/ and ask a volunteer to blend the two parts. Repeat with other short **e** words, such as /**w**/-/**eb**/, /**m**/-/**en**/, /**m**/-/**et**/.

Phonograms

Materials: Punchout Letter Cards

- Have children use their punchout letter cards to make the phonogram **et**. Read it aloud with children. Then have them place the letter **p** before **et**, leaving space between the two word parts. Tell children to run their finger from left to right beneath the word parts as you say together /**p**/-/**et**/ and then **pet**.

- Explain that other words can be made with the **et** phonogram by changing the initial consonant. Have children replace **p** with **b**, **g**, **j**, **l**, **m**, **n**, **s**, **v**, and **w** and blend the word parts to read the words.

- Continue with other short **e** phonograms, such as **en**, **eg**, and **ed**.

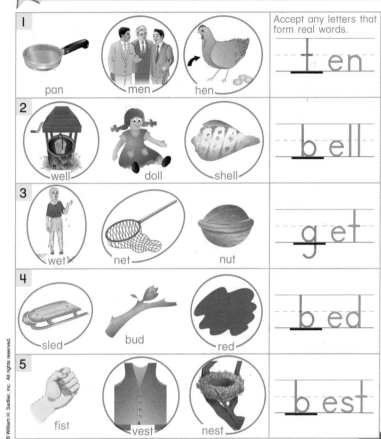

★ Say the name of each picture. In each row, circle two pictures that have rhyming names. Then make a new rhyming word.

Accept any letters that form real words.

1. pan | men | hen — **ten**
2. well | doll | shell — **bell**
3. wet | net | nut — **get**
4. sled | bud | red — **bed**
5. fist | vest | nest — **best**

UNIVERSAL ACCESS
Meeting Individual Needs

Auditory • Kinesthetic

Say the word **hen** and point out the short **e** sound. Tell children to bend their arms at the elbows, flap their "wings," and cluck like a hen when they hear other words with /**e**/. Then say **ten, bat, sit, fun, let, red, get, can, sun, mess, mop**.

Visual • Auditory

Materials: Sadlier Phonics Picture Cards for **net, pen, red, jet, web**

Have children form a circle and pass around a picture card. Have the first child say the picture name by separating the first sound from the rest of the word. Have the others say rhyming words. Repeat for each card.

Extra Support

Remind children that the words **set** and **let** end with the phonogram **et** and rhyme. Draw a ladder on the board and write **set** on the first rung. Help children write a rhyming word on each rung by changing the first letter.

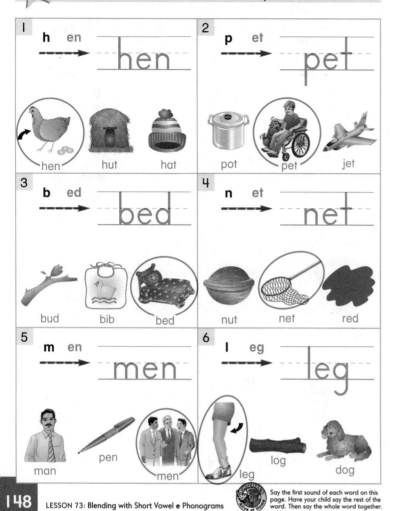

1. h en — hen
   hen   hut   hat

2. p et — pet
   pot   pet   jet

3. b ed — bed
   bud   bib   bed

4. n et — net
   nut   net   red

5. m en — men
   man   pen   men

6. l eg — leg
   leg   log   dog

148

LESSON 73: Blending with Short Vowel **e** Phonograms

Say the first sound of each word on this page. Have your child say the rest of the word. Then say the whole word together.

Practicing the Skill

• Read aloud the directions on page 147. Work on the first item together. Point out that many possible answers could be written in each blank. Make sure children know to write a rhyming word and not a picture name in each blank. Identify all pictures before having children complete the page.

• Read aloud the directions for page 148. Do item 1 together. Then identify all pictures before having children finish the page.

Curriculum Connections

Spelling Connection

Materials: Punchout Letter Cards

Read aloud the words and sentences below. Call on volunteers to use letter cards to spell each word.

hen	The **hen** digs in the dirt.
let	I **let** the bug go free.
vet	We took our sick pup to the **vet**.
sell	Will you **sell** lemonade?
yes	John said **yes**, he'd like to go.

Theme Activity: Science/Art

• Tell children that we would need "super" powers to do many of the things that bugs do. For example, ants carry objects that are several times their own weight; fleas jump long distances.

• Ask children to imagine they have "bug power." Then ask how they would use that power. They might fly as fast as a **jet**, for example. Record responses on a chart and have volunteers circle short **e** words.

• Direct children to make "Bug Power!" cartoons featuring short **e** words. Help them print captions or speech balloons and underline the short **e** words. Display cartoons on a "Bug Power!" bulletin board.

Portfolio

When the cartoons are removed from the bulletin board, have children add them to their portfolios.

English Language Learners/ESL

Remember that children are actually building English vocabulary as they learn phonics skills. As they complete lesson pages, make sure children name aloud all the possible choices before choosing their answers. Provide assistance as needed, as they may misinterpret a picture and call it something else (e.g., they may say **hand** instead of **fist**) or they may mispronounce a word, which would prevent them from identifying the rhyming words.

Challenge

Provide children with a story starter using words with short **e**. For example, you might say: *Have you met my pet Chet, yet? He begs, has six legs, and can fly.* Ask children to write a few sentences to finish the story and circle short **e** words used.

Special Strategies

For Universal Access activities see page 77F.

148

Short Vowel e

Objectives
- To substitute initial sounds
- To use phonograms to read short **e** words
- To build short **e** words

Warming Up

Reviewing Short Vowels

Read aloud the sentences below. Have children identify the short vowel sound common to all the words in each sentence.

That ant ran fast. (short **a**)

Sis hid Kim's mitt. (short **i**)

Tom hops on rocks. (short **o**)

Judd's bug just jumped up. (short **u**)

Teaching the Lesson

Phonemic Awareness: Substitute Initial Sounds

Say the phonogram **est**. Remind children that /**est**/ is only part of a word and that it needs a consonant sound at the beginning. Add /**t**/ to make the word **test**. Ask: *What happens when you change the /**t**/ in **test** to /**b**/?* Then say: *You get **best**.* Ask: *What happens when you change the /**b**/ in **best** to /**v**/?* Have volunteers add other beginning consonants to make words such as **nest**, **west**, **pest**, **rest**.

Phonograms

- On the board, write **ed** and read the phonogram. Add a **b** to **ed**, leaving a space between word parts. Tell children you will blend the two parts to read a word. Slide a finger from left to right as you say /**b**/-/**ed**/ and then **bed**.
- Ask a volunteer to circle the word part **ed**. Tell children that other words can be made with this word part. Replace **b** with **r** and have children blend /**r**/ with /**ed**/ and read the new word, **red**.
- Build more words by replacing the initial consonant with **f, l, w, N,** and **T**.

149

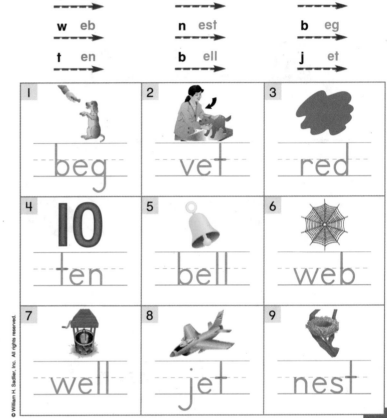

Trace the line as you blend the sounds together to say each word. Then print the word under the picture it names.

v et →

w eb →

t en →

w ell →

n est →

b ell →

r ed →

b eg →

j et →

1. beg
2. vet
3. red
4. ten
5. bell
6. web
7. well
8. jet
9. nest

LESSON 74: Blending with Phonograms 149

U N I V E R S A L A C C E S S
Meeting Individual Needs

Visual • Auditory
Materials: envelopes, index cards

On envelopes, write **ell, en, est, et.** On separate index cards, write a different short vowel word that ends with one of the above phonograms. Have children read a word and put it in the matching phonogram envelope.

Visual • Kinesthetic
Materials: Sadlier Phonics Picture Cards (6 short **e**; 2 each for short **a, i, o**)

Arrange cards face down. Have children turn over two cards and name them, listening for matching vowel sounds. If the cards match, children keep them; if not, the cards are put back. Continue until no cards remain face down.

Extra Support

Help children make the phonogram **en** using their letter cards. Say the phonogram **en** with them. Show them how to place **t** in front of **en** and read the word. Have them make and read new words using the letters **d, h, m, p.** Repeat with **et** and **b, g, j, l, m, n, p, s, w.**

149

Say each word part. Say the name of each picture. Print the word on the line. Then add your own rhyming word and picture.

_en	_et	_ell
1 men	4 jet	7 yell
2 hen	5 vet	8 shell
3 Accept any letters that form real words.	6 Accept any letters that form real words.	9 Accept any letters that form real words.

LESSON 74: Word Building with Short Vowel **e** Phonograms

With your child, use two words from any column in a short rhyme like this: **Let's hop on a jet and visit a vet.**

Practicing the Skill

● Read aloud the directions on page 149. Guide children as they trace the lines to say the words. Identify pictures together; then have children complete the page.
● Read aloud the directions for page 150 and help children identify the pictures. Be sure children understand that words in each column should rhyme. Do item 1 together; then have children complete the page.

Curriculum Connections

Spelling Connection
Read aloud each word and sentence below. Have one child spell each word orally and another print it on the board.

test	Are you ready for the **test**?
red	I like your new **red** shirt.
pet	This dog is my **pet**.
tell	Did you **tell** Ben the good news?
hen	The **hen** sits on her eggs.

Theme Activity: Art/Science
Materials: construction paper, string, tacks, crayons

● Point out that spiders use their webs to catch and eat bugs. Then share the theme book listed below.
● Cover a bulletin board with dark paper. Distribute long pieces of string. Have children work together to tack string to the board to make a web.
● Ask children to cut from construction paper shapes of bugs that might get caught in the class web. Write various short **e** phonograms on the board. Guide children to use the phonograms to build a short **e** word to write on each bug shape. Then attach the bugs to the web.

Theme Book

Carle, Eric. *The Very Busy Spider.* New York: Philomel Books, 1984. Touchable pictures add another dimension to the story of a spider and her web.

English Language Learners/ESL
Use the theme book, *The Very Busy Spider,* to prompt a discussion about legs in order to help children develop English vocabulary. Point out that **legs** has a short **e** sound. Say: *How many legs does a spider have?* (**8**) *How many legs does a bug have?* (**6**) *How many legs does a dog have?* (**4**) *How many legs do you have?* (**2**) Write **2 legs, 4 legs, 6 legs,** and **8 legs** on the board. Invite children to name other animals or insects and tell you under which category to list them.

Challenge
Tell children they've been invited to a ladybug party and will be wearing red vests for the occasion. Remind children that the words **red** and **vest** have the short **e** phonograms **ed** and **est**. Direct them to draw a picture of themselves in a red vest at a ladybug party and then write a brief story to go with the illustration. Ask children to underline the short **e** phonograms in their stories.

Special Strategies
For Universal Access activities, see page 77F.

Observational Assessment
*Note which children have difficulty thinking of short **e** words.*

Writing Short Vowel e

Objectives

- To substitute medial sounds
- To recognize short **e** words
- To write short **e** words

Warming Up

Reviewing Short e and Short i

Materials: **Sadlier Phonics Picture Cards** for short **e** and short **i** words

Remind children that **ten** is a short **e** word and that **bib** is a short **i** word. Have children work in pairs to sort the picture cards according to whether the picture name has the short **e** or short **i** vowel sound.

Teaching the Lesson

Phonemic Awareness: Substitute Medial Sounds

- Say **bag**. Point out that **bag** has the short vowel **a** sound, /**a**/, in the middle. Tell children that we can sometimes make new words by changing the vowel sound in the middle. Model changing **bag** to **beg**. Say /b/-/a/-/g/ **bag**; /b/-/e/-/g/ **beg**. Have children repeat after you.
- Tell children to change the middle sound in these words: **cat**–change /**a**/ to /**u**/ (**cut**), **tin**–change /**i**/ to /**e**/ (**ten**), **pet**–change /**e**/ to /**i**/ (**pit**).

Sound to Symbol

- Say **net**, **beg**, **red**. Point out that these words have the short vowel **e** sound, /**e**/, in the middle.
- Write each word on the board, circling the **e**. Explain that **e** stands for the /**e**/ that children hear in **net**, **beg**, and **red**.
- Print the following on the board:

  b_g　　l_t　　m_n
  n_t　　r_d　　y_s

Have volunteers print **e** in each blank, say the word, and name its vowel sound.

151

Circle the word that names each picture.

1 (net) not nut	2 (ten) tin tan	3 pit (pet) pot
4 (belt) bat bell	5 nuts rest (nest)	6 pen (pin) pan
7 rid rod (red)	8 ten (tent) tint	9 (beg) big bag
10 will (well) went	11 hem (ham) hum	12 jam jot (jet)
13 (pup) pep pop	14 (vest) van vet	15 bad bid (bed)

LESSON 75: Practicing Short Vowel **e**　　**151**

UNIVERSAL ACCESS
Meeting Individual Needs

Auditory • Visual

Remind children that the word **red** has the sound of short vowel **e**. Have children play "I Spy" by "spying" in the room things that are red. Give children 10 points for spying a red object; give 20 points if its name also has the short **e** sound.

Auditory • Kinesthetic

Write the lyrics to "The Farmer in the Dell" on the board, and have children sing the song. Have children suggest short **e** words for key words in the song. For example, the farmer could take a **hen** or a **pet** instead of a wife. Cross out words in the song, and write the replacements. Have children sing and act out the new lyrics.

Extra Support

Remind children that the middle sound in **jet** is /**e**/. Tell children that they can make more short **e** words by changing the first or last letter. Have them replace **j** with **n** and read **net**. Continue changing letters to form and read **pet**, **pen**, **men**, **met**, **let**, **leg**, **beg**, **bed**.

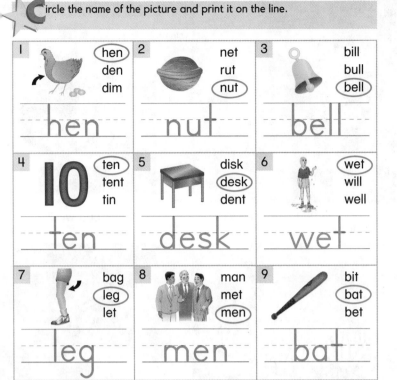

Circle the name of the picture and print it on the line.

1	hen (circled) / den / dim	2	net / rut / nut (circled)	3	bill / bull / bell (circled)
	hen		nut		bell
4	ten (circled) / tent / tin	5	disk / desk (circled) / dent	6	wet (circled) / will / well
	ten		desk		wet
7	bag / leg (circled) / let	8	man / met / men (circled)	9	bit / bat (circled) / bet
	leg		men		bat

Trace the words in the sentence and use a short **e** word to complete it.

The red bug
is wet .

Randomly read words on this page.
Have your child hold up ten fingers
when he or she hears a short **e** word.

152 LESSON 75: Writing Short Vowel **e**

Practicing the Skill

- Read the directions at the top of page 151. Help children identify the pictures. Model completing the first item before having children proceed.
- Read aloud the directions on page 152 and identify the pictures together. Discuss the bug pictured at the bottom of the page. Point out that the sentence they will trace and complete begins with an uppercase letter and ends with a period. Then have them complete the page.

Curriculum Connections

Spelling Connection
Read aloud each word and sentence below. Call on a volunteer to spell each word and print it on the board.

cents A dime is ten **cents**.

leg Len fell and hurt his **leg**.

mess The kitchen is a **mess**.

pet A cat makes a good **pet**.

net The ball went into the **net**.

Theme Activity: Language Arts/Art
- Brainstorm with children words they might use when talking about bugs and picnics (e.g., **pest**, **ants**, **bees**, **rain**, **tent**, **wet**). List the words on the board. Have volunteers circle the short **e** words.
- Have children use the circled words to write about a picnic at which the picnickers were bothered by bugs. Have children illustrate their stories.

Portfolio Have children add their picnic stories to their portfolios.

Sadlier Reading
Little Books and Big Books
Read *The Best Place* (nonfiction) for more practice with short **e**.

Observational Assessment
*Note whether children can distinguish short **e** words from short **i** words.*

English Language Learners/ESL
Tell children they are going to play the Echo Game. Write the word **echo** on the board. Point out that the first sound of that word is /e/. Tell them that **echo** means to repeat, so if they hear /e/ in any of the words you call out, they should echo, or repeat, the word; otherwise they are to be silent. Say the words on pages 151–152, and have children respond accordingly.

Challenge
Have children choose a short **e** word and another word from pages 151 or 152. The other word might also be a short **e** word. Direct children to use both words to print a sentence that tells something about bugs. (e.g., "The red bug flew into the net."). Then have them exchange sentences with a partner and circle the short **e** word or words in each other's sentences.

Special Strategies
For Universal Access activities, see page 77F.

Short Vowel e Decodable Reader

Objectives
- To read short **e** words and high-frequency words in context
- To fluently read the story
- To classify objects

Introducing the Story Words

Short e Decodable Words   Remind children that the sound of short **e** is /e/. On the board, write **tell**. Model blending the sounds /t/-/e/-/l/ to read the word. Then write **wet**, **net**, **red**, **get**, **fed**, **yet**, and **pet**. Ask volunteers to blend the sounds of the letters to read each word.

High-Frequency Words   *Materials:* index cards

Write the words **is**, **this**, **be**, **a**, **jump**, **like**, **you**, **me**, and **by** on a word wall and on index cards. Read the list with children. Give cards to volunteers and ask them to read the card, spell the word, and then match the card to a word on the word wall.

Reading the Book

Reading Together   Have children remove pages 153 and 154. Show them how to cut and fold the pages into a book. Read aloud the title "Tell Me." Explain that this book asks questions about bugs. Have children follow along as you read aloud.

Responding   Ask children to provide an answer for each question in the story.

Reading for Fluency   Have children read the story along with you. Direct partners to alternate reading pages. Finally, have children read the story independently.

Observational Assessment

Note whether children can decode the short e words and fluently read the story.

Name _____

Tell Me

Can this bug jump like you?
8 Tell me.

Is this bug wet?

Can this bug be a pet?
6

Is this bug red?
3

Directions: Cut and fold the book. Then read the story. Talk about other things that are wet, red, or found in a net.

LESSON 76: Short Vowel e Decodable Reader
Comprehension: Classifying Objects

153

U N I V E R S A L   A C C E S S
Meeting Individual Needs

Auditory • Tactile
Materials: chart paper, audio-tape, tape player

On chart paper, list the words **is, this, be, a, jump, like, you, me, by, will**. Play an audio-tape of you reading the list and point to each word as it is said. Put the list and tape in the listening center for children to work with on their own.

Visual • Kinesthetic
Materials: flashlight

On the board, write the short **e** story words in large letters. Shine the flashlight on each letter as you blend the sounds to read each word. Give volunteers the flashlight and have them read the list in the same way.

Extra Support
Materials: story words on index cards

Read the word cards with children. Point out the short **e** sound. Give the cards to children. Tell a silly story that includes the words. Have children show their words as you say them.

Is this bug in a net?

Can this bug buzz by you?

2

7

Will this bug get fed?

Did this bug dig yet?

4

5

154

LESSON 76: Short Vowel **e** Decodable Reader
Comprehension: Classifying Objects

Comprehension Strategy

Classifying Objects   Explain to children that grouping similar things together can help them see connections between things. Guide children in reviewing the illustrations that go with the story. Ask them to name other things that are red, that get fed, that can dig, that can be a pet, or that can jump.

Phonics and Decoding

Learning About Short e   On the board, write these story words: **wet, red**. Read the words aloud and ask children to find them in the story. Help children notice that each word has the short **e** sound. Then lead children in playing a game called "Tell Me." Say: *Tell me if this word sounds like /e/.* Write on the board a list of short vowel words, such as **bed, pet, fed, on, up, yet, dog, bell, mitt, nut**. Call on volunteers to read a word and clap if it has the short **e** sound.

Word Building   *Materials:* net, Punchout Letter Cards

Place punchout letter cards displaying the phonogram **et** in a pocket chart. Hang the net and put the other letters in the net. Direct volunteers to draw a card from the net and put it in front of the phonogram to build and read the word. Ask children to use the word they read in a sentence.

Curriculum Connections

Writing and Sharing   Ask children to use short **e** words to write a question about bugs. Have children trade papers with a partner and write an answer to the question. Then ask partners to read their questions and answers to the class.

English Language Learners/ESL
After children have assembled their *Decodable Readers*, work with them to discuss the pictures and to sound out the words in each sentence. Help them see that they can often use cues from the pictures to help them "read." For example, for page 1, elicit that the bug is in a pool of water. Say: *When you are in water, are you wet? Is this bug wet?* Relate your final question to the text on the page.

Challenge
Ask children to use short **e** words to write questions they could ask a bug. Then have them write the answers a bug might give. Ask volunteers to share their questions and answers with the class. Direct the class to identify the short **e** words.

Special Strategies
For Universal Access activities, see page 77F.

Short Vowel e in Context

Objectives
- To match words
- To complete sentences by writing short **e** words
- To recognize short **e** words in context

Warming Up

Reviewing Initial Consonants

On the board print the phonograms **ed**, **eg**, **en**, and **et**. Have children add initial consonants to make rhyming words. List the words beside their phonograms. Have children make up rhymes with their words. List rhyming words on the board as children say them.

Teaching the Lesson

Phonemic Awareness: Match Words

Tell children that you are going to say a word and then say that word in a sentence. Ask them to clap when they hear that word in the sentence. Use these sentences:

leg	That cat has a white spot on each **leg**.
pest	A bug can be a **pest** in your home.
red	A ladybug is **red** with black spots.
net	The boy caught a butterfly in a **net**.
pet	Your **pet** may have fleas in its fur.

Phonics in Context

Write this sentence on the board: The ___ sits on a nest. Write the words **pen**, **hen**, **jet** next to the sentence. Read aloud the sentence and the word choices. Then read the sentence three times, each time filling in the blank with one of the word choices. Circle the word **hen**, and tell children that it best completes the meaning of the sentence. Now have children complete this sentence: My cat Mimi is a fun ___. (**bed**, **bug**, **pet**)

Look at each picture. Circle the word that completes the sentence. Then print it on the line.

1. Can a bug be a _pet_ ?
   pat / **pet** / pot

2. _Yes_ , it can.
   Yes / Yet / Jet

3. It can be the _best_ pet.
   list / **best** / rest

4. It will not be a _pest_ .
   last / past / **pest**

5. It will not make a _mess_ .
   mess / miss / moss

6. But it must be _fed_ .
   fan / fin / **fed**

LESSON 77: Short Vowel e in Sentences **155**

U N I V E R S A L   A C C E S S
Meeting Individual Needs

Auditory • Kinesthetic

Materials: hen outline, oaktag, crayons, scissors, tape

Have children work in teams to trace, color, and cut out a hen shape. Use tape to mark off on the floor spaces leading to a finish line. A hen can move one space forward each time its team member takes a turn and says a short **e** word.

Visual • Kinesthetic

Materials: slips of paper, paper bag

Print on slips of paper short **e** words such as **belt**, **hen**, **jet**, **neck**, **pen**, **red**, and **yell**. Fold the slips in half and put them in a paper bag. Have children take turns drawing a slip of paper out of the bag and acting out what it names while the class guesses the word.

Extra Support

Say the word **red** and write it on the board. Tell children that it has the short **e** sound. Say the words **pet** and **bag** and ask which word also has the short **e** sound. Continue with other word pairs such as **pin/web; den/top**.

Listen as the poem is read aloud. Circle each thing the bugs run past. Then use short **e** words to complete the sentences.

The Big Bug Race

Get set, bugs.
Run past the hen.
Run past the pen.
Run past the men.
Run, bugs, run.
Run to the end.

1. The bugs run past the ___hen___.

2. They run past the ___pen___.

3. They run past the ___men___.

4. They run to the ___end___.

156

LESSON 77: Short Vowel **e** in Context
Comprehension: Retelling a Story

Have your child walk through your home and draw or name things he or she sees that have short **e** names.

● Read the directions on page 155 together. Ask children what kinds of clues, such as illustrations or context clues, they can use to help them choose the correct word. Then have them complete the page.

● Read aloud the directions and poem on page 156. Then read the sentences at the bottom of the page. Tell children to use short **e** words from the poem to complete each sentence.

Curriculum Connections

Spelling Connection

Read aloud each word and sentence below. Have a child spell the word orally. Have another child print the word on the board.

pen   Will you lend me a **pen**?

wet   The **wet** bee buzzed angrily.

best   My dog is the **best** pet.

men   The **men** waited for the bus.

tent   A moth flew into the **tent**.

Theme Activity: Multicultural

● Explain that in the United States, some people think it is good luck when a ladybug flies to them. In China, some families keep a pet cricket in a cage for good luck.

● Read the theme book listed below aloud and share the pictures. Point out the short **e** sound in **insects**. Then discuss how some bugs are helpful.

● Have children imagine his or her own "good luck" bug, and ask them to draw it. Have children write sentences about their bugs and circle short **e** words.

Theme Book

Fowler, Allan. It's a Good Thing There Are Insects. Chicago: Children's Press, 1990. Helpful, harmful—the world needs insects.

English Language Learners/ESL

Storytelling and/or retelling stories are excellent ways for children to build fluency. Have children engage in such activities either before or after they complete the lesson. Cover the words on both pages of the lesson, and have children tell or retell the stories in their own words using only pictures.

Challenge

Tell children to imagine a race involving bugs such as ladybugs or grasshoppers and draw a picture of the race. Have children pretend to be spectators and write sentences telling what they would say to cheer on the racers, for example, "Get moving, Red!" Have children use and circle short **e** words in their cheers.

Special Strategies

For Universal Access activities, see page 77F.

Note children's use of context, picture clues, and letter/sound association.

Assessing Short Vowel e Reviewing Short Vowels a, i, o, u, and e

Objectives
- To identify and complete words with short **e**
- To build sentences containing short vowel words

Warming Up

Reviewing Initial Consonants

Write the following sentences on the board. Point to a word with an initial consonant and say the word. Have children repeat the word, name the beginning sound and the letter that stands for the sound.

Butterflies and **l**adybugs,

Such **n**ice, **p**retty **b**ugs!

Soaring, **f**lying **w**ay up **h**igh.

Teaching the Lesson

Short Vowel e

Say **ten** and **leg**. Remind children that in these words, **e** stands for the short **e** sound. Write on the board the short **e** phonogram **et**. Have children add beginning consonants to form words. (**get, net, pet, set, jet, let, bet, vet**) Repeat for **eg** to form **beg, leg, peg**. Have children circle the **e** in each word they formed.

Short Vowels a, i, o, u, e

Print the following chart on the board:

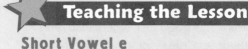

A pig	sat	to the man.
My dog	ran	in the pen.
The hen	hid	in the sun.

Model how to write a sentence using one choice from each box (e.g., The dog ran to the man.). Point out that a sentence begins with an upper case letter and ends with a period. Have children use the other choices to say and write two more sentences. Then have children name the short vowel sound in **pig, dog, hen, sat, ran, hid, man, pen,** and **sun.**

157

 Check-Up Say the name of each picture. Print **e** on the line to complete the picture name if it has the short **e** sound.

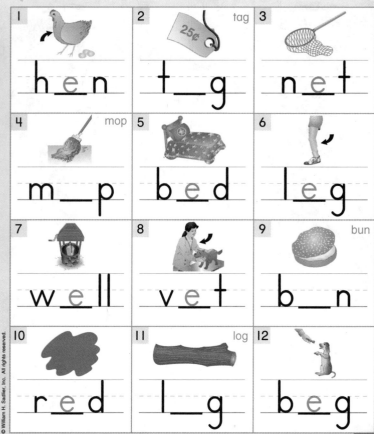

1. h e n
2. t _ g (tag)
3. n e t
4. m _ p (mop)
5. b e d
6. l e g
7. w e ll
8. v e t
9. b _ n (bun)
10. r e d
11. l _ g (log)
12. b e g

UNIVERSAL ACCESS
Reteaching Activities

Activity 1

Materials: **Sadlier Phonics Picture Cards** for **bed, jet, pen, ten, web, pin, log, bat, rug**

Remind children that the short **e** sound is the vowel sound they hear in **get**. Have children name all the pictures and find the five with names that have the short **e** sound. Then help children print the short **e** words on the board.

Activity 2

Materials: Punchout Letter Cards

Review short vowel sounds using the words **bag, wet, pig, dog,** and **cup**. Divide the class into five groups and assign each group a vowel. Have each group arrange their letter cards into words with their assigned vowel. Tell children to keep a list of the words they make. Then have them read their list to the class.

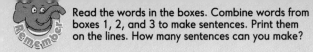

Read the words in the boxes. Combine words from boxes 1, 2, and 3 to make sentences. Print them on the lines. How many sentences can you make?

1	2	3
Six bugs	had fun	at the pond.
A frog	will jump	in the sun.
The pet	can hop	on the bud.

Possible responses:

Six bugs will jump on the bud. A frog had fun in the sun. The pet can hop at the pond.

Accept any combination of sentence parts that forms a real sentence.

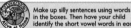

Make up silly sentences using words in the boxes. Then have your child identify the short vowel words in each.

158   LESSON 78: Reviewing Short Vowels **a, i, o, u, e**

Assessing the Skill

Ask volunteers to name the pictures on page 157. Read aloud the directions, and do the first item together. Then have children complete the page independently.

Cumulative Review

Go over the directions on page 158, and model how to use the phrases to build sentences. Point out the uppercase letters in box 1 and the periods in box 3. Remind children that their sentences should begin with uppercase letters and end with periods.

Observational Assessment   Observe which children have difficulty recognizing short vowel sounds as well as reading short vowel words. Make notes for use in reteaching.

Dictation   Tell children you are going to say some short **a** words. Have them write the short **a** words as you dictate them. Say **has**, **vat**, **ran**, **wag**, **ban**. Repeat the activity with short **i** words (**fit**, **lips**, **him**, **dig**, **dip**); short **o** words (**mop**, **hog**, **log**, **nod**, **jot**); short **u** words (**bun**, **cut**, **gum**, **hut**, **nut**); and short **e** words (**get**, **pep**, **peg**, **hem**, **wet**).

Student Skills Assessment   Use the checklist on Student Edition pages 321–322 to record your observations of individual children.

Guided Instruction	
Skills	**Resources**
Short vowel **a**	Instruction on pages 79–90 Little Book *Alexander Ant Cools Off*
Short vowel **i**	Instruction on pages 93–106 Little Book *All Mixed Up*
Short vowel **o**	Instruction on pages 109–122 Little Book *How to Make a Crocodile*
Short vowel **u**	Instruction on pages 127–140 Little Book *What Bear Cubs Like to Do*
Short vowel **e**	Instruction on pages 143–156 Little Book *Don't Tell!*
Short vowels **a, i, o, u, e**	Phonemic Awareness Activities on pages 77H–77I

Connecting Spelling, Writing, and Speaking

Objectives

- To identify and isolate medial sounds
- To say, spell, sort, and write short vowel words
- To write descriptive sentences using spelling words from a list

★ Teaching the Lesson

Phonemic Awareness: Identify and Isolate Medial Sounds

Say the word **pan**. Tell children the middle sound in **pan** is short **a**. Say: /p/-/a/-/n/ **pan** and have children repeat after you. Say the following words and have children identify the middle sound for each: **red**, /e/; **bib**, /i/; **pot**, /o/; **bug**, /u/.

Spelling

Materials: Punchout Letter Cards

- Write the following rhyme on the board:
   A bug in a hat!
   How about that?

Read the rhyme together. Have volunteers name the words with the short **a** sound (**hat**, **that**) and the short **u** sound (**bug**).

- Say each spelling word listed on page 159, and ask a child to repeat the word and spell it. Direct the class to hold up the letter cards for the vowel sounds they hear. Then have the class use each spelling word in a sentence.

Practicing the Skill

Read the directions and spelling list on page 159 aloud. Explain to children that they will sort the words by vowel sound. Together work through the first two items before having children complete the page

Observational Assessment

As children hold up the letter cards, note who needs help with a particular short vowel.

159

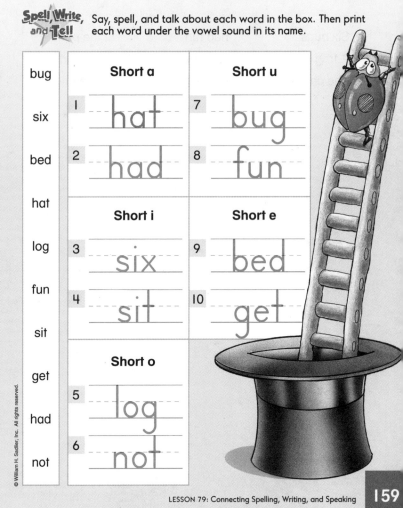

Spell, Write, and Tell, Say, spell, and talk about each word in the box. Then print each word under the vowel sound in its name.

bug
six
bed
hat
log
fun
sit
get
had
not

Short a
1 hat
2 had

Short u
7 bug
8 fun

Short i
3 six
4 sit

Short e
9 bed
10 get

Short o
5 log
6 not

LESSON 79: Connecting Spelling, Writing, and Speaking   **159**

U N I V E R S A L   A C C E S S
Meeting Individual Needs

Tactile • Visual

Materials: drawing paper, tube of glue, sand

Help children use a tube of glue to print a spelling word on drawing paper and to sprinkle sand over it. Let it dry, and shake off excess sand. Direct children to say and spell their words as they trace over the sand letters with their fingers.

Kinesthetic • Auditory

Materials: oaktag, marker, masking tape

Print each vowel on a ten-inch oaktag square, and tape the squares to the floor. Have a group of children line up in front of the squares. As you say a short vowel word, ask a child to jump onto the letter that stands for the vowel sound. Use words such as: **cat, get, sit, hop, bug.**

Extra Support

Say the words **fan** and **van**. Tell children that both words have the short **a** sound and rhyme. Have a volunteer say another short **a** word that rhymes with **fan**. Continue with other short vowel words: **pen, men; dig, wig; hot, cot; bun, sun.**

Write a sentence about each picture. Use one or more of your new spelling words in each sentence. Then tell about what you wrote.

bug	bed	log	sit	had
six	hat	fun	get	not

1 Accept any sentences that contain at least one spelling word.

2

LESSON 79: Connecting Spelling, Writing, and Speaking

Take turns reading the spelling words with your child. Then have him or her spell each word.

The Writing Process

Tell children that they will be writing sentences to describe pictures. Together, read the directions on page 160.

Brainstorm Before asking children to write, have them share ideas about the pictures. Ask questions such as: *What do the bugs look like?* and *What are the bugs doing?*

Write Have children write first drafts on writing paper.

Revise Have children reread their sentences to make sure the sentences say what they want them to say before writing on the page. Then tell children to check that each of their sentences begins with an uppercase letter and ends with a period and check that their spelling is correct.

Publish Have each child choose one sentence and then write it neatly. Have children underline spelling words they used. Post sentences on a bulletin board under a sign that says **Write**!

Speak After children have completed the page, invite them to share their sentences orally.

Extending the Skills

Have children think like a bug. Use the pictures on page 160 to discuss what it might be like to be a bug in a bed or a bug on a log. Talk about what the bugs on the log might do all day. Then have children pretend to be a bug and write two sentences describing what they would do during the day. Tell children to use one or more of the spelling words in their sentences. Suggest a sentence starter such as: *If I were a bug, I would. . . .*

Portfolio Have children add their writing to their portfolios.

English Language Learners/ESL
Materials: Sadlier Phonics Picture Cards for short vowel words

Some children may have difficulty distinguishing among short vowel sounds, especially if those sounds do not exist in their native language or are associated with other letters. Have children work in small groups. Give each group 10 picture cards, including two pictures for each short vowel. Have children name and sort the pictures by short vowel sound.

Challenge
Have children choose two spelling words on page 159 that have the same vowel sound in the middle — for example, **six** and **sit**. Help children print a sentence about bugs for each word; for example:

I see **six** bugs.

I can **sit** next to the bugs.

Have children read their sentences to a partner, and have the partner tell which two words have the same vowel sound in the middle (other than **bugs**).

Special Strategies
For Universal Access activities, see page 77F.

Integrating the Language Arts

Objectives

- To count words in a spoken sentence
- To use oral and written language to extend the theme concept
- To demonstrate recognition of short vowel sounds

⭐ **Teaching the Lesson**

Phonemic Awareness: Count the Words in a Spoken Sentence

Materials: counters

Tell children you are going to count words in a sentence. Give children five counters. Say: *I like bugs very much.* Pause and put down a counter after you say each word. Add the counters. Tell children there are **5** words in the sentence. Repeat the sentence and tell children to put down a counter each time you say a word. Ask children how many words they heard. Repeat the process using these sentences:

Some bugs have wings. (**4**)

The ant digs a hole. (**5**)

Spiders make webs. (**3**)

Skills in Context

Read the text on page 161 aloud. Then read it again, and have children join in. Read the photo captions, and have children find each hidden insect. Ask why it is helpful for insects to blend in with their surroundings. Read the question, and discuss other things bugs do. Record children's comments on chart paper. Challenge children to find all the short vowel words on the page.

Comprehension Skill: Recognizing Facts

Explain that a fact is something that is known to be true. For example, a bee is a bug that flies. Ask children to name facts they know about bugs.

Listen as the page is read aloud. Look at the pictures. Then talk about what you see.

Can you spot the bugs?
Don't let them trick you.
They can see you just fine.
Lots of bugs blend in well with rocks, plants, and sticks.
The bugs can sit still for a very long time. This helps them hide and stay safe.

What can bugs do?

Possible responses: Some bugs can fly; some crawl; some sting or bite; bees make honey.

Treehopper

Walkingstick

Katydid

LESSON 80: Short Vowels in Context
Comprehension: Recognizing Facts

161

UNIVERSAL ACCESS
Meeting Individual Needs

Reading and Writing Connection

Materials: paper, crayons, including one yellow crayon

Have children illustrate an interesting fact about a bug. Have them print or dictate a caption for their illustrations. Tell children to highlight the short vowel words in their captions with yellow crayon. Bind children's pages together to make a class Bug Book. Read the book together. Encourage children to sign the book out and share it with their families.

Science Connection

Explain that camouflage (disguise) is important to many animals. Ask children to tell about other bugs and animals that camouflage themselves. Talk about these animals' natural environments.

Because coloring is so important to the concept of camouflage, have children paint pictures of the named animals in their environments. Tell children to camouflage a short vowel word somewhere in their pictures and to challenge a partner to find the hidden word.

The words in the box are often used in sentences. Use one of the words to complete each sentence. Then practice reading the sentences aloud.

and	help	it	No	see	will

1. Do you **see** a bug by the ?

   tree

2. Is **it** on the 🌼 ?

   flower

3. **No** , that bug is by the 🚧 .

   fence

4. You can **help** me stop that bug.

5. I **will** run with you.

6. You **and** I will get that bug!

LESSON 81: Reading High-Frequency Words

 Print each word from the box on an index card. Have your child practice reading the words every day for a week.

High-Frequency Words

Objectives
- To recognize and read high-frequency words
- To write high-frequency words to complete sentences

Teaching the Lesson

Materials: index cards

- Write the word **and** on the board. Point to the word, say it, spell it, and say the word again. Have children repeat after you and then trace the word in the air. Repeat the process with the words **help**, **it**, **no**, **see**, and **will**.
- Write these sentences on the board:

  Did you ever see a ladybug?

  It is red and black.

  Ladybugs help gardens grow.

  They will eat bad bugs.

  There is no reason to fear ladybugs!

List the words **and**, **help**, **it**, **no**, **see**, and **will** in mixed-up order beside the sentences. Say the words with the class. Help children read the sentences aloud, and ask volunteers to underline each high-frequency word. Then say one of the words and call on a volunteer to spell it aloud, circle the word in the sentence, and draw a line from that word to the matching word in the list. Repeat with the remaining words.

Practicing the Skill

Read aloud the directions at the top of page 162. Have children read each word in the box. Be sure children can read the sentences before having them complete the page.

Extra Practice

Write the words **and, help, it, no, see,** and **will** in a row on the board, placing each word in a box. Tell children they can be grasshoppers and hop across the board, reading and spelling each word in a box. Call on a volunteer to place a finger under the first box, read and spell the word, then "jump" to the next box. Continue having other children "jump" from word to word.

Review

Materials: ten index cards, chart paper

Write the words **by, let, ride, stop,** and **walk** on index cards so that there are two cards for each word. Distribute the cards and have children find their partner—a classmate with the same word. Ask each pair to make up a sentence with their word. As they say their sentence, help them write it on chart paper. Repeat the activity with other children as necessary. Help the class reread the sentences on the chart, and ask volunteers to underline the review word in each sentence.

Assessing Short Vowels
a, i, o, u, e

Objectives
• To demonstrate recognition of short vowel words

Warming Up

Reviewing Rhyming Words

Review with children that rhyming words have the same ending sound, such as **mop/hop** and **red/bed**. Make up rhymes like the ones below. Tell children to name each pair of rhyming words and the short vowel sound.

Watch out for the **pup**.

It's going to jump **up**! (**pup/up**; short **u**)

Don't touch that **pot**!

It's very **hot**. (**pot/hot**; short **o**)

Teaching the Lesson

Short Vowels a, i, o, u, e

Materials: **Sadlier Phonics Picture Cards** for **ham, pin, pot, rug, bed**

• Show children the picture cards. Have children say each picture name and identify its short vowel sound.

• Write **ham**, **hem**, and **him** on the board. Have children read the word choices. Then display the **ham** picture card. Have a volunteer circle the correct word for the picture and name its middle sound again. Repeat the activity with the following word choices: **pan, pen, pin (pin)**; **pat, pet, pot (pot)**; **rag, rig, rug (rug)**; **bad, bed, bud (bed)**.

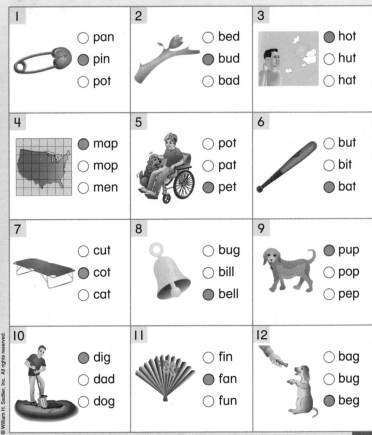

Check-Up Fill in the circle next to the name of each picture.

1	pan ○ / pin ● / pot ○	2	bed ○ / bud ● / bad ○	3	hot ● / hut ○ / hat ○
4	map ● / mop ○ / men ○	5	pot ○ / pat ○ / pet ●	6	but ○ / bit ○ / bat ●
7	cut ○ / cot ● / cat ○	8	bug ○ / bill ○ / bell ●	9	pup ● / pop ○ / pep ○
10	dig ● / dad ○ / dog ○	11	fin ○ / fan ● / fun ○	12	bag ○ / bug ○ / beg ●

LESSON 82: Assessing Short Vowels **a, i, o, u, e**   **163**

U N I V E R S A L   A C C E S S
Reteaching Activities

Activity 1

Materials: large box, index cards

Use the words **pat**, **sit**, **pot**, **tug**, and **pen** to review short vowel sounds. Have each child write one of the short vowel words from pages 163–164 on an index card and put the card in the box. Then have children take turns drawing a word, reading it, identifying the short vowel and using it in a sentence.

Activity 2

Review the short vowel sounds of /**a**/, /**i**/, /**o**/, /**u**/ and /**e**/. Then say each pair of rhyming words shown below aloud. Have children name the short vowel sound. Then write the words on the board and have a volunteer circle the vowel that stands for the sound.

hat, **cat** (short **a**), **fin**, **win** (short **i**), **hop**, **pop** (short **o**), **bug**, **dug** (short **u**), **pet**, **net** (short **e**).

1.
- ○ bag
- ○ dig
- ● dog

2.
- ● hat
- ○ hot
- ○ hit

3.
- ○ rug
- ○ rap
- ● rip

4.
- ○ beg
- ● bug
- ○ bit

5.
- ● pen
- ○ pin
- ○ pan

6.
- ○ not
- ○ net
- ● nut

7.
- ● lips
- ○ laps
- ○ tops

8.
- ○ cap
- ○ cob
- ● cup

9.
- ○ pat
- ● pot
- ○ pet

10.
- ○ fog
- ● bag
- ○ big

11.
- ○ bid
- ○ bad
- ● bed

12.
- ● mop
- ○ map
- ○ mud

13.
- ○ sit
- ● wet
- ○ wag

14.
- ○ fin
- ○ vet
- ● van

15.
- ● pig
- ○ peg
- ○ pan

Review this Check-Up with your child.

Guided Instruction

Skills	Resources
Short vowel **a**	Instruction on pages 79–90 Little Book *Who Can Run Fast?*
Short vowel **i**	Instruction on pages 93–106 Little Book *Look at the Pictures*
Short vowel **o**	Instruction on pages 109–122 Little Book *Stop by a Pond*
Short vowel **u**	Instruction on pages 127–140 Little Book *Funny Bugs*
Short vowel **e**	Instruction on pages 143–156 Little Book *The Best Place*
Short vowels **a, i, o, u, e**	Phonemic Awareness Activities on pages 77H–77I

Assessing the Unit

Check-Up *Materials: Sadlier Phonics Picture Card* for **bug**

Say a word for each short vowel sound (e.g., **gas, lid, top, sun, pet**), and have children identify the vowel sound. Then read aloud the directions on page 163. Model how to answer the questions by printing **bus**, **bug**, and **rug** on the board with a circle in front of each word. Hold up the picture card for **bug**. Have a volunteer read the choices and fill in the circle that names the picture.

Observational Assessment Review the observational notes you recorded about children's mastery of and participation in the Unit 3 skill and theme activities. Use the notes to help you assess children's overall performance and progress.

Portfolio Assessment Have each child choose a writing sample from his or her portfolio for a writing conference. Ask children how their writing has improved. Ask if there are any corrections they would make now that they have learned about short vowels. See the Writing Rubrics on page 77C.

Dictation Tell children you are going to say some short **a** words. Have children write the short **a** words as you dictate them. Say **cat, tag, had, fan, jam**. Continue the activity with short **i** words (**wig, did, pin, fix, bib**); short **o** words (**pop, sock, fox, dog, top**); short **u** words (**bun, cut, tug, rug, tub**); and short **e** words (**pet, red, men, pen, web**).

Student Skills Assessment Use the checklist on Student Edition pages 321–322 to record your observations of the progress of individual children.

Take-Home Book Remind children to complete at home the *Take-Home Book* page for Unit 3.

Additional Assessment See pages 77C–77E.

Save Our Earth
Reduce! Reuse! Recycle!

Long Vowels

READING/LANGUAGE ARTS STANDARDS

✪ Respond to a poem in a way that reflects understanding
✪ Distinguish long and short vowel sounds in orally stated single-syllable words
✪ Generate sounds from letters and letter patterns and blend those sounds into recognizable words
✪ Recognize and use knowledge of spelling patterns, including sounds represented by single letters and vowel digraphs
✪ Spell basic short vowel and long vowel words
✪ Read simple one-syllable and high-frequency words

OBJECTIVES

▶ To enjoy a poem about recycling
▶ To develop phonemic awareness by identifying, matching, segmenting, blending, and manipulating sounds in spoken words
▶ To recognize long **Aa, Ii, Oo, Uu, Ee**
▶ To discriminate between long and short vowel sounds
▶ To identify long vowel words
▶ To use long vowel concepts to decode words
▶ To read and write short and long vowel words and high-frequency words in context

LESSONS

Thematic Teaching

In Unit 4 children learn long vowel sounds as they learn what Earth does for them and what they can do for Earth. Phonics skills include discriminating, reading, and writing long vowel words alone and in context.

Display the "Yesterday's Paper" **Unit 4 Classroom Poster** near the Art Center so that children make the connection between reusing and recycling found materials and helping keep our planet clean.

Curriculum Integration

Spelling A *Spelling Connection* appears in most lesson plans. Children also practice spelling long vowel high-frequency words on page 258.

Writing Meaningful writing activities appear on pages 172, 176, 188, 196, and 252.

Optional Learning Activities

Multisensory Activities
Opportunities for visual, auditory, tactile, and kinesthetic learning occur regularly.

Multicultural Connection
Help children learn about cultural diversity by enjoying together the multicultural activities on pages 166, 172, 204, 218, and 246.

Learning Centers
Learning Centers actively involve children in phonics and ecology. Children become sculptors and experiment with making collages in the Art Center. The Science Center is both an air pollution lab and the staging area for Cleanup Day.

Thematic Activities
Motivate children with the engaging thematic activities in the *Curriculum Connections* section of many lesson plans.

Author's Corner

Mabel Watts
Mabel Watts was born in London in 1906 but eventually moved with her family to Canada and the United States. Ms. Watts did not begin to write until after she became a mother. To encourage her four-year-old daughter to eat, she promised to read to her. She read so many children's books that she soon decided to write her own.

✓ Assessment Strategies
Assessment is an ongoing process. Multiple strategies in the Student Edition as well as the Teacher's Edition and regular use of the *Skills Assessment Checklist* on pages 321–322 will help you monitor children's progress in reading and writing words with long vowels.

UNIT RESOURCES

Sadlier Reading

Phonics Picture Cards

Classroom Poster

Little Books and Big Books

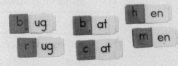

Student Manipulatives

Other Books by Mabel Watts
Watts, Mabel, and Kurt Werth. *Molly and the Giant.* New York: Parents Magazine Press, 1973. Available in local libraries.

Watts, Mabel. *The Narrow Escapes of Solomon Smart.* New York: Parents Magazine Press, 1966. Available in local libraries.

Theme-Related Resources
Silver, Donald M. *Backyard: One Small Square.* New York: McGraw Hill, 1997. How much nature is in one small piece of our own backyard? In this book children will learn to observe nature firsthand.

Carlson, Laurie. *EcoArt! Earth-Friendly Art and Craft Experiences for 3- to 9-year-olds.* Charlotte, VT: Williamson, 1993. Recycling projects for teachers.

Recycle It. Wheeling, Illinois: film ideas, inc., 1993. The World Patrol Kids give recycling tips.

In Unit 4 children focus on recognizing and spelling long vowel sounds. The assessment ideas on this page are for use throughout the unit.

Pretests/Posttests

The tests on pages 165D–165E serve as a formal end-of-unit assessment of children's mastery of long vowel sounds. In some cases you may choose to use them as pretests to help you identify a starting point for instruction for individual children. You will find that the Phonemic Awareness Test on page 165J also serves as a pretest.

Observational Assessment

Specific opportunities to observe children's progress with long vowel sounds are highlighted in the lesson plans. The *Student Skills Assessment Checklist* on pages 321–322 of the Student Edition will help you keep track of students' progress.

Dictation

Dictate the following words and have children write each word on a sheet of paper: **lake**, **right**, **snow**, **June**, **boat**, **seed**, **blue**, **hive**, **rain**, **leaf**. Then have children write the following sentences: The little **goat** sat down. Please put the **vase** here. In addition to assessing long vowels, observe whether children begin each sentence with an uppercase letter and end with a period.

Using Technology

The activities on pages 165O–165P may also be used to evaluate children's progress.

Performance Assessment

Set up a station in the Arts Center with a poster titled "We Reduce, Reuse, and Recycle!" showing a picture from a newspaper, book, or magazine of people working to help the environment. Encourage children to make a collage of something they can do to help the environment, such as picking up a piece of litter on the street or turning off lights when they leave a room. Display children's collages around the room, and discuss ways children can work together to help the environment. Use the *Student Skills Assessment Checklist* on pages 321–322 to record your observations.

Answer Key

Page 165D		Page 165E
1. rake	7. rope	1. (n)ice
2. bow	8. seal	2. (s)uit
3. tie	9. fly	3. (t)oes
4. bike	10. goat	4. (w)ave
5. mail	11. glue	5. (k)eep
6. hay	12. night	

Portfolio Assessment

The portfolio icon in the lesson plans indicates portfolio opportunities throughout the unit. Post the rubrics for Unit 4 on a chart when you begin the unit, and review the criteria with children. Discuss with children how they can select work from their portfolios that best represents their progress in a given area. Suggest that children put the date on each piece of written work as they complete it. This will enable them to compare the work they did in the beginning of the unit with the work they did at the end of the unit.

Name _____

Writing Rubrics	Sometimes	Never	Always
Phonics Skills			
Associates long vowel sounds with their corresponding letters			
Su___es rhyming words with a given long vowel sound			
Distinguishes between long and short vowel words			
Reads long vowel words in context			
Writing Skills			
Forms legible letters			
Uses initial, medial, and final sounds to spell words phonetically			
Spells long vowel words, using two vowels when appropriate, and high-frequency words appropriate to grade level			
Formulates and writes sentences using long vowel words			
Uses spaces to separate words			
Begins sentences with uppercase letters and uses correct punctuation			

 Say the name of each picture. Circle the word and print it on the line.

1	rock rain rake

2	box bay bow

3	toe tie tail

4	bake bike back

5	mail mill mile

6	hat hay hoe

7	rope ripe rap

8	sail sell seal

9	fly flow flip

10	gave got goat

11	gum glue glow

12	nut neat night

Read each sentence. Fill in the circle in front of the missing letters. Print the letters on the line.

1 It is **n**_____ at the lake.	○ ose ○ ice ○ ame
2 I wear my swimming **s**_____.	○ uit ○ at ○ eat
3 We dip our **t**_____ in the water.	○ ime ○ oes ○ une
4 We can make a big **w**_____.	○ eek ○ ise ○ ave
5 Let's **k**_____ the lake clean.	○ eep ○ ite ○ id

In Unit 4 children learn the sounds of long vowels and encounter different letter combinations that can stand for each long vowel sound. Difficulty in decoding long vowel words individually or in context, or in spelling long vowel words, may be caused by visual/perceptual/memory problems, attention deficit disorder (ADD), or spatial relationship problems. Below are some strategies you can use to help children cope with these problems.

Visual/Perceptual/Memory

Children with visual, perceptual, or memory problems may reverse the letters in vowel pairs such as **oa**, **ie**, **ea**, **ui**, and **ai**. They may also have trouble remembering which spelling to use when writing long vowel words. The techniques below may help these children as they work through the unit.

- Make word cards for words with long vowel letter combinations such as **goat**, **pie**, **read**, **suit**, and **rain**. Focusing on one word at a time, help children read the word and name the vowel sound. Then have them trace the first letter in the vowel combination with red crayon and name that letter. Point out that the letter that is the same as the name of the long vowel is usually the first vowel in the vowel pair.

- Post a list of words with long vowel combinations, and have children form the words with three-dimensional alphabet letters. Have children say the word, trace the letters with their fingers, spell the word aloud, close their eyes and spell it again, and then write the word without looking at the chart.

Attention Deficit Disorder (ADD)

Children who have ADD are often easily distracted and may have difficulty following directions, especially directions involving more than one step. Try these techniques to help children focus on directions:

- Have children look at the directions as you read them, pointing to each word as you say it.

- Tell children to circle important words, such as *read, circle,* and *write.* Remind them that they can look back at the circled words if they forget what to do next.

- After reading the directions, have volunteers explain in their own words exactly what they need to do.

Spatial Relationships

Children who have difficulty orienting things in space may also have difficulty following the sequence of letters in words and of words in sentences. Try these techniques to help children read words, sentences, and stories:

- To help children remember the concept of *left,* have children who do *not* reverse the letter **L** hold both fists in front of them and then open their index finger and thumb. The index finger and thumb on their left hand will form a perfect **L** for **left**.

- For those children who do reverse letters, practice patterning with them. Give them practice with copying patterns with beads, shapes, and colors. Make sure children always begin at the left and move toward the right.

- After children form patterns with beads, move on to patterns with letters. Have children sequence Punchout Letter Cards to match words.

- Children who can read words in isolation may have difficulty when confronted with a group of words in a sentence. Have children begin by focusing on one word at a time, covering the other words in the sentence with their fingers. After children have read each individual word, they can read the complete sentence, pointing to each word as they read it. Have children continue to reread the sentence until they can say it in a natural way. Encourage children to eliminate the single word stage when they feel ready.

- Write sentences from the decodable readers on sentence strips, and cut apart the words. Using the cards as flashcards, have children read the individual words in the order in which they appear in each sentence. Then give children the cards for the first sentence in the story, and have them arrange the words from left to right to match the sentence. Have children say "first word, second word," and so on as they lay down each card. Then have children read the complete sentence from the cards and, finally, directly from the reader.

The chart below identifies problems that children may manifest as they learn the concepts and skills presented in this unit. The chart also identifies strategies to use with children who have not yet mastered the key concepts in the unit.

SKILL	Silent e	Discriminating Long Vowel Sounds	Final y
Observation	Child does not recognize silent **e** as a long vowel signal.	Child confuses the long vowel sounds.	Child confuses the two long vowel sounds **y** can stand for.
Intervention	• Use Punchout Letter Cards to form these short vowel words in a pocket chart: **at**, **hid**, **hop**, **cut**. • Tell child to form the words with her or his own cards at her or his seat. • Have child read the words. • Have child add **e** to the end of one of the words, read the new word, and compare and contrast the way the two words look and sound. • Continue in a similar fashion with the remaining words.	• Remind child that long vowels have the same sound as the name of the letter. • Have child make a reference card to help her or him remember the long vowel sounds. Tell child to print each vowel on a sentence strip and draw a picture of a word that has that long vowel sound beside the letter. • Have child tape the reference card to her or his desk and keep it there until she or he feels comfortable with all the long vowel sounds.	• On index cards write words with final **y** from pages 249 to 252. • Read the words aloud with the child. • Have child sort the word cards according to the vowel sound **y** stands for. • Help child conclude that in a longer word with more than one vowel sound, such as **bunny**, **y** usually stands for long **e**, but that when **y** is the only vowel sound, it usually stands for the long **i** sound, such as **sky**.

These activities are designed to augment the lessons in the unit with engaging exercises that reinforce skills and encourage creativity.

Identify and Count Phonemes

Break It Up

Remind children that words are made up of separate sounds. Say /t/-/ō/-/d/ **toad**. Have children repeat after you and hold up fingers to count each segmented sound as they say it. Then ask a volunteer how many sounds are heard in **toad**. Repeat with the words **peel** and **hide**.

Say a word, and point to a child. Have that child stand and say the first sound in the word. Have a second child stand and say the second sound. Continue for each sound in the word. Then have the class say the whole word and count the standing children to find the number of sounds. Use these words: **game**, **go**, **he**, **cute**, **race**, **toe**, **hide**, **say**, **eat**, **read**.

Segment and Blend Onsets and Rimes

Farm Sing-Along

Sing one verse of "Old MacDonald." Instead of using an animal sound, say the animal's name as an onset and rime and then the two parts blended together. For example, you might sing:

Old MacDonald had a farm.

E-I-E-I-O.

And on this farm he had a pig.

E-I-E-I-O.

With a /p/-/ig/ **pig** here,

And a /p/-/ig/ **pig** there,

Here a **pig**, there a **pig**, everywhere a /p/-/ig/, etc.

Have children sing more verses, using animal names such as **dog**, **cat**, **duck**, **goat**.

Segment Onsets and Rimes

Word Parts

Materials: **Punchout Cards**, picture side up, for **cake**, **leaf**, **seal**, **hive**, **kite**, **mule**, **goat**, **five**, **note**

Tell children to spread out the picture cards on their desks so that they can see all the cards at the same time. Have children hold up the picture for **five**. Model how to segment the first sound from the rest of the word: /f/-**ive**. Have children repeat the complete word and then the segmented word.

Then ask them to find and hold up a picture card with a name that has the same rime, or ending sound, as **five** (**hive**). Have them say the word. Repeat with **goat** so that children hold up and name **note**. Then say the following words; have children segment the onset and rime before finding a picture with the same rime: **real** (/r/-**eal seal**); **rake** (/r/-**ake cake**); **boat** (/b/-**oat goat**).

Finally, say the following words; have children again say the onset and rime but this time find a picture with the same *onset* or beginning sound: **name** (/n/-**ame note**); **king** (/k/-**ing kite**); **Mike** (/m/-**ike mule**); **light** (/l/-**ight leaf**).

Blend Onsets and Rimes

What's the Word?

Have children play a word game that allows them to blend onsets and rimes. Model by saying *What's the word that begins like* **cap** *and ends like* **boat**? *(coat)* Continue with other questions, such as:

What's the word that begins...

like **fat** and ends like **lace**? (**face**)

like **mop** and ends like **tile**? (**mile**)

like **hot** and ends like **rose**? (**hose**)

like **rat** and ends like **mule**? (**rule**)

like **sun** and ends like **neat**? (**seat**)

Count Words in a Spoken Sentence

Word Count

Materials: 10 counters for each child

Say the sentences below one at a time. Have children slide a counter away from a pile on their desks each time you say a word. Then say the sentence again and have a volunteer count aloud the number of words. Have children check their counters to verify each total.

Mary had a little lamb.

Jack and Jill went up the hill.

Humpty Dumpty sat on a wall.

Do you know the muffin man?

Substitute Medial Sounds

Look in the Middle

Tell children you will say some silly sentences. Direct them to listen for the word that is a mistake and to correct it by saying a word with a different middle sound. Model by saying: *I like to ride my* **bake**. Point out that **bake** is the incorrect word. Have a volunteer change the middle sound to /ī/ to form the word **bike**. Have the class repeat the correct sentence. Continue with these sentences:

Letter carriers deliver the **mile**. (**mail**)

Hurray! I made the soccer **time**. (**team**)

I have a pet **gate**. (**goat**)

We sang a happy **teen**. (**tune**)

Name _____ Date _____

Directions: Give this assessment orally to each child. The correct answers are boldfaced.

Blend Onsets and Rimes

Say: *I will break apart a word and say the parts. You blend the sounds together and say the whole word.* Circle each word the child blends correctly.

1. /r/ -ead	**read**		6. /l/ -eaf	**leaf**
2. /k/ -ube	**cube**		7. /hw/ -y	**why**
3. /m/ -ule	**mule**		8. /b/ -ite	**bite**
4. /k/ -oat	**coat**		9. /s/ -uit	**suit**
5. /n/ -ight	**night**		10. /r/ -ain	**rain**

Segment Onsets and Rimes

Say: *I will say a word such as* **tame**. *You break the word apart, for example,* /t/ **-ame**. Circle each word the child segments correctly.

11. rain	/r/ **-ain**		16. light	/l/ **-ight**
12. like	/l/ **-ike**		17. wave	/w/ **-ave**
13. tune	/t/ **-une**		18. weave	/w/ **-eave**
14. see	/s/ **-ee**		19. jeep	/j/ **-eep**
15. gave	/g/ **-ave**		20. cone	/k/ **-one**

Identify and Count Phonemes

Say: *I will say a word. You say each sound in the word and tell how many sounds the word has. For example, if I say* **beet**, *you say "/b/-/ē/-/t/, 3 sounds."* Circle the word if the child correctly identifies and counts the phonemes.

21. pail	/p/ - /ā/ - /l/	**(3)**	26. heel	/h/ - /ē/ - /l/	**(3)**
22. no	/n/ - /ō/	**(2)**	27. road	/r/ - /ō/ - /d/	**(3)**
23. side	/s/ - /ī/ - /d/	**(3)**	28. leap	/l/ - /ē/ - /p/	**(3)**
24. tube	/t/ - /oo/ - /b/	**(3)**	29. safe	/s/ - /ā/ - /f/	**(3)**
25. sight	/s/ - /ī/ - /t/	**(3)**	30. pay	/p/ - /ā/	**(2)**

GAME TIME

Recycle the Rhymes

Blackline Master 19
p. 165L

Objective
To identify long vowel rhyming words

Players
Pairs

Materials
• scissors
• index cards

■ Duplicate and distribute Blackline Master 19 to each pair.

■ Read each rhyme with the class, and identify the picture beside it. Point out that the pictures and rhymes do not belong together.

■ Ask the children in each pair to cut and separate the pictures and rearrange them so that each appears beside the corresponding rhyme.

■ Extend the activity by having pairs make up new rhymes for the pictures and print the rhymes on index cards. Have pairs ask each other to match the new rhymes with the pictures.

Ten Questions

Blackline Master 19
p. 165L

Objective
To use phonetic and semantic clues to guess a long vowel word

Players
Groups of three or four

Materials
• box or bag
• picture cards used in "Recycle the Rhymes"

■ Distribute the picture cards used in "Recycle the Rhymes" to each group.

■ Have children fold the picture cards in half and place them in a box or bag. Direct group members to take turns choosing one picture without letting the others see it.

■ Have group members ask up to ten questions that can be answered with either "yes" or "no" to help them guess each child's picture.

■ Model how to phrase questions by saying: *Does the name of the picture have the sound of long i?* or *Is it something that is alive?*

Reusable Endings

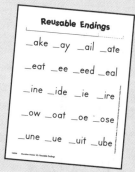

Blackline Master 20
p. 165M

Objective
To add initial consonants to long vowel phonograms to build words

Players
Small groups

Materials
• Punchout Letter Cards
• glue, scissors
• construction paper

■ Duplicate and distribute Blackline Master 20 to each group.

■ Have one child in each group remove the consonants from his or her set of Punchout Letter Cards. Ask another child to glue Blackline Master 20 onto construction paper and cut out the game cards.

■ Assign a group member to be the recorder. Tell children to combine the punchout letters with the word endings to see how many words they can make in ten minutes.

■ When time is up, have each group share its word list with the class.

Recycle the Rhymes

Can you tell me why
Earth needs bugs like the _____?

Wouldn't a goat
Look odd in a _____?

On nice days I like
To ride my _____.

The boy looks cute
in his little _____.

Here is the rule.
Don't feed the gray _____.

It made my day
To see the blue _____.

"Beep! Beep! Beep!"
Says the _____.

Can you bake
A carrot _____?

Reusable Endings

__ake	__ay	__ail	__ate
__eat	__ee	__eed	__eal
__ine	__ide	__ie	__ire
__ow	__oat	__oe	__ose
__une	__ue	__uit	__ube

Spelling Sentences

Materials: index cards, pocket chart

Make sentences that use the Unit 4 spelling words. Write all the words—except the spelling words—on index cards, and arrange the cards in order in a pocket chart. Replace each spelling word with scrambled letter cards. Have volunteers unscramble the letters, place them in the correct order, and then read the completed sentences. Encourage children at their seats to use their own letter cards to unscramble each word. Use sentences like these:

The **alef** has turned red. (**leaf**)

Jane's pet **bynun** is pink. (**bunny**)

I see the sun in the **ysk**. (**sky**)

Did you ever plant a **dese**? (**seed**)

A blue **jya** made a nest in the tree. (**jay**)

Do you have your **wno** skates? (**own**)

What color do you **klie** best? (**like**)

I **vage** my mom a gift. (**gave**)

Get the **oshe** and water the plants. (**hose**)

Do you want to **esu** my red crayon? (**use**)

You can **epek** the key. (**keep**)

Turn **girht** at the big tree. (**right**)

Long Vowel Webs

Have children work in pairs. Tell each pair to take out one letter card for each vowel, as well as cards with these pictures: **cake, leaf, seal, ride, queen, hive, goat, five, kite, jeans, note, mule, soap,** and **hose**. Direct children to make webs by placing the long vowel pictures in circles around the appropriate vowel letter cards.

Rebus Sentences

Materials: sentence strips, paper clips

Have children use the picture sides of long vowel Punchout Cards to compose rebus sentences. Ask each child to take out these pictures: **cake, leaf, seal, ride, queen, hive, goat, five, kite, jeans, note, mule, soap,** and **hose**. Then give out sentence strips, and challenge children to print on their strip a sentence that includes one or two of the picture names. Have children paper clip appropriate pictures to their strips instead of printing the picture names. You might suggest that children practice printing their sentences on scrap paper first. Circulate to help with difficult words. When children have completed their rebus sentences, encourage class sharing.

Memory Challenge

Materials: construction paper

Tell children they can use the picture sides of long vowel Punchout Cards to test their memory. To model the process, place three pictures on a desk, and give children a few seconds to study the pictures. Then cover the cards with a sheet of construction paper, and call on volunteers to name the pictures. Remove the paper to check their memory. Then have children work in pairs to play the game themselves. Encourage them to identify the long vowel sound in each picture name.

SAVE THE EARTH SIGNS

Objectives

- To help children recognize and use words with long vowel sounds in context
- To use a writing and painting program such as Kid Pix Studio® Deluxe* to make Save the Earth signs

Preparation

- Read aloud the poem "Recycle Today" on page 180. Then share a book about saving Earth with the class, such as *Long Live Earth* by Maighan Morrison.
- Ask children to name ways they can help Earth live a long life. List their ideas on the board or on chart paper. Suggestions might include "plant a **tree**;" "**clean** up a **lake**;" "**recycle**;" "**reuse** plastic bags." Have children identify words on the list that have long vowel sounds.

One Step at a Time

1. Write the following on the board, filling in the blanks with information comparable to that in the sample:

   How can you stop waste today?

   Robert has a way.

   Bring your lunch in a lunch box, instead of a paper bag.

2. Tell children to combine their names with the list of ideas to complete the sentences.

3. Then have them use a writing and drawing program such as Kid Pix Studio® Deluxe. Have them select the Typewriter icon in "Kid Pix" and then input the sentences as the text for their signs.

4. Have children select the drawing tools in the side toolbar or the options in the "Goodies" menu to illustrate their Save the Earth signs.

5. Have children print their illustrated signs.

Class Sharing

Have children share their ways of stopping waste one at a time. Display the signs on a bulletin board.

> Robert has a way to save the earth.
> Bring your lunch in a lunch box, instead of a paper bag.

I SPY DRAWINGS

Objectives

- To enable children to identify animals whose names have long vowel sounds
- To use a painting program such as Kid Pix Studio® Deluxe* to draw a picture of an animal

Preparation

Guide the class in brainstorming a list of animals having names that contain long vowel sounds. The list might include **bee** for long **e**, **toad** for long **o**, **lion** for long **i**, **jay** for long **a**, and **mule** for long **u**. Write the list on the board.

*All software referred to in this book is listed under Computer Resources on page 348.

One Step at a Time

1. Have each child choose an animal from the list on the board.

2. Instruct children to open Kid Pix to access the paint tools.

3. Have children use the tools and colors available to draw a picture of the animal.

4. Guide children to use the Typewriter icon from the side menu to enter the name of the animal.

5. Instruct children to print their animal drawings.

6. Direct children to say their animal's name and underline with a crayon the long vowel in the name.

7. Have children repeat the process for each long vowel.

Class Sharing

Display children's animal drawings on a bulletin board. Invite the class to play "I Spy."

Model the process by saying: *I spy, with my two eyes, an animal that has* (name the long vowel sound in the animal's name and a characteristic of the animal). For example, you might say: *a long **u** and long ears.* (**mule**) Have volunteers reply by repeating the characteristic mentioned in the clue: "You spy a (**mule**) because it has (a long **u** and long ears)." Continue the game until every picture has been identified.

RECITE A RHYME

On the board write the rhyme shown at the right. Read the rhyme several times, and have children join in. Have children work with a partner. Tell them to use an audiocasette recorder to tape themselves reciting the rhyme.

Listen to the recordings as a class. Invite volunteers to identify long vowel words and to write the letter on the board that stands for the long vowel sound in each word.

> Eeny, meeny, miney, mo.
> Catch a tiger by the toe.
> If he hollers, you can say,
> "Quiet, please, or go away."

Literature Introduction to Long Vowels

Objectives

- To enjoy a poem about recycling
- To match medial sounds
- To identify long vowels **a**, **i**, **o**, **u**, **e**

Starting with Literature

Read aloud "Yesterday's Paper." Lead children to see how the poem relates to recycling. Ask: *Why is recycling a good idea? How else can we take care of Earth?* Reread the poem, directing the class to read along.

Developing Critical Thinking

Discuss the Critical Thinking questions on page 165. Display children's responses on a chart reminding them to recycle.

Introducing the Skill

Phonemic Awareness: Match Medial Sounds

Say **boat** and **cone**, and have children repeat the words. Explain that both words have /ō/ in the middle. Tell children to listen as you say pairs of words. Direct them to raise their hands if both words in a pair have the same sound in the middle. Say **cage/cup**, **rice/kite**, **toad/bone**, **mule/make**, **jeep/team**.

Long Vowels

- Print **a**, **i**, **o**, **u**, **e** on the board. Remind children that these letters are called *vowels* and that they already know one sound for each. Explain that each vowel has a *long* sound as well. Point to the words **boat** and **plane** on the Unit 4 Classroom Poster. Say each as an example of a long vowel sound.
- In another column, write **take**, **bike**, **toad**, **mule**, **tree**. Read aloud the words. Have volunteers compare the vowel sound in each word with that vowel's name.

Yesterday's Paper

Yesterday's paper makes a hat,
　Or a boat,
　Or a plane,
　Or a playhouse mat.

Yesterday's paper makes things
　Like that—
And a very fine tent
For a sleeping cat.

Mabel Watts

Critical Thinking Possible responses: car, mountain, tunnel.
What else could you make out of old newspapers?
How might you recycle other things? Use plastic bottles to make dolls; save paper scraps to make pictures or puzzles.

LESSON 83: Long Vowels
Phonemic Awareness: Rhyme

165

Theme Words

Recycling Our Words Reread the poem "Yesterday's Paper." Hold up a copy of yesterday's newspaper. Ask: *What happens to newspapers when everyone is finished reading them?*

Print the word **recycle** on a word wall. Direct a volunteer to explain the word's meaning. Ask: *What else can be recycled besides newspapers?* As children respond, add key words to the wall. Continue adding to the word wall and referring to it throughout the unit.

Print **a**, **i**, **o**, **u**, **e** on the wall and print the words **cane**, **ride**, **rode**, **tube**, **feed** under the appropriate vowels. Point out that the words have, in a way, been "recycled." They have been changed from short vowel words to long vowel words, as in **can/cane**, **rid/ride**, **rod/rode**, **tub/tube**, and **fed/feed**. Challenge children to think of rhyming words for the "recycled" long vowel words and add those to the word wall, as well.

Name _____

Dear Family,

As your child learns about our environment in this unit, he or she will also be learning the sounds of the long vowels. You can participate by trying these activities together at home.

• Look at the pictures below. Say each letter and picture name with your child. Listen for the long vowel sounds. (Long vowels say their own name.)

Apreciada Familia:

Mientras aprenden sobre el medio ambiente los niños también aprenderán el sonido largo de las vocales. Pueden participar de estas actividades en el hogar.

• Miren los siguientes cuadros. Pronuncien cada letra y el nombre del objeto. Escuchen el sonido largo de las vocales. (El sonido es el de su nombre.)

a	i	o	u	e
lake	hive	boat	mule	tree

• Read the poem "Yesterday's Paper" on the reverse side of this page and talk about ways to recycle.

• Help your child find long vowel words in the poem, such as **paper**, **makes**, **boat**, **plane**, **playhouse**, **like**, **fine**, and **sleeping**. Also find words that rhyme. (hat/mat/that/cat)

• Lean el poema "Yesterday's Paper" en la página 165 y hablen sobre formas de recircular.

• Ayuden al niño a encontrar vocales de sonido fuerte en el poema, tales como: **paper**, **makes**, **boat**, **plane**, **playhouse**, **like**, **fine** y **sleeping**. También busquen palabras que rimen. (hat/mat/that/cat)

PROJECT

Recycle an old shoe box and some used magazines or catalogs. Help your child cut out magazine pictures of things that have long vowel sounds in their names. Put the pictures in the box. Ask your child to sort the pictures according to the different long vowel sounds.

PROYECTO

Recirculen una caja de zapatos. Pida al niño recortar de revistas fotos de cosas que tengan vocales de sonido largo en sus nombres. Pongan las fotos en la caja. El niño puede ordenarlas de acuerdo a los diferentes sonidos.

66 LESSON 83: Long Vowels—Phonics Alive at Home

Phonics Alive at Home

• The *Phonics Alive at Home* page for Unit 4 provides activities for children and their families. These activities focus on the unit theme, "Save Our Earth," and long vowels.

• Have children remove page 166 from their books and take the page home to share with family members.

• Throughout the unit, set aside class time for children to share projects completed at home. Ask children and their families to collect clean, recyclable materials—such as foil scraps, egg cartons, and cardboard—and bring them to school for use in class projects.

Make a plan for storing the materials until you need them.

 Direct children to additional activities on Sadlier-Oxford's web site: www.sadlier-oxford.com.

Sadlier Reading
Little Books and Big Books

Read the poem "My Name" on page 7 in Worlds of Poetry *Families, Families* and have children listen for words with long vowels.

Families, Families

Poems Selected by Lee Bennett Hopkins

Multicultural Connection

Explain that Native American cultures have long been concerned with taking care of Earth. Read aloud a Native American story, such as *Brother Eagle, Sister Sky* by Susan Jeffers (NAL-Dutton, 1993). Explain that in many Native American cultures, people paint their faces. Have children think of symbols that could represent life on Earth, such as a tree or stream. Have the class choose one symbol that has a long vowel sound and use tempera paint to put it on paper or cardboard masks. Another option is to mix tempera paint with water and hand lotion, and have children paint the symbol on a partner's face.

Take-Home Book

The Take-Home Book for Unit 4, *We Can Take Care of the Earth*, is found on student pages 329–330. This fold-up book reinforces long vowel phonics skills taught in this unit. Use this take-home component as a culminating activity for the unit or send the book home at another appropriate time.

Phonemic Awareness /ā/

Objectives

- To match medial sounds
- To identify words with /ā/
- To discriminate between words that do and do not have /ā/

Warming Up

Reviewing Short a

Write the following on the board:

n_p   c_n   h_t   b_g

g_s   d_d   l_p   m_n

Have volunteers print **a** in each word, say the word, and identify its vowel sound.

Teaching the Lesson

Phonemic Awareness: Match Medial Sounds

Say **rake** and **face**. Ask children to repeat the words after you. Explain that /ā/ is the sound in the middle of both words. Demonstrate by slowly saying /r/-/ā/-/k/, and then /f/-/ā/-/s/. Repeat with children. Ask them to raise both hands when they hear two words that have /ā/ in the middle. Say: **save/cage; cave/coat; lake/tape; pace/pine; late/paid.**

The Sound of Long a

- Say /ā/. Have children repeat it. Tell children this sound is long **a**. Say: *The word cake has the long a sound.* Read aloud the following words and ask children to pretend to blow out candles on a birthday **cake** each time they hear a word with the long **a** sound: **bake, sit, rain, fan, lace, dog, sheep, take, pay, whale.**
- Tell children you will read some sentences that include long **a** words. Ask them to clap their hands each time they hear a long **a** word. Say:

   I **ate** a piece of **cake.**

   We **made** a present for **Jake.**

   We **played games** and **stayed** up **late.**

Listen Listen as the page is read aloud. Talk about the long **a** words you hear, such as **make** and **plate.** Then answer the questions in the rhyme.

What Can You Make?

What can you **make**
From a torn **paper plate,**
Or a **faded** lamp **shade,**
Or a big wooden **crate?**

What can you **save**
To use in new **ways**
To **make** things to **play** with
On cold **rainy days?**

Discuss what can be made from recycled materials.

Critical Thinking

What are some good things to save for rainy days?

Possible responses: You can save paper plates, crates, and lamp shades.

LESSON 84: Phonemic Awareness: /ā/

167

UNIVERSAL ACCESS
Meeting Individual Needs

Auditory • Kinesthetic

Have children form two teams, with each team standing in a line facing you. Alternating between teams, ask each child to say a long **a** word. If the child responds correctly, he or she takes one step forward. The first team to have all its members step forward wins.

Visual • Kinesthetic

Materials: **Sadlier Phonics Picture Cards** for ten long **a** words and one each for short **a, i, o, u, e**

Hold up a card, and have a volunteer say the name of the picture. Direct the rest of the class to wave their right hands if the name of the picture has the sound of long **a**, as in the word **wave.**

Extra Support

Remind children /ā/ is the long **a** sound. Explain that **plate** has the long **a** sound. Read each sentence below, and have children name the long **a** words.

   Dan **made** a **game** to **play.**

   A **train came** past the **lake.**

   Who **ate** that **cake** on the **tray?**

Lake has the long **a** sound. Color the space ⟨⟩ if the name of the picture has the long **a** sound. What do you see?

bed

pot

bag

bus

cage (yellow)

train (yellow)

whale (yellow)

skate (yellow)

cane (yellow)

pig

hill

bell

tray (yellow)

tail (yellow)

cup

168

LESSON 84: Phonemic Awareness: /ā/

Ask your child to explain how he or she used the small pictures to decide which spaces to color.

Practicing the Skill

● Read aloud the directions on page 167. Remind children to listen for long **a** words as you read aloud the poem. Recite the poem again, this time pausing after each line so that children can identify and repeat the long **a** words they hear. Then discuss the Critical Thinking question.

● Read aloud the directions on page 168, and identify the pictures together. Have children complete the page independently and then name the picture they see (**an airplane**).

Curriculum Connections

Theme Activity:
Language Arts/Science
Materials: poster board, markers

● Discuss with children what we can do that is good for Earth. Explain that recycle means "use again." Ask what things can be recycled (e.g., newspapers, cans, glass).

● Have children work in small groups to make up slogans about ways to keep Earth clean. Tell them to use long **a** words in their slogans. For example:

Use your **brain** to think of **ways** to recycle.

Keep the **lake** clean!

Save cans in a recycling bin.

● Have each group choose a slogan and make a poster illustrating it. Then have groups share their posters.

Sadlier Reading
Little Books and Big Books

Read *Wake Up, Sleepyheads!* (fiction) for more practice with long **a**.

English Language Learners/ESL
Materials: a plate, a crate, a toy train, a cane, a skate

Help children listen for the sound of long **a**. Hold up the plate, identify it, say the word three times, and then use it in a sentence, e.g. a **plate**; **plate, plate, plate**; I put food on my **plate**. Have children repeat the word and the sentence after you. Then repeat the activity for each of the other objects.

Special Strategies
For Universal Access activities, see page 165F.

Challenge
Brainstorm with children things they could make from recycled materials. Items might include a bird feeder (milk carton), hats (newspaper), or dolls (plastic bottles). Have children illustrate the items and then talk about them using at least one long **a** word (e.g., "Birds **take** seeds from my feeder." or "I **play** a **game** with this egg carton."). Have children say their sentences to partners, who then name the long **a** words.

Sound to Symbol /ā/ a_e

Objectives

- To identify and isolate medial sounds
- To recognize that **a_e** stands for /ā/
- To spell words with /ā/ **a_e**

Teaching the Lesson

Phonemic Awareness: Identify and Isolate Medial Sounds

- Tell children that the middle sound in the words **gave** and **make** is /ā/. Say /g/-/ā/-/v/ **gave** and /m/-/ā/-/k/ **make**. Have children repeat after you.
- Tell children you will say some words. Ask them to repeat the middle sound if a word you say has the same long **a** sound as in **gave** or **rake**. Use **lake**, **hum**, **cat**, **cage**, **wet**, **game**, **fit**, **tape**.

Sound to Symbol

Materials: **Sadlier Phonics Picture Cards** for **lake**, **tape**, **rake**, **cake**

- Say the words **base** and **safe**. Remind children that the middle sound in **base** and **safe** is long a, /ā/. Long **a** can be spelled with the letters **a_e**. Point out that the **e** is silent.
- Display the picture cards and have children identify them. List the picture names on the board under **a_e** and have volunteers underline the **a** and **e** in each word.

Practicing the Skill

- Read aloud the directions on page 169. Have children find the picture cue at the top. Ask: *Which letters in **lake** stand for the long **a** sound?* (a_e) *Which letter is silent?* (e) Do the first three items together. Then have children complete the page.

Observational Assessment

*Note whether children correctly add **e** at the end of /ā/ a_e words.*

169

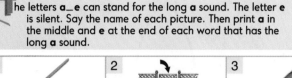

The letters **a_e** can stand for the long **a** sound. The letter **e** is silent. Say the name of each picture. Then print **a** in the middle and **e** at the end of each word that has the long **a** sound.

lake

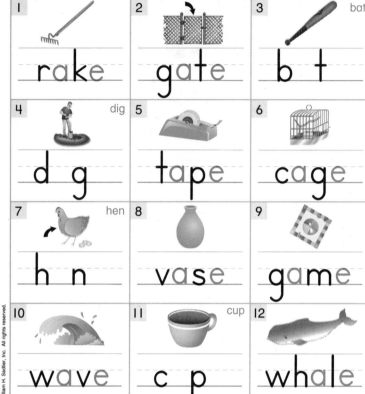

1. rake
2. gate
3. b_t   bat
4. d_g   dig
5. tape
6. cage
7. h_n   hen
8. vase
9. game
10. wave
11. c_p   cup
12. whale

LESSON 85: Connecting Sound to Symbol: /ā/ a_e

169

UNIVERSAL ACCESS
Meeting Individual Needs

English Language Learners/ESL

Materials: realia of **game, tape, vase, cage, rake, cake**

On a table, spread out realia for some of the things children will encounter in the lesson pictures. Point to each object as you say its name; have children repeat. Change the position of the objects on the table and ask, *Where is the _____?* Have children answer using the name of the object (e.g., "Here's the ___.") and pointing.

Challenge

Materials: drawing paper, crayons

Tell children to pretend they are exploring a cave. Have them work with partners and write sentences about their adventure, using at least one /ā/ a_e word. Have children read their sentences aloud, and ask volunteers to name the long **a** words that they hear. Then have children illustrate their sentences.

Extra Support

Materials: **Sadlier Phonics Picture Cards** for **cake, wave, lake, rake, grapes**

Display the picture cards. Draw five large circles as a bunch of grapes. Have children name the pictures. Write the words in the circles. Children "pick" a grape, say the word, and underline the **a_e** phonogram.

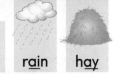

The letters **ai** and **ay** can stand for the long **a** sound. Say the name of each picture. Circle the word. Then print **ai** or **ay** on the line.

rain   hay

1	name / **nail**	2	**jay** / nail	3	**pay** / pat
	n a i l		j a y		p a y
4	take / **train**	5	**mail** / map	6	**hay** / ham
	t r a i n		m a i l		h a y
7	sale / **snail**	8	**tail** / tap	9	**rain** / rake
	s n a i l		t a i l		r a i n
10	same / **sail**	11	**tray** / tan	12	pal / **pail**
	s a i l		t r a y		p a i l

LESSON 86: Connecting Sound to Symbol: /ā/ **ai** and **ay**

Read the long **a** words aloud. Then help your child write the words in two columns under the headings **ai** and **ay**.

Sound to Symbol: /ā/ ai and ay

Objectives
- To identify and isolate medial sounds
- To recognize that **ai** and **ay** stand for /ā/
- To spell words with /ā/ **ai** and **ay**

Teaching the Lesson

**Phonemic Awareness:
Identify and Isolate Medial Sounds**
- Tell children that the middle sound in **rain** is /ā/. Say: /r/-/ā/-/n/ **rain**. Have children repeat after you.
- Tell children you will say some words. Ask them to repeat the middle sound and pretend to open an umbrella if a word you say has the same sound as the /ā/ in **rain**. Use **lane, pat, dip, pot, train, lap, sail**.

Sound to Symbol
Materials: three pairs of **Sadlier Phonics Picture Cards**: **pail** and **jay**, **rain** and **hay**, and **train** and **spray**
- Say the word **nail**. Remind children that the vowel sound in **nail** is long **a**, and is spelled with the letters **ai**. Then say: *The vowel sound in **day** is also long **a**, which is spelled with the letters **ay**.*
- Display the picture cards for **pail** and **jay**, and have children identify them.
- List the picture names on the board under **ai** or **ay**, and have volunteers underline the long **a** letters.

Practicing the Skill

- Read the directions on page 170 with children. Call their attention to the picture cues at the top. Tell children to use these as clues to complete the page. Have children complete the page independently.

English Language Learners/ESL
Materials: realia of **mail, snail, pay, tray, nail, pail**

On a table, spread out realia for some of the things children will encounter in the lesson pictures. Point to each object as you say its name; have children repeat. Change the position of the objects on the table and ask, *Where is the _____?* Have children answer using the name of the object (e.g., "Here's the ___.") and pointing.

Challenge
Provide children with a story starter using words with long **a**. For example, you might say: **Today**, we collected **rain** in a **pail**. Ask children to write two or three sentences to finish the story. Identify long **a** words spelled with **ay** or **ai**.

Extra Support
Materials: Sadlier Phonics Picture Cards for **jay, hay, spray, pail, rain**

Draw a pail and a haystack. Have children name the pictures. Write the **ai** words in the pail and the **ay** words in the haystack. Have children underline the **ai** and **ay** letters.

Student Pages 171–172

Long Vowel a Phonograms

Objectives

- To substitute initial sounds
- To recognize long **a** phonograms
- To build words with long **a** phonograms

Warming Up

Reviewing Initial Consonant Sounds

Read the tongue twisters below aloud. Ask volunteers to identify the repeated initial consonant sounds.

We will walk to West Wooster. (**w**)

Ron and Ray recycled the red rags. (**r**)

Gail gave Gabe good green grapes. (**g**)

Teaching the Lesson

Phonemic Awareness: Substitute Initial Sounds

Say the word **lake** and then /l/-/āk/. Point out that the beginning sound in **lake** is /l/; the rest of the word is /āk/. Tell children that by changing the beginning sound in a word, we can sometimes make a new word. Repeat /l/-/āk/ **lake**. Then say /b/-/āk/ **bake**. Point out that you changed the /l/ to /b/ to make a new word. Repeat the process, changing the beginning sounds in the words **date**, **pail**, **cage**, **day**.

Phonograms

Materials: Punchout Letter Cards

- Have children use their letter cards to make the phonogram **age**. Read it aloud. Have children place the letter **p** in front of **age**, leaving a space between **p** and **age**. Tell children to run their finger beneath the word parts as you say together /p/-/āj/ **page**.
- Explain that other words can be made with the **age** phonogram by changing the initial consonant. Tell children to replace the **p** with **c**. Have a volunteer read the word by blending /k/ with /āj/.
- Repeat the process with phonograms **ate**, **ail**, **ake**, **ay**.

171

Say the name of each picture. In each row, circle two pictures that have rhyming names. Then make a new rhyming word. Check your answers by saying the rhyming words with a partner.

Accept any answer that is a real word.

1 lake pail snake   c ake

2 cap gate skate   l ate

3 snail pail cake   mail

4 stage can cage   p age

5 rain jay hay   s ay

LESSON 87: Long Vowel **a** Phonograms **171**

UNIVERSAL ACCESS
Meeting Individual Needs

Visual • Kinesthetic

Materials: beanbag; Sadlier Phonics Picture Cards for **hay, jay, lake, rake, pail, rain**

Place the long **a** picture cards face up on the floor. Have children take turns tossing the beanbag to land on a picture. Ask each child to name the picture and say a rhyming word.

Kinesthetic • Auditory

Have children listen as you say a series of sentences with rhyming words. Tell children to shout "Hooray!" after they hear a long **a** rhyme. Say these sentences:

*Earth wants to **say**, "Help me each **day**."*

Don't be rude — litter is crude!

*Have a **sale** to save the **whale**.*

*Don't ever **fail** to help a **snail**.*

Extra Support

Write the phonograms **ake, ate, ail, age,** and **ay** on index cards. Dictate long **a** words, and have children use their Punchout Letter Cards to build the words.

Say the name of each picture. Color each box that has a word that rhymes with the picture name.

1. **jay**
   | day | say |
   | game | hay |

2. **sail**
   | mail | vase |
   | pail | tail |

3. **lake**
   | tape | cake |
   | bake | take |

4. **cave**
   | wave | gave |
   | Dave | nail |

5. **gate**
   | snail | skate |
   | date | late |

6. **rain**
   | train | brain |
   | safe | gain |

7. **stage**
   | cage | cape |
   | age | page |

8. **game**
   | tame | same |
   | came | vase |

LESSON 87: Long Vowel **a** Phonograms

Help your child cut apart the word squares. Then mix them up and match the rhyming words together.

Practicing the Skill

● Have children turn to page 171. Read the directions together and identify the pictures. Model how to do the first item before having partners complete the page.

● Read the directions on page 172. Do the first item with children, then have them complete the page.

Curriculum Connections

Spelling Connection
Materials: Punchout Letter Cards
Read aloud each word and sentence. Ask a volunteer to spell the long **a** word aloud or use the letter cards.

make	Did Dad **make** the cake?
game	Make a **game** of picking up litter.
came	Jake **came** over to play.
page	The story starts on **page** ten.

Theme Activity: Multicultural/Science
Materials: world map

● Explain that in hot and rainy places in the world there are rain forests. Tell children that certain plants and animals live there and nowhere else. Point out Costa Rica and your state on a world map. Tell children that there is a special Children's Rainforest in Costa Rica. Explain that children from many countries have raised money to take care of it. Tell children that they can learn about the plants and animals in their own area.

● Take children for a walk around the school. Have them notice birds, insects, flowers, trees, and other animals and plants.

● Back in the classroom, have children illustrate what they saw and add sentence captions. Suggest they use long **a** words (i.e., **rain**, **ladybug**, **shade**, **snail**, **jay**). Display the pictures under the sign "Save Our Earth." List the long **a** words on the board.

English Language Learners/ESL
Materials: index cards

To combine or isolate parts of a word is a skill that some children may find difficult. Write the phonograms found on page 171 on the board (e.g., ake, ate, ail, age, ay). On index cards, write consonants that will be used in this lesson to form words. Model how to say each phonogram and how to add consonants to the phonograms to build words. Have children match consonant cards and word endings to make words and to read them aloud.

Special Strategies
For Universal Access activities, see page 165F.

Challenge
Write **lake** on the board and draw a wavy line for a shoreline around it. Write long **a** words (that children dictate) around the "lake" to make a web. Have children use a web word in a sentence that tells something they think will help save our Earth. Have them share their sentences with the class. Ask volunteers to say the long **a** word from the web and any other long **a** words used in a sentence.

Observational Assessment

Note whether children can spell long a words with the a_e pattern.

Long Vowel a Phonograms

Objectives
- To blend onsets and rimes
- To build words with long **a** phonograms
- To discriminate long **a** words from other words

Warming Up

Reviewing Rhyme
Say long **a** word pairs: **hay**, **pay**; **tame**, **take**; **main**, **train**; **nail**, **pail**; **may**, **cave**. Have children identify words that rhyme.

Teaching the Lesson

Phonemic Awareness: Blend Onsets and Rimes
Say the word parts **/p/-age**. Tell children you are going to blend these two parts to say a word. Model by saying **/p/-age page**. Now say **/k/-age**, and ask a volunteer to blend the two parts (**cage**). Repeat with **/t/-ail**, **/m/-ake**, and **/h/-ay**.

Phonograms
Materials: **Sadlier Phonics Picture Cards** for **lake, hay, pail**

- On the board write the phonogram **ake**. Under it write **make, cake,** and **bake**. Read aloud the phonogram and then each word. Ask children to circle **ake** in each word. Point out that all the words end with the **ake** phonogram.
- Write **ake** on the board. Show the **lake** picture, and say its name. Explain that to write **lake** you need to add the letter that stands for **/l/** to the beginning of **ake**. Write **l** in front of **ake**, then read the word together. Repeat this procedure with the phonograms **ay** and **ail** using the corresponding picture cards.

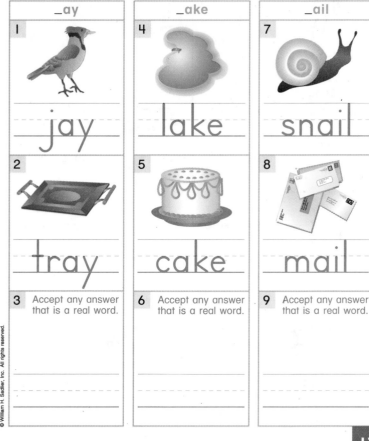

Say each word part. Say the name of each picture. Print the word on the line. Then add your own rhyming word and picture.

_ay

1. jay
2. tray
3. Accept any answer that is a real word.

_ake

4. lake
5. cake
6. Accept any answer that is a real word.

_ail

7. snail
8. mail
9. Accept any answer that is a real word.

LESSON 88: Word Building with Long Vowel **a** Phonograms   **173**

UNIVERSAL ACCESS
Meeting Individual Needs

Kinesthetic • Auditory
Materials: index cards

Print on cards long **a** words that can be acted out, for example, **bake, pay, skate**. Have children take turns picking a card and acting out the word for the class to guess. Remind children to guess only long **a** words.

Auditory • Kinesthetic
Tell children you are going to say a name, pronouncing the first sound separately from the rest of the name. Say **/j/-ane** for **Jane**. Have two volunteers repeat the segmented sounds, blend the sounds together to say the name, and shake hands if the name has the long **a** sound. Continue with **Dave, May, Gail, Jack, Ray, Dale, Pam, Val, Jake**.

Extra Support
Review that **a_e, ai,** and **ay** are spelling patterns for long **a**. Write **pail** and **pal** on the board. Remind children that only **pail** has the long **a** sound. Continue with **tack/take, bat/bait, pan/pain, man/may**. Have children identify the long **a** word in each pair.

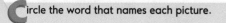

Circle the word that names each picture.

1. ran (rain) rail	2. (frame) from fan	3. cake can (cage)
4. will (whale) wait	5. (hay) hat hill	6. (safe) same sat
7. (plate) late pat	8. (stage) stain age	9. rock ram (rake)
10. (tape) tap tip	11. top (train) tan	12. jet pay (jay)
13. saw sell (sail)	14. (tray) trap trip	15. can (cane) cot

Read aloud all of the words on the page. Let your child shout "Hooray!" after each long a word.

174   LESSON 88: Practicing Long Vowel a

Practicing the Skill

● Read aloud the directions on page 173. Be sure children understand that each word they write should end with the letters printed above the column. Together, do item 1. Help children identify all pictures before having them complete the page.

● Read the directions on page 174. Remind children to use blending to read the words. Together, do item 1 and identify all pictures; then have children complete the page.

Curriculum Connections

Spelling Connection
Materials: Punchout Letter Cards

Read aloud each word and sentence. Ask a volunteer to spell the long **a** word orally or use letter cards to spell the word.

wade It's fun to **wade** in clean water.

cane Grandpa walks with a **cane.**

gate Close the **gate** in the fence.

lace The baby's cap is made of **lace**.

safe "**Safe**!" yelled the umpire.

Theme Activity: Math Center
Materials: drawing paper, crayons

● Read aloud the theme book cited below. Then have children brainstorm a list of animal names. Include names that have the long **a** sound, such as **crane**, **crayfish**, **quail**, **snail**, **snake**, and **whale**.

● Have small groups of children write and illustrate their own counting book featuring an animal that has the long **a** sound in its name. Page one should have one of the animal; page two, two of the animal; and so on. Display the books in the Math Center or Library Corner.

Theme Book Owens, Mary Beth. *Counting Cranes.* Boston: Little, Brown and Company, 1993. Children practice counting and learn the story of the endangered whooping crane.

English Language Learners/ESL
Materials: Punchout Letter Cards; index cards with the phonograms **ail, ame, ape, ain, ay, ake**

Model for children how to add an initial consonant to a phonogram to build a word. *I can add /s/ to ail and make the word* **sail**. Help children use the letter cards to build the words **snail, mail, tail, rail**, and so on. Have children say the word after they build it. Then do the same for all the phonograms listed above.

Challenge
Discuss with children how oil spills in the ocean can kill plants and animals living there. Then have them think of other events that are harmful to the environment, such as forest fires or traffic on the highway. Have children write two sentences about one such event. Tell them to use and underline long **a** words in their sentences. Have volunteers share their sentences with the class.

Special Strategies
For Universal Access activities, see Page 165F.

Observational Assessment

Note which children have difficulty writing the long a phonogram in the animal names.

Long a and Short a

Objectives

- To blend phonemes in a word
- To write long **a** words
- To discriminate long **a** words from short **a** words

Warming Up

Reviewing Initial Consonants

Materials: **ate**, **ail**, **ay**, **ame** on index cards

Give sets of phonogram cards to groups of children. Model adding /l/ to **ate** to get **late**. Have groups add initial consonants to make long **a** words.

Teaching the Lesson

Phonemic Awareness: Blend Phonemes in a Word

Materials: **Sadlier Phonics Picture Cards** for **lake** and **rake** and three counters

Display the picture cards. Explain that to say each picture name, we blend together the sounds in the word. Move three counters, one at a time, as you say /l/-/ā/-/k/. Then bring the counters together as you say **lake**. Have children use counters as they repeat what you said and did and point to the appropriate picture card. Repeat for **rake**.

Sound to Symbol

- Say the words **tape** and **tap**. Remind children that **tape** has the long **a** sound and that **tap** has the short **a** sound. Say **cake**, **map**, **play**, and **hat**. Have children tell whether each word has a long **a** or short **a** sound.
- Write the following words on the board: **cave**, **pail**, **may**, **can**, **mat**. Remind children that **a_e**, **ai**, and **ay** can stand for the long **a** sound. Then say each word, and have children repeat after you. Have volunteers identify whether each word has a long **a** or short **a** sound and underline the letter or letters that stand for the vowel sound.

175

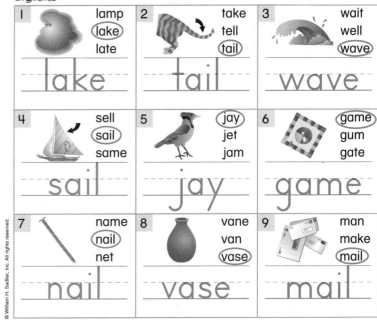

Say the name of each picture with a partner. Then circle the word and print it on the line.

1. lamp / (lake) / late — **lake**
2. take / tell / (tail) — **tail**
3. wait / well / (wave) — **wave**
4. sell / (sail) / same — **sail**
5. (jay) / jet / jam — **jay**
6. (game) / gum / gate — **game**
7. name / (nail) / net — **nail**
8. vane / van / (vase) — **vase**
9. man / make / (mail) — **mail**

Write a sentence about one picture using a long **a** word.

Accept any sentence that contains a long **a** word.

Possible response:

I have a game.

UNIVERSAL ACCESS
Meeting Individual Needs

Auditory • Visual

Have partners think of a long **a** or short **a** word and tell you (but not the class) what it is. Then have them draw on the board a picture of the word for classmates to guess. They may give a clue by telling whether they've drawn a long **a** or short **a** word.

Kinesthetic • Auditory

Show children how to use their bodies to depict "long" by stretching their arms up and standing on tiptoe. Then have them crouch to become as "short" as they can. Slowly say a list of both short **a** and long **a** words. Tell children to stretch when they hear a long **a** word and to crouch when they hear a short **a** word.

Extra Support

Materials: **Sadlier Phonics Picture Cards** for long **a** and short **a** words

Review the long and short sounds of **a**. Have children draw and name picture cards, repeat the sound of the **a**, and then place long and short **a** cards in separate piles.

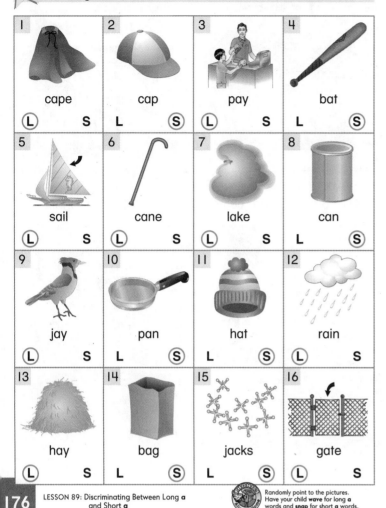

Read the name of each picture. Circle **L** if the name has the sound of long **a**. Circle **S** if the name has the sound of short **a**.

1 cape Ⓛ S	2 cap L Ⓢ	3 pay Ⓛ S	4 bat L Ⓢ
5 sail Ⓛ S	6 cane Ⓛ S	7 lake Ⓛ S	8 can L Ⓢ
9 jay Ⓛ S	10 pan L Ⓢ	11 hat L Ⓢ	12 rain Ⓛ S
13 hay Ⓛ S	14 bag L Ⓢ	15 jacks L Ⓢ	16 gate Ⓛ S

176

LESSON 89: Discriminating Between Long **a** and Short **a**

Randomly point to the pictures. Have your child **wave** for long **a** words and **snap** for short **a** words.

Practicing the Skill

- Read aloud the directions at the top of page 175 and help children identify the pictures. Go over the writing directions. Write an example sentence on the board and point out the uppercase letter and period. Then have children complete the page.
- Read aloud the directions on page 176. Clarify that "L" stands for *long* and "S" for *short*. Do the first four items with the class. Then identify the remaining pictures and have children work on their own.

Curriculum Connections

Spelling Connection

Read aloud each word and sentence below. Ask one child to spell the word aloud and another to print it on the board.

tail   A tiger has stripes on its **tail**.

main   The **main** gate of the zoo was open.

pail   A cub ate food out of a **pail**.

rain   The **rain** made the bear's fur wet.

Computer Connection

Have children play Word Munchers™ (MECC) to identify words that have the long **a** or short **a** sound. Before children play, access "Content" under Management Options to activate words with long **a** or short **a** sounds. Then instruct children to direct the Muncher to "eat" words that match the vowel sound displayed at the top of the screen.

Theme Activity: Language Arts

Materials: **Unit 4 Classroom Poster**

Hold up the "Yesterday's Paper" poster. Have children print a sentence telling what they think one of the children might be saying. Tell them to use at least one long **a** word. Display the sentences in a "Save Earth" display. Have the class point out any long **a** and short **a** words.

Sadlier Reading

Little Books and Big Books

Read *Space Camp* (nonfiction) for more practice with long **a**.

English Language Learners/ESL

Materials: Sadlier Phonics Picture Cards for **bat, ham, tag, van, hay, lake, rain, rake**

Help children practice the distinction between long and short vowel sounds. Remind children that /ā/ is the long vowel **a** sound and /a/ is the short vowel **a** sound. Tell children to watch how you shape your mouth differently for each **a**. Have children repeat the sound and have them notice how the shape of their mouths changes as they say long **a** versus short **a**. Show children the picture cards one at a time. Then have children repeat long **a** and short **a** words after you.

Challenge

Together come up with a list of long **a** words children might use when writing about protecting Earth. You might include **save, take, away, ways, replace, make, safe, aid, mail, lake, trail, rain, bay, jay,** and **today**. Have children print and illustrate two tips to follow to protect Earth. Add the tips to the "Save Earth" display from the *Theme Activity*.

Special Strategies

For Universal Access activities, see page 165F.

Long Vowel a Decodable Reader

Objectives
- To read long **a** words and high-frequency words in context
- To read the story fluently
- To compare and contrast

Introducing the Story Words

Decodable Words Remind children that the sound of long **a** is /ā/. On the board, write **take**, **game**, **day**, **make**, **cave**, **safe**, **mail**, **sail**, **lake**, **bake**, **cake**. Review how **a_e**, **ai**, and **ay** can make the long **a** sound. Together, read the words on the board. Ask volunteers to underline the two letters in each word that make the long **a** sound.

High-Frequency Words Write the high-frequency words **I**, **this**, **a**, **you**, **the**, **for**, **be**, **my** on the board. Read the list with the class. Direct children to write five of the words on a piece of paper, put their papers in envelopes, and "mail" them to a classmate to read and spell aloud.

Reading the Book

Reading Together Show children how to cut and fold pages 177 and 178 into a book. Read aloud the title, "Game Day Box." Discuss with children how they might play with a big box. Tell them to listen to the story to see whether the boy does some of the same things. Have children follow along in their books as you read aloud.

Responding Ask children to describe what kind of game day box they'd like to make.

Reading for Fluency Have children follow along as you read. Then direct partners to echo read the story. Finally, have children read the story independently.

Observational Assessment

Note whether children can decode the long a words and fluently read the story.

Name _____

Game Day Box

8 Will you make up a game?   I will take this box.

6 I will sail on the lake.   I will make a cave.

Directions: Cut and fold the book. Then read the story. Tell how the boy makes the box look different for each game.

LESSON 90: Long Vowel **a** Decodable Reader
Comprehension: Comparing and Contrasting

177

UNIVERSAL ACCESS
Meeting Individual Needs

Auditory • Kinesthetic
Seat children in a circle, with pairs sitting back-to-back. Have a child say a long **a** word, then have the partner sitting in back say a rhyming word. Have the next child in the circle say a new long **a** word. Continue until every child has said a long **a** word. Write the words on the board.

Visual • Tactile
Materials: strips of construction paper

On the board, write the long **a** story words and read the list with children. Direct each child to choose several of the words and write them on the strips of paper. Show children how to loop the strips together to make a long **a** chain. Then have children read aloud the words on their chain.

Extra Support
Read the long **a** story words with children, pointing out the long **a** spelling patterns **a_e**, **ai**, **ay**. Then have children read the list to you, spell each word, and name the two letters that make the long **a** sound. Have children sort words under the headings **a_e**, **ai**, **ay**.

2   It will be my game day box.   I will bake a cake.   7

4   I will make a safe.   I will make a box for mail.   5

178   LESSON 90: Long Vowel a Decodable Reader
      Comprehension: Comparing and Contrasting

Comparing and Contrasting   Explain to children that it can help them understand a story to notice how characters, events, and things are alike and how they are different. Lead children in a discussion comparing and contrasting their own experiences playing with boxes to that of the boy in the story. Also compare and contrast the different uses for the box the boy found.

Phonics and Decoding

Learning About Long a   *Materials:* index cards

On the board, write the long **a** story words. Have children read them aloud. Ask them to name the vowel sound in each word. (/ā/) Ask children to circle the two letters in each word that make the long **a** sound. (**a_e**, **ai**, **ay**)

Word Building   On the board, draw a word web with a long **a** phonogram in the center, such as **ake**. Direct children to add beginning consonants such as **b,c,f,l,r,w** to the phonogram to form words. Add the words to the web. Repeat with other long **a** phonograms, such as **ay** and **ail.**

Curriculum Connections

Writing and Sharing   *Materials:* large box

Ask children to write a group story entitled, "How To Make a Game Day Box." Write the title on the board and read it aloud. Guide the class in writing a group story. Write the story on the board. Direct volunteers to read aloud sentences from the story while a partner uses the box to demonstrate.

English Language Learners/ESL
Materials: index cards, markers, tape

Write this sentence frame on the board: I will _____ a _____. Write long **a** words (**take, game, day, make, cave, safe, mail, bike, cake**) from the *Decodable Reader* on individual index cards. Read aloud each word and then read the words as a group. Invite volunteers to tape word cards in the blank spaces on the board and to read the entire sentence. For each sentence, ask: *Does this make sense?*

Challenge
Materials: large box, paper, markers

Have children work in pairs to think of ways that a box could be used to help Earth, such as collecting used cans for recycling. Direct the pairs to write their ideas on paper, and read their ideas to the class. Have them point out long **a** words they used. Then have the class decide which idea to do in their classroom. Tape the written idea to the outside of the box. Encourage children to use the box for its stated purpose.

Special Strategies
For Universal Access activities, see page 165F.

Long Vowel a in Context

Objectives

- To divide words into syllables
- To identify long **a** words to complete sentences
- To write long **a** words in context

Warming Up

Reviewing Final Consonants, Final Blends

Say the rhyme below. Have volunteers name the final consonant sound(s) that each final blend or final consonant stands for.

Love the <u>land</u>—/Give it a <u>hand</u>./Please keep it <u>clean</u>/And keep the <u>dream</u>.

Teaching the Lesson

Phonemic Awareness: Divide Words into Syllables

Tell children that words are made up of one or more syllables or word parts, with each syllable having one vowel sound. Clap your hands to model syllables as you say **Jay** and **May** (one) and **Lanie** and **Jacob** (two). Then say the following word pairs, and have children repeat the word that has two syllables: **gate/baseball, face/away, rainbow/lace.**

Phonics in Context

Materials: Sadlier Phonics Picture Cards for **rake, hay, pail**

Display the picture cards, and have children identify each. Then write this sentence on the board: The horse had ___ for lunch. Write the words **rake, hay,** and **pail** next to the sentence. Model reading the sentence, each time substituting a word choice for the blank. Guide children to realize that **hay** best completes the meaning of the sentence.

Comprehension Skill: Identifying Problem/Solution

Look at each picture. Circle the word that completes the sentence. Then print it on the line.

1	Don't __waste__ paper scraps.	win / wet / (waste)
2	Take an old picture __frame__.	(frame) / from / flat
3	__Paste__ scraps onto it.	Pass / Pat / (Paste)
4	Draw your __face__.	(face) / fan / fin
5	__Tape__ it in the frame.	Tap / (Tape) / Tip
6	Hang it in a good __place__.	(place) / pal / plate

LESSON 91: Long Vowel **a** in Sentences **179**

UNIVERSAL ACCESS
Meeting Individual Needs

Visual • Kinesthetic

Materials: Sadlier Phonics Picture Cards for five long **a** and fifteen short vowel words

Have partners draw two cards. If both cards have long **a** names, the partners keep them and take another turn. If not, two other partners take a turn. The partners with the most cards win.

Auditory • Kinesthetic

Review that **brain** is a long **a** word. Tell children to use their brains to figure out which of the words you will say are long **a** words. Have children point to their heads whenever they hear a long **a** word. Use such words as **base, waste, walk, cape, cap, fake, fame, tap, play, tail, state, sat,** and **jay.**

Extra Support

Materials: Sadlier Phonics Picture Cards for **cake, game, snail, pail, hay**

Remind children that the vowel sound in **plate** and **say** is long **a**. On the board write the names of the pictures. Have a child draw a card, say the name and its vowel sound, and point to the name on the board.

listen as the poem is read aloud. Then use long **a** words to complete the sentences.

Recycle Today

How can you stop waste today?
Tate and Miss Jay have a way.

They say, "Save your lunch trays.
Don't toss them away.

Use them when you work
Or when you play.

Or use them to make gifts
For your friend's birthday!"

1. We need to stop ___waste___ .

2. Tate and Miss Jay save lunch ___trays___ .

3. They use them when they ___work___ .

4. Use a tray to make a ___birthday___ gift.

180   LESSON 91: Long Vowel **a** in Context
Comprehension: Identifying Problem/Solution

Help your child read labels on cans of food you have at home. Talk about any long **a** words you find.

● Have children tell what is happening in the sequence of pictures on page 179. Then tell children to use the pictures to help them decide which word belongs in each sentence. Model this process by doing the first item with children. Read the remaining word choices together, and have children complete the page.

● Read aloud the poem on page 180; then reread it together. Have children suggest answers to the question in the first line of the poem and then complete the page.

Curriculum Connections

Spelling Connection

Read aloud each word and sentence below. Ask a child to spell the word aloud and another child to print the word on the board.

sail   The gray boat has a white **sail**.
rail   Hold onto the stair **rail**.
stain   The spilled jam left a **stain**.
brain   You use your **brain** to think.
train   Did you ever ride on a **train**?

Theme Activity: Science/Language Arts

Materials: globe, water, pan, food coloring

● Have children look at a globe and notice the areas of water. Demonstrate how water pollution travels by dropping food coloring into a pan of water. Discuss how the "spreading" of food coloring is similar to what happens when waste is put into lakes, streams, or oceans.

● List on the board long **a** words that children used in the discussion (e.g., **lake**, **save**, **place**, **waste**, **make**). Have children write a sentence about pollution, using a long **a** word, and illustrate it.

Portfolio   Have children add their sentences and illustrations about pollution to their portfolios.

Observational Assessment

Note children's use of letter-sound association as well as context and picture cues.

English Language Learners/ESL

Preview the poem on page 180. Discuss the pictures on the page by pointing to different areas and asking: *What is happening?* Read the poem aloud, and ask the meaning of words or phrase such as **waste, save, toss-away,** and **gifts.** Help children to think of synonyms to increase their vocabulary. Then invite volunteers to make up sentences using those words.

Challenge

Remind children that the theme of the unit is "Save Our Earth." Then have children clap once for each syllable they hear as you say the following multisyllable words: **wildlife, pollution, ecosystem, recycle, environment, endangered, resources.**

Special Strategies

For Universal Access activities, see page 165F.

Student Pages 181–182

Reviewing and Assessing Long Vowel a

Objectives
- To identify the letters that stand for long **a**
- To complete long **a** words

Warming Up

Reviewing Short Vowel a

Write short **a** phonograms on the board, and challenge children to add consonants to make short **a** words.

-ab (**cab, dab, gab, lab, nab, tab**)

-ad (**dad, fad, had, mad, pad, sad**)

-an (**can, fan, man, pan, ran, van**)

As children suggest words, list them on the board. Have volunteers use the words in sentences. Repeat with other phonograms such as **-am** and **-ap**.

Teaching the Lesson

Long Vowel a

Materials: **Sadlier Phonics Picture Cards** for **hay, jay, lake, pail, rain, bike, boat, mule,** and **tree**; pocket chart

- Remind children that the sound of long **a** can be spelled in different ways. Say the words **day**, **wait**, and **take**. On the board, write the headings **ay**, **ai**, and **a_e**. Have children repeat after you as you write the words under the appropriate headings.

- Place three picture cards in the pocket chart. Choose two cards with pictures that have the long **a** sound and one that does not. Have volunteers say the long **a** words. Help children spell the words. Then write the words on the board. Continue the process with different picture groups.

- Have children turn to page 181. Read the directions aloud and help children name each picture. Do the first game with children. Then have them complete the page independently.

In each game, score a tic-tac-toe by drawing a line through three pictures that have names with the sound of long **a.** Print the letters that stand for the long **a** sound in each game on the whale.

1. hat | cake | web
rope | game | bag
leaf | wave | map

2. kite | can | six
suit | tag | cup
mail | rain | nail

3. jay | hay | tray
bat | sun | tube
pig | fan | cape

1 a_e
2 ai
3 ay

LESSON 92: Reviewing Long Vowel **a** 181

U N I V E R S A L A C C E S S
Reteaching Activities

Activity 1

Materials: tape dispenser

Show children the tape dispenser and remind them that **tape** has the sound of long **a**. Then have them sit in a circle and pass around the tape. The child holding the tape says one long **a** word. For children who have difficulty thinking of words, give clues such as "What word names something you play?" (**game**) and "What dessert do you eat on your birthday?" (**cake**)

Activity 2

Materials: three outlines of railroad cars for each child

Remind children that **ay, ai,** and **a_e** can stand for the long **a** sound. Then have each child write **ay, ai,** and **a_e** on three separate railroad car outlines. Have children write long **a** words on the appropriate cars. Tape cars together to make a train display.

Say the name of each picture. If the picture name has the long **a** sound, find the letters in the box to complete the word. Print the letters on the line.

| a_e | ai | ay |

1. lake
2. bat — b _ t
3. gate
4. dog — d _ g
5. pay
6. sail
7. hay
8. vase
9. man — m _ n
10. rain
11. lid — l _ d
12. tape

LESSON 92: Assessing Long Vowel **a**

Review this Check-Up with your child.

Assessing the Skill

Check-Up   Before children begin the written assessment on page 182, conduct a final class review of the three long **a** spelling patterns. Write **a_e**, **ai**, and **ay** on the board. Have volunteers say three long **a** words with **a_e** (e.g., **game**, **take**, **cane**). Write the words on the board under **a_e**. Repeat for **ai** and **ay**.

Ask children to turn to page 182. Read aloud the directions. Help children name the pictures. Suggest that they draw an **X** beside pictures with names that do not have the long **a** sound. Then have children complete the page on their own.

Observational Assessment   As children complete the Check-Up activity, note whether children use the correct spellings for the long **a** sound.

Dictation   Tell children you are going to say some long **a** words. Have them write the long **a** words as you dictate them. Say these words: **game, tray, rain, wave, nail**. Tell children that you are going to say a sentence. Have them write the sentence as you dictate it and underline any long **a** words. Use this sentence: **Jay** will **sail** on the **lake**.

Student Skills Assessment   Use the checklist on Student Edition pages 321–322 to record your observations of individual children.

Guided Instruction

Skills	Resources

Long vowel **a**	Instruction on pages 167–180
	Phonemic Awareness Activities
	   on pages 165H–165I
	Little Books *Wake Up, Sleepyheads!*;
	   Space Camp

Student Pages 183–184

Phonemic Awareness /ī/

Objectives
- To match medial sounds
- To identify words with /ī/
- To discriminate between words that do and do not have /ī/

Warming Up

Reviewing Short i

Remind children that short **i** is the sound they hear in the word **sit**. Ask them to stand by their chairs. Then say the following groups of words: **nice, nut, knit; sand, sox, six; bit, bite, bus; fox, fix, fast**. Have children sit when they hear a word with the short **i** sound.

Teaching the Lesson

Phonemic Awareness: Match Medial Sounds

Say **hive** and **tile** and have children repeat after you. Explain that both words have the same middle sound of long **i**. Have children say /ī/. Then have children wave "hi" when they hear a word that has /ī/ in the middle. Say: **dive, mile, big, hide, make, wide, might, pot, bite**.

The Sound of Long i

- Say /ī/. Tell children this sound is long **i**. Say the words **ice, side**, and **night** and tell children that these words have the long **i** sound.

- Explain that you will read sentences that include words with the long **i** sound. Ask children to pretend their fingers are bees and to fly them high in the sky when they hear a long **i** word. Say:

  Bees are **wise** and small in **size**.

  A bee sat **high** on a **vine**.

  There were **nine** bees in a **line**.

Long i

Listen as the page is read aloud. Talk about the long **i** words you hear, such as **five** and **vine**. Then circle the five bees.

Five in the Hive

Five bees wake up.
They leave the **hive**.
They see a **vine**,
And down they **dive**.

I **like** bees.
They're very **wise**.
Bees do **fine** work
For their small **size**.

Critical Thinking
What kind of work do bees do?

Possible answer: They help plants grow.

LESSON 93: Phonemic Awareness: /ī/

183

UNIVERSAL ACCESS
Meeting Individual Needs

Auditory • Kinesthetic

Have children form a line. Say a group of words, including some with long **i** such as: **bite, vine, sit, knife, mile, cape, bike, nice, jump**. Tell children to step out of line when they hear a word with the long **i** sound.

Auditory

Say the following groups of words and have children identify the pattern they hear. (Two long **i** words and one other long vowel word.) Say: **lie, tie, tape; right, might, rope; hide, side, seed; dime, lime, day**. Then have children continue the pattern.

Extra Support

Materials: Sadlier Phonics Picture Cards for **bike, hive, kite, pie, rice, tie, cake, hat, net**, and **fox**

Review that /ī/ is long **i**, as in the word **time**. Then display the picture cards, and have children identify the picture names. Have children sort the cards into two groups: long **i** words and non-long **i** words.

Hive has the long **i** sound. Circle and color each picture that has the long **i** sound in its name.

1 hive	2 nine	3 bike	4 bib
5 light	6 bride	7 lake	8 tie
9 slide	10 snail	11 dime	12 ribbon
13 pig	14 pie	15 vine	16 tire

184

LESSON 93: Phonemic Awareness: /ī/

Have your child say **hive** before each picture name (**hive/nine**) and tell if the vowel sounds are the same.

Practicing the Skill

● Read aloud the poem about bees on page 183. Have children study the picture.

● Read the direction for page 183, and discuss the Critical Thinking question. Tell children to complete the page.

● Have children turn to page 184 and read the directions together. Be sure children can properly identify each picture. Tell children to complete the page.

Curriculum Connections

Theme Activity: Science

Materials: nature magazines, drawing paper, markers

Have children look through nature magazines for things they might see on a hike. Then have children draw a picture of the plants and animals illustrated in the magazines. Place the drawings on a bulletin board display. Use the illustrations to talk about ways to take care of plants and animals. Have children use long **i** words such as: **nice**, **pine**, **side**, **slide**, **light**, **night**, **sight**, **bright**, **hike**, **white**, **dive**. You may want to begin by saying: *Don't step on flowers. Hike on trails. Don't cut down pine trees. It's time to help the wildlife.*

English Language Learners/ESL

Before presenting the rhyme on page 183, say **five**, **hive**, **vine**, and **dive**, stressing the medial long **i** sound. Have children repeat each word as you say it. Tell them that each word has the long **i** sound. Then draw a **hive** and a **vine** at different ends of the board. Say the first four lines of the rhyme, and act them out as children pantomime your actions from their seats. (Make a fist with one hand, and then suddenly extend your fingers to show the five bees waking up. Flutter your fingers as the "bees" leave the **hive**, see a **vine**, and **dive**.)

Challenge

Ask children to work in pairs to create a skit about bees. Challenge children to include long **i** words such as **hive**, **alive**, **arrive**, **mile**, **five**, and **time**. Allow each pair to act out its skit. Have the rest of the children raise their hands each time they hear a long **i** word.

Special Strategies

For Universal Access activities, see page 165F.

Sound to Symbol /ī/ i_e

Objectives
- To identify and isolate medial sounds
- To recognize that **i_e** stands for /ī/
- To spell words with /ī/ **i_e**

★ Teaching the Lesson

Phonemic Awareness:
Identify and Isolate Medial Sounds

- Tell children that the middle sound in the words **dime** and **hive** is /ī/. Say /d/-/ī/-/m/ **dime**; /h/-/ī/-/v/ **hive**. Have children repeat after you.
- Tell children you will say some words. Ask them to buzz like a bee each time they hear a word that has the same long **i** sound in the middle as in the words **dime** and **hive**. Then say **bike**, **cave**, **ride**, **bit**, **pine**, **dive**, **lid**, **nine**.

Sound to Symbol
Materials: **Sadlier Phonics Picture Cards** for bike, rice, kite, hive

- Say the words **hide** and **Mike**. Tell children that the middle sound in **hide** and **Mike** is long **i**, /ī/. Long **i** can be spelled with the letters **i_e**. Point out that the **e** is silent.
- Display the picture cards, and have children identify them. List the picture names on the board under **i_e**, and have volunteers underline the **i** and **e** in each word.

Practicing the Skill

- Together, read the directions on page 185. Direct children to the picture cue. Be sure children notice that **e** is silent in **kite**. Identify the pictures together.
- Do the first three items together. Then have children complete the page independently.

185

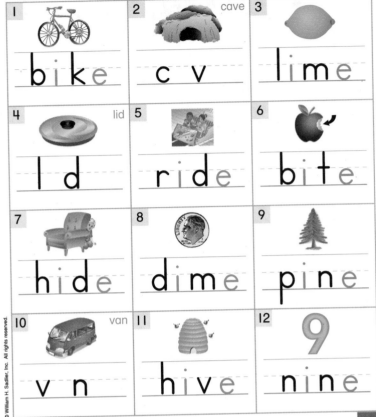

The letters **i_e** can stand for the long **i** sound. The letter **e** is silent. Say each picture name. Then print **i** in the middle and **e** at the end of each word that has the long **i** sound.

k<u>i</u>t<u>e</u>

1 b i k e	2 cave c v	3 l i m e
4 lid l d	5 r i d e	6 b i t e
7 h i d e	8 d i m e	9 p i n e
10 van v n	11 h i v e	12 n i n e

LESSON 94: Connecting Sound to Symbol: /ī/ i_e   **185**

U N I V E R S A L   A C C E S S
Meeting Individual Needs

English Language Learners/ESL
Have children review the pictures with you and name each one. Direct them to put an "x" through the pictures that do _not_ have the long **i** sound as they name them. Help children focus their attention entirely on the **i_e** spelling of the long **i** sound. Then, direct children to complete the remaining words with the letters **i** and silent **e**.

Challenge
Challenge partners to write three sentences and include words with **i_e**. The sentences might be about clean air, or about trees or flowers, or about endangered animals. (e.g., I like to fly my kite in the clear, clean air. Mike and I ride our bikes under tall trees. If I saved a tiger, I would call him Spike.) Invite children to illustrate their sentences.

Extra Support
Draw a kite with a long tail on the board. Display **Sadlier Phonics Picture Cards** for **kite**, **hive**, and **bike**. Have children name the pictures. List the picture names on the kite tail. Then have children underline the **i** and **e** in each word.

The letters **igh** and **ie** stand for the long **i** sound.

night   pie

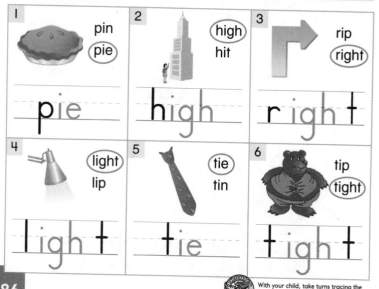

Say the name of each picture. Circle the word. Then print **igh** or **ie** on the line.

1	2	3
pin / (pie)	(high) / hit	rip / (right)
pie	high	right

4	5	6
(light) / lip	(tie) / tin	tip / (tight)
light	tie	tight

LESSON 95: Connecting Sound to Symbol: /ī/ **igh** and **ie**

With your child, take turns tracing the letters that stand for the long i sound in each word.

Sound to Symbol
/ī/ igh, ie

Objectives
- To identify and isolate medial sounds
- To recognize that **igh** and **ie** stand for /ī/
- To spell words with /ī/ **igh**, **ie**

Teaching the Lesson

Phonemic Awareness:
Identify and Isolate Medial Sounds
Tell children that the middle sound in the word **right** is /ī/. Have children repeat after you: /r/-/ī/-/t/ **right**. Tell children you will say some words. They will repeat the middle sound and raise their right hand if it has the same long **i** sound as in the word **right**. Say: **cake, seat, sight, bib, hope, night, gum, might**.

Sound to Symbol
- Draw a large crescent moon on the board. Beside it draw an outline of a man's tie. Say the word **night**. Tell children that the vowel sound in **night** is long **i** and is spelled with the letters **igh**. Write the word **night** in the crescent moon.
- Say the word **tie**. Tell children that the vowel sound in **tie** is also long **i**, and is spelled with the letters **ie**. Write the word **tie** in the outline of a tie. Tell children that the **e** is silent.
- Have volunteers say the words and underline the long **i** letters.

Practicing the Skill

Together, read the directions on page 186, and call attention to the two picture cues. Do the first item together. Then have children complete the page independently.

Observational Assessment

*Note children who can classify the words formed as either **igh** or **ie** words.*

English Language Learners/ESL
Have children review the pictures with you and name each one. Direct them to put an "x" through the pictures that do _not_ have the long **i** sound as they name them. Help children focus their attention entirely on the **igh** spelling of the long **i** sound. Then, direct children to complete the remaining words with the letters **igh**.

Extra Support
Display **Sadlier Phonics Picture Cards** for **pie, tie, night,** and **light**. Draw a pie that is cut into four pieces. Write the picture names in the pie sections, and have children underline letters that stand for the long **i** sound.

Challenge
Brainstorm the names of animals that are active when it is light out (dog, bird) and those that are active at night (owl, bat). Point out that **light** and **night** have long **i** spelled with the letters **igh**. Then have groups of children write sentences about one of the animals you discussed and include at least one word with long **i** spelled **igh**. Have children present their sentences to the class.

Long Vowel i Phonograms

Objectives

- To add initial sounds
- To recognize long **i** phonograms
- To build words with long **i** phonograms

Warming Up

Reviewing Initial Consonant Sounds

Provide riddles like those below. Ask children to name each word.

It rhymes with **lit** and begins with **p**. (**pit**)

It rhymes with **box** and begins with **f**. (**fox**)

It rhymes with **day** and begins with **s**. (**say**)

Teaching the Lesson

Phonemic Awareness: Add Initial Sounds

Say the word **ice** and have children repeat after you. Explain that they can make a new word by adding /**r**/ to the beginning of **ice**, making /**r**/-**ice rice**. Ask children to add /**d**/, /**l**/, /**m**/, /**n**/ to **ice** to make new words.

Phonograms

Materials: Punchout Letter Cards

- Have children use their letter cards to make the phonogram **ive**. Read it aloud with children. Then have them place the letter **h** in front of **ive**, leaving a space between **h** and **ive**. Tell children to run their finger from left to right under the word parts as you say together /**h**/-/**īv**/ **hive**.

- Explain that other words can be made with the **ive** phonogram by changing the initial consonant. Have children replace the **h** with **f**. Ask a volunteer to read the word by blending /**f**/ with /**īv**/ (**five**).

- Ask children to suggest other words with the phonogram **ive**. Repeat the process using the phonograms **ine**, **ide**, **ight**.

Say the name of each picture. In each row, circle two pictures that have rhyming names. Then make a new rhyming word. Check your answers with a partner's. Are they the same or different?

Possible answers

1. h ive
2. h ide
3. v ine
4. t ight

LESSON 96: Long Vowel i Phonograms **187**

U N I V E R S A L   A C C E S S
Meeting Individual Needs

Kinesthetic • Visual

Materials: catalogs, scissors, play-money dimes

Have each child cut out five items from catalogs that have the long **i** sound such as **pie, bike, light,** and **bride**. Then give five "dimes" to each child to buy objects from others. Have children display and name their long **i** purchases.

Visual • Kinesthetic

Materials: Sadlier Phonics Picture Cards for long **i** words (e.g., **bike, hive, kite, rice**)

Have children sit in a circle on the floor. Place the picture cards facedown in the middle, and ask a child to pick a card and name the picture. In turn have each child say a word that rhymes with the picture name. When no one can think of a rhyme, a new card is chosen.

Extra Support

Write the phonograms **ive, ide, ine, ight** on the board. Remind children that these letters can stand for long **i**. Guide children as they place different consonant letter cards in front of each phonogram to form words. Have children read the words aloud.

Add each letter in the hive to the word part below it. Say the word. If the word is real, print it on a line.

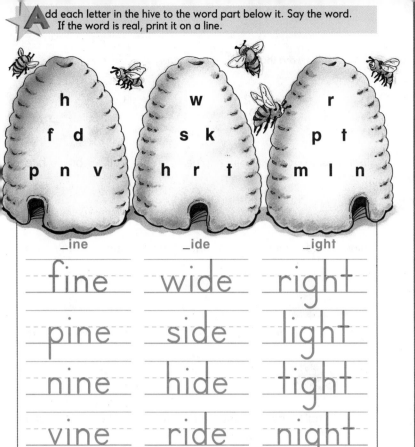

_ine

fine

pine

nine

vine

dine

_ide

wide

side

hide

ride

tide

_ight

right

light

tight

night

might

LESSON 96: Word Building with Long Vowel **i** Phonograms

With your child, build words by adding letters to _ime and _ile.

Practicing the Skill

● Review the directions on page 187 together, and identify the pictures. Then have children complete the page.

● Read aloud the directions and discuss the format on page 188. Remind children how to make new words by adding a beginning consonant to a word ending. Model how the example word **fine** was formed. Then have children complete the page.

Curriculum Connections

Spelling Connection

Read aloud each word and sentence below. Ask a volunteer to spell the word.

bite Did the bug **bite** you?

mile I walk a **mile** to school.

lie Mike would not tell a **lie**.

hive Bees live in a **hive**.

tire Maria can change a **tire**.

Theme Activity: Science

● Have children imagine they are an animal or plant. Discuss why Earth is important to that animal or plant and what they would say if they could talk. Have children include what their animal or plant can do for people and what people can do for it.

● Have each child print sentences telling what their animal or plant would say. Help them think of long **i** words for their sentences by giving them sentence frames like these:

I am a ____. People **like** me because I ____.

I am **nice** to the Earth. I ____.

● After children have finished, have volunteers share the long **i** words they used with the class. Then ask children to read their sentences aloud.

Have children place their completed sentences in their portfolios.

English Language Learners/ESL

Some children need help distinguishing real words from nonsense words. Write the phonogram **ide** on the board and say it. Write an **r** in front and say the word **ride**. Act out **ride**, and make the point that it is a real action and therefore a real word. Change the **r** to **g** and say: *Gide. Gide is not a real word. It's a non-sense word.* Combine **ide** with other initial sounds, and help children decide if each word is a nonsense or real word by having the group try to act it out or draw a picture of it.

Special Strategies

For Universal Access activities, see page 165F.

Challenge

Materials: drawing paper, crayons

Tell children they will compose two-line rhymes about nature. Model a rhyme by saying:

*First we sat under the **pine**.
Then we swung on a long **vine**.*

Have children use other rhyming long **i** words in their rhymes, print them on drawing paper, and illus-trate them. Ask children to say the long **i** rhyming words they used and then read their rhymes aloud.

Sadlier Reading

Little Books and Big Books

Read *Niles Likes to Smile* (fiction) for more practice with long **i**.

Student Pages 189–190

Practicing and Writing Long Vowel i

Objectives
- To segment phonemes in a word
- To recognize long **i** words
- To write long **i** words

Warming Up

Reviewing Long and Short Vowels

Have a volunteer print all five vowels in a column on the left side of the board. Call on children to print words with that vowel sound to the right of each vowel. Have children indicate whether each word has a long or short vowel sound.

Teaching the Lesson

Phonemic Awareness: Segment Phonemes in a Word

Say the word **kite**. Remind children that words are made up of separate sounds. Tell children that there are three sounds in the word **kite**. Segment the word by saying: /k/-/ī/-/t/ **kite** and have children repeat after you. Repeat the process using the following words: **hide**, /h/-/ī/-/d/; **right**, /r/-/ī/-/t/.

Sound to Symbol
- Say the words **pine**, **bite**, **sight**. Remind children that the middle sound in each of these words is long **i**.
- Write **bike**, **lie**, **fight**, **fine**, **light**, and **pie** on the board. Read the words aloud and have children repeat them after you. Remind children that **i_e**, **igh**, and **ie** stand for the long **i** sound. Then have volunteers go to the board and circle the letters that can stand for the long **i** sound.

Circle the word that names each picture.

1. net (nine) nail
2. (pin) pine pen
3. bait bit (bite)
4. (hide) had high
5. brain brick (bride)
6. ripe (rain) rip
7. (fire) fin fan
8. (kite) kit kiss
9. tip tape (tie)
10. nip (night) nail
11. mine men (man)
12. (slide) slid slip
13. (tape) tap tight
14. bake big (bike)
15. (pie) pay pit

LESSON 97: Practicing Long Vowel **i**   **189**

U N I V E R S A L   A C C E S S
Meeting Individual Needs

Auditory • Kinesthetic
Materials: "diploma" made from rolled-up paper tied with ribbon

Explain that this "diploma" shows that the person who receives it is **wise**. Have children sit in a circle. Then pass the diploma, and ask each "wise" child to name a word with the same long **i** sound as **wise**.

Auditory
Say the following groups of words, and have children identify the pattern they hear (e.g., two long **i** words and one short **i** word).

like, hike, dip

ride, side, lid

bite, kite, fin

Then have children continue the pattern.

Extra Support
Review that **i_e**, **igh**, and **ie** are spelling patterns for long **i**. Write pairs of words on the board. Have children identify and segment the long **i** word in each pair. Say: **hill, pie; pen, ride; hike, hay; leaf, light.**

Use the picture clues and words in the box to complete the puzzle. Print one letter in each box. Then write a sentence about one picture using a long **i** word.

hive	night	vine	tie	nine

ACROSS ➡

DOWN ⬇

Crossword puzzle:

	¹n	i	²g	h	t		³t
			i				i
	¹n		⁴v	i	n	e	
	i		e				
	n						
	e						

Possible answer

I sleep at night.

LESSON 97: Writing Long Vowel **i**

Have your child name each picture clue and point to the word in the puzzle.

Practicing the Skill

• Ask children to turn to page 189. Review the directions together and identify the pictures. Have children complete the page on their own.

• Read aloud the directions for page 190. Guide children in filling out 1 across. Name each of the pictures with them. Ask children to complete the page.

Curriculum Connections

Spelling Connection

Materials: Punchout Letter Cards

Read aloud each word and sentence below. Ask a volunteer to spell the word aloud, to print it on the board, or to use letter cards.

line   Can you draw a straight **line**?
ride   It's fun to **ride** a bike.
time   What **time** is it?
wise   Owls look very **wise**.
kite   Let's go fly a **kite**.

Art Center

Materials: recycled aluminum foil, yarn, newspaper, fabric scraps, poster board, glue

• Have children collect clean, recyclable materials from school and home.

• Set the clean materials on the floor or on a table. Have children identify any materials that have the long **i** sound in their name such as a pie plate or a wire hanger.

• Have small groups of children use the recyclable materials to make creatures with names that have the long **i** sound. When children have completed their projects, have them share what they made.

• Ask children to make up things their creatures do using words with the long **i** sound. (**hide, bite, slide, ride**)

English Language Learners/ESL

Materials: jigsaw puzzle, light, tie

Children may not be familiar with different kinds of puzzles. Display a jigsaw puzzle and help children name it. Then explain that there is another kind of puzzle called a *crossword puzzle*. On the board, draw a row of three boxes across and three down with the middle box intersecting. Hold up a light. Have a volunteer write the word in the boxes across, one letter per box. Next hold up a tie. Ask another child to write the word in the boxes going down to complete the puzzle.

Challenge

Tell children to make a poster about a park where they can play, hide, slide, bike, and fly a kite. Ask children to write a few sentences about the park. Tell children to underline the long **i** words they use. Then display their posters.

Special Strategies

For Universal Access activities, see page 165F.

Observational Assessment

*Observe whether children are able to identify long **i** words.*

190

Student Pages 191-192

Long i and Short i

Objectives

- To identify and isolate medial sounds
- To write long **i** words
- To discriminate long **i** words from short **i** words

Warming Up

Reviewing Initial Consonants

Say the tongue twisters below. Have volunteers identify the repeated initial consonant sounds.

> **Dine** on **dinner** at a **diner** for a **dime**.
>
> **Has Hal hopped home** or **has he hiked?**
>
> **Polly Peacock put pie** in her **purse**.

Teaching the Lesson

Phonemic Awareness:
Identify and Isolate Medial Sounds

- Say the words **right** and **fine** and ask children to repeat both words. Point out that the middle sound in both words is the long **i** sound /ī/.
- Ask children to listen carefully and hold up their right hand and say **I** each time they hear a word with the long **i** sound in the middle. Then say: **bite, toad, mine, lime, beet, night, lake**

Sound to Symbol

- Say **bite** and **bit**. Remind children that **bite** has the long **i** sound and **bit** has the short **i** sound. Say **fine, fin, hit, hive, hip**. Have children tell whether each word has a long **i** or short **i** sound.
- Write **lid, lie, tin, time, like, lit**, and **night** on the board. Remind children that **i_e, igh**, and **ie** are spelling patterns that can stand for the long **i** sound. Then say each word and have children repeat after you. Have volunteers identify whether each word has a long **i** or short **i** sound and underline the letter or letters that stand for the vowel sound.

191

Say the name of each picture. Print the word on the line. Then check your answers with a partner.

1 kite	2 bike	3 tie
4 five	5 right	6 vine
7 hive	8 dime	9 bite
10 line	11 pie	12 light

LESSON 98: Writing Long Vowel i   **191**

U N I V E R S A L   A C C E S S
Meeting Individual Needs

Auditory • Kinesthetic
Materials: magic slates

Dictate long **i** words pictured on pages 191 and 192 and have children print them on magic slates. Ask volunteers to spell the words on the board so children can check and revise their own spellings.

Kinesthetic • Auditory

Have children listen for the medial sound of long **i** in the word **time**. Then say a list of words with various vowel sounds children have studied. Have children raise their hands when they hear a word with the long **i** sound. Use words such as **find, slide, sled, tent, hid, bike, tire, crib, vine, bride**.

Extra Support

Say: *I like rice.* Point out that each word in the sentence has the long **i** sound. Say these sentences:

> These **five bikes** are **mine**.
>
> The airplane is **nine miles high**.

Have children clap when they hear a word that has the long **i** sound.

Say the name of each picture. If the word has the sound of long **i**, print it on the long **i** bin. If the word has the sound of short **i**, print it on the short **i** bin.

Long **i**	Short **i**
bike	pin
dive	kit
tight	bib
lime	six
tie	dig

192

LESSON 98: Discriminating Between Long **i** and Short **i**

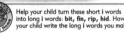 Help your child turn these short **i** words into long **i** words: **bit, fin, rip, hid**. Have your child write the long **i** words you make.

Practicing the Skill

● Read aloud the directions on page 191. Point out that each picture has the long **i** sound. Identify the pictures together. Then have children complete the page.

● Read aloud the directions on page 192. Have volunteers identify the pictures and tell in which bin each word belongs and why. Remind children of the **i_e**, **igh**, and **ie** spellings of long **i**. Then have them print the words on their own to complete the page.

Curriculum Connections

Spelling Connection

Read aloud each word and sentence below. Ask volunteers either to spell the words aloud or print them on the board.

hide	Let's **hide** behind the tree.
mine	That hat you found is **mine**.
pie	Would you like some **pie**?
rice	I like **rice**.
wipe	I can **wipe** the dishes.

Science Center

(Note: In advance, ask family volunteers to participate in a Clean-Up Day.)

Materials: construction paper, crayons, gloves for each child, garbage bags

● Help the class plan a Cleanup Day for picking up litter in the schoolyard or neighborhood. (Make sure that children wear gloves and are closely supervised.)

● Model making invitations to send to family volunteers. On the board print the message: "It is time to protect Earth!" Fold a sheet of paper in half and copy the message on the front page. Work together to come up with a few sentences to add inside the folded invitation. Include long **i** words such as **nice**, **right**, **pride**, **sight**, **time**, **fine**, **invite**. Ask volunteers to identify all the long **i** words. Be sure children include the time and place of the Cleanup Day.

Observational Assessment

*Note whether children can identify long **i** words in their messages.*

Long Vowel i
Decodable Reader

Objectives
- To read long **i** words and high-frequency words in context
- To read the story fluently
- To draw conclusions

Introducing the Story Words

Long i Decodable Words On the board write the words **time, Mike, pile, tire, tie, pie, kite, fine, ride.** Read the list together. Point out that all the words have the long **i** sound. Explain that the letters **i_e,** and **ie** can stand for /ī/. Have volunteers choose a word and give clues about it so classmates can guess the word.

High-Frequency Words Write the words **is, for, the, and, a** on the board and on index cards. Read aloud the list. Distribute the cards. Have each child read the word card, circle the matching word on the board, and spell the word in the air.

Reading the Book

Reading Together Have children remove pages 193 and 194, and show them how to cut and fold the pages into a book. Read aloud the title, "A Fine Sale." Explain that this story tells what two children do with things from a yard sale. Then read the story aloud as children follow along in their books.

Responding Discuss which of Mike and Jen's projects children like best.

Reading for Fluency Have children track the print as you read. Have partners do a choral reading of the story. Then have children read the story independently.

Observational Assessment

*Notice whether children are able to decode the long **i** words and read the story fluently.*

Your child has read this book in school. Ask him or her to read it to you. Then have him or her find, read, and spell all of the long **i** words.

Name _____

A Fine Sale

Mike and Jen let Dad make the pie!

8

It is time for the sale.

1

Mike and Jen make a kite.

6

Mike and Jen get a tire.

3

Directions: Cut and fold the book. Then read the story. Tell how you think Mike and Jen made each thing.

I Can Read LESSON 99: Long Vowel **i** Decodable Reader
Comprehension: Drawing Conclusions

193

UNIVERSAL ACCESS
Meeting Individual Needs

Auditory • Kinesthetic
Materials: long **i** objects, other vowel sounds objects

Put objects such as a **tie,** a **kite,** a **dime,** and **dice** in a pile. Also include objects that have other vowel sounds, such as a **pen, tape, cup,** and **bag.** Direct children to name and group together the long **i** objects.

Visual • Tactile
Materials: construction paper

On the board write the words **is, for, the, and, a,** and read them aloud. Demonstrate how to fold half a sheet of construction paper to make a "tent." Point to the words on the board, and tell children to read and then to write them on the tents. Have them keep their tents in their work area to refer to.

Extra Support
Materials: magnetic letters

Write the long **i** story words on the board, and read them aloud. Point out the long **i** spelling patterns: **i_e, ie.** Have children use the letters to build the words. After they read each word, have them mix up the letters and build more words.

Mike and Jen dig in
a big pile.

Mike and Jen make
a fine ride.

7

Mike and Jen get a mop
and a tie.

4

Mike and Jen get a pie tin.

5

✂

194

LESSON 99: Long Vowel **i** Decodable Reader
Comprehension: Drawing Conclusions

Comprehension Strategy

Drawing Conclusions Explain to children
that sometimes writers don't tell readers everything and that readers sometimes have to put
things together to understand what is happening in a story. Guide children in using the illustrations to draw conclusions about how Mike
and Jen used their yard sale purchases.

Phonics and Decoding

Learning About Long i On the board
write the story words **fine** and **tie**. Read the
words, and point out the spelling patterns **i_e**
and **ie** for long **i**. Then write **r_d_, p_ _, p_l_,
k_t_,** and **t_m_** on the board. Say a word, and
ask a volunteer to add the missing letters to
complete the word.

Word Building *Materials:* construction
paper, scissors

Direct children to make a long **i** pie. Show
them how to cut a paper circle into fourths.
Have them write the pattern **ie** on each of the
four pieces. Ask them to write the consonants
d, l, p, and **t** at the beginning of each pie
piece to build words. Then have children flip
the pieces over and write the phonogram **ine**
on each piece. Have them write consonants **f,
d, l, m,** and **p** to build words.

Curriculum Connections

Writing and Sharing Direct children to
make yard sale signs advertising long **i** items
for sale. Have children show their signs and
read them to classmates.

English Language Learners/ESL

Materials: play money, play cash register,
common items having names with a long
i sound

Build background about yard sales by
role playing one in the classroom.
Have children pretend to buy and
sell items that have the long **i**
sound, such as **bike, kite, tie.**
Help children increase their
vocabulary by modeling:
*How much is this? How many
do you have? That will be
____ dollars. Here's your
change.*

Special Strategies

For Universal Access activities,
see page 165F.

Challenge

Point out that recycling, or finding new uses for things, is a good
way to help Earth. Have partners
make a list of long **i** objects and
write about ways to reuse the
objects, much as Jen and Mike
did in the story. Then have
them share their ideas with
the class.

194

Long Vowel **i** in Context

Objectives

- To divide sentences into words
- To identify long **i** words to complete sentences
- To write long **i** words in context

Warming Up

Reviewing Long and Short a

Display these word pairs on the board: **cap/cape, vane/van, pain/pan, rat/rate, man/main**. Have volunteers choose a word pair, say the words, then write an **L** above the word with the long **a** sound and **S** above the word with the short **a** sound.

Teaching the Lesson

Phonemic Awareness: Divide Sentences into Words

Explain to children that sentences are made up of words. Say: *The light was very bright.* Pause briefly after each word and clap once. Then say the sentence again, and have children clap after each word. Repeat the process with another sentence such as: *We had a fine hike.*

Phonics in Context

Write this sentence on the board: I will _____ down the hill. Write the words **hire, hike, hail** next to the sentence. Read aloud the sentence and the word choices. Then read the sentence three times, each time filling in the blank with one of the word choices. Circle the word **hike**, and tell children that it best completes the meaning of the sentence. Now have children complete this sentence: Turn _____ at the corner. (**ride, bike, right**)

Comprehension Skill: Recognizing Main Idea and Details

Look at each picture. Circle the word that completes the sentence. Then print it on the line.

1. It is a ___fine___ day.　(fine) fin fail
2. We ___ride___ to Pine Lake.　(ride) red rake
3. It is on the ___right___.　rate rig (right)
4. We ___hike___ and swim.　high (hike) him
5. Mom makes a ___fire___.　fan fill (fire)
6. It is ___time___ to go!　tail tie (time)

LESSON 100: Long Vowel **i** in Sentences　**195**

UNIVERSAL ACCESS
Meeting Individual Needs

Visual • Auditory

Have children draw a large circle to represent a pie. Then have them draw ingredients in the pie that have the /ī/ sound. Suggest real ingredients, like **lime**, or silly ones, like **kite**. Print on the board: "I made a pie and put in a _____." Have children fill in the blank with their ingredients.

Kinesthetic • Visual

Materials: Sadlier Phonics Picture Cards for long **i** words, such as **bike, kite, hive, rice, prize, vine**; other picture cards

Divide the cards among groups of children. Have them sort the cards, placing pictures with names that have the sound of long **i** in a line on the floor. After the cards have been sorted, challenge children to walk along the line, naming each word as they pass it.

Extra Support

Remind children that we can often complete a sentence by looking at the other words in the sentence. Write the following on the board: Ride your _____ safely. Write the words **hive, kite, bike** next to the sentence. Have children choose the word that best completes the sentence. Then have them write their own sentences for each word.

I Like the Earth

Day and night,
I like the earth.
I like tall pines,
And buds that smile
On leafy vines,
And fine, clear lakes
Where I can dive,
And bees that buzz
Inside their hive.

1. Tall _pines_ are nice.

2. Buds can grow on _vines_.

3. It's fun to _dive_ right in to lakes.

4. Bees buzz inside a _hive_.

196   LESSON 100: Long Vowel **i** in Context
Comprehension: Recognizing Main Idea and Details

Help your child draw a line under all of the long **i** words in the poem.

Practicing the Skill

● Ask children to turn to page 195. Have them describe the pictures and talk about how the family is enjoying the outdoors. Model the first sentence for the class. Then have children complete the page.

● Read the poem on page 196 as a class. Discuss the poem's story. Help children pick out the long **i** words, and have them complete the sentences independently.

Curriculum Connections

Spelling Connection

Read aloud each word and sentence below. Ask a volunteer either to spell the word or print it on the board.

line	I waited in **line** for tickets.
fire	We cooked out over a **fire**.
wide	The stream is deep and **wide**.
five	One nickel is worth **five** pennies.

Theme Activity: Language Arts

● Reread the poem on page 196. Ask children to tell what makes Earth a special place for them. Then ask what they would change in the poem or add to it.

● Have children print the sentence "I like _____ about Earth" at the top of a page. Then have them fill in the blank by naming something that makes Earth special. Then have children draw a picture to illustrate their sentences and circle any long **i** words they may have used. Bind all the pages together to make a class book. Read the book aloud to remind children why Earth is a special place and how we should care for it.

Sadlier Reading

Little Books and Big Books

Read *Nice Vine, Quite Fine* (nonfiction) for more practice with long **i**.

Nice Vine, Quite Fine

English Language Learners/ESL

Call attention to the pictures on pages 195 and 196. Invite children to identify and discuss each illustration. Ask questions with *who, what, where, when,* and *why*. Then read the poem several times and have children join in when they can.

Challenge

Ask children to think about the family outing shown on page 195. Ask them to write a friendly letter telling the family how to care for Earth while enjoying the day. Challenge children to use long **i** words in their letters. For example:

Dear Family,

Hike on the path. Put out your fire. Do not hang on vines.

Provide time for sharing letters and identifying long **i** words.

Special Strategies

For Universal Access activities, see page 165F.

Observational Assessment

*Notice whether children are able to identify long **i** words as they complete their sentences about why Earth is a special place.*

Assessing Long Vowel i Reviewing Long Vowels a and i

Objectives

- To identify and complete words with long **i**
- To use long **a** and long **i** words to complete a puzzle

Warming Up

Reviewing Short i

Materials: shoe box, index cards

Say **mix** and point out the short **i** sound. Write **in**, **it**, **ill**, **ip**, **ig** on the board. Have children add beginning sounds to make words, write the words on cards, and toss the cards into the shoe-box "recycling bin." Call on volunteers to recycle the words by choosing one to read aloud.

Teaching the Lesson

Long i

Materials: word cards for **five**, **bike**, **hide**, **high**, **night**, **light**, **pie**, **tie**, **lie**; pocket chart

Say **kite** and point out the long **i** sound. Write **i_e**, **igh**, **ie** on the board and review that these letter combinations can stand for the long **i** sound. Mix the word cards and stack them facedown. Have children choose a card and read the word. Then have children sort the words in a pocket chart according to their long **i** spelling.

Long a and i

Materials: Punchout Letter Cards **a**, **i**

- Tell children **day** has the long **a** sound and **five** has the long **i** sound. Have them name the vowel sound repeated in these sentences: *Jake takes the bait to the lake; Mike likes to ride a bike.*

- Write on the board: **b_ke**, **_ce**, **l_ke**, **l_ne**, **m_le**, **t_le**, **p_le**, **r_ce**, **t_me**, **w_de**. Have children place the **a** and then the **i** card in the blank and read each word.

197

Say the name of each picture. If the picture name has the long **i** sound, find the letters in the box to complete the word. Print the letters on the line.

i_e	igh	ie

1	2	3 cape
pie	hive	c__p

4	5 wig	6
night	w__g	lime

7	8 sun	9
nine	s__n	tie

10 fin	11	12
f__n	ride	high

LESSON 101: Assessing Long Vowel i **197**

UNIVERSAL ACCESS
Reteaching Activities

Activity 1

Materials: Sadlier Phonics Picture Cards for **rice, hive, bike, kite, pie, tie, vine, ride, prize, lake, rain, jay, pig, six, hill, pin**

Write the numeral 9 on the board. Say the word and identify the long **i** vowel sound in **nine**. Mix the picture cards. Have children name the pictures and sort them according to whether the picture name has the long **i** sound or a different vowel sound.

Activity 2

Say **wave** and **dive**. Point out that **wave** has the long **a** sound and **dive** has the long **i** sound. Then model waving and making a stationary diving motion. Tell children you will say words that have the long **a** sound or the long **i** sound. Direct children to **wave** when they hear a word with the long **a** sound and pretend to **dive** when they hear a word with a long **i** sound. Say: **rain, ripe, live, sail, save, nine, time, lake, bike, take, pie, rake, stage, pine.**

Print **a** or **i** in each empty box to make two words.
Read the words across and down.

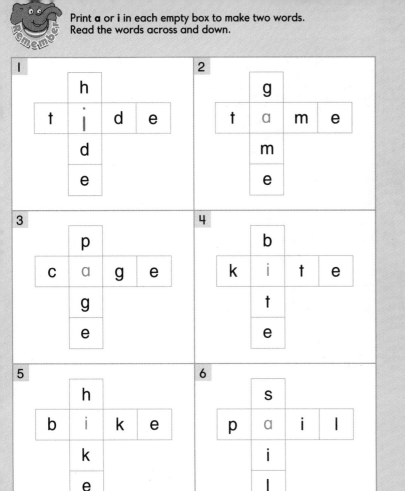

1.
```
  h
t i d e
  d
  e
```

2.
```
  g
t a m e
  m
  e
```

3.
```
  p
c a g e
  g
  e
```

4.
```
  b
k i t e
  t
  e
```

5.
```
  h
b i k e
  k
  e
```

6.
```
  s
p a i l
  i
  l
```

LESSON 101: Reviewing Long Vowels **a** and **i**

Read the words in each puzzle. Ask your child to tell whether he or she hears long **a** or long **i**.

Read aloud the directions on page 197. Help children identify the pictures and remind them that they should only complete words if the picture name has a long **i** sound. Work through the first three items together; then have children complete the page.

Cumulative Review

Remind children that they have done puzzles similar to the one on page 198 before. Then read aloud the directions. Stress that the letter children write must complete a word both across and down. Go over item 1 as an example. For item 2, have volunteers try both **a** and **i**. Work through as many items together as necessary. Have children complete the remaining items independently.

Observational Assessment   As children complete the crosswords, note whether they form the letters **a** and **i** correctly.

Dictation   Tell children you are going to say some long **a** words. Have them write the long **a** words as you dictate them. Say these words: **lake, day, sail, rain, game**. Repeat the activity with these long **i** words: **night, lie, bike, high, kite**. Then tell children you are going to say a sentence. Have them write the sentence as you dictate it and underline any long **a** and long **i** words. Use this sentence: **Jake likes** to **bike** to the **lake**.

Student Skills Assessment   Use the checklist on Student Edition pages 321–322 to record your observations of individual children.

Guided Instruction

Skills	Resources
Long vowel **a**	Instruction on pages 167–180 Little Book *Wake Up, Sleepyheads!*
Long vowel **i**	Instruction on pages 183–196 Little Book *Niles Likes to Smile*
Long vowels **a, i**	Phonemic Awareness Activities pages 165H–165I

LESSON 102 • UNIT 4
Student Pages 199–200

Phonemic Awareness /ō/

Objectives

- To match medial sounds
- To identify words with /ō/
- To discriminate between words that do and do not have /ō/

Warming Up

Reviewing Short o

Say groups of words such as **pot/Pat/pit**, **let/lie/log**, **Bob/bake/bet**, **sat/sock/sit**, **tap/top/tip**, **mitt/man/mop**. Be sure to include at least one short **o** word in each group. Have volunteers identify the short **o** words.

Teaching the Lesson

Phonemic Awareness: Match Medial Sounds

Say **boat**, and have children repeat the word after you. Tell children /ō/ is the sound they hear in the middle of **boat**. Have children say /ō/. Have children clap each time they hear two words that have /ō/ in the middle. Say: **boat/nose**, **hat/cap**, **road/hose**, **pet/leg**, **goat/rope**, **nine/five**.

The Sound of Long o

- Say /ō/. Tell children this is the sound of long vowel **o**. They can hear the long **o** sound in **snow**. Say the following words, and ask children to flutter their fingers like falling snow each time they hear a word with the long **o** sound: **hole**, **pin**, **bone**, **toe**, **top**, **note**, **cat**, **lake**, **rose**, **coat**, **bike**, **bow**.
- Tell children you will say some sentences that include long **o** words. Ask them to make an **o** with their arms each time they hear a long **o** word. Say:

  I **hope** it **snows**.
  Let's **coast** down the **road**.
  Can we **go** to **Joe's**?

Long o

Listen as the page is read aloud. Talk about the long **o** words you hear, such as **snow** and **coat**. Then draw a **nose**, **bow**, and **coat** on the snowman.

nose

bow

coat

Let It Snow

I grab my **coat**
And out I **go**
To make a **snowman**
In the **snow**.

I'll **coast** down hills,
And make a fort.
A **snowy** day
Is much too short!

Accept any drawing of a nose, bow, and coat.

Critical Thinking
Possible answers:
Boots, hat, coat, gloves.
What should you wear to play in the snow?

© William H. Sadlier, Inc. All rights reserved.

LESSON 102: Phonemic Awareness: /ō/

199

UNIVERSAL ACCESS
Meeting Individual Needs

Visual • Kinesthetic
Materials: Sadlier Phonics Picture Cards for long **o** words (e.g., **boat**, **rose**, **snow**) and for short vowel words

Explain that water from melting snow nourishes spring seeds. Have children crouch and imagine that they are seeds. Have them "grow" a bit each time you show a long **o** picture.

Auditory • Kinesthetic
Have children form a line and march around the room as you say the following list of words: **pop**, **hat**, **oak**, **fin**, **loaf**, **rose**, **sail**, **goat**, **robe**, **line**, **toad**, **nose**. When they hear a word with the long **o** sound, such as **slow**, they should march very slowly until you say a word with a different sound.

Extra Support
Remind children that **snow** has the long **o** sound. Say the following words, and ask children to say rhyming long **o** words: **snow** (bow, tow, low); **goat** (boat, coat, moat); **rose** (hose, nose)

199

Rose has the long **o** sound. Circle and color each picture that has the long **o** sound in its name.

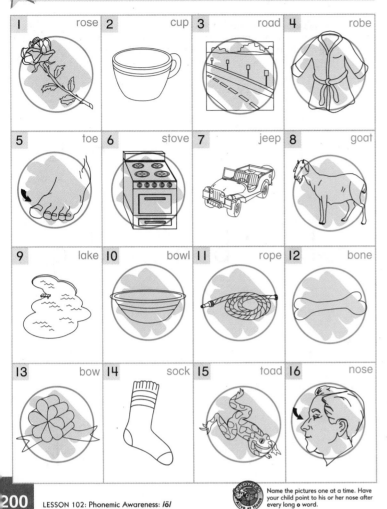

1 rose	2 cup	3 road	4 robe
5 toe	6 stove	7 jeep	8 goat
9 lake	10 bowl	11 rope	12 bone
13 bow	14 sock	15 toad	16 nose

LESSON 102: Phonemic Awareness: /ō/

Name the pictures one at a time. Have your child point to his or her nose after every long **o** word.

Practicing the Skill

• Read aloud the long **o** words in boldface type in the poem on page 199. Ask a volunteer to tell what vowel sound they have in common. Then read the directions aloud. As you read the poem, tell children to make an **o** with their arms each time you say a long **o** word. Then have children complete the picture and discuss the Critical Thinking question.

• Have children identify the pictures on page 200. Read the directions together. Then have children complete the page.

Curriculum Connections

Theme Activity: Art
Materials: light blue construction paper, crayons, glue, cotton balls

• Talk about the different things children do when it snows. Build knowledge by sharing the theme books.

• Have children draw pictures of themselves playing in the snow. Have them glue on pieces of cotton to represent snow.

• Have children include pictures that show long **o** words, such as **snow** and **coat**.

Theme Books

Hoban, Julia. *Amy Loves the Snow.* New York: Harper & Row, 1989. Building a snowman is even more fun when you and your parents do it together.

Komoda, Beverly. *The Winter Day.* New York: Harper Collins, 1991. Rabbit children like snow, too. But they don't build a snowman; they build a giant snow rabbit.

Portfolio

Have children place their snow drawings in their portfolios.

English Language Learners/ESL
Materials: pictures of snow

For children who have never lived in a *cold* climate, show pictures of snow falling or on the ground. Point out to children that **snow** and **cold** both have the long **o** sound. Tell children to repeat each word stretching out the /ō/. Then have children look at the poem on page 199, and help them find other words that contain the word **snow**. (**snowman, snowy**) Ask: *Can you think of other words that begin with* **snow**? (**snowfall, snowflake, snowstorm, snowball**)

Challenge
Point out that when it snows some people use wood-burning stoves, which sends smoke into the air. Help children think of other related environmental issues to be aware of when it snows (e.g., smoke from exhausts polluting the snow and litter thrown on the snowy ground). Challenge groups to create posters showing how to care for Earth during snowy weather. Ask children to share their posters and point out any objects with the long **o** sound.

Special Strategies
For Universal Access activities, see page 165F.

Observational Assessment

*Note whether children are able to identify correctly pictures that represent long **o** words in their snow drawings.*

Sound to Symbol /ō/ o_e

Objectives
- To identify and isolate medial sounds
- To recognize that **o_e** stands for /ō/
- To spell words with /ō/ **o_e**

Teaching the Lesson

Phonemic Awareness:
Identify and Isolate Medial Sounds

- Say **rose** and **bone,** and ask children to repeat each word. Point out that the middle sound in each word is the long **o** sound /ō/. Say **rose** /ō/ and **bone** /ō/ and have children repeat after you.
- Ask children to listen carefully and to hold up two fingers rounded in the shape of **o** and say /ō/ each time they hear a word with the long **o** sound in the middle. Then say **hop**, **hope, stone, cake, hide, joke, fun, globe**.

Sound to Symbol

- Remind children that the sound of long **o** is /ō/. Have children listen for a long **o** word in this sentence: *We left a note for Mom.* Ask a volunteer to name the long **o** word.
- Write **note** on the board. Say the word, and have children repeat it. Circle the **o** and the **e**. Tell children that these letters stand for the long **o** sound in **note.** Say the word again, and point out that the **e** at the end is silent.
- Repeat the process, using **home** and this sentence: *Mom is at home.* Then review that the **o_e** pattern stands for the long **o** sound.

Practicing the Skill

Read aloud the directions at the top of page 201. Point out the Key Picture Cue and its label, **cone,** and complete the first item together. Have children complete the rest of the page.

201

The letters **o_e** can stand for the long **o** sound. The letter **e** is silent. Say the name of each picture. Then print **o** in the middle and **e** at the end of each word that has the long **o** sound.

cone

1	2 vase	3
cone	v_s	note
4	5	6 dog
robe	bone	d_g
7 bun	8	9
b_n	stove	rope
10	11 dive	12
hose	d_v	smoke

LESSON 103: Connecting Sound to Symbol: /ō/ o_e

201

UNIVERSAL ACCESS
Meeting Individual Needs

English Language Learners/ESL
Review "silent **e**" words from previous lessons with children before they move on to words with **a_e**. Write **tap** on the board, and ask children to say that word. Point out that **tap** has the short **a** sound. Add an **e** to make **tape,** and direct children to say the new word. Point out that **tape** has the long **a** sound. Ask what happened when you added the **e** at the end. Tell children that adding the "silent **e**" changed the sound of the vowel from short to long. Continue with long and short **i** words and then long and short **o**.

Challenge
Point out that just as we need to care for our planet, we need to care for our homes and families. Then have children work in pairs to write two sentences about fire safety. Suggest that children use some of these long **o** words: **home, stove, smoke, hose, pole.**

Extra Support
Materials: Punchout Letter Cards

Remind children that **o_e** can stand for the long **o** sound. Help children use letter cards to spell long **o** words such as **rope, cone,** and **note.** Ask them to point out the silent **e** in each word.

The letters **oa** and **ow** can stand for the long **o** sound. Say the name of each picture. Circle the word. Then print **oa** or **ow** on the line.

b**oa**t sn**ow**

1	2	3
(toad) top	box (bow)	(road) rod
t o a d	b o w	r o a d
4	5	6
(row) rob	(goat) got	bop (bowl)
r o w	g o a t	b o w l
7	8	9
(soap) sob	(mow) mop	cot (coat)
s o a p	m o w	c o a t

202

LESSON 104: Connecting Sound to Symbol: /ō/ **oa** and **ow**

Randomly read aloud the words on the page. Have your child stand on his or her tiptoes when he or she hears a long o word.

Sound to Symbol /ō/ oa and ow

Objectives

- To identify and isolate medial sounds
- To recognize that **oa** and **ow** stand for /ō/
- To spell words with /ō/ **oa** and **ow**

Teaching the Lesson

Phonemic Awareness: Identify and Isolate Medial Sounds

Materials: **Sadlier Phonics Picture Cards** for **boat, toad, rain, pail, rose, smoke**

- Say **soap** and **bowl**. Point out that the sound in the middle of each word is /ō/. Have children repeat after you: **soap** /ō/ and **bowl** /ō/.
- Display the picture cards. Have children choose the picture cards that have the long **o** sound /ō/ in the middle. Have children say the names and then repeat them, isolating the /ō/ (e.g., **boat** /ō/).

Sound to Symbol

- Remind children that the sound of long **o** is /ō/. Say: *The **goat** **rows** the big **boat**.* Have children name all the words that have the long **o** sound.
- Write **goat** on the board, and circle the **oa**. Tell children that the letters **oa** stand for the long **o** sound in **goat**. Repeat with **rows**, circling the **ow**. Help children recognize that both **oa** and **ow** can spell the long **o** sound.
- Write **snow, boat, bowl,** and **soap** on the board. Read each word aloud. Have a volunteer circle the **oa** or **ow** in each one.

Practicing the Skill

Together read the directions on page 202. Call attention to the Key Picture Cues, and work with children on the first item. Then have them complete the page.

English Language Learners/ESL

Print on the board **oa** and **ow**. Tell children that **oa** and **ow** can stand for the long **o** sound. Point to each spelling and say /ō/. Demonstrate for children how to say /ō/, and have them repeat /ō/ after you. Then write on the board the words that identify the pictures on page 202. Point to each of the long **o** spellings as you say each word and have children repeat them after you. Tell the children to turn to page 202. Identify each picture and tell children to say the word.

Challenge

Materials: paper, crayons

Tell children that oceans and other bodies of water cover almost three-quarters of Earth. Make a list of water-related long **o** words, including **boat, float, row, foam, flow,** and **coast**. Have children draw watery scenes and label their pictures using as many long **o** words as possible.

Extra Support

Remind children that **ow** and **oa** can stand for the long **o** sound. Help children use Punchout Letter Cards to spell **low** and then **mow**. Repeat with **goat/coat** and **road/toad**. Have children point out the **ow** or **oa** in each new word.

Student Pages 203–204

Long Vowel o Phonograms

Objectives

- To distinguish rhyming words from non-rhyming words
- To recognize long o phonograms
- To build words with long o phonograms

Warming Up

Reviewing Initial Consonants

Point to consonants on an ABC chart. Then call on volunteers to complete the chant "___, my name is ___ and I like ___" with the given consonant and words that begin with that consonant (e.g., "**B**, my name is **Bobby** and I like **bananas**.").

Teaching the Lesson

Phonemic Awareness: Distinguish Rhyming Words from Non-Rhyming Words

Say **boat** and **float**, and have children repeat the words. Tell children that **boat** and **float** rhyme because they have the same ending sound /ōt/. Then say the following long **o** word pairs. Tell children to raise both hands when they hear a rhyming pair. Say: **rope/soak, coat/float, pose/rose, lone/load,** and **row/mow.**

Phonograms

- On the board, write the phonogram **ow**. Under it, write **row, low, mow**. Read aloud the phonogram and then each word. Point out that all the words end with the phonogram **ow**. Ask children to circle **ow** in each word.
- Write **ow** on the board. Say the word **tow**. Explain that to write **tow**, you need to add the letter that stands for /**t**/ to the beginning of **ow**. Write **t** in front of **ow**, and read the word together. Repeat this with other long **o** phonograms such as **oat** (**boat, coat, moat**) and **oad** (**load, road,** and **toad**).

Help Joe recycle. Say the name of each picture. Color the newspapers that have pictures with rhyming names the same color.

1. hose — Color 1 and 12 the same color
2. bone — Color 2 and 9 the same color
3. robe — Color 3 and 7 the same color
4. snow — Color 4 and 11 the same color
5. soap — Color 5 and 10 the same color
6. boat — Color 6 and 8 the same color
7. globe
8. coat
9. cone
10. rope
11. bow
12. nose

LESSON 105: Long Vowel o in Rhyming Words **203**

UNIVERSAL ACCESS
Meeting Individual Needs

Visual • Kinesthetic

Materials: index cards, tape

Have children choose a long o phonogram and print on index cards words that rhyme with the phonogram. Then tape cards to the floor to make "roads." Have children pretend to "drive" toy vehicles from road to road, reading each word as they cross it.

Auditory • Kinesthetic

Say a series of sentences. Ask children to say "Ho! Ho! Ho!" and hop after each sentence in which they hear the sound of long o. Use sentences like these:

The **foal** has **oats** on its **nose**.

The fox ran in the woods.

Can a **toad croak**?

Don't **poke** a **hole** in the balloon.

Did Max say hi to you?

I like to **row** my **boat**.

Extra Support

Review that the phonograms **ow, ose, oad,** and **oat** can stand for the long **o** sound. Say words with long **o** phonograms, such as **moat, road, pose, tow**. Ask children to name words that rhyme with each given word.

203

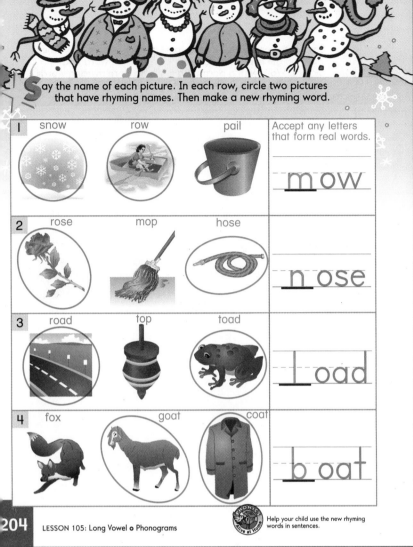

Say the name of each picture. In each row, circle two pictures that have rhyming names. Then make a new rhyming word.

1	snow	row	pail	Accept any letters that form real words.
				m ow
2	rose	mop	hose	n ose
3	road	top	toad	t oad
4	fox	goat	coat	b oat

204

LESSON 105: Long Vowel **o** Phonograms

Help your child use the new rhyming words in sentences.

- Ask children to turn to page 203. Read the directions together, and identify the pictures. Have a volunteer tell two pictures that should be colored the same, and explain why. Then have children complete the page.

- Have children read the phonograms on page 204 aloud. Ask children to name words that end with each phonogram. Then read the directions aloud, and have children complete the page.

Curriculum Connections

Spelling Connection

Read aloud each word and sentence below. Then call on volunteers to spell the words aloud or print them on the board.

home	Jim went **home** after the game.
hope	I **hope** my key works.
robe	I like my nice warm **robe**.
woke	The loud noise **woke** me.

Multicultural Connection

- Tell children that George Washington Carver was an African American agriculturist (a person who studies the production of crops). Carver researched ways to restore nutrients to overplanted farmland through the planting of soil-enriching crops (e.g., peanuts, soybeans, and sweet potatoes).

- Then have children name and illustrate "nutrients" (healthful foods and health-enhancing habits) that can help them to grow and stay healthy. Have children share their work. List any long **o** words that children may have used.

 Portfolio

Have children place their drawings in their portfolios.

English Language Learners/ESL

Review rhyming words by playing a pantomime guessing game. Remind children that rhyming words have the same ending sound, such as **toe** and **row**. Tell children that you are going to say a long **o** word and then pantomime a word that rhymes with it. They have to listen and watch to guess the rhyming word you are acting out. Use rhyming words from the lesson pages. For example, say the word **goat** and then pantomime putting on your **coat**.

Special Strategies

For Universal Access activities, see page 165F.

Challenge

Have each child work with a partner to write a list of rules that help protect Earth and keep it beautiful. (e.g., Pick up litter that may **blow** away. **Close** all garbage can lids.)

Provide time for children to share their "rules." Tell the class to vote for any rule they hear that includes a long **o** word by raising their hands.

Observational Assessment

*Note whether children have difficulty building words with particular long **o** phonograms, such as **oat** or **oad**.*

Long Vowel o Phonograms

Objectives
- To substitute medial sounds
- To build words with long **o** phonograms
- To discriminate long **o** words from other words

Warming Up

Reviewing Long a Phonograms

Materials: index cards, **Sadlier Phonics Picture Cards** for **cake**, **jay**, and **rain**

On index cards write words that end with **ake**, **ay**, and **ain**. Place the picture cards in a pocket chart. Ask children to name each picture. Then have volunteers place the rhyming words under the appropriate picture card.

Teaching the Lesson

Phonemic Awareness: Substitute Medial Sounds

Say **ripe**, and ask children to repeat the word. Then segment the word: /r/-/ī/-/p/ **ripe**; have children repeat. Explain that /ī/ is the middle vowel sound in **ripe**. Tell children that they can change the middle sound in a word to make a new word. Model how to change the middle vowel /ī/ in **ripe** to /ō/ to make **rope**. Change **cane** to **cone**, **pike** to **poke**, and **sale** to **sole**.

Phonograms

Materials: **Sadlier Phonics Picture Card** for **rose**

• On the board, write the phonogram **ose**. Under it write **nose**, **pose**, **hose**. Read aloud the phonogram and then each word. Point out that all the words end with the phonogram **ose**.

• Write **ose** on the board. Show the **rose** picture card, and say its name. Explain that to write **rose**, you need to add the letter that stands for /r/ to the beginning of **ose**. Write **r** in front of **ose**, and read the word together. Repeat this with other long **o** phonograms such as **ow** and **one**.

205

Say each word part. Say the name of each picture. Print the word on the line. Then add your own rhyming word and picture. Work with a partner to make up more rhyming words.

_ose	_oat	_ow
1 rose	4 goat	7 snow
2 nose	5 coat	8 bow
3 Accept any answer that is a real word.	6 Accept any answer that is a real word.	9 Accept any answer that is a real word.

LESSON 106: Word Building with Long Vowel **o** Phonograms

205

UNIVERSAL ACCESS
Meeting Individual Needs

Visual • Kinesthetic

Materials: yarn, scissors, glue, chart paper

Glue a piece of yarn in the shape of a large **O** onto chart paper. Have children write words with the long **o** sound in the large **O**. Then have them glue yarn around each long **o** phonogram.

Auditory • Kinesthetic

Tell children that a **crow** is a black bird that makes a "caw" sound. Then say words, including some with long **o** phonograms, such as **bowl**, **toad**, **poke**, **train**, **like**, **soak**, **rose**, and **same**. Have children flap their wings like a crow when they hear a long **o** word.

Extra Support

Review that the phonograms **oat**, **one**, **ope**, and **ose** all have the long **o** sound. Then write the phonograms on separate index cards. Have children choose a card, make a word by adding a consonant sound to the beginning of the phonogram, and blend the sounds to say the word.

Circle the word that names each picture.

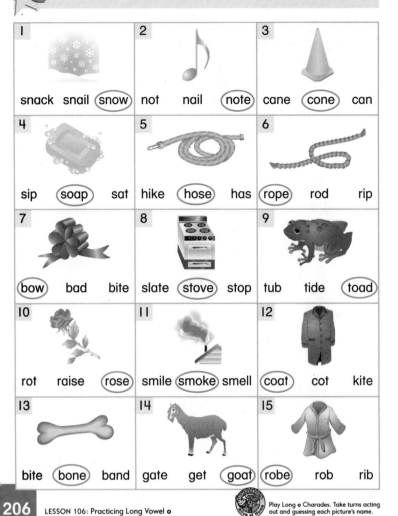

1. snack snail (snow)	2. not nail (note)	3. cane (cone) can
4. sip (soap) sat	5. hike (hose) has	6. (rope) rod rip
7. (bow) bad bite	8. slate (stove) stop	9. tub tide (toad)
10. rot raise (rose)	11. smile (smoke) smell	12. (coat) cot kite
13. bite (bone) band	14. gate get (goat)	15. (robe) rob rib

206 LESSON 106: Practicing Long Vowel o

Play Long o Charades. Take turns acting out and guessing each picture's name.

● Ask children to turn to page 205. Read the directions together, and identify the pictures in each column before having children complete the page.

● Read aloud the directions on page 206. Then ask what strategy children can use to read the words on the page. (Look for word parts; then blend the initial consonant or consonants with the phonogram.) Have children complete the page independently.

Curriculum Connections

Spelling Connection

Read aloud each word and sentence below. Then call on a volunteer to spell the word or print it on the board.

hose Water leaked from the **hose**.

row I sat in the **row** behind you.

coat My **coat** keeps me warm.

bow Can you tie a **bow**?

Theme Activity: Science/Math

Materials: newspapers, yardstick, tape

● Tell children that paper is made from the wood of trees. Explain that people can save trees by recycling newspapers and other paper products.

● Designate an area in the class for collecting newspapers. Help children tape a horizontal line on a wall four feet above the floor. Have children stack and bundle newspapers in the designated area. Tell children that for every four-foot stack of newspapers they recycle, one seventeen-foot tree is saved. For every four-foot stack, have children draw a picture of a tree and tape it to the wall.

● Have children write a story about recycled paper and trees. Have children circle any long o words they use.

 Portfolio Have children include their recycling story in their portfolios.

Sadlier Reading

Little Books and Big Books

Read *Joey's Rowboat* (fiction) for more practice with long **o**.

English Language Learners/ESL

Preview the pictures on lesson pages 205 and 206. Then make up and say a sentence using the pictures on page 205, for example, *I smell a rose with my nose.* Write the sentence on the board, and invite a volunteer to underline the two words that rhyme. Invite another child to act out the sentence. Encourage children to make up other rhyming sentences and to act them out.

Challenge

Display a picture of a sapling and explain that it is a young plant. Have children write a first, next, and last sequence of steps on how to plant the sapling. Brainstorm a list of words, such as **hole, hoe, pole, hose**. Have children circle any long **o** words used in their sequence.

Special Strategies

For Universal Access activities, see page 165F.

Student Pages 207–208

Long o and Short o

Objectives
- To identify and isolate medial sounds
- To write long o words
- To discriminate long o words from short o words

Warming Up

Reviewing Long i
Materials: **Sadlier Phonics Picture Cards** for **bike, hive, kite, pie, rice, tie**

Place the cards in a pocket chart. Ask a child to pick a card, say the word, and print it on the board. Repeat until all long **i** words have been printed on the board. Then have the class say each word.

Teaching the Lesson

Phonemic Awareness: Identify and Isolate Medial Sounds

Say **coat** and have children repeat the word. Explain that /ō/ is the middle sound in the word **coat**. Say the following words, and have children identify the middle sound for each: **deep** (/ē/), **poke** (/ō/), **same** (/ā/), **bone** (/ō/), **read** (/ē/), **moat** (/ō/).

Sound to Symbol
Materials: **Sadlier Phonics Picture Cards** for long and short **o** words

- Have children listen for long and short **o** words in this sentence: *The **odd toad** jumped on the **boat**.* Explain that the vowel sound /ō/ in **toad** and **boat** is long **o** and that the vowel sound /o/ in **odd** and **on** is short **o**. Have children repeat these word pairs: **toad/boat** /ō/; **odd/on** /o/.
- Write the word pairs on the board to serve as cues for long and short **o** sounds. Then distribute picture cards. Have children name each picture and write the word under the appropriate word pair on the board.

207

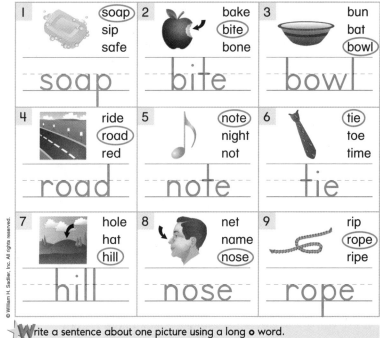

Say the name of each picture with a partner. Then circle the word and print it on the line.

1	soap / sip / safe	2	bake / bite / bone	3	bun / bat / bowl
	soap		**bite**		**bowl**
4	ride / road / red	5	note / night / not	6	tie / toe / time
	road		**note**		**tie**
7	hole / hat / hill	8	net / name / nose	9	rip / rope / ripe
	hill		**nose**		**rope**

Write a sentence about one picture using a long **o** word.

Accept any sentence about a picture.

UNIVERSAL ACCESS
Meeting Individual Needs

Visual • Auditory
Materials: notebook, pencil

Have small groups of children hunt for classroom objects with names that have the sound of long **o**. Have children say the name of the object and then record their findings in their notebooks. Possible entries include **globe, coat, envelope, notebook,** and **telescope**.

Kinesthetic • Auditory
Materials: index cards

Assign the roles of "driver" and "toll collector" to children. Give each driver several index cards with long **o** words on them. The drivers then go around the room, stop at each toll, and pay with a long **o** card. The toll collector reads the long **o** word aloud.

Extra Support
Remind children that the vowel sound in **hop** is short **o** and in **blow** is long **o**. Say the following list of words: **stop, road, rot, box, cone, rose, sock, snow, bowl, cot**. If the word has the short **o** sound, children hop. If the word has a long **o** sound, children pretend to blow out candles.

Read the name of each picture. Circle **L** if the name has the sound of long **o**. Circle **S** if the name has the sound of short **o**. Then color each picture that has the long **o** sound in its name.

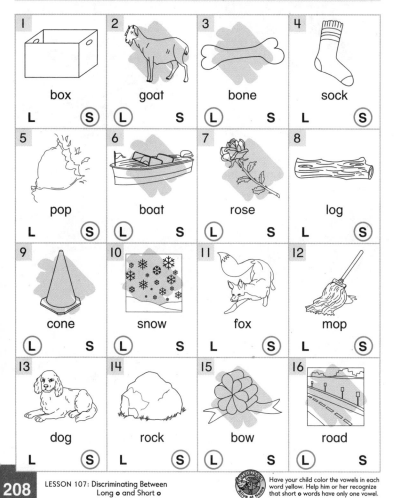

1 box — L (S)	2 goat — (L) S	3 bone — (L) S	4 sock — L (S)
5 pop — L (S)	6 boat — (L) S	7 rose — (L) S	8 log — L (S)
9 cone — (L) S	10 snow — (L) S	11 fox — L (S)	12 mop — L (S)
13 dog — L (S)	14 rock — L (S)	15 bow — (L) S	16 road — (L) S

LESSON 107: Discriminating Between Long **o** and Short **o**

Have your child color the vowels in each word yellow. Help him or her recognize that short **o** words have only one vowel.

Practicing the Skill

● Read aloud the directions on page 207, and identify the pictures. Make sure children notice the arrows in items 2, 7, and 8. Go over the writing directions. Point out that a sentence begins with an uppercase letter and ends with a period. Then have children complete the page.

● Read aloud the directions on page 208, and identify the pictures together. Ask a volunteer to explain what the letters **L** and **S** stand for. Then have children complete the page.

Curriculum Connections

Spelling Connection
Read aloud each word and sentence below. Then call on volunteers to spell the words or print them on the board.

bone The pup hid the **bone**.

goat I saw a **goat** on the farm.

rose The **rose** smelled sweet.

road The car went up the **road**.

bow I put a **bow** on the gift.

Theme Activity: Music
● Sing "Row, Row, Row Your Boat" with the class. Explain that rowing is an earth-friendly way to travel over water (no fuel or fumes to pollute the environment).

● Write "**Row**, **Row**, **Row** Your **Boat**" on the board. Have a volunteer replace the words **Row**, **row**, **row**, and **boat** with other words, using at least one word with the sound of long **o**. Write the replacements in the appropriate places, and have children sing their "silly" songs. Use the following as examples:

Sow, sow, sow, your **oats**

Grow, grow, grow your **toe**

Portfolio — Have children include some of their songs in their portfolios.

Sadlier Reading
Little Books and Big Books
Read *Did You Know?* (nonfiction) for more practice with long **o**.

English Language Learners/ ESL
Materials: pocket mirrors

Give each child a pocket mirror, and have children repeat the following word pairs: **rod/road, box/boat, got/goat, sock/soak, hop/hope.** Ask them to watch the movement of their mouths as they say each short **o** word and then each long **o** word. Model the correct formation of each letter for those children having difficulty.

Challenge
Discuss how people around the world are supporting farming policies that encourage farmers to use natural ways to control pests and to enrich the soil. Have children describe an earth-friendly farm. Encourage children to use long **o** words, such as **mow, row, sow, grow,** and **grove,** in their descriptions.

Special Strategies
For Universal Access activities, see page 165F.

Long Vowel o
Decodable Reader

Objectives
- To read long **o** words and high-frequency words in context
- To read the story fluently
- To understand cause and effect

Introducing the Story Words

Long o Decodable Words Remind children that the sound of long **o** is /ō/. Write **toad** on the board. Explain that **toad** has the sound of long **o**. Underline **oa**, and say that **oa** can stand for /ō/. Repeat with **boat** and **Joan**. Point out that the letters **o_e** and **ow** can also stand for /ō/. Write **home**, **pole**, and **row** on the board. Read the words with children.

High-Frequency Words List the words **the**, **a**, **this**, **is**, **for**, **and**, **jump**, **help**, and **with** on the board. Read them with children. Then call out words, and have children spell each word aloud and write it in the air.

Reading the Book

Reading Together Have children remove pages 209 and 210, and show them how to cut and fold the pages into a book. Read aloud the title, "Joan and the Toad." Then read the story aloud as children follow along.

Responding Ask children to tell what Joan did to save the toad's home.

Reading for Fluency Together read the story aloud. Have partners read the story aloud. One partner reads only sentences with the word **toad**. Then have children read the story independently.

Observational Assessment

*Notice whether children are able to decode the long **o** words and read the story fluently.*

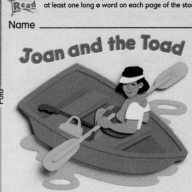

Your child has read this book in school. Ask him or her to read it to you. Then have him or her find at least one long **o** word on each page of the story.

Name _____

Joan and the Toad

This home is fun for Joan and the toad!

8

Joan can row the boat.

1

The toad will jump in the lake.

6

Joan can see a mess.

3

Directions: Cut and fold the book. Then read the story. Tell why Joan needed to help the toad.

LESSON 108: Long Vowel **o** Decodable Reader Comprehension: Understanding Cause and Effect

209

UNIVERSAL ACCESS
Meeting Individual Needs

Visual • Auditory
Materials: index cards

Write each of these words on an index card: **Joan, row, boat, home, toad, pole.** Distribute the cards. Write the headings **oa**, **o_e**, and **ow** on the board. Ask each child to read his or her word and write it under the correct heading on the board.

Auditory • Kinesthetic
Materials: index cards

Write each high-frequency word—**the, a, this, is, for, and, jump, help, with**—on an index card. Distribute the cards. Write the same words on the board. Read aloud a word, and have the child with the matching card circle the word on the board, spell it, and use it in a sentence.

Extra Support
Remind children that **home** has a long **o** sound. Then print **home, Joan,** and **row** on the board. Tell children that long **o** can be represented by **o_e, oa,** or **ow**. Have children find and circle the letters that stand for the long **o** sound in "Joan and the Toad."

Joan can see a toad.

Joan will jump in the lake.

2

7

Can Joan save the home for the toad?

4

Joan can help with a bag and a pole.

5

LESSON 108: Long Vowel **o** Decodable Reader
Comprehension: Understanding Cause and Effect

Comprehension Strategy

Understanding Cause and Effect
Materials: balance scale, weight

Explain that sometimes one thing makes something else happen. Put a weight in one pan of a balance scale. Say: *What did I do? What happened when I put a weight in one pan?* (The scale tipped so that the pan with the weight dropped while the other pan rose.) Relate this concept to the story by posing these questions: *What happened when Joan saw a mess in the lake?* (She cleaned it up.) *What happened after Joan cleaned up the mess?* (Joan and the toad could swim in the lake and have fun.)

Phonics and Decoding

Learning About Long o Write on the board and read aloud the sentence on page 1: **Joan** can **row** the **boat**. Call on a child to underline the words that have the sound of long **o**. (**Joan, row, boat**) Have other volunteers circle the letters that make up each long **o** sound. (**oa, ow, oa**) Repeat the activity with sentences on pages 4, 5, and 8.

Word Building Write the word **toad** on the board. Circle the letters **oad**. Have children think of another word with the **oad** phonogram. (**road, load**) Continue with the phonograms **oat** (**coat, goat**), **ole** (**hole, mole**), and **ow** (**how, bow**).

Curriculum Connections

Writing and Sharing Write this rhyme on the board, and read it with children:

Joan and the **toad** have a **load** of fun.

They play in the lake.

They play in the sun.

They _____ and have fun, fun, fun.

Have children work in pairs. Tell them to copy the rhyme, add one thing they think Joan and the toad might do that involves at least one long **o** word (e.g., "ride in a **boat**"), and complete the rhyme. Have children read aloud their completed rhymes.

English Language Learners/ESL
Have children predict the story of *Joan and the Toad* using only the pictures as clues. Show children a copy of the *Decodable Reader* with the words cut off or covered. Discuss each picture with them. Ask questions such as: *What is happening here? What does Joan see? What does Joan do?* Then help them read the story, and have them compare the story with their predictions.

Challenge
Ask children to recall what Joan did to clean up the lake. Then have children brainstorm things they could do to clean up their neighborhoods. If possible, each idea should contain a long **o** word (e.g., tie up newspapers with a **rope** or pick up trash from the **road**). Record their ideas, and have children identify each long **o** word.

Special Strategies
For Universal Access activities, see page 165F.

210

Long Vowel o in Context

Objectives
- To identify and isolate medial sounds
- To identify long **o** words to complete sentences
- To write long **o** words in context

Warming Up

Reviewing Short a and Short i
Play "stand up, sit down" to review short **a** and short **i** sounds. Say short **a** and short **i** words, such as **mat, in, cat, tip, knit, win, dad.** Tell children to stand when they hear a short **a** word, and to sit when they hear a short **i** word.

Teaching the Lesson

Phonemic Awareness: Identify and Isolate Medial Sounds
Materials: **Sadlier Phonics Picture Cards** for **boat, rain, lake, nose, jeep**
Say the word **robe.** Tell children that /ō/ is the middle sound in **robe.** Have children repeat **robe** /ō/. Display the picture cards; then have children choose the ones whose names have the long **o** sound in the middle. Have children say the names and repeat the middle sound (e.g., **rose** /ō/).

Phonics in Context
Write this sentence on the board: The ___ is in the barn. Write the words **goal, goat, glow** next to the sentence. Read the sentence and word choices aloud. Then read the sentence three times, each time filling in the blank with one of the word choices. Circle the word **goat,** and tell children that it best completes the meaning of the sentence. Now have children complete this sentence: I used __ to tie the box. (**rope, rose, row**)

Comprehension Skill: Comparing and Contrasting

Look at each picture. Circle the word that completes the sentence. Print it on the line. Then take turns reading the sentences with a partner.

1. Look at the __snow__.
   - snip
   - snake
   - (snow)

2. It is __so__ white at first.
   - (so)
   - say
   - sock

3. There is dirt on the __road__.
   - rope
   - rake
   - (road)

4. It is from __smoke__.
   - smile
   - (smoke)
   - smell

5. Snow __soaks__ up dirt.
   - soaps
   - (soaks)
   - sacks

6. Our __coats__ do, too!
   - cots
   - cast
   - (coats)

LESSON 109: Long Vowel **o** in Sentences

211

UNIVERSAL ACCESS
Meeting Individual Needs

Visual • Tactile
Materials: construction paper, white glue

Have children print words with the sound of long **o** on construction paper. Then have them trace over the letters that stand for the long **o** sound with white glue. After the glue has dried, tell children to trace the letters with their fingers. Have children make up sentences using their words.

Kinesthetic • Auditory
Have children crouch down like a toad with their hands between their feet. Say a list of words, such as **fox, goat, pet, toad, zone, gate, hop, pole,** and **home.** When children hear a long **o** word, the "toads" hop in place. When they hear a word that does not have the long **o** sound, they stay still.

Extra Support
Remind children that **goat** has the long **o** sound. Show children word cards for **toe, hot, coat, row, rod,** and **joke.** Ask children to read each word and to say if it has a long **o** sound. If the word has the long **o,** have children use it in a sentence.

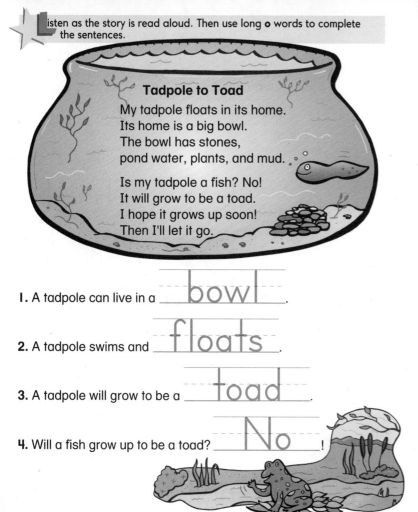

Listen as the story is read aloud. Then use long **o** words to complete the sentences.

Tadpole to Toad

My tadpole floats in its home.
Its home is a big bowl.
The bowl has stones,
pond water, plants, and mud.

Is my tadpole a fish? No!
It will grow to be a toad.
I hope it grows up soon!
Then I'll let it go.

1. A tadpole can live in a _____ bowl _____ .

2. A tadpole swims and _____ floats _____ .

3. A tadpole will grow to be a _____ toad _____ .

4. Will a fish grow up to be a toad? _____ No _____ !

212

LESSON 109: Long Vowel **o** in Context
Comprehension: Comparing and Contrasting

Have your child find long **o** words
in the story with these spellings:
o_e, oa, ow, and o.

Practicing the Skill

- Have children turn to page 211. Read aloud the directions and talk about the pictures. Complete the first item with the class. Read aloud the remaining sentences, and tell children to complete the page.
- Read aloud the directions and the story on page 212. Help children find the long **o** words. Read aloud the sentences, and help children complete the first item using a long **o** word from the story. Then have children complete the remaining sentences.

Curriculum Connections

Spelling Connection

Read aloud each word and sentence below. Call on volunteers to spell the words or to print them on the board.

loaf Grandma baked a **loaf** of bread.

hose Use a **hose** to water the garden.

road Look before you cross the **road**.

tow Here comes a big **tow** truck.

Science Center

Materials: coffee filters

- Reread the story on page 211 and talk about pollution. Then have children perform this simple experiment to observe air pollution. Tell them to dampen white coffee filters. Fasten the filters outside a classroom window so that they can be easily seen from inside the classroom.
- Have children check the filters once a day for a week.
- Help children write sentences to describe how the filters changed during the week. Encourage children to include long **o** words in their sentences.

Portfolio Have children include their observations from the Science Center in their portfolios.

English Language Learners/ESL

Materials: simple diagram of life cycle of a toad, drawing paper, crayons

Build background knowledge about tadpoles and toads by displaying a diagram, preferably with photographs, that shows the life cycle of a toad. Discuss with children how the eggs turn into tadpoles and the tadpoles into toads that lay eggs. Have children draw life cycle pictures of toads and label them. Suggest that they add these pictures to their portfolios.

Challenge

Discuss different kinds of weather, such as cold, hot, snow, rain, fog. Ask children what type of weather they like the best. Help them write a story describing what they like to do during their favorite kind of weather and why. Then have children trade papers, read their classmates' stories, and circle every long **o** word they find.

Special Strategies

For Universal Access activities, see page 165F.

Student Pages 213-214

Assessing Long Vowel o
Reviewing Long Vowels a, i, o

Objectives
- To identify and complete words with long **o**
- To write sentences with long **a**, **i**, and **o** words

Warming Up

Reviewing Short o
Tell children the vowel sound in **box** is short **o**. Then have them name and write the short **o** words in these sentences:

Mom and **Ron jog** to the lake.

They **stop** to eat lunch from a **box**.

Ron and **Mom** sit **on** a **log**.

It is **hot**, but **not** too **hot** to eat.

Teaching the Lesson

Long o
Read aloud the silly sentences below. Have children listen for long **o** words as you reread the sentences.

I **spoke** to a **crow** who **posed** in the **snow**.

Joe told a **joke** about a **goat** in a **boat**.

Write the long **o** words on the board. Have volunteers add other rhyming long **o** words.

Long a, i, o
Say **sail**, **kite**, **soap** and identify the long **a**, **o**, and **i** vowel sounds. Then ask the riddles below. Begin with a clue stating the vowel sound of each answer.

Long **a**: You can carry water in it to water a tree. What is it? (**pail**)

Long **i**: This tree has long needles. What is it? (**pine**)

Long **o**: You dig one in the ground to plant a tree. What is it? (**hole**)

213

 Check-Up Say the name of each picture. If the picture name has the long **o** sound, find the letters in the box to complete the word. Print the letters on the line.

o_e	oa	ow

1	2 kite	3
rope	k t	bowl

4 wave	5	6
w v	toad	hose

7	8 pot	9
cone	p t	soap

10 pop	11	12
p p	note	mow

LESSON 110: Assessing Long Vowel **o** **213**

UNIVERSAL ACCESS
Reteaching Activities

Activity 1
Materials: paper strips, envelopes

Write the sentences below on paper strips, cut them into individual words, and place each sentence in a separate envelope.

Bob **Jones rows** the **boat**.

Joan hopes the **rose** will **grow**.

The **snow froze** my **nose**.

Get some **soap** and a big **bowl**.

The **goat** is in the **road**.

Review the long **o** sound and its different spellings. Then give out the sentence envelopes to pairs of children. Direct them to unscramble the sentences, read them aloud, and identify the long **o** words.

Activity 2
Materials: yellow, white, gray construction paper; straws; scissors; glue; black crayon

Say the words **gray**, **white**, and **yellow** and point out the long **a**, **i**, and **o** sound in each. Then have children cut large flower shapes from construction paper of each color. Direct them to print long **a** words on the gray flowers, long **i** words on the white flowers, and long **o** words on the yellow flowers. Then have children glue their flowers onto straw "stems" and read their words aloud. Make the class garden grow by fastening the flowers onto the bulletin board.

Read the words in the boxes. Combine words from boxes 1, 2, and 3 to make sentences. Print them on the lines. Then go back and underline the long vowel words in the sentences.

1	2	3
Kate and Jay	hike	to the lake.
Joan and Mike	race	down the road.
Five men	rode	to the right.

Possible responses:

Kate and Jay race to the right. Five men rode down the road. Joan and Mike hike to the lake.

LESSON 110: Reviewing Long Vowels **a, i, o**

Help your child make up endings to these sentences: Mike likes to ____. Mrs. Dole bakes ____.

Assessing the Skill

Read aloud the directions on page 213 and have volunteers identify the pictures. Make sure children realize that they should complete only words that have the long **o** sound. Suggest that they put a mark beside each long **o** word before completing any words. Point out the boxed spelling guide and do items 1 and 2 together. Then have children complete the page.

Cumulative Review

Read aloud the directions on page 214. Explain that they can use phrases from the three boxes to form sentences. Model this example: *Kate and Jay race to the lake.* Point out the uppercase letters in column 1 and the periods in column 3. Remind children that their sentences should begin with uppercase letters and end with periods. Have children write sentences and read them aloud.

Observational Assessment   As children read aloud, note how well they decode words with the sounds of long **a**, **i**, and **o**.

Dictation   Tell children you are going to say some long **a**, **i**, and **o** words. Have them write the words as you dictate them. Say **cave**, **wait**, **side**, **might**, **grow**, **coal**. Then tell children you are going to say a sentence. Have them write the sentence as you dictate it and underline any long **a**, **i**, and **o** words. Use this sentence: **Joe likes** to **ride** the **train**.

Student Skills Assessment   Use the checklist on Student Edition pages 321–322 to record your observations of individual children.

Guided Instruction

Skills	Resources
Long vowel **a**	Instruction on pages 167–180 Little Books *Wake Up, Sleepyheads!*; *Space Camp*
Long vowel **i**	Instruction on pages 183–196 Little Books *Niles Likes to Smile*; *Nice Vine, Quite Fine*
Long vowel **o**	Instruction on pages 199–212 Little Books *Joey's Rowboat*; *Did You Know?*
Long vowels **a, i, o**	Phonemic Awareness Activities pages 165H–165I

Assessing Long Vowels a, i, o

Objectives
- To read words with long **a, i, o**
- To write words with long **a, i, o**

Warming Up

Reviewing Phonograms

Write the phonogram **an** on the board. Review that a consonant can be added to the beginning of a phonogram to make words. Write **p** in front of **an** to make the word **pan**. Then have a volunteer read the word aloud. Erase the **p** and ask children to think of other consonants that could be added to **an** to form a new word. (**b, c, D, f, p, r, t, v**) Repeat using the phonograms **it** and **ug**.

Teaching the Lesson

Long a, i, o

- Say: **Ride a bike.** Tell children that **ride** and **bike** both have the long **i** sound. Say: **Race in place.** Tell children that **race** and **place** both have the long **a** sound. Then say: **Hose the rose.** Ask what long vowel sound is heard in **hose** and **rose**. (long **o**) Ask children to name the repeated long vowel sounds in these sentences:

  Take a **break.**

  The **rope broke.**

  I **like limes.**

- Whisper to each volunteer a long **a**, **o**, or **i** word to act out for the class to guess. Tell the volunteer to name the word's long vowel sound as a clue before starting. Use words such as **face, bake, hide, bike, snow, goat.**

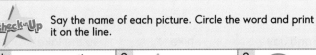

Say the name of each picture. Circle the word and print it on the line.

1	tip / **tape** / tap — tape
2	cane / can / **cone** — cone
3	name / **nine** / note — nine
4	**road** / rod / ride — road
5	joke / jam / **jay** — jay
6	box / **bow** / bike — bow
7	tag / tile / **tail** — tail
8	**night** / not / nail — night
9	**wave** / wove / wait — wave
10	rob / **robe** / rib — robe
11	time / **tie** / top — tie
12	**high** / hit / hope — high

UNIVERSAL ACCESS
Reteaching Activities

Activity 1

Say /ā/, /ī/, /ō/ and remind children that these are the sounds of long vowels **a, i, o.** Then review letter combinations that can spell each sound: **a_e, i_e, o_e, ai, ie, oa, ay, igh, ow.** Write on the board long vowel **a, i, o** phonograms such as **ale, ice, one, ain, oat, ay, ow, ight, ie.** Model adding **p** to **ale** to make **pale.** Then have children add consonants to turn the phonograms into words. Help them check that they have made real words.

Activity 2

Materials: Sadlier Phonics **Picture Cards** for **hay, lake, rain, bike, pie, tie, boat, rose, snow, toe; Punchout Letter Cards**

Show the **hay, bike,** and **rose** picture cards. Write each picture name on the board and beneath the name write the letters **ay, i_e,** and **o_e.** Review other spellings for long **a, i, o.** Show children the remaining picture cards. Ask volunteers to name each picture while classmates use letter cards to spell the words. Have children name the letters that spell the long vowel sound.

Check-Up Say the name of each picture. Circle the word and print it on the line.

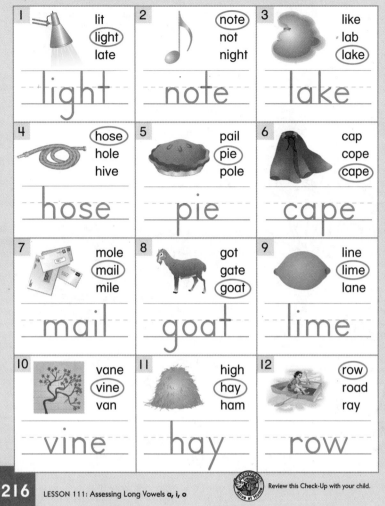

1. lit
   (light)
   late

   light

2. (note)
   not
   night

   note

3. like
   lab
   (lake)

   lake

4. (hose)
   hole
   hive

   hose

5. pail
   (pie)
   pole

   pie

6. cap
   cope
   (cape)

   cape

7. mole
   (mail)
   mile

   mail

8. got
   gate
   (goat)

   goat

9. line
   (lime)
   lane

   lime

10. vane
    (vine)
    van

    vine

11. high
    (hay)
    ham

    hay

12. (row)
    road
    ray

    row

216   LESSON 111: Assessing Long Vowels **a, i, o**   Review this Check-Up with your child.

Guided Instruction

Skills	Resources
Long vowel **a**	Instruction on pages 167–180 Little Books *Wake Up, Sleepyheads!*; *Space Camp*
Long vowel **i**	Instruction on pages 183–196 Little Books: *Niles Likes to Smile*; *Nice Vine, Quite Fine*
Long vowel **o**	Instruction on pages 199–212 Little Books *Joey's Rowboat*; *Did You Know?*
Long vowels **a, i, o**	Phonemic Awareness Activities pages 165H–165I

Assessing the Skills

Check-Up Review that the letters **a_e**, **ai**, **ay** can stand for the long **a** sound; that the letters **i_e**, **igh**, **ie** can stand for the long **i** sound; that the letters **o_e**, **oa**, **ow** can stand for the long **o** sound.

Read aloud the directions on page 215. Together identify all pictures and do the first item. Explain that the directions for page 216 are exactly the same as those for page 215. Remind children to select each picture name, circle it, and print it in the space. Then have them complete both pages.

Observational Assessment As children write, notice whether they use a combination of two vowels to spell words with long vowel sounds.

Portfolio Assessment Have children review their portfolios and choose favorite selections to discuss in a writing conference. Ask children to point out long **a**, **i**, and **o** words in their work and to consider how they might edit or revise specific pieces in light of what they've learned about those long vowel sounds and spellings. At the end of the conference, have each child write one or two notes on what to work on in future writing and add the notes to his or her portfolio. See the Writing Rubrics on page 165C.

Dictation Tell children you are going to say some long **a** words. Have them write the long **a** words as you dictate them. Say: **take, rail, say, bait, mate**. Continue the activity with long **i** words: **sigh, mine, lies, dine, sight**. Repeat with these long **o** words: **pole, bow, coal, Joan, robe**. Then tell children you are going to say a sentence. Have them write the sentence as you dictate it and underline any long **a**, **i**, and **o** words. Use this sentence: **Gail likes** to jump **rope**.

Student Skills Assessment Use the checklist on Student Edition pages 321–322 to record your observations of individual children.

Phonemic Awareness
/ŌŌ/ and /yŌŌ/

Objectives
- To match medial sounds
- To identify words with /ŌŌ/ and /yŌŌ/
- To discriminate between words that do and do not have /ŌŌ/ and /yŌŌ/

Warming Up

Reviewing Short u
Remind children that **pup** and **up** have the sound of short **u**. Say the following sentences. Have children hold their hands up when they hear a short **u** word.

Gus is a **pup**. **Gus** stepped on **gum**.

Gus tugged. But **Gus** was **stuck**!

Teaching the Lesson

Phonemic Awareness: Match Medial Sounds
- Have children say the words **suit** and **cube** together with you. Explain that each word has a slightly different long **u** sound in the middle. Tell children that the middle sound of **suit** is /ŌŌ/ and that the middle sound of **cube** is /yŌŌ/.
- Tell children to listen as you say pairs of words. Direct them to make a **U** with their arms if both words in a pair have the sound of long **u** in the middle. Then say: **suit/fruit, cab/cute, mule/cute, fruit/tube, June/jay, red/rude, juice/prune**.

The Sound of Long u
Say **cube**, **fruit**, and **true**, and have children repeat after you. Point out that each word has the sound of long **u**. Then say these sentences. Have children name the words that have the sound of long **u**.

Sue has a **huge tuba**.

She will play a **tune**.

June has paper, **glue**, and a **ruler**.

She will make a **blue cube**.

217

Listen Listen as the page is read aloud. Talk about the long **u** words, such as **blue** and **fruit**. Then tell one thing you like about June.

June
Bright **blue** skies,
Bathing **suits**,
Inner **tubes**,
Fresh, ripe **fruit**,

Sandy **dunes**,
Happy **tunes**,
Barbecues—
I love **June**!

Critical Thinking Possible Answer: They are putting their garbage in the trash and using the recycle bins.
How are people in the picture making the beach a safe and clean place?

LESSON 112: Phonemic Awareness: /ŌŌ/   **217**

UNIVERSAL ACCESS
Meeting Individual Needs

Auditory • Kinesthetic
Have children pretend to be a marching band. Tell them they will play **tubas** as they march. They will say "Oompa-pa" each time they hear a long **u** word. Say the words **mule, boat, true, tune, feet, glue, wet, hide, tube, June, suit, nail, mop**.

Visual • Kinesthetic
Materials: Sadlier Phonics Picture Cards for long **u**, including **blue, fruit, June, mule, suit, tube**; other picture cards

Show the cards one at a time, and name each picture. Have children act out drinking a glass of **juice** when they hear a long **u** word.

Extra Support
Ask riddles like the following. Point out that the answers are long **u** words.

I am sticky. I rhyme with **blue**. (**glue**)

You hum me. I rhyme with **June**. (**tune**)

June has the long **u** sound. Circle and color each picture that has the long **u** sound in its name.

1 June	2 juice	3 rain	4 suit
5 tube	6 cub	7 pine	8 ruler
9 tune	10 tuba	11 glue	12 rope

218   LESSON 112: Phonemic Awareness: /o͞o/ and /yo͞o/

Help your child cut apart the pictures. Take turns finding the ones with long **u** in their names.

Practicing the Skill

● Read aloud the poem on page 217, and ask children to name the long **u** words they hear. Ask children to tell what they like best about **June**. Then read aloud the Critical Thinking question, and discuss how the people in the picture are making the beach safe and clean.

● Together read the directions on page 218 and identify the pictures. Remind children that long **u** words can have the sound /o͞o/ or /yo͞o/. Have them complete the page.

Curriculum Connections

Theme Activity: Science
Materials: paper bags, markers

● Poll children to find how many bring lunch to school in a paper bag. Ask those children to tell what they do with their bags after eating lunch.

● Explain that paper bags are made from trees and that each cut tree makes about 700 bags.

● Tell children that reusing lunch bags helps save trees. Point out that **reusing** has the long **u** sound. Ask children to think of things a tree might say to encourage people to reuse their lunch bags (e.g., "**Use** your bag again!" "I'll sing a happy **tune** if you **reuse** your bag."). Have children identify the long **u** words.

● Distribute paper bags, and have children decorate them to illustrate one of their ideas. Invite children to reuse the bags for lunches or another purpose.

English Language Learners/ESL
Materials: a calendar

Review the months of the year. Before introducing the verse on page 217, display a calendar. Show June's page and talk about things that happen in that month (school ends, weather is warm). Have children name all the months with you. Talk about what things happen in each month. Tell them that if they hear another month with the same long **u** sound as in **June** (**January, February, July**), they should hum a tune. Discuss the day and date with children on a regular basis to reinforce these concepts.

Special Strategies
For Universal Access activities, see page 165F.

Challenge
Materials: index cards with long **u** words, one to a card; a paper bag

Tell children they will make up a silly story using four long **u** words. Have each child pick four words from the bag. Have children make up a story using their four words and any other words they need. For example, one story might go like this: A sad **tuba** went for a walk. He met a **flute** riding a **mule**. They made lots of **music** together!

Sound to Symbol /o͞o/ u_e and /yo͞o/ u_e

Objectives

- To identify and isolate medial sounds
- To recognize that **u_e** stands for /o͞o/ and /yo͞o/
- To spell words with /o͞o/ **u_e** and /yo͞o/ **u_e**

Teaching the Lesson

Phonemic Awareness: Identify and Isolate Medial Sounds

- Say **June**. Explain that /o͞o/ is the sound in the middle of **June**. Say /j/-/o͞o/-/n/ **June** and have children repeat after you. Then say **mule** and have children repeat after you. Explain that /yo͞o/ is the sound in the middle of **mule**. Have children repeat after you as you say /m/-/yo͞o/-/l/ **mule**.
- Tell children you will say some words. Ask them to clap if the middle sound is the same as the /o͞o/ in **June**, or to make "**mule** ears" with their fingers if the middle sound is the same as the /yo͞o/ in **mule**. Say **nose, cube, flute, bike, cute, tune, tape**.

Sound to Symbol

Materials: **Sadlier Phonics Picture Cards** for **June, mule, tube**

- Say **tune** and **cube**, and ask children to repeat after you. Explain that /o͞o/ as in **tune** and /yo͞o/ as in **cube** stand for a long **u** sound. Write the words **tune** and **cube** on the board; point out the **u_e** spelling for both sounds of long **u**. Note that the **e** is silent.
- Display the picture cards, and have children identify them. List the words on the board under **u_e**, and have volunteers underline the **u** and **e** in each word.

Practicing the Skill

On page 219, direct children to look at the Key Picture Cue and say the word **tube**. Read aloud the directions together. Model the first item, and have children complete the page.

219

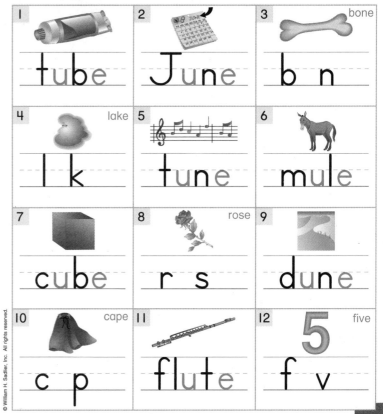

The letters **u_e** can stand for the long **u** sound. The letter **e** is silent. Say the name of each picture. Then print **u** in the middle and **e** at the end of each word that has the long **u** sound.

tube

1. tube	2. June	3. bone — b__n__
4. lake — l__k__	5. tune	6. mule
7. cube	8. rose — r__s__	9. dune
10. cape — c__p__	11. flute	12. five — f__v__

LESSON 113: Connecting Sound to Symbol: /o͞o/ u_e and /yo͞o/ u_e   **219**

UNIVERSAL ACCESS
Meeting Individual Needs

English Language Learners/ESL

Review with children vocabulary words from page 219. Encourage children to write a funny story about a mule. Tell children that one spelling for long **u** is **u_e**. Model for children: *June cannot play the flute. June cannot sing a tune!* Have children read their stories to the rest of the class.

Challenge

Have children describe what Earth-friendly activities they enjoy taking part in during the summer. Encourage children to use long **u** words in their descriptions (e.g., **June** picnics, **tube** rides on a lake, listening to **cute** parade **tunes**). Have children underline any words with **u_e**.

Extra Support

Materials: **Sadlier Phonics Picture Cards** for **bug, June, sun, mule, tube**

Draw a long tube. Help children name the pictures, and list the words on the tube. Have children underline the **u** and **e** in each word.

The letters **ui** and **ue** stand for the long **u** sound.

fruit   blue

Say the name of each picture. Circle the word. Then print **ui** or **ue** on the line.

1	2	3
bud (blue)	(suit) sun	gum (glue)
blue	suit	glue

4	5	6
(fruit) fume	(juice) June	sub (Sue)
fruit	juice	Sue

220

LESSON 114: Long Vowel **u** Spelling Patterns: **ui** and **ue**

First have your child point to and read all of the words with **ui**. Then have him or her do the same for the **ue** words.

Sound to Symbol /ōō/ ui and ue

Objectives

• To identify and isolate medial sounds

• To recognize that **ui** and **ue** stand for /ōō/

• To spell words with /ōō/ **ui** and **ue**

Teaching the Lesson

Phonemic Awareness: Identify and Isolate Medial Sounds

• Say **flute**, **rule**, and **juice**. Tell children that all these words have the sound of /ōō/ in the middle. Have them repeat after you: **flute** /ōō/, **rule** /ōō/, **juice** /ōō/.

• Tell children that you are going to say pairs of words. Ask children to hold up one finger if the first word in each pair has the same middle sound as **flute**, **rule**, and **juice**, or two fingers if the second word has the same sound. Say **jug/June; skate/use; suit/seat; fruit/fun**.

Sound to Symbol

• Say: *What's this* **blue fruit**? Point out that **blue** and **fruit** both have the sound of long **u**. Say /ōō/ several times, and have children repeat after you.

• Write **fruit** and **blue** on the board. Circle the **ui** and **ue**. Tell children that **ui** and **ue** can spell the long **u** sound.

• Write **suit**, **glue**, **juice**, and **Sue** on the board. Have children tell you which words have the long **u** sound spelled **ui** and which have the long **u** sound spelled **ue**.

Practicing the Skill

On page 220, have children look at the Key Picture Cues and say **fruit** and **blue**. Together read the directions and identify each picture. Complete the first item together. Then have children finish the page independently.

English Language Learners/ESL

Materials: suit, fruit, juice, Punchout Letter Cards

Display the objects in the Reading Center. Identify each object for children. Say the word and stretch the medial sound. Then label the object and explain that one way to spell the long **u** sound is **ui**. Have children use their letter cards to spell all the words. Then write on the board the words **Sue**, **blue**, and **tune**. Say the words and underline **ue**. Tell children that **ue** is another way to spell the long **u** sound. Have children use their letter cards to spell these words.

Challenge

Tell children that one way to recycle is to make new objects from old bottles, boxes, and cans. Ask children to write directions for making a pencil holder from a used can. Have children include as many of the following words in their directions as possible: **fruit, juice, glue, blue.**

Extra Support

Write the letters **ui** and **ue** on the board and remind children that they stand for /ōō/. Dictate long **u** words and have children use their punchout letter cards to build and then say the words. Use the words: **juice, fruit, glue, blue, Sue.**

Long Vowel **u** Phonograms

Objectives

- To identify rhyming words
- To recognize long **u** phonograms
- To recognize rhyming words with long **u** phonograms

Warming Up

Reviewing Short u Phonograms

Materials: **Sadlier Phonics Picture Cards** for **sun**, **bug**, **rug**, **cub**, and **cup**

Display the picture cards. Have children say the picture name and the sound of the final letters. Have children list or dictate other rhyming words for the short **u** phonograms **un**, **ug**, **ub**, and **up**.

Teaching the Lesson

Phonemic Awareness: Identify Rhyming Words

Say **fruit** and **suit**, and have children repeat the words. Explain that **fruit** and **suit** rhyme because they have the same ending sound: /$\overline{oo}$t/. Then say the following words, and tell children to name the two words in each group that rhyme. Say **tone**, **dune**, **tune**; and **cute**, **mute**, **mark**.

Sound to Symbol

Say **June** and **tune**. Tell children that these words rhyme because they have the same ending sound: /$\overline{oo}$n/. Then write the phonogram **une** on the board and the words **June** and **tune** beneath it. Circle the **une** part in each word. Tell children that these are the parts of the words that rhyme. Then say **dune**. Ask what sound can you add to **une** to make the rhyming word **dune**. Then write the **d** and blend the word /d/-/$\overline{oo}$n/ **dune**. Repeat the process with the phonogram **ue** and the words **blue**, **Sue**, and **glue**.

Look at the calendar page. Color six pictures that have the long **u** sound in their names. Check your work with a partner to see if you colored the same pictures.

Children should pick any six of these colored items.

LESSON 115: Recognizing Long Vowel **u** 221

UNIVERSAL ACCESS
Meeting Individual Needs

Auditory • Kinesthetic

Have children stand and hum a **tune** only when they hear a long **u** word. Say such words as **fuse**, **glue**, **duck**, **true**, **van**, **pet**, **tube**, **chute**, **coat**, and **hug**.

Visual • Auditory

Materials: **Sadlier Phonics Picture Cards** for **blue**, **June**, **mule**, **suit**, and **tube**

Give each child a picture card for a long **u** word. Have children make up riddles for their words and share them aloud. For example, they may say: I am thinking of a word that rhymes with **blue**. It is sticky. (**glue**)

Extra Support

Remind children that the vowel sounds in **fruit** /$\overline{oo}$/ and **cube** /y$\overline{oo}$/ are long **u**. Have children name the long **u** word in each of the following pairs: **suit**/**seat**, **blow**/**blue**, **us**/**use**, **road**/**rule**.

In each row, circle the word that rhymes with the name of the picture in the box.

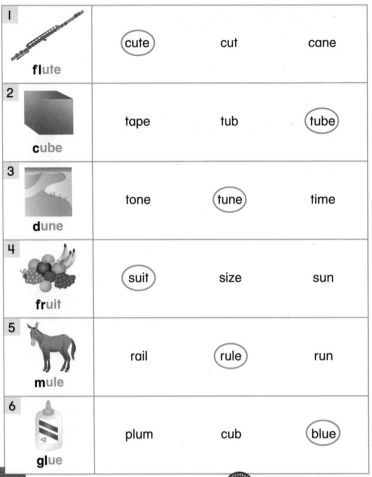

1	flute	(cute)	cut	cane
2	cube	tape	tub	(tube)
3	dune	tone	(tune)	time
4	fruit	(suit)	size	sun
5	mule	rail	(rule)	run
6	glue	plum	cub	(blue)

LESSON 115: Long Vowel **u** in Rhyming Words

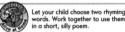 Let your child choose two rhyming words. Work together to use them in a short, silly poem.

Practicing the Skill

● Have children turn to page 221, and discuss the illustration. Read the directions aloud, and have children color the pictures that name long **u** words. Suggest that the children check their work by identifying the items they colored.

● Together, read the directions on page 222. Have a volunteer explain how to do the first item. Then have children complete the page independently.

Curriculum Connections

Spelling Connection
Read aloud each word and sentence below. Call on volunteers to spell the words or print them on the board.

mule Can you ride on a **mule**?
suit What a nice bathing **suit**!
tune Luke sang a pretty **tune**.
cute The puppy is so **cute**.

Theme Activity: Science/Health
Materials: construction paper, scissors, chart paper

● Discuss how land is an important natural resource used for growing crops such as fruits and vegetables.

● Ask children to name their favorite fruit. Distribute paper, and have children cut out different fruit shapes, each large enough to write a word on. On the cutouts, have children print long **u** words such as **fruit**.

● Draw an outline of a large fruit bowl on chart paper. Have children attach their fruit cutouts to the bowl and say their long **u** words aloud.

English Language Learners/ESL
Materials: index cards

Reinforce the sound of long **u** pronounced as /$\overline{oo}$/ and /$y\overline{oo}$/ with a concentration card game. Write the six words from the left side of page 222 on index cards, two cards for each word. Add **juice** and **blue** for a total of 16 cards. Spread the cards out facedown. Have children take turns turning over two cards and reading the words to see if they match. Children keep matches and return non-matches to the game. Continue until all the cards have been matched.

Challenge
Materials: chart paper

On chart paper, list this title: *Rules for Being Kind to Earth*. Have children work in pairs and add an entry to the list. Encourage children to include a long **u** word in their entries. (e.g., "Always **use** the front and back of writing paper." "**Reuse** shoe boxes to hold toys.")

Special Strategies
For Universal Access activities, see page 165F.

Long Vowel u Phonograms

Objectives
- To blend onsets and rimes
- To build words with long **u** phonograms
- To discriminate long **u** words from other words

Warming Up

Reviewing Long o Phonograms

Ask children to use the following clues to name long **o** words.

You put one on a gift. It rhymes with **low**. (**bow**)

It is the place where you live. It rhymes with **dome**. (**home**)

Cars drive on it. It rhymes with **toad**. (**road**)

Teaching the Lesson

Phonemic Awareness: Blend Onsets and Rimes

In a rhythmic way, say: *I say /t/-/ōōn/; you say* ***tune***. Have children repeat after you. Then point to yourself as you say additional onsets and rimes, such as **/k/-/yōōb/** **cube**, and **/k/-/yōōt/** **cute**. Point to children to signal them to blend the word parts and say the word.

Phonograms

Say the word **tune**. Have children repeat the word. Tell children that the letters **une** form the ending sound in **tune**. Write the phonogram **une** on the board. Tell children that a **t** can be added to **une** to form **tune**. Then add a **t** to **une** on the board. Help children blend the parts and say the word. Next, erase the initial **t** and substitute **d**. Read the rhyming word together. (**dune**) Repeat the activity, adding consonants to the phonograms **ute** and **ube**.

Say each word part. Say the name of each picture. Print the word on the line. Then work with a partner to add your own rhyming words.

1 _une	2 _uit	3 _ube
June	fruit	cube
Possible answers:		
tune	suit	tube

4 _ue	5 _ute	
glue	flute	
Possible answers:		
blue	cute	

© William H. Sadlier, Inc. All rights reserved.

LESSON 116: Word Building with Long Vowel **u** Phonograms — 223

UNIVERSAL ACCESS
Meeting Individual Needs

Visual • Auditory
Write this silly rhyme on the board:

Little Boy **Blue**,
Come play your **flute**.
The cow's acting **rude**,
And the **mule** wears a **suit**.
Sheep are breaking **rules**.
And you're not being **cute**!

Read the rhyme aloud. Have children circle long **u** words and list them by phonogram.

Visual • Tactile
Materials: paper, glue, sand

Have children place the paper on a flat surface. Ask them to print long **u** words on the paper with glue and then to sprinkle sand over the glue. After the glue dries, have children shake off the excess sand. Then have them say and spell each word as they trace over the letters with their fingers.

Extra Support
Remind children that the vowel sound in **cute** /yōō/ and **suit** /ōō/ is long **u**. Ask children to stand and make a **cute** face when they hear a word with a long **u** sound. Say **fruit, fly, cage, cube, dune, duck, tub, tune**.

Circle the word that names each picture.

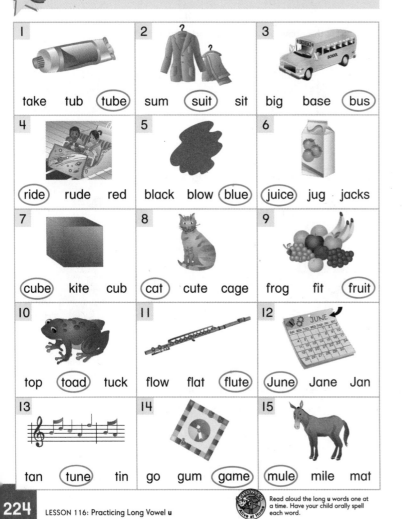

1 take tub (tube)	**2** sum (suit) sit	**3** big base (bus)
4 (ride) rude red	**5** black blow (blue)	**6** (juice) jug jacks
7 (cube) kite cub	**8** (cat) cute cage	**9** frog fit (fruit)
10 top (toad) tuck	**11** flow flat (flute)	**12** (June) Jane Jan
13 tan (tune) tin	**14** go gum (game)	**15** (mule) mile mat

224

LESSON 116: Practicing Long Vowel **u**

Read aloud the long u words one at a time. Have your child orally spell each word.

Practicing the Skill

● Read aloud the directions on page 223, and help children identify the pictures. Ask volunteers to model completing the first item. Then have children complete the page with a partner.

● Review the directions on page 224. Ask children to describe a strategy for reading the word choices beneath each picture. (e.g., look for word parts; blend initial consonant or consonants with the phonogram) Model the strategy with the first item. Then have children complete the page.

Curriculum Connections

Spelling Connection
Materials: Punchout Letter Cards

Read aloud each word and sentence below. Have children use their letter cards to spell the words at their desks.

Sue	**Sue** is my best friend.
tube	The **tube** is long.
clue	Can you give me a **clue**?
huge	The elephant is **huge**.
glue	Please pass me the **glue**.

Computer Connection

Use Word Munchers™ (MECC) to help children identify and recognize words that have long or short vowel sounds. Access "Content" under Management Options to modify the game to activate only words that have either a long or a short vowel sound. Then ask children to direct the Muncher to "eat" words that match the vowel sound shown at the top of the screen.

Sadlier Reading
Little Books and Big Books

Read *A Hippo in June's Tub* (fiction) for more practice with long **u**.

English Language Learners/ ESL
Materials: index cards, Punchout Letter Cards

Write the phonograms from page 223 on index cards and distribute sets to pairs of children. Read aloud the phonograms and then ask children to do the same. Have children work together to use their letter cards to add to the index cards to form words. Have them blend each word they make, and think of and say a sentence using that word.

Challenge
Ask children to think of long **u** words that relate to nature, such as **fruit**, **mule, prune**, and **dune**. Write the words on the board, and have the children write their own long **u** rhyming words for them. Then have children use their long **u** words to make silly sentences, such as "The **mule** wore a **suit** in **June**."

Special Strategies
For Universal Access activities, see page 165F.

Long u and Short u

Objectives

- To identify and isolate medial sounds
- To write long **u** words
- To discriminate long **u** words from short **u** words

Warming Up

Reviewing Long a, i, o

Have children answer each question below and name the long vowel sound in the answer.

Can you ride a page, a bike, or a cone?
(**bike**, long **i**)

Can you eat a cake, a five, or a bowl?
(**cake**, long **a**)

Does your face have a game, a kite, or a nose? (**nose**, long **o**)

Teaching the Lesson

Phonemic Awareness:
Identify and Isolate Medial Sounds

Say **tube**, and have children repeat the word. Segment the word /t/-/o͞o/-/b/ **tube**, and have children repeat the medial sound /o͞o/. Explain that /o͞o/ is the middle sound in **tube**. Then say the following word pairs, and have children identify those with the same middle sound. **June/tune** (long **u**), **rake/late** (long **a**), **cut/cute** (short **u** and long **u**) **rose/dome** (long **o**), and **suit/sat** (long **u** and short **a**).

Sound to Symbol

- Say **cute** and **cub**, and have children repeat after you. Tell children that **cute** has the sound of long **u** and that **cub** has the sound of short **u**.
- Write this sentence on the board: *The cute cub sang a tune in the tub*. Have volunteers circle words with **u** and tell which words are long **u** and which are short **u**. Have volunteers list rhyming words beneath the long and short **u** words.

225

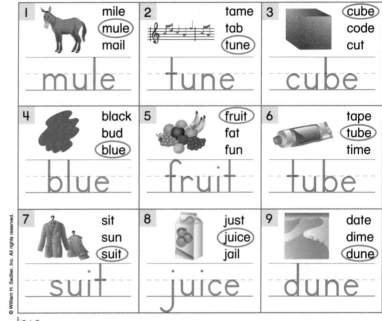

Circle the name of the picture and print it on the line.

1	mile **(mule)** mail	2	tame tab **(tune)**	3	**(cube)** code cut
	mule		tune		cube
4	black bud **(blue)**	5	**(fruit)** fat fun	6	tape **(tube)** time
	blue		fruit		tube
7	sit sun **(suit)**	8	just **(juice)** jail	9	date dime **(dune)**
	suit		juice		dune

Write a sentence about one picture using a long **u** word.

Accept any answer using a long **u** word.
Possible response:

I like fruit.

LESSON 117: Writing Long Vowel **u** 225

UNIVERSAL ACCESS
Meeting Individual Needs

Auditory • Kinesthetic
Materials: cubes

Have children draw a large **U** on a sheet of paper. Tell them to write words with the long **u** sound within the letter. Then have children trade "U's" and read the words.

Visual • Kinesthetic
Materials: Sadlier Phonics Picture Cards for **blue, bug, tub, fruit, duck, cup, June, sun, mule, suit, cub, tube, bus, rug**

Show the picture cards one at a time. Have children use their arms to make a **U** when they see a picture name with a short **u**.

Extra Support
Review that **dune** has a long **u** sound and that **run** has a short **u** sound. Then have children work in pairs to write two words that rhyme with each word.

Say the name of each picture. If the word has the sound of long **u**, print it under the long **u** tube. If the word has the sound of short **u**, print it under the short **u** tube.

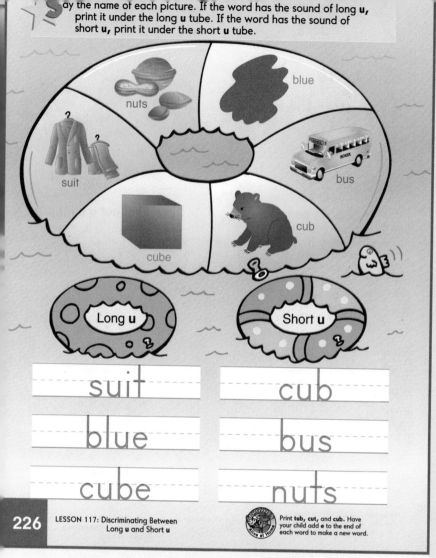

Long u	Short u
suit	cub
blue	bus
cube	nuts

LESSON 117: Discriminating Between
Long **u** and Short **u**

Print **tub**, **cut**, and **cub**. Have your child add **e** to the end of each word to make a new word.

Practicing the Skill

● Read the directions on page 225 aloud. Ask volunteers to identify the pictures. Complete the first item with children. Before children begin writing the sentence, remind them that a sentence begins with an uppercase letter and ends with a period.

● Read aloud the directions on page 226, and identify the pictures. Tell children to mark the pictures in the inner tube with "L" for long **u** or "S" for short **u** before they write the picture names on the lines. Then have children complete the page.

Curriculum Connections

Spelling Connection

Materials: Punchout Letter Cards

Read aloud each word and sentence below. Have children use their letter cards to spell the words at their desks.

Luke	**Luke** is my uncle's name.
true	Is that really **true?**
reuse	I try to **reuse** things.
reduce	I recycle to **reduce** trash, too.

Theme Activity: Science/Language Arts

Materials: large index cards

● Help children learn more about helping Earth by reading aloud the theme book cited below.

● Have children use an index card to create a postcard. On one side of the card, have them write a message about protecting Earth; on the other side, have them illustrate their message.

● Tell children to use at least two long **u** words in their message. Then have children exchange postcards, read the messages, and underline any long **u** words used.

Theme Book

Stewart, Sarah, and Small, David. *The Gardener.* New York: Farrar, Straus & Giroux, 1997. Shows the difference one small individual can make.

Portfolio

Have children add their postcards to their portfolios.

English Language Learners/ESL

Materials: Sadlier Phonics Picture Cards for **sun** and **mule**, rubber bands

Display the picture card for **sun** and remind children that this has the short **u** sound; do the same for **mule**, and point out that this has a long **u** sound. Then give each child a rubber band. Direct children to stretch it when they hear a long **u** word and to make it into the shape of a **U** when they hear a short **u** word. Use these words: **cube, cub, suit, tube, tub, bus, bug, blue, fruit, nut.**

Challenge

Have children write "What Am I?" nature riddles for words with a long **u** sound. For example, they may write, "I am the color of the sky. What am I?" (**blue**) Have children exchange and solve one another's riddles.

Special Strategies

For Universal Access activities, see page 165F.

Long Vowel u
Decodable Reader

Objectives
- To read long **u** words and high-frequency words in context
- To read the story fluently
- To distinguish fantasy/reality

Introducing the Story Words

Long u Decodable Words   Remind children that the sound of long **u** is /o͞o/ or /yo͞o/. On the board write **mule**, **cute**, **Duke**, **June**, **rude**, **rule**, **Sue**, **suit**. Explain that all the words have the sound of long **u**. Read the words with children. Underline the two letters in each word that can stand for the long **u** sound. (**u_e**, **ui**, **ue**) Point to a word, and have a volunteer read it.

High-Frequency Words   List the high-frequency words on the board: **will**, **a**, **do**, **not**, **run**, **and**, **be**, **help**, **for**, and **up**. Then read them aloud. Ask partners to come to the board. One person points to a word, reads it, and spells it, and the partner uses it in a sentence. Then have partners switch roles for the next word.

Reading the Book

Reading Together   Have children remove pages 227 and 228, and show them how to cut and fold the pages into a book. Read aloud the title, "A Pet Mule." Ask children to tell anything they know about mules. Read the story aloud as children follow along.

Responding   Ask children to tell something Sue did for the mule.

Reading for Fluency   Read the story aloud, and have children read with you. Then have partners read the story. One person reads pages 1–4, and the partner reads pages 5–8. Then have children read the story independently.

Your child has read this book in school. Ask him or her to read it to you. Then have him or her find and read all of the long u words.

Name _____

A Pet Mule

In June, Sue got a pet mule.   1

Sue will help Duke.   8

Do not run and be rude!   6

Sue made a cute suit for Duke.   3

Directions: Cut and fold the book. Then read the story. Tell whether or not you think this story can really happen.

LESSON 118: Long Vowel **u** Decodable Reader
Comprehension: Distinguishing
Fantasy/Reality   **227**

UNIVERSAL ACCESS
Meeting Individual Needs

Visual • Auditory
Write the headings **u_e**, **ui**, **ue** on the board. Ask children to find long **u** words from the story, read them aloud, and write them under the correct heading.

Auditory • Kinesthetic
Write the high-frequency words **a, do, and, be, help,** and **for** on the board. Have children take turns walking to the board, closing their eyes, and touching a word on the board. Have them open their eyes, say the word they chose, spell it, and then use it in a sentence.

Extra Support
Materials: word cards for **mule, June, Sue, cute, suit, Duke, rude, rule**

Read aloud each card, and place it face-down in a pile. Then have a child draw a card, name the two letters that stand for /o͞o/ or /yo͞o/, and read the word.

Sue gave him a name. | Duke will help Sue.

7

Duke ran and made a mess. | Sue made up a rule for Duke.

5

LESSON 118: Long Vowel **u** Decodable Reader
Comprehension: Distinguishing Fantasy/Reality

Comprehension Strategy

Distinguishing Fantasy/Reality Tell children that some stories are about fantasy, or make-believe, and that some are about things that can really happen. Help children point out things in "A Pet Mule" that can really happen and things that are made up. Write responses on the board.

Phonics and Decoding

Learning About Long u Write the sentences below on the board. Read the sentences, and have children circle the long **u** word(s) and underline the two letters in each word that can stand for the long **u** sound.

> **Sue** named her pet **Duke**.
>
> **Duke** looked **cute** in the **suit**.
>
> **Duke** was **rude** to make a mess.
>
> **Sue** sat down and wrote a **rule**.

Word Building Write the word **June** on the board. Have children think of another word with the **une** phonogram. (**tune**) Continue with the phonograms **ule** (**rule**), **uit** (**suit**), and **ue** (**Sue**).

Curriculum Connections

Writing and Sharing Write this rhyme on the board, and read it to children:

> **Duke** helps plant flowers now.
>
> **Sue** took time to show him how.
>
> **Sue** taught **Duke** to play the **flute**.
>
> He _____.

Tell children to copy the rhyme and finish the last line about Duke (e.g., "plays a **tune** and wears a **suit**"). Tell them to use a long **u** word. Have children share their rhymes.

English Language Learners/ESL

Help children identify the decodable words in their readers before they read the story. Review the long **u** sound and the different ways it can be spelled. Use words with the **u_e, ui,** and **ue** spellings, and write them on the board. Ask for another example word for each spelling. Then direct children to look through their readers and circle every word that they believe is a long **u** word. Ask children to share the words they circled with their classmates.

Challenge

Have children choose a long **u** word and another word from the story. (The other word may also be a long **u** word.) Help children use both words to write a sentence about something that they would do with a pet outdoors (e.g., I **gave** my **cute** puppy a ride in my wagon.). Have children exchange sentences with a partner and circle the long **u** word or words in the partner's sentence.

Special Strategies

For Universal Access activities, see page 165F.

Observational Assessment

*Notice whether children are able to decode the long **u** words and read the story fluently.*

Long Vowel **u** in Context

Objectives

- To identify and count syllables
- To identify long **u** words to complete sentences
- To write long **u** words in context.

Warming Up

Reviewing Long and Short i

Have children answer the following riddles and tell whether the answer has a long or short vowel sound.

It's when a fruit is ready to eat. (**ripe**)

What holds things together? (**pin**)

It's a kind of tree. (**pine**)

What is a small hole? (**rip**)

Teaching the Lesson

Phonemic Awareness: Identify and Count Syllables

Review that words are made up of one or more syllables, or word parts, and that each syllable has one vowel sound. Clap the appropriate number of times to model identifying and counting syllables. Use **help** (one vowel sound, one syllable) and **music** (two vowel sounds, two syllables). Have children repeat the process using these words: **tree**, **apple**, **fruit**, **blue**, **pencil**, **number**.

Phonics in Context

Write this sentence on the board: The sky above is ___. Write the words **rude**, **fruit**, **blue** next to the sentence. Read aloud the sentence and word choices. Then read the sentence three times, each time filling in the blank with a word choice. Circle the word **blue**, and tell children that it best completes the meaning of the sentence. Now have children complete this sentence: Can you hum a ___? (**tune**, **huge**, **cute**)

Comprehension Skill: Recalling Details

Look at each picture. Circle the word that completes the sentence. Print it on the line. Then explain to a partner how to make a cardboard flute.

1. Sue will make a _flute_ . — fun, (flute), flat
2. She will use a _tube_ . — tub, tape, (tube)
3. She will paint it _blue_ . — blow, (blue), bug
4. Luke will bring his _tuba_ . — (tuba), tag, tug
5. June will _use_ an old box. — (use), us, as
6. They will play a _tune_ . — toad, tan, (tune)

LESSON 119: Long Vowel **u** in Sentences

229

U N I V E R S A L   A C C E S S
Meeting Individual Needs

Auditory • Kinesthetic

Tell children a tuba makes an "OOM-pa-pa" sound. As you read these sentences aloud, have them stand and sing "OOM-pa-pa" when they hear a long **u** word:

I like to hear fast **music**.
I dance to catchy **tunes**.
I put coins in a **jukebox**.
I listen for a **tuba**.

Auditory • Tactile

Have children guess the long **u** word that each sentence describes:

I may be made of ice. (**cube**)
I am an orange drink. (**juice**)
Some people wear me to work. (**suit**)
I look like a horse. (**mule**)

Extra Support

Have children think of long **u** words. Write them on the board under **ui**, **ue**, or **u_e**. (Accept **oo** words, but do not list them.) Have children copy the list, using a blue crayon to print the letters that spell the long **u** sound.

What Am I?

I have blue skies,
huge seas,
lively beasts,
ripe fruit,
soft winds that sound
like flutes,
and beauty everywhere.

Rude people pollute me.
My true friends salute me.
What am I? *Earth*

1. Earth's friends like ___blue___ skies.

2. Earth's friends like ripe ___fruit___.

3. Earth's friends do not ___pollute___.

4. Earth's true friends ___salute___ it.

230

LESSON 119: Long Vowel **u** in Context
Comprehension: Recalling Details

Ask your child to read aloud the clues that helped him or her answer the riddle.

Practicing the Skill

● Together read aloud the directions on page 229. Ask volunteers to describe the activities shown in the pictures. Model completion of the first item before having children complete the sentences.

● Read aloud the directions on page 230. Discuss what is happening in the picture. Read the riddle aloud and have children solve it. Then have children complete the page.

Curriculum Connections

Spelling Connection

Read aloud each word and sentence below. Then call on volunteers to spell the words or print them on the board.

glue I will **glue** the yarn on the card.

use We can **use** this bowl.

rules We follow the **rules** for recycling.

due Your homework is **due** now.

flute Can Sue play the **flute**?

Theme Activity: Music

Materials: boxes of various sizes, rubber bands, dried beans or small stones, tissue paper, cardboard tubes, other recyclable materials

● Ask children to look at the pictures and sentences on page 229. Explain that Sue is recycling materials to make a flute. Then display the materials listed above, and have children work together to make their own musical instruments.

● Focus on long **u** words by asking: *What did you make with the* **tube**? *Who made a* **flute**? Allow children to play their instruments for the class.

Sadlier Reading

Little Books and Big Books

Read *Amazing Blue Animals* (nonfiction) for more practice with long **u**.

Observational Assessment

*Note whether children recognize that only long **u** words in the riddle are used to complete the sentences.*

[English Language Learners/ ESL

Materials: ripe and unripe fruit (bananas or peaches); pictures of the sea, a beast (any large four-footed animal), pollution, and a soldier saluting

Pre-teach the vocabulary for the riddle on page 230. Use the fruit and the pictures to introduce and explain the vocabulary words. Write the words on the board and invite children to locate them in the riddle.

Challenge

Ask children to look at the riddle on page 230 and make a list of all the long **u** words. Have them work with a partner to write a riddle using one word from the list. Have children take turns solving each other's riddles.

Special Strategies

For Universal Access activities, see pages 165F.

Assessing Long Vowel u
Reviewing Long Vowel a, i, o, u

Objectives

- To identify and complete words with long **u**
- To unscramble words to write sentences

Warming Up

Reviewing Short u

Say **up** and point out the short **u** sound. Ask children to name other short **u** words. Have them move their arms to imitate a bird flying and tell them to "fly **up**" when they hear a short **u** word. Say: **hush, mile, pup, cub, show, red, duck, run, mule.**

Teaching the Lesson

Long u

Materials: **Sadlier Phonics Picture Cards** for **blue, fruit, mule, suit, tube**

Say **cube** and **fruit** and remind children both words have the sound of long **u**. Review the letters that stand for long **u**: u_e, ui, ue. Display and name the picture cards. On the board print **bl _ _, fr _ _ t, m _ l _, s _ _ t, t _ b _.** Have children write the letters to complete each picture name, read the word aloud, and identify the matching picture.

Long a, i, o, u

Say: *The **baby** has a **nice snowsuit**.* Point out the sounds of long **a, i, o, u** in the sentence. Then write on the board the sentences below, read them with children, and identify the long vowel words.

Cute baby animals **play.**

The soft **rain** is warm in **May.**

Sue played a **fine tune.**

I can't **wait** for the **roses** to **grow.**

Have children fold a sheet of paper into four sections; label them long **a, i, o,** and **u**; and write the long vowel words from the sentences in the appropriate sections.

231

Say the name of each picture. If the picture name has the long **u** sound, find the letters in the box to complete the word. Print the letters on the line.

u_e	ui	ue

1 tune	2 glue	3 jug · j_g
4 cube	5 row · r_w	6 suit
7 blue	8 dune	9 light · l_t
10 cup · c_p	11 fruit	12 mule

LESSON 120: Assessing Long Vowel u **231**

UNIVERSAL ACCESS
Reteaching Activities

Activity 1

Materials: **Sadlier Phonics Picture Cards** for **fruit, June, mule, suit, tube, bug, lake, bike, toad, rug;** pieces of blue cloth or paper

Remind children that long **u** has the /ōō/ sound in **blue** and /yōō/ sound in **cube**. Ask volunteers to name other words that have a long **u** sound. Give each child a piece of blue cloth or paper. Show one picture card at a time. As volunteers name each picture, have the class wave their blue cloth or paper when a picture name has a long **u** sound.

Activity 2

Materials: **Sadlier Phonics Picture Cards** for long vowel **a, i, o, u** words

Say: *Mike made his **blue coat**.* Identify the long **a, i, o,** and **u** words. Then have children work in groups of four. Assign one long vowel sound (**a, i, o, u**) to each child in the group. Place the picture cards facedown. Have children draw one card at a time, name the picture and its long vowel sound, and keep the card if it has the sound they've been assigned. Other cards should be placed in a discard pile, reshuffled, and used again.

Unscramble the words to make a sentence. Print the sentence on the line. Then go back and circle the long vowel words.

1. June. in nice is Earth

Earth is (nice) in (June)

2. blue. sky is The

Some students may circle sky. Accept this as a correct answer.

The sky is (blue).

3. on logs. Toads play

(Toads) (play) on logs.

4. There snow. no is

There is (no) (snow).

5. coats away. our We put

(We) put our (coats) (away).

6. ride We bikes day. all

(We) (ride) (bikes) all (day).

232 LESSON 120: Reviewing Long Vowels a, i, o, u

Have your child read the sentences to you. Then take turns finding the long a, i, o, and u words.

Ask volunteers to name the three different ways to spell the long **u** sound. (**u_e**, **ui**, **ue**) Print the three spellings on the board and have children think of a long **u** word that exemplifies each. Then read aloud the directions on page 231 and name the pictures together. Go over the first item. Remind children to use the spelling clues in the box to complete the rest of the long **u** words on the page.

Cumulative Review

Read aloud the directions on page 232. Ask children to share tips for unscrambling sentences. (Start with a word that begins with an uppercase letter. Put the word with the period at the end.) Do the first item together. Make sure children remember to circle the long vowel words. Have children complete the page independently.

Observational Assessment Ask children to read aloud from an easy reader. Observe to see whether they easily recognize long vowel words.

Dictation Tell children you are going to say some long **a**, **i**, **o**, and **u** words. Have them write the words as you dictate them. Say: **make, play, sight, wide, slow, tone, suit, true**. Then tell children you are going to say a sentence. Have them write the sentence as you dictate it and underline any long **a**, **i**, **o**, and **u** words. Use this sentence: *Joey watched the blue kite sail high*.

Student Skills Assessment Use the checklist on Student Edition pages 321–322 to record your observations of individual children.

Guided Instruction

Skills	Resources
Long vowel **a**	Instruction on pages 167–180 Little Books *Wake Up, Sleepyheads!*; *Space Camp*
Long vowel **i**	Instruction on pages 183–196 Little Books *Niles Likes to Smile*; *Nice Vine, Quite Fine*
Long vowel **o**	Instruction on pages 199–212 Little Books *Joey's Rowboat*; *Did You Know?*
Long vowel **u**	Instruction on pages 217–230 Little Books *A Hippo in June's Tub*; *Amazing Blue Animals*
Long vowels **a, i, o, u**	Phonemic Awareness Activities on pages 165H–165I

232

Phonemic Awareness /ē/

Objectives

- To match medial sounds
- To identify words with /ē/
- To discriminate between words that do and do not have /ē/

Warming Up

Reviewing Short e

Say a list of words such as **Jen, let, red, boat, ten, pin, mess, wax, well, tent, pop, sail,** and **vet.** Ask children to clap when they hear a word with the sound of short **e.**

Teaching the Lesson

Phonemic Awareness: Match Medial Sounds

Say **neat** and **green** and ask children to repeat after you. Explain that /ē/ is the sound in the middle of both words. Have children say /ē/. Ask children to raise both hands when they hear two words that have /ē/ in the middle. Say: **meet, mole; teach, beach; pole, peach; seal, team.**

The Sound of Long e

Say /ē/ and point out to children that this is the sound of long vowel **e.** Say the words **peel, eat,** and **seat** and explain that each word has the sound of long **e.** Then say the sentences below and have children pretend to **peel** and **eat** a banana each time they hear a long **e** word. Say: *I **need** to **keep** the **peach.** **Please peel** the **green** tape off the **wheel.***

Long e

Listen Listen as the page is read aloud. Talk about the long **e** words you hear, such as **green** and **trees.** Then complete the picture by drawing a person or animal.

Green Trees

Green trees,
Green trees!
They give us wood
And things to **eat.**
Branches hold
Our swing's **seat.**
We think **trees**
Are really **neat!**

Critical Thinking Possible responses: desk, pencil, paper
What things made from trees do you see in your classroom?

LESSON 121: Phonemic Awareness: /ē/

233

UNIVERSAL ACCESS
Meeting Individual Needs

Visual • Kinesthetic

Materials: Sadlier Phonics Picture Cards for long **e** (such as **bee, tree, jeans, jeep, team**)

Ask children to show how they would use a broom to **sweep** a floor. Show the picture cards and have children make a "sweeping" motion when they see any picture whose name has the sound of long **e.**

Auditory • Kinesthetic

Have children identify the long **e** sound in **sleep.** Ask them to pretend they are going to sleep each time you say a long **e** word. When you say a word with any other vowel sound, children should sit up. Use **tree, jeans, train, cheek, geese, life, peace, lock, queen, lap, win, seed, hope, hop, dream,** and **sit.**

Extra Support

Remind children that /ē/ is the middle sound in the word **trees.** Then ask them to make a "thumbs up" gesture when you say a word that has a long **e** sound. Use **bees, nose, rude, feet, knees, not, seed, white, need, cat.**

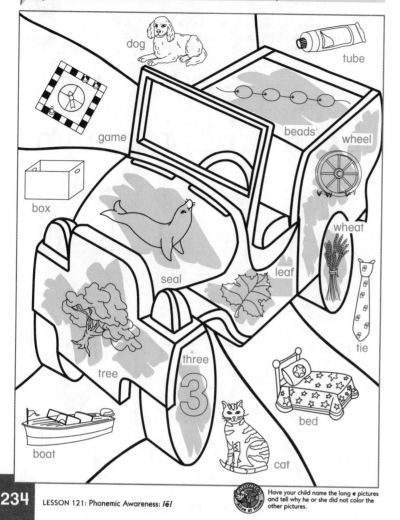

Jeep has the sound of long e. Color the space ▭ if the name of the picture has the long e sound. What do you see?

dog
tube
game
beads
wheel
box
wheat
seal
leaf
tree
three
tie
boat
bed
cat

LESSON 121: Phonemic Awareness: /ē/

Have your child name the long e pictures and tell why he or she did not color the other pictures.

● Read the aloud the directions on page 233. After you read the poem, ask children to name the long **e** words they heard. Guide children in recognizing that **ee** and **ea** both have the sound of long **e**. Then have children complete the page.

● Together read the directions on page 234. Have children complete the page.

Curriculum Connections

Theme Activity: Science/Art
Materials: paper, crayons, pencils, yarn

● Share books, such as the theme books cited below, that help children identify and describe trees.

● Have children bring in leaves from trees in their neighborhoods. Have them use the leaves to make individual tree scrapbooks by tracing the leaves and coloring the tracings. Help children group leaf tracings by type of tree. Have children make a cover. Then bind and staple the pages together.

Theme Books Althea. *Trees and Leaves.* Mahwah, NJ: Troll, 1990. Identifies different trees and explains their importance.

Arnosky, Jim. *Crinkleroot's Guide to Knowing the Trees.* New York: Simon and Schuster, 1992. Identifies trees by their bark and leaves.

English Language Learners/ ESL
Materials: a leaf, a tie, glue, a bead, a wheel, a peach, a pencil, a game, a bean

To help children identify the long **e** sound and distinguish it aurally from other vowel sounds, play a vocabulary sorting game with real objects such as those listed above. Tell children that the long **e** sound is like the beginning sound in **eat**. Then help them name the items. Ask them to group together any objects that contain the long **e** sound.

Challenge
Ask children to make up sentences about their favorite tree. Have children say their sentences aloud. Listeners should stand each time they hear a long e word. Children can illustrate their sentences. Post the drawings on the bulletin board under the heading Our Favorite Trees.

Special Strategies
For Universal Access activities, see page 165D.

Sound to Symbol /ē/ ea

Objectives

- To identify and isolate medial sounds
- To recognize that **ea** stands for /ē/
- To spell words with /ē/ **ea**

⭐ Teaching the Lesson

Phonemic Awareness:
Identify and Isolate Medial Sounds

- Tell children that the middle sound in the word **leaf** is /ē/. Say /l/-/ē/-/f/ **leaf** and have children repeat after you. Repeat the process with the word **read**.
- Tell children to listen as you say pairs of words. Have them pretend to read a book if the middle sound is the same as in **read** and to put their hands down if it is not. Say **milk/meat, peach/pot, bed/bean, seat/suit, bake/beak, peak/poke.**

Sound to Symbol

On the board draw a branch with leaves. Say the word **leaf**. Explain to children that the middle sound in **leaf** is /ē/, spelled **ea**. Write **ea** on the board and say /ē/. Have children repeat /ē/, then write **leaf** in one of the leaves. Tell children some other words whose middle sound is /ē/, spelled **ea**, are **neat** and **seat**. Write these words in the other leaves. Have volunteers underline the long **e** letters.

Practicing the Skill

Together, read aloud the directions on page 235 and point out the picture cue. Remind children that they are only to write **ea** if the picture name has the long **e** sound. Do the first item together, and then have children complete the page.

Observational Assessment

*Note which children have difficulty differentiating **ea** words from words with other medial sounds.*

235

The letters **ea** can stand for the long **e** sound. Say the name of each picture. Print **ea** in the middle of each word that has the long **e** sound.

leaf

1. bean	2. b___t (boat)	3. team
4. s___t (suit)	5. meat	6. beak
7. seal	8. r___n (rain)	9. wheat
10. seat	11. peach	12. g___t (goat)

LESSON 122: Connecting Sound to Symbol: /ē/ ea   **235**

U N I V E R S A L A C C E S S
Meeting Individual Needs

English Language Learners/ESL
Materials: **bean, meat, seat, peach**

Display objects in the Reading Center. Identify each of the objects and point out that the sound in the middle of the words is /ē/. Have children say each word and then say the middle vowel sound. Model for children: **bean,** /ē/-/ē/-/ē/. Then write the word on the board and underline **ea.** Tell the children that the **ea** can stand for /ē/. Have children turn to page 235. Then identify each picture on the page and have children repeat the word after you. Help children identify which words have the **ea** spelling for /ē/.

Challenge

Have children pretend they live on a farm. Tell partners to make a list of **ea** words such as **wheat, beans, peach, leaves, meal, eat, peas,** and **heat.** Then have them write three sentences about ways they help things grow on a farm (e.g., I water the **beans**. I give the animals food to **eat**. I keep the garden **neat**.). Have children choose one sentence to illustrate.

Extra Support

Display Sadlier Phonics Picture Cards for **leaf, peas, seal, jeans, team, wheat, wreath.** Have children name the pictures. Then write the words on the board. Have volunteers underline the long **e** letters.

The letters **ee** can stand for the long **e** sound. Say the name of each picture. Print **ee** in the middle of each word that has the long **e** sound.

tree

1	2	3 coat
p e e l	f e e t	c __ __ t
4 rain	**5**	**6**
r __ __ n	h e e l	s e e d
7	**8** mail	**9**
j e e p	m __ __ l	g r e e n
10	**11** blue	**12**
w h e e l	b l __ __	s l e e p

236   LESSON 123: Connecting Sound to Symbol: /ē/ ee

Write the letters **ee** five times on a sheet of paper. Have your child add letters to make new words.

Sound to Symbol /ē/ ee

Objectives
- To identify and isolate medial sounds
- To recognize that **ee** stands for /ē/
- To spell words with /ē/ **ee**

Teaching the Lesson

Phonemic Awareness:
Identify and Isolate Medial Sounds
Tell children the middle sound in **sleep** and **feet** is /ē/. Say: /sl/-/ē/-/p/ **sleep**. Then say /f/-/ē/-/t/ **feet** and have children repeat after you. Direct children to pretend to sleep if the middle sound in a word you say is the same as in **sleep**. Say: **joke/jeep; need/nail; street/straight.**

Sound to Symbol
Materials: **Sadlier Phonics Picture Cards** for **jeep, queen, green, teeth, sheep**

- Draw a large bicycle wheel on the board. Say **wheel**, /hw/-/ē/-/l/ and tell children the middle sound in **wheel** is /ē/, spelled **ee**. Write **ee** on the board and say /ē/. Have children repeat /ē/. Under the drawing write **wh__l**. Say the word again and print **ee** on the line.
- In the spaces between the wheel's spokes, write **j__p, qu__n, gr__n, t__th, sh__p**. Direct children to choose and name a picture card, find the matching beginning and ending sounds on the wheel, and print the letters **ee** in the blank. Then say each word and have children repeat it after you.

Practicing the Skill

Read aloud the directions on page 236. Go over the picture names, making sure children understand the arrows in items 1, 5, and 6. Then have children complete the page.

Observational Assessment

*Note whether children confuse the spellings of homonyms (e.g., **meet, meat**).*

English Language Learners/ESL
Draw a tree on the board. Write **tree** under the drawing. Underline the letters that stand for the vowel sound. Then tell children that the **ee** in **tree** makes the sound of long **e**. Say **tree** and have children repeat after you. Then write the following words on the board and have children underline the letters that stand for the long **e** sound and say the word. Use the following words: **heel, knee, sheep, green, jeep, sleep.**

Extra Support
Write the letters **ee** on the board and remind children that they stand for the long **e** sound as in **tree**. Dictate long **e** words and have children use their punchout letter cards to build and then say the words. Use these words: **feel, heel, seed, weed, deep, keep.**

Challenge
Materials: oaktag sheets, markers

Have children work with a partner to make posters that tell ways to keep the classroom clean. Help children think of words spelled with **ee**, such as **need, keep, sweep, feet.** Write these on the board. Then brainstorm slogans, such as, "Wipe Your **Feet** to **Keep** Our Room Neat." Have partners write their slogans and illustrate them to make posters.

Long Vowel e Phonograms

Objectives

- To produce rhyming words
- To recognize rhyming long **e** words
- To build words with long **e** phonograms

Warming Up

Reviewing Final Consonant Sounds

Give children the following clues and ask them to name the words described:

It grows on a tree. It ends with /f/. (**leaf**)

It shines and keeps our Earth warm. It ends with /n/. (**sun**)

It is a small, wild animal that looks like a dog. It ends with /ks/. (**fox**)

Teaching the Lesson

Phonemic Awareness: Produce Rhyming Words

Say the words **feel** and **heel** and write them on the board. Remind children that **feel** and **heel** rhyme because they have the same ending sound /ēl/. Ask children to name a rhyming word for each word below.

seed (e.g., **need**) **green** (e.g., **queen**)

peel (e.g., **wheel**) **sleep** (e.g., **sheep**)

Phonograms

Materials: Punchout Letter Cards

- Have children use their letter cards to make the phonogram **eep**. Read it aloud. Have children place the letter **j** in front of **eep**, leaving a space between **j** and **eep**. Tell children to run their finger beneath the word parts as you say together /j/-/ēp/ **jeep**.
- Explain that other words can be made with the **eep** phonogram by changing the initial consonant. Tell children to replace the **j** with **k**. Have a volunteer read the word by blending /k/ with /ēp/ **keep**.

237

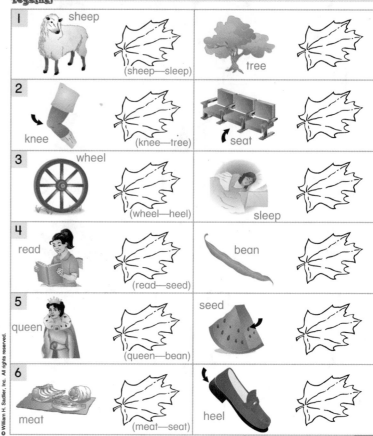

 Work with a partner to find each pair of pictures that have rhyming names. Color their leaves the same color.

1. sheep (sheep—sleep) tree
2. knee (knee—tree) seat
3. wheel (wheel—heel) sleep
4. read (read—seed) bean
5. queen (queen—bean) seed
6. meat (meat—seat) heel

LESSON 124: Long Vowel **e** in Rhyming Words **237**

UNIVERSAL ACCESS
Meeting Individual Needs

Auditory

Say words with long vowel phonograms, such as **sheep, goat, bee, race, nail, peel, mule, queen, feed, beet.** Ask children to "baa" like a sheep when they hear a long **e** word.

Visual • Auditory

Materials: Sadlier Phonics Picture Cards for **bee, green, team, feet, jeep**

Have children sit in a circle. Give one child a picture card. Ask him or her to name the picture and pass the card to the next child, who names a rhyming word. After each child has had a turn, hand out another card.

Extra Support

Materials: Sadlier Phonics Picture Cards for **jeep, team, feet;** word cards for **jeep, team, feet**

Display the picture cards. Tell children that the picture names end with a long **e** phonogram. Have children match the word cards to the pictures, say the picture name, and underline each phonogram.

Say each word part. Say the name of each picture. Print the word on the line. Then add your own rhyming word and picture.

_ee	_eep	_eat
1 tree	4 jeep	7 meat
2 bee	5 sleep	8 seat
3 Accept any rhyming answer that is a real word.	6 Accept any rhyming answer that is a real word.	9 Accept any rhyming answer that is a real word.

238 LESSON 124: Word Building with Long Vowel e Phonograms

Read one of the words on the page. Have your child name words that rhyme with the word you read.

Long Vowel e Phonograms

Objectives
- To substitute medial sounds
- To build words with long **e** phonograms
- To discriminate long **e** words from other words

Warming Up

Reviewing Initial Consonant Sounds

Write a **b** on the board. Then ask volunteers to say a word that begins with **b** and names something children might see outdoors (e.g., **bug, bee, berry, bunny**). Continue with other initial consonants.

Teaching the Lesson

Phonemic Awareness: Substitute Medial Sounds

Tell children they can make new words by changing the middle sound in a word. Model by saying: *If I change the /ē/ in* **seat** *to /a/, what word do I make? I make the word /s/-/a/-/t/* **sat**. Tell children to change the middle sound in these words: **bat**—change /a/ to /ē/ (**beat** or **beet**); **bead**—change /ē/ to /e/ (**bed**); **seal**—change /ē/ to /ā/ (**sail** or **sale**).

Phonograms

- Say: *A fish is a tasty **meal** for a **seal***. Tell children that the words **meal** and **seal** end with the long **e** phonogram **eal**. Point out that we can use a phonogram, or word part, to help us read words. Then write the word **meal** on the board, read it together, and underline the phonogram. Erase the **m** and substitute **s**. Have children read the new word.
- Repeat the activity for words that end with the phonograms, or word parts, **ee** and **eed**. Ask children to identify the letters that stand for the long **e** phonogram in each word.

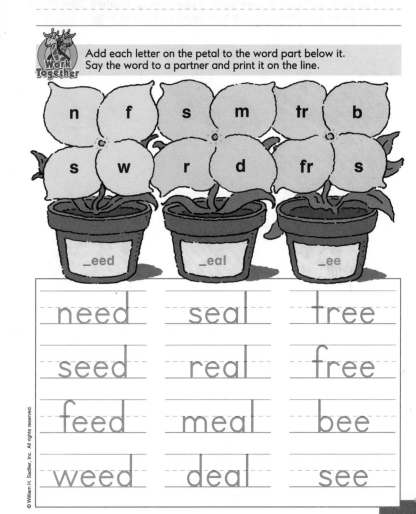

Add each letter on the petal to the word part below it. Say the word to a partner and print it on the line.

| n | f | s | m | tr | b |
| s | w | r | d | fr | s |

_eed	_eal	_ee
need	seal	tree
seed	real	free
feed	meal	bee
weed	deal	see

LESSON 125: Word Building with Long Vowel e Phonograms

239

UNIVERSAL ACCESS
Meeting Individual Needs

Auditory • Kinesthetic
Prepare a word list with both long **e** words and other words (e.g., **weed, green, grin, sell, seal**). Have children crouch down and imagine they are weeds. Tell them to rise a little each time they hear a word with the sound of long **e**. Read aloud the words. Continue until the "weeds" are fully grown.

Visual • Kinesthetic
Draw a tic-tac-toe grid on the board. Have children form two teams, and let each choose a long **e** phonogram, such as **eam** or **eed**. Have teams take turns sending players to fill in squares with words that have the appropriate phonogram. The first team to fill in three boxes in a row, column, or diagonal with rhyming long **e** words wins the game.

Extra Support
Write the phonograms **eed, eal**, and **ee** on the board and remind children that they stand for long **e**. Dictate long **e** words and have children use their punchout letters cards to build and then say long **e** words. Use these words: **need, seed, deal, seal, see, free**.

Circle the word that names each picture.

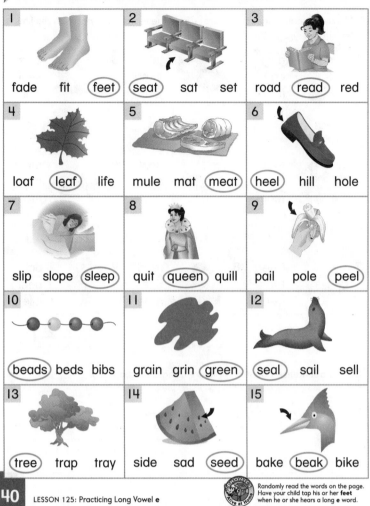

1 fade fit (feet)	**2** (seat) sat set	**3** road (read) red
4 loaf (leaf) life	**5** mule mat (meat)	**6** (heel) hill hole
7 slip slope (sleep)	**8** quit (queen) quill	**9** pail pole (peel)
10 (beads) beds bibs	**11** grain grin (green)	**12** (seal) sail sell
13 (tree) trap tray	**14** side sad (seed)	**15** bake (beak) bike

LESSON 125: Practicing Long Vowel **e**

Randomly read the words on the page. Have your child tap his or her **feet** when he or she hears a long **e** word.

Practicing the Skill

● Together, read the directions on page 239 and say each word part. Then build the first word for each word part together. Have partners complete the page.

● Read the directions on page 240 with the class. Note the arrows and the objects they point to. Do the first item together, and then have children complete the page.

Curriculum Connections

Spelling Connection

Read aloud each word and sentence below. Ask one child to spell the word aloud and another to write it on the board.

bees	The farmer keeps **bees**.
feeds	He **feeds** his animals.
green	He plants **green** beans.
peas	He also plants **peas**.
need	We **need** farmers to grow our food.

SCIENCE CENTER

Materials: vegetable seeds, soil, paper cups, notebooks, pencils

● Ask children what they would like to learn about seeds and write their questions on the board. Explain that a hypothesis is a guess about what might happen in a given situation. As applicable, turn children's questions into hypotheses. For example, you can say that seeds grown in the sun will sprout before seeds grown in the shade, or that seeds that get water will sprout first. Have children form two teams and then choose two hypotheses that they will test.

● Have children plant the seeds in cups and label the cups Team A and Team B. After children have observed the seeds for a week, help them print a report describing their results. Have children refer to their reports to make a long **e** science word chart. Display the reports and the chart in your Science Center.

English Language Learners/ESL
Materials: index cards

Write the phonograms **eed, eal, ee** and three sets of the consonants and blends from page 239 on index cards. Have children work in three teams, and give a set of the consonant/blend cards and one of the phonograms to each team. Invite teams to use their cards to make words and to read and record those words. Then have children exchange phonogram cards and continue until all teams have worked with all phonograms. Have teams share their results with the rest of the class.

Challenge
Materials: paper, markers

Have each child draw the outline of a daisy on a sheet of paper. Inside the center circle, have children write a long **e** phonogram, such as **eed, eat,** or **eel.** Then have them label each petal with a word containing the phonogram.

Special Strategies
For Universal Access activities, see page 165F.

Student Pages 241–242

Long e and Short e

Objectives

- To identify and isolate medial sounds
- To write long **e** words
- To discriminate long **e** words from short **e** words

Warming Up

Reviewing Short e

Write the phonograms **ed, eg, en,** and **et** on the board. Ask volunteers to add initial consonants to make words. Have children say their word aloud and write it on the board.

Teaching the Lesson

Phonemic Awareness:
Identify and Isolate Medial Sounds

Say the words **beep** and **seal** and have children repeat each word. Point out that /ē/ is the middle sound in **beep** and **seal**. Ask children to "beep" each time they hear a word with the long **e** sound in the middle. Then say: **speed, lake, tune, seat, blue, neat, queen.**

Sound to Symbol

- Say **weed** and **wed.** Remind children that **weed** has the long **e** sound and **wed** has the short **e** sound. Say **pen, meat, seed, set, sleep.** Have children tell whether each word has a long **e** or short **e** sound.
- Remind children that **ee** and **ea** can stand for the long **e** sound. Then write the following words on the board: **peep, hen, met, feet, beg, deal, knee, bead, neat.** Say each word and have children repeat after you. Have volunteers identify whether each word has a long **e** or short **e** sound and underline the letter or letters that stand for the vowel sound.

Say the name of each picture. Circle the word and print it on the line.

1	eat (egg) it	eat
2	jet jump (jeep)	jeep
3	sale (seal) sell	seal
4	tame time (team)	team
5	bow (bee) bay	bee
6	mule mitt (meat)	meat
7	true trip (tree)	tree
8	(read) ride rude	read
9	pal (peel) pile	peel

Write a sentence about one picture using a long **e** word.

Accept any answer using a long **e** word. Possible response:

I like to read.

LESSON 126: Writing Long Vowel e   **241**

UNIVERSAL ACCESS
Meeting Individual Needs

Auditory • Kinesthetic

Have children listen as you read a list of words. Tell them to touch their **knee** when they hear a long **e** word and hold up **ten** fingers when they hear a short **e** word. Say **seat, shell, web, weep, tree, bed, pen, nest, keep, clean.**

Visual • Kinesthetic

Tell children you are going to give them directions for drawing pictures. Write the boldface words on the board and have children use them to label the pictures.

1. Draw a **tree** with **green leaves**.
2. Put a **bee** on one **leaf**.
3. Add a **sheep** under the branches.
4. Draw some **geese** flying by.

Extra Support

Materials: **Sadlier Phonics Picture Cards** for long **e** and short **e** words

Review the long and short sounds of **e**. Have children draw and name picture cards, repeat the sound of **e**, and then place long and short **e** cards in separate piles.

Read the name of each picture. Circle **L** if the name has the sound of long **e**. Circle **S** if the name has the sound of short **e**. Then color each picture that has the long **e** sound in its name.

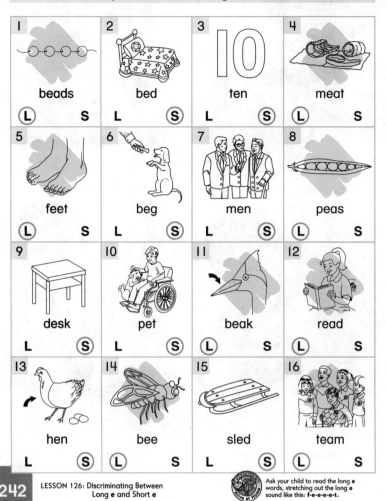

1 beads (L) S	2 bed L (S)	3 ten L (S)	4 meat (L) S
5 feet (L) S	6 beg L (S)	7 men L (S)	8 peas (L) S
9 desk L (S)	10 pet L (S)	11 beak (L) S	12 read (L) S
13 hen L (S)	14 bee (L) S	15 sled L (S)	16 team (L) S

242

LESSON 126: Discriminating Between Long e and Short e

Ask your child to read the long e words, stretching out the long e sound like this: f-e-e-e-t.

Practicing the Skill

● Help children read the directions at the top of page 241. Together, identify the pictures and complete the first item. Then direct children's attention to the directions at the bottom. As a model, write: I like to read.

● Read aloud the directions on page 242, and identify the pictures together. Do the first two items together. Have children complete the page on their own.

Curriculum Connections

Spelling Connection

Read aloud each word and sentence below. Ask one child to spell each word aloud and another to print it on the board.

trees I like apple **trees**.

deep The plant has **deep** roots.

see Do you **see** birds in the sky?

peep Baby birds **peep** from a nest.

beak I can see one bird's **beak**.

Theme Activity: Math/Language Arts

Materials: assorted wooden blocks

● Share the theme book cited below, and have children tell the story.

● Have children choose blocks and work with partners to make shapes like the dolls did in the story. Then have pairs tell a story about their shapes.

● Help children print and illustrate their stories. Have them underline long **e** words.

Hutchins, Pat. *Changes, Changes.* New York: Aladdin, 1987. A doll couple reuses blocks to build useful things.

Have children make copies of their stories for their portfolios.

English Language Learners/ESL

Materials: Sadlier Phonics Picture Cards for **bed, egg, jet, ten, web, jeans, green, tree, jeep, team**

Help children practice discriminating between with short **e** and long **e** sounds. Hide the picture cards around the classroom. Then divide your group into two teams, the "short **e**'s" and the "long **e**'s." Tell children they will go on a scavenger hunt—teams will search the classroom for the five picture cards that represent their sound. The first team to find and correctly name all of its cards is the winner.

Challenge

Ask children to make up riddles for which the answers are long **e** words. Use the following riddles as models:

Fish live in me. You can swim in me? What am I? (**sea**)

I have one eye. I am very sharp. What am I? (**needle**)

As children print their riddles, tell them to put the answers on the back of the paper. Compile these in a Riddle Book for the classroom.

Special Strategies

For Universal Access activities, see page 165F.

242

Long Vowel e Decodable Reader

Objectives

- To read long **e** words and high-frequency words in context
- To read the story fluently
- To identify steps in a process

Introducing the Story Words

Long e Decodable Words   Remind children that the sound of long **e** is /ē/. Write **bean** on the board, and explain that **bean** has the sound of long **e**. Point out that the letters **ea** stand for /ē/. Repeat with **leaf**. Then explain that the letters **ee** also stand for /ē/. Write the words **deep**, **keep**, **see**, and **seed** on the board. Ask children to read the words and then circle the letters that stand for /ē/.

High-Frequency Words   Write the words **a**, **the**, **you**, **it**, **will**, **can**, and **with** on the board. Read them together. Have children use one or more of the words in a sentence.

Reading the Book

Reading Together   Have children remove pages 243 and 244, and show them how to cut and fold the pages into a book. Read aloud the title, "A Bean Seed." Have volunteers tell what they would do with a bean seed. Then read "A Bean Seed" aloud as children follow along.

Responding   Ask children to compare what they said they would do with a bean seed with what was done with the bean seed in the story.

Reading for Fluency   Read the story aloud with children. Direct groups of six to read the story, each child reading a page and then all reading the last two pages in unison. Then have children read the story independently.

Observational Assessment

Notice whether children are able to decode the long e words and read fluently.

I Can Read   Your child has read this book in school. Ask him or her to read it to you. Then have your child read and spell each long e word in the story.

Name _____

A Bean Seed

8   Can you see a leaf yet?   Take a bean seed.   I

6   Keep the seed wet.   Make a deep hole.   3

Directions: Cut and fold the book. Then read the story. Tell how to plant and take care of a bean seed.

I Can Read   LESSON 127: Long Vowel e Decodable Reader
Comprehension: Identifying Steps in a Process   **243**

UNIVERSAL ACCESS
Meeting Individual Needs

Tactile • Auditory
Materials: Punchout Letter Cards

Read aloud a sentence from "A Bean Seed." Ask a volunteer to name the long e word(s) in the sentence. Then have children spell the word with their letter cards. Have a child print the word on the board for the others to check spelling.

Auditory • Visual
Materials: index cards

Write the high-frequency words **a, the, you,** and **with** on index cards. Review how to read them. Then place the cards facedown in a pile. Ask volunteers to pick two words, read them, and then use them both in one sentence.

Extra Support
Remind children that **ea** and **ee** can both stand for the long **e** sound. Write the headings **ea** and **ee** on a piece of paper. Ask children to find long **e** words in "A Bean Seed," read them aloud, and then write them under the correct heading.

2 Fill a pot with mud.   It will pop up.   7

4 Add the bean seed.   Set the pot in the sun.   5

LESSON 127: Long Vowel **e** Decodable Reader
Comprehension: Identifying Steps in a Process

Comprehension Strategy

Identifying Steps in a Process   Explain to children that some of the things they read tell the steps needed to do or make something. Then explain that the steps are given in the order in which you should do them. Print each step depicted on pages 1 to 6 on an oaktag strip, and have children take turns putting the steps in the correct order.

Phonics and Decoding

Learning About Long e   Write on the board and read aloud the sentence on page l: Take a **bean seed**. Call on a volunteer to underline the words that have the sound of long **e**. (**bean**, **seed**) Have children circle the letters that stand for the long **e** sound. (**ea**, **ee**) Repeat the activity with the sentences on pages 3, 6, and 8.

Word Building   Write the word **bean** on the board. Have children think of another word with the **ean** phonogram. (**mean**) Write the word. Continue with the words and phonograms **seed/eed** (**feed**) and **deep/eep** (**peep**).

Curriculum Connections

Writing and Sharing   Write the words **bean**, **seed**, **deep**, **keep**, **see**, and **leaf** on the board. Ask groups of children to write and illustrate a story about a bean using these words. Have each group share its story with the class.

English Language Learners/ESL

Materials: bean seeds or other kind of seeds, planting pot, potting soil, hand shovel, water

Assess children's prior knowledge of how to grow a seed. Show children some seeds and ask questions such as: *How can I grow these seeds? What do I need? What do I do first? Second? Next? Finally?* Encourage children to talk through the sequence of the planting and growing process or to show you with actions. Finally, have children pretend to be a bean seed sprouting out of the ground.

Special Strategies

For Universal Access activities, see page 165F.

Challenge

Materials: paper, scissors

Have children write a list of three or four steps to complete a task, such as feeding a pet. Tell children to use a long **e** word in at least two of the steps. Have them cut apart the steps and exchange them with partners. Direct them to arrange each other's steps in the correct order and circle the long **e** words.

Long Vowel e in Context

Objectives
- To identify and isolate medial sounds
- To identify long **e** words to complete sentences
- To read long **e** words in context

Warming Up

Reviewing Long a
Read aloud the sentences given below. Ask children to clap when they hear a word with a long **a** sound.

> **Jane** has an apple tree by the **lake**.
>
> She **takes** care of it every **day**.
>
> She **rakes** the leaves that fall.

Teaching the Lesson

Phonemic Awareness: Identify and Isolate Medial Sounds
Tell children that the middle sound in the words **week** and **meal** is /ē/. Say /w/-/ē/-/k/ **week**; /m/-/ē/-/l/ **meal**, and have children repeat after you. Then say the following words, and have children identify the middle sound for each: **seat** /ē/, **peel** /ē/, **bake** /ā/, **deal** /ē/, **bone** /ō/.

Phonics in Context
Write this sentence on the board: I saw a nest in the ___. Write the words **weed**, **beach**, **tree** next to the sentence. Read aloud the sentence and the word choices. Then read the sentence three times, each time filling in the blank with one of the word choices. Circle the word **tree**, and tell children that it best completes the meaning of the sentence. Now have children complete this sentence: My ___ won the race. (**team**, **seat**, **peel**)

Comprehension Skill: Summarizing

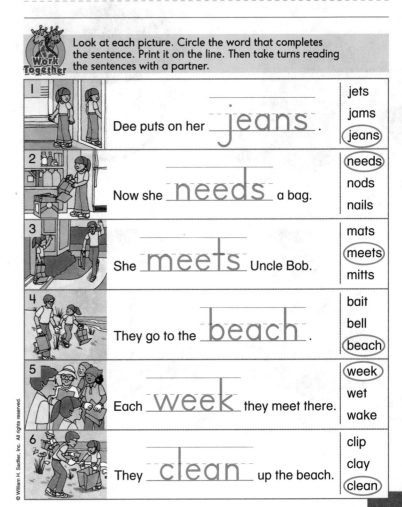

Look at each picture. Circle the word that completes the sentence. Print it on the line. Then take turns reading the sentences with a partner.

1. Dee puts on her **jeans**. — jets / jams / (jeans)
2. Now she **needs** a bag. — (needs) / nods / nails
3. She **meets** Uncle Bob. — mats / (meets) / mitts
4. They go to the **beach**. — bait / bell / (beach)
5. Each **week** they meet there. — (week) / wet / wake
6. They **clean** up the beach. — clip / clay / (clean)

LESSON 128: Long Vowel **e** in Sentences **245**

UNIVERSAL ACCESS
Meeting Individual Needs

Visual • Tactile
Materials: paper, crayons

On the board, write a list of long **e** words, such as **bead, bee, green, leaf, pea, seed, sheep,** and **tree**. Have each child print one word on paper in large letters. Ask children to decorate the letters that spell the sound of long **e** using crayons.

Auditory • Visual
On the board, write the following:

> I know words that have long **e**.
>
> They have the same vowel sound as **tree**.
>
> ___ and ___ and ___ and ___,
>
> ___ and ___ and ___ and ___.

Have children fill in the blanks with words that rhyme with **tree**. Then sing the words to the tune of "The Alphabet Song."

Extra Support
Draw a large tree on the board, and tell children that the word **tree** has the sound of long **e**. Tell them to sway like trees in the wind when they hear you say a long **e** word. Say: **rake, leaf, hill, seed, breeze, sun, mop, bead.**

Listen as the story is read aloud. Then use long **e** words to complete the sentences.

In the Big Tree

Last week Dad and I
saw a big tree.
Dad said, "Stay still, Lee.
Listen to the birds peep."

I looked up and saw
three baby birds in a nest.
Dad said, "Their mother will
bring them a nice meal."

1. Last ___week___ we saw a big tree.

2. We could hear the birds ___peep___.

3. ___Three___ baby birds were in a nest.

4. Their mother will bring them a ___meal___.

246

LESSON 128: Long Vowel e in Context
Comprehension: Summarizing

With your child, name three things you can do together that have the long e sound in their names.

Practicing the Skill

● Read aloud the directions on page 245. Discuss what is happening in the pictures. Do the first item together. Then have partners complete the page and take turns reading the sentences.

● Read the story on page 246. Remind children that they will use long **e** words from the story to complete the sentences. Have them complete the page independently.

Curriculum Connections

Spelling Connection

Read aloud each word and sentence below. Ask a child to spell each word. Ask another volunteer to print the word on the board.

free   Animals are **free** in the forest.

jeep   The scientist drove her **jeep**.

leaf   Is a bug hiding on the **leaf**?

seat   Rob's **seat** was in the first row.

Multicultural Connection

Explain that many people are concerned about the destruction of **trees** in the rain forests. On a map of the world, point out the large rain forest areas in South America and in Africa. Tour a rain forest by sharing a video such as *The Rain Forest* (Schlessinger Video Productions, 1993).

Theme Activity: Language Arts

Materials: brown construction paper, old magazines, scissors, glue, paper circles

● Post a construction paper "tree" on a bulletin board.

● Have children scan old magazines for pictures whose names have the sound of long **e.** Have children glue the pictures onto paper circles and print the name of each picture on the back of the circle.

● Have each child attach a circle to the tree and say the picture name.

Sadlier Reading

Little Books and Big Books

Read *Peach Tree Street* (fiction) for more practice with long **e.**

Assessing Long Vowel e
Reviewing Long Vowels a, i, o, u, e

Objectives

• To identify and complete words with long **e**

• To write sentences with long vowel words

Warming Up

Reviewing Short i

Say **wig** to point out the short **i** sound. Tell children to **wiggle** their fingers when they hear a short **i** word in this poem:

A **fish** has **fins**.

A cushion has **pins**.

Porcupines have **quills**,

And doctors have **pills**.

Some people have **wigs**;

A few have **pigs**.

Did the goat have a **kid**?

Yes, **it did**.

Teaching the Lesson

Long e

Materials: word cards for **tree**, **seem**, **feet**, **week**, **seed**, **team**, **meat**, **pea**, **eat**, **leaf**

Say **bee** and **beach**, and write the words on the board. Point out that **ee** in **bee** and **ea** in **beach** stand for the long **e** sound. Have children read the word cards and sort them by long **e** spelling.

Long a, i, o, u, e

Materials: **Sadlier Phonics Picture Cards** for long vowels **a, i, o, u, e**

Use picture cards for **hay**, **kite**, **rose**, **suit**, **tree** to review long vowel sounds. Then give each child a new long vowel card. Direct children to gather with classmates whose pictures match theirs in vowel sound. Have groups name more words with their vowel sound. List the words then read them aloud.

247

Check-Up Say the name of each picture. If the picture name has the long **e** sound, find the letters in the box to complete the word. Print the letters on the line.

ea	ee

1 t e a m	2 rain r __ __ n	3 s e e d
4 jay j __	**5** p e e l	**6** m e a t
7 boat b __ t	**8** b e a n	**9** j e e p
10 f e e t	**11** pie p __	**12** s e a l

LESSON 129: Assessing Long Vowel e   **247**

U N I V E R S A L   A C C E S S
Reteaching Activities

Activity 1

Materials: pictures of **ee** and **ea** words such as **jeep, tree, bee, sea, team, beach, peach**

Create a two column chart and label one side **ee** and the other **ea**. Insert key words **seed** and **team** in the corresponding column on the chart. Remind children of the long **e** spellings in **seed** and **team**. Then display the long **e** pictures. Call on a child to choose a picture, name it, and spell the name aloud. Have classmates check the spelling before the child writes the picture name on the board under the appropriate column.

Activity 2

Materials: 5-by-5 grid cards, counters

Distribute cards and counters. Have children print the vowels **a, i, o, u, e** in each square on the card until the entire card is filled. Call out long vowel words such as **tree, clean, sail, lake, grain, blue, mule, row, boat, pine, wise.** Have children use the counters to cover on their cards the letters that stand for the vowel sounds in the words they hear. Tell children to call out when they have covered an entire row of spaces.

Remember

Read the sentences. First number the sentences in order to tell the story. Then print the sentences in order on the lines.

_3_ Then, she gave it water.

_2_ Next, she put a pine tree in it.

_4_ She waits for it to grow.

_1_ First, June made a hole.

1. First, June made a hole.

2. Next, she put a pine tree in it.

3. Then, she gave it water.

4. She waits for it to grow.

248 LESSON 129: Reviewing Long Vowels a, i, o, u, e
Comprehension: Comparing and Contrasting

Have your child read the sentences. Ask him or her to point out words with long vowel sounds.

Guided Instruction

Skills	Resources
Long vowel **a**	Instruction on pages 167–180 Little Books _Wake Up, Sleepyheads!_; _Space Camp_
Long vowel **i**	Instruction on pages 183–196 Little Books _Niles Likes to Smile_; _Nice Vine, Quite Fine_
Long vowel **o**	Instruction on pages 199–212 Little Books _Joey's Rowboat_; _Did You Know?_
Long vowel **u**	Instruction on pages 217–230 Little Books _A Hippo in June's Tub_; _Amazing Blue Animals_
Long vowel **e**	Instruction on pages 233–246 Little Books _Come Meet Some Seals_; _Peach Tree Street_
Long vowels **a, i, o, u, e**	Phonemic Awareness Activities pages 165H–165I

Assessing the Skill

Have children turn to page 247, and read aloud the directions. Ask volunteers to name the pictures. Suggest that children star all the long **e** words before writing any letters. Remind them to use only the spelling choices in the box. Then have children complete the page.

Cumulative Review

Ask children to recall what they have done so far today and to list the events in time-order sequence. Together, write a sample list on the board using the words _first, next,_ and _then._

Read aloud the directions and sentences on page 248. Together decide on the best order for the sentences, and have children number them. Then have children complete the page by writing the sentences in order. Point out the numbers beside each ruled space.

Observational Assessment As children complete written work during the day, note whether they use correct spellings for long vowel sounds.

Dictation Tell children you are going to say some long **a** words. Have them write the long **a** words as you dictate them. Say these words: **gave**, **late**, **train**, **pay**, **clay**. Repeat the activity with long **i** words (**mine**, **tried**, **high**, **vine**, **tile**); long **o** words (**hole**, **home**, **loaf**, **goal**, **glow**); long **u** words (**true**, **rule**, **dune**, **flute**, **suit**); and long **e** words (**seem**, **dream**, **neat**, **deal**, **weed**). Then tell children you are going to say a sentence. Have them write the sentence as you dictate it and underline any long **a, i, o, u,** and **e** words. Use this sentence: _Can **Sue take** the **green bike home**?_

Student Skills Assessment Use the checklist on Student Edition pages 321–322 to record your observations of individual children.

Sounds of Final y as a Vowel

Objectives
- To identify and count syllables
- To identify the sounds of final **y** as long **i** and long **e**
- To write words with final **y** as a vowel

Warming Up

Reviewing Long i and e

Write these words on index cards: **beans, geese, hives, mice, peaches, peas, pines**. Have children read the words aloud, and identify the vowel sounds. Then have them sort the cards as /ī/ or /ē/ words.

Teaching the Lesson

Phonemic Awareness: Identify and Count Syllables

- Remind children that words are made up of one or more word parts, called *syllables*, and that each syllable has one vowel sound. Say and clap each syllable for the words **fly** and **bun-ny**. Point out that **fly** has one syllable and **bunny** has two. Then repeat the words with children and have them say and clap each syllable.
- Say the words **pen-ny, cher-ry, my, fif-ty, buy, hap-py, twen-ty, dry**. Have children say and clap the syllables for each word. Then have children identify the number of syllables in each word.

The Sound of Final y

- Tell children that **y** at the end of a word can have two different sounds. Explain that the ending sound in **happy** has the long **e** sound spelled with a **y** and that the ending sound in **cry** has the long **i** sound and is also spelled with a **y**.
- Say the words **my, thirty, merry, shy, funny, try, pony**. Tell children to smile if the ending sound is the same as **happy** and to pretend to cry if the ending sound is the same as **cry**.

249

When **y** is at the end of a word, it can have the sound of long **i**, as in **sky**, or the sound of long **e**, as in **bunny**. Listen for the sounds of **y** in the rhyme.

sky   bunny

Up in the sky,
See the clouds fly by.
One looks like a bunny,
Isn't that funny?

Circle the picture if the **y** in its name has the long **i** sound. Draw a line under the picture if the **y** in its name has the long **e** sound.

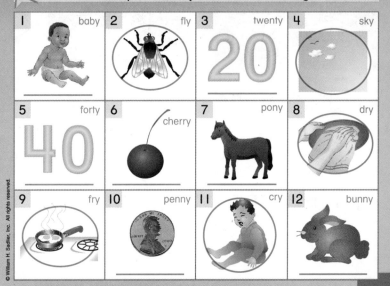

LESSON 130: Sounds of Final y as a Vowel   **249**

U N I V E R S A L   A C C E S S
Meeting Individual Needs

Visual • Kinesthetic
Materials: Sadlier Phonics Picture Cards for **bunny, strawberry, thirty, cherry, fly, cry, fry, sky**

Have children make a sun by forming a circle with their arms. Tell them to make the room **sunny** when they see a picture whose name ends with the sound of long **e**.

Visual • Auditory
Write these sentences on the board:

Jim told **many funny** jokes.

The **bunny** went hopping **by**.

I will **try** to **carry** the box.

Read the sentences aloud. When you say a word with final **y**, have children say /ē/ or /ī/ to show which sound the **y** has.

Extra Support
Materials: Sadlier Phonics Picture Cards for **sky** and **cherry**

Hold up each picture card, and say its name. Ask children to say a rhyming word for **sky** (buy, my, fly) and for **cherry** (very, berry, merry).

Say the name of each picture. Circle the word and print it on the line.

1. cherry / (cry) **cry**	2. (daisy) / day **daisy**	3. (buggy) / by **buggy**
4. 50 (fifty) / fly **fifty**	5. (candy) / cry **candy**	6. silly / (sky) **sky**
7. (penny) / pry **penny**	8. play / (fly) **fly**	9. (pony) / spy **pony**
10. handy / (dry) **dry**	11. (baby) / bay **baby**	12. gray / (fry) **fry**

250 LESSON 130: Writing Final **y**

Count by tens to 100. Have your child repeat number words that end with the long e sound of **y**, such as **twenty**.

Practicing the Skill

● Read aloud the sentence and poem at the top of page 249. Point out the two Key Picture Cues. Read the directions together, and do the first two items with the class.

● Together read the directions and identify each picture on page 250. Complete the first item together. Then have children complete the page.

Curriculum Connections

Theme Activity:
Science/Language Arts
Materials: paper patterns of butterfly and daisy, crayons, markers, scissors

● Share the theme books cited below, which explain why bugs are important.

● Ask children why we are lucky there are bugs, and list their ideas on the board. Have children copy words with final **y** from the list and add the words to their word banks.

● Have children trace and cut out a paper daisy and butterfly. Then ask children to print a word with the long **e** sound of final **y** on the daisy and a word with the long **i** sound of final **y** on the butterfly. Post daisy and butterfly cutouts on a wall mural.

Theme Books Ling, Mary, and Taylor, Kim. *See How They Grow: Butterfly.* London: Dorling Kindersley, 1992. The story is told from the point of view of the changing and growing swallowtail butterfly.

Souza, Dorothy. *Insects in the Garden.* New York: Carolrhoda Books, 1991. Learn about the insects living in your garden.

English Language Learners/ ESL
Materials: Sadlier Phonics Picture Cards for **sky, fly, cry, fry, bunny, strawberry, cherry,** and **thirty**

Help children practice with the different sounds of **y** at the end of words. Present the picture cards in random order, and identify each picture with children. As children name a picture, record the word on the board. Ask what sound children hear at the end of each word, and tell children that sometimes the **y** sounds like /ē/ and sometimes like /ī/. Have children sort the cards into two piles according to their ending sounds.

Challenge
Brainstorm a list of words that have final **y** with the sound of long **i** and long **e**. Then have each child write two sentences about nature, using the two final **y** sounds in each sentence (e.g., **My puppy** ate the **daisy. Why** does a **bunny** have long ears?). Have children illustrate their sentences.

Special Strategies
For Universal Access activities, see page 165F.

Observational Assessment

Ask children to explain how they have organized their word banks and to read aloud some of their words.

Final y in Context

Objectives
- To combine syllables to form words
- To discriminate between final **y** as long **e** and long **i**
- To write words in context

Warming Up

Reviewing Initial Consonant y

Ask children to name a word that begins with **y** based on the clues given below.

A sweater is made of this. (**yarn**)

It is the opposite of **me**. (**you**)

It is the opposite of **no**. (**yes**)

Teaching the Lesson

Phonemic Awareness:
Combine Syllables to Form Words

Materials: two magnets

Remind children that words can be made up of one or more syllables and that a syllable is a word or word part with one vowel sound. Hold two magnets together and say **magnet**. Pull the magnets apart and say **mag-net**. Put the magnets back together and say **magnet**. Repeat the process and have children model with you. Use these words:

rock-et	**pin-wheel**	**pup-pet**
skate-board	**foot-ball**	**cray-on**

Sound to Symbol

- Remind children that **y** can have the sound of long **i** as in **sky** or long **e** as in **pony**. Write the words **sky** and **pony** on the board. Explain that the last sound in **sky** is /ī/. Point to the letter **y** and tell children that **y** stands for long **i**. Repeat with **pony** to show that **y** stands for /ē/.
- Write the following list of words on the board. Read the words together. Have volunteers say a word and then the final sound in the word. Then have children circle the letter that stands for the final sound. Use these words: **pretty, many, shy, lady, try, candy, fry**.

Read the name of each picture. Listen for the ending sound. Circle **i** if the **y** has the sound of long **i**. Circle **e** if the **y** has the sound of long **e**.

1 city — i (e)	2 dry — (i) e	3 daisy — i (e)	4 candy — i (e)
5 fry — (i) e	6 cherry — i (e)	7 sky — (i) e	8 forty — i (e)
9 buggy — i (e)	10 penny — i (e)	11 pony — i (e)	12 fly — (i) e
13 fifty — i (e)	14 cry — (i) e	15 bunny — i (e)	16 baby — i (e)

LESSON 131: Discriminating Between Final y as Long e and Long i **251**

UNIVERSAL ACCESS
Meeting Individual Needs

Visual • Tactile
Materials: Sadlier Phonics Picture Cards for **fly, cry, strawberry, sky, cherry, thirty, jay, hay**

Have children work alone or with a partner to say the names of the picture cards. Tell children to arrange the cards into piles that represent the same ending sound.

Visual
Materials: Sadlier Phonics Picture Cards for **fly, cry, sky**

Write these sentences on the board:

Air pollution makes me ___. (**cry**)

A clear ___ is pretty. (**sky**)

A spider caught a ___. (**fly**)

Display the picture cards and ask children to print the word that completes each sentence.

Extra Support

Display Sadlier Phonics Picture Cards for **fly, sky, strawberry, cherry**. Have children identify the pictures. Write the names under long **i** or long **e**, and underline the **y**. Have children make up sentences using the final **y** words.

Listen as the page is read aloud. Use a word from the box to complete each sentence. Then print the word on the line.

fuzzy	sky	happy	windy	cry	baby

1. It was **windy** outside.

2. But the **sky** was sunny and blue.

3. Billy's baby sister started to **cry**.

4. Billy put the **baby** in the buggy.

5. He put the **fuzzy** bear in, too.

6. They were **happy** to be outside.

252   LESSON 131: Final **y** in Context
Comprehension: Identifying Problem/Solution

Talk about the weather. Help your child list and read weather words that end with y.

252

Connecting Spelling, Writing, and Speaking

Objectives
- To identify and isolate medial sounds
- To say, spell, sort, and write long vowel words
- To write and say sentences using spelling words

Teaching the Lesson

Phonemic Awareness: Identify and Isolate Medial Sounds

- Remind children that the middle sound in **bike** is /ī/. Say /b/-/ī/-/k/ **bike**. Have children repeat after you as you isolate the medial sounds in **cape**, **rose**, **seed**, **June**, **cute**.

- Tell children they will play a game called Hot Potato. Explain that you will say a word and throw a ball to someone. The person who catches the ball says the middle sound in the word. As you say another word, the person with the ball throws it to someone else. Repeat until everyone has had a turn. Use the following words: **gave**, **juice**, **hose**, **weed**, **Mike**, **note**, **take**, **tune**, **teach**, **bow**, **night**, **pail**.

Spelling

On the board write all the spelling words shown in the box on page 253, but leave spaces for the letter(s) that stand for the long vowel sound (e.g., **r__t** for **right**). Say each spelling word, spell the word, and repeat the word. Have children identify the vowel sound they hear and print the missing letter(s) to complete the word. Then have volunteers use each spelling word in a sentence.

Practicing the Skill

- Read the directions and spelling list on page 253 aloud. Do the first item together. Explain to children that they will sort words by vowel sound. Go over the first item before having children complete the page.

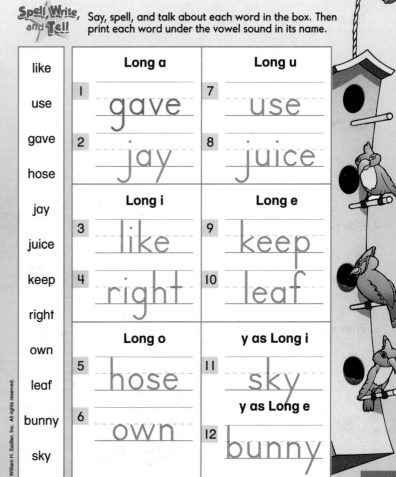

Spell, Write, and Tell Say, spell, and talk about each word in the box. Then print each word under the vowel sound in its name.

| like | use | gave | hose | jay | juice | keep | right | own | leaf | bunny | sky |

Long a	Long u
1 gave	7 use
2 jay	8 juice

Long i	Long e
3 like	9 keep
4 right	10 leaf

Long o	y as Long i
5 hose	11 sky
	y as Long e
6 own	12 bunny

LESSON 132: Connecting Spelling, Writing, and Speaking   253

UNIVERSAL ACCESS
Meeting Individual Needs

Auditory • Visual
Materials: index cards, crayons

Write each spelling word on an index card. Ask a child to choose a card, say and spell the word, and identify its long vowel sound. Ask another child to use the word in a sentence. Continue until all cards have been used.

Tactile • Auditory
Draw the shapes of the long **a** words **gave** and **jay**.

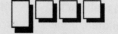

Have children copy the shapes. Then say the words. Ask children to spell each word by writing a letter in each rectangle. Repeat for other pairs of long vowel words.

Extra Support
Display Sadlier Phonics Picture Cards for **rake**, **jeep**, **kite**, **smoke**, and **tube**. As children name the cards, write the words on the board. Underline the long vowel letters. Ask children for words that rhyme, and repeat the process for those.

Write to Jake and Lane and tell them how they can be kind to the Earth. Use one or more of your spelling words. Then talk about what you wrote.

like	gave	jay	keep	own	right
use	hose	juice	bunny	leaf	sky

Possible responses:

To Jake: Use water carefully. Turn off the hose.

To Lane: Keep empty cans and juice boxes in a bin.

254   LESSON 132: Connecting Spelling, Writing, and Speaking

With your child, think of one way your family can be kinder to the Earth. Use one of the spelling words in your idea.

The Writing Process

Tell children that they will be writing sentences to Jake and Lane telling them how they can help care for Earth. Together read the directions on page 254.

Brainstorm   Talk about the picture and encourage children to share ideas. Ask: *What is Jake doing? What is Lane doing?*

Write   Have children write first drafts on a sheet of paper.

Revise   Have children reread their sentences to make sure the sentences say what they want them to say before writing them on the page. Then tell children to check that each of their sentences begins with an uppercase letter and ends with a period and check that their spelling is correct.

Publish   Have children print the corrected sentences on page 254 and underline any spelling words they used.

Speak   Ask children to role-play a conversation with Jake and Lane. Possible topics include explaining why everyone should help care for Earth and what happens to Earth when people are not kind to it.

Extending the Skills

Set up a letter exchange with children in another school. Have children write to pen pals in another school asking them to describe one thing that they do in school to help Earth (e.g., use both sides of writing paper). Encourage children to use one or more of the spelling words in their letters.

Portfolio   Have children add their writing to their portfolios.

English Language Learners/ESL
After discussing the picture on page 254 with the class, help children orally generate sentences to write to Jake and Lane using the spelling words at the top of the page. First model saying some sentences you might write. Then call on children to say sentences, and help them print the sentences on their lesson page. Make sure children know that Lane is the name of the girl pictured on the page and that Jake is the name of the boy.

Challenge
Materials: large oaktag sheets, markers

Have the class work in five groups. Assign one long vowel to each group, and have groups brainstorm ideas for a slogan urging people to take care of Earth (e.g., **Save** Our **Lakes, Keep** the **Beach Clean,** It's **No Joke—Recycle,** We **Like** Our **Trees,** Make a **Tube** into a Toy). Have children print their slogans and illustrate them. Display children's work.

Special Strategies
For Universal Access activities, see page 165F.

Assessing Long Vowels a, i, o, u, e, and Final y

Objectives

- To demonstrate recognition of long vowel words

Warming Up

Reviewing y as a Vowel

Materials: **Sadlier Phonics Picture Cards** for **cry**, **fry**, **sky**, **strawberry**, **thirty**, **cherry**

Remind children that **y** can have the long **i** sound, as in **dry**, or the long **e** sound, as in **berry**. Then hold up the picture cards for children to name and sort into two groups according to the sound of **y**.

Teaching the Lesson

Long a, i, o, u, e, and Final y

Materials: **Sadlier Phonics Picture Cards** for long vowels **a**, **i**, **o**, **u**, **e**, and final **y** (two for each sound); pocket chart

- Remind children of the five long vowel sounds studied in this unit. Show a picture card for each sound, starting with **rain** for long **a**. Have children repeat after you the picture name and the name of its long vowel sound.
- Place several long vowel picture cards in the pocket chart. Point to one picture for each sound. Ask volunteers to identify each picture and long vowel sound and then choose another picture that has the same long vowel sound. List the word pairs on the board as children identify them.
- Have one child choose a picture card from the pocket chart and another circle the matching word on the board, read it, and use it in a sentence. Continue until all words have been circled.

255

Check-Up Fill in the circle next to the name of each picture.

1	● sail ○ seal ○ sell	2	○ glum ● glue ○ glow	3	○ rate ● right ○ rat
4	○ pile ○ pal ● peel	5	○ fit ○ fat ● fifty	6	○ gate ● game ○ gum
7	○ tame ● team ○ ten	8	● suit ○ sit ○ seat	9	○ mile ● mule ○ mail
10	○ high ○ heat ● hay	11	● rose ○ raise ○ rise	12	○ pea ○ pay ● pie
13	○ cot ● coat ○ cute	14	● bike ○ beak ○ bake	15	○ bill ○ bail ● bowl

LESSON 133: Assessing Long Vowels
a, i, o, u, e, and Final y   **255**

UNIVERSAL ACCESS
Reteaching Activities

Activity 1

Materials: **Sadlier Phonics Picture Cards** for long vowels, drawing materials

Hold up an appropriate picture card to review the long vowel sounds **a, i, o, u, e**, and final **y**. Display other long vowel cards and have children sort them according to their vowel sound. Then have each child name a new long vowel word, draw a picture of the word, and print the word beneath the picture. Have children share pictures and help correct one another's spelling. Finally, have them sort the pictures according to spelling.

Activity 2

Materials: **Sadlier Phonics Picture Cards** for long vowels

To review long vowels, say each isolated long vowel sound followed by a word with that sound. Then display the picture cards. Give clues, such as those below, describing long vowel words that name the pictures. Have children select the picture, name it, identify the long vowel sound, and write the picture name on the board.

It has two wheels. (**bike**, long **i**)

This month starts summer vacation. (**June**, long **u**)

You can swim or boat here.
(**lake**, long **a**)

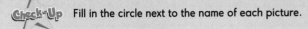
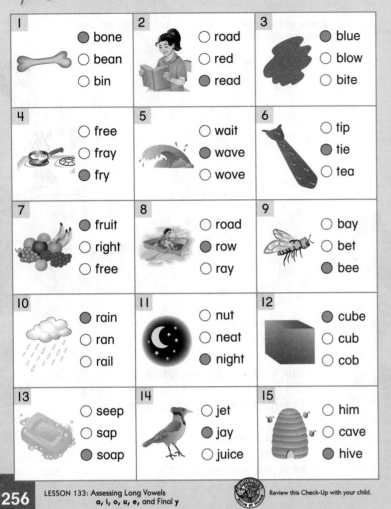

1 ● bone ○ bean ○ bin	**2** ○ road ○ red ● read	**3** ● blue ○ blow ○ bite
4 ○ free ○ fray ● fry	**5** ○ wait ● wave ○ wove	**6** ○ tip ○ tie ● tea
7 ● fruit ○ right ○ free	**8** ○ road ● row ○ ray	**9** ○ bay ○ bet ● bee
10 ● rain ○ ran ○ rail	**11** ○ nut ○ neat ● night	**12** ● cube ○ cub ○ cob
13 ○ seep ○ sap ● soap	**14** ○ jet ● jay ○ juice	**15** ○ him ○ cave ● hive

256

LESSON 133: Assessing Long Vowels
a, i, o, u, e, and Final y

Review this Check-Up with your child.

Guided Instruction

Skills	Resources
Long vowel **a**	Instruction on pages 167–180 Little Book *Space Camp*
Long vowel **i**	Instruction on pages 183–196 Little Book *Nice Vine, Quite Fine*
Long vowel **o**	Instruction on pages 199–212 Little Book *Did You Know?*
Long vowel **u**	Instruction on pages 217–230 Little Book *Amazing Blue Animals*
Long vowel **e**	Instruction on pages 233–246 Little Book *Peach Tree Street*
Final **y** as a vowel	Instruction on pages 249–252
Long vowels **a, i, o, u, e;** Final **y**	Phonemic Awareness Activities on pages 165H–165I

Assessing the Unit

Check-Up Say a word for each long vowel sound (e.g., **rake**, **kite**, **cone**, **June**, **leaf**, **sky**, **bunny**), and have children identify the vowel sound. Read aloud the directions on page 255 and point out that the same directions apply to page 256 as well. Do the first item with the class. Make sure children understand the meaning of the arrow in the picture. Together identify the rest of the pictures on both pages and remind children to think of long vowel spellings as they fill in the circle that names each picture. Then have children complete both pages.

Observational Assessment Have children read aloud the long vowel words on pages 255 and 256. Observe how well they recognize different long vowel sounds with and without a picture cue.

Portfolio Assessment Hold writing conferences to review the contents of each child's portfolio. Ask what improvements the child feels he or she has made in writing since your last conference. Help the child set goals for the next conference. See the Writing Rubrics on page 165C.

Dictation Tell children you are going to say some long **a**, **i**, **o**, **u**, **e**, and final **y** words. Have them write the words as you dictate them. Say: **cave, date, nine, pie, home, coat, tune, suit, green, team, penny, cry**. Tell children you are going to say a sentence. Have them write the sentence as you dictate it and underline any long **a**, **i**, **o**, **u**, **e**, and final **y** words. Use this sentence: ***Tony gave* this *blue bike* to *me*.**

Student Skills Assessment Use the checklist on Student Edition pages 321–322 to record your observations of individual children.

Take-Home Book Remind children to complete at home the Take-Home Book for Unit 4.

Additional Assessment See pages 165C–165E.

Integrating the Language Arts

Objectives

- To match words in spoken sentences
- To use oral and written language to extend the theme concept
- To demonstrate recognition of long vowel sounds

Teaching the Lesson

Phonemic Awareness:
Match Words in Spoken Sentences

Tell children that you will say a word. Then ask children to listen for that word in a sentence and clap when they hear it. Model the process with a volunteer. Use these words and sentences:

litter Don't drop **litter** in the park.

trash We picked up all the **trash**.

bin Mark has a **bin** for cans.

new Old papers can make **new** paper.

glass People can recycle broken **glass**.

clean Plants help **clean** the air.

Skills in Context

- Read aloud the text on page 257. Discuss the "nice things" mentioned in the text. Have children suggest other things they appreciate about Earth (e.g., the ocean, beach, and sunshine).
- Read the questions and discuss what the children in the pictures are doing. Ask children to suggest other things people might do to take care of Earth. Then challenge children to identify short and long vowel words as you reread the page together.

Comprehension Skill:
Making Inferences

Discuss why people recycle paper products. Ask what would happen if people didn't recycle paper.

Look and Learn
Listen as the page is read aloud. Look at the pictures. Then talk about what you see.

Earth is our home.
It gives us nice things
like pine trees, blue lakes,
fruit to eat, and green grass.
We must take care of Earth.
We must keep it safe and clean.
They are giving us more plants;
they are recycling.
How are the people in the pictures helping Earth?
How can you help Earth?
Possible responses: not litter, recycle, use water wisely, plant trees. LESSON 134: Long Vowels in Context
Comprehension: Making Inferences

257

UNIVERSAL ACCESS
Meeting Individual Needs

Reading and Writing Connection

Have children study the pictures on page 257 and think about environmental projects they have talked about or participated in. Have children make a sign showing what people can do to take care of Earth. Then have children label their sign with a caption. Post signs around the classroom.

Social Studies Connection

Materials: globe, glass bowl, water, food coloring

Have children examine a globe. Point out how water and land are shown. Have children trace a water path around the globe with their fingers to show how oceans are connected. Then have children place a teaspoon of food coloring in a glass bowl. Point out how the whole water becomes colored. Talk about how water pollution affects us all.

The words in the box are often used in sentences. Use one of the words to complete each sentence. Then practice reading the sentences aloud.

| down | How | little | Please | Put | said |

1. I said, "__Please__ help the sea 🐢."
   turtle

2. Keep the __little__ 🐢🐢 safe.
   turtles

3. Mom __said__, "Please help the 🦅."
   eagle

4. Do not cut __down__ 🌳🌳.
   trees

5. __How__ can you help save the 🐿🐿?
   squirrels

6. __Put__ that 🗑 in a bin.
   trash

258   LESSON 135: Reading High-Frequency Words

Randomly point to the words in the box and have your child read them. Repeat this activity frequently.

High-Frequency Words

Objectives
- To recognize and read high-frequency words
- To write high-frequency words to complete sentences

Teaching the Lesson

- Write the word **down** on the board. Point to the word, say it, spell it, and say the word again. Have children repeat after you and then trace the word in the air. Repeat the process with the words **how**, **little**, **please**, **put**, and **said**.

- Write these sentences on the board:
   Do you know ___ to fly a kite?
   Would you ___ teach me?
   My big sister ___ it was easy.
   My kite keeps falling ___.
   I ___ a tail on it.
   Now my ___ kite is flying.

Help children read the sentences aloud. Point out that most sentences end with a period. However, when the sentence asks a question, it ends with a question mark. Then write a ? on the board. Ask volunteers to choose the word (from those listed on the board) that best completes the meaning of the sentence, and write it in the sentence. Then say one of the high frequency words and call on a child to spell it aloud and circle the word in the sentence. Repeat with the remaining words.

Practicing the Skill

Read aloud the directions at the top of page 258, and call on children to read the words in the box. Be sure children can read the sentences and identify the rebus pictures before they complete the page. Remind children that the first word in a sentence begins with an uppercase letter.

Extra Practice
Materials: index cards, container

Write the words **down, how, little, please, put,** and **said** on index cards and place them in a container. Have children play "spill and spell" by shaking the container and spilling out the cards. Children should read, say, and spell aloud each word that lands faceup, use the word in a sentence, and then return the cards to the container and pass it to the next player.

Review
Materials: index cards

Write the words **be, do, for, me,** and **so** on index cards. Then ask volunteers to come to the board. Spell out each word so that children can write it on the board as you say each letter. Ask volunteers to read the words children wrote and to use the words in sentences. Then distribute the word cards. Ask a child holding a card to read the word, to circle the matching word on the board, and to spell it. Repeat until all the children have had a chance to come to the board.

Reviewing and Assessing Short and Long Vowels

Objectives

• To read, identify, and write short and long vowel words

Warming Up

Reviewing Medial Consonants

Materials: Punchout Letter Cards for **b**, **g**, **t**, **m**, **v**, **d**

On the board write **robot**, **wagon**, **water**, **camel**, **seven**, and **spider**, substituting dashes for the medial consonants. Have children hold up the letter card that stands for the missing middle sound.

Teaching the Lesson

Short and Long Vowels

Materials: **Sadlier Phonics Picture Cards** for **van**, **six**, **log**, **cup**, **web**, **lake**, **pie**, **boat**, **tube**, **jeep**

• Review that **a**, **i**, **o**, **u**, **e** can have a long or short sound. On the board, write: **man**, **main**; **pill**, **pile**; **hop**, **hope**; **cut**, **cute**; **men**, **mean**. Read each word pair, and identify the long and short sounds.

• Display picture cards. On the board, write the headings Short and Long. Have partners name the pictures, sort them by long and short vowel sound, and write the names under the proper headings.

• Read aloud the directions on page 259. Help children name each picture. Then have them complete the page.

Say the name of each picture. Circle the word. Then circle **L** if the name has a long vowel sound or **S** if the name has a short vowel sound.

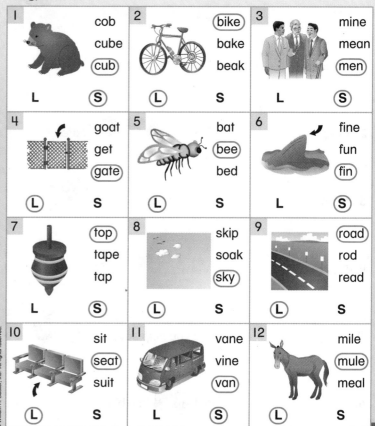

1. cob / cube / (cub) — L (S)	2. (bike) / bake / beak — (L) S	3. mine / mean / (men) — L (S)
4. goat / get / (gate) — (L) S	5. bat / (bee) / bed — (L) S	6. fine / fun / (fin) — L (S)
7. (top) / tape / tap — L (S)	8. skip / soak / (sky) — (L) S	9. (road) / rod / read — (L) S
10. sit / (seat) / suit — (L) S	11. vane / vine / (van) — L (S)	12. mile / (mule) / meal — (L) S

LESSON 136: Reviewing Short and Long Vowels **259**

UNIVERSAL ACCESS
Reteaching Activities

Activity 1

Materials: **Sadlier Phonics Picture Cards** for **lamp**, **game**, **sled**, **jeans**, **bib**, **bike**, **doll**, **boat**, **rug**, **suit**; Punchout Letter Cards for **L** and **S**.

On the board write the five vowels and the following: **a_e, ai, ay; i_e, igh, ie; o_e, oa, ow; u_e, ui, ue; ea, ee**. Review the long and short vowel sound that each spelling pattern stands for. Then show children the picture cards. Have them hold up the **L** card when they see a picture whose name has a long vowel sound and the **S** card when they see a picture whose name has a short vowel sound.

Activity 2

Materials: index cards, marker, Punchout Letter Card **e**

Review long and short vowel sounds using the following word pairs: **tag/face, tip/nine, top/road, tug/fruit (cube), bed/seat**. Then write the following words on index cards: **cap, at, mat, man, bit, fin, hid, kit, pin, hop, not, cut, hug**. Have children work in groups; give each group a set of cards. Have children add silent **e** to turn short vowel words into long vowel words. Have children print sentences using short or long vowel words.

259

Say the name of each picture. Circle **long** if the name has a long vowel sound or **short** if the name has a short vowel sound. Then print the name of the picture on the line.

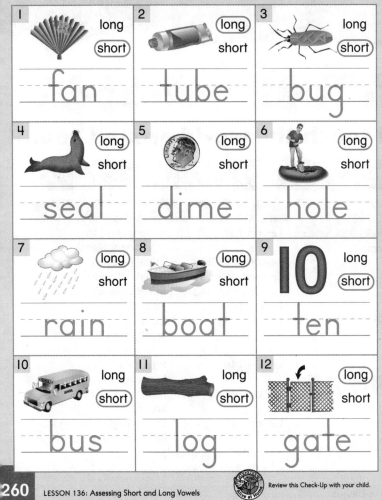

1 long / (short) fan	2 (long) / short tube	3 long / (short) bug
4 (long) / short seal	5 (long) / short dime	6 (long) / short hole
7 (long) / short rain	8 (long) / short boat	9 long / (short) ten
10 long / (short) bus	11 long / (short) log	12 (long) / short gate

LESSON 136: Assessing Short and Long Vowels

Review this Check-Up with your child.

Assessing the Skills

Check-Up Remind children that vowels can have short and long sounds. On the board write **bat, hit, pot, cut, pet**. Review each short vowel sound and have children name another word with the same short vowel sound. Repeat with long vowel sounds using these words: **cake, night, goat, glue, tree**. Have children turn to page 260. Read aloud the directions and together identify the pictures. Do the first item together before having children complete the page.

Observational Assessment As children complete the Check-Up activity, note whether they confuse long and short vowel spellings.

Dictation Tell children you are going to say some short vowel words. Have children write the short vowel words as you dictate them. Say: **sat, did, hop, mud, get**. Continue with long vowel words: **day, time, boat, cute, weed**. Then tell children you are going to say a sentence with short and long vowel words. Have them write the sentence as you dictate it. Use this sentence: ***Lin put* a *blue coat*** in a ***box***.

Student Skills Assessment Use the checklist on Student Edition pages 321–322 to record your observations of individual children.

Guided Instruction

Skills	Resources
Short vowels	See Unit 3 pages 79–90, 93–106, 109–122, 127–140, 143–156 Little Books Level A Set 1 and Level AA Set 1
Long vowels	See Unit 4 pages 167–180, 183–196, 199–212, 217–230, 233–246, 249–252 Little Books Level A Set 2 and Level AA Set 2
Short and Long vowels	Phonemic Awareness Activities on pages 77H–77I, 165H–166I

Sensational Senses

Smell, see, hear, taste, and touch the world around you.

Consonant Blends

READING/LANGUAGE ARTS STANDARDS

- ✪ Respond to a poem in a way that reflects understanding
- ✪ Recognize and identify initial and final consonant blends in words
- ✪ Read high-frequency words and words with blends
- ✪ Write words with consonant blends

OBJECTIVES

- ▶ To enjoy a poem about the pleasant and not-so-pleasant sounds around us
- ▶ To develop phonemic awareness by identifying, matching, segmenting, blending, and manipulating sounds in spoken words
- ▶ To recognize initial **l**-blends, **r**-blends, and **s**-blends
- ▶ To recognize final blends
- ▶ To use consonant blends to decode words
- ▶ To read and write words with consonant blends and high-frequency words in context

LESSONS

Lesson 137	Introduction to Consonant Blends
Lessons 138–139 . . .	Initial **l**-Blends
Lessons 140–141 . . .	Initial **r**-Blends
Lessons 142–143 . . .	Initial **s**-Blends
Lesson 144	Final Blends
Lesson 145	Connecting Spelling, Writing, and Speaking
Lesson 146	Integrating the Language Arts
Lesson 147	High-Frequency Words
Lesson 148	Reviewing/Assessing Initial and Final Blends

- Take-Home Book: *Making Sense*

Thematic Teaching

In Unit 5 children learn the sounds of consonant blends as they focus on using their senses both to get information about the world around them and to appreciate that world.

Display the "Ears Hear" **Unit 5 Classroom Poster** in a prominent place in the classroom. As you progress through the unit, point out the many words with consonant blends.

Curriculum Integration

Spelling A *Spelling Connection* appears in most lesson plans. A special focus on spelling high-frequency words appears on page 280.

Science Children learn how their senses help them get information about the world around them as they complete the activities on pages 264, 266, 270, 272, and 279.

Art Children have the opportunity to express their ideas creatively through art activities on pages 264 and 274.

Optional Learning Activities

Multisensory Activities
Multisensory activities that foster visual, auditory, tactile, and kinesthetic learning are a regular feature of the phonics lessons.

Multicultural Connection
Focus on the contributions of diverse cultural groups by inviting students to participate in the activity on page 262.

Thematic Activities
Use the thematic activities in *Curriculum Connections* to enrich children's phonics experiences.

Author's Corner

Lucia and James L. Hymes, Jr.
Lucia Manley Hymes and her husband, James L. Hymes, Jr., make a good team. Both are poets who have also been teachers. James Hymes has written books for parents and for teachers to help them become more effective in the classroom.

 Assessment Strategies

Assessment is an ongoing process. Multiple strategies in the Student Edition as well as the Teacher's Edition and regular use of the *Student Skills Assessment Checklist* on pages 321–322 will help you monitor children's progress in discriminating consonant blends.

UNIT RESOURCES

Sadlier Reading

Classroom Poster

Phonics Picture Cards

Little Books and Big Books

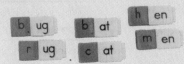

Student Manipulatives

Other Poems by Lucia and James L. Hymes, Jr.
Oodles of Noodles, and Other Hymes' Rhymes. Young Scott Books, 1964. Available in local libraries.

Theme-Related Resources

Animal Senses. Dorling Kindersley, 1996. Learn the sensory abilities of many animals.

Pandell, Karen. *By Day and By Night.* Tiburon, CA: H.J. Kramer, Inc., 1991. Familiar things seem different at night. This rhyme shows how the five senses help sort it all out.

Seuss, Dr. *Mr. Brown Can Moo, Can You?* New York: Random House, 1989. Children will enjoy attempting to imitate all the sounds Mr. Brown makes!

5 ✓ ASSESSMENT

In Unit 5 children focus on developing the ability to recognize consonant blends. The assessment ideas on this page are for use throughout the unit.

Pretests/Posttests

The tests on pages 261D–261E can serve as a formal end-of-unit assessment of children's mastery of consonant blends. In some cases you may choose to use them as pretests to help you identify a starting point for instruction for individual children. The Phonemic Awareness Test on page 261J also serves as a pretest.

Observational Assessment

Specific opportunities to observe children's progress with recognizing consonant blends are highlighted in the lesson plans. The *Student Skills Assessment Checklist* on pages 321–322 of the Student Edition will help you keep track of students' progress.

Dictation

Review consonant blends by dictating words to children and having them write the letters that stand for the sound they hear in these words: at the beginning of **stop**, **glass**, **brick**, **slide**, **clown**; at the end of **desk**, **tent**, **lamp**, **wink**, **nest**.

Then have children write the following sentences: **Scrub** the pot. The **king** has a **mask**. The **ring** is by the **lamp**. In addition to assessing the consonant blends, observe whether children begin each sentence with an uppercase letter and end with a period.

Using Technology

The activities on pages 261O–261P may also be used to evaluate children's progress.

Performance Assessment

Tell children to think about the last time they were in the school cafeteria. On large sheets of construction paper, post the following in the Writing Center: SEE, HEAR, SMELL, TASTE, FEEL. Direct children to use all their senses to picture the cafeteria. Then have children write sentences to describe the school cafeteria. You might have children illustrate their sentences. Use the *Student Skills Assessment Checklist* on pages 321–322 to record your observations.

Portfolio Assessment

The portfolio icon in the lesson plans indicates portfolio opportunities throughout the unit. Post the rubrics for Unit 5 on a chart when you begin the unit, and review the criteria with children. Discuss with children how they can select work from their portfolios that best represents their progress in a given area. For example, for the rubric "spells words with final blends," model posing questions such as: *What work in my portfolio has words I've written that end with blends? Did I spell those words correctly? Did I write those words so someone else can read them?*

Answer Key

Page 261D
1. **cl**oud
2. hu**mp**
3. **tr**ain
4. te**nt**
5. **bl**ocks
6. **sm**oke
7. **fl**ag
8. **cr**ab
9. **sn**ake
10. ki**ng**
11. **sk**ate
12. **gr**ill

Page 261E
1. The band plays a song.
2. Cold snow covers the grass.
3. The buzzing bees may sting.
4. Brad claps his hands.
5. Birds sing in the nest.
6. The train sits on the track.

Name _____

Writing Rubrics

	Sometimes	Never	Always
Phonics Skills			
Associates consonant blends with their corresponding letters			
Identifies final blends			
Reads and writes words with blends in context			
Writing Skills			
Spells words beginning with **l-**, **r-**, and **s**-blends			
Spells words with final blends			
Spells sight words appropriate to grade level			
Conveys a clear message through writing			
Organizes ideas coherently and logically			
Demonstrates awareness of sentence structure			
Writes from left to write and from top to bottom			
Spaces letters, words, and sentences appropriately			

Say the name of each picture. Fill in the circle in front of the letters that stand for the missing blend. Print the blend on the line.

1	○ cl
	○ br
	○ sn

_____oud

2	○ sk
	○ ng
	○ mp

hu_____

3	○ sm
	○ pr
	○ tr

_____ain

4	○ sk
	○ nt
	○ nk

te_____

5	○ dr
	○ nt
	○ bl

_____ocks

6	○ sm
	○ sp
	○ tr

_____oke

7	○ cl
	○ fl
	○ fr

_____ag

8	○ cl
	○ br
	○ cr

_____ab

9	○ sw
	○ dr
	○ sn

_____ake

10	○ nt
	○ sk
	○ ng

ki_____

11	○ sn
	○ sk
	○ pr

_____ate

12	○ gr
	○ fr
	○ st

_____ill

Read the sentences. Fill in the circle in front of the one that tells about the picture.

1		○ The band sits down.
		○ The band plays a song.
2		○ Cold snow covers the grass.
		○ Green leaves are on the grass.
3		○ The ants make a sand hill.
		○ The buzzing bees may sting.
4		○ Brad claps his hands.
		○ Brad tastes some fruit.
5		○ Birds sing in the nest.
		○ The birds have left the nest.
6		○ The plane flies in the sky.
		○ The train sits on the track.

I n Unit 5 children learn the sounds of consonant blends. Children who struggle with this unit may be manifesting visual discrimination or memory problems, and/or attention deficit disorder (ADD). The following techniques can be a starting point from which to develop more needs–specific techniques.

Visual Discrimination

Children with visual discrimination difficulties may be unable to detect similarities and/or differences in material presented visually. For example, these children may have difficulty seeing a difference between the blends **gl** and **pl** or **dr** and **br**. The following techniques may benefit such children as they proceed through the unit.

- Use of tactile word cards allows children to employ their nonvisual sense of touch when learning blends. Make several pairs of word cards with blends that children commonly confuse (e.g., **brain**, **drain**). Have children trace each word with glue. When the glue dries, have children trace the raised lines with their fingers as they say the sound of each letter. Children should then draw a line with their finger from left to right beneath the letters as they blend the sounds together to say the word.

- Enlarge the Student Edition pages on a photocopier and have children highlight the consonant blends. You might try creating a "window" for children to allow them to selectively view parts of an exercise. To make a window, cut a rectangle in a large index card. Instruct children to put the window opening on top of one word at a time. This cuts down on potentially distracting peripheral material. As children's tracking begins to improve, have them replace the window with a ruler; finally, have them use their fingers to track letters and words.

Memory

Children may be unable to retain information presented either orally or visually. In this unit children could have trouble remembering particular blends from day to day. The following techniques may help children cope with such memory problems.

- As you progress through the unit, have children brainstorm a list of words containing the consonant blends presented in a lesson. Record the words, organized by blend, in a cumulative list on a wall chart. Children should both hear and read the words as they are added to the list. As each word is written and said, call attention to its blend. Display the list in a prominent place, and each day have children parade around the room saying the words.

- To promote visual memory, have children read a paragraph that contains many words with blends. As children read, have them underline each blend.

- To promote auditory memory, say an alliterative sentence with a consonant blend being studied. For example, ***Clara clapped*** *when the* ***clown climbed*** *the* ***clock***. Name the blend, and have children repeat the sentence.

Attention Deficit Disorder (ADD)

When learning consonant blends, children will need to tune in to the information presented and filter out the unwanted sounds in the environment. Children who have ADD may have difficulty focusing on the relevant information because they are easily distracted by external and internal stimuli. It is important for these children to develop good listening skills so that they can tune out the continuous barrage of sounds competing for their attention. The following strategies may help these children sharpen their listening skills.

- Teach these children what listening looks like. Explain that they should look at the person presenting the information. They should also sit as still and as quietly as possible. Once they understand these things, teach them to monitor their own listening behavior.

- While teaching, observe the inattentive children and gently tap their desks occasionally as a reminder to listen and focus.

- Incorporate children's interests into the lessons. For example, if trains are popular with children, motivate them by presenting consonant blend words related to **trains** (e.g., **track**, **stop**, and **smoke**).

- Try to alternate physical and mental activities.

- Give simple, concrete instructions one time only so as not to lose children's attention. To prevent further distraction, have children keep their desks clear except for the materials they need to complete the assignment.

The chart below identifies problems that children may manifest as they learn the concepts and skills presented in this unit. The chart also identifies strategies to use with children who have not yet mastered the key concepts in the unit.

SKILL	Identifying Beginning Blends	Forming Beginning Blends	Writing Final Blends
Observation	Child has difficulty identifying beginning blends in spoken words.	Child has difficulty combining the correct consonants to spell beginning blends in words.	Child consistently omits the **g** when spelling words with the final **ng** blend.
Intervention	• Slowly say words with and without beginning blends. Point out the different beginning sounds of the words. • On the chalkboard write a list of words with **l**-blends using colored chalk: **clock**, **glass**, **plate**, **fly**, **block**. Stretch out each word as you say it (e.g., /**kl**/-/**o**/-/**k**/). Use a different colored chalk to circle each blend as you say the word. Have child stretch the word out after you and then underline the blend with different colored chalk. • As you slowly say a word, have the child give a thumbs-up signal if he or she hears a beginning blend or a thumbs-down signal if the word does not contain a blend.	• Have child use magnetic letters to spell words with blends. Put the nonblend letters in position and tell child that the beginning blend is missing. Start with **ide** for **slide**. Say **slide**, and have child locate the **s** and **l** and put them in the correct position to complete the word. Then say **glide**, and have child locate **g** and **l** and position them in place of the **sl** blend. Continue with **bride**, **pride**, and other blend words. • In a row in random order, place magnetic letters for a word with a beginning blend, plus a few extra letters. Say the word; then have child pull down the letters to spell the word.	• Say a word with the final **ng** blend, such as **ring**. Have child repeat the word, segmenting it into sounds. Tell child the word has four letters. Have child spell the word, reminding child to include enough letters. • Teach child to check his or her own spelling. Have child write a word with an **ng** final blend and then slowly slide a finger beneath the letters as he or she says each sound. Tell child to listen carefully for the /**ng**/.

These activities are designed to augment the lessons in the unit with engaging exercises that reinforce skills and encourage creativity.

Blend Phonemes

Little Fly
Read aloud the following poem. As you say the segmented words, articulate the sounds separately and slowly. Have children blend the sounds together and say the words. Once children know the words, teach them the accompanying motions. Then recite the poem together.

I saw a little /fl/-/ī/ go /h/-/o/-/p/, hop, hop.

(bounce two fingers of one hand on the palm of the other hand)

I told the little fly to /st/-/o/-/p/, stop, stop.

(shake first finger)

I /kr/-/e/-/pt/ to the window to say, "How do you do?"

(bow)

He /st/-/u/-/k/ out his wings

(spread arms like wings)

And away he /fl/-/oo/.

(flap arms)

Magic Trick
Materials: Sadlier Phonics Picture Cards for **block, fly, clap, sink, ring, smell, plane, mask, sky, lamp**; a bag

Place the picture card for **block** in the bag without showing it to children. Say the sounds of the word separately: /bl/-/o/-/k/. Have children blend the sounds together and say the word. If they say the word correctly, pull the picture out of the bag and show it to the children. Repeat with the other picture cards.

Segment Phonemes

Materials: a piece of string for each child

Teach children the following poem:

Noses are **crazy**!

Some are **long** and some are **flat**.

Some are **pretty** and some are fat!

Use your nose when you **smell** a **bloom**.

Try not to use it when you use a **broom**.

The **dust** might make you **sneeze**.

Use a **cloth** if you **sneeze, please**.

When all children know the poem, have them recite it while holding a piece of string. For each word with a blend, have children spread out the string as they say each sound in the word.

Have children hold hands to form a circle. Tell them to keep their elbows close to their bodies. Together, recite the poem. As children say the sounds of the words with blends, have them stretch the circle out until their arms are fully extended and then close the circle again.

Add Initial Sounds

Materials: a ball

Have children sit in a circle around you. Say the word **ice**, and have children repeat it. Ask what new word is formed when you add /n/ to the word **ice**. Roll the ball to one of the children. Have that child say the new word and roll the ball back to you. Repeat with other words and sounds. You may want to include: **lay**, add /p/ (**play**); **each**, add /t/ (**teach**); **at**, add /fl/ (**flat**); **oil**, add /sp/ (**spoil**); **lake**, add /f/ (**flake**); **mall**, add /s/ (**small**); **last**, add /b/ (**blast**).

Identify Rhymes

My Eyes
Read the poem "My Eyes" to children.

♫ Here are my eyes,

Bright and blue.

I make them blink.

So can you.

When they're open,

I can see my friend Jack.

When they're closed

Everything's all black.

Read the poem again and have children act it out. Then say it a third time, and have children identify the rhyming words. Finally, have children repeat the poem again, beginning in a loud voice. As they say each line, they should speak more softly, ending the poem in a whisper.

Guess the Rhyme
Have children work in small groups. Have each group act out its assigned rhyme, and have the rest of the class try to guess which one it is. When the rhyme has been identified, recite it together. Have children identify the rhyming words. Use rhymes such as "Humpty Dumpty," "Little Miss Muffet," "Rock-A-Bye, Baby," "Hickory, Dickory, Dock," and "Jack and Jill."

Match Words

*Materials: **Sadlier Phonics Picture Cards** for **star**, **mask**, **drum**, **hand**, **clap**, **truck**, **spoon**, **band**, **green**; five blocks for each child*

Display the first five picture cards on the chalk ledge, and have children identify each picture. Read the first paragraph of the following story. Each time children hear the word for one of the pictures, they should place one of the blocks on their desk.

My mother took my sister and me to the circus. When we walked in, we each got a **star** sticker. I put mine on my **hand**. Everyone started to **clap** when a man rode out on a horse. My sister was afraid of the **mask** the man wore. I couldn't believe he could play a **drum** and ride the horse at the same time!

Have children clear their desks of the blocks. Display the last four picture cards on the chalk ledge, and have children identify each one. Read the last paragraph of the story, and again have children place a block on their desk each time they hear one of the picture card words.

My favorite part of the circus was when a very small **green truck** appeared. The driver was a clown. He was honking the horn. Ten clowns climbed out of that small **truck**. I don't know how they all fit in there! Each clown had a funny musical instrument. One of the clowns tried to play a **spoon**! They started to march and play. It was the worst **band** I'd ever heard!

Name _____ Date _____

Directions: Give this assessment orally to each child. The correct answers are boldfaced.

Blend Phonemes in a Word

Say: *I will say some sounds. Listen to the sounds and tell me what word
you get when you blend the sounds together.* Write the word the child says.

1. /kr/ - /ī/ _____ **cry**   6. /pl/ - /ā/ _____ **play**

2. /sw/ - /i/ - /m/ _____ **swim**   7. /fl/ - /i/ - /p/ _____ **flip**

3. /pl/ - /ā/ - /n/ _____ **plain**   8. /l/ - /a/ - /mp/ _____ **lamp**

4. /sk/ - /i/ - /p/ _____ **skip**   9. /bl/ - /o/ - /k/ _____ **block**

5. /tr/ - /ē/ _____ **tree**   10. /d/ - /e/ - /sk/ _____ **desk**

Segment Phonemes in a Word

Say: *I will say a word. Say each of the sounds you hear in the word.*
Write the sounds the child says.

11. snow _____ **/sn/ - /ō/**

12. blue _____ **/bl/ - /o͞o/**

13. spot _____ **/sp/ - /o/ - /t/**

14. hand _____ **/h/ - /a/ - /nd/**

15. truck _____ **/tr/ - /u/ - /k/**

16. clap _____ **/kl/ - /a/ - /p/**

17. sleep _____ **/sl/ - /ē/ - /p/**

18. smell _____ **/sm/ - /e/ - /l/**

19. went _____ **/w/ - /e/ - /nt/**

20. gift _____ **/g/ - /i/ - /ft/**

Stack Up

Blackline Master 24
p. 261L

Objective
To build words with initial blends

Players
Pairs

Materials
- glue
- construction paper
- scissors

- Duplicate and distribute Blackline Master 24 to each group.

- Have children glue the blackline master onto construction paper, cut the cards apart, and sort them by size.

- Instruct children to display the word cards faceup and to stack the blend cards facedown. Have the first player turn the top blend card faceup and read the sound of the blend. The partner then places that blend card over the blend on each word card and reads the resulting word until a word the child knows is formed.

- Tell children to alternate roles and continue play until all of the word cards have been used.

Sensible Riddles

Blackline Master 25
p. 261M

Objective
To use phonograms with final blends to answer riddles

Players
Pairs

Materials
- construction paper
- glue
- scissors

- Duplicate and distribute Blackline Master 25 to each pair.

- Together, name the rebus pictures and read the riddles and the answer words. Have children glue the blackline master onto construction paper and cut the cards apart.

- Tell children to stack the answer cards facedown; also have them stack the riddle cards facedown. Ask children to take turns choosing and reading aloud a riddle, spelling the ending phonogram, and turning over an answer card.

- Explain that if children turn up the answer to the riddle, they keep both cards; if they do not, they place the riddle card at the bottom of the pile, shuffle the answer cards, and let the other player take a turn.

- The game ends when there are no more cards to choose.

Blend Bloopers

Objective
To use phonetic and aural clues to identify words

Players
Pairs

Materials
- sheets of paper
- scissors

- On a sheet of paper, print several sentences, each containing a word that does not make sense in that context, but does begin with the same blend as the correct word. Examples:

  The skunk is sunny and blue. (**sky**)

  I watered the green plays. (**plants**)

  Give a copy to each pair.

- On another sheet of paper, print the correct words. Give a copy to each pair, and have children cut the words apart and place them faceup in a row.

- Tell the children in each pair to take turns choosing a sentence, reading it aloud, identifying the word that does not make sense, and finding the appropriate word to replace it.

Stack Up

clock	grow	snail	brake
skate	flag	glue	train
stick	play	frame	cry
swing	spill	drop	sleep

cl	gl	pl	fl	bl	sl
fr	cr	tr	dr	br	pr
gr	st	sw	sp	sk	sn

Sensible Riddles

It's something to taste. It ends like

Use your voice to make music. It ends like

It hurts when bees do this. It ends like

If something is wet, it feels this way. It ends like

It feels good to a baby bird. It ends like

This group makes loud music. It ends like

It's a color you can see. It ends like

It doesn't smell good. It ends like

It helps you with your sense of touch. It ends like

nest	**damp**	**skunk**
band	**hand**	**sing**
drink	**sting**	**pink**

Consonant Review

Have children work in pairs. Tell the children in each pair to stack, picture side down, the following Punchout Cards: **fan**, **leaf**, **pig**, **net**, **seal**, **ride**, **queen**, **fox**, **doll**, **cap**, **bug**, **hive**, **goat**, **five**, **kite**, **pen**, **note**, **mule**, **soap**, **rug**, **box**, **van**, **cup**, **yell**, **ten**, and **six**. Then have partners divide between them all the consonants from their remaining complete set of Punchout Cards. Direct them to turn up

one picture at a time and locate the letter cards that stand for the beginning and ending sounds of the picture name. Tell children to place the beginning consonant to the left of the picture and the ending consonant to the right.

Adapt this activity to include a review of final consonant blends by adding the cards with the cards: **gift**, **mask**, **tent**, **lamp**, **king**, and **ant**.

Word Guess

Materials: pocket chart

On the board, list some beginning blends from Unit 5; you might include **cl**, **gr**, and **sm**. Ask children to think of words that begin with the listed blends and to take out the letter cards needed to spell those words. Display a pocket chart on the chalk ledge. Have a volunteer place the first letter of one of his or her words in the chart and then call on classmates to guess the remaining letters in order. As each letter is correctly named, have the original volunteer place it in the pocket chart. Ask the child who completes the word to lead the next round. Change the beginning blends periodically. Use blend groups such as: **gl**, **fr**, **st**; **pl**, **cr**, **sw**; **fl**, **tr**, **sp**; **bl**, **dr**, **sk**; **sl**, **br**, **sn**.

Ribbons of Rhymes

Materials: strips of ribbon, index cards

Attach each of the following Punchout Picture cards to the top of a separate strip of ribbon that is held vertically: **ant**, **king**, **mask**, **tent**, and **lamp**. Have volunteers print each picture name on an index card, underline the final blend, and attach the name card just below the corresponding picture. Then invite children to think of words that rhyme with the name of each picture. As volunteers name rhyming words, give them index cards so that they can add the words to the ribbons. Read each final string of words with the class, and attach the ribbons to a wall for reference.

Spelling Crossword Puzzles

Have children work in pairs to make Punchout Card crossword puzzles that feature their spelling words. Direct one child in each pair to position letter cards in a vertical column to spell a spelling word. Direct remaining partners to build another spelling word across the first so that the two words share one letter card, crossword style. You might draw an example on the board. Encourage children to extend their crosswords with as many words as possible.

```
      W
      E
B A N D
      T
```

STINKY STORIES

Objectives

- To help children recognize and use words that contain consonant blends in context
- To use a writing program such as Storybook Weaver® Deluxe* to write a "stinky" story

Preparation

- Focus on the sense of smell by sharing the book *Mucky Moose* by Jonathan Allen. It is a story about a very smelly moose and a tricky wolf. Help children retell the story. Ask children to name other smelly animals.

- Write the following words on the board:

stinky	beast	broom
smell	dragon	forest
tree	smoke	stable
skunk	king	brave
slime	sniff	breath

- Read the list of words to the class, and have volunteers identify initial or final consonant blends. Lead children to see that these words are words they might include in a "stinky" story. Read aloud the following example:

  A **stinky smell** came from the **stable**. The **brave king** went to take a look. He found a **skunk**!

One Step at a Time

1. Using Storybook Weaver® Deluxe, direct children to select "Start a New Story" from the opening screen.

2. Have children select "Title" and enter "My Stinky Story." Then have them select "Author" to enter their names and "Border" to include a border for their title pages.

3. Tell children to use words from the list to make up sentences for their "stinky" stories. Have them select "Picture and Text" to enter their stories.

4. Have children choose from "Scenery," "Objects," and "Color" to illustrate their stories. Inform them that they can also add music or sound effects to accompany each page by selecting the Musical Note icon.

5. Direct children to print their stories.

Class Sharing

Encourage volunteers to read their "stinky" stories to the class. You may also wish to choose "Read a Story" from the opening screen and use an LCD (liquid crystal display) plate and overhead projector to display their stories for the class.

A **stinky smell** came from the **stable**.
The **brave king** went to take a look.
He found a **skunk**.

WHAT'S MY BLEND

All software referred to in this book is listed under Computer Resources on page 348.

One Step at a Time

1. Have children work in small groups. Have them use Kid Pix® Studio, and tell them to select "Moopies" from the opening screen.

2. Direct groups to use the drawing tools and color palette from the side menu to draw objects having names that begin with their assigned consonant blend.

3. Instruct each group to select the Dancing Alphabet Text tool and to make wiggling words from those words listed on the board that contain their assigned consonant blend.

4. Have groups search the Rubber Stamps for objects having names that contain the group's assigned consonant blend, and have children place them in their drawings. For example, to illustrate the blend **dr**, children may choose the animated rubber stamps of a **dr**um and a **dr**ip.

5. Encourage children to add sound to their "Moopies" by selecting "Pick a Sound" under the Goodies menu.

6. Have groups save their "Moopies."

Class Sharing

Ask each group to present its "Moopies" to the class. If possible, use an LCD (liquid crystal display) plate and overhead projector to enhance the presentations. After each presentation, direct the class to identify the consonant blend that is illustrated.

 SING A SONG

Write on the board and sing the song "If You're Happy and You Know It" (shown at right).

If you're happy and you know it, Clap your hands.

If you're happy and you know it, Clap your hands.

If you're happy and you know it, And you really want to show it,

If you're happy and you know it, Clap your hands.

Invite children to sing with you. When all have learned the words, have them substitute the following phrases for "Clap your hands," and sing the song again.

Stamp your feet.

Blink your eyes.

Brush your teeth.

Tape-record the class singing the song. As you play back the recording, direct children to listen for action words that demonstrate initial consonant blend sounds.

Literature Introduction to Consonant Blends

Objectives

- **To enjoy a poem about what we hear**
- **To identify rhyming words**
- **To identify consonant blends**

Starting with Literature

Read aloud "Ears Hear." Ask children to identify what sounds are being made in the illustration. Reread the poem and ask children to imitate the sounds mentioned.

Developing Critical Thinking

Read aloud the Critical Thinking questions on page 261. As children respond, make lists of both pleasant and unpleasant sounds.

Introducing the Skill

Phonemic Awareness: Identify Rhyming Words

Say the following rhyme.

> Do you **hear** something **near**?
>
> I think it's a **cat**.
>
> Or is it a **bat**?

Have children repeat the rhyming words. Then ask volunteers to substitute other rhyming words for the boldface words and repeat the rhyme.

Consonant Blends

- Print **s** and **l** on the board. Remind children that /s/ stands for **s** and /l/ stands for **l**.
- Print the word **slam** by the letters. Underline **sl**. Explain that when two consonants appear together their sounds are often blended together. Tell the class they will learn more about consonant blends in Unit 5, but for now they can look and listen for them at the beginning or end of words. Reread "Ears Hear" on the **Unit 5 Classroom Poster** and help children find words with consonant blends.

Ears Hear

Flies buzz,
Motors roar.
Kettles hiss,
People snore. both
Dogs bark, both
Birds cheep.
Autos honk: Beep! Beep!

Winds sigh,
Shoes squeak.
Trucks honk,
Floors creak.
Whistles toot,
Bells clang,
Doors slam: Bang! Bang!

Kids shout,
Clocks ding. both
Babies cry,
Phones ring. both
Balls bounce, both
Spoons drop.
People scream: Stop! Stop!

Lucia and James L. Hymes, Jr.

Critical Thinking
Which sounds are loud? soft? Loud sounds circled in poem; soft sounds underlined
What sounds make you feel happy? Children might suggest sounds mentioned in poem.

LESSON 137: Consonant Blends
Phonemic Awareness: Rhyme

261

Theme Words

Word Sense Reread the poem "Ears Hear" and have children list words that describe sounds. Write those words on a word wall. Then write the words **sight, hearing, taste, touch,** and **smell** on the word wall. Have children pretend they are in a restaurant and then have them name things associated with each sense. Write their responses under the appropriate sense word. Refer to the word wall and add to it throughout the unit.

As headings on a separate chart, write the words **plate, tray, skate,** and **hand** as examples of initial and final consonant blends. Throughout the unit, have children work in groups to find magazine pictures of items with names that have consonant blends that match those in the words on the chart. Direct children to cut out the pictures and glue them to the appropriate place on the chart. Have children write sentences about the pictures to post near the chart.

Name _____

Dear Family,

In this unit about our five senses, your child will learn the sounds of consonant blends. As your child progresses through this unit, you can try these activities together at home.

• Say the name of each picture below with your child. Listen to the sounds of the consonant blends.

l blend l principio	r blend r principio	s blend s principio	final blend final
 clown	 fruit	 stop	 band

• Read the poem "Ears Hear" on the reverse side of this page.

• Find words with consonant blends in the poem, such as **flies**, **snore**, **honk**, **trucks**, **clang**, **clocks**, **cry**, **ring**, **spoons**, **drop**, **scream**, and **stop**.

• Then find the rhyming words. (roar/snore, cheep/Beep, squeak/creak, clang/Bang, ding/ring, drop/Stop)

Apreciada Familia:

En esta unidad se enseñarán los cinco sentidos y los sonidos de dos consonantes juntas. Ustedes pueden hacer estas actividades juntos en la casa.

• Con su niño pronuncien los nombres de los objetos en los cuadros. Escuchen los sonidos de las consonantes al principio de la palabra.

• Lea el poema "Ears Hear" en la página 261.

• Encuentren sonidos de dos consonantes juntas en el poema, tales como: **flies**, **snore**, **honk**, **trucks**, **clang**, **clocks**, **cry**, **ring**, **spoons**, **drop**, **scream** y **stop**.

• Después encuentren las palabras que riman. (roar/snore, cheep/Beep, squeak/creak, clang/Bang, ding/ring, drop/Stop)

PROJECT

Be very quiet, close your eyes for a short time, and listen carefully. Then make a list of sounds you heard in your home or outside. Also list the things that made the sounds. Circle any consonant blends you use.

tick tick tick tick

PROYECTO

Rápido cierren los ojos por poco tiempo y escuchen con cuidado. Luego hagan una lista de los sonidos que escucharon afuera y en la casa. Hagan una lista de lo que hizo el sonido y encierren en un círculo cuando aparezcan dos consonantes juntas.

262 LESSON 137: Consonant Blends—Phonics Alive at Home

Phonics Alive at Home

• The *Phonics Alive at Home* page provides activities so that families may share in their children's language progress. The Unit 5 page focuses on the unit theme, "Sensational Senses," and consonant blends.

• Have children remove page 262 from their books and take it home. Encourage them to complete the activities with family members and report back to you on those they enjoyed.

• Throughout the unit, set aside class time for children to share photos or drawings of sound makers that they bring in from home.

Sadlier Reading
Little Books and Big Books

Read several poems in *Mother Goose Through the Seasons* to listen for consonant blends.

Direct children to additional activities on Sadlier-Oxford's web site: www.sadlier-oxford.com.

Multicultural Connection

Explain to children that people in cultures all over the world enjoy using their sense of hearing while singing and making music. Lead children in singing popular folksongs from different cultures, such as "Frère Jacques" or "De Colores." If you are not familiar with such songs, check out a recording from a library. Print the English translation of the song on the board. Call attention to words with consonant blends as you read the translation.

Take-Home Book

The Take-Home Book for Unit 5, *Making Sense*, is found on student pages 331–332. This fold-up book reinforces the consonant blend phonics skills taught in this unit. Use this take-home component as a culminating activity for the unit or send the book home at another appropriate time.

Recognizing Initial l-Blends

Objectives
- To blend phonemes in a word
- To identify words with the same initial **l**-blend
- To sort words by initial blends

Warming Up

Reviewing Initial l
- Say **leaf**, and have children repeat it. Remind children that leaf begins with /**l**/. Have children drop their hands like falling leaves when they hear you say a word that begins with /**l**/. Say this poem:

  I **like** to **look** at **lions** in the zoo.

  I do! Do you?

  I **like leopards**, and **lizards**, too.

  I do! Do you?

Teaching the Lesson

Phonemic Awareness: Blend Phonemes in a Word
Tell children that words are made up of different sounds. Say the sounds /**fl**/-/**a**/-/**g**/ and then blend them to say **flag**. Then have children repeat after you. Continue in the same way with **plan**, **click**, **black**, and **globe**.

Sound to Symbol
- Say /**kl**/-**ean, clean**. Have children repeat after you. Explain to children that /**k**/ and /**l**/ together make /**kl**/. Say these sounds, and then have children repeat them and tell you the words they make: /**kl**/-**ock** (**clock**); /**pl**/-**ay** (**play**); /**bl**/-**ue** (**blue**).
- Explain to children that when two consonants appear together in a word, and you hear both sounds, the sounds you say together are called a blend.
- Write on the board, point to, and say these blends: **bl, cl, fl, gl,** and **pl**. Have children repeat after you. Then list **clock, globe, flutter, play,** and **blue** in a column. Read each word, and ask volunteers to write the words under the correct blend headings.

Play starts with the **l** blend **pl**. Listen for the sounds of **l** blends in the rhyme.

When I play ball, it's noisy.

I slide and the fans all clap.

But please be quiet now.

I'm going to take a nap.

In each row, circle and color each picture that has the same **l** blend at the beginning of its name as the picture in the box.

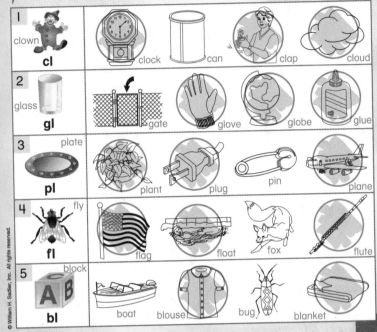

1 clown **cl**	clock	can	clap	cloud	
2 glass **gl**	gate	glove	globe	glue	
3 plate **pl**	plant	plug	pin	plane	
4 fly **fl**	flag	float	fox	flute	
5 block **bl**	boat	blouse	bug	blanket	

LESSON 138: Phonemic Awareness: Sounds of **l** Blends **263**

UNIVERSAL ACCESS
Meeting Individual Needs

Visual • Auditory
Materials: Sadlier Phonics Picture Cards for **fly, glass, plane, cloud**

Display the picture cards. Give hints to help children choose the correct cards.

I can hold juice. (**glass**)

I am in the sky when it rains. (**cloud**)

People fly in this. (**plane**)

I am an insect. (**fly**)

Auditory • Kinesthetic
Say **clap/lap**. Point out that you hear the blend /**kl**/ at the beginning of **clap**, but **lap** begins with /**l**/. Have children clap when they hear a word that begins with an **l**-blend and put their hands in their laps when a word does not. Say these words: **clown, lift, plant, pan, late, plate, flag, clock, back, black.**

Extra Support
Remind children that some words begin with a blend. Tell children to pick the words that begin with **l**-blends in order to answer these questions:

Do you wear a **love** or a **glove**?

What tells time, a **lock** or a **clock**?

Is this crayon **back** or **black**?

Blue, glue, plane, and flag begin with l blends. Color the pictures if their names begin with **bl** 🖍, **gl** 🖍, **pl** 🖍, **fl** 🖍.

bl	**gl**	**pl**	**fl**

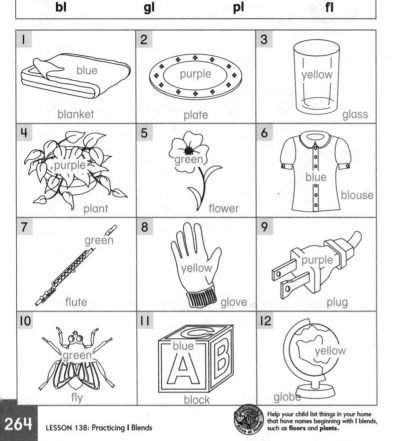

1 blue / blanket	2 purple / plate	3 yellow / glass
4 purple / plant	5 green / flower	6 blue / blouse
7 green / flute	8 yellow / glove	9 purple / plug
10 green / fly	11 blue / block	12 yellow / globe

264

LESSON 138: Practicing l Blends

 Help your child list things in your home that have names beginning with l blends, such as **floors** and **plants**.

Practicing the Skill

● Read aloud the instructions on top of page 263 before you read the rhyme. Help children name the pictures. Then read the directions for completing the page.

● Read aloud the directions on page 264. Have children color each picture with the correct color. Help children name the pictures.

Curriculum Connections

Spelling Connection

Read aloud each word and sentence below. Have a volunteer spell the word—either aloud, on the board, or with Punchout Letter Cards.

plop   **Plop** went the frog in the pond.
globe   A **globe** is a round map of the world.
plant   The **plant** has red flowers.

Theme Activity: Science/Art

Materials: chart paper

● Have children talk about their favorite sights and sounds of nature. List their favorites on chart paper. Include words with l-blends, such as **flowers**, **bluebirds**, **clover**, **plants**, **blossoms**, and **flamingoes**.

● Read aloud the theme book. Have children add any new l-blend words to the list.

● Ask children to draw a picture of a pond that includes animals and plants. Help children label objects that begin with l-blends.

Theme Book Fleming, Denise. *In the Small, Small Pond.* New York: Henry Holt, 1998. A glimpse of the sights and sounds at a pond.

Portfolio Have children add their pond pictures to their portfolios.

Sadlier Reading
Little Books and Big Books

Read *Stop by a Pond* (non-fiction) to learn more about who lives in a pond.

English Language Learners/ESL

Materials: a glass, a glove, a flag, a flower, a paper clip, clay, a plant, a plug, a block, and a blouse

Provide extra practice hearing words with l-blends. Hold up one item at a time, and give a clue, such as: *I use this to hold my papers together.* It is called a /**kl**/-/**i**/-/**p**/ *clip, a paper clip.* Have children say **clip**. Write **clip** on the board. Complete the activity using all objects.

Challenge

Materials: paper, pencils

Have children choose an l-blend and write it in very large letters on the left side of a sheet of paper. Ask them to make new words by listing as many phonograms as they can to the right of the blend (e.g., **fl: op, ip, ag, at, oat**). Have children illustrate two of the words.

Special Strategies

For Universal Access activities, see page 261F.

Writing I-Blends in Context

Objectives
- To add initial sounds
- To write words with **l-blends**
- To read words with **l-blends** in context

Warming Up

Reviewing c, g, p, f, b
- Write the consonants **c**, **g**, **p**, **f**, and **b** in columns on the board. Have children write or dictate a list of words with each initial sound. Then have children use the words in each list to tell a silly story.

Teaching the Lesson

Phonemic Awareness: Add Initial Sounds
Say the word **ate**. Tell children that they can make a new word by adding /**pl**/ before **ate**. Say /**pl**/-**ate**, **plate**, and have children repeat after you. Ask children what word can be made by adding /**sl**/ to **ate**. Have them repeat after you: /**sl**/-**ate**, **slate**. Repeat the process by having children add /**cr**/ and /**fl**/ to **ash** (**crash**, **flash**).

Phonics in Context
- Write this sentence on the board: I will play a tune for you on the ___. Write the words **floor**, **flute**, and **flow** next to the sentence. Read aloud the sentence and the word choices. Then read the sentence three times, each time filling in the blank with one of the word choices. Circle the word **flute**, and tell children that it best completes the sentence because it makes sense. Now have children complete this sentence: You use a ___ to tell time. (**clay**, **cloth**, **clock**)

Comprehension Skill: Making Generalizations

Say the name of each picture with a partner. Then circle the word and print it on the line.

1 <u>flat</u> fit feet → **flat**	2 bell bee <u>blue</u> → **blue**	3 cape <u>clap</u> cap → **clap**
4 back bake <u>block</u> → **block**	5 pine <u>plane</u> pan → **plane**	6 <u>flute</u> fell fin → **flute**
7 <u>club</u> cub cube → **club**	8 late pat <u>plate</u> → **plate**	9 <u>flag</u> frog fig → **flag**

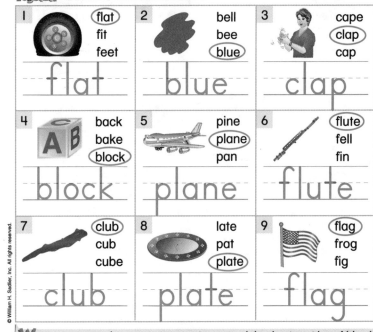

Write a sentence about one picture using a word that begins with an I blend.

Accept any sentence that contains an l-blend word.

UNIVERSAL ACCESS
Meeting Individual Needs

Auditory • Kinesthetic
Have children play Clarence Says. Tell them to follow directions only when a command includes an l-blend word. Give directions such as these:

Clarence says:
Blink your eyes.
Stamp your feet.
Flap your arms.
Jump.
Clap twice.

Visual • Tactile
Materials: index cards, masking tape

On a wall, affix two vertical strips of masking tape with the length of an index card between them. Have children search printed materials for initial l-blend words to print on index cards. Then tape the cards on the wall to form rungs on a ladder. Have children **"climb"** by reading each word from the bottom rung up.

Extra Support
Remind children that some words begin with two consonants to form a blend. Ask children to answer riddles with l-blends, such as: *Rhymes with **boat** and begins with fl* (**float**), *rhymes with **pack** and begins with bl* (**black**), *rhymes with **map** and begins with cl* (**clap**).

Our Senses

Hear the wind <u>blow</u>.
See the <u>blue</u> sky.
Hear the <u>clock</u> tick
And the loud, buzzing <u>fly</u>.

Feel the smooth <u>glass</u>.
Smell the sweet <u>flower</u>.
Hear the <u>plane</u> roar
As it <u>flies</u> by the tower.

1. What can you smell?

I can smell a sweet flower.

2. What can you feel?

I can feel the smooth glass.

266   LESSON 139: Words with l Blends in Context
Comprehension: Making Generalizations

Sit with your child and talk about what you hear, see, feel, smell, and taste. Write down any words that start with an l blend.

Practicing the Skill

● Read aloud the directions on page 265. Ask volunteers to identify the pictures. Together complete the first item. Before children write a sentence with a word that begins with an **l**-blend, remind them that the first word of a sentence begins with an uppercase letter and ends with a period.

● Recite the poem on page 266. Model the first item. Then have children complete the page individually or in pairs.

Curriculum Connections

Spelling Connection

Read aloud each word and sentence. Have a volunteer spell the word on the board and spell the word aloud.

fly	I hear a **fly** buzzing.
blink	The bright light made me **blink**.
glove	This **glove** keeps my hand warm.
flame	A **flame** is very hot.
clay	The **clay** feels lumpy.

Theme Activity: Language Arts

Materials: paper bag; objects with **l**-blend names, such as **block**, pipe **cleaner**, **clip**, **clay**, **cloth**, **flashlight**, **flower**, **glove**, toy **plane**, paper **plate**; index cards

● Place objects with **l**-blend names into a bag. Invite volunteers to reach in the bag and, without looking, touch one object and describe its characteristics without naming it. Have the class guess the object described.

● When children guess correctly, write the name of the object on the board. Beneath the name, list the words used to describe the object. Circle those that begin with **l**-blends.

● Have children use index cards to make a label for each object. Display labeled objects.

Sadlier Reading
Little Books and Big Books

Read *Why Coyote Howls at Night* (fiction) for more practice with initial consonant **l**-blends.

English Language Learners/ESL
Materials: sentence strips

Point to the **flag** in the classroom and say /fl/-/fl/-/fl/ **flag**. Tell children to listen for the **f** and the **l**. Write **flag** on the board and underline **fl**. Then **clap** your hands, point to words in the classroom that have an l-blend, and display pictures of words with l-blends to help children recognize l-blend words. Then display these fill-in sentences on sentence strips and read them with children: We _____ our hands. I play a _____. The _____ waves outside our school. Have children choose from the pictures on page 265 to complete the sentences. Invite volunteers to fill in the blanks with the l-blend words.

Challenge
Have children write phrases describing a spring day. Tell them to include l-blends in their sensory details (e.g., "clear blue sky," "sweet-smelling blooms," "the blowing wind," "soft, fluffy clouds"). Have children read their phrases aloud. Then have them select and illustrate a phrase.

Special Strategies
For Universal Access activities, see page 261F.

Recognizing Initial r-Blends

Objectives
- To blend phonemes in a word
- To identify words with the same initial **r**-blend
- To match words with the same initial **r**-blend

Warming Up

Reviewing Initial r
- Say **rabbit** and have children repeat the word. Remind children that **rabbit** starts with /**r**/.
- Say a word, and have children give a rhyming word that begins with /**r**/. For **sun**, children should respond **run**. Say these words: **bug**, **cake**, **pan**, **nice**, **lace**, **hope**.

Teaching the Lesson

Phonemic Awareness: Blend Phonemes in a Word
Materials: **Sadlier Phonics Picture Cards** for **drum**, **fruit**, **train**, and other **r**-blends

Display the picture cards. Model how to blend sounds in a word by holding up the **drum** card and saying each sound slowly: /**dr**/-/**u**/-/**m**/ **drum**. Continue with **fruit** and **train**. Have children name the other pictures and blend the sounds in each word.

Sound to Symbol
Say: /**fr**/-/**o**/-/**g**/ **frog**. Have children repeat after you. Remind children that two consonants that appear together are often consonant blends. Tell children that **r** often combines with another letter to make an **r**-blend. On the board write these words in two columns: **frog**, **grizzly**, **crow** and **caw**, **croak**, **growl**. One at a time, point to each word, say the word, and where possible underline the **r**-blend. Have children repeat the word and the **r**-blend. Have volunteers draw a line from an animal to its sound and underline the **r**-blends.

267

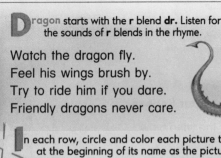

Dragon starts with the **r** blend **dr**. Listen for the sounds of **r** blends in the rhyme.

Watch the dragon fly.
Feel his wings brush by.
Try to ride him if you dare.
Friendly dragons never care.

In each row, circle and color each picture that has the same **r** blend at the beginning of its name as the picture in the box.

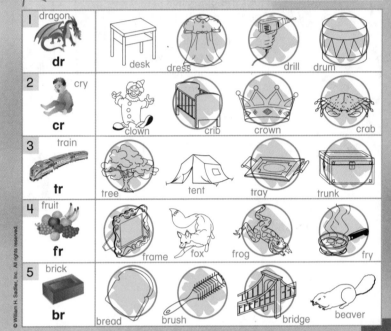

LESSON 140: Phonemic Awareness: Sounds of r Blends **267**

U N I V E R S A L A C C E S S
Meeting Individual Needs

Visual • Kinesthetic
Materials: index cards on which are printed **br, fr, tr, dr, ip, ain, y, im**

Distribute blend and word-ending cards. Have a child from each group stand at the front and hold up the group's cards. If the letters make a word, have the two children shake hands. Write the word on the board.

Auditory
Tell children they are going to go "grocery shopping" for **r**-blends. Ask them to call out, "What a treat!" when they hear a word that begins with an **r**-blend. Then name these foods: **bread, milk, fruit, grapes, meat, cranberries, chicken, gravy, pretzels, eggs, crackers.**

Extra Support
Help children recognize both initial consonant sounds in **r**-blend words. Say a word, and have children isolate the initial blend. Say **train**, and help children respond /**tr**/-**ain**. Then say other words such as **bring, crunch, grin, trick, tree, drop, grouch.**

Say the sound each **r** blend makes. Draw a line from each blend to the picture with a name that begins with that blend.

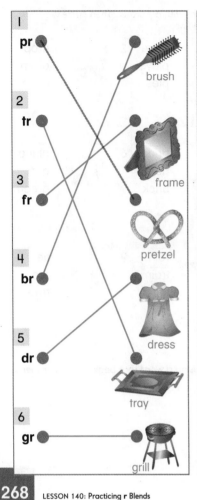

1 **pr**

2 **tr**

3 **fr**

4 **br**

5 **dr**

6 **gr**

brush

frame

pretzel

dress

tray

grill

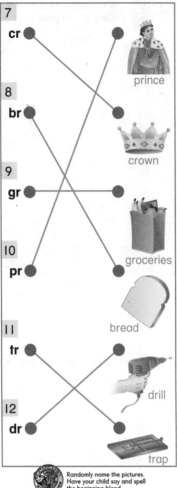

7 **cr**

8 **br**

9 **gr**

10 **pr**

11 **tr**

12 **dr**

prince

crown

groceries

bread

drill

trap

LESSON 140: Practicing r Blends

 Randomly name the pictures. Have your child say and spell the beginning blend.

● Read aloud the rhyme on page 267. Have the children identify the **r**-blend words as you reread it. Read aloud the directions. Talk about the dragon, and help children name the pictures. Have children complete the page.

● Make sure children understand the directions on page 268. Help children name the pictures before completing the page.

Curriculum Connections

Spelling Connection

Read aloud each word and sentence. Have a volunteer spell the word aloud, on the board, or with Punchout Letter Cards.

frog   We heard the **frog** croak.

drum   The **drum** made a loud noise.

grass   Mowed **grass** smells good.

Theme Activity: Language Arts/Art

Materials: chart paper

● Discuss sounds children might hear at night. Help them make a list of sounds, including words with **r**-blends (**crying** babies, **creaking** floors, **dripping** water, **trucks**, **traffic**).

● Read aloud the theme book. Have children listen for **r**-blend words to add to the list.

● Ask children which of the things that keep Owl awake also keep children awake. Ask children to draw something that keeps them awake, print a caption, and circle **r**-blend words.

Theme Book   Hutchins, Pat. *Good-Night, Owl!* New York: Aladdin, 1990. The day is too noisy for Owl to sleep, but at night he gets revenge.

Portfolio   Have children add their night pictures to their portfolios.

English Language Learners/ESL

Materials: **fruit, brick,** toy **train,** toy **dragon, frying** pan, **crown, drum, bread**

Display objects in front of the classroom. Hold up each object, identify it, stretch the word out, and say it again. Model: *This is a* **crown**. (You might want to wear the crown and point to it.) /kr/-/kr/-/kr/-ow-/n/-/n/-/n/ **crown**. Have children say the word after you. Then do the same for all the articles listed. You might also want to include any other objects in and around the classroom that begin with an **r**-blend. Label each of the items after children have identified them.

Special Strategies

For Universal Access activities, see page 261F.

Challenge

Materials: index cards, on which are printed the following **r**-blends: **cr, br, dr, fr, gr, pr, tr**

Have children choose a card and then list words that begin with the letters. Children may look through books for words. Have them try to use three or more of their words in a single sentence.

Sadlier Reading

Little Books and Big Books

Read *The Tongue Twister Prize* (fiction) for more practice with initial consonant **r**-blends.

Writing r-Blends in Context

Objectives

- To add initial sounds
- To write words with **r**-blends
- To read words with **r**-blends in context

Warming Up

Reviewing Rhyming Words

Ask children to identify rhyming words as you read aloud this poem:

My fuzzy kitten feels so soft.

Her face is black and white.

And even though she has sharp teeth,

She'd never, ever bite.

Teaching the Lesson

Phonemic Awareness: Add Initial Sounds

Review with children that we can add one or more beginning sounds to a word or word part to make a new word. Model an example by saying **an**, adding /**f**/ to the beginning of it, and then saying the whole word: **fan**. Repeat the procedure using /**kr**/ and the word part **ab** to make **crab**. Then have children form new words using the following: /**t**/ -**ime**, /**fr**/ -**og**, /**dr**/ -**ill**, and /**br**/ -**ick**.

Phonics in Context

Say the following rhyme:

A tree frog sits in a tall, green tree,

While rain drip-drops on a crab by the sea.

Ask children to listen for **r**-blends as you reread the rhyme, and to croak like a frog when they hear an **r**-blend word. Then write the rhyme on the board and have children read it with you. Point out that when two consonants appear together at the beginning of a word, they keep their own sounds to make a blend. Have children circle the **r**-blend in each **r**-blend word.

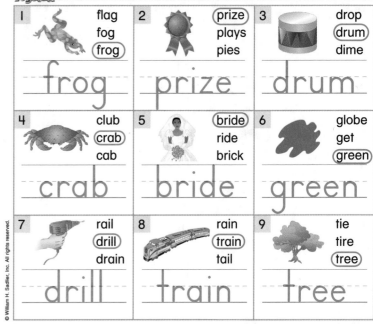

Say the name of each picture with a partner. Then circle the word and print it on the line.

1 flag / fog / (frog) frog	2 (prize) / plays / pies prize	3 drop / (drum) / dime drum
4 club / (crab) / cab crab	5 (bride) / ride / brick bride	6 globe / get / (green) green
7 rail / (drill) / drain drill	8 rain / (train) / tail train	9 tie / tire / (tree) tree

Write a sentence about one picture using a word that begins with an **r** blend.

Accept any sentence using an **r**-blend word shown above.

UNIVERSAL ACCESS
Meeting Individual Needs

Auditory • Kinesthetic

Have children stand in a line to form a train. Tell the "train" to move forward one step each time children hear a word that begins with an **r**-blend. Some words to use are: **track, grow, drop, bug, brook, crumb, prize, fun, boat,** and **breakfast**.

Visual • Kinesthetic

Materials: Punchout Letter Cards **r, b, c, d, f, g, p, t**

Say: *"The Three Billy Goats Gruff" is about three goats who face a troll before they cross a bridge.* Appoint a "troll." As each child approaches, the troll holds up an **r** and another letter. Children must say a word that begins with that blend.

Extra Support

Materials: Punchout Letter Cards **t, r, i, d, p, m, u**

Help children make the word **trim** with the cards. Help them use the cards to make new words as you say them slowly: **trip, drip, drum**.

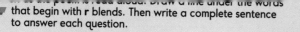

... that begin with **r** blends. Then write a complete sentence to answer each question.

Tasty <u>Treats</u>

I like the taste of <u>bread</u> and jam,
And <u>crunchy</u> <u>pretzels</u>, <u>fruit</u>, and ham,
Refried <u>frijoles</u>—tacos, too.
And I love <u>fresh</u>, <u>green</u> <u>grapes</u>, don't you?
And <u>frozen</u> yogurt—what a <u>treat</u>!
It's <u>great</u> to end with something sweet.

Sample sentences given.

1. Which of the treats are crunchy?

Pretzels are crunchy.

2. Which of the treats are sweet?

Frozen yogurt and
jam are sweet.

270
LESSON 141: Words with **r** Blends in Context
Comprehension: Classifying Objects

Help your child make a list of healthy treats. Have him or her circle any words that begin with **r** blends.

- Read aloud the directions on page 269, and help children identify the pictures. Do the first item with children. Read the direction at the bottom of the page so that partners can go on to write their sentences. Remind children that a sentence begins with a capital letter and ends with a period.
- Read aloud the directions and then the poem on page 270. Have children answer the questions orally before they write.

Curriculum Connections

Spelling Connection
Read aloud each word and sentence below. Have a volunteer spell the word aloud, on the board, or with Punchout Letter Cards.

trail	We can hike up the **trail**.
prize	Our team won a **prize**.
bride	The **bride** carried flowers.
crib	The baby sleeps in a **crib**.
from	Take a cookie **from** the jar.

Theme Activity: Science/Language Arts
Materials: bite-sized samples of different foods such as apples, carrots, pretzels, pickles, crackers, bread; paper napkins

(Note: Before beginning this activity, check to determine whether any children have allergies to any of the foods.)

- Wrap the food samples in paper napkins.
- Have children take turns closing their eyes and tasting one food sample. Ask each child to describe the food and to guess its name. Record on the board the descriptive comments and the food name. Review the words on the board, having children look for **r**-blend words.
- Help children realize that it is easier to name and describe food when it is seen as well as tasted. Help them understand that the five senses all work together.

English Language Learners/ESL
Materials: **pretzels, jam, grapes, yogurt, crackers, bread** (Check if any children have food allergies.)

Talk about how food tastes and different food textures to expand children's vocabulary. Have children sample a food item, and help children identify each. Talk about each item's taste and texture—salty, sweet, crunchy, smooth, dry, chewy, juicy, and so on. Write on the board all the words children use to describe the foods. Ask children about their favorite foods and encourage them to describe the taste and texture of those foods.

Challenge
Materials: paper plates, markers

Have children draw on a paper plate some foods that begin with **r**-blends. Ask children to print the name of each food. Have children show their plates and describe the taste, smell, and feel of the foods.

Special Strategies
For Universal Access activities, see page 261F.

Observational Assessment

Watch to see that children identify each letter as they read each food name.

Student Pages 271–272

Recognizing and Practicing Initial s-Blends

Objectives
- To blend phonemes in a word
- To blend words with initial **s**-blends
- To sort words by their initial blends

Warming Up

Reviewing Initial Consonant s
Remind children that **seal** begins with /s/. Have them clap like a seal, keeping their arms straight, each time they hear an **s** word in this story:

I like to **see seals** at the zoo. They beg for **some** fish. They **sit** in the warm **sun**.

★ Teaching the Lesson

Phonemic Awareness:
Blend Phonemes in a Word
Materials: **Sadlier Phonics Picture Cards** for **sled, smell, sky, spray, strawberry**, and other **s**-blend words

Display the picture cards. Model blending by holding up the **sled** card and saying slowly /sl/-/e/-/d/ **sled**. Continue with /sm/-/e/-/l/ **smell** and /spr/-/ay/ **spray**. Have children name the other pictures and blend the sounds in each word.

Sound to Symbol
- Say /sk/-ate **skate**. Have children repeat after you. Explain that **skate** begins with two consonant sounds blended together, /sk/. Write **skate** on the board and underline the **sk**. Review that two or three consonant sounds blended together are called a *consonant blend*. Then have children repeat these sounds and tell you the word they make: /sn/-/ail/, /skw/-/eak/, /sk/-/ared/, /spr/-/ing/.
- Write on the board **skate, snail, squeak, scared, spring**. Read them with children and have volunteers underline the consonant blend in each word.

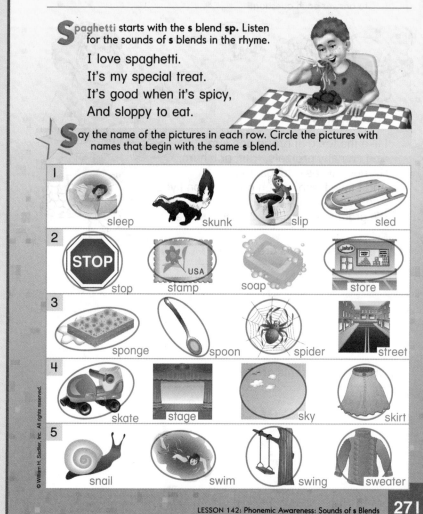

Spaghetti starts with the **s** blend **sp.** Listen for the sounds of **s** blends in the rhyme.

I love spaghetti.
It's my special treat.
It's good when it's spicy,
And sloppy to eat.

Say the name of the pictures in each row. Circle the pictures with names that begin with the same **s** blend.

1	sleep	skunk	slip	sled
2	stop	stamp	soap	store
3	sponge	spoon	spider	street
4	skate	stage	sky	skirt
5	snail	swim	swing	sweater

LESSON 142: Phonemic Awareness: Sounds of s Blends

271

UNIVERSAL ACCESS
Meeting Individual Needs

Visual • Kinesthetic
Materials: eight Sadlier Phonics Picture Cards for **s**-blend words and eight other cards with names that do not begin with blends

Mix up the cards. Hold up one card at a time, and have children touch their noses only if the picture begins with an **s**-blend.

Visual • Kinesthetic
Materials: Sadlier Phonics Picture Cards for **s**-blends

Write these **s**-blends on the board: **sk, st, scr, squ, sm, sl, sn, sp, spr, str, sw.** Display the picture cards. Have children select a picture, say its name, and place it on the chalk ledge under the appropriate blend.

Extra Support
Materials: Sadlier Phonics Picture Cards for **snow, smoke,** and other **s**-blend words

Display cards. Hold up the **snow** card and remind children that **snow** begins with /sn/. Have volunteers name the pictures. Write the words on the board and underline the blends.

Say the name of each picture. Circle the letters that stand for the beginning **s** blend in the picture name.

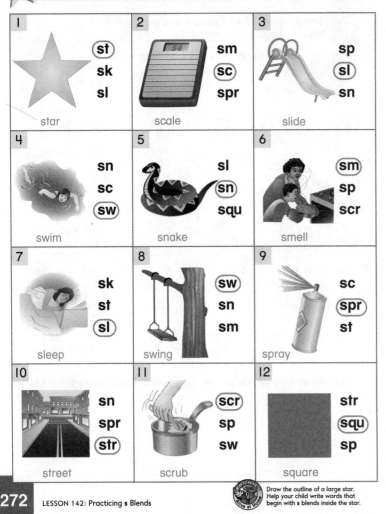

1 ⟨st⟩ sk sl — star	**2** sm ⟨sc⟩ spr — scale	**3** sp ⟨sl⟩ sn — slide
4 sn sc ⟨sw⟩ — swim	**5** sl ⟨sn⟩ squ — snake	**6** ⟨sm⟩ sp scr — smell
7 sk st ⟨sl⟩ — sleep	**8** ⟨sw⟩ sn sm — swing	**9** sc ⟨spr⟩ st — spray
10 sn spr ⟨str⟩ — street	**11** ⟨scr⟩ sp sw — scrub	**12** str ⟨squ⟩ sp — square

272

LESSON 142: Practicing **s** Blends

- Read aloud the rhyme directions on page 271. Help children name the pictures, and then have them complete the page.
- Read aloud the directions on page 272. Be sure children can name the pictures before having them complete the page.

Curriculum Connections

Spelling Connection

Read aloud each word and sentence. Have a volunteer spell the word aloud, on the board, or with Punchout Letter Cards.

sniff We can **sniff** the flowers.

skin The wind was cold on my **skin**.

slice Mom can **slice** the apple.

smell Do you **smell** the skunk?

snug My new coat is **snug** and warm.

Theme Activity: Science

- Tell children that crocodiles are reptiles that live in swampy regions and are able to swim and stay under water for a long time. Display and talk about the cover of the theme book. Ask children to predict how other animals might deal with a mean crocodile. Then establish a slow, steady clapping beat. Read aloud the theme book to the clapping rhythm, and encourage children to clap along.
- Direct children to listen for initial **s**-blend words as you read the book again. Help them identify **sleeps**, **splash**, **screech**, **swoop**, **swish**, **snake**, **stomping**, and **snap**.
- *Crocodile Beat* lends itself to dramatization. Help children choreograph and practice movements for a choral reading.

Theme Book

Jorgense, Gail, and Patricia Mullins. *Crocodile Beat*. New York: Bradbury Press, 1989. Animals outwit a mean crocodile; children keep the beat.

English Language Learners/ESL

Materials: **stamps, stickers**, a **stool**, pictures of a **stop sign, sled, snake**

Some children might have difficulty pronouncing initial **s**-blends. Point to objects in the classroom such as **stamps, stickers**, a **stool**, and so on. As you point to each item say the word, stretch out the word, and say the word again. Have children repeat these steps. Model how your mouth makes the two sounds that form each of the **s**-blends. Use other examples of the **s**-blend to help children increase vocabulary and pronounce words correctly. Again model for children how to form their mouths as they say different words: **shut, shout**. Display a list of all the words in the Reading Center.

Challenge

Materials: Sadlier Phonics Picture Cards for **s**-blends and other cards

List the five senses on the board: taste, touch, sight, smell, and sound. Have children work in small groups. Ask each group to use the picture cards to make a list of words that are associated with each of the five senses. Tell the groups to find as many **s**-blend words as possible.

Special Strategies

For Universal Access activities, see page 261F.

Observational Assessment

As children sound out words with consonant blends, notice whether they include all the consonant sounds.

Student Pages 273–274

Recognizing s-Blends

Objectives
- To add initial sounds
- To write words with **s**-blends
- To read words with **s**-blends in context

Warming Up

Reviewing Initial l- and r-Blends
Materials: squares of blue and brown paper;
Unit 5 Classroom Poster

Write the words **blue** and **brown** on the board. Help children identify the consonants that form the blend in each word. Distribute blue and brown squares. Read "Ears Hear" from the poster. Have children hold up a blue square when they hear an **l**-blend word and a brown square when they hear an **r**-blend word.

Teaching the Lesson

Phonemic Awareness: Add Initial Sounds
Say **age**, and have children repeat after you. Tell them that they can make a new word by adding /**p**/ to the beginning of **age**, to make /**p**/-age **page**. Ask children to add /**r**/, /**c**/, /**w**/, and /**st**/ to **age** to make new words. (**rage, cage, wage, stage**)

Phonics in Context
- Write this sentence on the board: The long ___ showed its fangs. Write the words **star**, **snake**, and **spray** next to the sentence. Read aloud the sentence and the word choices. Then read the sentence three times, each time filling in the blank with one of the word choices. Circle the word **snake**, and tell children that it best completes the sentence.
- Have children complete this sentence: The ___ moved back and forth. (**spill, star, swing**)

Say the name of each picture with a partner. Then circle the word and print it on the line.

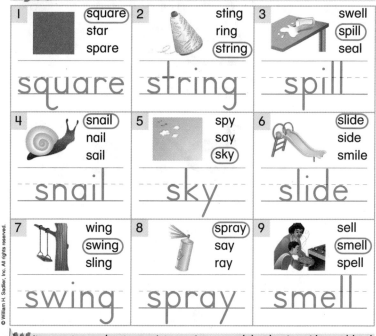

1	square / star / spare	square
2	sting / ring / string	string
3	swell / spill / seal	spill
4	snail / nail / sail	snail
5	spy / say / sky	sky
6	slide / side / smile	slide
7	wing / swing / sling	swing
8	spray / say / ray	spray
9	sell / smell / spell	smell

Write a sentence about one picture using a word that begins with an **s** blend.

Accept any answer that contains an **s**-blend word.

UNIVERSAL ACCESS
Meeting Individual Needs

Auditory • Kinesthetic
Have children put their heads on their desks. Direct them to "snap awake" by sitting up when they hear a word with an **s**-blend. Slowly say words such as **spider, glass, summer, smile, wing, start, lock, sport, try, name, scare, bug, sleep.**

Visual • Tactile
Materials: cardboard, glue

Have children pick an **s**-blend (**sk, st, str, sm, sl, sn, sp, spr, sw**) and name a word beginning with that blend. Have them print the word on cardboard and go over the letters with glue. When the letters dry, have children exchange papers and trace the letters with their fingers as they spell the words aloud.

Extra Support
Review that the blend **st** stands for /**st**/ as in **stove**. Ask children to change the initial sound in the following words to /**st**/ and say the new word: **pool** (changes to **stool**), **bar** (changes to **star**), **mop** (changes to **stop**), **far** (changes to **star**).

Listen as the story is read aloud. Draw a line under the words that begin with **s** blends. Then use words that begin with **s** blends to complete the sentences.

A Scarecrow Speaks

I like to <u>stand</u> in one <u>spot</u>.
I see <u>spiders</u> <u>spin</u> webs.
I hear the gate <u>squeak</u>.
Sometimes I <u>sneak</u> a <u>sweet</u> <u>strawberry</u>.
Some days rain <u>sprinkles</u> on me.
I like what I see, hear, taste, feel, and <u>smell</u>.
Oh, no! I do not like it now!
A <u>smelly</u> <u>skunk</u> is <u>strolling</u> my way.
<u>Stop</u>, <u>skunk</u>, <u>stop</u>!

1. The scarecrow sees spiders ____spin____ webs.

2. The scarecrow hears the gate ____squeak____.

3. The scarecrow sneaks a ____sweet____ strawberry.

4. The scarecrow will not like the ____smell____ of a skunk.

274

LESSON 143: Words with **s** Blends in Context
Comprehension: Making Predictions

Have your child draw a picture of a scarecrow. Talk about the things you would use to make it.

Practicing the Skill

- Read aloud the directions on page 273. Help children name the pictures. Then have them complete the page. Remind children that sentences always begin with an uppercase letter and end with a period.
- Read aloud the directions and story on page 274. Then read the sentences at the bottom of the page. Have children use **s**-blend words to complete each sentence.

Curriculum Connections

Spelling Connection
Read aloud each word and sentence below. Have a volunteer spell the word aloud or print it on the board.

snap	Can you **snap** your fingers?
speak	We **speak** softly at the library.
step	Don't **step** in the mud.
skip	Casey can **skip** very fast.
slip	Try not to **slip** and fall.

Theme Activity: Language Arts/Art
Materials: index cards

- Remind children of the five senses: sight, hearing, touch, taste, and smell. On index cards, print phrases about using each of the senses. Include words with **s**-blends (e.g., see a **snake/spider**, hear a **scream/snore**, feel something **smooth/scratchy**, taste something **sweet**, smell a **skunk**).
- Read the phrases aloud. Then have children choose a phrase to illustrate. Ask them to print the phrase as a caption under the picture. Bind the pictures into a class book entitled "Using Our Senses."

Sadlier Reading
Little Books and Big Books
Read *Ah-choo!* (fiction) for more practice with initial consonant **s**-blends.

Observational Assessment

As children pronounce words with consonant blends, listen to be sure they include all the consonant sounds.

English Language Learners/ESL
Materials: pictures of scarecrows, spiders, strawberries, skunk, crow

First show pictures of a scarecrow and tell children how it is made and what it is used for. Break apart the compound word **scare + crow = scarecrow** to help children understand the meaning. Tell children that the **scarecrow** was meant to **scare** away **crows** from eating anything in a garden. Show a picture of a **crow**. Have children say the word. Help children practice **s**-blend words in the poem on page 274. Use the pictures to identify a **spider**, a **strawberry**, and a **skunk**. Use TPR to demonstrate the following for children: **standing** in one spot, chalk **squeaking**, and so on.

Special Strategies
For Universal Access activities, see page 261F.

Challenge
Materials: large index cards

Have children use their five senses to describe a park scene. Children may describe the sights and sounds of people having fun, the smells and tastes of food, and the feel of things in nature. Tell children to create a postcard of the scene by drawing a picture on one side of an index card and writing a message on the back. Have children use **s**-blend words in their messages.

Recognizing and Writing Final Blends

Objectives

- To blend phonemes in a word
- To identify and write final blends in words

Warming Up

Reviewing Final Consonants

Materials: Punchout Letter Cards **b, d, l, n, p, t, s**

Display the letters. Tell children to listen for the ending sound as you say some words such as **rub, head, ball, pen, top, cut, glass**. After each word have a volunteer hold up the letter that stands for the last sound.

Teaching the Lesson

Phonemic Awareness: Blend Phonemes in a Word

Materials: **Sadlier Phonics Picture Cards** for **king, mask, nest**; three counters

Display the picture cards. Remind children that to say each picture name, we blend together the sounds in the word. Move three counters, one at a time, as you say /**k**/-/**i**/-/**ng**/. Then bring the counters together as you say **king**. Have children use counters to repeat what you said and did. Ask a child to point to the appropriate picture card. Repeat for **mask** /**m**/-/**a**/-/**sk**/ and **nest** /**n**/-/**e**/-/**st**/.

Sound to Symbol

Remind children that blended sounds can come at the end of a word. Say **king**, and have children repeat after you. Explain that the letters **n** and **g** heard at the end of **king** stand for the ending sound /**ng**/. Write this sentence on the board: Sing a song to the king. Have children repeat each **ng** word as volunteers underline the letters that stand for the final /**ng**/.

Band ends with the blend **nd**. **R**ing ends with the blend **ng**. Other blends can end words, too. Listen for final blends in the rhyme.

Listen to the band.
Hear the music ring.
Give the band a hand.
Then join in and sing.

Say the name of each picture. Circle the letters that stand for the final blend in each picture name.

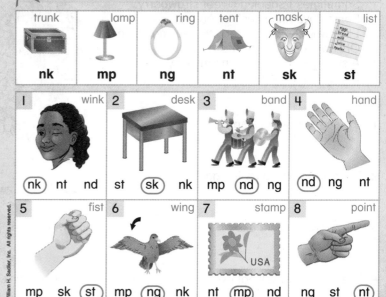

trunk	lamp	ring	tent	mask	list
nk	**mp**	**ng**	**nt**	**sk**	**st**

1 wink	2 desk	3 band	4 hand
(nk) nt nd	st (sk) nk	mp (nd) ng	(nd) ng nt

5 fist	6 wing	7 stamp	8 point
mp sk (st)	mp (ng) nk	nt (mp) nd	ng st (nt)

LESSON 144: Phonemic Awareness: Sounds of Final Blends

275

UNIVERSAL ACCESS
Meeting Individual Needs

Auditory • Kinesthetic

Materials: Sadlier Phonics Picture Cards for **band, desk, lamp, list, ring, sink**

Have children pick a card and say only the ending blend. Then children get their classmates to guess the word by pantomiming actions related to the word.

Auditory • Kinesthetic

Materials: Sadlier Phonics Picture Cards for **band, desk, giant, lamp**

Place one card on each side of the room. Have children stand. Ask them to turn to face the picture that ends with the same sound as each word you say: **hand, plant, stamp, task, hunt, stump, grand, mask, hump, hint, land**.

Extra Support

Materials: index cards

Ask children to write the blends **mp, nt, nk, ng, st, nd** on index cards. Have children hold up the appropriate card representing the final blend for each of the following words: **mist, land, mink, damp, sing, dent**.

Say the name of each picture with a partner. Then circle the word and print it on the line.

1	hint had (hand)	2	kiss (king) cone	3	(desk) dime dent
	hand		king		desk

4	win (wink) wig	5	(tent) team ten	6	let (list) lid
	wink		tent		list

7	land lime (lamp)	8	mist (mask) make	9	(band) bad bat
	lamp		mask		band

 Write a sentence about one picture using a word that ends with a blend.

Accept any answer that contains a blend.

_____

_____

LESSON 144: Writing Final Blends

Help your child write words that rhyme with some of the picture names. Circle the final blend in each word.

Practicing the Skill

● Read aloud the directions on page 275, identify the pictures together, and read the rhyme. Go over the first item before having children complete the page.

● Read aloud the directions on page 276. Have children name the pictures. Before children write a sentence with a word that ends in a blend, remind them that sentences always begin with an uppercase letter and end with a period. Then have children complete the page.

Curriculum Connections

Spelling Connection

Read aloud each word and sentence. Have a volunteer spell the word aloud or print it on the board.

nest The bird made a strong **nest**.

wing What color is the bird's **wing**?

tent We went camping in a **tent**.

list I have the grocery **list**.

Computer Connection

Have children use Reading Robot's video studio in Sound It Out Land 2™ (Conexus). Have them listen to the Robot Blend song. Then have them match a picture with the word the robot displays.

Theme Activity: Language Arts

● Discuss what children know about snow—how it feels, sounds, and looks.

● Display the theme book cover, and have children predict what might happen in the story. Read the book aloud. Ask what the boy and dog saw, heard, and felt.

● Reread the book, and have children listen for words with final blends.

● Ask children to illustrate a snowy day and write a caption for their pictures that includes a final blend.

 Theme Book

Shulevitz, Uri. *Snow*. New York: Farrar, Strauss, and Giroux, 1999. Celebrates the joy of a boy and a dog as snow blankets the city.

English Language Learners/ESL

Materials: word cards for **ant, bunk, lamp, ring**

Help children see that consonant blends can appear at the beginning as well as the end of words. Write **plant, skunk, stamp,** and **string** on the board. Have volunteers circle each initial blend and say it. Then point out that there are also two consonants next to each other at the end of each word. Circle those blends using a different colored chalk, and help children say each word emphasizing each final blend. Hand out the word cards, and have children write their word on the board next to the word with which it rhymes.

Challenge

Have children use the words **first, best,** and **last** to describe sensory experiences. Children might use sentence starters such as these: "The first thing I saw today was ___." "The best thing I ate today was ___." "The last thing I heard today was ___." Have children circle any final blend words they used.

Special Strategies

For Universal Access activities, see page 261F.

Connecting Spelling, Writing, and Speaking

Objectives
- To match words in spoken sentences
- To say, spell, sort, and write words with consonant blends
- To write a thank-you note using spelling words

★ Teaching the Lesson

Phonemic Awareness:
Match Words in Spoken Sentences

Tell children that you will say a word. Then ask children to listen for that word in a sentence and clap when they hear it. Model the process with a volunteer. Use these words and sentences:

snap	Can you **snap** your fingers?
please	Always say **please** and thank you.
slip	You might **slip** on an icy walk.
glass	Pour the milk into the **glass**.
clock	The **clock** tells the right time.

Spelling

- On the board write: Blue is the color of the summer sky. Have children read the sentence with you, and then have a volunteer underline the word that begins with an **l**-blend. (**blue**) Have children say, spell, and repeat the word.
- Write each spelling word from page 277 on the board. Tell children to say, spell, and say again each word. Have volunteers underline the beginning or ending blend in each word.
- Have children use each spelling word to ask a question, such as "What is blue?" or "What foods can you cook on a grill?"

Practicing the Skill

Read aloud the directions on page 277. Have children read the spelling words before they complete the page. Be sure children understand how to name and sort the blends.

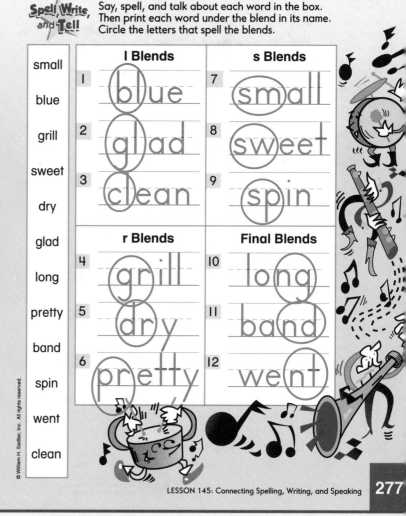

Spell, Write, and Tell

Say, spell, and talk about each word in the box. Then print each word under the blend in its name. Circle the letters that spell the blends.

| small | blue | grill | sweet | dry | glad | long | pretty | band | spin | went | clean |

l Blends
1 blue
2 glad
3 clean

s Blends
7 small
8 sweet
9 spin

r Blends
4 grill
5 dry
6 pretty

Final Blends
10 long
11 band
12 went

LESSON 145: Connecting Spelling, Writing, and Speaking

277

UNIVERSAL ACCESS
Meeting Individual Needs

Kinesthetic • Visual
Materials: index cards

Have children work in groups. Tell each group to write each of the spelling words from page 277 on a card. Then have them sort the cards into any groups they choose. Ask each group to explain its categories.

Visual • Kinesthetic
Materials: cards, scissors, envelopes

Write each spelling word from page 277 on a card, and then cut each card into individual letters. Place the letters for each word into a separate envelope, and lightly write the word inside the flap. Have children choose an envelope and unscramble the letters to spell the word.

Extra Support
Display Sadlier Phonics Picture Cards for **block, clap, band, lamp, drum**

Write the picture names on the board, with a blank for each blend. As children name the pictures, fill in the blend that completes each word. Have volunteers underline the blends.

Spell, Write, and Tell Write a note to thank a friend for a great party. Use some of your spelling words. Then tell about what you wrote.

| small | grill | dry | long | band | went |
| blue | sweet | glad | pretty | spin | clean |

Dear _____,

You may want to list word combinations or phrases that include spelling words. The following are examples:

clean grill   sweet cupcake
pretty balloons   long time
small table   great band

Your friend,

LESSON 145: Connecting Spelling, Writing, and Speaking

Help your child write and mail or e-mail a note to a friend or relative.

The Writing Process

Read aloud the directions on page 278. Tell children to pretend they went to a party, and ask them to write a thank-you note.

Brainstorm Talk with children about the parties they have attended. Ask them what they liked best about the parties. List their responses on the board. Model writing a thank-you note. Include how to write a greeting, such as "Dear Betsy," and the closing, such as "Your friend, Josh."

Write Distribute paper, and ask children to write a first draft of a thank-you note. Remind them to try to use some of the spelling words in the note.

Revise Have children reread their sentences to be sure their thank-you notes say what they want them to say before copying them onto the page. Then tell children to check that each of their sentences begins with an uppercase letter and ends with a period and check that their spelling is correct.

Publish Have children copy their thank-you notes onto page 278 and underline the spelling words they used.

Speak Have children read aloud their thank-you notes to classmates.

Extending the Skills

Model how to address an envelope. Help children address an envelope to a friend. You might invent an address for children to use.

Portfolio Have children add their thank-you notes to their portfolios.

English Language Learners/ESL
To help children complete the writing task on page 278, review the meaning of each spelling word with pantomime and/or pictures. Then ask which words have something to do with a party, and have children think of sentences that use those words. Begin by modeling an example such as: *At the party, I cooked lots of hot dogs on the grill.* Then help children think of sentences using some of the other words in the context of a party, for example: *The pretty cake had blue icing.*

Challenge
Draw a railroad track across the board. Then move a cutout train along the track. Tell children to pretend they are on a little train through a very big supermarket. Have them write sentences describing what they see, hear, taste, touch, and smell. Tell children to use consonant blends in their descriptions. Then as children read their descriptions, draw objects along the track to illustrate children's details.

Special Strategies
For Universal Access activities, see page 261F.

Observational Assessment
Observe which children have difficulty using the spelling words in oral and written sentences, as well as those who have difficulty sorting and spelling words with l-, s-, r- blends and final blends.

Integrating the Language Arts

Objectives
- To combine syllables to form words
- To use oral and written language to extend the theme concept
- To demonstrate recognition of words with consonant blends in context

Teaching the Lesson

Phonemic Awareness: Combine Syllables to Form Words

Remind children that words can be made up of one or more syllables and that a syllable is a word or word part with one vowel sound. Then tell children you will say some words. Hold your fists together and say **peanut**. Move your fists apart and say **pea-nut**. Put your fists back together and say **peanut**. Repeat the process and have children do it with you. Use these words:

pick-le	pop-corn	gro-cer
pen-cil	sand-wich	drag-on

Skills in Context

- Have children look at the pictures on page 279 and name things they can taste, see, hear, smell, and feel.
- Read aloud the text. Discuss what game is being played. Ask what other sounds, sights, smells, or tastes children might experience at a ball game.
- Challenge children to find the words containing blends in the text. (**smell**, **green**, **blue**, **pretend**, **crowd**, **smooth**, **crunchy**, **drink**, **try**)

Comprehension Skill: Classifying Objects

Name the following: a crowd cheering, a baseball mitt, home plate, music playing. Ask which of these can you hear at a baseball game.

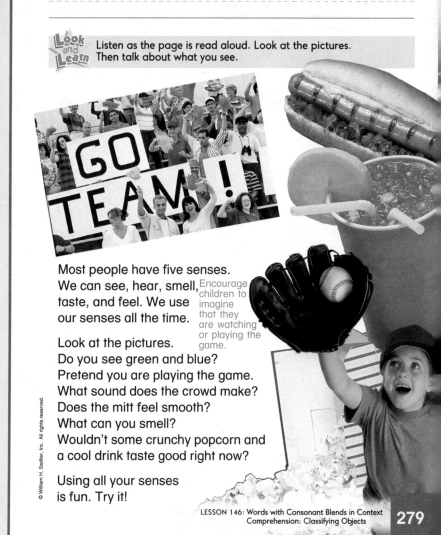

Look and Learn Listen as the page is read aloud. Look at the pictures. Then talk about what you see.

Most people have five senses. We can see, hear, smell, taste, and feel. We use our senses all the time.

Encourage children to imagine that they are watching or playing the game.

Look at the pictures.
Do you see green and blue?
Pretend you are playing the game.
What sound does the crowd make?
Does the mitt feel smooth?
What can you smell?
Wouldn't some crunchy popcorn and a cool drink taste good right now?

Using all your senses is fun. Try it!

LESSON 146: Words with Consonant Blends in Context
Comprehension: Classifying Objects
279

UNIVERSAL ACCESS
Meeting Individual Needs

Reading and Writing Connection
Materials: paper, pencils

Have children work in four groups and assign each group a sense: sight, sound, smell, touch. Ask each group to observe the classroom and contribute to a list of things they find in the room that relate to their sense. Have children share their ideas as one group member jots them down.

Have the groups use their notes to write several sentences that describe the classroom. Ask each group to read their sentences aloud. Collect the pages into a book for the class to share.

Science Connection
Materials: paper bags, objects of different textures, paper, pencils

Collect ten objects with different textures, such as sandpaper, a silk scarf, a wool mitten, an orange, a stuffed animal, a plastic baggie, a rubber toy, and a wood block. Place each object in a paper bag.

Have children number a sheet of paper from 1 to 10. Have them reach into each bag and examine the object using only their sense of touch. On their paper, have them describe how each object feels. Then reveal the objects and have children read their words.

Ready to Read

The words in the box are often used in sentences. Use one of the words to complete each sentence. Then practice reading the sentences aloud.

| again | ate | big | Look | to | yellow |

1. Glen and Brad rode a bus _____to_____ the .
   city

2. Brad said, "I see a _____big_____ ."
   skyscraper

3. Glen said, "I see a _____yellow_____ ."
   cab

4. Glen said, "_____Look_____ at the ."
   store

5. Brad said, "I _____ate_____ a ."
   pretzel

6. Glen and Brad will ride the bus _____again_____ .

LESSON 147: Reading High-Frequency Words

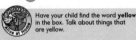 Have your child find the word **yellow** in the box. Talk about things that are yellow.

Extra Practice

Materials: index cards, container

Write the words **again, ate, big, look, to,** and **yellow** on index cards, and place the cards in a container. Have children stand in a circle and pass the container from child to child until you say "stop." The child holding the container er should select a card, read aloud the word, spell it for the group, and use it in a sentence. Return the card to the container, shake it, and continue the process.

Review

Materials: index cards

Write the words **stop, jump, please,** and **and** on index cards. Hold up each card, read it aloud, and have the class repeat it after you. Then place the cards face down in a pile. Have children take turns selecting a card, reading the word, and spelling it. Ask children to identify the consonant blend in each word. (**stop/st**), (**jump/mp**), (**please/pl**), (**and/nd**) Then have children try to make up a sentence that uses at least two of the words. For example, they may say: **Please stop** running. I like to **jump and** skip.

High-Frequency Words

Objectives

- To recognize and read high-frequency words
- To write high-frequency words to complete sentences

Teaching the Lesson

Materials: sentence strips, index cards

- Write the word **again** on the board. Point to the word, say it, spell it, and say the word again. Have children repeat after you and then trace the word in the air. Repeat the process with the words **ate**, **big**, **look**, **to**, and **yellow**.

- Write these sentences on sentence strips:
  Tom went _____ school.
  He rode on a small _____ bus.
  He likes to _____ out the window.
  His mom made him a _____ lunch.
  Tom said, "I _____ my lunch."
  After class, Tom went home _____.

Write **again**, **ate**, **big**, **look**, **to**, and **yellow** on index cards. Place the cards and the strips face down in piles. Have children take turns choosing one strip and one card. They should read aloud the sentence (provide help as needed) and insert the chosen word. Point out to children that quotation marks are placed around words someone speaks. Then have them tell whether the sentence makes sense. If it does, remove the sentence and word from the pile. If not, have the child continue picking words until he or she picks the correct word.

Practicing the Skill

Read aloud the directions at the top of page 280. Ask volunteers to read the words in the box. Be sure children can read the sentences and identify the rebus pictures before they complete the page.

Reviewing and Assessing Initial and Final Blends

Objectives
- To use words with consonant blends to complete a puzzle
- To write words with consonant blends

Warming Up

Reviewing Initial Consonants

Say /t/-aste and /t/-ouch. Tell children that both words have the same initial consonant sound, /t/, the sound of **t**. On the board print this poem, leaving blanks for the letters in parentheses:

"Bow (**w**)ow," (**b**)arked the big brown dog.

It was so (**l**)oud, it scared the frog.

The frog (**d**)ove in the deep blue stream.

"Wow!" (**h**)e said. "That dog is (**m**)ean!"

He (**s**)aw his lily (**p**)ad. "I think it would be best,

To (**j**)ust (**g**)o there and rest!"

Read the poem aloud and have children print the letters to complete the poem.

Teaching the Lesson

- Remind children that some words begin or end with two consonant sounds blended together. Tell them **smell** begins with the **s**-blend /**sm**/. Point out that some words end with blends as with /**sk**/ in **mask**. Return to the rhyme from *Warming Up*, and have children name the words with blends and tell whether the blend is an initial **l**-, **r**-, or **s**-blend or a final blend.
- Read aloud the directions on page 281. Point out how the numbers indicate where to print the words. Together identify the pictures and do item 1 together. Then have children complete the puzzle.

Use the picture clues to fill in the puzzle.
Print one letter in each box.

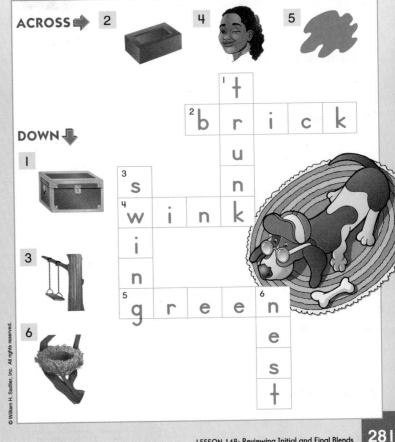

ACROSS ➡ 2   4   5

DOWN ⬇ 1

LESSON 148: Reviewing Initial and Final Blends   **281**

U N I V E R S A L   A C C E S S
Reteaching Activities

Activity 1

Materials: star cutouts, magazines, glue, scissors

Remind children that the word **print** begins with the **r**-blend /**pr**/. Tell them that **find** ends with the blend /**nd**/. Have children work in pairs. Give each pair two stars: one labeled with an initial blend, the other with a final blend. Have partners cut from magazines words with their assigned blends. Instruct them to glue the words onto the appropriate star. Have pairs share their stars with the class.

Activity 2

Materials: adding-machine tape

Say the words **plane** and **list** and point out the initial and final blends. Then tell children they will make a **list** of words with blends. Give rolls of adding-machine tape to groups of children. Have them skim classroom reading materials for words with initial or final blends. Direct them to unroll the tape, print on it the words they find, and then reroll the tape. Have groups take turns unrolling one another's tapes and reading the list of words.

Say the name of each picture. Print the letters that stand for the missing blend on the lines.

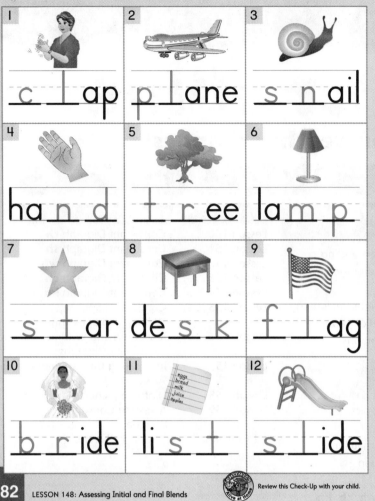

1 c l ap	2 p l ane	3 s n ail
4 ha n d	5 t r ee	6 la m p
7 s t ar	8 de s k	9 f l ag
10 b r ide	11 li s t	12 s l ide

LESSON 148: Assessing Initial and Final Blends

Review this Check-Up with your child.

Guided Instruction

Skills	Resources
l-blends	Instruction on pages 263–266
r-blends	Instruction on pages 267–270
s-blends	Instruction on pages 271–274
Final blends	Instruction on pages 275–276
Initial and Final blends	Phonemic Awareness Activities on pages 261H–261I Game Time on pages 261K–261M Punchout Cards on page 261N Technology on pages 261O–261P Take-Home Book *Making Sense*

Assessing the Unit

Check-Up Explain to children that cooks often blend two or more ingredients together, just as we often put two consonants together to form a blend. Direct children to make a stirring motion with their hands when they hear you say a word with an initial or final blend. Say **block**, **cat**, **desk**, **clap**, **zoo**, **wind**, **toy**, **swim**. Then have children turn to page 282. Read aloud the directions and have volunteers identify each picture. Finally, instruct children to complete the page.

Observational Assessment Use notes taken during your teaching of the unit to help assess each child's progress with consonant blends.

Portfolio Assessment Ask children to review their portfolios in preparation for a writing conference and to consider which pieces are most successful. In conference discuss how certain pieces might be edited or revised in light of what has been learned in this unit on consonant blends. See the Writing Rubrics on page 261C.

Dictation Tell children you are going to say some words with initial and final blends. Have them write the words as you dictate them. Say **train**, **blue**, **skip**, **grass**, **ring**, **band**, **lamp**, **list**. Then tell children you are going to say a sentence with blend words. Have them write the sentence as you dictate it and underline the words with blends. Use this sentence: *Clap hands* for the *bride*.

Student Skills Assessment Use the checklist on Student Edition pages 321–322 to record your observations of individual children.

Take-Home Book Remind children to complete at home the *Take-Home Book* for Unit 5.

Additional Assessment See pages 261C–261E.

Rain or Shine
Watch for weather changes!

Consonant Digraphs

READING/LANGUAGE ARTS STANDARDS

⚙ Respond to a poem in a way that reflects understanding

⚙ Blend initial consonant digraph sounds with common vowel spelling patterns to read words

⚙ Recognize and use knowledge of spelling patterns, including sounds represented by single letters and vowel digraphs

⚙ Spell correctly basic words with consonant digraphs

OBJECTIVES

▶ To enjoy a poem about using imagination to see pictures in clouds

▶ To develop phonemic awareness by identifying, matching, segmenting, blending, and manipulating sounds in spoken words

▶ To recognize initial consonant digraphs **th, sh, wh, ch, kn**

▶ To use consonant digraphs to decode words

▶ To read and write words with consonant digraphs and high-frequency words in context

LESSONS

Thematic Teaching

In Unit 6 children learn the sounds of consonant digraphs while becoming aware of signs of change in the weather. Phonics skills include reading and writing words with **th, sh, wh, ch**, and **kn**.

Display the "Clouds" **Unit 6 Classroom Poster** near a window so children will be reminded to think of words with consonant digraphs whenever they look outside.

Curriculum Integration

Spelling A *Spelling Connection* appears in most lesson plans. Children also practice spelling high-frequency words involving digraphs on page 300.

Writing Meaningful writing activities appear on pages 290 and 292.

Science On page 290 children create wind socks and use them to record daily weather observations.

Art On page 288 children make and decorate paper bag "shirts." On pages 294 and 298 they make cloud pictures with consonant digraph words.

Optional Learning Activities

Multisensory Activities
Multisensory activities that appeal to children with different learning styles—visual, auditory, tactile, and kinesthetic—are a regular feature of the phonics lessons.

Multicultural Connection
Extend children's world with the multicultural activities on pages 284, 286, and 292. On page 284 children make traditional Mexican "tin" ornaments.

Thematic Activities
Activities in *Curriculum Connections* give children opportunities to apply their newly acquired phonics skills.

Christina Rossetti

Author's Corner

Christina Rossetti died more than a hundred years ago, but her poems live on. She grew up in London and came from a creative family. Her brother Dante illustrated some of her poems. Christina's first known poem was written when she was twelve. By the time Christina was seventeen, several of her poems had been published. Christina used the pen name Ellen Alleyne.

Assessment Strategies

Assessment is an ongoing process. Multiple strategies in the Student Edition as well as the Teacher's Edition and regular use of the *Student Skills Assessment Checklist* on pages 321–322 will help you monitor children's progress in reading and writing words with consonant digraphs.

UNIT RESOURCES

Sadlier Reading

Classroom Poster

Little Books and Big Books

Phonics Picture Cards

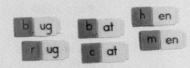

Student Manipulatives

Other Poems by Christina G. Rossetti

Goblin Market and Other Poems. New York: Dover Publications, 1994.

Sing-Song: A Nursery Rhyme Book. New York: Dover Publications, 1969.

Theme-Related Resources

Branley, Franklyn M. *Flash, Crash, Rumble, and Roll.* New York: HarperCollins Juvenile Books, 1999. Children learn safety tips and the real story behind thunder and lightning.

Clouds: Nature's Sprinklers. Wheeling, Illinois: film ideas, inc., 2000. A simple explanation of the water cycle gives children a reason to be glad when it rains.

Macmillan, Bruce. *The Weather Sky.* New York: Farrar, Straus & Giroux, 1991. Photos and illustrations reveal cloud secrets.

In Unit 6 children focus on consonant digraphs. The assessment ideas on this page are for use throughout the chapter.

Pretests/Posttests

The tests on pages 283D–283E serve as a formal end-of-unit assessment of children's mastery of consonant digraphs. In some cases you may choose to use them as pretests to identify the starting point for individual instruction. The Phonemic Awareness Test on page 283J also serves as a pretest.

Observational Assessment

Specific opportunities to observe children's progress with consonant digraphs are highlighted in the lesson plans. The *Student Skills Assessment Checklist* on pages 321–322 of the Student Edition will help you keep track of students' progress.

Dictation

Dictate the following words. Tell children to write each word and to circle the digraphs: **think**, **shell**, **wheel**, **why**, **chair**, **knife**, **knob**, **shave**, **thin**, **chin**. Then dictate the following sentences: My mom can **knit**. I see a **chick**. See the **ship**. In addition to assessing the consonant digraphs, observe whether children begin each sentence with an uppercase letter and end with a period.

Using Technology

The activities presented on pages 283O–283P may also be used to evaluate children's progress.

Performance Assessment

Model for children a story you wrote about what you do when you have a day off. Include as many consonant digraphs as you can. Display your story in the Writing Center. Tell children to write a story about what they do on their day off or when they go outside to play. Direct children to practice reading the story and then have them share it with the rest of the class. Provide time for children to share their stories. Encourage children to use props such as baseball gloves, games, soccer balls, and so on when they give their talks. Use the *Student Skills Assessment Checklist* on pages 321–322 to record your observations.

Portfolio Assessment

The portfolio icon in the lesson plans indicates portfolio opportunities throughout the unit. Post the rubrics for Unit 6 on a chart when you begin the unit, and review the criteria with children. Discuss with children how they can select work from their portfolios that best represents their progress in a given area. For example, for the rubric *"Ends sentences with the appropriate punctuation mark,"* have children read each sentence in their written work for the unit and tell why they chose the punctuation mark at the end.

Name _____ **Writing Rubrics**	Sometimes	Never	Always
Phonics Skills			
Shows awareness that consonant digraphs have their own special sound			
Recognizes consonant digraphs			
Reads words with consonant digraphs in context			
Writing Skills			
Correctly spells both words with consonant digraphs and high-frequency words appropriate to grade level			
Ends sentences with the appropriate punctuation mark			
Recognizes that writing has a purpose			
Writes sentences that others can read			
Writes descriptive sentences			

Answer Key

Page 283D
1. **ch**in
2. **kn**ot
3. **thr**ow
4. **sh**ip
5. **wh**iskers
6. **sh**ell
7. **kn**it
8. **th**imble
9. **ch**urch
10. **sh**apes
11. **ch**ain
12. **wh**ale

Page 283E
1. know
2. chill
3. shine
4. whistles
5. thunder

Say the name of each picture. Fill in the circle in front of the letters that stand for the missing beginning digraph. Print the digraph on the line.

1	○ kn	2	○ kn	3	○ sh
	○ th		○ th		○ th
	○ ch		○ wh		○ kn
_____ in		_____ ot		_____ row	

4	○ kn	5	○ ch	6	○ sh
	○ th		○ th		○ kn
	○ sh		○ wh		○ wh
_____ ip		_____ iskers		_____ ell	

7	○ kn	8	○ ch	9	○ wh
	○ wh		○ th		○ sh
	○ th		○ wh		○ ch
_____ it		_____ imble		_____ urch	

10	○ sh	11	○ kn	12	○ wh
	○ wh		○ sh		○ th
	○ th		○ ch		○ ch
_____ apes		_____ ain		_____ ale	

Use a word from the box to complete each sentence.
Print the word on the line.

thunder

whistles

shine

chill

know

1. I _____ it will rain today.

2. There is a _____ in the air.

3. The sun will not _____ today.

4. The wind _____ in the trees.

5. Is that _____ I hear?

In Unit 6 children learn the sounds of consonant digraphs. Children who have auditory or oral discrimination problems, who perseverate, or who have attention deficit disorder (ADD) may have difficulty working through the unit. Below are some strategies you can use to help children cope with these problems.

Auditory/Oral Discrimination

Children who have difficulty saying the **th** sound or who are unable to distinguish the sounds /**s**/, /**sh**/, and /**ch**/ may also have problems saying and spelling words with consonant digraphs. The techniques below may help these children as they work through the unit.

- Focus attention on what children are doing with their tongue, teeth, and lips as they say words that begin with different consonant digraphs. Have children look in a mirror as they say the words. Ask them to explain in their own words how their lips and tongue form each digraph.

- Focus on each sound separately. Have children make a collage of pictures and words that begin with consonant digraph **th**. Then have children point to and name each **th** word, saying /**th**/ **thing,** /**th**/ **thimble,** and so on. Repeat the activity for each consonant digraph with which children have trouble.

- Focus on several consonants and consonant digraphs together. Take every opportunity to have children sort pictures and word cards. Include pictures and words that begin with single consonants that children may confuse with a consonant digraph, such as **t** and **s**.

- Give children their own special secret key words for consonant digraphs **th**, **ch**, and **sh**, such as **thumb**, **chin**, and **shirt**. Tell them that when they encounter a new word that begins with one of the digraphs, they should look at their **thumb** or touch their **chin** or **shirt** and then say the key word and the new word together (e.g., **thumb—thimble**). Tell children to pay close attention to the beginning sounds and to how they are formed to check whether the sounds are the same.

Perseveration

Children with perseveration problems may have difficulty switching to a new activity. As children participate in independent or small group activities, such as those in *Theme Activity, Curriculum Connections,* and *Reteaching Activities,* they may wish to continue the activity rather than move on to the next one. Try these techniques to help children move from one activity to the next.

- Make the transition easier by telling children before they start how they will know when an activity is over.

- In some cases you will want to set a time limit. Begin by telling children how long they will have to complete the activity. A few minutes before the activity is to end, remind children of how much time they have left.

- If an activity does not have a time limit but requires the completion of a product, such as a drawing with a caption or a list of words, periodically check on children who are likely to perseverate. Direct children to the next step with comments such as: *I think your picture is complete. What will you say in your caption?*

Attention Deficit Disorder (ADD)

Children with ADD are likely to have difficulty staying on task. Try these techniques to help children stay focused:

- Watch for children who are fidgeting, looking away from their papers, or indicating distraction in some other way. Walk to their desks to quietly check on their progress. Recap and acknowledge the work they have completed. Watch as they begin the next item.

- Have children with ADD sit near your desk so that you can monitor their work. Begin by having children show you each item as it is completed. Give immediate feedback by praising accuracy or by helping to correct a wrong answer. Gradually increase the number of items a child must complete before showing you his or her work. Progress toward having the child complete the whole page independently.

The chart below identifies problems that children may manifest as they learn the concepts and skills presented in this unit. The chart also identifies strategies to use with children who have not yet mastered the key concepts in the unit.

SKILL	Saying Consonant Digraphs	Spelling Words with **kn**	Spelling Words with **wh**
Observation	Child attempts to say two sounds instead of using the new sound of the consonant digraph, for example, /**k**/-/**h**/-/**o**/-/**p**/ instead of /**ch**/-/**o**/-/**p**/.	Child has difficulty remembering to include the silent **k** when spelling words.	Child has difficulty determining when to use **wh** in words that begin with **w**.
Intervention	• Use Punchout Letter Cards to form a one-syllable consonant digraph word in a pocket chart. • Separate letters that stand for phonemes. The word **chain** would appear: **ch ai n**. • Have child form the word with her or his own letter cards and then blend the phonemes to say the word. • Continue in this manner to have child form and say words with consonant digraphs until she or he masters the skill.	• Ask child to recall **kn** words from the unit. List the words. • Tell child you are going to say the words in a silly way. Then say, for example, /**k**/—**nob** and /**k**/—**night.** Have child repeat each silly word after you. Together, say the words correctly. Point out the difference. • Tell child that whenever she or he hears a word beginning with **kn**, she or he can use this trick of saying the word in a funny way silently in order to help her or him remember the **k** when spelling the word.	• Tell child that since it is difficult to hear a difference between /**w**/ or /**hw**/ she or he will need to memorize /**hw**/ words. • Have child use her or his phonics book and children's dictionaries to find familiar /**hw**/ words. List the words on chart paper as child names them. Post the chart in the Writing Center. • Have child copy each word in the list onto a separate reference card and to keep the cards at her or his desk.

These activities are designed to augment the lessons in the unit with engaging exercises that reinforce skills and encourage creativity.

Identify and Isolate Initial Sounds

Hear That Train?

Tell children to line up facing in one direction, one behind another, and to put their hands out straight in front of them to form a train. Say: *The train says /ch/ chug.* Have children repeat the sentence. Explain that you will say more sentences. Tell children to repeat each sentence and say the beginning sound in the final word. For each beginning sound they repeat correctly, the "train" can move one step forward. Use sentences ending with words with digraphs. For example:

The train hauls **/th/ things**.

The train hauls **/hw/ whales**.

The train hauls **/sh/ shoes**.

The train hauls **/n/ knapsacks**.

The train hauls **/ch/ children**.

The train hauls **/ch/ chimps**.

The train hauls **/hw/ wheat**.

The train hauls **/sh/ shirts**.

The train hauls **/n/ knives**.

The train hauls **/th/ thimbles**.

Once children understand the game, invite volunteers to make up their own sentences. If time allows, continue the activity until children have traveled all the way around the classroom.

Match Initial Sounds

What Picture Is It?

Materials: **Sadlier Phonics Picture Cards** for **sheep, shorts, whale, wheat, chair, cherry, thermometer, thirty, knee, knot**; masking tape

Tape one of the picture cards to a volunteer's back without letting the child see the picture. Have the child turn his or her back to show the picture to the rest of the class. Then have the child call on class members to give clues that will help her or him figure out the name of the picture. Tell children that the clues can be other words that begin with the same sound or can be about what the picture on the card is or does. Give these clues for the picture card **shorts** as examples:

The picture begins with the same sound as **shoe**.

The picture shows something you wear in the summer.

Continue the activity with other volunteers and other pictures.

Identify and Count Syllables

Cloudy with a Hint of Rain

Talk about television weather forecasters and the words they use in their daily forecasts. Then call on volunteers to give their own weather forecasts, such as: **wet and rainy, fair and mild, sunny and warm, tornado warning, hurricane watch**.

Have children slowly repeat each phrase the "forecasters" use and clap as they say the syllables in each word. After each word, call on one child to tell how many syllables the word has.

Segment Phonemes in a Word

That Cloud Looks Like...

Materials: blue construction paper, crayons, glue, cotton balls

Reread "Clouds" on page 283, and tell children they will make pictures of clouds like the ones Christina Rossetti wrote about in the poem. Give each child a sheet of blue construction paper. Tell children to draw an outline of something a cloud might look like and to fill in the outline with glue. Have them complete their pictures by filling the glued surface with cotton balls.

Allow time for children to share their pictures and to tell the class in one word what their "cloud" looks like to them (e.g., **sheep**). Have the class repeat the word the artist says and segment it into individual phonemes. For **sheep**, children would say /**sh**/-/ē/-/**p**/. Display the cloud pictures around the classroom.

Substitute Initial Sounds

What Do I Spy?

Write **sh**, **ch**, **wh**, **th**, and **kn** on the board, and tell children they will play I Spy. Explain that you will give a clue and that children will substitute one of the digraphs on the board for the initial sound of the clue word to tell what you "spy." Give this example: *I spy something that is young and alive and looks like you. It rhymes with* **wild**. Model how to try out the different consonant digraph sounds in the initial position to find the answer, **child**. Continue with these clues:

I spy something on a hand. It rhymes with **crumb**. (**thumb**)

I spy something people sit in. It rhymes with **bear**. (**chair**)

I spy something on a car. It rhymes with **meal**. (**wheel**)

I spy something on a shoelace. It rhymes with **hot**. (**knot**)

I spy something on a foot. It rhymes with **you**. (**shoe**)

Name _____ Date _____

Directions: Give this assessment orally to each child. The correct answers are boldfaced.

Identify and Isolate Initial Sounds

Say: *I will say a word. You say the sound that comes at the beginning.*
Write the beginning sound that the child identifies.

1. shoe	_____	**/sh/**
2. whale	_____	**/hw/**
3. knife	_____	**/n/**
4. chimp	_____	**/ch/**
5. chop	_____	**/ch/**
6. think	_____	**/th/**
7. white	_____	**/hw/**
8. shine	_____	**/sh/**
9. shirt	_____	**/sh/**
10. thumb	_____	**/th/**
11. knock	_____	**/n/**
12. what	_____	**/hw/**
13. chain	_____	**/ch/**
14. thorn	_____	**/th/**
15. knit	_____	**/n/**

Substitute Initial Sounds

Say: *I will say a beginning sound and then say a word. Use the beginning sound to make a word that rhymes with the word I said.* Say the sounds and words below. Circle the item if the child correctly substitutes the initial sound and names the rhyming word. Model the first item.

16. **/ch/**	lamp:	**champ**	24. **/hw/**	pen:	**when**
17. **/th/**	sing:	**thing**	25. **/th/**	bank:	**thank**
18. **/hw/**	sip:	**whip**	26. **/sh/**	well:	**shell**
19. **/n/**	job:	**knob**	27. **/sh/**	tip:	**ship**
20. **/hw/**	my:	**why**	28. **/th/**	bird:	**third**
21. **/sh/**	nut:	**shut**	29. **/ch/**	time:	**chime**
22. **/ch/**	mess:	**chess**	30. **/n/**	hot:	**not**
23. **/n/**	low:	**know**			

Wonderful Weather

Blackline Master 29
p. 283L

Objective
To identify beginning consonant digraphs in words

Players
Pairs or small groups

Materials
• small objects for game pieces
• number cubes or pennies

■ Duplicate and distribute Blackline Master 29 to each group along with game pieces and a number cube or a penny.

■ Tell children to roll the number cube to determine the number of spaces they should move their game pieces on each turn. (If they are using a penny, have them move two spaces if the penny lands on heads and one if it lands on tails.)

■ Have children begin on the storm cloud and try to outrun the rain to reach the sunny weather.

■ Direct each player to name the picture on which he or she lands and to identify its beginning digraph. Players who name the correct digraph stay on the new space; those who don't answer correctly return to their previous space.

Shifty Sheep

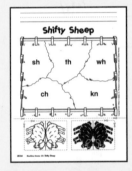

Blackline Master 30
p. 283M

Objective
To identify beginning consonant digraphs

Players
Pairs

Material
• scissors

■ Duplicate and distribute Blackline Master 30 to each pair.

■ Have each child cut out a sheep card and fold it on the solid line to make the sheep stand up.

■ Tell children to take turns being the sheep and the shepherd. Have the shepherds tell the sheep where to move by giving directions such as "Move to the field that has the beginning sound in (**shoe**)." The other child moves the sheep into the correct field and replies, "(**Shoe**) begins with (**sh**)." After a few turns, have children switch roles.

■ The shepherds can get ideas for words from their books or the Wonderful Weather game board.

Pass Words

Objective
To match consonant digraphs and phonograms to build words

Players
Small groups

Materials
• index cards
• scissors
• markers

■ Write each word on an index card for each group: **think, thing, ship, sheep, shell, white, whale, chop, chin, chain, knee, knock**.

■ Have children cut apart each index card between the digraph and the phonogram. Then have a child deal the phonogram cards and stack the digraph cards facedown.

■ Tell children to place their phonogram cards faceup. Have a child pick a digraph card, combine it with one of his or her phonogram cards, and sound out the word. If the combination spells a known word, tell the child to print the word on the board. Let each child have a turn. Then have the next child pick another digraph and proceed in the same way.

■ Stop the game after ten minutes; then have the class compare word lists.

Wonderful Weather

Shifty Sheep

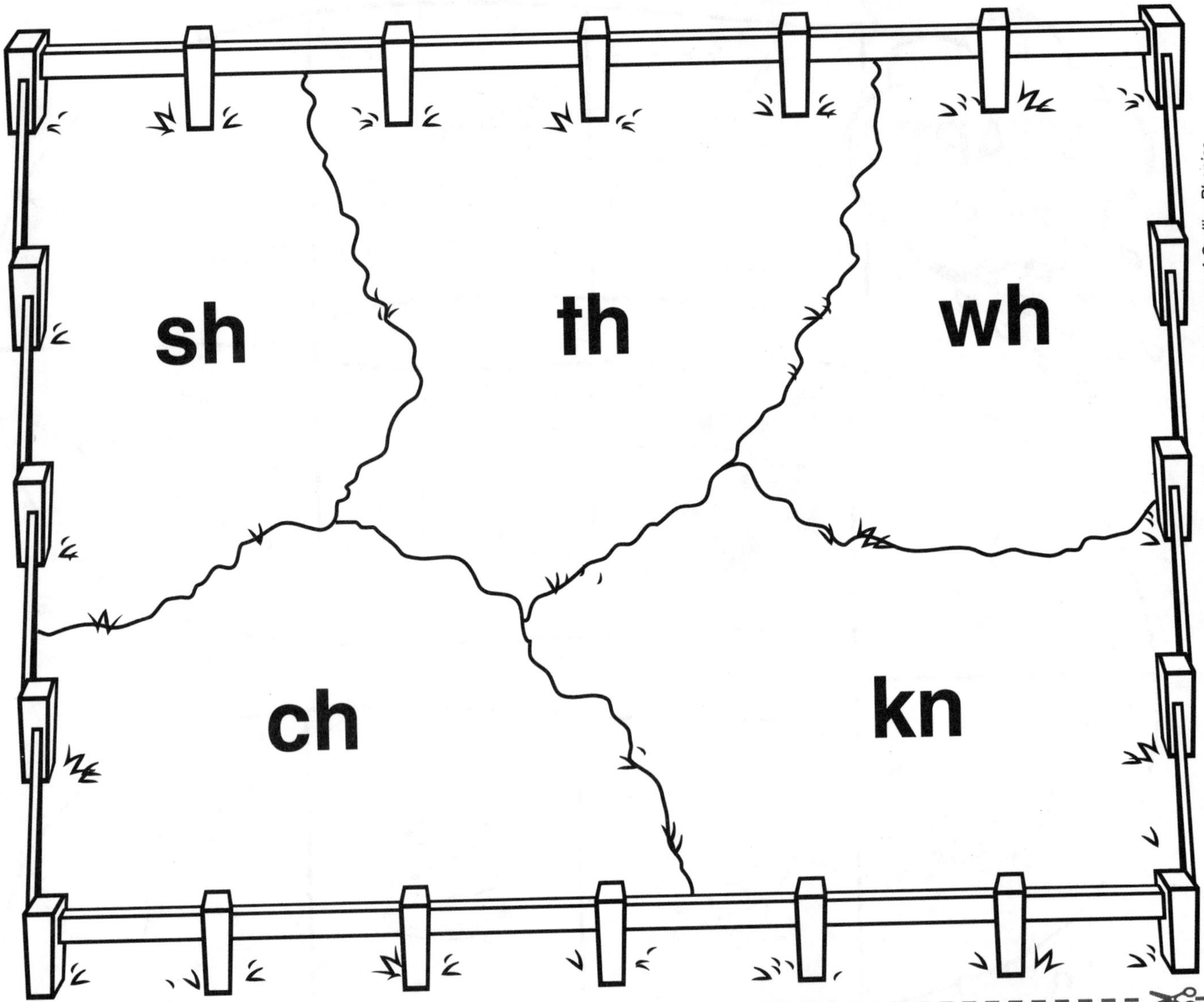

sh

th

wh

ch

kn

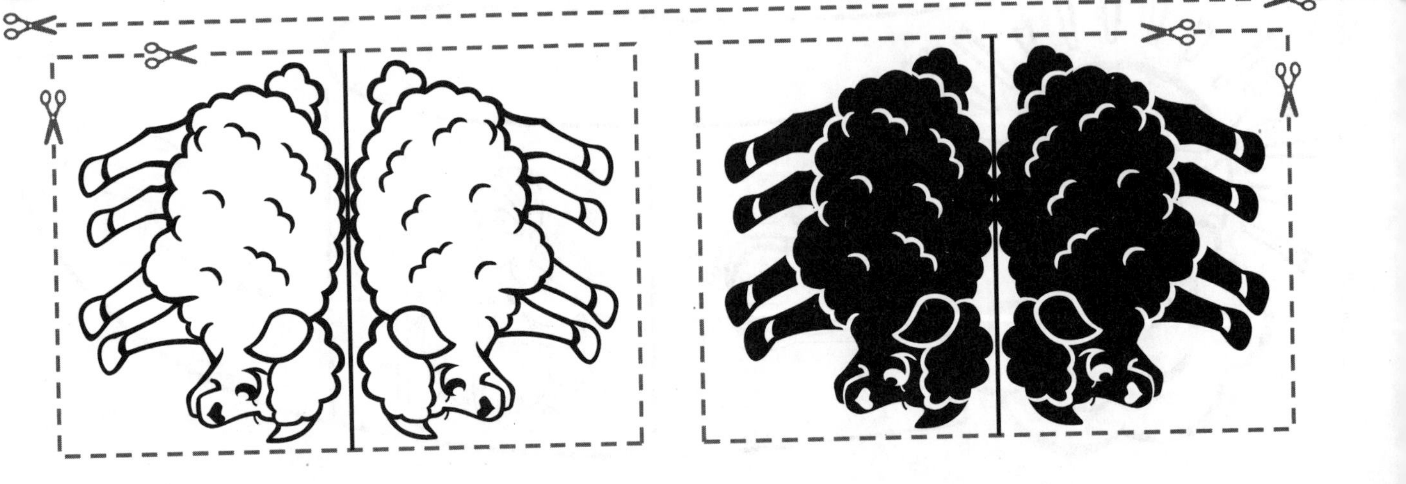

Blackline Master 30: Shifty Sheep

Say and Spell

Have children work in pairs. Explain that you are going to give clues to describe spelling words from Unit 6. Direct the pairs to identify each word and to spell it with their letter cards. You might use these clues:

This animal gives us wool. (**sheep**)

If it's not thick, it's like this. (**thin**)

You turn this to open a door. (**knob**)

It's a word you use to talk about a girl or woman. (**she**)

It's what triangles, circles, and squares are called. (**shapes**)

The part of your face below your mouth is called this. (**chin**)

If it's not a person, place, or animal, its this. (**thing**)

It's a question word you use when you can't find something. (**where**)

It's like a rope, but it's made of metal links. (**chain**)

It's what you do with your brain. (**think**)

This sounds like the opposite of yes, but it's not spelled the same. (**know**)

It's the opposite of black. (**white**)

Riddle and Rhyme

Materials: sentence strips, index cards

On separate sentence strips write: **I start with**; **I rhyme with**; **I am**. Then print these words on separate cards: **shake**, **chant**, **thorn**, **shift**, **thing**, **chug**, **white**, **when**, **chose**, **shell**, and **champ**. Have the class work in small groups. Give each group a word card, and direct children to spell the word's initial digraph using letter cards. Then have them find a picture card with a name that rhymes with their word (e.g., **shake**: **sh**, **cake**). Then have each group complete the first two chart sentences by inserting the letter cards and picture card. Have each group call on classmates to guess the group's word and then place the word card in the last sentence. Tell the class to use the sentence starters from the previous rhyme activity to make riddle books.

What's the Word?

Have the class work in groups of three or four to use their letter cards to spell words with digraphs. Direct children to take turns laying down two letters that stand for a consonant digraph. The rest of the group should then add letters to make a word that begins with the digraph. Give the groups ten minutes to make and record words. Then have children share their lists.

DIGRAPH CHIP COOKIE

Objectives

- To help children write and illustrate words that contain consonant digraph sounds

- To use a paint program such as Kid Pix Studio® Deluxe* to illustrate words with consonant digraph sounds

Preparation

- Cut a piece of butcher paper in a cookie shape, and place it on a wall along with the title "Digraph Chip Cookie."

- Read the title aloud. Point out that the cookie has no chips. Tell children that the "chips" will be words or pictures with names that have consonant digraph sounds. Have children brainstorm words having these sounds and then list them on the board. Suggest: **shark**, **thumb**, **sheep**, **whale**, **cherry, and knot**.

One Step at a Time

1. Have children select "Kid Pix" from the opening screen. Guide them in clicking on the Typewriter icon in the side menu to enter a word with a consonant digraph sound at the top of the screen. Have children refer to the list on the board.

2. Instruct children to use the paint tools from the side menu to illustrate each word.

3. Have children select "Pick a Stamp Set" under "Goodies" to access different sets of stamps. Tell them to scan through the sets of stamps for pictures of the word chosen. Have children include these stamps in their illustrations.

4. Have children print their digraph "chips." If possible, have them do so on different color paper.

Class Sharing

Invite volunteers to take turns presenting the chips to the class. Have children cut their chips into different shapes and glue them onto the cookie.

WEATHER FORECASTS

Objectives

- To help children recognize and use words with consonant digraph sounds in context
- To use a writing and painting program such as Kid Pix Studio® Deluxe* to write and illustrate a weather forecast

Preparation

Focus on the unit theme by sharing the book *Cloudy with a Chance of Meatballs* by Judi Barrett. After several readings of part of the book, have volunteers forecast the weather for the town of Chewandswallow using words that contain consonant digraph sounds such as **cheese** or **shapes**. List all forecasts on the board.

One Step At A Time

1. Have children select "Kid Pix" and then click on the Type-writer icon to enter their weather forecast. Provide assistance as needed.

2. Direct children to use the drawing and paint tools to illustrate their forecasts.

3. Tell children to print their illustrated forecasts.

4. Have children use crayons to circle the consonant digraphs.

All software referred to in this book is listed under Computer Resources on page 348.

Class Sharing

Have children present their weather forecasts to the class. You might want children to use the Speech feature so that the computer recites children's forecasts in a digitized voice. Display each forecast on a bulletin board entitled "Forecasts for Chewandswallow."

RED SKIES

Explain to children that people often use folklore to explain different kinds of weather. Tell them that the folk poem you will read is one of many that address weather, then read this folk poem to the class:

Red sky at night
Sailor's delight.
Red sky in the morning
Sailor's warning!

Show children *Skywatching: A Video Guide to the Daytime Sky* (Purple Crayon Productions). Have them retell the folktales in the video. Write their responses on a chart. Have volunteers circle all the consonant digraphs they recognize. Tell children to choose one folktale and illustrate it. Then ask them to present their folktales to the class.

Tell children that they are going to have a "Weather Folklore Day." Children may dress up as a character in their weather folktales or use their illustrations to present their tales to another class or to parents.

Literature Introduction to Consonant Digraphs

Objectives
- **To enjoy a poem about clouds**
- **To match initial sounds**
- **To identify consonant digraphs**

Starting with Literature

Read aloud the poem "Clouds." Ask children to count how many "sheep clouds" they see in the illustration. Reread the poem together.

Developing Critical Thinking

Ask the Critical Thinking questions on page 283. Discuss the different appearances and meanings of clouds. Have children look out a window to look for images in clouds.

Introducing the Skill

Phonemic Awareness: Match Initial Sounds

Materials: **Sadlier Phonics Picture Cards** for **sheep, shorts, whale, wheat, chair, cherry;** pocket chart

Hold up cards for **sheep** and **shorts**, say the two words, and point out the common initial sound. Place all cards, facing backward, in a pocket chart. Have volunteers choose two cards, identify them, and say whether the names have the same beginning sounds. Those that do should be displayed.

Consonant Digraphs

- Print **sun, hop, sheep** on the board. Underline the initial consonants of **sun** and **hop**. Have children say the words.
- Underline the **sh** in **sheep**. Read the word aloud. Point out that the beginning sound is not /**s**/ or /**h**/. Explain that sometimes two letters combine to make one sound that is different from the sounds of each letter. Tell children they will learn about consonant digraphs in Unit 6. Point to the word **sheep** on the **Unit 6 Classroom Poster** while the class repeats /**sh**/-**eep sheep**.

283

CLOUDS

White sheep, white sheep
On a blue hill,
When the wind stops
You all stand still.
When the wind blows
You walk away slow.
White sheep, white sheep,
Where do you go?

Christina G. Rossetti

Possible responses: Clouds would be dark. Fluffy clouds indicate good weather. Feathery clouds indicate weather change.

Critical Thinking

How would the clouds look on a stormy day? What do the different kinds of clouds tell you about the weather?

LESSON 149: Consonant Digraphs
Phonemic Awareness: Initial Sounds
283

Theme Words

Picturing Words Mention that clouds are often associated with a dreamy feeling. Ask children to close their eyes and picture the poem "Clouds" as you reread it to them. Together identify words with consonant digraphs in the poem and use these to begin a word wall on the theme of weather. Ask children to name other weather-related words that begin with consonant digraphs, such as **thunder** and **shine**. Write these words on the word wall. Continue to add to the wall and use it as a reference throughout the unit.

Sometime during the unit, guide children to play Beat the Clock. Have them work in groups, using dictionaries to locate as many words with initial digraphs as they can within a ten-minute span. The group with the most words wins. Add new words to the word wall.

Name _____

Dear Family,

 n this unit about weather, your child will learn the sounds of consonant digraphs. You can participate with your child by doing these home activities.

• Say the name of each picture below with your child. Listen to the sounds of the beginning consonant digraphs **th**, **sh**, **wh**, **ch**, and **kn**.

th	sh	wh	ch	kn
thumb	sheep	whale	cherry	knot

• Read the poem "Clouds" on the reverse side of this page.

• Talk about the shapes of clouds you see in the sky. What do they remind you of?

• Help your child find words with consonant digraphs in the poem, such as **white**, **sheep**, **when**, and **where**. Then find the rhyming words. (hill/still, slow/go)

Apreciada Familia:

E n esta unidad se hablará del tiempo y se enseñarán los sonidos dígrafos de las consonantes. Pueden practicarlos con su hijo haciendo estas actividades en la casa.

• Pronuncien el nombre de los objetos en los cuadros. Escuchen los sonidos dígrafos de las consonantes al principio de las palabras, **th**, **sh**, **wh**, **ch** y **kn**.

• Lean el poema "Clouds" en la página 283.

• Hablen de las diferentes formas de las nubes en el cielo. ¿Qué te recuerdan?

• Ayuden al niño a encontrar consonantes de sonido dígrafo en el poema, tales como: **white**, **sheep**, **when** y **where**. Después encuentren las palabras que riman. (hill/still, slow/go)

PROJECT

With your child, read and answer these questions about weather. **Wh**at is the weather like **wh**ere you live? Can you **th**ink of the sound that **th**under makes? Can you find a **sh**adow during a rain **sh**ower? If you had the **ch**ance, how would you **ch**ange the weather?

PROYECTO

Haga las siguientes preguntas sobre el tiempo al niño. ¿Cómo es el tiempo en el lugar donde vives? ¿Puedes imaginar el ruido que hace un trueno? ¿Puedes ver una sombra durante un aguacero? Si tienes la oportunidad ¿cómo puedes cambiar el tiempo?

284   LESSON 149: Consonant Digraphs—Phonics Alive at Home

Phonics Alive at Home

• The *Phonics Alive at Home* page is an opportunity for family members to monitor and share in their child's language learning progress. For Unit 6, the page provides activities focused on the unit theme, "Rain or Shine," and consonant digraphs.

• Have children remove page 284 from their books and take the page home to share with family members. Encourage them to complete the activities and report back to the class on those they enjoyed.

• Throughout the unit, provide opportunities during class for children to share their experiences of completing the activities at home with family.

Sadlier Reading
Little Books and Big Books

Read poems in Worlds of Poetry *Around the Neighborhood* and have children identify words with initial and final consonant digraphs.

 Direct children to additional activities on Sadlier-Oxford's web site: www.sadlier-oxford.com.

Multicultural Connection

Explain to children that making tin ornaments is a traditional craft in Mexico and Central America and that a beaming sun is a popular design for these ornaments. Guide children in making tin ornaments. First have them glue a sheet of tinfoil to a piece of oaktag. Then provide a pattern and have them cut out a sun shape. Together, write instructions for making the tin ornaments. Underline words with consonant digraphs.

Take-Home Book

The Take-Home Book for Unit 6, *Weather Changes*, is found on student pages 333–334. This fold-up book reinforces the consonant digraph phonics skills taught in this unit. Use this take-home component as a culminating activity for the unit or send the book home at another appropriate time.

Consonant Digraph th

Objectives
- To match initial sounds
- To identify and write words that begin with consonant digraph **th**

Warming Up

Reviewing Long and Short Vowels
Materials: **Sadlier Phonics Picture Cards** for **ham, egg, cake, mix, rice, jam, peas**

Have children name each card. Then give clues for each word, such as: *This short **e** word names something you break.* (**egg**) Have volunteers choose the correct card.

Teaching the Lesson

Phonemic Awareness: Match Initial Sounds
Materials: **Sadlier Phonics Picture Cards** for **toys, tub, hat, horn, thermometer, thirty, king, kitten**

- Say **seven** and **seal**. Point out that the words have the same initial sound, /**s**/.
- Display the cards, and have children name each picture. Place the cards face down. Have children take turns choosing pairs of cards and telling whether the words have the same initial sound.

Sound to Symbol
- Say: *I put a **thimble** on my **thumb**.* Tell children that /**th**/ is the sound at the beginning of **thimble** and **thumb**. Have children say /**th**/ along with you. Then have them say the words that begin with /**th**/.
- Write **th** on the board. Tell children that **th** is a digraph—a letter combination that stands for one sound. The consonant digraph **th** stands for /**th**/.
- Write: *My rose has **thirty thorns**.* Read the sentence aloud. Have children name the words that begin with the consonant digraph **th**.

285

Th

Thunder starts with the sound of the consonant digraph **th**. Listen for the sound of **th** in the rhyme.

Think about thick clouds,
Think about thunder.
Think of some big things,
You can hide under.

Circle the picture if its name begins with the sound of **th**.

1 thumb	2 fire	3 thirty	4 thin
5 thimble	6 ten	7 sun	8 think
9 thick	10 thorn	11 doll	12 thermometer

LESSON 150: Phonemic Awareness: Initial /th/ **285**

UNIVERSAL ACCESS
Meeting Individual Needs

Visual • Auditory
Materials: **Sadlier Phonics Picture Cards** for **thermometer, thirty, thread**, and cards with names that do not begin with **th**

Have children name each picture. Ask them to use each **th** word to fill in the blank in the following sentence:

I think ___ begins with **th**.

Auditory • Kinesthetic
Have children tap their fingertips on their desks to suggest the sound of thunder. Then say a list of words such as **think, thunder, talk, thump, ten, type, thorn, tree, thing, ten, thin, thick**. Have children make the sound of thunder when they hear a word that begins with consonant digraph **th**.

Extra Support
Materials: index cards with **think, thin, thumb, thorn, thread, thick, thirty, thimble**; flashlight

Tack the cards on a bulletin board and dim the classroom lights. Flash the light on one word at a time and call on volunteers to read the word.

Say the name of each picture. Circle **th** or **t** for each beginning sound. Then print the word from the box that names the picture.

think	tape	thirty	tube	thorn
	thumb	top	thick	ten

1 (th / t)	2 (th / t)	3 (th / t)
thumb	tape	ten

4 (th / t)	5 (th / t)	6 (th / t)
thorn	top	think

7 (th / t)	8 (th / t)	9 (th / t)
thirty	thick	tube

Write a sentence about one picture using a **th** word.

Accept any sentence that contains a **th** word from items 1–9.
Remind children that a sentence begins with an uppercase letter and ends with a period.

286   LESSON 150: Writing Consonant Digraph **th**

Read the words in the box. Ask your child to give the "thumbs up" sign after each **th** word.

Practicing the Skill

- Read aloud the introduction and the rhyme on page 285. Ask children to name the words in the rhyme that begin with the sound of **th**. Do the first item together before children complete the page.
- Read aloud the words in the box on page 286. Point out that even though they all start with **t**, their initial sounds are different. Then read the directions aloud and complete the first item together. Have children complete items 2–9 before doing the bottom section of the page with them.

Curriculum Connections

Spelling Connection
Materials: Punchout Letter Cards

Read aloud each word and sentence below. Have a child spell the word aloud. Ask another to spell it with the letter cards.

three	The storm is **three** miles away.
think	I **think** the clouds look like sheep.
thumb	I hit my **thumb** with the hammer.
thick	The clouds are **thick** and gray.

Theme Activity: Multicultural
Tell children that people in different parts of the world have long told stories about what causes thunder. The Dutch, for example, told stories about elf-like characters who made thunder when they knocked over wooden pins with a bowling ball. Have children draw pictures to illustrate this traditional story. Also have them write captions that include the word **thunder**.

Portfolio   Have children add their pictures and captions to their portfolios.

Sadlier Reading
Little Books and Big Books

Read the poem "Thinking Time" on page 16 in Worlds of Poetry *Families, Families* and have children listen for the words that begin with initial consonant digraph **th**.

Families, Families

English Language Learners/ ESL
Some children might have difficulty pronouncing /th/. Say the word **think** and the beginning sound /th/. Model for children how to place the tip of their tongue between their teeth to form the **th** sound. Have children practice making the **th** sound. On the board, one at a time, write the **th** words from pages 285 and 286. Say the word, model how you make the **th** sound, and then say the word again. Have children repeat each word after you. You might also have children say the word in a simple sentence. Model: *I have a* /th/-/th/-/th/-**thumb**. *I can* /th/-/th/-/th/-**think**.

Challenge
Write these words on the board: **three, thirty, thermometer, thunder, thick, thaw**. Have children work in pairs to write questions and answers about the weather, using the **th** words (e.g., What goes boom in a storm? **thunder**). Have each pair present its questions to the class.

Special Strategies
For Universal Access activities, see page 283F.

286

Consonant Digraph sh

Objectives
- To identify and isolate initial sounds
- To identify and write words that begin with consonant digraph **sh**

Warming Up

Reviewing s-blends

Write the following rhyme on the board and read it aloud. Have children name the words that begin with **s**-blends.

A red **sky** at night

Is a sailor's delight.

But a **scarlet sky** in the morning

Gives sailors **stern** warning.

Teaching the Lesson

Phonemic Awareness:
Identify and Isolate Initial Sounds

- Say **sheep**. Repeat the word, isolating the initial sound: /sh/-/sh/-/sh/ **sheep**. Tell children that the sound at the beginning of **sheep** is /sh/.
- Tell children to listen for /**sh**/ in this song, set to the tune of "Frére Jacques":

Listen closely, listen closely,

To these words, to these words.

What is their beginning sound?

What is their beginning sound?

Sheep, shoe, shirt; sheep, shoe, shirt.

Sound to Symbol

- Say /**sh**/, and have children repeat after you. Tell them that /**sh**/ is the beginning sound in **shell**.
- Write **shell** on the board, and circle the **sh**. Explain that the digraph **sh** stands for /**sh**/. Review that *digraph* means two letters that combine to make one sound.
- Write: I saw a **shell** and a **ship** at the **shore**. Read the sentence. Have children point out the words that begin with **sh**.

sh

Shovel starts with the sound of the consonant digraph **sh**. Listen for the sound of **sh** in the rhyme.

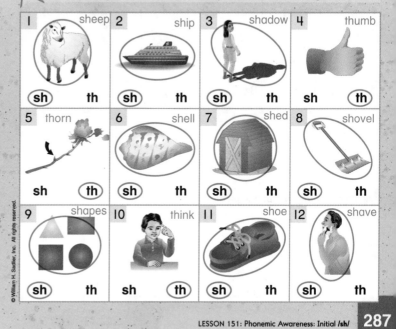

The sun is shining.
Shout hooray!
Grab a shovel.
Be on your way.

Say the name of each picture. Circle the letters that stand for the beginning sound. Then circle the picture if its name begins with **sh**.

1 sheep	2 ship	3 shadow	4 thumb
(sh) th	(sh) th	(sh) th	sh (th)

5 thorn	6 shell	7 shed	8 shovel
sh (th)	(sh) th	(sh) th	(sh) th

9 shapes	10 think	11 shoe	12 shave
(sh) th	sh (th)	(sh) th	(sh) th

LESSON 151: Phonemic Awareness: Initial /sh/

287

UNIVERSAL ACCESS
Meeting Individual Needs

Auditory • Visual

Materials: yellow construction paper, scissors

Have children cut out yellow suns. Say a list of words such as **show, Sue, thumb, shovel, sheep, thin, shape, shoe, sock.** Have children make their suns **shine** by holding them up when they hear a word that begins with **sh**.

Auditory • Kinesthetic

Tell children that they are going to play Show Me! They should act out only the actions that include a word that begins with **sh**. Say: *Show me how to....*

shovel snow; *dance;* **shine** *your shoes;* **shut** *a door; climb stairs;* **shake** *hands; ride a bike;* **sharpen** *a pencil.*

Extra Support

Remind children that the digraph **sh** stands for /**sh**/. Write several word pairs on the board (e.g., **shine/soak, sea/shop, shower/soap, save/shape, sheet/seven**. Have children say each word and circle the initial **sh** words.

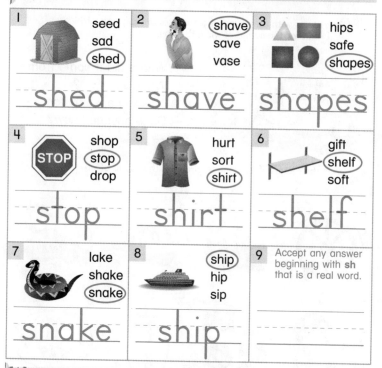

ay the name of each picture. Circle the name and print it. In the last box, draw a picture of a word that begins with **sh**. Print the word.

1	seed sad (shed)	2	(shave) save vase	3	hips safe (shapes)
	shed		shave		shapes
4	shop (stop) drop	5	hurt sort (shirt)	6	gift (shelf) soft
	stop		shirt		shelf
7	lake shake (snake)	8	(ship) hip sip	9	Accept any answer beginning with **sh** that is a real word.
	snake		ship		

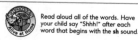

Write a sentence about one picture using an **sh** word.

Accept any sentence that contains an **sh** word.

Remind children that a sentence begins with an uppercase letter
and ends with a period.

288 LESSON 151: Writing Consonant Digraph **sh**.

Read aloud all of the words. Have
your child say "Shhh!" after each
word that begins with the **sh** sound.

Practicing the Skill

● Read aloud the introduction and the rhyme on page 287. Ask children to name the words in the rhyme that begin with the sound of **sh**. Together read the directions and do the first item. Have children complete the page.

● Together read the directions on page 288. Make sure children understand they should draw a picture in the last box and print the picture name. Complete the first item together. Have children finish items 2–9. Then do the bottom section of the page with them.

Curriculum Connections

Spelling Connection
Read aloud each word and sentence below. Have a child spell the word aloud. Have another child print the word on the board.

shirt	In the summer I can wear a short-sleeved **shirt**.
sheep	Look at the fluffy white **sheep**.
shell	I found this **shell** on the beach.
ship	The sailor left the **ship**.
shake	Let's **shake** hands and be friends.

Theme Activity: Art/Language Arts
Materials: brown paper grocery bags, markers, magazines, scissors, glue

● Ask children to name words that begin with consonant digraph **sh**. Then list the responses on the board.

● Have children make sunshine shirts from grocery bags. Cut a hole in the bottom of each bag large enough to fit over the child's head, and cut armholes in the sides. Have each child draw and color a smiling sun on his or her shirt. Then have children cut out and glue pictures of **sh** words onto the bags.

Sadlier Reading
Little Books and Big Books

Read *Getting to Know Sharks* (nonfiction) and have children listen for words that begin with the initial consonant digraph **sh**.

English Language Learners/ ESL
Materials: large **shopping** bag, items that begin with /sh/ such as **shell**, **shirt**, **shovel**, **shoe**, toy **shed**, **shaving** cream, **shelf**, **shapes**

Place all objects in the **shopping** bag. **Shake** the **shopping** bag. Tell children that you are /**sh**/-/**sh**/-/**sh**/-aking the /**sh**/-/**sh**/-/**sh**/-opping bag. Explain that **shaking** and **shopping** begin with /**sh**/ and that the letters **sh** stand for /**sh**/. Model for children how to make the sound **sh**. Then have each child take a turn reaching into the bag and taking out an item. Help the child name the item.

Challenge
Write the following tongue twister on the board: The sun **shines** and **shimmers** on the **sharp shells** on the **shore**. Have a volunteer repeat the tongue twister three times. Then have children create their own tongue twisters from words that begin with consonant digraph **sh**. Have them share their tongue twisters with the class.

Special Strategies
For Universal Access activities, see page 283F.

288

Consonant Digraph wh

Objectives
- To match initial sounds
- To identify and write words that begin with consonant digraph **wh**

Warming Up

Reviewing Digraphs th and sh

Write **thunder** and **ship** on the board. Ask children to name the beginning sound of each word. Have them thump their feet when they hear a word that begins with **th** and whisper "Shhh!" when they hear a word that begins with **sh**. Then say **thumb, thirty, shout, sheep, think, shave, shop, thorn.**

Teaching the Lesson

Phonemic Awareness: Match Initial Sounds

Materials: **Sadlier Phonics Picture Cards** for **fish, valentine, queen, whale, wheat**

- Ask children to listen as you say **wheel, white, when**. Point out that the words all have the same beginning sound, /**hw**/.
- Display the cards. Have children choose the pictures whose names begin like **wheel, white,** and **when** and say the picture names.

Sound to Symbol

- Say: *My cat has **white whiskers**.* Point out that **white** and **whiskers** have the same beginning sound: the sound is /**hw**/.
- Write the words on the board. Underline the initial **wh** in each one.
- Explain that **wh** is the consonant digraph that stands for /**hw**/ in **white** and **whiskers**. Tell children that they need to look carefully at words that begin with /**hw**/ to remember how to spell them.

wh

White starts with the sound of the consonant digraph **wh**. Listen for the sound of **wh** in the rhyme.

Where did it come from?
When will it go?
This white whirly fog,
Does anyone know?

Circle the picture if its name begins with the sound of **wh**.

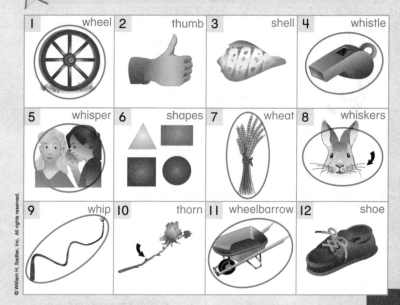

1 wheel	2 thumb	3 shell	4 whistle
5 whisper	6 shapes	7 wheat	8 whiskers
9 whip	10 thorn	11 wheelbarrow	12 shoe

LESSON 152: Phonemic Awareness: Initial /hw/   **289**

U N I V E R S A L   A C C E S S
Meeting Individual Needs

Auditory
Have children sit in a large circle. Whisper an initial **wh** word to the first child (e.g., **whale, when, whisper, wheat, wheel, where, whiskers, why, whistle, white, whine, what**). Have each child in turn whisper it to the next child. The last child stands and says the word aloud.

Visual • Tactile
Materials: blue paper, glue, cotton

Together make a list of words that begin with **wh**. Then tell children that they are going to make "word clouds." Have each child choose a word, print it on paper with glue, and cover the glue with cotton. After the glue dries, have children trace their words with their fingers.

Extra Support
Materials: Punchout Letter Cards

Remind children that **what, when,** and **why** begin with **wh**. Have them make up questions using these words. Then have them use the letter cards to spell the **wh** words.

Use a **wh** word from the box to complete each sentence. Print the word on the line. Then read the sentences to a partner.

white	What	whipped	When	Why

1. "__What__ a bad weather day!"

2. __When__ I woke up, it was sunny.

3. Then the __white__ clouds turned gray.

4. The wind __whipped__ the leaves around.

5. "__Why__ does it have to storm?" I whined.

LESSON 152: Writing Consonant Digraph **wh**

Take turns with your child asking each other questions that begin with **What**, **When**, and **Why**.

Practicing the Skill

• Together read the introduction and the rhyme on page 289. Ask children to name the words that begin with /**hw**/. Then read the directions and do the first item together. Have children complete the page.

• Ask volunteers to read the words on the top of page 290. Then read the directions and discuss which word completes each sentence. Have children print the words. Read the finished story together.

Curriculum Connections

Spelling Connection

Read aloud each word and sentence below. Have a child spell the word aloud. Ask another child to print the word on the board.

white Some **white** clouds are fluffy.

whale The **whale** lives in the sea.

what **What** is your favorite season?

wheel Ernesto broke the wagon **wheel**.

Theme Activity: Science

Materials: picture of a wind sock, whale cutouts, blue construction paper, glue, tape, crepe paper, twine, sticks

• Show children a picture of a wind sock. Tell them that a wind sock shows the direction the wind is blowing.

• Have children make their own whale wind socks. Give each child a whale cutout to glue onto blue construction paper. Help children tape together the long ends of the paper to make cylinders. Have them tape crepe paper streamers to one end. Attach the wind socks to twine and the twine to sticks.

• Place the wind socks outside in a location where children can observe them easily. Have children record daily observations in a class log and circle the words beginning with consonant digraph **wh**.

Sadlier Reading
Little Books and Big Books

Read *Getting to Know Sharks* (nonfiction) and have children listen for words that begin with the initial consonant digraph **wh**.

English Language Learners/ESL

Materials: whistle, wheel, whipped cream, toy **wheelbarrow**, toy **whale**, four posters with one of the following words written on each: **when, where, what, why**

Display all objects. Pick up and blow the whistle. Tell children that this is a /**hw**/-/**hw**/-/**hw**/-**istle**. On the board write the word **whistle** and underline **wh** as you say /**hw**/-**istle**. Model for children how to form their mouths as they say /**hw**/. Identify the other objects, repeating the procedure. Then read each question word on the posters, point out the beginning sound /**hw**/, and explain the meaning of each word. Then help children form questions using the question words and the object. Model: *What is a wheelbarrow? Where is the wheelbarrow?*

Challenge

Show children a **whirligig** and explain that it is a garden decoration with movable parts. These parts move when the wind blows. Have children sketch designs for their own whirligigs on paper. Then have them write a sentence about the wind, using one or more **wh** words (e.g., The wind **whirls** and **whips** up the leaves).

Special Strategies

For Universal Access activities, see page 283F.

Consonant Digraph ch

Objectives
- To identify and isolate initial sounds
- To identify and write words that begin with consonant digraph **ch**

Warming Up

Reviewing Initial Consonant c
- Write **cave** and **card** on the board, and read the words aloud. Remind children that in these words, the sound of **c** is /k/.
- Read aloud the following sentence: **Carrie** and her **cousin Calvin can call** a **cab**. Ask children to form a **c** with their hands whenever they hear a word that begins with **c**.

Teaching the Lesson

Phonemic Awareness: Identify and Isolate Initial Sounds
- Sing the following to the tune of "Twinkle, Twinkle, Little Star":

    Tell me, tell me what you heard.

    What's the sound that starts each word?

    Chair and **chalk** and **chop** and **cheer**,

    Cherry, **chilly**, **chief**, and **chin**.

- Say /**ch**/ several times. Point out that /**ch**/ is the beginning sound in **chair**, **chalk**, **chop**, **cheer**, **cherry**, **chilly**, **chief**, and **chin**.

Sound to Symbol
- Say /**ch**/ and then /**ch**/-/**ch**/ **chilly**. Tell children that the sound at the beginning of **chilly** is /**ch**/.
- Write **chilly** on the board, and underline the initial **ch**. Tell children that **ch** is a consonant digraph; when put together, the two letters in this digraph stand for /**ch**/.
- Write this sentence on the board and read it aloud: **Chad** has **chalk** on his **cheeks** and **chin**. Have a volunteer point out the words that start with /**ch**/. Have another circle the **ch** in each one.

ch

Chilly starts with the sound of the consonant digraph **ch**. Listen for the sound of **ch** in the rhyme.

The air is so chilly,
It makes my teeth chatter.
But weather keeps changing,
So what does it matter?

Circle the picture if its name begins with the sound of **ch**.

1 chick	2 cat	3 checkers	4 chair
5 chimney	6 cheese	7 church	8 cloud
9 camel	10 check	11 chopsticks	12 chipmunk

LESSON 153: Phonemic Awareness: Initial /**ch**/   **291**

UNIVERSAL ACCESS
Meeting Individual Needs

Visual • Kinesthetic
Materials: Sadlier Phonics Picture Cards for **cake, chair, cherry, cub, chick, cup, horn, sheep, shorts**

Show the cards one at a time. Have children clasp their hands over their heads as a **champion** would if the name of the picture begins with **ch**.

Auditory
On index cards, write fictitious book titles that contain the consonant digraph **ch** and titles that do not have the digraph. Have children take turns selecting a card and reading the title aloud. Have listeners say "Check it out!" when they hear a title containing a word that begins with the sound of **ch**.

Extra Support
Tell children that the word **cheep** begins with the sound /**ch**/. Ask them to cheep like birds when they hear a word that begins with the digraph **ch**. Say **chum, chalk, cent, chain, chart, circle, chop, chip**.

Say the name of each picture. Circle **ch** or **c** for each beginning sound. Then print the word from the box that names the picture.

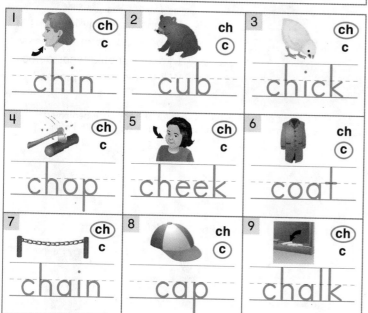

chain	cap	cheek	chin	chop
chalk	coat	chick	cub	

1 (ch) c — chin	2 ch (c) — cub	3 (ch) c — chick
4 (ch) c — chop	5 (ch) c — cheek	6 ch (c) — coat
7 (ch) c — chain	8 ch (c) — cap	9 (ch) c — chalk

Write a sentence about one picture using a **ch** word.

Accept any sentence that contains a **ch** word from items 1–9. Remind children that a sentence begins with an uppercase letter and ends with a period.

292

LESSON 153: Writing Consonant Digraph **ch**

Have your child read the sentence to you. Then work together to make up sentences about other pictures.

Practicing the Skill

● Read aloud the introduction and the rhyme on page 291. Ask children to name the words that begin with the sound of **ch**. Then read the directions and identify each picture. Have children complete the page.

● Ask volunteers to read the words at the top of page 292. Point out that even though they all begin with **c**, their initial sounds are different. Then read the directions and have children complete the page.

Curriculum Connections

Spelling Connection

Read aloud each word and sentence below. Have a child spell the word aloud. Have another child print the word on the board.

chop	Dad will **chop** wood for the fire.
cherry	The **cherry** trees are blooming.
cheese	Do you like **cheese** sandwiches?
children	Some **children** like storms.

Multicultural Connection

● Tell children that Cherrapunji, India, receives the greatest amount of rainfall in the world, while a desert in Chile receives the smallest amount. Point out Cherrapunji and Chile both begin with **Ch**.

● Point out the rainiest and driest places on a map of the world. Ask children which place they would rather live.

Theme Activity: Language Arts

● Discuss the expression "It's raining cats and dogs" with children. Ask what it would be like if the expression were true.

● Have children imagine what it would be like if strange things, such as **chairs**, **chickens**, or **chalk,** fell from the sky during a storm. Ask children to write a story about a strange storm. Have them circle the initial **ch** words they used.

Sadlier Reading

Little Books and Big Books

Read the poems "My Baby Brother" on page 9 and "By the Sea" on page 14 in Worlds of Poetry *Families, Families* and have children identify words that begin with initial consonant digraphs.

English Language Learners/ESL

Materials: magazine pictures of a **chick**, a **church**, a **chipmunk**, a **chimney**, a **chain**

Point to a **chair** in the classroom and say /**ch**/-/**ch**/-/**ch**/-**air**. Have children repeat the word after you. Write the word **chair** on the board and underline the **ch**. Model for children how to form their mouths to say /**ch**/. Then point to your **chin** and repeat the process. Continue using objects in the classroom such as **chalk** and **child**.

One at a time show the pictures and identify each picture for children. Label all the **ch** objects in the classroom. Have children say them on a daily basis.

Challenge

Have children work in pairs. Ask each pair to prepare and deliver a TV weather report about a blizzard. Have them include as many initial **ch** words as possible (e.g., **check, chilly, cheeks, chin, chop, chain**). Afterward have children write weather-related sentences that include the words.

Special Strategies

For Universal Access activities, see page 283F.

Consonant Digraph kn

Objectives
- To identify and isolate initial sounds
- To identify and write words that begin with consonant digraph **kn**

Warming Up

Reviewing Consonant k
- Remind children that **kite** begins with the sound of **k**. Say these sentences, and have children make an "OK" sign with their thumb and index finger when they hear a word that begins with the sound of **k**.

   Do you like **kites**? Do you like **kittens**?

   How about **kangaroos** holding up **keys**?

   All **kinds** of things are A-OK with me.

Teaching the Lesson

Phonemic Awareness: Identify and Isolate Initial Sounds
- Have children point to their **knuckles** and their **knees**. Say each word, and point out that the sound at the beginning of each is /**n**/. Then say /n/-/n/-/n/ **knees**; /n/-/n/-/n/ **knuckles**.
- Tell children to listen carefully and put their hands on their knees when they hear a word that begins with /**n**/. Then say **name**, **kite**, **clown**, **knife**, **note**.

Sound to Symbol
- Say: *I knock and turn the knob.* Explain that /**n**/ is the sound at the beginning of **knock** and **knob**. Have children repeat after you: /n/-/n/ **knock**; /n/-/n/ **knob**.
- Write **knock** and **knob** on the board. Underline the initial **kn** in each word.
- Explain that **kn** is a consonant digraph. The sound of **kn** is /**n**/. Point out that the **k** at the beginning of **knock** and **knob** is silent. Write **knight**, **king**, **kite**, and **knit** on the board. Have children name the words that begin with consonant digraph **kn**.

293

---

kn

Knit starts with the sound of the consonant digraph **kn**. The **k** is silent. Listen for the sound made by **kn** in the rhyme.

> Mittens warm my knuckles.
> Wool pants warm my knees.
> I know I should wear a cap.
> Will you knit one, please?

Say the name of each picture. Circle **kn** or **k** for each beginning sound. Then circle the picture if its name begins with **kn**.

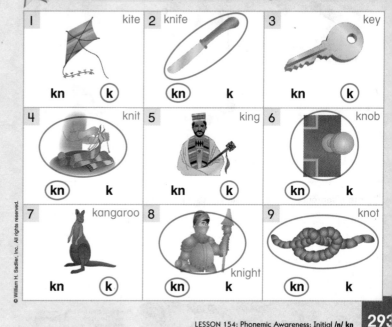

1 kite	2 knife	3 key
kn (k)	(kn) k	kn (k)
4 knit	5 king	6 knob
(kn) k	kn (k)	(kn) k
7 kangaroo	8 knight	9 knot
kn (k)	(kn) k	(kn) k

LESSON 154: Phonemic Awareness: Initial /n/ **kn**

293

U N I V E R S A L A C C E S S
Meeting Individual Needs

Visual • Kinesthetic
Materials: Sadlier Phonics Picture Cards for **knee, knot, cherry, chair, thread, thirty, king, kitten, shorts**

Show the cards one at a time, and have volunteers name each picture. Have listeners knock on their desks when they hear a word that begins with the sound of digraph **kn**.

Auditory • Kinesthetic
Read each riddle below, and have children respond by pantomiming and naming the correct **kn** word.

When you open a door, you may have to turn me first. What am I? (**knob**)

I am the part of your body in the middle of your leg. What am I? (**knee**)

You use me to cut your food. What am I? (**knife**)

Extra Support
Remind children that **knit** begins with digraph **kn** and that these two letters combine to make /**n**/. Write **ife, ob, ot, ow**, and **ee** in a column on the board. Have children add **kn** to each and say the word that is formed.

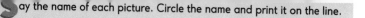
ay the name of each picture. Circle the name and print it on the line.

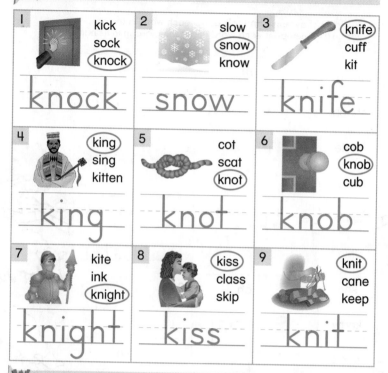

1	kick sock (knock)	2	slow (snow) know	3	(knife) cuff kit
	knock		snow		knife
4	(king) sing kitten	5	cot scat (knot)	6	cob (knob) cub
	king		knot		knob
7	kite ink (knight)	8	(kiss) class skip	9	(knit) cane keep
	knight		kiss		knit

Write a sentence about one of the pictures using a **kn** word.

Accept any sentence about a pictured **kn** word.
Remind children that a sentence begins with an uppercase letter and ends with a period.

294 LESSON 154: Writing Consonant Digraph **kn**

 Play "I Know a Word." Take turns with your child naming words that begin with **kn**.

Practicing the Skill

● Together read aloud the introduction and the rhyme on page 293. Then read the directions and do the first item together. Have children complete the page.

● Read the directions on page 294. Have volunteers identify the pictures. Complete the first item together before having children do items 2–9. Then complete the bottom section of the page with children.

Curriculum Connections

Spelling Connection

Read aloud each word and sentence below. Have a child spell the word aloud. Have another child print the word on the board.

know   I **know** her name.
knot   The **knot** in my shoelace is tight.
knob   Turn the **knob** to open the door.
knife   Be careful with that sharp **knife**!

Computer Connection

For practice with identifying digraphs, have children enter the Wooden Blocks Room in *Beginning Reading(c)* (Sierra). Explain that they will see blocks with two-letter sound combinations; Bananas, the talking chimpanzee, pronounces and shows pictures for the sounds. Have children find consonant digraphs on the blocks.

Theme Activity: Art

Materials: drawing paper, white crayons, blue or gray paint, brushes, smocks

● Have children become cloud artists and "hide" a picture of something whose name begins with **kn** in a picture of the sky.

● Tell children to draw their **kn** pictures with white crayon on paper. Then have them paint over the entire paper. The paint will not stick to the crayon, so their cloud art will show through.

● Have children add captions. Model: "It looks like a cloud, but I know it is a _____."

English Language Learners/ESL

Tell children that words that begin with **kn** have the beginning sound /n/. **Knock** on the door or the window and explain to children that you are **knocking**. Have children **knock** on their desks. Write **knock** on the board and underline the **kn**. Tell children to trace **k** and **n** in the air. Then say words that begin with **kn** such as **knee, knob, kneel**. Write each word on the board and make sure children recognize that the **kn** makes the sound /n/.

Challenge

Write this paragraph on the board:

It was a nasty November day. The fog was so thick, you could cut it with a _____. The chilly air made my _____ numb and my _____ _____ together. If only I _____ how to _____! I would make myself a nice, warm scarf.

Help children read it aloud. Have them fill in the blanks using this list of **kn** words: **knees, knew, knife, knuckles, knit, knock.**

Special Strategies

For Universal Access activities, see page 283F.

294

Connecting Spelling, Writing, and Speaking

Objectives
- To segment initial sounds
- To say, spell, sort, and write words with consonant digraphs
- To write a pilot's log entry using spelling words

Teaching the Lesson

Phonemic Awareness: Segment Initial Sounds

Model for children how to separate the beginning sound from the rest of the word. Say /sh/-/sh/-/sh/-ape, **shape**. Say it again, and have children repeat after you. Repeat the process using the following words /**ch**/-ain, **chain**; /**hw**/-ite, **white**; /**sh**/-eep, **sheep**; /**th**/-in, **thin**; /**n**/-ob, **knob**; /**ch**/-art, **chart**; /**n**/-ow, **know**; /**hw**/-ere, **where**.

Spelling
- Direct children's attention to the **Unit 6 Classroom Poster**, "Clouds." Ask a volunteer to point out the words that begin with **wh** (**white**, **when**, **where**). Ask another child to point out the word that begins with **sh** (**sheep**).
- On the board write the digraphs **th**, **sh**, **wh**, **ch**, and **kn**. Say each spelling word with children, spell it, and say it again. Then ask volunteers to print each word on the board under its initial diagraph.

Practicing the Skill

Read aloud the directions on page 295. Do the first item together. Then have children complete the page independently.

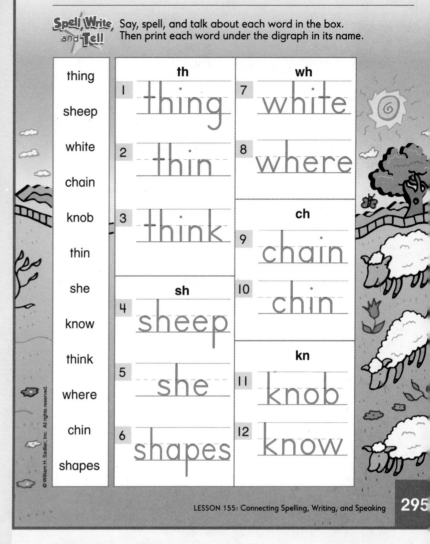

Spell, Write, and Tell Say, spell, and talk about each word in the box. Then print each word under the digraph in its name.

word list	th	wh
thing	1 thing	7 white
sheep	2 thin	8 where
white	3 think	**ch**
chain	**sh**	9 chain
knob	4 sheep	10 chin
thin	5 she	**kn**
she	6 shapes	11 knob
know		12 know
think		
where		
chin		
shapes		

LESSON 155: Connecting Spelling, Writing, and Speaking **295**

UNIVERSAL ACCESS
Meeting Individual Needs

Auditory • Tactile

Ask children to print the spelling word for each clue that you give. Begin by saying: *I'm thinking of a word that begins like . . . .* End the sentence with phrases such as:

where and names a color. (**white**)

thing and is the opposite of **thick**. (**thin**)

Visual • Tactile

Materials: Punchout Letter Cards

Have children work in pairs. One child selects a word from the list on page 295. The child scrambles the letter cards that form the word and gives them to his or her partner to unscramble. Children trade roles and repeat the activity.

Extra Support

Place **Sadlier Phonics Picture Cards** for the digraphs **th**, **sh**, **wh**, **ch**, **kn** (e.g., **knee**, **whale**, etc.) facedown on a table. Have children pick a card, name the picture, and say the digraph sound. Write the word and circle the digraph.

Spell, Write, and Tell!

Pretend you are the pilot of a plane. Write about one of your trips in your pilot's log. Use one or more of your spelling words. Then tell about what you wrote.

thing
sheep
white
chain
knob
thin
she
know
think
where
chin
shapes

Date: _____

Encourage the children to write two or three sentences about an imaginary trip.

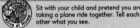

LESSON 155: Connecting Spelling, Writing, and Speaking

Sit with your child and pretend you are taking a plane ride together. Tell each other what you see.

296

The Writing Process

Tell children that a log is a type of journal. A pilot keeps track of what happens during a plane trip in the log. Then read aloud the directions on page 296.

Brainstorm   Talk about flying on a plane. Encourage children who have taken an airplane trip to share their experiences. Discuss what a pilot might see, hear, and feel while flying a plane.

Write   On a sheet of paper, have children write about an imaginary flight. Remind them to imagine they are pilots and to use the word **I**.

Revise   Have children work with partners to check each other's sentences. Remind them to check spelling and punctuation. Have children underline spelling words they have used.

Publish   On a separate sheet of paper have children write their final draft for the pilot log. Compile the papers and make a Pilot Journal for the Reading Center.

Speak   Invite children to make construction-paper goggles to wear as they read their entries to the class.

Extending the Skills

Share Charles G. Shaw's _It Looked Like Spilt Milk_ (HarperCollins, 1992). Then have children write their own cloud books. Write this sentence frame on the board: "On ___, the clouds looked like ___." For one week, have children observe clouds and write a page in their books. On the last day, have them add a cover. Help children bind their books and place them in the Reading Center.

Portfolio   Have children add their cloud books to their portfolios.

English Language Learners/ESL
Materials: Sadlier Phonics Picture Cards for **thirty, sheep, whale, chick,** and **knot.**

Review the consonant digraph sounds before reading and writing the spelling words. Write **th, sh, wh, ch,** and **kn** on the board. Have children practice saying the digraphs. Then arrange the picture cards for **thirty, sheep, whale, chick,** and **knot** on the chalk ledge. Invite volunteers to choose a picture and say the word and the beginning sound. Encourage children to think of additional words for each digraph.

Challenge
Have children work in pairs to make a list of other words that contain the initial consonant digraphs in the word box. Then have children pretend to be TV weather reporters and to use as many digraph words as they can to write three sentences about what the weather might be like tomorrow. Have children underline the words with the digraphs. Some words they might use: **thermometer, thirty, thunder, shirt, shorts, shining, beach, fish, shoes.**

Special Strategies
For Universal Access activities, see page 283F.

Observational Assessment
Note which children are misspelling words that begin with digraphs.

296

Student Pages 297–298

Reviewing and Writing Consonant Digraphs

Objectives

- To segment phonemes in a word
- To write words with consonant digraphs
- To read and write words with consonant digraphs in context

Warming Up

Reviewing Long Vowel e

Read aloud the rhyme below. Have children name words with the long **e** sound.

I look out over the **tree**.

What do I **see**?

A **sheep** and a **bee**

And a **chimpanzee**.

Teaching the Lesson

Phonemic Awareness: Segment Phonemes in a Word

Say the word **sheep**. Remind children that words are made up of separate sounds. Tell children that there are three sounds in the word **sheep.** Segment the word by saying /**sh**/-/ē/-/p/ **sheep**, and have children repeat after you. Repeat the process using **chop** /**ch**/-/o/-/p/ and **white** /**hw**/-/ī/-/t/.

Sound to Symbol

Say the words **thirty**, **whale**, **chilly**, **sheep**, **knit**. Remind children that each word begins with a digraph. Have children say with you each word and the initial digraph: **thirty** /**th**/, **whale** /**hw**/, **chilly** /**ch**/, **sheep** /**sh**/, **knit** /**n**/. Next write the words on the board, and underline each beginning digraph as you say /**th**/, /**hw**/, /**ch**/, /**sh**/, /**n**/. Then say **thick**, **wheat**, **chop**, **ship**, and **knob**. Have children repeat each initial digraph and then write the letters for the sound on the board.

Read the riddles. Print the answers on the lines. The picture clues will help you. Then circle the words with consonant digraphs.

1. I grow on a tree. I am a fruit.

   I am a ___cherry___.

2. I swim in the sea, but I am not a (shark.)

   I am a ___whale___.

3. I may prick you (when) you pick a rose.

   I am a ___thorn___.

4. I am black or (white.) I graze in the (shade) with my flock.

   I am a ___sheep___.

5. Open the door with me. (Then) use me to (shut) it.

   I am a ___knob___.

LESSON 156: Reviewing Consonant Digraphs

297

U N I V E R S A L   A C C E S S
Meeting Individual Needs

Visual • Tactile

Materials: construction paper strips, glue

Give each child paper strips. Have children print a word with an initial consonant digraph on each strip. Then have them glue the strips, with the words on the outside, into interlocking circles to make a chain.

Auditory • Kinesthetic

Materials: Sadlier Phonics Picture Cards for **thermometer, thirty, sheep, shorts, whale, wheat, chair, cherry, knee, knot**

Have children work in pairs. Give each pair the picture cards. Have partners say each picture name and sort the cards by the sound of the consonant digraph. Tell children to print the digraph in the air.

Extra Support

Remind children that a digraph combines two consonants to make one new sound, as with the letters **c** and **h** in **chain**. Write **op, ip, in,** and **ore** on the board. Have children add the digraphs **sh** and **ch** to the beginning of each and say the words.

⭐ **W**rite about and draw a picture of each day's weather. Circle any consonant digraphs you use.

Yesterday it was	Accept any answers that accurately complete the sentences. On the board, you may want to list the following consonant digraph words to use in the sentences:
_____ _____ _____ _____ _____	white — when thick — where then — thirty thin — shady sharp — shapes whipped — chilly change
Today it is _____ _____ _____ _____	
I think tomorrow will be _____ _____ _____ _____	

298   LESSON 156: Writing Words with Consonant Digraphs

 Watch a television weather report with your child. Listen for words he or she wrote on this page.

Practicing the Skill

● Read aloud the directions and riddles on page 297. Remind children to use the pictures to solve the riddles. Do the first item together. Then have children complete the page.

● Go over the directions on page 298. Ask children to write sentences describing the weather. Tell them to use words that begin with the digraphs **th**, **sh**, **wh**, and **ch** (e.g., **thick**, **then**, **thin**, **sharp**, **shady**, **white**, **change**, **chilly**). Then have children draw a picture for each day's weather.

Curriculum Connections

Spelling Connection

Read aloud each word and sentence below. Have a child spell the word orally. Ask another child to print the word on the board.

chew — Always **chew** your food carefully.

knee — Your **knee** is part of your leg.

show — Please **show** me your new book.

whip — Mara will **whip** up a snack for us.

think — Can you **think** of the answer?

Theme Activity:
Language Arts/Science

Materials: magazines or catalogs, scissors, glue, cloud shapes made from construction paper, crayons

Tell children to look through magazines or catalogs and cut out pictures of objects with names that begin with a consonant digraph. Have children glue each picture onto a cloud shape and print the consonant digraph on the back. Ask each child to show her or his cloud and say the picture name. Have the group name each initial consonant digraph.

Sadlier Reading

Little Books and Big Books

Read *The Trash Can Band* (fiction) for more practice with consonant digraphs.

English Language Learners/ESL

To help children understand and practice riddles in preparation for the lesson, play a guessing game involving common objects in the classroom that they can see or touch. Help children identify consonant digraph words naming classroom objects, such as a **chart**, **shades**, **chair**, or **thumbtack**. Then present riddles such as those on page 297 to give clues from the first-person perspective. Invite volunteers to answer with "I am a ____."

Challenge

Tell children that they will work in groups to make a word web for each season. Have groups write the name of each season in the center of a separate sheet of paper and circle the word. Then have them write words that describe the season and draw lines to connect words that relate. Have children include words with consonant digraphs in their word webs.

Special Strategies

For Universal Access activities, see page 283F.

Integrating the Language Arts

Objectives

- To identify and count syllables
- To use oral and written language to extend the theme concept
- To demonstrate recognition of words with consonant digraphs

★ Teaching the Lesson

Phonemic Awareness: Identify and Count Syllables

Remind children that a syllable is a word or word part with one vowel sound, and that words can have one or more syllables. Tell children that you will say some weather words. Say the words slowly and have them repeat each word after you. Then ask them to tap out the word on their desk, one syllable at a time, as you say the word together. Ask volunteers to tell how many syllables are in each word. Use these words: **sky, thunder, lightning, tornado, snowflake, rain, hurricane, humidity, sunshine**.

Skills in Context

- Have children study the pictures on page 299 and then look for clouds outside. Ask if any of the clouds they see look like the ones in the pictures.
- Read aloud the text. Point out each kind of cloud as it is mentioned. Pay special attention to long or scientific words such as **cumulus**, **cirrus**, and **stratus**.
- Challenge children to find the words on the page that begin with consonant digraphs.

Comprehension Skill: Recognizing Facts

Explain that a fact is something that is known to be true. For example, ice is frozen water. Ask children to name facts they know about clouds.

 Listen as the page is read aloud. Look at the pictures. Then talk about what you see.

You know there are many kinds of clouds. They come in different shapes and colors.

Cumulus clouds are white and fluffy. You see them when the sun shines. Cirrus clouds look like feathers. When they are in the sky, the weather may change soon. A layer of stratus clouds can cover the sky. Stratus clouds may be gray. They often bring rain.

Cumulus Clouds

Cirrus Clouds

Stratus Clouds

When you go outside, look up. What are clouds telling you about the weather?

LESSON 157: Words with Consonant Digraphs in Context
Comprehension: Recognizing Facts

299

UNIVERSAL ACCESS
Meeting Individual Needs

Reading and Writing Connection

Have children look through the classroom library for books that show clouds, and then have them decide what the clouds tell about the weather.

Ask children to write a short weather forecast based on the pictures. Then challenge children to deliver a television-type weather forecast by showing the pictures and reading their forecast at the front of the room.

Science Connection

Materials: paper, crayons

Talk about ways the weather in your area changes during the year. Write the names of the four seasons on the board and use a calendar to show children which months are part of each season.

Have children fold a sheet of paper into four sections. Ask them to draw a picture that shows one season in each section. Then guide them to print the name of the season under each picture.

The words in the box are often used in sentences. Use one of the words to complete each sentence. Then practice reading the sentences aloud.

| come | find | open | out | want | We |

1. I _____want_____ to plan a .
   picnic

2. Dad and Gran will _____come_____, too.

3. _____We_____ want to see if it will rain.

4. Gran can _____find_____ out on [TV].
   TV

5. Dad can find _____out_____ in the [newspaper].
   newspaper

6. I can _____open_____ the [window] to find out.
   window

300

LESSON 158: Reading High-Frequency Words

Write each word in the box on a piece of paper. Ask your child to read each word and use it in a sentence.

LESSON 158 • UNIT 6
Student Page 300

High-Frequency Words

Objectives

- To recognize and read high-frequency words
- To write high-frequency words to complete sentences

Teaching the Lesson

Materials: index cards

- Write these sentences on the board: The door is _____ . I _____ to play. You cannot go _____ in the rain. The dog wants to _____ a bone. _____ work hard at school. Can you _____ to my house?

Write the words **come, find, open, out, want,** and **We** on the board. Point to each word, read it, and ask the class to repeat it. Have a volunteer choose a sentence from the board for you to read aloud, and another to select a word from the board to complete the sentence. Print the word in the blank. Remind children that the first word in a sentence begins with an uppercase letter.

- Write the words **come, find, open, out, want,** and **We** on index cards, and place the cards in a pile. Then write these sentences on the board or on a chart:

  We eat all our vegetables. I like to come to school. Will you open the door so we can go out? Cheryl cannot find her hat. What do you want to do?

Read the sentences with the children. Have them take turns choosing a card and finding the matching word in one of the sentences.

Practicing the Skill

Read aloud the directions at the top of page 300 and call on children to read the words in the box. Read aloud the sentences and identify the rebus pictures. Then have them complete the page.

Extra Practice

Materials: Punchout Letter Cards **c, f, o, w**

Write these word parts on the board, omitting the first letter of each word: _ome, _pen, _ant, _e, _ut, _ind. Display the letter cards, and tell children to listen as you say the words **come, open, want, we, out,** and **find,** one at a time. Call on volunteers to make each word you say by placing the correct letter card in front of each word part. Have the rest of the class print each word as it is completed.

Review

Materials: index cards

Write the words **funny, stop, no, down,** and **little** on index cards. Make rebus cards for these words: **up**—an arrow pointing up; **go**—a green traffic light; **yes**—a hand showing a "thumbs-up" signal; **sad**—a sad face; **big**—a child looking up at a big elephant. Help children understand the word that each rebus card represents. Display the rebus cards on the chalk ledge. Then hold up each word card, read it aloud, and ask the class to repeat it after you. Have children take turns choosing a word card and matching it with the rebus card that has the opposite meaning. Have them say each pair of opposites and spell the word on the card.

Student Pages 301–302

Assessing Consonant Digraphs

Objectives
- To recognize consonant digraphs
- To write words with consonant digraphs

Warming Up

Reviewing Final Consonants

Materials: Punchout Letter Cards for all the consonants

Remind children that words are made up of different sounds. Say /w/-/i/-/g/ **wig**, and tell children that the letter **g** stands for /g/, the ending sound in **wig**. Have children choose a consonant at random, name it, and sound it out. Then have them name a word that ends with the sound of the consonant

---

Teaching the Lesson

Materials: 16 index cards, each with one of the following words printed on it: **shadow, shirt, shoe, shave, throw, think, thumb, wheel, whistle, chop, chair, chin, check, knee, knit, knock**

- Remind children that when two letters combine to make a new sound, they form a digraph (e.g., the letters **s** and **h** in **ship**). Then write **ship, chain, wheat, think,** and **knit** on the board. Tell children that each word begins with a digraph. Circle each digraph, and say each sound (/**sh**/, /**ch**/, /**hw**/, /**th**/, /**n**/). Have children repeat after you.
- Have children play charades using the words on the index cards. Explain that one child chooses a card at random and acts out the word without speaking. Then the class guesses the word. The child who guesses correctly writes the digraph on the board and draws the next card.

Check-Up Say the name of each picture. Fill in the circle next to the letters that stand for the beginning digraph.

1 knife	2 checkers	3 whisper
● kn / ○ sh / ○ th	● ch / ○ sh / ○ wh	○ th / ○ ch / ● wh
4 check	**5 thirty**	**6 knock**
○ kn / ○ sh / ● ch	● th / ○ kn / ○ sh	○ wh / ○ ch / ● kn
7 whistle	**8 shoe**	**9 chair**
○ ch / ○ th / ● wh	● sh / ○ kn / ○ ch	○ th / ● ch / ○ wh
10 thumb	**11 whiskers**	**12 knight**
○ ch / ○ sh / ● th	○ sh / ● wh / ○ kn	● kn / ○ th / ○ ch
13 ship	**14 thimble**	**15 shovel**
○ ch / ● sh / ○ th	○ sh / ● th / ○ kn	○ th / ○ wh / ● sh

UNIVERSAL ACCESS
Reteaching Activities

Activity 1

Materials: magazines or catalogs, scissors, glue, crayons, large construction paper shapes for **cherry, shell, knob, thimble, wheel**

Distribute shapes for each digraph to groups of children. Have children name each shape and label it with its digraph. Then have children look through magazines and cut out pictures of objects that begin with each digraph. Tell them to paste the pictures on the back of the corresponding shape. Have children present their shapes to the class and say the picture names.

Activity 2

Materials: overhead projector, construction paper, markers

Remind children that some words begin with digraphs. Ask them to identify the beginning consonant digraph in the word **shadow**. Using an overhead projector to cast shadows, have children work in pairs to trace each other's shadows on construction paper. Have them cut out the shadow shapes. Ask children to decorate their shadows with beginning digraph words. Then have volunteers share their words with the class. Make a bulletin board display of the shadows.

Say the name of each picture. Find the letters in the box that stand for the missing digraph. Then print the letters on the lines.

| th | sh | wh | ch | kn |

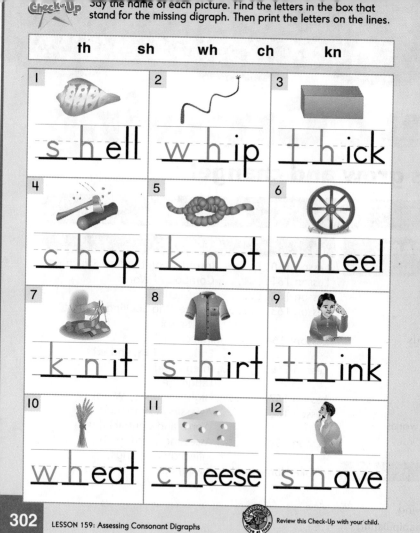

1. s h ell
2. w h ip
3. t h ick
4. c h op
5. k n ot
6. w h eel
7. k n it
8. s h irt
9. t h ink
10. w h eat
11. c h eese
12. s h ave

302

LESSON 159: Assessing Consonant Digraphs

Review this Check-Up with your child.

Assessing the Unit

Check-Up Use pages 301 and 302 to assess children's mastery of consonant digraphs. Page 301 also prepares them for standardized tests. Together read the directions on page 301 and identify each picture. Review with children how to indicate their answers by filling in the circles. Then read aloud the directions on page 302, and identify the pictures. Go over the first item together. Then have children complete both pages.

Observational Assessment Review your observational notes about children's mastery of consonant digraphs and participation in the unit's skill and theme activities. Use these notes to help assess performance and progress.

Portfolio Assessment Discuss with each child any portfolio pieces that he or she would like to revise. Review the goals set at your last conference, and determine whether the child has achieved them. Work together to set new goals. See the Writing Rubrics on page 283C.

Dictation Tell children you are going to say some words with consonant digraphs. Have them write the words as you dictate them. Say: **thorn**, **shape**, **white**, **knit**, **chain**. Then tell children you are going to say a sentence. Have them write the sentence as you dictate it and underline any words with consonant digraphs. Say: *The **wheel** is in the **shed***.

Student Skills Assessment Use the checklist on Student Edition pages 321–322 to record your observations of individual children.

Take-Home Book Remind children to complete at home the *Take-Home Book* for Unit 6.

Additional Assessment See pages 283C–283E.

Guided Instruction

Skills	Resources
Consonant digraph **th**	Instruction on pages 285–286
Consonant digraph **sh**	Instruction on pages 287–288
Consonant digraph **wh**	Instruction on pages 289–290
Consonant digraph **ch**	Instruction on pages 291–292
Consonant digraph **kn**	Instruction on pages 293–294
Consonant digraphs	Phonemic Awareness activities on pages 283H–283I Game Time on pages 283K–283M Punchout Cards on page 283N Technology on pages 283O–283P

All About Growing

Watch things grow and change!

Word Structure

READING/LANGUAGE ARTS STANDARDS

- ❂ Respond to a poem in a way that reflects understanding
- ❂ Read compound words
- ❂ Use knowledge of individual words in unknown compound words to predict their meanings
- ❂ Identify and use contractions in writing and speaking
- ❂ Read inflectional forms and root words

OBJECTIVES

- ▶ To enjoy a poem about a seed that grows
- ▶ To develop phonemic awareness by identifying, matching, segmenting, blending, and manipulating sounds in spoken words
  - ▶ To read and write compound words
  - ▶ To read and write contractions
  - ▶ To read and write words with the inflectional endings **s, ing**, and **ed**
- ▶ To read and write compound words, contractions, words with inflectional endings, and high-frequency words in context

LESSONS

- Take-Home Book: *Growing Up*

Thematic Teaching

In Unit 7 children learn to use word structure to decode longer words as they watch how things grow and change. They work with compound words, contractions, and words with inflectional endings **s, ing**, and **ed**. The poem "Tommy" exemplifies how nature, in verse and in the real world, can delight children with its surprises.

Choose activities from the lesson plans to complement children's interests. Display the "Tommy" **Unit 7 Classroom Poster** where children can refer to it as they discuss changes they have observed in plants and animals.

Curriculum Integration

Spelling The *Spelling Connection* appears in most lesson plans. In the lesson on page 316, children practice spelling high-frequency words.

Writing Children practice meaningful writing on pages 308, 310, 312, 314, and 315.

Science Children learn about growth and change as they complete the activities on pages 312 and 314.

Optional Learning Activities

Multisensory Activities
Multisensory activities are a regular feature of the phonics lessons and appeal to all learning styles—visual, auditory, tactile, and kinesthetic.

Multicultural Connection
Broaden children's understanding of places around the world with the activities on pages 304, 306, and 312.

Thematic Activities
Activities in *Curriculum Connections* allow children to apply their new phonics skills as they build upon the theme of the unit.

Gwendolyn Brooks

Author's Corner

Gwendolyn Brooks started making up rhymes when she was seven. Her proud parents were sure she would grow up to become a writer, and they were right! At thirteen she published a poem in a children's magazine, and at sixteen she was publishing poetry regularly in a Chicago newspaper. In 1950 she won the Pulitzer Prize in poetry.

✔ Assessment Strategies

Assessment is an ongoing process. Multiple strategies in the Student Edition as well as the Teacher's Edition and regular use of the *Student Skills Assessment Checklist* on pages 321–322 will help you monitor children's progress in using compound words, contractions, and words with inflectional endings.

UNIT RESOURCES

Sadlier Reading

Classroom Poster

Phonics Picture Cards

Little Books and Big Books

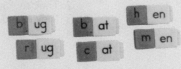

Student Manipulatives

Books by Gwendolyn Brooks

Bronzeville Boys and Girls. New York: HarperCollins Children's Books, 1967.

The Tiger Who Wore White Gloves: Or What You Are You Are. Chicago: Third World Press, 1974.

Theme-Related Resources

Flowers, Plants, and Trees. Prism Entertainment, 1994. Questions about plant life are explored in this thirty-minute video.

Raffi. *Everything Grows.* New York: MCA Records, 1998. Singing along with this tape will help children make connections among all kinds of growth.

Wilkes, Angela. *See How I Grow.* New York: DK Publishing, 1994. Children are led to think about their own growing experiences.

UNIT 7 ✓ ASSESSMENT

In Unit 7 children focus on word structure: compound words, contractions, inflectional endings, and base words. The assessment ideas on this page are for use throughout the chapter.

Pretests/Posttests

The tests on pages 303D–303E serve as a formal end-of-unit assessment of children's mastery of inflectional endings and contractions. In some cases you may choose to use them as pretests to help you identify a starting point for instruction for individual children. The Phonemic Awareness Test on page 303J may also be used as a pretest.

Observational Assessment

Specific opportunities to observe children's progress in using word structure to recognize compound words, contractions, inflectional endings, and base words are highlighted in the lesson plans. The *Student Skills Assessment Checklist* on pages 321–322 of the Student Edition will help you keep track of students' progress.

Dictation

Dictate the following words and have children write them on a sheet of paper: **isn't**, **reading**, **plays**, **raincoat**, **it's**, **you're**, **mailbox**, **backpack**, **mixed**, **walking**. Then have children write the following sentences: I **walked** with Mom. We **don't** see the plant. The puppy **plays** with the **shoelace**. In addition to assessing the compound words, contractions, and inflectional endings, observe whether children begin each sentence with an uppercase letter and end with a period.

Using Technology

The activities on pages 303O–303P may also be used to evaluate children's progress.

Performance Assessment

On a bulletin board display the title Now and When I'm Ten! Brainstorm with children about the things they can do now and the things children can do when they are ten. Tell children to write three things they can do now and then write three things they'll be able to do when they are ten. Remind children to write in complete sentences. Have children illustrate one thing they'll do at age ten. Display children's sentences and illustrations on the bulletin board. Use the *Student Skills Assessment Checklist* on pages 321–322 to record your observations.

Portfolio Assessment

The portfolio icon in the lesson plans indicates portfolio opportunities throughout the unit. Post the rubrics for Unit 7 on a chart when you begin the unit, and review the criteria with children. Discuss with children how they can select work from their portfolios that best represents their progress in a given area. For example, for the rubric "correctly forms contractions," model by posing questions such as: *Did I put the apostrophe where letters are left out?*

Name _____

Writing Rubrics

	Sometimes	Never	Always
Phonics Skills			
Forms compound words			
Forms contractions			
Uses inflectional endings			
Reads compound words, contractions, and words with inflectional endings in context			
Writing Skills			
Writes sentences using compound words			
Writes sentences using contractions			
Writes sentences using words with inflectional endings			
Produces sample writing with a beginning, middle, and end			
Writes fluently and independently			
Edits for punctuation and spelling			

Answer Key

Page 303D		Page 303E	
1. aren't	4. I'm	1. plant	4. watching
2. They're	5. It's	2. happened	5. playing
3. they'll	6. don't	3. water	6. turned

Read each sentence. Fill in the circle in front of the contraction that stands for the underlined words.

1	The kittens <u>are</u> <u>not</u> very big.	○ doesn't ○ aren't ○ isn't
2	<u>They</u> <u>are</u> sleeping by their mother.	○ You're ○ They'll ○ They're
3	Soon <u>they</u> <u>will</u> wake up.	○ they'll ○ you'll ○ they're
4	<u>I</u> <u>am</u> going to play with them.	○ I'll ○ They're ○ I'm
5	<u>It</u> <u>is</u> surprising how fast they grow.	○ Isn't ○ It's ○ I'm
6	But <u>do</u> <u>not</u> let them go outside yet!	○ don't ○ doesn't ○ isn't

Pre/Posttest   Read each sentence. Fill in the circle in front of the missing word.

1 Did you ever _____ a seed?	○ plant ○ planted ○ planting
2 What _____ to it?	○ happen ○ happened ○ happening
3 Did you _____ it every day?	○ water ○ watered ○ watering
4 Did you enjoy _____ it grow?	○ watch ○ watched ○ watching
5 It grew while you were _____.	○ play ○ played ○ playing
6 The seed _____ into a plant.	○ turn ○ turned ○ turning

In Unit 7 children learn about compound words, inflectional endings, base words, and contractions. Children who have difficulty with this unit may be exhibiting problems with spatial discrimination or memory, or they may be showing signs of attention deficit disorder (ADD). Presented here are some beginning strategies that you can use to help these children cope with such difficulties.

Spatial Discrimination

Compound Words

Children with spatial discrimination problems may have difficulty dealing with print on a page (e.g., the spatial relationship between and among letters and words). In the formation of compound words, it may be hard for these children to see that two words are "put together" to make a new word. The following techniques may help these children work through this unit.

- In each hand hold a picture card for one of the two words in a compound word (e.g., **mail** and **box**). Say each word separately. Then move the cards together and say the two words together as a compound word. Display a picture of a **mailbox**, and guide children to see that the new word combines the meaning of each word—"a box for mail." After children have practiced forming compounds that carry the meaning of both words, guide them to understand that sometimes a new word formed from putting two words together may have a different meaning. Use a picture of a **butterfly** and the words **butter** and **fly** as an example.

- Write the word for each picture on an index card and repeat the above activity. Review the meaning of each word and then the meaning of the new word formed after putting the two words together.

Words with Inflectional Endings

Children with spatial discrimination problems may have difficulty attaching inflectional endings to verbs. These techniques are helpful in such cases.

- Have a child walk to the board. Have others describe what the child is doing: "Sue is **walking** to the board." Write **walking** on the board, and have children say the word. Then have them describe what Sue did: "Sue **walked** to the board." Write **walked** on the board, and have children say the word. Continue with other actions, using words with inflectional endings such as **jump, jumping, jumped**.

Memory

Contractions

Children with memory problems may have difficulty retaining the contractions presented in this unit. Such children may benefit from activities that involve repetition, recurring patterns, rules, and reminders.

- As a reference, display on a bulletin board the contractions presented in the unit that are similar to the form of **is + not = isn't**.

- Have children with memory problems work with partners who are good at recall in an activity using contractions. Have each pair of children work together to say and write sentences that involve a contraction. Have them give the two separate words first, followed by the contraction, in their sentences (e.g., "**We will**—**we'll**—dress up in pioneer clothes.").

Attention Deficit Disorder (ADD)

Children with ADD vary in the specific traits as well as in the severity of their condition. A common problem for many of these children is an inability to follow directions. Use the following strategy with these children.

- List on the board contractions that children have encountered in their lessons. Then dictate, one at a time, a numbered list of directions, such as the list below. Allow time for children to complete each step.

  1. Number your paper 1, 2, and 3.

  2. Beside number 1 print one of the contractions.

  3. Beside number 2 print the first word that the contraction stands for.

  4. Beside number 3 print the second word that the contraction stands for.

  5. Put your paper in the box on the table.

When children have finished, have them tell the steps they followed in the correct order.

The chart below identifies problems that children may manifest as they learn the concepts and skills presented in this unit. The chart also identifies strategies to use with children who have not yet mastered the key concepts in the unit.

SKILL	Compound Words	Contractions	Inflectional Endings **s**, **ing**, **ed**
Observation	Child does not recognize that the meaning of a compound word can often be inferred from the meaning of the two words that comprise it.	Child does not understand that in a contraction an apostrophe replaces a letter or letters left out from the two words that make up the contraction.	Child has difficulty adding inflectional endings **s**, **ing**, and **ed** to indicate whether something is happening now or has already happened.
Intervention	• Write these words on the board: **dollhouse, doghouse, bathtub, bathmat, mailbox, lunchbox, hairbrush, and toothbrush**. Say the words, and have child identify the two words that make up each compound word. To help child infer the meaning of each word, write on the board: *A **house** for a **doll** is called a ___.* Have child say and print the missing word and then draw a vertical line between the two smaller words that form it. Have child write a similar sentence for each word.	• Write these words on the board: **you are** and **you're**. Have child circle the letter that has been left out in the contraction (**a**), and explain how it relates to the apostrophe. Repeat with other contractions. • Have child work with a partner. Tell each child to print sentences using contractions. Have partners exchange papers, print the words for which the contractions stand, and circle the letters that have been left out.	• Have child classify words with inflectional endings, such as **laughs, laughing, laughed**, under the headings *What's Being Done Now* and *What Was Done in the Past*. If child needs help, say: *The teacher **laughs** [laugh]. I am **laughing** [laugh while saying the sentence].* Then pause for a minute, and say: *I **laughed** a minute ago.* • Help child make up sentences about what is shown in a picture, such as the one shown on this page, using words with inflectional endings. For example: *The baby **smiles**. The dog is **rolling** the ball. It **rained** earlier.*

These activities are designed to augment the lessons in the unit with exercises that reinforce skills and encourage creativity.

Produce Rhyming Words

A Poet—and You Know It!

Say the rhyme "Jack and Jill went up the hill." Then ask what word rhymes with **Jill**. (**hill**) Say other familiar rhymes, such as those given below, and have children supply the final rhyming word. Then have children think of other rhyming words not in the rhyme. Have children make up their own version of the last two lines of each rhyme using one of the words they suggest.

Rain, Rain,

Go away;

Come again another day.

All the children want to play.

Star light, Star bright,

First star I see tonight,

I wish I may,

I wish I might,

Have this wish

I wish tonight.

Three little kittens, they lost their mittens,

And they began to cry,

"Oh Mother, dear, we sadly fear,

Our mittens we have lost."

"What? Lost your mittens?

You naughty kittens,

Then you shall have no pie."

Humpty Dumpty sat on a wall,

Humpty Dumpty had a great fall.

All the King's horses and all the King's men

Couldn't put Humpty Dumpty together again.

"This Land Is Your Land"

Lead children in singing "This Land Is Your Land." Then have them pretend they are in the woods, at the seashore, or in some other natural setting suggested by the song. Tell them to close their eyes and imagine the sights and sounds and activities around them.

After a few minutes ask children to share things they saw, heard, or did in their imagination. Make the activity into a game by having each child name one thing and then say a word that rhymes. Challenge children to include compound words and words with inflectional ending, such as: **seashore**, **roar**; **hiked**, **biked**; **swims**, **trims**; **mountain**, **fountain**; **waterfall**, **tall**; **fishing**, **wishing**; **riverboat**, **goat**. Then have the class add other rhyming words to the list.

Identify and Count Syllables

Syllables in Pet Names
Materials: drawing paper, crayons, magic marker

Have the class talk about the importance of being kind to all living creatures, including pets. Tell children to draw a picture of a pet they have or would like to have. Tell children to share their pictures with a partner and to say the pet's name, clapping once for each syllable in the name as they say it. Have the partner identify the number of syllables in the pet's name.

Name That Tree!

Materials: colored construction paper, scissors

Introduce children to different kinds of trees, either through a nature walk or through books and other materials. Tell children the names of the different kinds of trees they see. The different kinds might include **apple**, **ash**, **banana**, **banyan**, **butternut**, **cedar**, **coconut**, **cottonwood**, **holly**, **maple**, **oak**, **pawpaw**, **persimmon**, **pine**, **sequoia**, **walnut**, and **willow**.

Say the name of one of the trees. Have children repeat the name of the tree and tap the desk with one hand for each syllable in the name.

Clap Your Name

Choose a volunteer, and say the child's first name, clapping once for each syllable as you say it. Have children take turns, following your model, saying their first name and clapping once for each syllable as they say it. (If there is not much variety in the number of syllables in children's first names, use their last names instead.)

Next clap once and have children with one-syllable names stand up, clap twice and have children with two-syllable names stand up, and so on. Follow the same procedure to have children sit back down, but mix up the sequence of the number of claps.

Combine Syllables

Play the game "I Went to the Mall." Model an example by saying: *I went to the mall and saw a* **mon**-**key**. (Say one syllable of **monkey** at a time, pausing between syllables.) Call on a volunteer to say the word for what you saw, combining the two parts of the word. Continue with *bought a* **basketball** and *ate a* **hamburger**.

Then have children take turns saying "I went to the mall and [saw, bought, ate, heard, and so on] a ___," completing the sentence with a word of more than one syllable, pausing after each syllable as you did in your model. Call on volunteers to say the word by combining the syllables.

Name _____ Date _____

Directions: Give this assessment orally to each child.

Identify and Count Syllables

Say: *Listen to each word I say. Repeat it after me, and tap lightly on your desk as you say each syllable. Then tell me how many syllables are in the word.* Circle the words that the child responds to correctly.

1. water	**(2)**	6. banana	**(3)**	11. apple	**(2)**
2. watermelon	**(4)**	7. rain	**(1)**	12. triangle	**(3)**
3. carrot	**(2)**	8. sunny	**(2)**	13. cherry	**(2)**
4. row	**(1)**	9. bicycle	**(3)**	14. vacation	**(3)**
5. gorilla	**(3)**	10. umbrella	**(3)**	15. caterpillar	**(4)**

Combine Syllables to Form Words

Say: *I am going to say the parts of a word. Listen, then put the parts together and say the word.* Circle the words that the child responds to correctly.

16. wag-on	24. ig-loo
17. sev-en	25. re-mem-ber
18. an-i-mal	26. ma-chine
19. nev-er	27. lem-on
20. chil-dren	28. val-en-tine
21. es-ca-la-tor	29. pic-ture
22. gi-ant	30. sal-ad
23. feath-er	

Words That Grow

Blackline Master 34
p. 303L

Objective
To build compound words by joining two words together

Players
Small groups

Materials
- small paper bags
- cardboard
- glue
- scissors

■ Duplicate Blackline Master 34, and give a copy to each group along with a small paper bag.

■ Have children glue the blackline master onto cardboard, cut the cards apart, and place them in the bag.

■ Tell children to take turns drawing two cards from the bag and making the two words "grow" into a compound word. If the two words can be combined to form a known word, tell the child who drew them to name the compound word, use it in a sentence, and keep the cards. If the two words do not form a compound word, tell the child to return the cards to the bag.

Flower Puzzle

Flower Puzzle

don't isn't she's it's he'll

you'll we're

they're you're I'm

Blackline Master 35
p. 303M

Objective
To identify the two words that make up a contraction

Players
Pairs or small groups

Materials
- scissors
- construction paper
- glue

■ Duplicate and distribute Blackline Master 35 to each group. Help children cut out the puzzle pieces along the dotted lines and turn them facedown.

■ Ask children to work together to make a jigsaw puzzle that pictures a flower in a pot. First, have one child choose a puzzle piece and read its contraction. Then have another child in the group name the two words the contraction represents. If the children are correct, tell them to add the piece to the puzzle.

■ As an alternative activity, give copies of Blackline Master 35 to all children. Have them cut out the pieces and paste them in position on construction paper. Invite children to take the flower home and practice reading contractions with their families.

Sentence Scramble

Objective
To read words with inflectional endings in sentences

Players
Pairs

Materials
- sentence strips
- scissors
- envelopes

■ Print the sentences below on sentence strips. Cut the words apart and place each cut-apart sentence in an envelope.

■ Have each pair choose an envelope and unscramble the words inside to make a sentence. Ask one child to read the sentence aloud. Have the other find the word with an **ed** or **ing** ending and name the base word. Use sentences such as:

The baby duck **quacked**.

It is **raining** on the flowers.

The white cat **jumped** on me.

Mom **cooked** meat on the grill.

Pat **planted** seeds in the garden.

Fish are **floating** in the pond.

Words That Grow

rain	shoe	news
pea	flash	wheel
back	straw	base
play	scare	grass
mail	pop	chop
pen	box	paper
ball	coat	corn
berry	light	chair
lace	sticks	pack
crow	nut	hopper

Flower Puzzle

don't

isn't

she's

it's

he'll

you'll

we're

they're

you're

I'm

Listen for Endings

Have children print **ing** on one blank Punchout Card and **ed** on another. Then direct them to hold up the **ing** card whenever they hear you say a word that ends with **ing,** and the **ed** card when they hear a word that ends with **ed.** Say sentences such as:

Five ducks were **swimming** in a nearby pond.
The ducks **wanted** something.
They **watched** us plant the seeds.
Soon, there was a **quacking** sound in the garden.
The ducks were **enjoying** our corn!

Invite children to continue the activity.

Constructing Compounds

Materials: index cards, chart paper

Have children take out the picture cards for **cake, pig, hive, yard, bug, apple,** and **box.** On the board, write **cup, pen, bee, back, lady, crab,** and **sand.** Read the words with the class, and have children copy each word onto an index card. Then challenge children to combine a word card and a picture card to make compound words, such as **cupcake** and **pigpen.** When children have completed the task, invite volunteers to share their words. List the words on chart paper, read them with the class, and have children use them in sentences.

Spelling Contractions

On the board, write these contractions presented in Unit 7: **I'm, she's, they're, doesn't, don't, they'll, it'll, we're, we'll, he's, you're,** and **isn't.** Read the words with the class, and ask volunteers to name the two words that make up each contraction. Then have children choose two contractions and think of a sentence for each. Ask them to print the sentences using the separate words instead of the contraction. Have children exchange sentences with partners and use letter cards to spell one another's chosen contractions. Tell them they will need to make an apostrophe on a blank Punchout Card.

Write and Review

Materials: poster board, tape

Have the class work in small groups to use all the phonics skills they have learned this year to write a story. Have each group spread out a set of Punchout Cards, picture side up, to inspire ideas for its story. Suggest to children that first they write a rough draft and then edit the draft until the entire group is satisfied.

Ask each group to publish its work by printing the story on poster board and taping on picture cards wherever the picture names occur. Encourage each group to read aloud its story. Have volunteers scan the stories for **ed** and **ing** endings, contractions, and compound words and circle them wherever they appear. Then display the story posters on a wall.

COMPOUND-WORD PICTURES

Objectives

- To help children identify and review compound words

- To use a drawing program such as Kid Pix Studio® Deluxe* to make a compound-word picture

Preparation

- Guide the class in brainstorming a list of compound words, such as **strawberry**, **raincoat**, **newspaper**, and **baseball**.

- Write the list on the board, and read the words aloud. Then have volunteers identify the two words that make up each compound word.

One Step at a Time

1. Have each child choose a compound word from the list on the board.

2. Direct children to select "Kid Pix" to access tools for making pictures.

3. Tell children to use the pencil tool to divide the screen in half vertically.

4. Have children click on the Typewriter icon. Then have them spell the first word of the compound on the left side of the screen and the second word on the right.

5. Direct children to use the drawing tool options to illustrate the word on each side of the screen.

6. Instruct children to use the Speech menu to pick a voice and hear their word said aloud.

7. Have children print their compound-word pictures.

Class Sharing

Invite children to present their compound-word pictures to the class. Ask volunteers first to identify the two individual words and then to name the compound word. Display the compound-word pictures on a bulletin board.

You may wish to extend this activity by having children cut along the vertical lines of their drawings to separate their compound words. Display the separate drawings along the chalk ledge. Then have the class work together to form new compound words, both real and invented, by pairing the pictures. List the new words on the board. Ask volunteers to identify the real words.

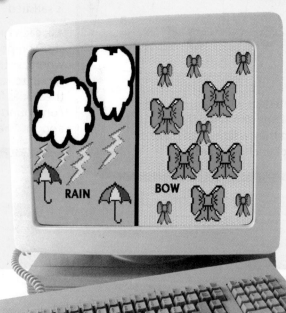

RHYMING STORIES

Objectives

- To help children recognize and identify words that make up a contraction
- To use a writing and painting program such as Kid Pix Studio® Deluxe*

Preparation

Help the class recall contractions made with the words **am**, **will**, **is**, **are**, and **not**. Write several contractions on the board. Have volunteers read them aloud and identify the words that comprise each one.

All software referred to in this book is listed under Computer Resources on page 348.

One Step at a Time

1 Write the following on the board, and fill in the blanks with information given by a volunteer:

> Hi, **I'm** <u>name of child</u>.
>
> When **I'm** older, **I'll** <u>name something he or she would like to do when she or he grows up</u>.
>
> **It'll** be fun!

2 Tell children to use their own names and something they would like to do when they grow up when writing their own sentences. Then guide children to use the Typewriter icon in "Kid Pix" to enter their sentences.

3 Have children access the following drawing tools in order to illustrate what they would like to do when they grow up: "Pick a Stamp Set" or "Pick More Pictures."

4 Have children print their illustrated sentences.

5 Suggest that they choose a voice from the Speech menu to listen to their sentences said aloud.

Class Sharing

Have children take turns presenting their illustrated sentences to the class. Display the illustrations on a bulletin board with the title "He'll-She'll."

SING A SONG

On the board write the song below. Sing the song several times with the class to the tune of "I've Been Working on the Railroad." Use an audiocassette recorder to tape the class singing. Listen to the recording as a class. Have volunteers identify and circle compound words, contractions, and words with the inflectional ending **ing**.

We'll be running 'round the playground,

All the livelong day.

We'll be talking with our schoolmates,

Just to pass the time away.

Can't you hear the children laughing?

Jumping, skipping on a sunny day.

Can't you hear the children singing?

"How we love to play!"

Teacher, may we play? Teacher, may we play?

Teacher, may we play today?

Teacher, may we play? Teacher, may we play?

Teacher, may we play all day?

Literature Introduction to Word Structure

Objectives

- To enjoy a poem about growing
- To identify compound words
- To identify contractions
- To identify words with inflectional endings **ed** and **ing**

Starting with Literature

Read aloud the poem "Tommy" on page 303. Discuss the illustration. Ask what the boy's name might be and what things are growing in the picture. Be sure children notice that the boy is growing, as well as the flower. Read the poem several times and have children join in.

Develop Critical Thinking

Read aloud the questions. Record ideas about seeds and plants on a flower cutout.

Introducing the Skill

Phonemic Awareness: Produce Rhyming Words

Remind children that words with the same ending sound rhyme, such as **grow** and **know**. Make a large sunflower drawing and fold it three times, accordion-style. Say the word **seed**. Hand a volunteer the folded picture. Have him or her unfold one section, say a word that rhymes with **seed**, and then pass the picture to a classmate, who repeats the process. When three rhyming words have been named, begin again with a new word.

Word Structure

- Print on the board: **I'll** be **watering** the **sunflower** soon. Tell children they will learn about compound words, contractions, and words with specific endings. Explain to children what each underlined word exemplifies.
- Point to the **Unit 7 Classroom Poster** and mention that "Tommy" contains some long, unfamiliar words. Have children share strategies for reading long words.

Read Aloud

Unit 7

TOMMY

I put a seed into the ground
And said, "I'll watch it grow."
I watered it and cared for it
As well as I could know.

One day I walked in my back yard
And oh, what did I see!
My seed had popped itself right out,
Without consulting me.

Gwendolyn Brooks

Critical Thinking   Possible responses: water it; provide nutrients and light
What would you do to help seeds grow?
What kind of seeds grow into big plants?   sunflower, acorns

LESSON 160: Word Structure
Phonemic Awareness: Rhyme

303

Theme Words

Word Growth Illustrate various stages of growth, using pictures of a baby, a child, and an adult. Have children share personal experiences of growth. Use key words and phrases from their responses to begin a word wall or a chart on growth. Also include words from the poem "Tommy." Explain that the word wall itself will "grow" as the class adds new theme words to it throughout the unit.

Draw a yardstick horizontally on the board. Write a base word above it. Add an ending and point out to children how the word "grew." Ask volunteers to say base words that name actions. Write them on the word wall. Have other volunteers make these words grow by orally adding **ed** or **ing** endings. Record the new words on the word wall.

Draw pictures of a sun and a flower on the board to illustrate the compound word **sunflower**. Elicit from children other compound words and add them to the word wall.

Name _____

Dear Family,

As your child progresses through this unit, you can help phonics come alive at home. Your child will learn about things that grow, as well as words that "grow" from other words—compound words, contractions, and words with endings.

• Help your child read the words below.

Apreciada Familia:

A medida que los niños avanzan en esta unidad ustedes pueden revivir los fonemas en la casa. Los niños aprenderán sobre el crecimiento de las cosas y también sobre palabras que "crecen", palabras compuestas, contracciones y terminaciones.

• Ayuden al niño a leer estas palabras.

Compound Word Palabra compuesta	Contraction Contracción	Ending **s** Terminación **s**	Ending **ing** Terminación **ing**	Ending **ed** Terminación **ed**
sunflower	I'll	sees	growing	planted

• Read the poem "Tommy" on the reverse side of this page.

• Talk about things that grow, such as **flowers, kittens,** and, of course, **children.**

• Help your child find compound words in the poem (itself, without), the contraction (I'll), and words with endings (watered, cared, walked, popped, consulting).

• Then make a list of words that rhyme with **grow.** (bow/go/hoe/mow/know/row/sow/toe)

• Lean el poema "Tommy" en la página 303.

• Hablen de las cosas que crecen como las **flores,** y por supuesto, **los niños.**

• Ayuden a su niño a encontrar palabras compuestas en el poema (itself, without) la contracción (I'll) y palabras con terminación (watered, cared, walked, popped, consulting).

• Después hagan una lista de palabras que riman con **grow.** (bow/go/hoe/mow/know/row/sow/toe)

PROJECT

Draw a flower on paper and print **ing** in the center. Help your child make the flower "grow" by printing words with that ending in the petals. Draw another flower using the ending **s.** Use the words in sentences.

PROYECTO

Dibujen una flor y escriban **ing** en el centro. Ayuden a su hijo a hacer "crecer" la flor escribiendo palabras con esa terminación en los pétalos. Dibujen otra flor usando la terminación **s.** Usen las palabras en oraciones.

304 LESSON 160: Word Structure—Phonics Alive at Home

Multicultural Connection

Explain that schoolchildren in Africa may tend gardens during their school day. Tomatoes, corn, and sweet potatoes are often grown. Start an indoor garden in a jar. Wash sweet potatoes and poke toothpicks in a single line around the center. Set one end of each potato in a jar half filled with water so that the toothpicks keep it straight. In about three weeks, green, leafy vines will sprout. Have children write predictions about growth in terms of color, size, shape, and number of sprouts. Record results, calling attention to word structure.

Take-Home Book

Both children and family members might enjoy the Unit 7 Take-Home Book, *Growing Up*, which can be found on student pages 335–336. This fold-up book reinforces newly learned phonics skills regarding inflectional endings and word structure. Use this take-home component to conclude the unit activity, or send the book home at some other appropriate time.

Phonics Alive at Home

• The *Phonics Alive at Home* page for Unit 7 provides children and their families with activities that focus on the unit theme "All about Growing" and that strengthen word-structure skills.

• After children have been introduced to the unit theme and phonics concepts, direct them to remove page 304 from their books and take the page home to share with family members.

• Ask children to bring to class something from home that shows how they have grown. This might be a photo taken when the child was younger or a piece of clothing that she or he has outgrown. Allow adequate time for brief presentations.

• Throughout the unit, provide opportunities for children to share in class their at-home experiences with the family activities. Encourage those who complete the flower project to bring in their flowers for display.

Sadlier Reading
Little Books and Big Books

Read the poem "Families, Families" on page 4 from Worlds of Poetry *Families, Families* to talk about different kinds of families. You might also point out the inflectional ending -**ing** in the poem.

Families, Families
Poems Selected by Lee Bennett Hopkins

Direct children to additional activities on Sadlier-Oxford's web site: www.sadlier-oxford.com.

Recognizing and Writing Compound Words

Objectives
- To join two words to form a compound word
- To write compound words

Warming Up

Reviewing Long Vowels

● Read this poem aloud several times until children can join in with you:

My baby brother's **only** one.

He can't talk and **he** can't run.

He can't **read** and **he** can't **write**.

He can't **stay** up **late** at **night**.

"**Don't feel blue**," **I** have to **say**.

"**You'll grow** big **like me someday**."

● When children can say the poem, read it again, one line at a time. Have them identify the words with long vowel sounds.

Teaching the Lesson

Word Structures

Materials: **Sadlier Phonics Picture Card** for **strawberry**

● Write this sentence on the board: The **strawberry** is red and sweet. Show children the picture card for **strawberry**. Underline **strawberry** on the board. Draw a line between the **w** and **b** in the word. Then write **straw** and **berry** on the board. Say each word and then say them as one word. Tell children that recognizing the two shorter words in **strawberry** helps them recognize the whole word.

● Write these compound words on the board. For each word draw a line between the two shorter words, say the two words, then say the compound word, and have children repeat the words after you.

bedtime, birthday, doghouse

sailboat, snowflake, toothbrush

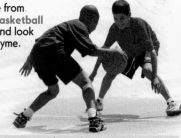

basket + ball = basketball

A compound word is a word made from two or more shorter words. Basketball is a compound word. Listen and look for compound words in the rhyme.

I crawled in my playpen,
When I was small.
Now I climb to the treetops
And play basketball.

Put two words together to make a compound word. Print the compound word on the line.

1		sun + flower =	sunflower
2		rain + coat =	raincoat
3		wheel + chair =	wheelchair
4		wish + bone =	wishbone
5		butter + fly =	butterfly

LESSON 161: Recognizing Compound Words **305**

U N I V E R S A L A C C E S S
Meeting Individual Needs

Visual • Kinesthetic
Materials: index cards, scissors

Write compound words on index cards. Cut the cards in two between the shorter words. Distribute the halves to children. Have them find another half that makes a compound word and write the word on the board.

Visual • Kinesthetic
On the board write the story below; then read it aloud. Have volunteers circle each compound word and draw a line between the two shorter words within it.

I planted a garden by my **sandbox**. It has **watermelons** and **sunflowers**. Warm **sunshine** makes the plants grow. One day **raindrops** watered the plants. Then came a **rainbow**.

Extra Support
Materials: backpack

Wear a **backpack** into class. Write the word on the board and explain the meaning by showing you have a **pack** on your back. On the board write: **baseball, flashlight, weatherman, shoelace, sidewalk.** Read the words and help children find the two words that make up the compound word.

Say the name of each picture with a partner. Find a word in Box 1 and join it with a word in Box 2 to name the picture. Print the word on the line.

Box 1			Box 2		
pop	rain	mail	chair	pack	lace
shoe	wheel	back	corn	coat	box

1. mailbox
2. raincoat
3. wheelchair
4. shoelace
5. popcorn
6. backpack

306   LESSON 161: Writing Compound Words

With your child, see how many compound words you can make using **man, snow, ball, foot,** and **base.**

● Read the directions on page 305 with the class. Then read the rhyme and have volunteers name the compound words. Do the first item together. Then have children complete the page.

● Read the directions on page 306. Then read the words in Boxes 1 and 2. Go over the answer to the first item before having children complete the page.

Curriculum Connections

Spelling Connection

Read aloud each word and sentence below. Ask one child to spell the word aloud and another child to print the word on the board.

sidewalk	I skate on the **sidewalk**.
blueberry	**Blueberry** pie is my favorite!
homework	Do your **homework** after school.
doorbell	Did I hear the **doorbell** ring?

Multicultural Connection

Materials: popcorn, popcorn popper

Explain that popcorn, like all corn, originally came from North and South America. Native Americans in both North and South America grew many different kinds of corn. European explorers took corn back to Europe from the Americas. Now it is an important food crop throughout most of the world. Ask children what two words form the compound word **popcorn**. Help them make popcorn to celebrate this popular food.

Computer Connection

Have children explore the Word Mine in *Reader Rabbit®* 2 (The Learning Company). Tell children to make compound words by combining shorter words.

Sadlier Reading
Little Books and Big Books

Read the poem "My Name" on page 7 from Worlds of Poetry *Families, Families* to practice compound words.

English Language Learners/ESL
Materials: sentence strips, index cards

Print common compounds such as **backpack, raincoat, homework, sunshine,** and **strawberry** on sentence strips. On index cards, print a set of the word parts for each child. Display the sentence strips, identify the compound words one at a time, and direct children to repeat the word after you. Then have children search among their cards to find the two smaller words. Tell volunteers to place the smaller words on top of the compound words, reading the parts and the whole.

Challenge
Materials: Sadlier Phonics Picture Cards for **bed, bird, boat, door, house, rain, snow, sun**

Display the picture cards, and write their names on the board. Then write **house + boat = houseboat.** Have children work with partners to form other compound words using one or two picture card names in each word. Tell partners to follow the model for **houseboat** to write the words on the board.

Special Strategies
For Universal Access activities, see page 303F.

Recognizing Contractions

Objectives
- To identify contractions formed with **is**, **are**, and **am**
- To identify contractions formed with **will** and **not**

Warming Up

Reviewing Initial Consonants

Write these rhymes on the board, with blanks for the words in parentheses.

That little green twig
    Is going to grow (**b**ig).
Will this tiny seed
    Be a flower or a (**w**eed)?
The chirp you heard
    Is a baby (**b**ird).

Read the rhymes aloud, and give the initial letter clue for each missing word. Have children fill in the correct word.

Teaching the Lesson

Word Structures

- Write this quotation from "Tommy" on page 303:

    "I'll watch it grow."

Tell children that **I'll** is written with a special symbol. Explain that this symbol is an *apostrophe* and that it takes the place of letters left out when certain words are combined. Tell children that these word combinations are called *contractions* and that **I'll** is a contraction for **I will**.

- Write the sentences below on the board. Read each sentence and have children repeat the sentence after you. Underline the contraction and tell children what two words make up the contraction. Direct children to repeat the contraction and the two words.

    It's raining on my plants. (**It is**)

    They'll like it a lot. (**They will**)

    Don't water them today. (**Do not**)

    I'm sure they are wet enough. (**I am**)

it + is = it's

A contraction is a short way of writing two words as one. One or more letters are left out. An apostrophe (') shows where the letters were. **Isn't** is a contraction. Look and listen for contractions in the rhyme.

Isn't that a flower bud?
Didn't that baby bird sing?
Everything is growing now.
Can't you tell—it's spring!

Color each leaf if the contraction stands for the other two words below it.

I am = I'm	she is = she's	we are = we're
	he is = he's	you are = you're
	it is = it's	they are = they're

1. I'm / I am
2. she's / she had
3. you're / you are
4. it's / it is
5. he's / he is
6. we're / I was
7. they're / they are
8. we're / we are
9. she's / she is

UNIVERSAL ACCESS
Meeting Individual Needs

Visual • Kinesthetic
Materials: oaktag, marker, masking tape

On a ten-inch oaktag square, print each contraction listed on pages 307 and 308. Tape the squares to the floor to make a path. Have children walk along the path and name each contraction, and the two words it stands for.

Visual • Tactile
Materials: index cards, two paper bags

On index cards make three copies each of **is** and **will**. Place them in a bag. Make two copies of **she**, **he**, and **it** on cards, and place them in another bag. Have children take a card from each bag, say the contraction that the words form, and write it on the board.

Extra Support
On the board write the sentences below. Have children name the contractions in each sentence and tell what words the contractions stand for.

    I **don't** think **I'll** pick the beans.

    Sam **doesn't** know if **they're** ripe.

Contractions can be made with **will** and **not**. Read the words on the flower petals. Color the petals with a contraction that is made from the word in the center of each flower.

he + will = he'll

is + not = isn't

I will = I'll	we will = we'll	is not = isn't
he will = he'll	you will = you'll	do not = don't
she will = she'll	they will = they'll	does not = doesn't
it will = it'll		are not = aren't

he'll she'll

They're **will** you'll

we'll I'm

don't it's

isn't **not** doesn't

I'll aren't

308 LESSON 162: Recognizing Contractions

Ask your child to read each contraction and name the two words from which it is made.

Practicing the Skill

● Together read the directions on page 307. Read the rhyme. Have volunteers name the contractions in the rhyme. Then read aloud the contractions in the box. Do the first two items together before children complete the page.

● Read the directions on page 308 with the class. Also read the contractions in the box and the words they stand for. Model the first item and have children complete the page.

Curriculum Connections

Spelling Connection

Read aloud each word and sentence below. Ask one child to spell the word aloud and another child to print the word on the board.

aren't **Aren't** you glad you're growing?

I'll **I'll** be taller soon.

it's **It's** fun to get bigger.

you'll **You'll** like being seven.

she'll I think **she'll** like it, too!

Theme Activity: Language Arts

● Share the theme book with the class. Then work together to find contractions in the story.

● On the board write a sentence starter such as, "When I'm old like Grandpa, I'll. . . ." Have children write sentences about things they might do when they are old. Tell them to try to use contractions.

Theme Book
Johnson, Angela. *When I Am Old with You.* New York: Orchard Books, 1990. A boy dreams about the things he and his grandfather might do together when they are both old.

Sadlier Reading

Little Books and Big Books

Read *Too Small Jill* (fiction) for more practice with contractions.

English Language Learners/ESL

Materials: Sets of cards for **I am, she is, you are, they are, do not, does not, I will,** and their contractions

Draw a large apostrophe on the chalkboard and explain that this is used in place of the letters that were taken out of the words. Write **you** and **are** on the board and then put them together, erasing the **a** and adding the apostrophe to make **you're**. Say the words and have children repeat them after you. Distribute a set of cards and have children match the contraction to its words. Repeat the activity for the rest of the contractions.

Challenge

Have partners make up riddles about things that grow using contractions such as, **I'm, it'll, it's, they're,** and **you'll.** For example:

You'll see me growing in the sun.
I'm big and round and yellow.
(**sunflower**)

Have partners share their riddles with the class. Ask volunteers to write on the board the contractions used in the riddles.

Special Strategies

For Universal Access activities, see page 303F.

308

Connecting Spelling, Writing, and Speaking

Objectives
- To say, spell, sort, and write contractions
- To write sentences using spelling words

Teaching the Lesson

Spelling

Materials: index cards

- Review that a contraction is a short way of writing two words as one, with an apostrophe added to represent letters left out. As an example, write on the board and read aloud: **I + am = I'm.** Remind children that they have also studied contractions made with **is**, **are**, **will**, and **not**.

- Write this poem on the board:

  Each day **I'm** getting older.

  Can't you tell? **Don't** you know?

  Each day **I'm** growing taller.

  I'm so lucky! Watch me grow!

Read the poem together. Ask a child to find and underline the contractions made from **am** and another word. (**I'm**) Ask another child to find and underline the contractions made from **not**. (**can't, don't**) Identify the word combined with **not** to form each contraction.

Practicing the Skill

Read aloud the directions on page 309. Do the first item together. Then have children complete the page.

Observational Assessment

Note children who need help identifying the words that make up a contraction.

309

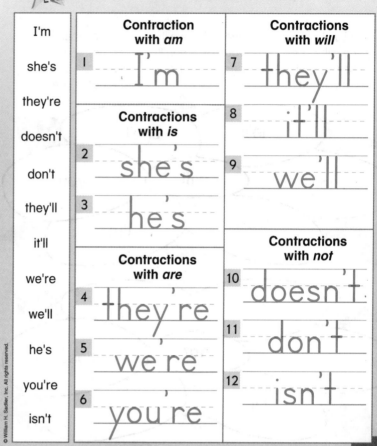

Spell, Write, and Tell — Say, spell, and talk about each word in the box. Then print each word under the correct heading.

I'm
she's
they're
doesn't
don't
they'll
it'll
we're
we'll
he's
you're
isn't

Contraction with *am*
1 I'm

Contractions with *is*
2 she's
3 he's

Contractions with *are*
4 they're
5 we're
6 you're

Contractions with *will*
7 they'll
8 it'll
9 we'll

Contractions with *not*
10 doesn't
11 don't
12 isn't

LESSON 163: Connecting Spelling, Writing, and Speaking 309

UNIVERSAL ACCESS
Meeting Individual Needs

Auditory • Visual
Materials: three-by-three grids, paper circles

Distribute grids and circles for "Contraction Bingo." Have children print spelling words in the grid spaces. Then call out contraction word pairs, bingo-style, as children cover corresponding words on their grids. Three in a row wins.

Auditory • Visual
On the board write **am, is, are, will, not.**

Direct children to answer each question you ask with a complete sentence that includes a contraction that ends with one of the words on the board. Ask questions such as: *Where are your friends today?* (**They're** *at school.*) Print contractions used to answer beneath the correct headings on the board.

Extra Support
Write the words **am, is, are, will, not** across the board. Yawn and say: *I'm sleepy.* Explain that **I'm** is the contraction for **I am.** Write **I'm** under **am** on the board. Make up other sentences with contractions for the other words and use actions as you say the sentences. Have children repeat the contractions and the two words after you.

My Summer Plans

Encourage children to write two or three sentences about summer plans.

I'm	they're	don't	it'll	we'll	you're
she's	doesn't	they'll	we're	he's	isn't

LESSON 163: Connecting Spelling, Writing, and Speaking

Ask your child to draw a picture showing one of the family activities he or she wrote about.

The Writing Process

Tell children they will write sentences about their summer plans. Then read the directions on page 310 together.

Brainstorm Look at the pictures on page 310 with children and talk about things that are fun to do in summer. Have volunteers tell what they plan to do by themselves, with friends, and with family.

Write For first drafts, have children write a few sentences about their summer plans on writing paper.

Revise Have children work with partners to check what they have written. Remind them to check their use of uppercase letters, apostrophes, and periods. Have them underline spelling words used and check these and all other words for correct spelling. Then have children print revised compositions in the space provided on page 310.

Publish Have each child choose a favorite sentence from her or his composition, print it on a paper strip, and make an illustration to go with the sentence. Post sentences and illustrations on a bulletin board under the title "Summer's Coming!"

Speak After children have completed the page, arrange for them to share sentences with the class or invite another class into your room for a more formal sharing.

Portfolio Have children add their corrected first drafts to their portfolios.

English Language Learners/ESL
Materials: Punchout Letter Cards, marker

Some languages do not have a counterpart for contractions, so children may have difficulty understanding the concept of contractions or the purpose and positioning of the apostrophe. Help children use letter cards to form each of the two words of the contractions presented on page 310. Make a bright-colored apostrophe out of a blank card. Explain that contractions are a short-cut way of saying two words. Show children how to put two words together to form a contraction and how to replace the omitted letters with the apostrophe.

Challenge
Tell children to think of a special place they would like to go in the summer. Have them write about their imaginary trips, using as many contractions as they can. For example: "**We're** on our way to the beach. **I'm** going to swim. **We'll** build a castle in the sand." or "**We're** going on a space ship. First, **it'll** go to Mars." Have them share their imaginary trip writings with the class.

Special Strategies
For Universal Access activities, see page 303F.

Extending the Skills

Have children work in small groups to write poems about summer fun. Provide sample first lines such as these:

We'll be hiking.

We'll be biking.

We'll be playing in the sun.

Ask each group to choose one child to print a final draft. Then have groups share their poems with the class.

Student Pages 311–312

Recognizing Inflectional Endings s, ing, and ed

Objectives

- To write words with inflectional endings **s**, **ing**, and **ed**
- To read words with inflectional endings in context

Warming Up

Reviewing Consonant Digraphs

- Read aloud the poem below. Then write **th, sh, ch, wh,** and **kn** on the board. Slowly reread the poem. Have children raise their hands when they hear a word that begins with one of the digraphs.

> I **know** my seeds need **three things**
> To help them **thrive** and grow:
> Water, soil, and **shining** sun,
> **Which** melts the **chilly** snow.

- Write the boldface words from the poem next to the appropriate digraphs. Have volunteers name other words that begin with each digraph. List these on the board.

★ Teaching the Lesson

Word Structures

Materials: index cards

- Write **cook, plant, rain, snow, spill, want, smell, talk, wait,** and **yell** on index cards. Place cards in a pocket chart. Explain that these words are base words to which we can add endings.
- Write **s, ing,** and **ed** on the board. Explain that the endings **s** and **ing** mean something is happening now and the ending **ed** means something has already happened.
- Ask volunteers to choose a word from the chart and add **s, ing,** or **ed**. Have them print the new word on the board. Have others use each new word in a sentence.

Thinks was made by adding **s** to the end of the base word **think**. Listen and look for words that end in **s** in the rhyme.

> "Oh no, rain!" Ann thinks.
> But the oak tree smiles.
> It drinks and drinks.

Add **s** to the base word in the box. Print the new word on the line.

1	Dad _____digs_____ in the yard.	dig
2	Adam ____plants____ the seeds.	plant
3	Tasha ____waters____ the plants.	water
4	The garden ____grows____.	grow
5	Gram ____picks____ the peas.	pick

© William H. Sadlier, Inc. All rights reserved.

LESSON 164: Recognizing Inflectional Ending **s**   **311**

U N I V E R S A L   A C C E S S
Meeting Individual Needs

Auditory • Kinesthetic

Read the sentences below. Tell children to act out those with a word ending in **ing**.

> I find a sunny spot.
> Now I am **raking** the soil.
> Now I am **digging** holes.
> I am **planting** seeds.
> I cover the seeds with dirt.
> I am **watering** my garden.
> I wait for plants to grow.

Auditory • Tactile

Materials: drawing paper, glue, seeds

Have each child use glue to print on drawing paper an **ed** word from *Teaching the Lesson*. Help children sprinkle seeds over their words. When the glue has dried, have children trace their words with their fingers. Ask each child to hold up his or her paper and say the word.

Extra Support

Have children decide whether a sentence tells something that is happening now or that has already happened. Use sentences such as:

> The children **planted** an apple tree.
> The apple tree is **blooming**.

Rowing and **rowed** were made by adding **ing** and **ed** to the end of the base word **row**. Listen and look for words that end in **ing** or **ed** in the rhyme.

Last year grandpa rowed,
But now I am rowing.
I'm learning new things
Because I am growing.

Look at each picture and read the base word in Column 1. Add **ing** to the base word in Column 2. Add **ed** to the base word in Column 3.

Column 1 Base Word	Column 2 + ing	Column 3 + ed
1 mix	mixing	mixed
2 kick	kicking	kicked
3 yell	yelling	yelled
4 crawl	crawling	crawled

312 LESSON 164: Recognizing Inflectional Endings **ing** and **ed**

Help your child add **ing** and **ed** to **walk**, **look**, and **play**. Then make up sentences for the new words.

English Language Learners/ESL
Use Total Physical Response activities to focus on the meaning of the inflectional endings **ing** and **ed**. For example, have a child pantomime washing his/her hands and say: _____ is **washing** his/her hands. Write **washing** on the board and underline the **ing**. When the child finishes, say: _____ **washed** his/her hands. He/She just **finished**. Write **washed** and **finished**, underlining the **ed**. Emphasize that **washing** was happening at the moment of speaking, while **washed** and **finished** were spoken after the action happened. Repeat using other verbs.

Challenge
Have children work in small groups to brainstorm ways people can plant a flower garden no matter where they live. Ask children to make drawings to show their ideas. Have them add captions, using verbs with **s**, **ing**, and **ed** endings. Write these sentences on the board as examples:

Mom **puts** up a window box.
A lily is **floating** in the pond.
We **planted** a rosebush.

Have the groups share their ideas.

Special Strategies
For Universal Access activities, see page 303F.

Practicing the Skill
● Together read the directions on page 311. Then read the rhyme. Have volunteers name the words made by adding **s** to the base word. Do the first item together. Then have children complete the rest.
● Follow the same procedure for page 312, but have children name the words that were made by adding **ing** or **ed**. Go over the first item; then have children complete the page.

Curriculum Connections
Spelling Connection
Read aloud each word and sentence below. Have one child spell the word aloud and another child print the word on the board.

waited   I **waited** for the seeds to grow.
growing They are **growing** right now.
smelled The girl **smelled** the lilacs.
picks   Peter **picks** the daisies.
handing He is **handing** them to Mom.

Multicultural Connection
Explain that the Japanese discovered a way to grow trees in very small spaces. They called these miniature trees *bonsai*. To keep the trees small, growers trim their branches and roots. Arrange for a florist to show children examples of bonsai.

Theme Activity:
Science/Language Arts
Have children find out how trees help the environment. Develop a class letter to an environmental organization. On the board write questions that children dictate. Have children copy the letter. Circle verbs that end with **s**, **ing**, and **ed**.

Portfolio   Have children add copies of their letters to their portfolios.

Sadlier Reading
Little Books and Big Books
Read the poem *"Sleep, Baby, Sleep"* on page 16 in *Mother Goose and Her Children* to practice verbs that end in **s**.

Base Words and Inflectional Endings

Objectives

- To recognize and write base words
- To read and write words with inflectional endings in context

Warming Up

Reviewing Blends

Materials: index cards

● Write the sentences below on the board, leaving a space for the blends in parentheses. Then write each blend on a separate card. Display the blend cards on the chalk ledge. Have children complete each sentence by inserting the missing blend.

Have you **pla(nt)ed** the seeds yet?

They will be **(spr)outing** soon.

The plants will be **(gr)owing**.

Then **(fl)ower** buds will pop out.

● Have volunteers read the completed sentences to the class.

Teaching the Lesson

Word Structures

● Write these sentences on the board.

The tiny plant **pushed** through the soil.

The plant **grows** bigger every day.

Now a rabbit is **eating** the leaves.

● Remind children that we can add endings to base words to make new words. Read each sentence, and underline the boldfaced word.

● Point out that in the first sentence, the ending **ed** was added to the base word **push**. Have a volunteer circle the ending and say the base word. Repeat the procedure for the other two sentences.

Comprehension Skill: Making Generalizations

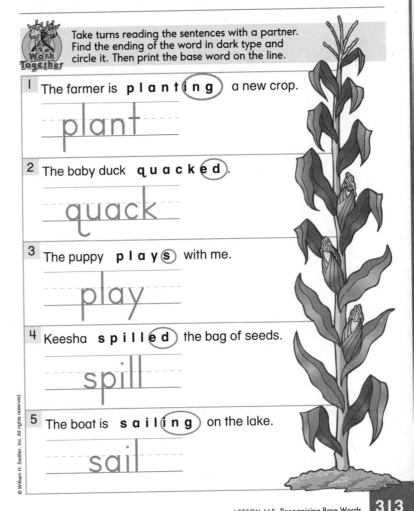

Take turns reading the sentences with a partner. Find the ending of the word in dark type and circle it. Then print the base word on the line.

1 The farmer is **p l a n t i n g** a new crop.

plant

2 The baby duck **q u a c k e d**.

quack

3 The puppy **p l a y s** with me.

play

4 Keesha **s p i l l e d** the bag of seeds.

spill

5 The boat is **s a i l i n g** on the lake.

sail

LESSON 165: Recognizing Base Words **313**

UNIVERSAL ACCESS
Meeting Individual Needs

Visual • Kinesthetic

On the board write:

I am think**ing** of a baby.

It hatch**ed** from an egg.

It run**s** after the hen.

What is it call**ed**?

It is call**ed** a chick.

Tell children to copy the riddle and answer, and then circle the endings **s, ed,** and **ing.** Then have them read the riddle aloud.

Visual • Kinesthetic

Materials: drawing paper, crayons

Ask children to draw pictures of themselves at different ages. Suggest that they begin with themselves as babies and end with a picture of themselves today. Have children write a caption for each picture and underline any words that have inflectional endings.

Extra Support

Have children name things baby birds do (e.g., **eat, sing, wait, look**). Write these verbs on the board (do not use inflectional endings). Have volunteers add **ing** to the words and use them in sentences.

listen as the poem is read aloud. Draw a line under the words that end with **ing** and **ed.** Then write a complete sentence to answer each question.

Living Things Grow

At first, baby Toyo crawled,
But soon he could walk.
He was playing and laughing
And learning to talk.

All living things grow up,
Not just me and you.
Seeds, trees, birds, and pups—
They're all growing, too.

1. How can you tell that something is growing up?

Possible response:
It is getting bigger and stronger.

_____

_____

2. What things have you learned since you were a baby?

Possible response:
I have learned how to walk, to talk, and to read.

_____

_____

314 LESSON 165: Words with Inflectional Endings **ing** and **ed** in Context
Comprehension: Making Generalizations

Tell your child what he or she was like as a baby. Talk about how your child has grown.

Practicing the Skill

- Write **planting** on the board, and say it aloud. Then erase the **ing**. Tell children that **plant** is the base word for **planting.** Read aloud the directions on page 313 before students complete the page.
- Together read aloud the poem on page 314. Model underlining the words ending in **ing** and **ed.** Then help children answer both questions using a word that ends with **ing** and/or **ed.**

Curriculum Connections

Spelling Connection

Read aloud each word and sentence below. Ask one child to spell the word aloud and another child to print the word on the board.

mowing	Mom is **mowing** the lawn.
planted	Dad has **planted** vegetables.
wants	José **wants** flowers, too.
tossed	He **tossed** seeds on the soil.
watering	He is **watering** the garden.

Theme Activity: Science/Language Arts

- Explain that a plant grows and produces seeds that fall to the ground. In the spring the seeds begin to grow into other plants that, in turn, produce more seeds.
- Share the theme book cited below to help children see how a pumpkin's life cycle is circular. Then reread it. Have children listen for words with inflectional endings (e.g., **planted, picked, carved, planting**). On the board, write the words in the order in which they appear in the book.

Theme Book

Titherington, Jeanne. *Pumpkin, Pumpkin.* New York: Greenwillow, 1986. A seed grows into a pumpkin and produces new seeds, starting the process all over again.

Sadlier Reading

Little Books and Big Books

Read *The Trash Can Band* (fiction) for more practice with inflectional endings and contractions.

English Language Learners/ESL

Materials: index cards, pocket chart

Write the base form of the verbs on page 313 on index cards and insert them into the pocket chart. Demonstrate **plant, quack, play, spill,** and **sail** with actions or pictures. Write **s, ed,** and **ing** on another set of index cards. Invite volunteers to choose a verb and an ending to put together in the pocket chart. Have them say the word and make an appropriate sentence to fit the inflectional ending.

Special Strategies

For Universal Access activities, see page 303F.

Challenge

Have a volunteer read aloud the poem "Living Things Grow," and ask children to listen for things that a baby does. Then have children work in groups to make a "busy baby" web. Have them draw a sketch of a baby in the center of the web and write "The baby is..." Have children use surrounding circles to write **ing** words from the poem, along with additional **ing** words, such as **sleeping, eating,** and **cooing.** Have each group present its web to the class.

Integrating the Language Arts

Objectives

- To identify and count syllables
- To use oral and written language to extend the theme concept
- To demonstrate the ability to write words with inflectional endings

Teaching the Lesson

Phonemic Awareness: Identify and Count Syllables

Review that each syllable in a word has one vowel sound. Have children repeat the word **animal** after you. Then have them say the word syllable by syllable, clapping on each syllable. Ask how many syllables they hear. Have them do the same for these words: **li-on, car-i-bou, duck-ling, el-e-phant, di-no-saur, dal-ma-tian, sal-a-man-der, chim-pan-zee**.

Skills in Context

- Read aloud the text on page 315. Have children match each baby picture with the adult. Discuss ways babies change as they grow.
- Challenge children to find the words on the page with **ed** and **ing** endings, contractions, and compound words.

Comprehension Skill: Comparing and Contrasting

Display two plants. Ask how they are alike and how they are different. For example, both plants are green; both grow in soil; both need water and light; one plant is taller; the plants have different-shaped leaves.

Look and Learn

Listen as the page is read aloud. Look at the pictures. Then talk about what you see.

All living things grow.
Sunflowers grow.
So do animals such as tigers.
You're growing, too. Aren't you?

Try matching the young plants and animals to the older ones.
How are they the same?
How are they different?
How do they change as they grow?

Look at a baby picture of yourself.
Don't you look different now?
How have you changed?

LESSON 166: Compound Words, Contractions, and Words with Endings in Context
Comprehension: Comparing and Contrasting

315

UNIVERSAL ACCESS
Meeting Individual Needs

Reading and Writing Connection

Write the word **autobiography** on the board, and tell children that an autobiography is a true story people write about themselves. Have children begin autobiographies by printing a few sentences about an early memory. Then have them print how they have changed. Provide a model sentence such as: "I know I'm growing because . . . ." Use photos as illustrations, or have children make their own drawings.

Mathematics Connection

Materials: strips of paper

Have children try to find out how long they were at birth, or use your own or your child's birth length as an example. Help children make a cutout figure about the length of a newborn—approximately 18–20 inches. Guide children to use their "babies" to see how many "babies tall" they are now. They may enjoy using the cutouts to measure classmates or other people in school or at home.

The words in the box are often used in sentences. Use one of the words to complete each sentence. Then practice reading the sentences aloud.

| ask | going | he | just | play | up |

1. "Tim can not walk __up__ the 🪜," said Tom.
   stairs

2. "Tim can not __ask__ for help yet," said Mom.

3. "Tim is __just__ a 👶," said Mom.
   baby

4. "Will Tim __play__ ⚾ with me?" asked Tom.
   baseball

5. "Will __he__ ride to the 🛝 with me?" asked Tom.
   park

6. "Tim is __going__ to need you, Tom!" said Mom.

316

LESSON 167: Reading High-Frequency Words

Together with your child, use the words in the box to make up sentences about the baby in the story.

High-Frequency Words

Objectives
- To recognize and read high-frequency words
- To write high-frequency words to complete sentences

Teaching the Lesson

- Write the words **ask**, **going**, **he**, **just**, **play**, and **up** on cards and place them along the chalk ledge. Point to each word, read it aloud, and ask children to repeat the word. Then write these sentences on the board:

  I am ___ to plant some seeds. (**going**)

  They ___ need water and sun. (**just**)

  Soon, little plants will come ___ . (**up**)

  Casey will come to ___ with me. (**play**)

  He will ___ what I am doing. (**ask**)

  Won't ___ be surprised! (**he**)

Read each sentence and have children choose the best card to complete each sentence. Ask them to spell each word aloud.

- Write these sentence parts on the board:

  up in the air.   just in time.

  My friend is going   If I play

  Did you ask   Matt said he

Point to the underlined words. Ask children to read them aloud and spell the word in the air. Read aloud each sentence part. Remind children that the first word in a sentence begins with an uppercase letter, and that a sentence ends with a period. Discuss whether each sentence part is the beginning or end of a sentence.

Practicing the Skill

Read aloud the directions at the top of page 316, and call on children to read the words in the box. Be sure children can read the sentences and identify the rebus pictures. Tell children that quotation marks are placed around the words someone says. Then have children complete the page.

Extra Practice
Materials: index cards and container for each pair of children

- Write the words **ask, going, he, just, play,** and **up** on index cards. Hold up and read aloud each card before placing it in a container. Have children work with a partner. Each child should draw one card from the container, read the word, and spell it. Then have the partners work together to make up one oral sentence that uses both words. Have partners return the cards to the container and continue as time permits.

Review
Materials: index cards

Write the words **help, look, jump, walk,** and **open** on index cards.

Make three columns, like those below, on a chart or on the board. Have children choose a word, read it, and write it in the first column. Then have volunteers write the word with the endings **ed** and **ing** in the next two columns, say the word, and use it in a sentence.

word	+ ed	+ ing

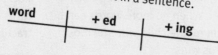

316

Assessing Compound Words and Contractions

Objectives
- To read and write compound words
- To read contractions

Warming Up

Reviewing Consonant Digraphs
Write the consonant digraphs **sh**, **th**, **wh**, **kn**, and **ch** on the board. Point to each digraph, and say the sound it stands for. Then write these word endings on the board: **ink**, **ob**, **ain**, **ine**, **eat**. Say **think**, **knob**, **chain**, **shine**, **wheat**. Have volunteers write the digraph to complete each word.

Teaching the Lesson

Compound Words
On the board write **base + ball = baseball**. Remind children that when you combine the two words **base** and **ball**, you get the compound word **baseball**. On the board write **rain**, **scare**, **shoe**, **sun**, **basket**, **flash**. For each word ask a volunteer to name a word that can be added to it to make a compound word. Write each compound word on the board, using a plus sign and an equals sign, as in the **baseball** example.

Contractions
Remind children that **I** and **will** are often joined with an apostrophe to make the word **I'll**. Explain that this kind of word is called a *contraction*. Call attention to the letters the apostrophe stands for in **I'll**. (**wi**) On the board write **aren't**, **you're**, **they'll**, **he's**. Have volunteers say the two words that make up each contraction.

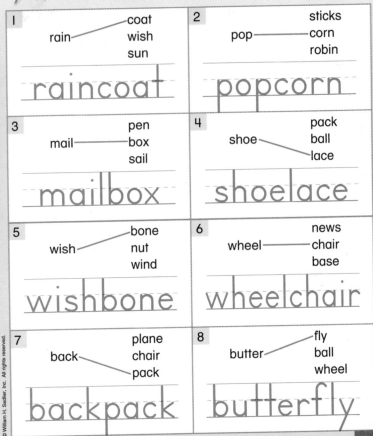

Make a compound word by drawing a line from the first word in the box to another word in the box. Print the compound word on the line.

1. rain — coat / wish / sun → **raincoat**
2. pop — sticks / corn / robin → **popcorn**
3. mail — pen / box / sail → **mailbox**
4. shoe — pack / ball / lace → **shoelace**
5. wish — bone / nut / wind → **wishbone**
6. wheel — news / chair / base → **wheelchair**
7. back — plane / chair / pack → **backpack**
8. butter — fly / ball / wheel → **butterfly**

LESSON 168: Assessing Compound Words   **317**

U N I V E R S A L   A C C E S S
Reteaching Activities

Activity 1
Materials: index cards

Review that a compound word is made up of two words. Write the words **base**, **ball**, **foot**, **mail**, **box**, **house**, **boat**, **dog**, **light**, **sun**, **flower**, **set**, **sail**, and **print** on index cards. Have children work in pairs with a set of cards placed facedown. Each child turns over two cards. If the words form a compound word, the child says the word and keeps the cards. If not, the cards are turned back over. When no more words can be formed, the child with the most cards wins.

Activity 2
Materials: index cards

Remind children that when certain words are combined to form a contraction, an apostrophe takes the place of one or two letters. Write **aren't**, and have children identify the two words that make up the contraction. (**are, not**) Write the contractions from page 318 on index cards. Have children work in pairs to sort the cards into these categories: **am/is, are, will, not**. Then have partners take turns naming the words each contraction represents.

Check-Up Circle the contraction that stands for the underlined words.

1			7			13		
she is	she'll		do not	(don't)		you are	you'll	
	(she's)			doesn't			they'll	
	isn't			aren't			(you're)	

2			8			14		
I will	we'll		it is	(it's)		he will	we're	
	(I'll)			it'll			he's	
	I'm			we'll			(he'll)	

3			9			15		
they will	(they'll)		are not	isn't		you will	you're	
	they're			it'll			(you'll)	
	I'll			(aren't)			he'll	

4			10			16		
they are	aren't		I am	I'll		she will	(she'll)	
	they'll			(I'm)			she's	
	(they're)			it's			he'll	

5			11			17		
is not	it's		we will	(we'll)		does not	don't	
	(isn't)			we're			aren't	
	I'll			they'll			(doesn't)	

6			12			18		
it will	(it'll)		he is	he'll		we are	we'll	
	it's			(he's)			you're	
	I'll			she's			(we're)	

Review this Check-Up with your child.

Guided Instruction

Skills	Resources
Compound words	Instruction on pages 305–306
Contractions	Instruction on pages 307–308
Compound words and contractions	Phonemic Awareness Activities on pages 303H–303I Technology on pages 303O–303P Games on pages 303K–303M Punchout Cards on page 303N

Assessing the Skills

Check-Up Read aloud the directions and the words in the boxes on page 317. Remind children that the line they draw to connect the two words will help them remember the compound word they will write. Do the first item together. Then have children complete the page independently.

Read aloud the directions on page 318. Then ask a volunteer to explain what the children will do. Have children complete the rest of the page independently.

Observational Assessment Review your observational notes about children's mastery of compound words and contractions. Watch as children complete the assessment pages, and make note of those who may need additional practice with either skill.

Dictation Tell children you are going to say some compound words and contractions. Have them write the words as you dictate them. Say **mailbox**, **newspaper**, **wishbone**, **he'll**, **it's**, **didn't**. Then tell children that you are going to say a sentence with a compound word and a contraction. Have them write the sentence as you dictate it. Use this sentence: *You'll like doing* **homework**.

Student Skills Assessment Use the checklist on Student Edition pages 321-322 to record your observations of individual students' progress.

Sadlier Reading
Little Books and Big Books

Read *Joey's Rowboat* (fiction) for more practice with compound words, contractions, and inflectional endings.

Assessing Words with Inflectional Endings

Objectives
● To read and write words with inflectional endings

Warming Up

Reviewing Compound Words

Materials: a basketball

Remind children that a compound word is made up of two smaller words as in the words **basket** and **ball** making **basketball**. Sit with children in a circle. Then say **foot**. Have children raise their hands if they know another word to add to **foot** to make a compound word. (**football**) Roll the basketball to one of those children. Have him or her say the word, then have the class say the compound word together. Repeat with other words such as: **mail**, **water**, **news**, **base**.

Teaching the Lesson

● Remind children that you can make a new word by adding **s**, **ed** or **ing** to a base word. Write the words **walks**, **walked**, **walking** on the board. As you say each word, circle the base word and underline the ending. Explain that the endings **s**, **ed**, and **ing** are added onto words to tell about actions.

● Then write the following sentences on the board: Mimi walks to school. Mimi walked to school. Mimi is walking to school. Have volunteers read each sentence, circle the base word, and underline the ending.

● Write these base words on the board: **yell**, **plant**, **look**, **jump**, **laugh**, **add**, **call**. Ask volunteers to write an ending (**s**, **ed** or **ing**) to each word and use the new word in a sentence.

 Check-Up Read each sentence. Circle the word that completes each sentence. Then print the word on the line.

1	It is _raining_ on my hat!	rain rained (raining)
2	I _yelled_ for Sam to come home.	yells (yelled) yelling
3	The man _waits_ here for the bus.	wait (waits) waiting
4	Dad is _mowing_ the grass.	mows mowed (mowing)
5	Jim _helped_ Sue bake a cake.	help (helped) helping
6	That boat _sails_ on the lake.	sail (sails) sailing

LESSON 169: Assessing Words with Inflectional Endings **319**

U N I V E R S A L   A C C E S S
Reteaching Activities

Activity 1

Materials: magazines, scissors, glue, drawing paper, crayons

Remind children that the word **talking** is made up of the base word **talk** and the ending **ing**. Ask them what base word and ending form the word **reads**. Have children search magazines and newspapers for words with the endings **s**, **ed**, and **ing**. Once children have cut out several words, have them construct sentences by pasting down their cut-out words and writing in their own words to complete the sentence.

Activity 2

Materials: matching pairs of index cards printed with words with inflectional endings (two for each word: **jumps, jumping, played, playing, talks, talked,** etc.)

Remind children that by adding **ed** to the base word **change**, you get the word **changed**. Have groups place the index cards facedown in rows. A child turns over two cards and reads the words aloud. If the words match, the player keeps the cards. Otherwise, the player replaces the cards and another player takes a turn. Have groups play until all cards have been matched.

Read each sentence. Circle the word that completes each sentence. Then print the word on the line.

1 The dog is _jumping_ up on me.	jumps jumped (jumping)
2 I _wanted_ to play with the cat.	wants (wanted) wanting
3 Dad _plays_ the flute.	play (plays) playing
4 I am _mailing_ you a big box.	mail mailed (mailing)
5 Jill _walks_ home with Tom.	walk (walks) walking
6 Mom _filled_ the pot to the top.	fill (filled) filling

320

LESSON 169: Assessing Words with Inflectional Endings

Review this Check-Up with your child.

Guided Instruction

Skills	Resources
Inflectional endings **s, ing, ed**	Instruction on pages 311–314
Compound words, contractions, and inflectional endings	Phonemic Awareness Activities on pages 303H–303I Game Time on pages 303K–303M Punchout Cards on page 303N Technology on pages 303O–303P Take-Home Book *Growing Up*

Assessing the Unit

Check-Up Read aloud the directions on page 319. Explain that the directions for page 320 are exactly the same as 319. Together read each sentence and its word choices. Go over the first item. Then have children complete both pages.

Observational Assessment Review your observational notes about children's mastery of word structure and their participation in the unit's skill and theme activities. Use these notes to help assess performance and progress.

Portfolio Assessment If you have taught the units in sequence, your class has just completed the final unit. Talk with children about how far they have progressed.

Compare each child's earlier work with his or her most recent work. Have the child talk about his or her own progress. Help focus the discussion by asking questions about troublesome words the child has learned to spell, certain sounds in words he or she now recognizes and remembers, and his or her use of punctuation and capitalization. See the Writing Rubrics on page 303C.

Dictation Tell children you are going to say some words ending in **s**. Have them write the words ending in **s** as you dictate them. Say these words: **rows, sleeps, jumps, claps, steps**. Repeat the activity with words ending in **ed: worked, cooked, fixed, marked, talked**; and words ending in **ing: pulling, painting, eating, locking, learning**.

Student Skills Assessment Use the checklist on Student Edition pages 321–322 to record your observations of individual children.

Take-Home Book Remind children to complete at home the *Take-Home Book* page for Unit 7.

Additional Assessment See pages 303C–303E.

Sadlier Reading
Little Books and Big Books

Read *Discovering Dinosaurs* (nonfiction) for more practice with inflectional endings **s, ed**, and **ing**.

STUDENT SKILLS ASSESSMENT CHECKLIST

☑ Assessed   ☒ Retaught   ⬛ Mastered

Unit 1 **Phonemic Awareness and Auditory Discrimination**
- ❑ Phonemic Awareness: Rhyming Sounds
- ❑ Phonemic Awareness: Initial Sounds

Unit 2 **Consonant Sounds**
- ❑ Initial Consonant **f**
- ❑ Initial Consonant **m**
- ❑ Initial Consonant **s**
- ❑ Final Consonants **f, ff, m, s, ss**
- ❑ Initial Consonant **t**
- ❑ Initial Consonant **h**
- ❑ Initial Consonant **b**
- ❑ Final Consonants **t, tt, b**
- ❑ Consonants **f, m, s, t, h, b**
- ❑ Initial Consonant **l**
- ❑ Initial Consonant **d**
- ❑ Initial Consonant **c**
- ❑ Final Consonants **l, ll, d, dd**
- ❑ Initial Consonant **n**
- ❑ Initial Consonant **g**
- ❑ Initial Consonant **w**
- ❑ Final Consonants **n, g, gg**
- ❑ Consonants **l, d, c, n, g, w**
- ❑ Initial Consonant **p**
- ❑ Initial Consonant **r**
- ❑ Initial Consonant **k**
- ❑ Final Consonants **p, r, k**
- ❑ Initial Consonant **j**
- ❑ Initial Consonant **q(u)**
- ❑ Initial Consonant **v**

Teacher Comments

❑ Final Consonant **v**
❑ Initial Consonants **y** and **z**
❑ Final Consonants **x** and **zz**
❑ Consonants **p, r, k, s, q(u), v, x, y, z**
❑ Double Final Consonants **ff, ss, tt, ll, dd, gg, zz**
❑ Medial Consonants
❑ Initial, Medial, Final Consonants
❑ High-Frequency Words **by, funny, let, ride, stop, walk**

Unit 3 Short Vowels

❑ Short Vowel **a**
❑ Short Vowel **i**
❑ Short Vowel **o**
❑ Short Vowel **u**
❑ Short Vowel **e**

❑ High-Frequency Words **and, help, it, no, see, will**

Unit 4 Long Vowels

❑ Long Vowel **a**
❑ Long Vowel **i**
❑ Long Vowel **o**
❑ Long Vowel **u**
❑ Long Vowel **e**
❑ Final **y** as a Vowel

❑ High-Frequency Words **down, here, little, please, put, said**

Unit 5 Consonant Blends

❑ **L** Blends
❑ **R** Blends
❑ **S** Blends
❑ Final Consonant Blends

❑ High-Frequency Words **again, ate, big, look, to, yellow**

Unit 6 Consonant Digraphs

❑ Consonant Digraph **th**
❑ Consonant Digraph **sh**
❑ Consonant Digraph **wh**
❑ Consonant Digraph **ch**
❑ Consonant Digraph **kn**

❑ High-Frequency Words **come, find, open, out, want, we**

Unit 7 Word Structure

❑ Compound Words
❑ Contractions
❑ Inflectional Endings **s, ing, ed**

❑ High-Frequency Words **ask, going, he, just, play, up**

Teacher Comments

322

Good Books

Fold

on the ranch or in the sea.

Fold

Draw a picture of a book you would like to share.

8

Fun adventures, silly rhymes!

6

Directions: Cut and fold the book.

Unit 1 Take-Home Book
Comprehension: Identifying the Setting

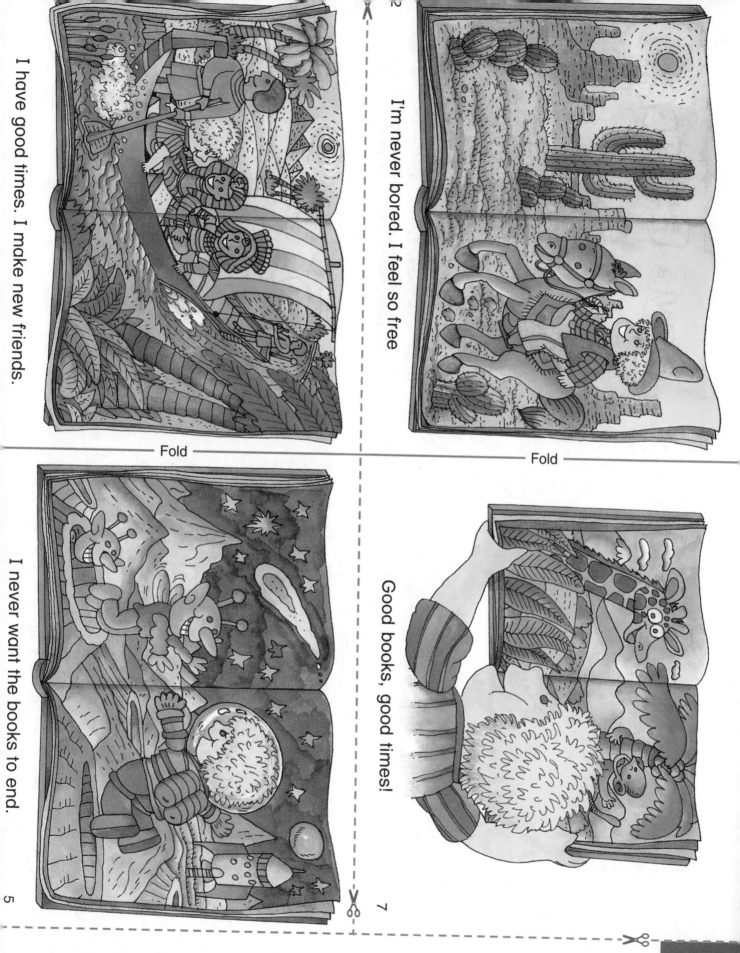

I'm never bored. I feel so free

I have good times. I make new friends.

Fold

Fold

Good books, good times!

I never want the books to end.

5

7

Name _____

I LOVE PARADES

Reading at Home: Read the book with your child. Listen for beginning and ending consonant sounds. Then ask your child to tell the story in order.

— Fold —

with funny clowns,

— Fold —

and me!
Draw a picture to show
what you do in the parade.

8

razzle-dazzle
floats that ride by,

6

Directions: Cut and fold the book.

325

Unit 2 Take-Home Book
Comprehension: Sequencing

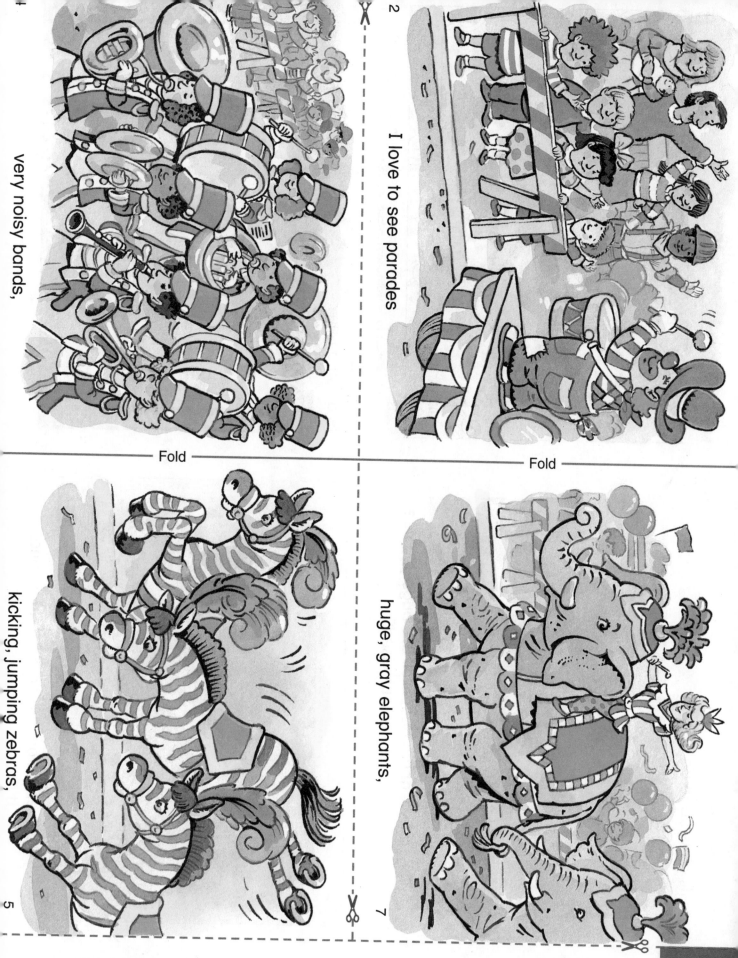

2

I love to see parades

very noisy bands,

Fold

Fold

huge, gray elephants,

kicking, jumping zebras,

4

5

7

Name _____

Is It a Bug?

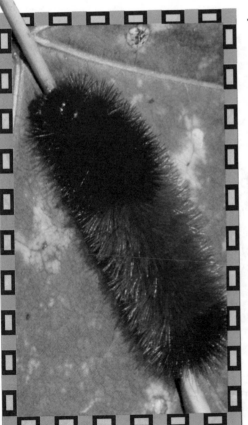

Reading at Home: Read the book together to find the answer to each question. Then look for short vowel words, such as **bug** and **digs**.

— Fold —

1

Is a lion a bug?

An ant lion is.

— Fold —

3

It will grow up to be a moth.

A lion, a fish, and a bear—all are bugs you see!
Were you surprised?

8

A silverfish bends like a fish in a pond.
It snacks on books or rugs.

6

327

Directions: Cut and fold the book.

Unit 3 Take-Home Book
Comprehension: Setting a Purpose for Reading

4

An ant lion digs a pit to make a trap. It gobbles up other bugs that drop in.

2

What is a bug?

I bet you'll be surprised.

Is a fish a bug?

A silverfish is.

5

Is a bear a bug?

A woolly bear is.

7

Name _____

We Can Take Care of the Earth

1

— Fold —

3

We can clean up a stream.
We can plant trees beside it.

— Fold —

President of the United States
The White House
Washington, DC 20502

We can learn the rules and tell what
we know. Please write to
someone who can help.

8

We can turn off the water while
we brush our teeth.

6

329

Directions: Cut and fold the book.

Unit 4 Take-Home Book
Comprehension: Retelling a Story

See how the earth looks.
It doesn't look nice.
What can we do?

We can try to save paper.
We can take bags to the grocery store.

We can recycle used toys.
We can put them on sale.

RECYCLING SALE

PUZZLE

We can be sure to turn off the lights when we go outside.

Making Sense

Name ——————

1

— Fold —

What sounds loud?

3

— Fold —

What smells good?

6

It looks ——————

It feels ——————

It is a ——————

8

331

Directions: Cut and fold the book.

Unit 5 Take-Home Book
Comprehension: Distinguishing Fact/Opinion

4

What tastes best to you?

Fold

2

What looks blue?

Fold

What feels soft?

5

Look! What is this?
Print your guess on the next page.

7

WEATHER CHANGES

Name _____

—✂ 1

Fold

Fold

© William H. Sadler, Inc. All rights reserved.

Weather changes.
Storms dash by.
Soon it should be
Warm and dry.

Thunder's knocking.
Crash and flash!
Rain is swishing.
Splish! Splash!

8 ✂

✂

333

Directions: Cut and fold the book.

Unit 6 Take-Home Book
Comprehension: Drawing Conclusions

Something's coming!
Check the sky—
No more white clouds
Rushing by.

Wind is whistling.
There's a chill.
Will it storm?
We know it will!

Fold

Fold

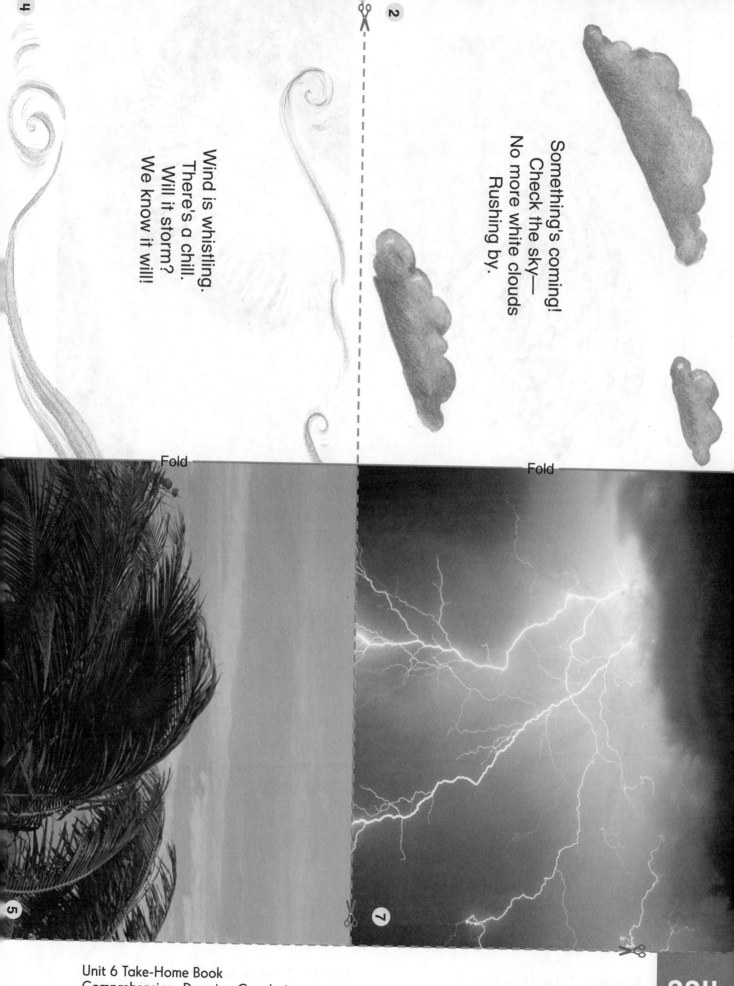

Unit 6 Take-Home Book
Comprehension: Drawing Conclusions

Growing Up

Name _____

Reading at Home: Read the book together. Talk about how a caterpillar and butterfly are alike and different. Then find compound words, contractions, and words with s and ing endings in the story.

Fold

— 1 —

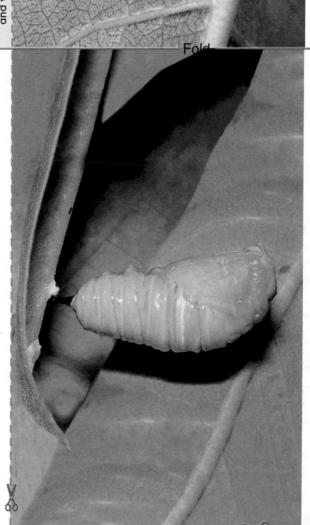

It starts eating and eating.

Fold

Growing up looks pretty good, don't you think?

Doesn't the bug's new home

8

335

Directions: Cut and fold the book.

Unit 7 Take-Home Book
Comprehension: Comparing and Contrasting

Someday this little bug is going
to be a butterfly.

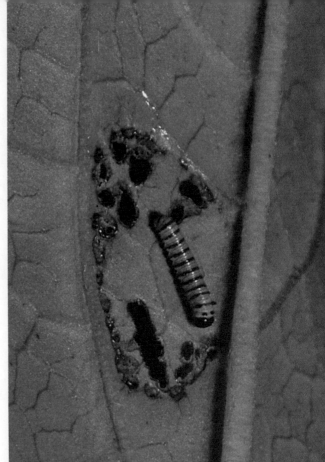

It grows bigger every day.

Fold   Fold

Soon the butterfly comes out.

Then it hangs upside down.

A B C D

E F G H

I J K L

M N O P

Q R S T

U V W X

Y Z a b

c d e f

g h i j

k l m n

o p q r

s t u v

341

w	x	y	z
a	e	i	o
u	a	e	i
o	u		

343

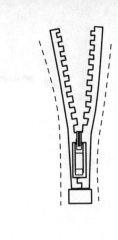  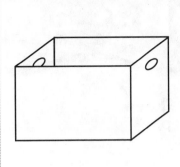 

ot ip ed at

in et ag ug

un op

344

Songs and Rhymes

Baa, Baa, Black Sheep
Baa, baa, black sheep,
Have you any wool?
Yes, sir, yes, sir,
Three bags full;
One for my master,
And one for my dame,
And one for the little boy
Who lives in the lane.

Down by the Station
Down by the station,
    early in the morning,
See the little pufferbellies all in a row,
See the engine driver pull
    the little throttle,
Chug, chug! Toot, toot! Off we go!

Mary Had a Little Lamb
Mary had a little lamb,
    little lamb, little lamb.
Mary had a little lamb,
    its fleece as white as snow.

It followed her to school one day,
    school one day, school one day.
It followed her to school one day,
    which was against the rule.

It made the children laugh and play,
    laugh and play, laugh and play.
It made the children laugh and play
    to see a lamb at school.

Merrily We Roll A-Long
Mer-ri-ly we roll a-long,
    roll a-long, roll a-long,
Mer-ri-ly we roll a-long,
    o'er the deep blue sea.

Little Boy Blue
Little Boy Blue, come blow your horn,
The sheep's in the meadow,
The cow's in the corn.
Where's the little boy that
    looks after the sheep?
Under the haystack, fast asleep!

Oh Where, Oh Where Has My Little Dog Gone?
Oh where, oh where has my
    little dog gone?
Oh where, oh where can he be?
With his ears cut short and his
    tail cut long,
Oh where, oh where can he be?

Rub-a-dub-dub
Rub-a-dub-dub,
Three men in a tub;
And who do you think they be?
The butcher, the baker,
The candlestick maker,
And all of them gone to sea.

Row, Row, Row Your Boat
Row, row, row your boat,
Gently down the stream,
Merrily, merrily, merrily, merrily,
Life is but a dream.

This Little Piggy
This little piggy went to market,
This little piggy stayed home;
This little piggy had roast beef,
This little piggy had none.
And this little piggy cried
"Wee, wee, wee,"
All the way home.

Twinkle, Twinkle, Little Star
Twinkle, twinkle, little star,
How I wonder what you are.
Up above the world so high,
Like a diamond in the sky.
Twinkle, twinkle, little star,
How I wonder what you are.

The Wheels on the Bus
The wheels on the bus go
    round and round,
Round and round, round and round.
The wheels on the bus go
    round and round,
All around the town.

The driver on the bus says,
"Move on back.
Move on back. Move on back."
The driver on the bus says,
"Move on back",
All around the town.

The people on the bus go
    up and down,
Up and down, up and down.
The people on the bus go
    up and down,
All around the town.

The babies on the bus go,
    "Wa, wa, wa,
Wa, wa, wa; wa, wa, wa"
The babies on the bus go,
    "Wa, wa, wa",
All around the town.

The Mulberry Bush
Here we go round the mulberry bush,
The mulberry bush, the mulberry bush,
Here we go round the mulberry bush,
So early in the morning.

Working On the Railroad
I've been working on the railroad,
All the live-long day.
I've been working on the railroad,
Just to pass the time away;
Can't you hear the whistle blowing, Rise up
so early in the morn;
Don't you hear the captain shouting,
"Dinah, blow your horn!"

Dinah, won't you blow,
Dinah, won't you blow,
Dinah, won't you blow your horn?
Dinah, won't you blow,
Dinah, won't you blow,
Dinah, won't you blow your horn?

Three Little Kittens
Three little kittens,
They lost their mittens,
And they began to cry:
"Oh, Mother dear, see here, see here,
Our mittens we have lost!"
"What, lost your mittens?
You naughty kittens!
Then you shall have no pie."
"Meow! Meow! Meow! Meow!"

Three little kittens,
They found their mittens,
And they began to cry:
"Oh, Mother dear, see here, see here,
Our mittens we have found!"
"What, found your mittens?
You darling kittens!
Then you shall have some pie."
"Meow! Meow! Meow! Meow!"

Helpful Hints
for children, teachers, and parents

Phonemic Awareness
Phonemic awareness is the awareness of the sounds (phonemes) that make up spoken words. For example, **fan** has three sounds: /f/-/a/-/n/.

Rhyming Words
Words that have the same ending vowel and consonant sounds are called rhyming words. **C<u>at</u>** and **b<u>at</u>** rhyme and so do **c<u>oat</u>** and **g<u>oat</u>**.

Consonants
The letters **b, c, d, f, g, h, j, k, l, m, n, p, q, r, s, t, v, w, x, y,** and **z** are consonants.

Vowels
The letters **a, i, o, u,** and **e** are vowels.

Short Vowels
If a syllable or word has only one vowel and it comes at the beginning or between two consonants, the vowel is likely to be short. **<u>A</u>nt, s<u>i</u>x, b<u>o</u>x, b<u>u</u>g,** and **b<u>e</u>d** are short vowel words.

Long Vowels
If there are two vowels in a one-syllable word, the first vowel is usually long and the second vowel is silent. **L<u>a</u>ke, h<u>i</u>ve, t<u>oa</u>d, J<u>u</u>ne,** and **tr<u>ee</u>** are long vowel words.

Phonogram
A **phonogram** is a syllable, a word, or the part of a syllable or word consisting of the vowel(s) and any consonants that follow: **<u>at</u>, t<u>op</u>, r<u>ake</u>, b<u>oat</u>**.

y as a Vowel
When **y** comes at the end of a word, it can have the sound of long **i,** as in **sk<u>y</u>,** or the sound of long **e** as in **bunn<u>y</u>**.

High-Frequency Word
A **high-frequency word** is a word that appears much more frequently than most other words in spoken or written language. **Let, it,** and **will** are high-frequency words.

Consonant Blend
A **consonant blend** is two or three consonants sounded together in a word so that each letter is heard. **<u>Cl</u>ap, <u>gr</u>apes,** and **<u>sm</u>ell** begin with consonant blends.

Consonant Digraph
A **consonant digraph** is two consonants together that stand for one sound. **<u>Th</u>umb, <u>sh</u>orts, <u>wh</u>ale, <u>ch</u>erry,** and **<u>kn</u>ee** begin with consonant digraphs.

Compound Word
A **compound word** is a word made by joining two smaller words. **Basketball** is a compound word.

Contraction
A **contraction** is a short way of writing two words as one. In a contraction, one or more letters are left out. An apostrophe (') shows where the letters were. **He'll** is a contraction for **he will**. **It's** is a contraction for **it is**.

Base Word
A **base word** is a word to which endings such as **s, ed,** and **ing** may be added to make new words: **<u>grows</u>, <u>jumped</u>, <u>planting</u>**.

Bailey's Book House is a registered trademark of:
Edmark Corporation
P.O. Box 97021
Redmond, WA 98073-9721
(1-800-691-2986)
www.edmark.com

Beginning Reading is a registered trademark of:
Sierra
3060 139th Ave. SE, Suite 500
Bellevue, WA 98005
(1-425-649-9800)
www.sierra.com

JumpStart Phonics is a registered trademark of:
Knowledge Adventure
4100 W. 190th St.
Torrance, CA 90504
(1-800-542-4240)
www.knowledgeadventure.com

Kid Pix Studio® Deluxe is a registered trademark of:
The Learning Company
500 Redwood Blvd.
Novato, CA 94947
(1-800-825-4420)
www.learningcompanyschool.com

Let's Go Read, An Island Adventure is a registered trademark of:
Edmark Corporation
P.O. Box 97021
Redmond, WA 98073-9721
(1-800-691-2986)
www.edmark.com

Reader Rabbit® I Can Read! with Phonics is a registered trademark of:
The Learning Company
500 Redwood Blvd.
Novato, CA 94947
(1-800-825-4420)
www.learningcompanyschool.com

Reader Rabbit® 2 Deluxe is a registered trademark of:
The Learning Company
500 Redwood Blvd.
Novato, CA 94947
(1-800-825-4420)
www.learningcompanyschool.com

Sound It Out Land is a registered trademark of:
99v Phonics Reading and Writing Programs
P.O. Box 500005
San Diego, CA 92150-0005
(1-800-998-8854)
www.99v.com

Storybook Weaver® Deluxe is a registered trademark of:
The Learning Company
500 Redwood Blvd.
Novato, CA 94947
(1-800-825-4420)
www.learningcompanyschool.com

Word Munchers® Deluxe is a registered trademark of:
The Learning Company
500 Redwood Blvd.
Novato, CA 94947
(1-800-825-4420)
www.learningcompanyschool.com

Credits

Photo

Harold Taylor Abipp: 327 *bottom right*; Diane Ali: 299 *top, background*, 331 *panel 6 top right*, 332 *left, panel 2 background, panel 5 center, bottom*, 333 *top left*; Animals/Animals, David Barnes: 315 *top right*, 336 *top right*; George Bernard: 153 *top right*; Stephen Dalton: 153 *top left*; Breck P. Kent: 161 *top, bottom left*, 331 *panel 3 top right*, 335 *bottom right*, 336 *top right*; James Balog: 327 *top right*; Myrleen Cate: 54 *top left*; Cate Photography: 299 *left*; E.R. Degginger: 328 *top right*; Earth Scenes, E.R. Degginger: 332 *panel 7*; Donald Specker: 331 *panel 6 center*; ENP Images, Gerry Ellis: 336 *bottom left*; Neal Farris: 243, 244; Kathy Ferguson: 331 *panel 3 top right*; Michael Fogden: 161 *right*; Zefa Hahn: 315 *center right*; Connie Hansen: 332 *panel 4 bottom* ; Hutchings Photography: T1–T38, T45–T55; Ken Karp: 5G, 11, 13I, 77G, 77I, 162, 245, 261G *bottom right*, 258, 280, 300, 316; Richard Kolar: 327 *bottom left*; Ross Harrison Koty: 331 *top center, left*; John Lemker: 299 *bottom right*; Renee Lynn: 331 *panel 6 bottom*; Raymond Mendez: 327 *top left*; Frank Moscati: 315 *center top*; Natural Selection, Steven M. Rollman: 153 *bottom right*, 154 *bottom right, bottom left*; Jose Pelaez: 315 *bottom center*; Frances Roberts: 81 *bottom right*; H. Armstrong Roberts: 279 *top right, center right, bottom*, 315 *bottom left, center*, 328 *bottom left*, 332 *panel 4 top, panel 2 top, bottom, panel 5 top,* 333 *bottom left,* 334 *left ;* J.H. Robinson: 328 *top left;* Kevin Schaefer: 315 *bottom right;* The Stock Market, Nadine Markova: 154 *top right;* Tony Stone Images: 315 *top left;* Stephen Studd: 333 *top right;* Chuck Savage: 279 *left;* A & J Verkaik: 299 *center right;* Steve Vidler/Nawrocki Stock Photography: 81 *top, bottom left;* Visuals Unlimited, Bill Beatty: 335 *top right;* John Gerlach: 335 *top left;* William S. Ormerod, Jr.: 153 *bottom left;* Dick Poe: 335 *bottom left,* 336 *top left;* Richard Walters: 336 *bottom right;* John Warden: 328 *bottom right;* Ralph Wetmore II: 334 *right;* David Young Wolff: 331 *top left.*

Art

Dirk Wunderlich: Cover

Bernard Adnet: 17; JoLynn Alcorn: 93, 106, 233; Shirley Beckes: 79, 90; Linda Bild: 43; Paige Billin-Frye: 223, 252, 266, 283; Lisa Blackshear: 162; Nan Brooks: 293; Jenny Campbell: 45, 89, 95, 105, 122, 140, 230, 246, 248, 254, 261; Terri & Joe Chicko: 5H, 13, 81, 165G, 220, 271, 283G; Bruce Day: 118, 136, 152; Denise & Fernando: 41, 53; Rob Dunlavey: 29, 39, 47, 305; Jim Durk: 103, 104, 249; Cameron Eagle: 35, 40, 65; Dagmar Fehlau: 25; Rusty Fletcher: 19, 186, 263; Arthur Friedman: 323, 324; Barbara Friedman: 109, 121, 277; Dave Garbot: 130, 181; Adam Gordon: 327, 328; Myron Grossman: 239, 296; Tim Haggerty: 59, 280; Susan Hall: 155; Laurie Hamilton: 124, 156; John Stephen Henry: 196, 274; Tim Huhn: 87, 88; Ann Iosa: 314; Megan Jeffrey: 179, 195, 221; Dave Jonason: 5H, 31, 77I, 96, 261H, 261I;Karol Kaminski: 7, 27, 51, 74, 300, 316; Andy Levine: 58, 63, 168, 187, 204, 212, 221, 226, 234, 278, 295, 308; Jason Levinson: 82, 83, 86, 101, 127, 159, 160, 183, 188, 199;Judy Dufour Love: 119, 120, 285; Ben Mahan: 61; Maria Pia Marrella: 257; Christine Mau: 258; Patrick Merewether: 143; Judy Moffatt: 209, 210, 312; John Nez: 325, 326; Olivia: 115, 310; Leah Palmer Preiss: 5; Mick Reid: 311;Bart Rivers: 291; BB Sams: 55; Alfred Schrier: 137, 138, 167; Stacey Schuett: 303, 329, 330; Clive Scruton: 287; Teri Sloat: 307; Jamie Smith: 15, 71, 165, 227, 228, 275, 289; Jackie Snider: 30, 37, 66; Sally Springer: 180, 203, 211, 229, 245, 270; Matt Straub: 192, 193, 194, 211H, 303I; Steve Sullivan: 6, 14, 84, 166, 262, 284, 304; Don Tate: 5I, 77H, 91, 108, 142, 253, 281, 283H, 303I, 313; Terry Taylor: 23; Neecy Twinem: 62, 267; Sally Vitsky: 48; Susan Williams: 290; Eddie Young: 165H, 165I, 177, 178, 261H, 303H; Jerry Zimmerman: 129, 139, 283I, 283N, 303H, 303I. Functional Art: Diane Ali, Sommer Keller, and Michael Woo.